Troubleshooting Oracle Performance

Christian Antognini

Apress®

Troubleshooting Oracle Performance

Copyright © 2008 by Christian Antognini

ISBN-13: 978-1-59059-917-4

ISBN-13 (electronic): 978-1-4302-0498-5

Printed and bound in the United States of America (POD)

Lead Editor: Jonathan Gennick
Developmental Editor: Curtis Gautschi
Technical Reviewers: Alberto Dell'Era, Francesco Renne, Jože Senegacnik, Urs Meier
Editorial Board: Clay Andres, Steve Anglin, Ewan Buckingham, Tony Campbell, Gary Cornell,
    Jonathan Gennick, Matthew Moodie, Joseph Ottinger, Jeffrey Pepper, Frank Pohlmann,
    Ben Renow-Clarke, Dominic Shakeshaft, Matt Wade, Tom Welsh
Project Manager: Sofia Marchant
Copy Editor: Kim Wimpsett
Associate Production Director: Kari Brooks-Copony
Production Editor: Laura Esterman
Compositor: Susan Glinert Stevens
Proofreader: Lisa Hamilton
Indexer: Brenda Miller
Artist: April Milne
Cover Designer: Kurt Krames
Manufacturing Director: Tom Debolski

Distributed to the book trade worldwide by Springer-Verlag New York, Inc., 233 Spring Street, 6th Floor, New York, NY 10013. Phone 1-800-SPRINGER, fax 201-348-4505, e-mail orders-ny@springer-sbm.com, or visit http://www.springeronline.com.

For information on translations, please contact Apress directly at 2855 Telegraph Avenue, Suite 600, Berkeley, CA 94705. Phone 510-549-5930, fax 510-549-5939, e-mail info@apress.com, or visit http://www.apress.com.

Apress and friends of ED books may be purchased in bulk for academic, corporate, or promotional use. eBook versions and licenses are also available for most titles. For more information, reference our Special Bulk Sales–eBook Licensing web page at http://www.apress.com/info/bulksales.

A dédichi chésto libro a
chí, che a rasón, i ga l'éva
sü con mí perché a gó metú
tròpp témp par scrival . . .

a Michelle, Sofia, e Elia.

Contents at a Glance

PART 1 ▪▪▪ Foundations

PART 2 ▪▪▪ Identification

PART 3 ▪▪▪ Query Optimizer

PART 4 ▪▪▪ Optimization

PART 5 ▦▦▦ Appendixes

Contents

PART 1 ■■■ Foundations

PART 2 ▪▪▪ Identification

PART 3 ▪▪▪ Query Optimizer

PART 4 ▪▪▪ Optimization

PART 5 ▪▪▪ Appendixes

Forewords

I think the best thing that has happened to Oracle performance in the past ten years is the radical improvement in the quality of the information you can buy now at the bookstore.

In the old days, the books you bought about Oracle performance all looked pretty much the same. They insinuated that your Oracle system inevitably suffered from too much I/O (which is, in fact, *not* inevitable) or not enough memory (which they claimed was the same thing as too much I/O, which also isn't true). They'd show you loads and loads of SQL scripts that you might run, and they'd tell you to tune your SQL. And that, they said, would fix everything.

It was an age of darkness.

Chris's book is a member of the family tree that has brought to us us . . . light. The difference between the darkness and the light boils down to one simple concept. It's a concept that your mathematics teachers made you execute from the time when you were about ten years old: *show your work*.

I don't mean show-and-tell, where someone claims he has improved performance at hundreds of customer sites by hundreds of percentage points so therefore he's an expert. I mean *show your work*, which means documenting a relevant baseline measurement, conducting a controlled experiment, documenting a second relevant measurement, and then showing your results openly and transparently so that your reader can follow along and even reproduce your test if he wants.

That's a big deal. When authors started doing that, Oracle audiences started getting a lot smarter. Since the year 2000, there has been a dramatic increase in the number of people in the Oracle community who ask intelligent questions and demand intelligent answers about performance. And there's been an acceleration in the drowning-out of some really bad ideas that lots of people used to believe.

In this book, Chris follows the pattern that works. He tells you useful things. But he doesn't stop there. He shows you *how he knows*, which is to say he shows you how *you can find out for yourself*. He shows his work.

That brings you two big benefits. First, showing his work helps you understand more deeply what he's showing you, which makes his lessons easier for you to remember and apply. Second, by understanding his examples, you can understand not just the things that Chris is showing you, but you'll also be able to answer additional good questions that Chris hasn't covered . . . like what will happen in the next release of Oracle after this book has gone to print.

This book, for me, is both a technical *and* a "persuasional" reference. It contains tremendous amounts of fully documented homework that I can reuse. It also contains eloquent new arguments on several points about which I share Chris's views and his passion. The arguments that Chris uses in this book will help me convince more people to do the Right Things.

Chris is a smart, energetic guy who stands on the shoulders of Dave Ensor, Lex de Haan, Anjo Kolk, Steve Adams, Jonathan Lewis, Tom Kyte, and a handful of other people I regard as heroes for bringing rigor to our field. Now we have Chris's shoulders to stand on as well.

Cary Millsap

Cary Millsap is chief executive of Method R Corporation, a software performance company. He wrote *Optimizing Oracle Performance* with Jeff Holt in 2003, which earned Cary and Jeff the *Oracle Magazine* 2004 Author of the Year award. You can find Cary at http://method-r.com or http://carymillsap.blogspot.com.

I started using the Oracle RDBMS a little more than 20 years ago, and it took about three years for me to discover that troubleshooting and tuning had acquired a reputation verging on the mystical.

One of the developers had passed a query to the DBA group because it wasn't performing well. I checked the execution plan, checked the data patterns, and pointed out that most of the work could be eliminated by adding an index to one of the tables. The developer's response was "But it doesn't need an index; it's a small table." (This was in the days of 6.0.36, by the way, when the definition of a "short" table was "no more than four blocks long.") So I created the index anyway, and the query ran about 30 times faster—and then I had a lot of explaining to do.

Troubleshooting does not depend on magic, mystique, or myth; it depends on understanding, observation, and interpretation. As Richard Feynmann once said, "It doesn't matter how beautiful your theory is; it doesn't matter how smart you are. If your theory doesn't agree with experiment, it's wrong." There are many "theories" of Oracle performance that are wrong and should have been deleted from the collective memory many years ago—and Christian Antognini is one of the people helping to wipe them out.

In this book, Christian Antognini sets out to describe how things really work, what type of symptoms you should be watching out for, and what those symptoms mean. Above all, he encourages you to be methodical and stick to the relevant details in your observation and analysis. Armed with this advice, you should be able to recognize the real issues when performance problems appear and deal with them in the most appropriate way.

Although this is a book that should probably be read carefully from cover to cover, I think different readers will benefit from it in different ways. Some may pick out the occasional special insight whilst browsing, as I did in Chapter 4 with the explanation of height-balanced histograms—after years of trying to find an intuitively clear reason for the name, Christian's description suddenly made it blatantly obvious.

Some readers may find short descriptions of features that help them understand why Oracle has implemented that feature and allow them to extrapolate from the examples to situations that are relevant in their applications. The description of "secure view merging" in Chapter 5 was one such description for me.

Other readers may find that they have a section of the book that they read time and again because it covers so many details of some particularly important, and relevant, feature that they are using. I'm sure that the extensive discussion of partitioning in Chapter 9 is something that many people will return to again and again.

There's a lot in this book—and it's all worth reading. Thank you, Christian.

Jonathan Lewis

Jonathan Lewis is the author of *Cost-Based Oracle: Fundamentals*, also published by Apress. You can find further examples of his work at http://jonathanlewis.wordpress.com.

About the Author

Since 1995, **CHRISTIAN ANTOGNINI** has focused on understanding how the Oracle database engine works. His main interests include logical and physical database design, the integration of databases with Java applications, the query optimizer, and basically everything else related to application performance management and optimization. He is currently working as a principal consultant and trainer at Trivadis (http://www.trivadis.com) in Zürich, Switzerland.

If Christian is not helping one of his customers get the most out of Oracle, he is somewhere lecturing on application performance management or new Oracle Database features for developers. In addition to classes and seminars organized by Trivadis, he regularly presents at conferences and user-group meetings. He is a proud member of the Trivadis Performance Team and of the OakTable Network (http://www.oaktable.net).

Christian lives in Ticino, Switzerland, with his wife, Michelle, and their two children, Sofia and Elia. He spends a great deal of his spare time with his wonderful family and, whenever possible, reading books, enjoying a good movie, riding one of his BMX bikes, or gliding down the Swiss alps on a snowboard.

About the Technical Reviewers

ALBERTO DELL'ERA has spent his entire professional life working in the Italian telecommunications sector since 1996, specializing in Oracle full-time since 1999. He currently works for Etnoteam S.p.A. (a Value Team S.p.A. company, a consultancy of 2600+ employees), where he is mainly responsible for all Oracle-related developments for the flagship customer web portal of one of the largest Italian mobile operators. He is a member of the OakTable Network (http://www.oaktable.net), the well-known organization of Oracle professionals, distinguished by its use of the scientific method (and ethics of the scientific community) for all its activities. He holds a degree in electronics engineering and can be contacted at alberto.dellera@gmail.com.

FRANCESCO RENNE was born in 1962 in Como, Italy. He studied computer sciences at the University of Milan, and after graduating, he joined Olivetti, working on the development of the Unix operating system. Francesco has been interested in performance since the beginning of his professional career and has worked on Unix internals and Oracle environments in order to achieve the best possible performance in different environments (new products, benchmarks, international real applications on production, and so on).

In 1994, he joined the Banca Popolare di Bergamo, the only bank in Italy that has rewritten its entire information system using Unix and Oracle. He has made major contributions to improve performance over the whole platform.

In 1999, he co-founded ICTeam and is now the company's CEO. He continues to work on performance, especially on Oracle data warehouse environments, for some of the largest companies in Italy.

Francesco lives near Bergamo, Italy, with his wife, Adria, and their two daughters, Viola and Veronica. When not striving to improve something, he enjoys staying with his family, listening to progressive music, and taking pictures.

JOŽE SENEGACNIK has 20 years experience in working with Oracle products. In 1988, he started working with Oracle version 4. Since 1992, he has been self-employed as a private researcher in the field of computer science. Most of his work time is dedicated to solving performance bottle-necks in different application solutions based on the Oracle Database. He is also an international speaker giving talks on the most important Oracle Database–related events worldwide. He conducts well-known performance tuning courses together with Oracle University.

URS MEIER works as an IT consultant and is cofounder of Trivadis, a European IT solution company. He has used Oracle over the past 20 years. During this time, query optimization became one of his favorite topics, since good SQL tuning was often mission-critical for his customers. IT architecture, application design, and agile design principles are his other main interests.

During his professional career, he has worked with many other database systems, but he still likes Oracle because of its cutting-edge technology.

Acknowledgments

Many people assisted me in writing the book you now have in your hands. I'm extremely grateful to all of them. Without their assistance, this piece of work wouldn't have seen the light of the day. While sharing with you the brief history of TOP (*Troubleshooting Oracle Performance*), let me thank the people who made it all possible.

Even though I didn't realize it at the time, this story began on July 16, 2004, the day of the kickoff meeting I had organized for a new seminar, Oracle Optimization Solutions, which I had planned to write with some colleagues of mine at Trivadis. During the meeting, we discussed the objectives and the structure of the seminar. Many of the ideas developed that day and while writing the seminar in the following months have been reused in this book. Big thanks to Arturo Guadagnin, Dominique Duay, and Peter Welker for their collaboration back then. Together, we wrote what, I'm convinced to this day, was an excellent seminar. In addition to them, I also have to thank Guido Schmutz. He participated in the kickoff meeting only but strongly influenced the way we approached the subjects covered in the seminar.

Two years later, in the spring of 2006, I started thinking seriously about writing this book. I decided to contact Jonathan Gennick at Apress to ask for his opinion about what I had in mind. From the beginning, he was interested in my proposal, and as a result, a few months later I decided to write the book for Apress. Thank you, Jonathan, for supporting me from the very beginning. In addition, thanks to all the people at Apress who worked on the book. I only had the pleasure of working with Sofia Marchant, Kim Wimpsett, and Laura Esterman, but I know that several others contributed to it as well.

Having an idea and a publisher are not enough to write a book. You also need time, a lot of time. Fortunately, the company I work for, Trivadis, was able to support me and the project in this way. Special thanks to Urban Lankes and Valentin De Martin.

In order to write a book, it is also essential to be surrounded by people who carefully check what you are writing. Great thanks go to the technical reviewers: Alberto Dell'Era, Francesco Renne, Jože Senegacnik, and Urs Meier. They helped me considerably in improving the quality of the book. Any remaining errors are, of course, my own responsibility. In addition to the technical reviewers, I would also like to thank Daniel Rey, Peter Welker, Philipp von dem Bussche-Hünnefeld, and Rainer Hartwig for reading part of the book and providing me with their comments on and impressions of the text.

Another person who played a central role is Curtis Gautschi. For many years, he has proofread and enhanced my poor English. Thank you so much, Curtis, for assisting me for so many years now. I know, I should really try to improve my English skills someday. Unfortunately, I find it much more interesting (and easier) to improve the performance of Oracle-based applications than foreign languages.

Special thanks also go to Cary Millsap and Jonathan Lewis for writing the forewords. I know that you spent a considerable amount of your valuable time writing them. I'm very much indebted to you both for that.

Another special thank goes to Grady Booch for giving me the permission to reproduce the cartoon in Chapter 1.

Finally, I would like to thank all the companies for which I have had the privilege to consult over the years, all those who have attended my classes and seminars and asked so many good questions, and all the Trivadis consultants for sharing their knowledge. I have learned so much from all of you.

Introduction

The Oracle database engine has become a huge piece of software. This not only means that a single human can no longer be proficient in using all the features provided in recent versions, but it also means that some of them will rarely be used. Actually, in most situations, it is enough to know and take advantage of a limited number of core features in order to use the Oracle database engine efficiently and successfully. This is precisely why in this book I will cover only the features that, based on my experience, are necessary to troubleshoot most of the database-related performance problems you will encounter.

Structure of This Book

This book is divided into five parts:

Part 1 covers some basics that are required to read the rest of the book. Chapter 1, "Performance Problems," explains not only why it is essential to approach performance problems at the right moment and in a methodological way but also why understanding business needs and problems is essential. Chapter 2, "Key Concepts," describes the operations carried out by the database engine when parsing and executing SQL statements. It also introduces some terms that are frequently used in the book.

Part 2 explains how to approach performance problems in an environment that is based on the Oracle database engine. Chapter 3, "Identifying Performance Problems," provides a detailed analysis road map for identifying performance problems. Several tools and techniques that can be used with it are also described.

Part 3 describes the component that is responsible for turning SQL statements into execution plans: the query optimizer. Chapter 4, "System and Object Statistics," describes what system statistics and object statistics are, how to gather them, and why they are important for the query optimizer. Chapter 5, "Configuring the Query Optimizer," covers a configuration road map that you can use to find a good configuration for the query optimizer. Chapter 6, "Execution Plans," describes in detail how to obtain, interpret, and judge the efficiency of execution plans. Chapter 7, "SQL Tuning Techniques," discusses the SQL tuning techniques that are available with the Oracle database engine.

Part 4 shows which features are provided by the Oracle database engine to execute SQL statements efficiently. Chapter 8, "Parsing," describes how SQL statements are parsed and how to identify, solve, and work around parsing problems. Chapter 9, "Optimizing Data Access," describes the methods available to access data and how to choose between them. Chapter 10, "Optimizing Joins," discusses how to join several sets of data together efficiently. Chapter 11, "Beyond Data Access and Join Optimization," describes advanced optimization techniques such as parallel processing and materialized views. Chapter 12, "Optimizing the Physical Design," explains why it is important to optimize the physical design of a database.

Part 5 provides a list of the files used through the book as examples. In addition, a bibliography, containing the sources I used while writing the book, is also provided.

Intended Audience

This book is intended for performance analysts, application developers, and database administrators who are involved in troubleshooting performance problems of applications based on the Oracle database engine.

No specific knowledge in optimization is required. However, readers are expected to have a working knowledge of the Oracle database engine and to be proficient with SQL. Some sections of the book cover features that are specific to programming languages such as PL/SQL, Java, C#, and C. These features are covered only to provide a wide range of application developers with specific information about the programming language they are using. You can pick out the ones you are using or interested in and skip the others.

Which Versions Are Covered?

The most important concepts covered in this book are independent of the Oracle database engine version you are using. It is inevitable, however, that when details about the implementation or provided features are discussed, that some information is version specific. This book explicitly discusses the versions currently available from Oracle9*i* Release 2 to Oracle Database 11*g* Release 1. They are as follows:

- Oracle9*i* Release 2, up to version 9.2.0.8

- Oracle Database 10*g* Release 1, up to version 10.1.0.5

- Oracle Database 10*g* Release 2, up to version 10.2.0.4

- Oracle Database 11*g* Release 1, version 11.1.0.6

If the text doesn't explicitly mention that a feature is available for a specific version only, this means that it is available for all these versions.

Online Resources

You can download the files used through the book as examples at http://top.antognini.ch. At the same URL, you will also find addenda and errata as soon as they are available. You can also send any type of feedback or questions about the book to top@antognini.ch.

About the OakTable Network

In and by itself, the OakTable network is just a bunch of people who like to talk to and be in contact with like-minded people—that is, people with a scientific approach (and inquiring mind) regarding Oracle's database technology.

It all started sometime in 1998 when a group of Oracle experts, including Anjo Kolk, Cary Millsap, James Morle, and a few others, started meeting once or twice a year, on various pretexts. Each would bring a bottle of Scotch or Bourbon and in return earn the right to sleep on the floor somewhere in my house.

We spent most of our time sitting around my dining table, with computers, cabling, paper, and other stuff all over the place, discussing Oracle, relaying anecdotes, and experimenting with new and better ways of working with the database. By the spring of 2002, the whole thing had grown. One evening, I realized that I had 16 world-renowned Oracle scientists sitting around my dining table. We were sleeping three or four to a room and even had to borrow the neighbor's shower in the mornings. Anjo Kolk suggested we call ourselves the "OakTable network" (after my dining table), and about two minutes later, http://www.OakTable.net was registered.

James Morle now maintains the website along with his wife Elain, and although it doesn't get updated with new content perhaps as often as it should, it is useful at least for providing the links, names, and such. We also use it for the Challenge questions and answers.

The Challenge is something we occasionally run during conferences. Ask us anything (technical) about Oracle, and if we can't find the answer (whether it be yes, no, or a solution) within 24 hours, the person who asked the question gets a T-shirt stating that he or she beat the OakTable.

The Challenge, though, is not used as much as we'd like, probably because it looks as if we want to be challenged with questions to which we cannot find answers. The opposite is actually true—the purpose is to answer questions from anybody, regardless of how "simple" or "easy" they might seem.

The Members

I recently read the book *Operation Certain Death*, about an operation in Sierre Leone by the British Special Forces. I want to make perfectly clear that in no way can the physical abilities of the OakTable members be compared to those of the Special Forces. In fact, not at all.

But somewhere in the book the author makes the observation that the Special Forces soldiers are all totally convinced of the maxim that anything can be done with two elastic bands and a piece of rope, if you think long and hard enough about it. In other words, never, ever, give up.

That struck me as something I also have observed with the OakTable members: they all believe that there's always one more option, always one more way of looking at things. It might take a chat with another member, maybe even a Chinese parliament, but the idea of giving up on a problem really is not acceptable, unless you're ordered to.

So, imagine bringing a bunch of people with that attitude (and a tremendous respect for each other) together for even just a few days. It's never boring, and you very rarely see them waiting on an idle wait event, as we put it.

Imagine standing on the cold, gray cement in the exhibition hall at OracleWorld in Copenhagen, realizing that we hadn't paid for carpeting or anything, just 6-by-6 meters of cement floor. Well, it turned out the Intel guys had spare super-quality AstroTurf carpet but needed beer. It was Gary Goodman who brokered that deal within half an hour.

Then Johannes Djernes saw the BMC guys bringing all their advanced exhibition stuff in, placed in two crates that each measured 2.5-by-1-by-1 meters. Two cases of beers later we had borrowed the empty crates. Then Johannes went out and bought various bits and pieces, and within a few hours we had the tallest tower (5 meters high) in the whole exhibition area. It was possibly also the ugliest, but people noticed it.

During the same event, James Morle fought like a lion to establish the World's Biggest Laptop RAC Cluster, using a NetApp filer, a Linux boot CD, and the laptops of anybody who happened to pass by. It was a huge success, but without the "never give up" attitude of James and of others like Michael Möller and Morten Egan, it would never have happened.

A committee, consisting of James Morle, Cary Millsap, Anjo Kolk, Steve Adams, Jonathan Lewis, and myself, review suggestions for new OakTable members. The number of members now exceeds 70, and I have no doubt we will continue to add members with the inquiring, scientific, "never give up" attitude that is the hallmark of this extraordinary group of humans.

The Politics

How often have you heard the phrase "Oracle says that . . ." or "Oracle Support promised . . ."? Well, most of the time it isn't Oracle as a corporation that "says" something but an individual who has an opinion or an idea. I know, because I spent ten years working for Oracle Support, and it is indeed a strange feeling to hear one's own words later repeated as the words of Oracle Corporation (or at least of Oracle Denmark).

It is the same with the OakTable. We don't act as a single body but as individuals. Some (technical) views might be shared, but that's just lucky coincidence. There are no guidelines regarding the individual member's conduct or attitude, except that ideas should be shared and guessing should be eliminated by constantly testing and pushing boundaries.

Sharing ideas openly between peers and striving for scientific methods is what the OakTable network is all about. On those aims there can and will be no compromise.

The Books

One day in Kenilworth, United Kingdom, during an Oracle SIG meeting, James Morle came up with the idea of the BAARF Party (Battle Against Any RAID Five/Four/and err . . . Free) while having a Larson cognac. That same evening we had dinner with Tony Davis from Apress, and that's when James came up with this idea of a press label called OakTable Press. Tony thought that was a splendid idea, and a few days later it was a reality.

The idea was to let OakTable members either write books or at least review books before they were published under this label. At least two OakTable members must review and OK a book before it can be published.

Along with the book you have in your hands now, the current catalog consists of the following:

Expert Oracle JDBC Programming: Oracle and Java expert R.M. Menon shows how to build scalable and highly performing Java applications that access Oracle through JDBC. Rather than take a database-agnostic approach, Menon shows you how to write JDBC code specific to Oracle, and to write it well, ensuring that you can take advantage of all the richness that the Oracle Database platform has to offer.

Mastering Oracle PL/SQL: Practical Solutions: Connor McDonald et al. show you how to write PL/SQL code that will run quickly and won't break in high load, multiuser environments.

Oracle Insights: Tales of the Oak Table: A bunch of OakTable members (including me) present a series of stories about our experiences (good and bad) using the Oracle software: where it's been, where it's going, how (and how not) to use it successfully, and some frightening tales of what can happen when fundamental design principals are ignored.

Peoplesoft for the Oracle DBA: David Kurtz provides a "survival guide" for any Oracle DBA charged with maintaining a PeopleSoft application. The book shows you how to effectively implement common Oracle database administration techniques using the PeopleSoft toolset, how to analyze application activity, and how to obtain the critical data that will allow you to track down the causes of poor performance.

We hope that every book published by OakTable Press will be imbued by the qualities that we admire: they will be scientific, rigorous, accurate, innovative, and fun to read. Ultimately, we hope that each book is as useful a tool as it can possibly be in helping make your life easier.

Mogens Nørgaard
managing director of Miracle A/S
(http://www.miracleas.dk)
and cofounder of the OakTable network

PART 1

■ ■ ■

Foundations

Chi non fa e' fondamenti prima, gli potrebbe con una grande virtú farli poi, ancora che si faccino con disagio dello architettore e periculo dello edifizio.

He who has not first laid his foundations may be able with great ability to lay them afterwards, but they will be laid with trouble to the architect and danger to the building.[1]

—Niccoló Machiavelli, *Il principe.* 1532.

---

1. Translated by W. K. Marriott. Available at http://www.gutenberg.org/files/1232/1232-h/1232-h.htm.

CHAPTER 1

■ ■ ■

Performance Problems

Too often, tuning begins when an application's development is already finished. This is unfortunate because it implies that performance is not as important as other crucial requirements of the application. Performance is not merely optional, though; it is a key property of an application. Not only does poor performance jeopardize the acceptance of an application, it usually leads to a lower return on investment because of lower productivity. In fact, as shown in several IBM studies from the early 1980s, there is a close relationship between performance and user productivity. The studies showed a one-to-one decrease in user think time and error rates as system transaction rates increased. This was attributed to a user's loss of attention because of longer wait times. In addition, poorly performing applications lead to higher costs for software, hardware, and maintenance. For these reasons, this chapter discusses why it is important to plan performance and how to know when an application is experiencing performance problems. Then the chapter covers how to approach performance problems on a running system.

Do You Need to Plan Performance?

In software engineering, different models are used to manage development projects. Whether the model used is a sequential life cycle like a waterfall model or an iterative life cycle like Rational Unified Process, an application goes through a number of common phases (see Figure 1-1). These phases may occur once (in the waterfall model) or several times (in the iterative model) in development projects.

Figure 1-1. *Essential phases in application development*

If you think carefully about the tasks to carry out for each of these phases, you may notice that performance is inherent to each of them. In spite of this, real development teams quite often forget about performance, at least until performance problems arise. At this point, it may be too late. Therefore, in the following sections, I'll cover what you should not forget, from a performance point of view, the next time you are developing an application.

Requirements Analysis

Simply put, a *requirements analysis* defines the aim of an application and therefore what it is expected to achieve. To do a requirements analysis, it is quite common to interview several stakeholders. This is necessary because it is unlikely that only one person can define all the business and technical requirements. Since requirements come from several sources, they must be carefully analyzed, especially to find out whether they potentially conflict. It is crucial when performing a requirements analysis to not only focus on the functionalities the application has to provide but also to carefully define the utilization of them. For each specific function, it is essential to know how many users[1] are expected to interact with it, how often they are expected to use it, and what the expected response time is for one usage. In other words, you must define the expected performance figures.

RESPONSE TIME

The time interval between the moment a request enters a system or functional unit and the moment it leaves is called *response time*. The response time can be further broken down into the time needed by the system to process the request, which is called *service time*, and the time the request is waiting to be processed, which is called *wait time*.

response time = service time + wait time

If you consider that a request enters a system when a user performs an action, such as clicking a button, and goes out of the system when the user receives an answer in response to the action, you can call that interval *user response time*. In other words, the user response time is the time required to process a request from the user's perspective.

In some situations, like for web applications, it is not common to consider user response time because it is usually not possible to track the requests before they hit the first component of the application (typically a web server). In addition, most of the time it is not possible to guarantee a user response time because the provider of the application is not responsible for the network between the user's application, typically a browser, and the first component of the application. In such situations it is more sensible to measure, and guarantee, the interval between the entry of requests into the first component of the system and when they exit. This elapsed time is called *system response time*.

Table 1-1 shows the performance figures for the actions provided by JPetStore.[2] For each action, the guaranteed system response times for 90 percent and 99.99 percent of the requests entering the system are given. Most of the time, guaranteeing performance for all requests (in other words, 100 percent) is either not possible or too expensive. It is quite common, therefore, to define that a small number of requests may not achieve the requested response time. Since the workload on the system changes during the day, two values are specified for the maximum

---

1. Note that a user is not always a human being. For example, if you are defining requirements for a web service, it is likely that only other applications will use it.
2. JPetStore is a sample application provided, among others, by the Spring Framework. See http:// www.springframework.org to download it or to simply get additional information.

arrival rate. In this specific case, the highest transaction rate is expected during the day, but in other situations—for example, when batch jobs are scheduled for nights—it could be different.

Table 1-1. *Performance Figures for Typical Actions Provided by a Web Shop*

Action	Max. Response Time (s)		Max. Arrival Rate (trx/min)	
	90%	**99.99%**	**0–7**	**8–23**
Register/change profile	2	5	1	2
Sign in/sign out	0.5	1	5	20
Search products	1	2	60	240
Display product overview	1	2	30	120
Display product details	1.5	3	10	36
Add/update/remove product in/from cart	1	2	4	12
Show cart	1	3	8	32
Submit/confirm order	1	2	2	8
Show orders	2	5	4	16

These performance requirements are not only essential throughout the next phases of application development (as you will see in the following sections), but later you can also use them as the basis for defining service level agreements and for capacity-planning purposes.

SERVICE LEVEL AGREEMENTS

A *service level agreement* (SLA) is a contract defining a clear relationship between a service provider and a service consumer. It describes, among others things, the provided service, its level of availability regarding uptime and downtime, the response time, the level of customer support, and what happens if the provider is not able to fulfill the agreement.

Defining service level agreements with regard to response time makes sense only if it is possible to verify their fulfillment. They require the definition of clear and measurable performance figures and their associated targets. These performance figures are commonly called *key performance indicators*. Ideally a monitoring tool is used to gather, store, and evaluate them. In fact, the idea is not only to flag when a target is not fulfilled but also to keep a log for reporting and capacity-planning purposes. To gather these performance figures, you can use two main techniques. The first takes advantage of the output of instrumentation code (see Chapter 3 for more information). The second one is to use a monitoring tool that checks the application by applying synthetic transactions (see the section "Response-Time Monitoring" later in this chapter).

Analysis and Design

Based on the requirements, the architects are able to design a solution. At the beginning, for the purpose of defining the architecture, it is essential to consider all requirements. In fact, an application that has to handle a high workload must be designed from the beginning to achieve this requirement. This is especially the case if techniques such as parallelization, distributed computing, or reutilization of results are implemented. For example, designing a client/server application aimed at supporting a few users performing a dozen transactions per minute is quite different from designing a distributed application aimed at supporting thousands of users performing hundreds of transactions per second.

Sometimes requirements also impact the architecture by imposing limits on the utilization of a specific resource. For example, the architecture of an application to be used by mobile devices connected to the server through a very slow network must absolutely be conceived to support a long latency and a low throughput. As a general rule, the architects have to foresee not only where the bottlenecks of a solution might be but also whether these bottlenecks might jeopardize the fulfillment of the requirements. If the architects do not possess enough information to perform such a critical estimation *a priori*, one or even several prototypes should be developed. In this respect, without the performance figures gathered in the previous phase, it is difficult to make sensible decisions. By sensible decisions, I mean those leading to an architecture/design that supports the expected workload with a minimal investment—simple solutions for simple problems, elegant solutions for complex problems.

Coding and Unit Testing

A developer should write code that has the following characteristics:

Robustness: The ability to cope with unexpected situations is a characteristic any software should have, based on the quality of the code. To achieve this, it is essential to perform unit testing on a regular basis. This is even more important if you choose an iterative life cycle. In fact, the ability to quickly refactor existing code is essential in such models. For example, when a routine is called with a parameter value that is not part of the list of allowed values, it must nevertheless be able to handle it without crashing. If necessary, a meaningful error message should be generated as well.

Clarity: Long-term readable and documented code is much simpler (and cheaper) to maintain than code that is poorly written. For example, a developer who packs several operations in a single line of cryptic code has chosen the wrong way to demonstrate his intelligence.

Speed: Code should be optimized to run as fast as possible, especially if a high workload is expected. For example, you should avoid unnecessary operations as well as inefficient or unsuitable algorithms.

Shrewd resource utilization: The code should make the best possible use of the available resources. Note that this does not always mean using the least resources. For example, an application using parallelization requires many more resources than one where all operations are serialized, but in some situations parallelization may be the only way to handle high workloads.

Instrumented: The aim of instrumentation is twofold. First, it allows for the easier analysis of both functional and performance problems when they arise—and they will arise to be sure. Second, it is the right place to add strategic code that will provide information about an application's performance. For example, it is usually quite simple to add code that provides information about the time taken to perform a specific operation. This is a simple yet effective way to verify whether the application is capable of fulfilling the necessary performance requirements.

Not only do some of these characteristics conflict with each other, but budgets are usually limited (and sometimes are *very* limited). It seems reasonable then that more often than not it is necessary to prioritize these characteristics and find a good balance between achieving the desired requirements within the available budget.

Integration and Acceptance Testing

The purpose of integration and acceptance testing is to verify functional and performance requirements as well as the stability of an application. It can never be stressed enough that performance tests have the same importance as function tests. For all intents and purposes, an application experiencing poor performance is no worse than an application failing to fulfill its functional requirements. In both situations, the application is useless. Still, it is possible to verify the performance requirements only once they have been clearly defined.

The lack of formal performance requirements leads to two major problems. First, the chances are quite high that no serious and methodical stress tests will be performed during integration and acceptance testing. The application will then go to production without knowing whether it will support the expected workload. Second, it will not always be obvious to determine what is acceptable and what is not in terms of performance. Usually only the extreme cases (in other words, when the performance is very good or very poor) are judged in the same way by different people. And if an agreement is not found, long, bothersome, and unproductive meetings follow.

In practice, designing, implementing, and performing good integration and acceptance testing to validate the performance of an application are not trivial tasks. You have to deal with three major challenges to be successful:

- Stress tests should be designed to generate a representative workload. To do so, two main approaches exist. The first is to get real users to do real work. The second is to use a tool that simulates the users. Both approaches have pros and cons, and their use should be evaluated on a case-by-case basis. In some situations, both can be used to stress different parts of the application or in a complementary way.

- To generate a representative workload, representative test data is needed. Not only should the number of rows and the size of the rows match the expected quantity, but also the data distribution and the content should match real data. For example, if an attribute should contain the name of a city, it is much better to use real city names than to use character strings like *Aaaacccc* or *Abcdefghij*. This is important because in both the application and the database there are certainly many situations where different data could lead to different behavior (for example, with indexes or when a hash function is applied to data).

- The test infrastructure should be as close as possible, and ideally the same, as the production infrastructure. This is especially difficult for both highly distributed systems and systems that cooperate with a large number of other systems.

In a sequential life cycle model, the integration and acceptance testing phase occurs close to the end of the project, which might be a problem if a major flaw in the architecture leading to performance problems is detected too late. To avoid such a problem, stress tests should be performed during the coding and unit testing phases as well. Note that an iterative life cycle model does not have this problem. In fact, in an iterative life cycle model, a stress test should be performed for every iteration.

Do You Have Performance Problems?

There is probably a good chance that sooner or later the performance of an application will be questioned. If, as described in the previous sections, you have carefully defined the performance requirements, it should be quite simple to determine whether the application in question is in fact experiencing performance problems. If you have not carefully defined them, the response will largely depend on who answers the question.

Interestingly enough, in practice the most common scenarios leading to questions regarding the performance of an application fall into very few categories. They are short-listed here:

- Users are unsatisfied with the current performance of the application.

- A system-monitoring tool alerts you that a component of the infrastructure is experiencing timeouts or an unusual load.

- A response-time monitoring tool informs you that a service level agreement is not being fulfilled.

The difference between the second point and the third point is particularly important. For this reason, in the next two sections I will briefly describe these monitoring solutions. After that, I will present some situations where tuning appears to be necessary but in fact is not necessary at all.

System Monitoring

System-monitoring tools perform health checks based on general system statistics. Their purpose is to recognize irregular load patterns that pop up as well as failures. Even though these tools can monitor the whole infrastructure at once, it is important to emphasize that they monitor only individual components (for example, hosts, application servers, databases, or storage subsystems) without considering the interplay between them. As a result, it is difficult, and for complex infrastructures virtually impossible, to determine the impact on the system response time when a single component of the infrastructure supporting it experiences an anomaly. An example of this is the high usage of a particular resource. In other words, an alert coming from a system-monitoring tool is just a warning that something could be wrong with the application or the infrastructure, but the users may not experience any performance problems at all (called a *false positive*). In contrast, there may be situations where users are experiencing performance problems but the system-monitoring tool does not recognize them (called a *false negative*). The most common, and simple, cases of false positive and false negative are seen while monitoring the CPU load of SMP systems with a lot of CPUs. Let's say you have a 16-CPU system (or a system with four quad-core CPUs). Whenever you see a utilization of about 75 percent, you may think that it is too high; the system is CPU-bounded. However, this load could be very healthy if the number of running tasks is much greater than the number of CPUs. This is a false positive. Conversely, whenever you see a utilization of about 8 percent of the CPU, you may think that everything is fine. But if the system is running a single task that is not parallelized, it is possible that the bottleneck for this task is the CPU. In fact, 1/16th of 100 percent is only 6.25 percent, and therefore, a single task cannot burn more than 6.25 percent of the available CPU. This is a false negative.

Response-Time Monitoring

Response-time monitoring tools (also known as *application-monitoring tools*) perform health checks based on synthetic transactions that are processed by *robots*. The tools measure the time taken by an application to process key transactions, and if the time exceeds an expected threshold value, they raise an alert. In other words, they exploit the infrastructure as users do, and they complain about poor performance as users do. Since they probe the application from a user perspective, they are able to not only check single components but, and more important, check the whole application's infrastructure as well. For this reason, they are devoted to monitoring service level agreements.

Compulsive Tuning Disorder

Once upon a time, most database administrators suffered from a disease called *compulsive tuning disorder*.[3] The signs of this illness were the excessive checking of many performance-related statistics, most of them ratio-based, and the inability to focus on what was really important. They simply thought that by applying some "simple" rules, it was possible to tune their databases. History teaches us that results are not always as good as expected. Why was this the case? Well, all the rules used to check whether a given ratio (or value) was acceptable were defined independently of the user experience. In other words, false negatives or positives were the rule and not the exception. Even worse, an enormous amount of time was spent on these tasks.

For example, from time to time a database administrator will ask me a question like "On one of our databases I noticed that we have a large amount of waits on latch X. What can I do to reduce or, even better, get rid of such waits?" My typical answer is "Do your users complain because they are waiting on this specific latch? Of course not. So, don't worry about it. Instead, ask them what problems they are facing with the application. Then, by analyzing those problems, you will find out whether the waits on latch X are related to them or not." I'll elaborate on this in the next section.

Even though I have never worked as a database administrator, I must admit I suffered from compulsive tuning disorder as well. Today, I have, like most other people, gotten over this disease. Unfortunately, as with any bad illness, it takes a very long time to completely vanish. Some people are simply not aware of being infected. Others are aware, but after many years of addiction, it is always difficult to recognize such a big mistake and break the habit.

---

3. This wonderful term was first coined by Gaya Krishna Vaidyanatha. You can find a discussion about it in the book *Oracle Insights: Tales of the Oak Table* (Apress, 2004).

How Do You Approach Performance Problems?

Simply put, the aim of an application is to provide a benefit to the business using it. Consequently, the reason for optimizing the performance of an application is to maximize that benefit. This does not mean maximizing the performance, but rather finding the best balance between costs and performance. In fact, the effort involved in an optimization task should always be compensated by the benefit you can expect from it. This means that from a business perspective, performance optimization may not always make sense.

Business Perspective vs. System Perspective

You optimize the performance of an application to provide a benefit to a business, so when approaching performance problems, you have to understand the business problems and requirements before diving into the details of the application. Figure 1-2 illustrates the typical difference between a person with a *business perspective* (that is, a user) and a person with a *system perspective* (that is, an engineer).

Figure 1-2. *Different observers may have completely different perspectives.* [4]

---

4. Booch, Grady, *Object-Oriented Analysis and Design with Applications*, page 42 (Addison Wesley Longman, Inc., 1994). Reproduced with the permission of Grady Booch. All rights reserved.

It is important to recognize that there is a cause-effect relationship between these two perspectives. Although the effects must be recognized from the business perspective, the causes must be identified from the system perspective. So if you do not want to troubleshoot nonexistent or irrelevant problems (compulsive tuning disorder), it is essential to understand what the problems are from a business perspective—even if more subtle work is required.

Cataloging the Problems

The first steps to take when dealing with performance problems are to identify them from a business perspective and to set a priority and a target for each of them, as illustrated in Figure 1-3.

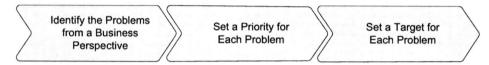

Figure 1-3. *Tasks to carry out while cataloging performance problems*

Business problems cannot be found by looking at system statistics. They have to be identified from a business perspective. If a monitoring of service level agreements is in place, the performance problems are obviously identified by looking at the operations not fulfilling expectations. Otherwise, there is no other possibility but to speak with the users or those who are responsible for the application. Such discussions can lead to a list of operations, such as registering a new user, running a report, or loading a bunch of data that is considered slow.

Once you know the problematic operations, it is time to give them a priority. For that, ask questions like "If we can work on only five problems, which should be handled?" Of course, the idea is to solve them all, but sometimes the time or the budget is limited. In addition, it is not possible to leave out cases where the measures needed to fix different problems conflict with each other. It is important to stress that to set priorities, the current performance could be irrelevant. For example, if you are dealing with a set of reports, it is not always the slowest one that has the highest priority. Possibly the fastest one is also the one that is executed more frequently. It might therefore have the highest priority and should be optimized first. Once more, business requirements are driving you.

For each operation, you should set a quantifiable target for the optimization, such as "When the Create User button is clicked, the processing lasts at most two seconds." If the performance requirements or even service level agreements are available, it is possible that the targets are already known. Otherwise, once again, you must consider the business requirements to determine the targets. Note that without targets you do not know when it is time to stop investigating for a better solution. In other words, the optimization could be endless. Remember, the effort should always be balanced by the benefit.

Working the Problems

Troubleshooting a whole system is much more complex than troubleshooting single components. Therefore, whenever possible, you should work one problem at a time. Simply take the list of problems and go through them according to their priority level.

For each problem, the three questions shown in Figure 1-4 must be answered:

Where is time spent? First, you have to identify where time goes. For example, if a specific operation takes ten seconds, you have to find out which module or component most of these ten seconds are used up in.

How is time spent? Once you know where the time goes, you have to find out how that time is spent. For example, you may find out that the application spends 4.2 seconds on CPU, 0.4 seconds doing I/O operations, and 5.1 seconds waiting for dequeuing a message coming from another component.

How can time spent be reduced? Finally, it is time to find out how the operation can be made faster. To do so, it is essential to focus on the most time-consuming part of the processing. For example, if I/O operations take 4 percent of the overall processing time, it makes no sense to start tuning them, even if they are very slow.

Figure 1-4. *To troubleshoot a performance problem, you need to answer these three questions.*

It is important to note that thanks to beneficial side effects, sometimes measures implemented to fix a particular problem will also fix another one. Of course, the opposite can happen as well. Measures taken may introduce new problems. It is essential therefore to carefully consider all the possible side effects that a specific fix may have. Clearly, all changes have to be carefully tested before implementing them in production.

On to Chapter 2

In this chapter, we looked at some key issues of dealing with performance problems: why it is essential to approach performance problems at the right moment and in a methodological way, why understanding business needs and problems is absolutely important, and why it is necessary to agree on what *good performance* means.

Before describing how to answer the three questions in Figure 1-4, it is essential that I introduce some key concepts that I'll be using in the rest of the book. For that purpose, Chapter 2 will describe the processing performed by the database engine to execute SQL statements. In addition, I'll define several frequently used terms.

CHAPTER 2

■■■

Key Concepts

The aim of this chapter is twofold. First, to avoid unnecessary confusion, I'll introduce some terms that are used repeatedly throughout this book. The most important include *selectivity* and *cardinality*, *soft* and *hard parses*, and *bind variable peeking* and *extended cursor sharing*. Second, I'll describe the life cycle of SQL statements. In other words, I'll describe the operations carried out in order to execute SQL statements. During this discussion, special attention will be given to parsing.

Selectivity and Cardinality

The *selectivity* is a value between 0 and 1 representing the fraction of rows filtered by an operation. For example, if an access operation reads 120 rows from a table and after applying a filter returns 18 of them, the selectivity is 0.15 (18/120). The selectivity can also be expressed as a percentage, so 0.15 can also be expressed as 15 percent. The number of rows returned by an operation is the *cardinality*. Formula 2-1 shows the relationship between selectivity and cardinality. In this formula, the value *num_rows* is the number of processed rows.

cardinality = selectivity · num_rows

Formula 2-1. *Relationship between selectivity and cardinality*

■**Caution** In some publications, the term *cardinality* refers to the number of distinct values stored in a particular column. I never use the term *cardinality* in this way.

Let's take a look at a couple of examples based on the script selectivity.sql. In the following query, the selectivity of the operation accessing the table is 1. This is because no WHERE clause is applied, and therefore, the query returns all rows stored in the table (10,000).

```
SQL> SELECT * FROM t;
...

10000 rows selected.
```

In the following query, the selectivity of the operation accessing the table is 0.2601 (2,601 rows returned out of 10,000):

```
SQL> SELECT * FROM t WHERE n1 BETWEEN 6000 AND 7000;
...

2601 rows selected.
```

In the following query, the selectivity of the operation accessing the table is 0 (0 rows returned out of 10,000):

```
SQL> SELECT * FROM t WHERE n1 = 19;

no rows selected.
```

In the previous three examples, the selectivity related to the operation accessing the table is computed by dividing the number of rows returned by the query with the number of rows stored in the table. This is possible because the three queries do not contain operations leading to aggregations. As soon as a query contains a GROUP BY clause or group functions in the SELECT clause, the execution plan contains at least one aggregate operation. The following query illustrates this (note the presence of the group function sum):

```
SQL> SELECT sum(n2) FROM t WHERE n1 BETWEEN 6000 AND 7000;

  SUM(N2)
----------
    70846

1 row selected.
```

In this type of situation, it is not possible to compute the selectivity of the access operation based on the number of rows returned by the query (in this case 1). Instead, a query like the following should be executed to find out how many rows are processed in order to execute the aggregate operation. Here, the selectivity of the access operation is 0.2601 (2,601/10,000).

```
SQL> SELECT count(*) FROM t WHERE n1 BETWEEN 6000 AND 7000;

  COUNT(*)
----------
     2601

1 row selected.
```

As you will see later, especially in Chapter 9, knowing the selectivity of an operation helps you determine what the most efficient access path is.

Life Cycle of a Cursor

Having a good understanding of the life cycle of cursors is required knowledge for optimizing applications that execute SQL statements. The following are the steps carried out during the processing of a cursor:

Open cursor: A memory structure for the cursor is allocated in the server-side private memory of the server process associated with the session, the *user global area* (UGA). Note that no SQL statement is associated with the cursor yet.

Parse cursor: A SQL statement is associated with the cursor. Its parsed representation that includes the execution plan (which describes how the SQL engine will execute the SQL statement) is loaded in the shared pool, specifically, in the library cache. The structure in the UGA is updated to store a pointer to the location of the shareable cursor in the library cache. The next section will describe parsing in more detail.

Define output variables: If the SQL statement returns data, the variables receiving it must be defined. This is necessary not only for queries but also for DELETE, INSERT, and UPDATE statements that use the RETURNING clause.

Bind input variables: If the SQL statement uses bind variables, their values must be provided. No check is performed during the binding. If invalid data is passed, a runtime error will be raised during the execution.

Execute cursor: The SQL statement is executed. But be careful, because the database engine doesn't always do anything significant during this phase. In fact, for many types of queries, the real processing is usually delayed to the fetch phase.

Fetch cursor: If the SQL statement returns data, this step retrieves it. Especially for queries, this step is where most of the processing is performed. In the case of queries, rows might be partially fetched. In other words, the cursor might be closed before fetching all the rows.

Close cursor: The resources associated with the cursor in the UGA are freed and consequently made available for other cursors. The shareable cursor in the library cache is not removed. It remains there in the hope of being reused in the future.

To better understand this process, it is best to think about each step being executed separately in the order shown by Figure 2-1. In practice, though, different optimization techniques are applied to speed up processing. (I'll provide additional information about these techniques in Chapter 8.) For the moment, just think that this is the way things generally work.

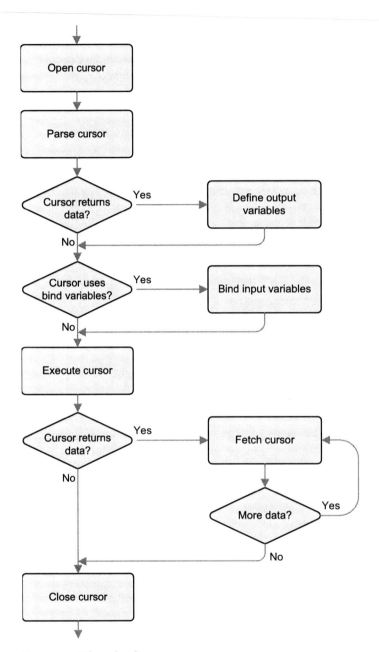

Figure 2-1. *Life cycle of a cursor*

Depending on the programming environment or techniques you are using, the different steps depicted in Figure 2-1 may be implicitly or explicitly executed. To make the difference clear, take a look at the following two PL/SQL blocks that are available in the script lifecycle.sql. Both have the same purpose (reading one row from table emp), but they are coded in a very different way.

The first is a PL/SQL block using the package dbms_sql to explicitly code every step shown in Figure 2-1:

```
DECLARE
  l_ename emp.ename%TYPE := 'SCOTT';
  l_empno emp.empno%TYPE;
  l_cursor INTEGER;
  l_retval INTEGER;
BEGIN
  l_cursor := dbms_sql.open_cursor;
  dbms_sql.parse(l_cursor, 'SELECT empno FROM emp WHERE ename = :ename', 1);
  dbms_sql.define_column(l_cursor, 1, l_empno);
  dbms_sql.bind_variable(l_cursor, ':ename', l_ename);
  l_retval := dbms_sql.execute(l_cursor);
  IF dbms_sql.fetch_rows(l_cursor) > 0
  THEN
    dbms_sql.column_value(l_cursor, 1, l_empno);
  END IF;
  dbms_sql.close_cursor(l_cursor);
END;
```

The second is a PL/SQL block taking advantage of an implicit cursor; basically, the PL/SQL block delegates the control over the cursor to the PL/SQL compiler:

```
DECLARE
  l_ename emp.ename%TYPE := 'SCOTT';
  l_empno emp.empno%TYPE;
BEGIN
  SELECT empno INTO l_empno
  FROM emp
  WHERE ename = l_ename;
END;
```

Most of the time, what the compiler does is fine. However, sometimes you need more control over the different steps performed during processing. Thus, you cannot always use an implicit cursor. For example, between the two PL/SQL blocks, there is a slight but important difference. Independently of how many rows the query returns, the first block does not generate an exception. Instead, the second block generates an exception if zero or several rows are returned.

How Parsing Works

While the previous section described the life cycle of cursors, this section focuses on the parse phase. The steps carried out during this phase, as shown in Figure 2-2, are the following:

Include VPD predicates: If Virtual Private Database (VPD, formerly known as *row-level security*) is in use and active for one of the tables referenced in the parsed SQL statement, the predicates generated by the security policies are included in its WHERE clause.

Check syntax, semantics, and access rights: This step makes sure not only that the SQL statement is correctly written but also that all objects referenced by the SQL statement exist and the current user parsing it has the necessary privileges to access them.

Store parent cursor in library cache: Whenever a shareable parent cursor is not yet available, some memory is allocated from the library cache, and a new parent cursor is stored inside it. The key information associated with the parent cursor is the text of the SQL statement.

Logical optimization: During this phase, new and semantically equivalent SQL statements are produced by applying different transformation techniques. In doing so, the amount of execution plans considered, the *search space*, is increased. The purpose is to explore execution plans that would not be considered without such transformations.

Physical optimization: During this phase, several operations are performed. At first, the execution plans related to each SQL statement resulting from the logical optimization are generated. Then, based on statistics found in the data dictionary or gathered through dynamic sampling, a cost is associated with each execution plan. Lastly, the execution plan with the lowest cost is selected. Simply put, the query optimizer explores the search space to find the most efficient execution plan.

Store child cursor in library cache: Some memory is allocated, and the shareable child cursor is stored inside it and associated with its parent cursor. The key elements associated with the child cursor are the execution plan and the execution environment.

Once stored in the library cache, parent and child cursors are externalized through the views v$sqlarea and v$sql, respectively. The cursors are identified in three columns: address, hash_value, and child_number. With address and hash_value, the parent cursors are identified; with all three values, the child cursors are identified. In addition, as of Oracle Database 10*g*, it is also possible, and it is more common as well, to use sql_id instead of the pair address and hash_value for the same purpose.

When shareable parent and child cursors are available and, consequently, only the first two operations are carried out, the parse is called a *soft parse*. When all operations are carried out, it is called a *hard parse*.

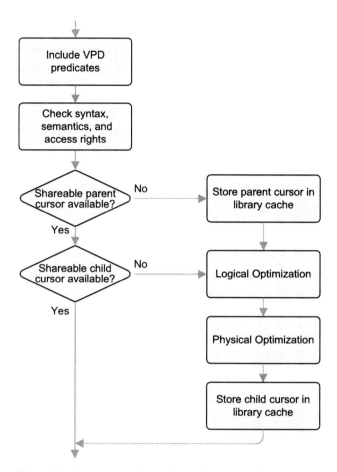

Figure 2-2. *Steps carried out during the parse phase*

From a performance point of view, you should avoid hard parses as much as possible. This is precisely the reason why the database engine stores shareable cursors in the library cache. In this way, every process belonging to the instance might be able to reuse them. There are two reasons why this leads to high costs for hard parses. The first is that the logical and physical optimizations are highly CPU-intensive operations. The second is that memory is needed for storing the parent and child cursors in the library cache. Since the library cache is shared over all sessions, memory allocations in the library cache must be serialized. In practice, one of the latches protecting the shared pool must be obtained before being able to allocate the memory needed for both the parent and child cursors. Even if the impact of soft parses is much lower than that of hard parses, it is desirable to avoid soft parses as well because they are also subject to some serialization. In fact, to search for a shareable parent cursor, you must obtain one of the latches protecting the library cache. In summary, you should avoid soft and hard parses as much as possible because they inhibit the scalability of applications.

Shareable Cursors

The result of a parse operation is a parent cursor and a child cursor stored in the library cache. Obviously, the aim of storing them in a shared memory area is to allow their reutilization and thereby avoid hard parses. Therefore, it is necessary to discuss in what situations it is possible to reuse a parent or child cursor. To illustrate how sharing parent and child cursors works, in this section I'll cover two examples based on the script sharable_cursors.sql.

The purpose of the first example is to show a case where the parent cursor cannot be shared. The key information related to a parent cursor is the text of a SQL statement. Therefore, several SQL statements share the same parent cursor if their text is exactly the same. This is the most essential requirement. There is, however, an exception to this that I'll describe in Chapter 8. In the following example, four SQL statements are executed. Two have the same text. Two others differ only because of lowercase and uppercase letters or blanks.

```
SQL> SELECT * FROM t WHERE n = 1234;

SQL> select * from t where n = 1234;

SQL> SELECT   *   FROM   t   WHERE   n=1234;

SQL> SELECT * FROM t WHERE n = 1234;
```

Through the view v$sqlarea, it is possible to confirm that three distinct parent cursors were created. Also notice the number of executions for each cursor.

```
SQL> SELECT sql_id, sql_text, executions
  2  FROM v$sqlarea
  3  WHERE sql_text LIKE '%1234';

SQL_ID        SQL_TEXT                                    EXECUTIONS
------------- ------------------------------------------- ----------
2254m1487jg50 select * from t where n = 1234                       1
g9y3jtp6ru4cb SELECT * FROM t WHERE n = 1234                       2
7n8p5s2udfdsn SELECT   *   FROM   t   WHERE   n=1234               1
```

The aim of the second example is to show a case where the parent cursor, but not the child cursor, can be shared. The key information related to a child cursor is an execution plan and the execution environment related to it. The execution environment is important because if it changes, the execution plan might change as well. As a result, several SQL statements are able to share the same child cursor only if they share the same parent cursor and their execution environments are compatible. To illustrate, the same SQL statement is executed with two different values of the initialization parameter optimizer_mode:

```
SQL> ALTER SESSION SET optimizer_mode = all_rows;

SQL> SELECT count(*) FROM t;
```

```
  COUNT(*)
----------
      1000

SQL> ALTER SESSION SET optimizer_mode = first_rows_10;

SQL> SELECT count(*) FROM t;

  COUNT(*)
----------
      1000
```

The result is that a single parent cursor (5tjqf7sx5dzmj) and two child cursors (0 and 1) are created. It is also essential to note that both child cursors have the same execution plan (the column plan_hash_value has the same value). This shows very well that a new child cursor was created because of a new individual execution environment and not because another execution plan was generated.

```
SQL> SELECT sql_id, child_number, sql_text, optimizer_mode, plan_hash_value
  2  FROM v$sql
  3  WHERE sql_id = (SELECT prev_sql_id
  4                  FROM v$session
  5                  WHERE sid = sys_context('userenv','sid'));

SQL_ID        CHILD_NUMBER SQL_TEXT                OPTIMIZER_MODE PLAN_HASH_VALUE
------------- ------------ ---------------------- -------------- ---------------
5tjqf7sx5dzmj            0 SELECT count(*) FROM t ALL_ROWS            2966233522
5tjqf7sx5dzmj            1 SELECT count(*) FROM t FIRST_ROWS          2966233522
```

To know which mismatch led to several child cursors, you can query the view v$sql_shared_cursor. In it you might find, for each child cursor (except the first one, 0), why it was not possible to share a previously created child cursor. For several types of incompatibility (60 of them in Oracle Database 11g), there is a column that is set to either N (no mismatch) or Y (mismatch). With the following query, it is possible to confirm that in the previous example, the mismatch for the second child cursor was because of a different optimizer mode. Note, however, that the view doesn't provide you with a reason in every situation:

```
SQL> SELECT child_number, optimizer_mode_mismatch
  2  FROM v$sql_shared_cursor
  3  WHERE sql_id = '5tjqf7sx5dzmj';

CHILD_NUMBER OPTIMIZER_MODE_MISMATCH
------------ -----------------------
           0 N
           1 Y
```

In practice, it is quite common to see too many hard parses caused by nonshared parent cursors than nonshared child cursors. In fact, more often than not, there are few child cursors for each parent cursor. If the parent cursors cannot be shared, it means that the text of SQL statements changes constantly. This happens if either the SQL statements are dynamically generated or literals are used instead of bind variables. In general, dynamically generated SQL statements cannot be avoided. On the other hand, it is usually possible to use bind variables. Unfortunately, it is not always good to use them. The following discussion of the pros and cons of bind variables will help you understand when it is good and not so good to use them.

Bind Variables

Bind variables impact applications in two ways. First, from a development point of view, they make programming either easier or more difficult (or more precisely, more or less code must be written). In this case, the effect depends on the application programming interface used to execute the SQL statements. For example, if you are programming PL/SQL code, it is easier to execute them with bind variables. On the other hand, if you are programming in Java with JDBC, it is easier to execute SQL statements without bind variables. Second, from a performance point of view, bind variables introduce both an advantage and a disadvantage.

Note In the following sections, you'll see some execution plans. I'll explain how to obtain and interpret execution plans in Chapter 6. You might consider returning to this chapter later if something is not clear.

Advantage

The advantage of bind variables is that they allow the sharing of cursors in the library cache and that way avoid hard parses and the overhead associated with them. The following example, which is an excerpt of the output generated by the script bind_variables.sql, shows three INSERT statements that, thanks to bind variables, share the same cursor in the library cache:

```
SQL> variable n NUMBER

SQL> variable v VARCHAR2(32)

SQL> execute :n := 1; :v := 'Helicon';

SQL> INSERT INTO t (n, v) VALUES (:n, :v);

SQL> execute :n := 2; :v := 'Trantor';

SQL> INSERT INTO t (n, v) VALUES (:n, :v);

SQL> execute :n := 3; :v := 'Kalgan';

SQL> INSERT INTO t (n, v) VALUES (:n, :v);
```

```
SQL> SELECT sql_id, child_number, executions
  2  FROM v$sql
  3  WHERE sql_text = 'INSERT INTO t (n, v) VALUES (:n, :v)';

SQL_ID         CHILD_NUMBER EXECUTIONS
-------------- ------------ ----------
6cvmu7dwnvxwj            0          3
```

There are, however, situations where several child cursors are created even with bind variables. The following example shows such a case. Notice that the INSERT statement is the same as in the previous example. Only the maximum size of the VARCHAR2 variable has changed (from 32 to 33).

```
SQL> variable v VARCHAR2(33)

SQL> execute :n := 4; :v := 'Terminus';

SQL> INSERT INTO t (n, v) VALUES (:n, :v);

SQL> SELECT sql_id, child_number, executions
  2  FROM v$sql
  3  WHERE sql_text = 'INSERT INTO t (n, v) VALUES (:n, :v)';

SQL_ID         CHILD_NUMBER EXECUTIONS
-------------- ------------ ----------
6cvmu7dwnvxwj            0          3
6cvmu7dwnvxwj            1          1
```

The new child cursor (1) is created because the execution environment between the first three INSERT statements and the fourth has changed. The mismatch, as can be confirmed by querying the view v$sql_shared_cursor, is because of the bind variables.

```
SQL> SELECT child_number, bind_mismatch
  2  FROM v$sql_shared_cursor
  3  WHERE sql_id = '6cvmu7dwnvxwj';

CHILD_NUMBER BIND_MISMATCH
------------ -------------
           0 N
           1 Y
```

What happens is that the database engine applies the *bind variable graduation*. The aim of this feature is to minimize the number of child cursors by graduating bind variables (which vary in size) into four groups depending on their size. The first group contains the bind variables with up to 32 bytes, the second contains the bind variables between 33 and 128 bytes, the third contains the bind variables between 129 and 2,000 bytes, and the last contains the bind variables of more than 2,000 bytes. Bind variables of datatype NUMBER are graduated to their maximum length, which is 22 bytes. As the following example shows, the view v$sql_bind_metadata displays the maximum size of a group. Notice how the value 128 is used, even if the variable of child cursor 1 was defined as 33.

```
SQL> SELECT s.child_number, m.position, m.max_length,
  2            decode(m.datatype,1,'VARCHAR2',2,'NUMBER',m.datatype) AS datatype
  3  FROM v$sql s, v$sql_bind_metadata m
  4  WHERE s.sql_id = '6cvmu7dwnvxwj'
  5  AND s.child_address = m.address
  6  ORDER BY 1, 2;

CHILD_NUMBER   POSITION MAX_LENGTH DATATYPE
------------ ---------- ---------- ----------------------------------------
           0          1         22 NUMBER
           0          2         32 VARCHAR2
           1          1         22 NUMBER
           1          2        128 VARCHAR2
```

It goes without saying that each time a new child cursor is created, an execution plan is generated. Whether this new execution plan is equal to the one used by another child cursor also depends on the value of the bind variables. This is described in the next section.

Disadvantage

The disadvantage of using bind variables in WHERE clauses is that crucial information is hidden from the query optimizer. In fact, for the query optimizer, it is much better to have literals instead of bind variables. With literals, it is able to improve its estimations. This is especially true when it checks whether a value is outside the range of available values (that is, lower than the minimum value or higher than the maximum value stored in the column) and when it takes advantage of histograms. To illustrate, let's take a table t with 1,000 rows that store, in the column id, the values between 1 (the minimum value) and 1,000 (the maximum value):

```
SQL> SELECT count(id), count(DISTINCT id), min(id), max(id) FROM t;

 COUNT(ID) COUNT(DISTINCTID)    MIN(ID)    MAX(ID)
---------- ----------------- ---------- ----------
      1000              1000          1       1000
```

When a user selects all rows that have an id of less than 990, the query optimizer knows (thanks to object statistics) that about 99 percent of the table is selected. Therefore, it chooses an execution plan with a full table scan. Also notice how the estimated cardinality (column Rows in the execution plan) corresponds to the number of rows returned by the query.

```
SQL> SELECT count(pad) FROM t WHERE id < 990;

COUNT(PAD)
----------
       989
```

```
---------------------------------------------
| Id  | Operation          | Name  | Rows  |
---------------------------------------------
|  0  | SELECT STATEMENT   |       |       |
|  1  |  SORT AGGREGATE    |       |     1 |
|  2  |   TABLE ACCESS FULL|  T    |   990 |
---------------------------------------------
```

When another user selects all rows that have an `id` of less than 10, the query optimizer knows that only about 1 percent of the table is selected. Therefore, it chooses an execution plan with an index scan. Also in this case, notice the good estimation.

```
SQL> SELECT count(pad) FROM t WHERE id < 10;

COUNT(PAD)
----------
         9
```

```
------------------------------------------------------------
| Id  | Operation                   | Name  | Rows  |
------------------------------------------------------------
|  0  | SELECT STATEMENT            |       |       |
|  1  |  SORT AGGREGATE             |       |     1 |
|  2  |   TABLE ACCESS BY INDEX ROWID|  T   |     9 |
|  3  |    INDEX RANGE SCAN         | T_PK  |     9 |
------------------------------------------------------------
```

Whenever dealing with bind variables, the query optimizer used to ignore their values. Thus, good estimations like in the previous examples were not possible. To address this problem, a feature called *bind variable peeking* was introduced in Oracle9*i*.

Caution Bind variables peeking is not supported by the JDBC thin driver distributed with Oracle9*i*. This restriction is documented in MetaLink note 273635.1.

The concept of bind variable peeking is simple. During the physical optimization phase, the query optimizer peeks at the values of bind variables and uses them as literals. The problem with this approach is that the generated execution plan depends on the values provided by the first execution. The following example, which is based on the script `bind_variables_peeking.sql`, illustrates this behavior. Note that the first optimization is performed with the value 990. Consequently, the query optimizer chooses a full table scan. It is this choice, since the cursor is shared (the `sql_id` and the child number are the same), that impacts the second query that uses 10 for the selection.

```
SQL> variable id NUMBER

SQL> execute :id := 990;

SELECT count(pad) FROM t WHERE id < :id;

COUNT(PAD)
----------
       989

SQL_ID  asth1mx10aygn, child number 0

---------------------------------------------
| Id  | Operation           | Name | Rows  |
---------------------------------------------
|   0 | SELECT STATEMENT    |      |       |
|   1 |  SORT AGGREGATE     |      |     1 |
|   2 |   TABLE ACCESS FULL | T    |   990 |
---------------------------------------------

SQL> execute :id := 10;

SQL> SELECT count(pad) FROM t WHERE id < :id;

COUNT(PAD)
----------
         9

SQL_ID  asth1mx10aygn, child number 0

---------------------------------------------
| Id  | Operation           | Name | Rows  |
---------------------------------------------
|   0 | SELECT STATEMENT    |      |       |
|   1 |  SORT AGGREGATE     |      |     1 |
|   2 |   TABLE ACCESS FULL | T    |   990 |
---------------------------------------------
```

Of course, as shown in the following example, if the first execution takes place with the value 10, the query optimizer chooses an execution plan with the index scan—and that, once more, occurs for both queries. Note that to avoid sharing the cursor used for the previous example, the queries were written in lowercase letters.

```
SQL> execute :id := 10;

SQL> select count(pad) from t where id < :id;

COUNT(PAD)
```

```
----------
        9

SQL_ID  7h6n1xkn8trkd, child number 0

-------------------------------------------------------
| Id  | Operation                     | Name  | Rows  |
-------------------------------------------------------
|   0 | SELECT STATEMENT              |       |       |
|   1 |  SORT AGGREGATE               |       |    1  |
|   2 |   TABLE ACCESS BY INDEX ROWID | T     |    9  |
|   3 |    INDEX RANGE SCAN           | T_PK  |    9  |
-------------------------------------------------------

SQL> execute :id := 990;

SQL> select count(pad) from t where id < :id;

COUNT(PAD)
----------
       989

SQL_ID  7h6n1xkn8trkd, child number 0
-------------------------------------------------------
| Id  | Operation                     | Name  | Rows  |
-------------------------------------------------------
|   0 | SELECT STATEMENT              |       |       |
|   1 |  SORT AGGREGATE               |       |    1  |
|   2 |   TABLE ACCESS BY INDEX ROWID | T     |    9  |
|*  3 |    INDEX RANGE SCAN           | T_PK  |    9  |
-------------------------------------------------------
```

It is essential to understand that as long as the cursor remains in the library cache and can be shared, it will be reused. This occurs regardless of the efficiency of the execution plan related to it.

To solve this problem, as of Oracle Database 11g, a new feature called *extended cursor sharing* (also known as *adaptive cursor sharing*) is available. Its purpose is to automatically recognize when the reutilization of an already available cursor leads to inefficient executions. To understand how this feature works, let's start by looking at the content of the view v$sql for the SQL statement used in the previous example. The following new columns are available as of Oracle Database 11g:

is_bind_sensitive indicates not only whether bind variable peeking was used to generate the execution plan but also whether the execution plan depends on the peeked value. If this is the case, the column is set to Y; otherwise, it's set to N.

is_bind_aware indicates whether the cursor is using extended cursor sharing. If yes, the column is set to Y; if not, it's set to N. If set to N, the cursor is obsolete, and it will no longer be used.

is_shareable indicates whether the cursor can be shared. If it can, the column is set to Y; otherwise, it's set to N. If set to N, the cursor is obsolete, and it will no longer be used.

In the following example, the cursor is shareable and sensitive to bind variables, but it is not using extended cursor sharing:

```
SQL> SELECT child_number, is_bind_sensitive, is_bind_aware, is_shareable
  2  FROM v$sql
  3  WHERE sql_id = '7h6n1xkn8trkd'
  4  ORDER BY child_number;

CHILD_NUMBER IS_BIND_SENSITIVE IS_BIND_AWARE IS_SHAREABLE
------------ ----------------- ------------- ------------
           0 Y                 N             Y
```

Something interesting happens when the cursor is executed several times with different values for the bind variable. After a few executions with the values 10 and 990, the information provided by the view v$sql is different. Notice that child number 0 is no longer shareable and that two new child cursors use extended cursor sharing.

```
SQL> SELECT child_number, is_bind_sensitive, is_bind_aware, is_shareable
  2  FROM v$sql
  3  WHERE sql_id = '7h6n1xkn8trkd'
  4  ORDER BY child_number;

CHILD_NUMBER IS_BIND_SENSITIVE IS_BIND_AWARE IS_SHAREABLE
------------ ----------------- ------------- ------------
           0 Y                 N             N
           1 Y                 Y             Y
           2 Y                 Y             Y
```

Looking at the execution plans related to the cursor, as you might expect, you see that one of the new children has an execution plan based on the full table scan, while the other is based on the index scan:

```
SQL_ID  7h6n1xkn8trkd, child number 0


----------------------------------------------
| Id  | Operation                  | Name  |
----------------------------------------------
|   0 | SELECT STATEMENT           |       |
|   1 |  SORT AGGREGATE            |       |
|   2 |   TABLE ACCESS BY INDEX ROWID| T   |
|   3 |    INDEX RANGE SCAN        | T_PK |
----------------------------------------------


SQL_ID  7h6n1xkn8trkd, child number 1
```

```
-------------------------------------
| Id  | Operation          | Name |
-------------------------------------
|   0 | SELECT STATEMENT   |      |
|   1 |  SORT AGGREGATE    |      |
|   2 |   TABLE ACCESS FULL| T    |
-------------------------------------
```

SQL_ID 7h6n1xkn8trkd, child number 2

```
----------------------------------------------
| Id  | Operation                  | Name  |
----------------------------------------------
|   0 | SELECT STATEMENT           |       |
|   1 |  SORT AGGREGATE            |       |
|   2 |   TABLE ACCESS BY INDEX ROWID| T    |
|   3 |    INDEX RANGE SCAN        | T_PK  |
----------------------------------------------
```

To further analyze the reason for the generation of the two child cursors, new dynamic performance views are available: v$sql_cs_statistics, v$sql_cs_selectivity, and v$sql_cs_histogram. The first shows whether peeking was used and the related execution statistics for each child cursor. In the following output, it is possible to confirm that for one execution, the number of rows processed by child cursor 1 is higher than for child cursor 2. Hence, in one case the query optimizer chose a full table scan and in the other an index scan.

```
SQL> SELECT child_number, peeked, executions, rows_processed, buffer_gets
  2  FROM v$sql_cs_statistics
  3  WHERE sql_id = '7h6n1xkn8trkd'
  4  ORDER BY child_number;

CHILD_NUMBER PEEKED EXECUTIONS ROWS_PROCESSED BUFFER_GETS
------------ ------ ---------- -------------- -----------
           0 Y               1             19           3
           1 Y               1            990          19
           2 Y               1             19           3
```

The view v$sql_cs_selectivity shows the selectivity range related to each predicate of each child cursor. In fact, the database engine does not create a new child cursor for each bind variable value. Instead, it groups values together that have about the same selectivity and, consequently, should lead to the same execution plan.

```
SQL> SELECT child_number, predicate, low, high
  2  FROM v$sql_cs_selectivity
  3  WHERE sql_id = '7h6n1xkn8trkd'
  4  ORDER BY child_number;
```

```
CHILD_NUMBER PREDICATE LOW        HIGH
------------ --------- ---------- ----------
           1 <ID       0.890991   1.088989
           2 <ID       0.008108   0.009910
```

In summary, to increase the likelihood that the query optimizer will generate efficient execution plans, you should not use bind variables. Bind variable peeking might help. Unfortunately, it is sometimes a matter of luck whether an efficient execution plan is generated. The only exception is when the new extended cursor sharing of Oracle Database 11g automatically recognizes the problem.

Best Practices

Any feature should be used only if the advantages related to its utilization outweigh the disadvantages. In some situations, it is easy to decide. For example, there is no reason for not using bind variables with SQL statements without a WHERE clause (for example, plain INSERT statements). On the other hand, bind variables should be avoided at all costs whenever histograms provide important information to the query optimizer. Otherwise, there is a high risk of being stung by bind variable peeking. In all other cases, the situation is even less clear. Nevertheless, it is possible to consider two main cases:

SQL statements processing little data: Whenever little data is processed, the parsing time might be close to or even higher than the execution time. In that kind of situation, using bind variables is usually a good thing. This is especially true for SQL statements that are expected to be executed frequently. Typically, such SQL statements are used in data entry systems (commonly referred to as OLTP systems).

SQL statements processing a lot of data: Whenever a lot of data is processed, the parsing time is usually several orders of magnitude less than the execution time. In that kind of situation, using bind variables is not only irrelevant for the whole response time, but it also increases the risk that the query optimizer will generate very inefficient execution plans. Therefore, bind variables should not be used. Typically, such SQL statements are used for batch jobs, for reporting purposes, or, in data warehousing environments, by OLAP tools.

Reading and Writing Blocks

To read and write blocks belonging to data files, the database engine takes advantage of several types of I/O operations (see Figure 2-3):

Logical reads: A server process performs a logical read when it accesses a block that is in the buffer cache. Note that logical reads are used for both reading and writing data to a block.

Physical reads: A server process performs a physical read when it needs a block that is not in the buffer cache yet. Consequently, it opens the data file, reads the block, and stores it in the buffer cache.

Physical writes: Server processes do not perform physical writes. They modify only the blocks that are stored in the buffer cache. Then, the database writer process (which is a background process) is responsible for storing the modified blocks (also called *dirty blocks*) in the data files.

Direct reads: In some particular situations, which I'll describe in Chapter 11, a server process is able to directly read blocks from a data file. When it uses this method, the blocks, instead of being loaded in the buffer cache, are directly transferred to the private memory of the process.

Direct writes: In some particular situations, which I'll describe in Chapter 11, a server process is able to directly write blocks into a data file.

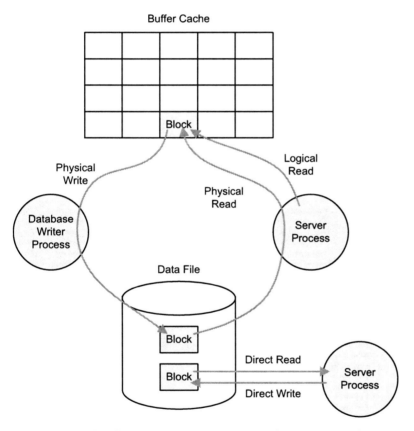

Figure 2-3. *The database engine takes advantage of several types of I/O operations.*

On to Chapter 3

This chapter described the operations carried out by the database engine when parsing and executing SQL statements. Particular attention was given to the pros and cons related to using bind variables. In addition, the chapter introduced some frequently used terms.

Chapter 3 is devoted to answering the first two questions posed in Figure 1-4:

- Where is the time spent?

- How is the time spent?

Simply put, the chapter will describe approaches to finding out where the problem is and what is causing it. Since failing to fix a performance problem is usually not an option, failing to correctly answer these questions is not an option either. Naturally, if you do not know what is causing a problem, you will find it impossible to fix it.

PART 2

■■■

Identification

Let's work the problem, people. Let's not make things worse by guessin'.

—Eugene F. Kranz[1]

The first thing to do when an application experiences performance problems is obvious: identify the root cause of the problem. Unfortunately, all too often this is where the real trouble starts. In a typical scenario where everyone is looking for the source of a performance problem, developers blame the database for poor performance, and the database administrators blame both the developers for misusing the database and the storage subsystem administrators because their very expensive piece of hardware ought to provide much better performance. And as the complexity of the application and infrastructure supporting it increases, so does the mess.

Chapter 3 presents different identification methods applicable to different software layers. The aim of this part is to introduce and employ a methodology that avoids guesswork and that will establish where the bottleneck is beyond any doubt.

---

1. This quote is from the movie *Apollo 13*, directed by Ron Howard. It can be heard about three minutes after the famous line "Houston, we have a problem."

CHAPTER 3

■ ■ ■

Identifying Performance Problems

Too often we hear things like "The database has performance problems!" Sometimes this is true, sometimes it is not. Personally, I have no problem with these kinds of statements. More often than not, however, people make such statements without looking into the problem first. In other words, the problem is arriving at a conclusion without careful analysis. To identify a performance problem, an open-minded approach is absolutely necessary. Instead of judging the actual situation based on opinions, feelings, and preconceptions, we must base our statements on evidence.

The aim of this chapter is to describe an analysis road map that you can use to find out where and how time is spent. In fact, this is the method I use myself when investigating my own customers' performance problems.

Divide and Conquer

Currently multitier architectures are the *de facto* standard in software development for applications needing a database like Oracle. In the simplest cases, at least two tiers (aka client/server) are implemented. Most of the time, there are three: presentation, logic, and data. Figure 3-1 shows a typical infrastructure used to deploy a web application. Frequently, for security or workload management purposes, components are spread over multiple machines as well.

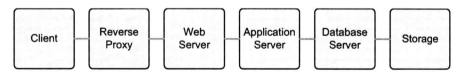

Figure 3-1. *A typical web application consists of several components deployed on multiple systems.*

The analysis of a performance problem should start by collecting end-to-end performance data about the execution of the request you are concerned with (remember, troubleshooting one problem at a time is much easier than troubleshooting a whole system). To be processed with a multitier infrastructure, requests may go through several components. However, not in all situations are all components involved in the processing of a specific request. For example, if caching at the web server level has been activated, a request may be served from the web server without being forwarded to the application server. Of course, the same also applies to an application server or a database server.

Ideally, to fully analyze a performance problem, we should collect detailed information about all components involved in the processing. In some situations, especially when many components are involved, it may be necessary to collect huge amounts of data, which may require significant amounts of time for analysis. For this reason, a *divide-and-conquer* approach is usually the only efficient[1] way to approach a problem. The idea is to start the analysis by breaking up the end-to-end response time into its major components (see Figure 3-2 for an example) and then to gather detailed information only when it makes sense. In other words, you should collect the minimum amount of data necessary to identify the performance problem.

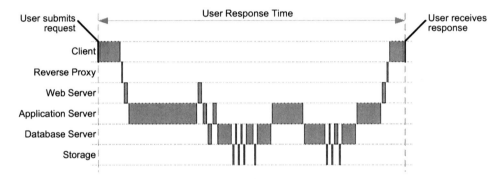

Figure 3-2. *The response time of a request broken up into all major components. Communication delays between components are omitted.*

Once you know which components are involved and how much time is spent by each of them, you can further analyze the problem by selectively gathering additional information only for the most time-consuming components. For example, according to Figure 3-2, you should worry only about the application server and the database server. Fully analyzing components that are responsible for only a very small portion of the response time is pointless.

---

1. While working on a performance problem, not only do you have to optimize the application you are analyzing, but you have to optimize your actions as well. In other words, you should identify and fix the problems as quickly as possible.

Depending on what tools or techniques you use to gather performance data, in many situations you won't be able to fully break up the response time for every component as shown in Figure 3-2. In addition, this is usually not necessary. In fact, even a partial analysis, as shown in Figure 3-3, is useful in order to identify which components may, or may not, be mainly responsible for the response time.

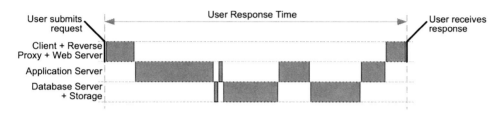

Figure 3-3. *The response time of a request partially broken up by components*

Now that you have seen why it is advisable to use a divide-and-conquer approach for identifying performance problems, let's look at a fairly detailed analysis road map that you can apply to that purpose.

Analysis Road Map

Figure 3-4 summarizes the analysis road map. Here the first analysis is performed either by taking advantage of the instrumentation capabilities of the application or with a concise profiling, typically at the call level, of the application code (as noted in the previous section, no detailed profiling is necessary initially). The aim is to break up the response time into three major categories:

- Application code not running in the database tier

- Database tier and its underlying storage

- All components supporting the application that are not covered in the first two categories (for example, network devices)

If the major time consumer is the application code, the analysis continues by taking a detailed profiling, typically at the line level, to find the component responsible for a large amount of the response time. If that analysis points to a small part of the code, you have found the part that needs tuning, and there is likely a straightforward way of fixing it. Otherwise, if the response time is distributed over a large part of the code, this usually means the problem is due to design decisions and, therefore, complete reengineering could be necessary. If the design itself is not a problem, then it is likely that the machine running the application is undersized.

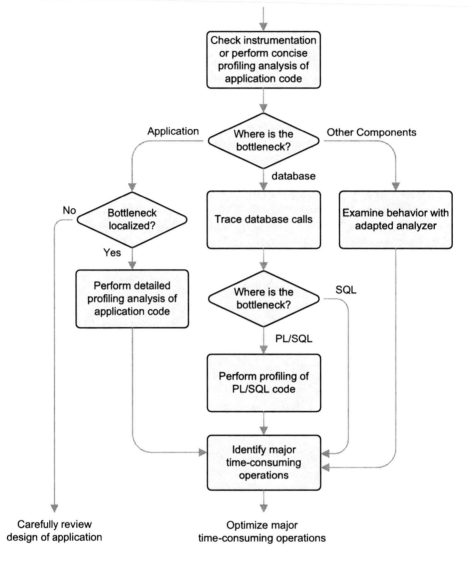

Figure 3-4. *The identification of performance problems consists of several steps that have to be executed in a specific order.*

If the major time consumer is the database, the analysis continues by tracing the database calls. In the first step, the purpose is to find out which kind of statements, either SQL or PL/SQL, are major contributors to the response time. If the analysis points to the SQL statements, then the trace files used in the first place to determine whether the problem is because of SQL or PL/SQL, already contain all the necessary information for a detailed analysis. Otherwise, if the PL/SQL is questioned, a profiling analysis of the PL/SQL code should be performed. The aim and the method used to profile and evaluate the results is basically the same as described earlier for the application code.

TIME MODEL STATISTICS

As of Oracle Database 10g, you are also able to identify which kind of database operation an application is spending most of its time on looking at the *time model statistics*. These are externalized at the instance and session levels through the views v$sys_time_model and v$sess_time_model, respectively. For example, the following query shows how a specific session spent its processing time: 78.8 percent of the time executing PL/SQL code and 20.8 percent of the time executing SQL statements. Notice how the percentages are computed based on the value DB time, which is the overall elapsed time spent processing user calls.

```
SQL> WITH
  2    db_time AS (SELECT sid, value
  3                FROM v$sess_time_model
  4                WHERE sid = 144
  5                AND stat_name = 'DB time')
  6  SELECT stm.stat_name AS statistic,
  7         trunc(stm.value/1000000,3) AS seconds,
  8         trunc(stm.value/tot.value*100,1) AS "%"
  9  FROM v$sess_time_model stm, db_time tot
 10  WHERE stm.sid = tot.sid
 11  AND stm.stat_name <> 'DB time'
 12  AND stm.value > 0
 13  ORDER BY stm.value DESC;

STATISTIC                                           SECONDS     %
--------------------------------------------------- --------  ------
DB CPU                                               15.150    85.5
PL/SQL execution elapsed time                        13.955    78.8
inbound PL/SQL rpc elapsed time                      13.955    78.8
sql execute elapsed time                              3.697    20.8
parse time elapsed                                    0.202     1.1
hard parse elapsed time                               0.198     1.1
connection management call elapsed time               0.025     0.1
```

This possibility is not included in the analysis road map described in Figure 3-4 because it gives only a general overview and, in practice, you need to trace the database calls to know exactly what is happening. In addition, the DB time is only the database processing time. Therefore, the time spent by the database waiting on user calls is not included. In other words, with the information provided by the time model statistics, you cannot know whether the problem is located inside or outside the database.

If the major time consumer is another component, the next step mostly depends on the type of the component. In any case, the idea is always the same: use a tool that provides timing information about what is going on with that specific component. For example, if communication between two machines is very slow, it would be advisable to monitor communication between them with a network analyzer. You could do this, for instance, to check whether the packets take the correct route and not a surprising detour. I will not discuss this type of analysis further since they are not that common and because the investigations are usually not performed by the people who are in charge of the performance of the application.

▓**Note** If you have the chance to use an end-to-end profiler that is able to put together detailed information coming from all tiers, it makes little sense to use this analysis road map. In fact, such profilers can easily break up the response time and drill down through tiers in an easy-to-use graphical user interface. That said, this kind of tool is often not available; therefore, different tools and techniques have to be applied to identify a performance problem. This is where the road map shown in Figure 3-4 is very helpful.

The rest of the chapter, while covering in detail the instrumentation, profiling analysis, and tracing capabilities available in the database engine, also provides examples of tools that you can use to support the analysis. Please notice that many other fine tools providing the same or similar functionalities exist. Although the choice of the tool is not essential, its utilization is. Ultimately the purpose here is to show you how such tools can enhance your ability to quickly and therefore efficiently identify performance problems.

Instrumentation vs. Profiling Analysis

To gather facts about performance problems, basically only the following two methods are available:

Instrumentation: When an application has been properly developed, it is instrumented to provide, among other things, performance figures. In normal circumstances, the instrumentation code is deactivated, or its output is kept to a minimum to spare resources. At runtime, however, it should be possible to activate or increase the amount of information it provides. An example of good instrumentation is Oracle's SQL trace (more about that later in this chapter). By default it is deactivated, but when activated, it delivers trace files containing detailed information about the execution of SQL statements.

Profiling analysis: A profiler is a performance analysis tool that, for a running application, records the executed operations, the time it takes to perform them, and the utilization of system resources (for example, CPU and memory). Some profilers gather data at the call level, others at the line level. The performance data is gathered either by sampling the application state at specified intervals or by automatically instrumenting the code or the executable. Although the overhead associated with the former is much smaller, the data gathered with the latter is much more accurate.

Generally speaking, both methods are needed to investigate performance problems. However, if good instrumentation is available, profiling analysis is less frequently used. Table 3-1 summarizes the pros and cons of these two techniques.

It goes without saying that you can take advantage of instrumentation only when it is available. Unfortunately, in some situations and all too often in practice, profiling analysis is often the only option available.

Table 3-1. *Pros and Cons of Instrumentation and Profiling Analysis*

Technique	Pros	Cons
Instrumentation	Possible to add timing information to key business operations. When available, can be dynamically activated without deploying new code. Context information (for example about the user or the session) can be made available.	Must be manually implemented. Covers single components only; no end-to-end view of response time. Usually, the format of the output depends on the developer who wrote the instrumentation code.
Profiling analysis	Always-available coverage of the whole application. Multitier profilers provide end-to-end view of the response time.	May be expensive, especially for multitier profilers. Cannot always be (quickly) deployed in production. Overhead associated with profilers working at the line level may be very high.

Instrumentation

Simply put, instrumentation code is implemented to externalize the behavior of an application. To identify performance problems, we are particularly interested in knowing which operations are performed, in which order, how much data is being processed, how many times operations are performed, and how much time they take. In some cases (for example, large jobs), it is also useful to know how many resources are used. Since information at the call or line level is already provided by profilers, with instrumentation you should focus particularly on business-relevant operations and on interactions between components (tiers). In addition, if a request needs complex processing inside the same component, it could be wise to provide the response time of the major steps carried out during the processing. In other words, to effectively take advantage of instrumentation code, you should add it to strategic positions in the code.

Let's look at an example. In the application JPetStore, which was briefly introduced in Chapter 1, there is an action called *Sign-on* for which Figure 3-5 shows the sequence diagram. Based on this diagram, the instrumentation should provide at least the following information:

- The system response time of the request from the perspective of the servlet[2] responding to requests (`FrameworkServlet`). This is the business-relevant operation.

- The SQL statement and response time of the interactions between the data access object (`AccountDao`) and the database. This is the interaction between middle tier and database tier.

- Timestamp of beginning and ending of both the request and the interaction with the database.

---

2. A *servlet* is a Java program that responds to requests coming from web clients. It runs in a J2EE application server.

With these values and the user response time, which you can easily measure with a watch if you have access to the application, you can break up the response time in a way similar to Figure 3-3.

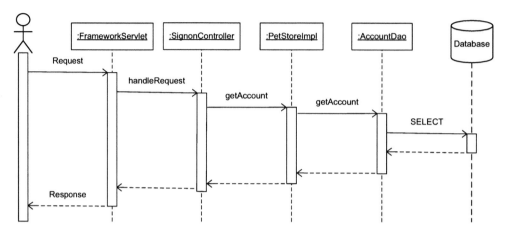

Figure 3-5. *Sequence diagram for the action Sign-on of JPetStore*

In practice, you cannot easily add the instrumentation code wherever you want. In the case of Figure 3-5, you have two problems. The first is that the servlet (FrameworkServlet) is a class provided by the Spring framework. Therefore, you do not want to modify it. The second is that the data access object (AccountDao) is just an interface used by the persistence framework (iBatis in this case). Therefore, you cannot add code to it either. For the first problem, you could create your own servlet that inherits from FrameworkServlet by simply adding the instrumentation code. For the second one, you could decide to instrument the call to the persistence framework for the sake of simplicity. This should not be a problem because the database itself is already instrumented and so, if necessary, you are able to determine the overhead of the persistence framework itself.

Now that you have seen how to decide where the instrumentation code should be added, you can take a look at a concrete example of how to implement it in the application code. Afterward, you will examine an Oracle-specific instrumentation of database calls.

Application Code

As mentioned in Chapter 1, every application should be instrumented. In other words, the question is not whether you should do it but *how* you should do it. This is an important decision that architects should make at the beginning of the development of a new application. Although the instrumentation code is usually implemented by taking advantage of the logging facility used for the rest of the application code, other techniques such as Java Management Extensions (JMX) might be used. If a logging facility is taken into consideration, the most efficient way is to use an already available logging framework. Since it is not easy to write a fast and flexible logging framework, this will actually save quite a lot of development time. In fact, the major drawback of logging is that it can slow down the application if not properly implemented. To avoid this, developers should not only be careful to limit the verbosity of logging but should also implement it with an efficient logging framework.

The Apache Logging Services Project[3] provides very good examples of logging frameworks. The core of the project is log4j, a logging framework written for Java. Because of its success, having been ported to other programming languages like C++, .NET, Perl, PHP, and PL/SQL, I will here provide an example based on log4j and Java. In fact, as for other tools I describe in this chapter, the purpose is to provide you with examples illustrating techniques you can use with other environments as well, not just full in-depth information about one specific tool.

For example, if you want to instrument the response time of the method handleRequest in the servlet SignonController described in Figure 3-5, you could write the following code:

```java
public ModelAndView handleRequest(HttpServletRequest request,
                                  HttpServletResponse response) throws Exception
{
    if (logger == null)
    {
        logger = Log4jLoggingHelper.getLog4jServerLogger();
    }

    if (logger.isInfoEnabled())
    {
      long beginTimeMillis = System.currentTimeMillis();
    }

    ModelAndView ret = null;
    String username = request.getParameter("username");

    // here the code handling the request...

    if (logger.isInfoEnabled())
    {
        long endTimeMillis = System.currentTimeMillis();
        logger.info("Signon(" + username + ") response time " +
                    (endTimeMillis-beginTimeMillis) + " ms");
    }

    return ret;
}
```

Simply put, the instrumentation code, which is highlighted in bold, gets a timestamp when the method begins, gets a timestamp when the method ends, and then logs a message providing the name of the user and the time it took to do it. In addition, it also checks whether the logger has already been initialized. Notice that the class Log4jLoggingHelper is specific to BEA WebLogic, not to log4j. This was used during the test.

---

3. See http://logging.apache.org for additional information.

Even if the code snippet is straightforward, there are some important points to note:

- Start measuring the time, in this case by calling the method `currentTimeMillis`, at the very beginning of the instrumented method. You never know what situations could cause even simple initialization code to consume time.

- The logging framework should support different levels of messages. In the case of log4j, the following levels are available (in increasing order of verbosity): fatal, error, warning, information, and debug. You set the level by calling one of the following methods: `fatal`, `error`, `warn`, `info`, and `debug`. In other words, each level has its own method. By putting messages in different levels, you are able to explicitly choose the verbosity of the logging by enabling or disabling specific levels. This could be useful if you want to enable the instrumentation only while investigating a performance problem.

- Even if the logging facility is aware of which levels the logging is enabled for, it is better to *not* call the logging method, in the example `info`, if the logging for that specific level is *not* enabled. It is usually much faster to check whether the logging for a specific level is enabled by calling a method like `isInfoEnabled` and then call the logging method only if necessary. That can make a huge difference. For example, on my test server, calling `isInfoEnabled` takes about 10 nanoseconds, while calling `info` and providing the parameters as shown in the previous code snippet takes about 350 nanoseconds (I used the class `LoggingPerf.java` to measure these statistics). Another technique for reducing the overhead of instrumentation would be to remove the logging code at compile time. This is, however, not the preferred technique because it is usually not possible to dynamically recompile the code in case the instrumentation is needed. Further, as you have just seen, the overhead of a line of instrumentation that does not generate any message is really very small.

- In this example, the generated message would be something like `Signon(JPS1907) response time 24 ms`. This is good for a human being, but if, for example, you plan on parsing the message with another program in order to check a service level agreement, a more structured form, such as XML, would be more appropriate.

Database Calls

This section describes how to instrument database calls properly in order to give information to the database engine about the application context in which they will be executed. Be aware that this type of instrumentation is very different from what you saw in the previous section. In fact, not only should database calls be instrumented like any other part of the application, but the database itself is also already able to generate detailed information about the database calls it executes. You will see more of this later in this chapter. The aim of the type of instrumentation described here is to provide the database with information about the user or the application using it. This is necessary since the database has generally little, and often no, information about the relationship between application code, sessions, and end users. Consider the following common situations:

- The database does not know which part of the application code is executing SQL statements through a session. For example, the database has no clue about which module, class, or report is running a specific SQL statement through a given session.

- When the application connects to the database through a pool of connections opened with a technical user and proxy users are not utilized, the end-user authentication is usually performed by the application itself. Therefore, the database ignores which end user is using which session.

For these reasons, the database engine provides the opportunity to dynamically associate the following attributes to a database session:

Client identifier: This is a string of 64 characters that identifies a client, albeit not unequivocally.

Client information: This is a string of 64 characters that describes the client.

Module name: This is a string of 48 characters that describes the module currently using the session.

Action name: This is a string of 32 characters that describes the action being processed.

As of Oracle Database 10g, for sessions opened through database links, only the attribute client identifier is automatically propagated to remote sessions. Therefore, in Oracle9*i* and for the other attributes as of Oracle Database 10g, it is necessary to explicitly set them.

Their values are externalized through the view v$session and the context userenv (module name and action name only as of Oracle Database 10g). Note that other views showing SQL statements, for example v$sql, also contain the columns module and action. One word of caution: the attributes are associated to a specific session, but a given SQL statement can be shared between sessions having different module names or action names. The values shown by the dynamic performance views are the ones that were set at parse time in the session that first parsed the SQL statement. This can be misleading if you are not careful.

Now that you have seen what is available, let's take a look at how you can set these values. The first method, PL/SQL, is the only one that doesn't depend on the interface used to connect the database. As a result, it can be used in most situations. The following three—OCI, JDBC, and ODP.NET—can be utilized only along with the specific interface. The main advantage of setting the attributes with these interfaces is that the values are added to the next database call instead of generating extra round-trips, which is what a call to PL/SQL does. Thus, the overhead of setting the attributes with them is negligible.

PL/SQL

To set the client identifier, you use the procedure set_identifier in the package dbms_session. In some situations, such as when the client identifier is used along with a global context and connection pooling, it could be necessary to clear the value associated with a given session. If this is the case, you can use the procedure clear_identifier.

To set the client information, the module name, and the action name, you use the procedures set_client_info, set_module, and set_action in the package dbms_application_info. For simplicity, the procedure set_module accepts not only the module name but also the action name.

The following example, which is an excerpt of the output generated by the script session_info.sql, shows not only how to set the four attributes but also how to query their content with the context userenv and the view v$session:

```
SQL> BEGIN
  2    dbms_session.set_identifier(client_id=>'helicon.antognini.ch');
  3    dbms_application_info.set_client_info(client_info=>'Linux x86_64');
  4    dbms_application_info.set_module(module_name=>'session_info.sql',
  5                                     action_name=>'test session information');
  6  END;
  7  /
```

```
SQL> SELECT sys_context('userenv','client_identifier') AS client_identifier,
  2         sys_context('userenv','client_info') AS client_info,
  3         sys_context('userenv','module') AS module_name,
  4         sys_context('userenv','action') AS action_name
  5  FROM dual;
```

```
CLIENT_IDENTIFIER      CLIENT_INFO    MODULE_NAME        ACTION_NAME
---------------------  -------------  -----------------  -------------------------
helicon.antognini.ch   Linux x86_64   session_info.sql   test session information
```

```
SQL> SELECT client_identifier,
  2         client_info,
  3         module AS module_name,
  4         action AS action_name
  5  FROM v$session
  6  WHERE sid = sys_context('userenv','sid');
```

```
CLIENT_IDENTIFIER      CLIENT_INFO    MODULE_NAME        ACTION_NAME
---------------------  -------------  -----------------  -------------------------
helicon.antognini.ch   Linux x86_64   session_info.sql   test session information
```

OCI

To set the attributes, you use the function OCIAttrSet. The third parameter specifies the value. The fifth parameter specifies, by means of one of the following constants, which attribute is set:

- OCI_ATTR_CLIENT_IDENTIFIER
- OCI_ATTR_CLIENT_INFO
- OCI_ATTR_MODULE
- OCI_ATTR_ACTION

Note that, except for OCI_ATTR_CLIENT_IDENTIFIER, these attributes are available as of Oracle Database 10g only.

The following code snippet shows how to call the function OCIAttrSet to set the attribute client identifier. The C program session_attributes.c provides a complete example.

```
text *client_id = "helicon.antognini.ch";
OCIAttrSet(ses,                         // session handle
           OCI_HTYPE_SESSION,           // type of handle being modified
           client_id,                   // attribute's value
           strlen(client_id),           // size of the attribute's value
           OCI_ATTR_CLIENT_IDENTIFIER,  // attribute being set
           err);                        // error handle
```

JDBC

To set the client identifier, module name, and action name, you use the method setEndToEndMetrics provided by the interface OracleConnection. No support is provided to set the attribute client information. One or more attributes are passed to the method with an array of strings. The position in the array, which is defined by the following constants, determines which attribute is set:

- END_TO_END_CLIENTID_INDEX

- END_TO_END_MODULE_INDEX

- END_TO_END_ACTION_INDEX

The following code snippet shows how to define the array containing the attributes and how to call the method setEndToEndMetrics. The Java class SessionAttributes.java provides a complete example.

```
metrics = new String[OracleConnection.END_TO_END_STATE_INDEX_MAX];
metrics[OracleConnection.END_TO_END_CLIENTID_INDEX] = "helicon.antognini.ch";
metrics[OracleConnection.END_TO_END_MODULE_INDEX] = "SessionAttributes.java";
metrics[OracleConnection.END_TO_END_ACTION_INDEX] = "test session information";
((OracleConnection)connection).setEndToEndMetrics(metrics, (short)0);
```

Note that the method setEndToEndMetrics is available in the JDBC driver as of Oracle Database 10g only and cannot be used with an Oracle9i database. In Oracle9i, you can use the method setClientIdentifier for the client identifier, although this same method has been deprecated in Oracle Database 10g with the introduction of the method setEndToEndMetrics.

ODP.NET

To set the client identifier, you use the property ClientId of the class OracleConnection. For all other attributes, no property is available. However, ODP.NET sets the module name automatically to the name of the executing assembly. ClientId is set to null when the method Close is called in order to prevent pooled connections from taking over ClientId settings. Note that this property is available as of Oracle Database 10g Release 2 only.

The following code snippet shows how to set the property `ClientId`. The C# class `SessionAttributes.cs` provides a complete example.

```
connection.ClientId = "helicon.antognini.ch";
```

Profiling Application Code

Every good development environment should provide an integrated profiler. Most of them do. The main problem is that not all profilers can be used in all situations. Either they do not support all components in the software stack or they simply do not support a required gathering mode. As a result, in practice it can happen that a profiler is used that is not integrated with the development environment. This is particularly true if you are not dealing with a client/server application.

Here are the key functionalities a profiler should provide:

- The ability to support distributed applications, such as J2EE components running on different servers. Note that this does not mean it should support end-to-end profiling analysis. It simply means that it has the ability to enable the profiler independently of where the code is executed.

- The ability to perform both call-level and line-level profiling analysis. The former is needed for concise profiling, the latter for detailed profiling.

- The ability to selectively enable or disable the profiler for part of the application code or for specific requests only. This is especially important for line-level profiling analysis.

The main purpose of the last two points is to avoid the higher overhead associated with a line-level profiler whenever possible. In fact, as described earlier in the section "Analysis Roadmap," line-level profiling analysis should be used only when either instrumentation or profiling analysis at the call level pinpoints a specific part of the code. This is especially important when the profiling analysis is directly performed on a production system already experiencing a lack of resources.

In the next two sections, you will examine two products that meet the requirements listed earlier. The first one is a profiler at the call level that supports, to some extent, end-to-end profiling analysis. The second one is a profiler used for gathering more detailed information for a specific part of the code. Remember, tools are not essential; techniques are. They are described here only to give you an idea of what such tools can do for you. If you are confronted with other tools in practical situations, this is not a problem. The principles are the same. To demonstrate this, the sample application JPetStore will be used again.

Concise Profiling

The profiler briefly described in this section, PerformaSure of Quest Software, is a J2EE performance diagnosis tool for analyzing transactions in distributed environments. It provides an end-to-end transaction-centric view of performance as experienced by end users. Even if it provides full details only for the Java stack, it allows for the breaking up of request response time for all components processing it. PerformaSure is very easy to use, and it has broad support for the most important operating systems, web servers, and application servers.

PerformaSure has been singled out here simply because of positive personal experience when using it to analyze performance problems for my own customers. Similar tools on the market, to name only a few, are Optimizeit Enterprise Suite (Borland), Vantage Analyzer (Compuware Corporation), dynaTrace Diagnostics (dynaTrace software), Grid Control (Oracle Corporation), and i^3 (Symantec Corporation).

PerformaSure Components

PerformaSure has three main components: the agents, the Nexus, and the Workstation.

The agents gather performance figures and send them to the Nexus. Since gathering profile information depends on the monitored component, three different agents are available:

- A *system agent* gathers performance figures about the operating system, such as the utilization of CPU, memory, disks, and network. It is deployed once for every machine.

- A *web server agent* gathers performance figures about a web server. For example, it gathers the requested pages and, for each page, the response time and the number of hits. It is deployed once for every web server.

- An *application server agent* gathers detailed performance figures about an application server, such as the number of active sessions, the response time and invocation rate of each servlet, the executed SQL statements, and the memory usage of the Java virtual machine. It is deployed once for every application server.

Each type of agent uses vendor-provided APIs to gather the performance figures about the monitored component. In addition, the application server agent uses bytecode instrumentation to gather call-level performance figures.

BYTECODE INSTRUMENTATION

Most of the time during the compilation of Java code, no native machine code is generated. In other words, no executable is available after the compilation. Instead, bytecode, which has to be interpreted by a Java virtual machine, is generated. This is what makes Java applications portable.

The aim of bytecode instrumentation is to inject code into an already compiled Java application. For example, if you want to know how much time it takes to execute a specific method, conceptually the original method is renamed, and in its place, a wrapper is injected that calls the original method and also contains instrumentation code.

The Nexus is the central component of PerformaSure. While gathering profiling information, not only does it store the performance figures received from the agents, but most important it reconstructs the end-to-end execution path for each request. When the gathering is over, the Nexus is used by the Workstation as an analysis engine.

The Workstation is the presentation tool of PerformaSure. It is used not only to manage and analyze the gathered data but also to start and stop the gathering of data and to manage users. To carry out the analysis, it provides different browsers.

Figure 3-6 shows how the different components are deployed in my test environment. On each of the three load-testing clients and on the server, there is a system agent (S). On the web server and application server, there is a web server agent (W) and an application server agent (A), respectively. The Nexus and the Workstation are installed on a separate machine. To stress the application with a real load, a load-testing tool called the Grinder is installed.

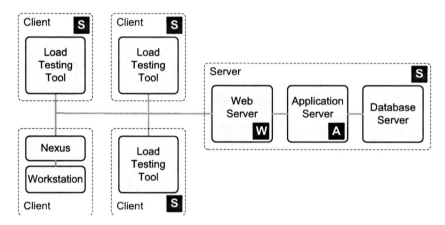

Figure 3-6. *Deployment of PerformaSure on the test infrastructure*

PerformaSure is not a monitoring tool. With it you cannot check the load on a system directly. Instead, the load has to be recorded for an interval of time, and when the recording is finished, the recorded information is analyzed through the Workstation. These two phases, the recording and the analysis, are further discussed in the next two sections.

THE GRINDER

The Grinder is a Java load-testing framework that is able, among other things, to simulate web browsers. Through a graphical console it is possible to coordinate several worker processes distributed over multiple machines. To generate the load, each worker process executes Jython test scripts in one or multiple threads. For the simulation used here, as shown in Figure 3-6, worker processes were started on three machines. On each of them, 10 worker processes each executing 10 threads were started. Basically, with such a configuration, 300 concurrent users working with JPetStore were simulated. It might seem like 100 users per machine is a very high number and hence that the client machines should be very big. In reality, a typical web user not only consumes little CPU time on the client but it also has a limited network bandwidth.

The Jython test scripts used for the load testing can be generated through a TCP Proxy, which is also provided by the framework. With it, the requests performed by real users are recorded and supplied as test scripts. In addition to the requests themselves, the test scripts also reproduce sleep intervals between requests and handle session information such as cookies. Naturally, you can modify the test scripts generated through the TCP Proxy to better simulate a real load. For example, my test script was recorded with a single account, but my database for JPetStore contains 100,000 accounts. To get around this, I modified the test script to randomly choose which account each thread has to use to perform the Sign-on action.

The Grinder is available under a BSD-style open-source license. For additional information, refer to http://grinder.sourceforge.net.

Recording a Session

Depending on where PerformaSure is used and on the amount of required information, you can configure it to record more or less data. This will have a direct impact on the overhead associated with the gathering. For example, if you are starting a new investigation on a production system, it makes sense to start by gathering relatively little information and, unless you know exactly what you are looking for, to gather information only about a selected number of requests. Remember, as discussed in Chapter 1, you need to know what the problems that you are investigating are. Then, based on this initial analysis, you can decide whether it is necessary to gather more in-depth information for all or only part of the system.

With PerformaSure, you can determine the amount of gathered information using these techniques:

- A recording level specifies which application classes are instrumented. Two levels are provided: component detail, which is the default, and full detail. With component detail, only a predefined set of core classes are instrumented. With full detail, all classes are instrumented.

- In addition to the recording level, specific classes or packages can be explicitly included or excluded from the instrumentation.

- When the number of requests entering the system is very high or when the recording interval is long, it isn't worth it to record every single request. In such cases, it is possible to perform sampling over the requests entering the system.

- Filtering between the agents and the Nexus can be activated to explicitly include or exclude specific requests. Such a filter is implemented by applying a regular expression to the URL of the requests.

In addition to reducing the amount of gathered information, the Nexus aggregates requests into time slices. The length of a time slice is configurable to a value between 1 second and 30 minutes. It is best to choose a length that provides a few hundred time slices. For example, if the recording lasts a few minutes, something in the range of 1–10 seconds could be fine. On the other hand, if the recording lasts one hour, something in the range of 30–60 seconds could be more appropriate.

For the recording of the session dealt with in the next section, I used a time slice of one second (the recording lasted five minutes), and I chose the component detail level. Note that I didn't define filtering of any kind for classes or requests.

Analyzing a Session

The analysis should start by examining the response time of the actions you are investigating. If you are not focusing on a specific request, which is not a good thing, you could take a look at the requests that on average take more time. For instance, Figure 3-7 shows the requests executed over 50 seconds, close to the beginning of the session. For each request, from left to right in Figure 3-7, the URL, the number of calls, the average response time, the maximum response time, and the total response time for all calls are shown. In this first overview, it is interesting to note the graphical representation for the average and total response time.

Two different colors (here shown in two shades of gray) are used for the two tiers involved in the processing: application tier and database tier. By moving the mouse over that graphical representation, you can obtain details about the time spent in the two tiers. For the slowest request (the action Sign-on), on average, 91.3 percent of the 781 milliseconds has been spent by the application tier and 8.7 percent by the database tier.

Name	Call Count	Avg Cumulative Time (s / req)	Max Cumulative Time (s)	Total Cumulative Time (s)
POST /jpetstore/shop/signon.do	290	0.781	1.867	226.557
GET /jpetstore/shop/viewProduct.do	270	0.163	1.084	44.123
POST /jpetstore/shop/searchProducts.do	49	0.153	0.643	7.512
GET /jpetstore/shop/viewCategory.do	137	0.129	1.501	17.677
GET /jpetstore/shop/viewItem.do	354	0.104	1.380	36.859
GET /jpetstore/shop/index.do	422	0.043	0.848	18.242
GET /jpetstore/shop/signonForm.do	280	0.042	0.860	11.851
GET /jpetstore/shop/listOrders.do	231	0.036	0.835	8.225
GET /jpetstore/shop/viewOrder.do	205	0.030	0.848	6.143
GET /jpetstore/shop/editAccount.do	270	0.023	0.824	6.143
GET /jpetstore	250	< 0.001	0.013	0.042
GET /_0sfdata/1	53	0.000	0.000	0.000

Figure 3-7. *Overview of the response time for all requests*

If you compare the response time provided by Figure 3-7 with the goals described in Table 1-1, you can see that the required performance figures are attained for all actions except for Sign-on. In such a case, the analysis should focus on the response time of this particular action only. This is exactly what Figure 3-8 shows: for each time slice (for each second in this case), a stacked bar shows how much time, on average, has been spent processing that specific action for all requests completed within that specific interval. This chart uses the same colors as Figure 3-7 to break up the response time between tiers. For example, for the selected (by the *slider*) time slice, the response time is 819 milliseconds, 86.5 percent of which is in the application tier and 13.5 percent in the database tier.

If necessary, you could also correlate the response time of a request with one of the many metrics gathered during the recording. Figure 3-9 shows the response time of the action Sign-on compared to the total number of requests processed by the system, the number of SQL statements executed by the database, and the load of the CPU of the server, all for the very same interval.

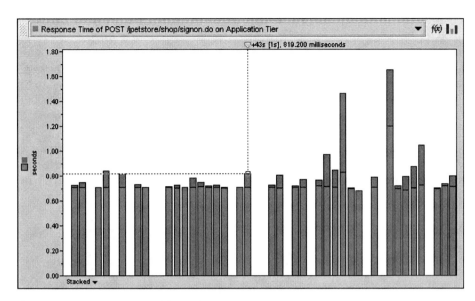

Figure 3-8. *Response time of the action Sign-on*

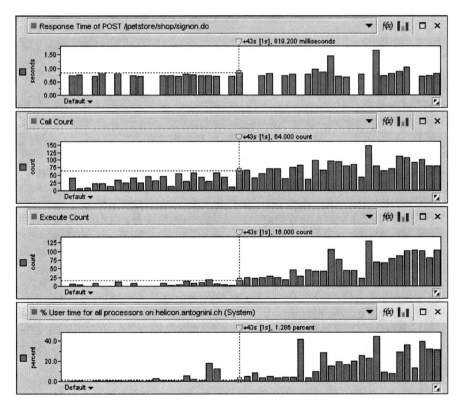

Figure 3-9. *Correlation of the response time for the action Sign-on with other metrics*

In practice, these correlations are of secondary interest, compared with getting detailed information about the execution of a specific request. For this purpose, it is also possible to see which operations are executed during the processing of a request or a time slice. This is called the *request tree*. Figure 3-10 shows the request tree of the action Sign-on. The root of the tree, which is called the entry point and in this case is an HTTP request, is on the left. The other nodes are either classes or SQL statements executed during the processing. Notice how for each class or SQL statement, you can see the executed methods. You can also see that the request is processed by a servlet with the method doPost, which in turn uses a database connection to execute one query. In this case, colors are also important. They show which tier an operation has been executed from, and they are used to highlight which operations are mainly responsible for the response time. A glance at the request tree should be enough to know which part of the application is slowing down the processing.

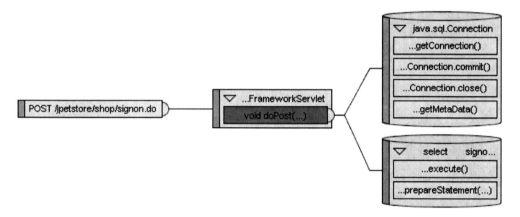

Figure 3-10. *Request tree of the action Sign-on*

By moving the mouse over the request, you can obtain details about each operation. Figure 3-11 shows the details for the method doPost and for the SQL statement. For a method, the response time and the number of executions per request are provided. For a SQL statement, the text of the SQL statement itself, the response time, and the number of executions per request are provided. In the request tree, it is also possible to show how many times a SQL statement was parsed and executed by looking at the number of executions of the methods prepareStatement and execute, respectively. This is very useful, since it is not unusual to see cases where specific SQL statements are unnecessarily parsed or executed over and over again.

In summary, checking the information provided by PerformaSure (Figure 3-7), you'll discover that on average a request for the action Sign-on took 781 milliseconds. From Figure 3-11, the largest part was taken by the method doPost: 774 milliseconds. The rest was spent by other operations. The SQL statement shown in Figure 3-11 took 3 milliseconds on average, for example. Since the bottleneck is clearly localized in the application tier, using the road map (Figure 3-4) as a guide, you can see that a detailed profiling analysis of the application at the line level is needed. This will be covered in the next section.

JDBC: select signon.username as userid, account.
email, account.firstname, account.
lastname, account.status, account.
addr1, account.addr2, account.city,
account.state, account.zip, account.
country, account.phone, profile.
langpref, profile.favcategory, profile.
mylistopt, profile.banneropt, bannerdata.
bannername from account, profile, signon,
bannerdata where account.userid = ? and
signon.password = ? and signon.username =
account.userid and profile.userid = account.
userid and profile.favcategory = bannerdata.
favcategory

Spring:	org.springframework.web.servlet.FrameworkServlet
	void doPost(HttpServletRequest, HttpServletResponse)

Tier: Application Tier

Time:

Avg Cumulative Time	0.774 s / req
Max Cumulative Time	1.390 s / req
Min Cumulative Time	0.661 s / req
Avg Exclusive Time	0.706 s / req

Counts:

Avg Call Count	1.000 / req
Called In Requests	290
Avg Exceptional Exits	-
Incomplete	-

Tier: Database Tier

Time:

Avg Cumulative Time	0.003 s / req
Max Cumulative Time	-
Min Cumulative Time	-
Avg Exclusive Time	0.003 s / req

Counts:

Avg Call Count	2.000 / req
Called In Requests	290
Avg Exceptional Exits	-
Incomplete	-

Figure 3-11. *Details for the action doPost and one SQL statement executed during the action Sign-on*

Detailed Profiling

Unfortunately, PerformaSure cannot help you with detailed profiling. In fact, it does not support line-level profiling. You'll need another tool. Quest Software proposes JProbe for this purpose, which includes Java tools for profiling code and analyzing memory allocation and code coverage. Note that PerformaSure and JProbe are only marginally integrated.

The next sections briefly describe the components constituting JProbe and how to record a session and analyze the gathered information.

JProbe Components

JProbe has two main components: the Analysis Engine and the Console. The Analysis Engine, which runs inside the Java virtual machine of the application, gathers profiling data with the Java Virtual Machine Tool Interface (JVMTI)[4] and sends it to the Console. In addition to providing the functionalities for enabling and disabling recording, you can use the JProbe Console for analyzing the gathered profiling data. As Figure 3-12 shows, in order to support distributed environments, JProbe separates the gathering and the presentation layers.

Note that to take full advantage of JVMPI, the Java code should be compiled with full debug information.

---

4. The JVMTI is a new interface available as of J2SE 1.5.0. Up to J2SE 1.4.2, JProbe uses the Java Virtual Machine Profiler Interface (JVMPI) instead.

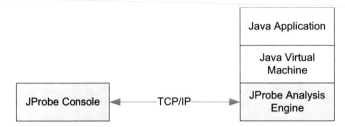

Figure 3-12. *The JProbe components: the Analysis Engine and the Console*

Recording a Session

With JProbe, you want to gather detailed information about a small part of the application. For this purpose, it is usually not necessary to stress the application with a real load. It is much better to manually execute the action to be profiled once or several times. In this case, the action Sign-on was executed just once while the recording was active.

Since in the previous section you already performed a concise profiling, you have also partially identified the performance problem. You can now limit the analysis to the classes shown in Figure 3-13:

- All methods the class identified by PerformaSure: `FrameworkServlet`. Notice that this class is part of the Spring framework. Because of this, only a method-level profiling analysis should be done.

- All classes in the package `org.springframework.samples.jpetstore`, which is the application code. For this part, a line-level profiling analysis is performed.

Data Collection Filters (package.class.method())	Action
☑ *.*.*()	Encapsulated
☑ org.springframework.web.servlet.FrameworkServlet.*()	Method Level
☑ org.springframework.samples.jpetstore.*.*()	Line Level

Figure 3-13. *JProbe allows for the selection of the classes and methods you need to profile data.*

Remember, limiting the scope of a profiling analysis is important to avoid unnecessary overhead, especially when you are dealing with line-level profiling analysis and CPU-bound operations.

Analyzing a Session

The analysis of a session starts by examining a call graph like the one shown in Figure 3-14. Basically, it is a much more detailed representation of Figure 3-10. With the zoom capabilities of the JProbe Console, it is also possible to get a more readable call graph. Like in PerformaSure, colors play an important role, highlighting the most time-consuming operations. In this way, even large call graphs can be effectively handled.

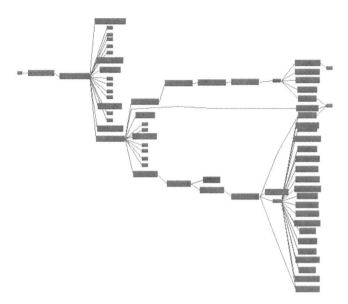

Figure 3-14. *Overall call graph for the action Sign-on*

To further simplify the analysis, a feature called Show Only Focus Path can automatically prune all calls that are not directly related to the most time-consuming calls. By applying it to the overall call graph (Figure 3-14), you get the resulting call graph and related statistics (Figure 3-15). The following information can be extracted:

- The method FrameworkServlet.doPost, as you have already seen with PerformaSure, receives the request. The processing takes about 0 milliseconds.

- The method FrameworkServlet.processRequest is called from the method FrameworkServlet.doPost. The processing takes about 2 milliseconds, which is about 0.3 percent of the overall response time.

- The method SignonController.handleRequest is called from the method FrameworkServlet.processRequest. The processing takes about 0 milliseconds.

- The method PetStoreFacade.getAccount is called from the method SignonController.handleRequest. The processing takes about 1 millisecond, which is about 0.1 percent of the overall response time.

- The method PetStoreImpl.getAccount is called from the method PetStoreFacade.getAccount. The processing takes about 0 milliseconds.

- The method Thread.sleep is called from the method PetStoreImpl.getAccount. The processing takes about 668 milliseconds, which is about 96.3 percent of the response time.

To locate the piece of code where the method sleep is called, you can view the source code and the statistics at line level of the method getAccount, as shown in Figure 3-16.

| FrameworkServlet doPost [0] | → | FrameworkServlet processRequest [2] | → | SignonController. handleRequest [0] □ | → | PetStoreFacade getAccount [1] | → | PetStoreImpl. getAccount [0] □ | → | Thread sleep [668] |

Name	Number of Calls	Cumulative ▾ Time	Method Time
FrameworkServlet.doPost(HttpServletRequest, HttpServletResponse)	1	694 (100.0%)	0 (0.0%)
FrameworkServlet.processRequest(HttpServletRequest, HttpServletResponse)	1	694 (100.0%)	2 (0.3%)
SignonController.handleRequest(HttpServletRequest, HttpServletResponse)	1	692 (99.7%)	0 (0.0%)
PetStoreFacade.getAccount(String, String)	1	671 (96.7%)	1 (0.1%)
PetStoreImpl.getAccount(String, String)	1	671 (96.6%)	0 (0.0%)
Thread.sleep(long)	1	668 (96.3%)	668 (96.3%)

Figure 3-15. *Call graph and related statistics for the critical path only*

Line # ▲	Number of Calls	Method Time	Cumulative Time	Source
105				public Account getAccount(String username, String password) {
106				// ***** lines added to slowdown the action sign-on
107				try {
108	1	0 (59.0%)	668 (99.6%)	java.lang.Thread.sleep(666);
109				}
110				catch (InterruptedException e) {
111	1	0 (13.1%)	0 (0.0%)	}
112				// *****
113	1	0 (27.9%)	3 (0.4%)	return this.accountDao.getAccount(username, password);
114				}

Figure 3-16. *Line-level statistics of the method* getAccount

In this case, I added the specific call to Thread.sleep to the original JPetStore application to simply slow down the action Sign-on. Be aware that this is an artificial example. In a real case, the profiler would point out, for example, a part of code executed over and over again because of a loop, a pause for accessing a synchronization point, or a call taking a long time. It is nevertheless useful to note that in our albeit artificial example, it was possible to quickly find not only the slowest action but also which lines of code were leading to this behavior.

Tracing Database Calls

Based on our road map described in Figure 3-4, if instrumentation or concise profiling analysis suggests that the bottleneck is situated in the database, it is necessary to take a closer look at the interactions between the application and the database. The Oracle database engine is a highly instrumented piece of software, and thanks to a feature called *SQL trace*, it is able to provide detailed trace files containing not only a list of executed SQL statements but also in-depth performance figures about their processing.

Figure 3-17 shows the essential phases involved in the tracing of database calls. The next sections, following an explanation of what SQL trace is, discuss each of these phases in detail.

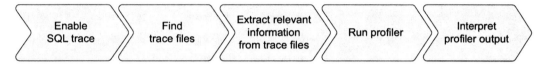

Figure 3-17. *Essential phases involved in the tracing of database calls*

SQL Trace

As described in Chapter 2, to process a SQL statement, the database engine (specifically, the SQL engine) carries out database calls (parse, execute, and fetch). For each database call, as summarized in Figure 3-18, the SQL engine either

- does some processing itself, by using CPU;

- makes use of other resources (for example, a disk); or

- has to go through a synchronization point needed to guarantee the multiuser capabilities of the database engine (for example, a latch).

The aim of SQL trace is twofold: first, to provide information in order to break up the response time between service time and wait time, and second, to give detailed information about the used resources and synchronization points. All this information regarding each interaction between the SQL engine and the other components is written in a trace file. Note that in Figure 3-18 the attribution of CPU, resource X, and synchronization point Y are artificial. The reason for this is to show that every call may use the database engine differently.

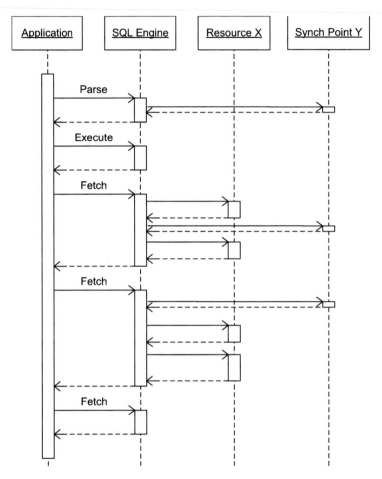

Figure 3-18. *Sequence diagram describing the interactions between the SQL engine and other components*

Although this will be covered in greater detail later in this chapter, let's briefly look at an example of the kind of information that is provided by SQL trace and that can be extracted by a tool (in this case, TKPROF). This includes the text of the SQL statement, some execution statistics, the waits occurred during the processing, and information about the parsing phase such as the generated execution plan. Note that such information is provided for each SQL statement executed by the application and recursively by the database engine itself.

```
SELECT CUST_ID, EXTRACT(YEAR FROM TIME_ID), SUM(AMOUNT_SOLD)
FROM SH.SALES
WHERE CHANNEL_ID = :B1
GROUP BY CUST_ID, EXTRACT(YEAR FROM TIME_ID)
```

call	count	cpu	elapsed	disk	query	current	rows
Parse	1	0.00	0.00	0	0	0	0
Execute	1	0.00	0.00	0	0	0	0
Fetch	164	1.12	1.90	2588	1720	0	16348
total	166	1.13	1.90	2588	1720	0	16348

```
Misses in library cache during parse: 0
Optimizer mode: ALL_ROWS
Parsing user id: 28  (SH)   (recursive depth: 1)


Rows   Row Source Operation
------ ---------------------------------------------------
 16348 HASH GROUP BY
540328  PARTITION RANGE ALL PARTITION: 1 28
540328   TABLE ACCESS FULL SALES PARTITION: 1 28
```

```
Elapsed times include waiting on following events:
  Event waited on                         Times   Max. Wait  Total Waited
  ----------------------------------------  Waited  ----------  ------------
  db file sequential read                   30     0.01       0.07
  db file scattered read                   225     0.02       0.64
  direct path write temp                   941     0.00       0.00
  direct path read temp                    941     0.01       0.05
```

As I have said, the previous sample is generated by a tool named TKPROF. It is not the output generated by SQL trace. In fact, SQL trace outputs text files storing raw information about the interactions between components. Here is an excerpt of the trace file related to the previous sample. Generally, for each call or wait, there is at least one line in the trace file.

```
...
...
PARSING IN CURSOR #1 len=142 dep=1 uid=28 oct=3 lid=28 tim=1156387084566620
hv=1624534809 ad='6f8a7620'
SELECT CUST_ID, EXTRACT(YEAR FROM TIME_ID), SUM(AMOUNT_SOLD) FROM SH.SALES
WHERE CHANNEL_ID = :B1 GROUP BY CUST_ID, EXTRACT(YEAR FROM TIME_ID)
END OF STMT
PARSE #1:c=0,e=93,p=0,cr=0,cu=0,mis=0,r=0,dep=1,og=1,tim=1156387084566617
BINDS #1:
kkscoacd
 Bind#0
  oacdty=02 mxl=22(21) mxlc=00 mal=00 scl=00 pre=00
  oacflg=03 fl2=1206001 frm=00 csi=00 siz=24 off=0
  kxsbbbfp=2a9721f070 bln=22  avl=02  flg=05
  value=3
```

```
EXEC #1:c=1000,e=217,p=0,cr=0,cu=0,mis=0,r=0,dep=1,og=1,tim=1156387084566889
WAIT #1: nam='db file sequential read' ela= 19333 file#=4 block#=211 blocks=1
obj#=10293 tim=1156387084610301
WAIT #1: nam='db file sequential read' ela= 2962 file#=4 block#=219 blocks=1
obj#=10294 tim=1156387084613517
...
...
WAIT #2: nam='SQL*Net message from client' ela= 978 driver id=1413697536 #bytes=1
p3=0 obj#=10320 tim=1156387086475763
STAT #1 id=1 cnt=16348 pid=0 pos=1 obj=0 op='HASH GROUP BY (cr=1720 pr=2588 pw=941
time=1830257 us)'
STAT #1 id=2 cnt=540328 pid=1 pos=1 obj=0 op='PARTITION RANGE ALL PARTITION: 1 28
(cr=1720 pr=1647 pw=0 time=1129471 us)'
STAT #1 id=3 cnt=540328 pid=2 pos=1 obj=10292 op='TABLE ACCESS FULL SALES PARTITION:
1 28 (cr=1720 pr=1647 pw=0 time=635959 us)'
WAIT #0: nam='SQL*Net message to client' ela= 1 driver id=1413697536 #bytes=1 p3=0
obj#=10320 tim=1156387086475975
```

In this excerpt, some tokens describing the kind of information that is provided are high-lighted in bold:

- PARSING IN CURSOR and END OF STMT enclose the text of the SQL statement.

- PARSE, EXEC, and FETCH for parse, execution, and fetch calls, respectively.

- BINDS for the definition and value of bind variables.

- WAIT for the wait events that occurred during the processing.

- STAT for the execution plans that occurred and associated statistics.

You can find a short description of the trace files' format in MetaLink note *Interpreting Raw SQL_TRACE and DBMS_SUPPORT.START_TRACE output* (39817.1). If you are interested in a detailed description and discussion of this topic, Millsap/Holt's book *Optimizing Oracle Performance* (O'Reilly, 2003) is worth reading.

Internally, SQL trace is based on debugging event 10046. Table 3-2 describes the supported levels, which define the amount of information provided in trace files. When SQL trace is used at a level higher than 1, it is also called *extended SQL trace*.

Table 3-2. *Levels of the Debugging Event 10046*

Level	Description
0	The debugging event is disabled.
1	The debugging event is enabled. For each processed database call, the following information is given: SQL statement, response time, service time, number of processed rows, number of logical reads, number of physical reads and writes, execution plan, and little additional information.
4	As in level 1, with additional information about bind variables. Mainly, the data type, its precision, and the value used for each execution.

Table 3-2. *Levels of the Debugging Event 10046*

Level	Description
8	As in level 1, plus detailed information about wait time. For each wait experienced during the processing, the following information is given: the name of the wait event, the duration, and a few additional parameters identifying the resource that has been waited for.
12	Simultaneously level 4 and level 8.

The next sections describe how to enable and disable SQL trace, how to configure the environment to our best advantage, and how to find the trace files it generates.

DEBUGGING EVENTS

A debugging event, which is identified by a numeric value, is the means used to set a type of flag in a running database engine process. The aim is to change its behavior, for example, by enabling or disabling a feature, by testing or simulating a corruption or crash, or by collecting trace or debug information. Some debugging events are not simple flags and can be enabled at several levels. Each level has its own behavior. In some situations, the level is an address of a block or memory structure.

You should use a debugging event with care and set it only when directed to do so by Oracle Support or if you know and understand what the debugging event is going to change. Debugging events enable specific code paths. Therefore, if a problem occurs when a debugging event is set, it is worth checking whether the same problem can be reproduced without the debugging event set.

Few debugging events are documented by Oracle. If documentation exists, it is usually provided through MetaLink notes. In other words, debugging events are generally not described in the official Oracle documentation about the database engine. You can find a complete list of the available debugging events in the file `$ORACLE_HOME/rdbms/mesg/oraus.msg`. Note that this file is not distributed on all platforms. The range from 10000 to 10999 is reserved for debugging events.

Enabling SQL Trace: The Legacy Way

Up to Oracle9*i*, the documentation (specifically the *Database Performance Tuning Guide and Reference* manual) describes three methods for enabling SQL trace: the initialization parameter `sql_trace`, the procedure `set_sql_trace` in the package `dbms_session`, and the procedure `set_sql_trace_in_session` in the package `dbms_system`. The important thing to notice about these three methods is that all of them are able to enable SQL trace only at level 1. That, unfortunately, is not enough in practice. If fact, in most situations you need to break up the response time completely to understand where the bottleneck is. For this reason, I won't describe these three methods here. Instead, I'll cover other undocumented[5] ways of enabling SQL trace at any level. Note that as of Oracle Database 10*g*, a documented and officially supported way of enabling

---

5. *Undocumented* here means that the official documentation of the database engine does not provide information about these methods. Some MetaLink notes, for example, *EVENT: 10046 "enable SQL statement tracing (including binds/waits)"* (21154.1), and many papers or books not published by Oracle do describe them in detail.

and disabling SQL trace has been introduced. Consequently, as of Oracle Database 10g, it is no longer necessary to use the methods described in this section. If, however, you are working with earlier releases, you can confidently take advantage of these methods since they have been successfully used over the years.

To enable and disable SQL trace at any level, there are two main methods. Either you set the parameter events by executing the SQL statement ALTER SESSION or you call the procedure set_ev in the package dbms_system. While the former can obviously enable SQL trace only for the session that executes it, the latter is able to enable SQL trace in any session by identifying it with a session ID and serial number. Here are some examples of use.

The following SQL statement enables SQL trace at level 12 for the session executing it. Notice how the event number and the level are specified.

```
ALTER SESSION SET events '10046 trace name context forever, level 12'
```

The following SQL statement disables SQL trace for the session executing it. Notice that this is *not* achieved by specifying level 0.

```
ALTER SESSION SET events '10046 trace name context off'
```

The following PL/SQL call enables SQL trace at level 12 for the session identified by ID 127 and serial number 29. No parameter has a default value. The last parameter then, even if it is not relevant in this case, must be specified.

```
dbms_system.set_ev(si => 127,    -- session id
                   se => 29,     -- serial number
                   ev => 10046,  -- event number
                   le => 12,     -- level
                   nm => NULL)
```

The following PL/SQL call disables SQL trace for the session identified by ID 127 and serial number 29. Notice that compared to the previous case, only the value of the parameter specifying the level has changed.

```
dbms_system.set_ev(si => 127,    -- session id
                   se => 29,     -- serial number
                   ev => 10046,  -- event number
                   le => 0,      -- level
                   nm => NULL)
```

You can list the session ID and serial number for every user connected to an instance by executing the following query:

```
SELECT sid, serial#, username, machine
FROM v$session
WHERE type != 'BACKGROUND'
```

You can also set the initialization parameter events by executing the SQL statement ALTER SYSTEM. The syntax is the same as for the SQL statement ALTER SESSION. In any case, there is usually no point in enabling SQL trace at the instance level. In addition, note that it takes effect only for sessions created after it is executed.

By default, the package `dbms_system` can be executed only by the user `sys`. If the privilege to execute it should be provided to other users, be careful because the package contains other procedures and the procedure `set_ev` itself can be used to set other events as well. If you really need to provide other users with the ability to enable and disable SQL trace in any session, it is advisable to use another package containing exclusively the procedures needed to enable and disable SQL trace. Such a package, `dbms_support`, is provided by Oracle but not installed by default. You should be aware that it is documented only in MetaLink notes *The DBMS_SUPPORT Package* (62294.1) and *Tracing Sessions in Oracle Using the DBMS_SUPPORT Package* (62160.1) and is not officially supported. Here are some examples.

To install the package `dbms_support`, create a public synonym for it, and grant to the role `dba` the permissions to execute it. You can use the following commands:

```
CONNECT / as sysdba
@?/rdbms/admin/dbmssupp.sql
CREATE PUBLIC SYNONYM dbms_support FOR dbms_support;
GRANT EXECUTE ON dbms_support TO dba;
```

This package really should not be used any longer as of Oracle Database 10*g*. You should use the techniques explained in the next section instead. Nevertheless, if you install it while the PL/SQL warnings are enabled (for example by setting the initialization parameter `plsql_warnings` to `enable:all`), the following warning is generated while creating the package body. You can simply ignore it.

```
PLW-05005: function CURRENT_SERIAL returns without value at line 29
```

The following PL/SQL call enables SQL trace at level 8 for the session identified by ID 127 and serial number 29. Notice that instead of specifying the level SQL trace has to be enabled at, with the third and fourth parameter you can specify whether you are interested in waits and bind variables, respectively. Although the first two parameters have no default value, the parameter `waits` defaults to `TRUE`, and the parameter `binds` defaults to `FALSE`.

```
dbms_support.start_trace_in_session(sid    => 127,
                                    serial => 29,
                                    waits  => TRUE,
                                    binds  => FALSE)
```

The following PL/SQL call disables SQL trace for the session identified by ID 127 and serial number 29. Both parameters have no default values.

```
dbms_support.stop_trace_in_session(sid    => 127,
                                   serial => 29)
```

Enabling SQL Trace: The Contemporary Way

As of Oracle Database 10*g*, for enabling and disabling SQL trace, the package `dbms_monitor` is provided. With this package, not only do you have an official way at last of taking full advantage of SQL trace, but more important, you can enable and disable SQL trace based on the session attributes (see the section "Database Calls"): client identifier, service name, module name, and action name. This means that if the application is correctly instrumented, you can enable and disable SQL trace independently of the session used to execute the database calls. Nowadays, this is particularly useful because in many situations connection pooling is used, so users are not tied to a specific session.

Here are some examples of using the package dbms_monitor for enabling and disabling SQL trace at the session, client, component, and database levels. Note that, by default, only the users with the role dba enabled are allowed to execute the procedures provided by the package dbms_monitor.

Session Level

To enable and disable SQL trace for a session, the package dbms_monitor provides the procedures session_trace_enable and session_trace_disable, respectively.

The following PL/SQL call enables SQL trace at level 8 for the session identified by ID 127 and serial number 29. All parameters have default values. If the two parameters identifying the session are not specified, SQL trace is enabled for the session executing the PL/SQL call. The parameter waits defaults to TRUE, and the parameter binds defaults to FALSE.

```
dbms_monitor.session_trace_enable(session_id => 127,
                                  serial_num => 29,
                                  waits      => TRUE,
                                  binds      => FALSE)
```

As of Oracle Database 10g Release 2, when SQL trace has been enabled with the procedure session_trace_enable, the columns sql_trace, sql_trace_waits, and sql_trace_binds of the view v$session are set accordingly. Warning: this happens only when the procedure session_trace_enable is used and at least one SQL statement has been executed by the session to be traced. For example, enabling SQL trace with the previous PL/SQL call will result in the following information being given:

```
SQL> SELECT sql_trace, sql_trace_waits, sql_trace_binds
  2  FROM v$session
  3  WHERE sid = 127;

SQL_TRACE       SQL_TRACE_WAITS SQL_TRACE_BINDS
--------------- --------------- ---------------
ENABLED         TRUE            FALSE
```

The following PL/SQL call disables SQL trace for the session identified by ID 127 and serial number 29. Be aware that both parameters have default values. If they are not specified, SQL trace is disabled for the session executing the PL/SQL call.

```
dbms_monitor.session_trace_disable(session_id => 127,
                                   serial_num => 29)
```

Note that if Real Application Clusters is used, the procedures session_trace_enable and session_trace_disable have to be executed on the instance where the session resides.

Client Level

To enable and disable SQL trace for a client, the package dbms_monitor provides the procedures client_id_trace_enable and client_id_trace_disable, respectively. Naturally, these procedures can be used only if the session attribute client identifier is set.

The following PL/SQL call enables SQL trace at level 8 for all sessions having the client identifier specified as a parameter. While the parameter client_id has no default value, the parameter waits defaults to TRUE, and the parameter binds defaults to FALSE. Be careful, because the parameter client_id is case sensitive.

```
dbms_monitor.client_id_trace_enable(client_id => 'helicon.antognini.ch',
                                    waits     => TRUE,
                                    binds     => FALSE)
```

The view dba_enabled_traces displays which client identifier SQL trace has been enabled for, and which parameters were used to enable it, through the procedure client_id_trace_enable. For example, after enabling SQL trace with the previous PL/SQL call, the following information is given:

```
SQL> SELECT primary_id AS client_id, waits, binds
  2  FROM dba_enabled_traces
  3  WHERE trace_type = 'CLIENT_ID';

CLIENT_ID               WAITS BINDS
--------------------    ----- -----
helicon.antognini.ch    TRUE  FALSE
```

The following PL/SQL call disables SQL trace for all sessions having the client identifier specified as a parameter. The parameter client_id has no default value.

```
dbms_monitor.client_id_trace_disable(client_id => 'helicon.antognini.ch')
```

Component Level

To enable and disable SQL trace for a component specified through a service name, module name, and action name, the package dbms_monitor provides the procedures serv_mod_act_trace_enable and serv_mod_act_trace_disable, respectively. To take full advantage of these procedures, you have to set the session attributes, module name, and action name.

The following PL/SQL call enables SQL trace at level 8 for all sessions using the attributes specified as a parameter. The only parameter without a default value is the first: service_name.[6] The default values of the parameters module_name and action_name are any_module and any_action, respectively. For both, NULL is a valid value. If the parameter action_name is specified, you must specify the parameter module_name as well. Failing to do so will result in an ORA-13859 to be raised. The parameter waits defaults to TRUE, and the parameter binds defaults to FALSE. If Real Application Clusters is used, with the parameter instance_name it is possible to restrict the tracing to a single instance. By default, SQL trace is enabled for all instances. Be aware

---

6. The *service name* is a logical name associated to a database. It is configured through the initialization parameter service_names. One database may have multiple service names.

that the parameters `service_name`, `module_name`, `action_name`, and `instance_name` are case sensitive.

```
dbms_monitor.serv_mod_act_trace_enable(service_name  => 'DBM10203.antognini.ch',
                                       module_name   => 'mymodule',
                                       action_name   => 'myaction',
                                       waits         => TRUE,
                                       binds         => FALSE,
                                       instance_name => NULL)
```

As for SQL trace at the client level, the view `dba_enabled_traces` displays which component SQL trace has been enabled for, and which parameters were used to enable it, through the procedure `serv_mod_act_trace_enable`. After enabling SQL trace with the previous PL/SQL call, you get the following information. Notice that if SQL trace is enabled without specifying all three attributes (that is, the service name, module name, and action name), the column `trace_type` will be set to either `SERVICE` or `SERVICE_MODULE` depending on which parameters are used.

```
SQL> SELECT primary_id AS service_name, qualifier_id1 AS module_name,
  2         qualifier_id2 AS action_name, waits, binds
  3  FROM dba_enabled_traces
  4  WHERE trace_type = 'SERVICE_MODULE_ACTION';

SERVICE_NAME             MODULE_NAME   ACTION_NAME   WAITS BINDS
---------------------    -----------   -----------   ----- -----
DBM10203.antognini.ch    mymodule      myaction      TRUE  FALSE
```

The following PL/SQL call disables SQL trace for all sessions using the session attributes specified as parameters. All parameters have the same default values and behavior as for the procedure `serv_mod_act_trace_enable`.

```
dbms_monitor.serv_mod_act_trace_disable(service_name  => 'DBM10203.antognini.ch',
                                        module_name   => 'mymodule',
                                        action_name   => 'myaction',
                                        instance_name => NULL)
```

Database Level

As of Oracle Database 10g Release 2, for enabling and disabling SQL trace for all sessions that connect to a database (except those created by background processes), the package `dbms_monitor` provides the procedures `database_trace_enable` and `database_trace_disable`, respectively.

The following PL/SQL call enables SQL trace at level 12 for a database. All parameters have default values. The parameter `waits` defaults to `TRUE`, and the parameter `binds` defaults to `FALSE`. In the case of Real Application Clusters, by using the parameter `instance_name`, it is possible to restrict the tracing to a single instance. If the parameter `instance_name` is set to `NULL`, which is also the default value, SQL trace is enabled for all instances. Again, note that the parameter `instance_name` is case sensitive.

```
dbms_monitor.database_trace_enable(waits         => TRUE,
                                   binds         => TRUE,
                                   instance_name => NULL)
```

As for SQL trace at the client and component levels, the view dba_enabled_traces displays which instance SQL trace has been enabled for, and which parameters it has been enabled with, through the procedure database_trace_enable.

```
SQL> SELECT instance_name, waits, binds
  2  FROM dba_enabled_traces
  3  WHERE trace_type = 'DATABASE';

INSTANCE_NAME    WAITS BINDS
---------------- ----- -----
                 TRUE  TRUE
```

The following PL/SQL call disables SQL trace for a database. If the parameter instance_name is set to NULL, which is also the default value, SQL trace is disabled for all instances.

```
dbms_monitor.database_trace_disable(instance_name => NULL)
```

Triggering SQL Trace

In the previous sections, you have seen different methods of enabling and disabling SQL trace. In the simplest case, you manually execute the shown SQL statements or PL/SQL calls in SQL*Plus. Sometimes, however, it is necessary to automatically trigger SQL trace. *Automatically* here means that code must be added somewhere.

The simplest approach is to create a logon trigger at the database level. To avoid enabling SQL trace for all users, I usually suggest creating a role (named sql_trace in the following example) and temporarily granting it only to the user utilized for the test. Naturally, it is also possible to define the trigger for a single schema or perform other checks based, for example, on the userenv context. Note that in addition to enabling SQL trace, it is good practice to set the other parameters related to SQL trace as well (more about them later in this chapter).

```
CREATE ROLE sql_trace;

CREATE OR REPLACE TRIGGER enable_sql_trace AFTER LOGON ON DATABASE
BEGIN
  IF (dbms_session.is_role_enabled('SQL_TRACE'))
  THEN
    EXECUTE IMMEDIATE 'ALTER SESSION SET timed_statistics = TRUE';
    EXECUTE IMMEDIATE 'ALTER SESSION SET max_dump_file_size = unlimited';
    dbms_monitor.session_trace_enable;
  END IF;
END;
/
```

Another approach is to add some code enabling SQL trace directly in the application. Some kind of parameterization triggering that code would need to be added as well. A command-line parameter for a fat-client application or an additional HTTP parameter for a web application are examples of this.

Timing Information in Trace Files

The dynamic initialization parameter timed_statistics, which can be set to either TRUE or FALSE, controls the availability of timing information such as the elapsed time and CPU time in the trace files. If it is set to TRUE, timing information is added to the trace files. If it is set to FALSE, they should be missing; however, depending on the port you are working on, they could be partially available as well. The default value of timed_statistics depends on another initialization parameter: statistics_level. If statistics_level is set to basic, timed_statistics defaults to FALSE. Otherwise, timed_statistics defaults to TRUE.

Generally speaking, if timing information is not available, the trace files are useless. So, before enabling SQL trace, make sure that the parameter is set to TRUE. You can do this, for example, by executing the following SQL statement:

```
ALTER SESSION SET timed_statistics = TRUE
```

DYNAMIC INITIALIZATION PARAMETERS

Some initialization parameters are static, and others are dynamic. When they are dynamic, it means they can be changed without bouncing the instance. Among the dynamic initialization parameters, some of them can be changed only at the session level, some only at the system level, and others at the session and system levels. To change an initialization parameter at the session and system levels, you use the SQL statements ALTER SESSION and ALTER SYSTEM, respectively. Initialization parameters changed at the instance level take effect immediately or only for sessions created after the modification. The view v$parameter, or more precisely the columns isses_modifiable and issys_modifiable, provide information about which situation an initialization parameter can be changed in.

Limiting the Size of Trace Files

Usually, you are not interested in limiting the size of trace files. If it is necessary to do so, however, it is possible to set at the session or system level the dynamic initialization parameter max_dump_file_size. A numerical value followed by a K or M suffix specifies, in kilobytes or megabytes, the maximum trace file size. If no limit is wanted, as shown in the following SQL statement, it is possible to set the parameter to the value unlimited:

```
ALTER SESSION SET max_dump_file_size = unlimited
```

Finding Trace Files

Trace files are produced by database engine server processes running on the database server. This means they are written to a disk accessible from the database server. Depending on the type of the process producing the trace files, they are written in two distinct directories:

- Dedicated server processes create trace files in the directory configured through the initialization parameter user_dump_dest.

- Background processes create trace files in the directory configured through the initialization parameter background_dump_dest.

Note that the following are considered background processes: processes listed in v$bgprocess, dispatcher processes (D*nnn*), shared server processes (S*nnn*), parallel slave processes (P*nnn*), job queue processes (J*nnn*), advanced queuing processes (Q*nnn*), MMON slave processes (M*nnn*), and ASM-related processes (O*nnn*). The process type is available in the column type of the view v$session.

As of Oracle Database 11*g*, with the introduction of the Automatic Diagnostic Repository, the initialization parameters user_dump_dest and background_dump_dest are deprecated in favor of the initialization parameter diagnostic_dest. Since the new initialization parameter sets the base directory only, you can use the view v$diag_info to get the exact location of the trace files. The following queries show the difference between the value of the initialization parameter and the location of the trace files:

```
SQL> SELECT value FROM v$parameter WHERE name = 'diagnostic_dest';

VALUE
--------------------------------------------------------------------
/u00/app/oracle

SQL> SELECT value FROM v$diag_info WHERE name = 'Diag Trace';

VALUE
--------------------------------------------------------------------
/u00/app/oracle/diag/rdbms/dbm11106/DBM11106/trace
```

The name of the trace file itself used to be version and platform dependent. As of Oracle9*i* and for the most-common platforms,[7] however, it has the following structure:

```
{instance name}_{process name}_{process id}.trc
```

Here's a breakdown:

instance name: This is the lowercase value of the initialization parameter instance_name. Notice that in a Real Application Clusters environment, this is different from the initialization parameter db_name. It is available in the column instance_name of the view v$instance.

process name: This is the lowercase value of the name of the process that is producing the trace file. For dedicated server processes, the name ora is used. For shared server processes, it is found in the column name of either the view v$dispatcher or v$shared_server. For parallel slave processes, it is found in the column server_name of the view v$px_process. For most other background processes, it is found in the column name of the view v$bgprocess.

process id: This is the process identifier at the operating system level. Its value is found in the column spid of the view v$process.

Based on the information here provided, it is possible to write a query like the following to find out which trace file name is associated with each user session (you can find the query in the script map_session_to_tracefile.sql). Notice that in the following output, the row with the server type is

---

7. This was explicitly checked on several AIX, HP-UX, Linux, Solaris, Tru64, and Windows systems. On more exotic platforms (for example, OpenVMS), there are differences.

equal to NONE. This happens when a session connected through a shared server process is not executing a SQL statement. As a result, it is not associated with a shared server process but with a dispatcher server process.

```
SQL> SELECT s.sid,
  2         s.server,
  3         lower(
  4           CASE
  5             WHEN s.server IN ('DEDICATED','SHARED') THEN
  6               i.instance_name || '_' ||
  7               nvl(pp.server_name, nvl(ss.name, 'ora')) || '_' ||
  8               p.spid || '.trc'
  9             ELSE NULL
 10           END
 11         ) AS trace_file_name
 12  FROM v$instance i,
 13       v$session s,
 14       v$process p,
 15       v$px_process pp,
 16       v$shared_server ss
 17  WHERE s.paddr = p.addr
 18  AND s.sid = pp.sid (+)
 19  AND s.paddr = ss.paddr(+)
 20  AND s.type = 'USER'
 21  ORDER BY s.sid;

      SID SERVER    TRACE_FILE_NAME
---------- --------- ----------------------------------------
      145 DEDICATED dbm10203_ora_24387.trc
      146 DEDICATED dbm10203_ora_24380.trc
      147 NONE
      149 DEDICATED dbm10203_ora_24260.trc
      150 SHARED    dbm10203_s000_24374.trc
```

As of Oracle Database 11*g*, for the current session, it is much easier to use the view v$diag_info as shown in the following query:

```
SQL> SELECT value FROM v$diag_info WHERE name = 'Default Trace File';

VALUE
------------------------------------------------------------------------
/u00/app/oracle/diag/rdbms/dbm11106/DBM11106/trace/DBM11106_ora_9429.trc
```

To find the right trace file easily, it is also possible to use the initialization parameter tracefile_identifier. In fact, with that parameter, you can add a custom identifier of up to 255 characters to the trace file name. With it, the trace file name structure becomes the following:

```
{instance name}_{process name}_{process id}_{tracefile identifier}.trc
```

Be aware that this method works only with dedicated server processes. It is also worth noting that every time a session dynamically changes the value of that parameter, a new trace file is automatically created. The value of the parameter `tracefile_identifier` is available in the column `traceid` of the view `v$process`. Be careful, though: this is true only for the very same session that set the parameter. All other sessions see the value `NULL`.

Now that you have seen what SQL trace is, how to configure, enable, and disable it, and where to find the trace files it generates, let's discuss their structure and some tools used to analyze, and consequently leverage, their content.

DO TRACE FILES CONTAIN CONFIDENTIAL INFORMATION?

By default, trace files are not accessible to everyone. This is good because they may contain confidential information. In fact, both the SQL statements, which may contain data (literals), and the values of bind variables end up in trace files. Basically, this means that every piece of data stored in the database could be written to a trace file as well.

For example, on Unix/Linux systems, the trace files belong to the user and group running the database engine binaries and by default have `-rw-r-----` as privileges. In other words, only users in the same group as the user running the database engine are able to read the trace files.

There is, however, really no good reason for preventing those that already have access to the data in the database from having access to the trace files, if they are required to perform a task. In fact, from a security point of view, trace files are a useful source of information only for those without access to the database. For this reason, the database engine provides an undocumented parameter named `_trace_files_public`. Per default, it is set to `FALSE`. If set to `TRUE`, the trace files are made readable to everyone having access to the system. Since the parameter is not dynamic, an instance bounce is necessary to change its value.

For example, on Unix/Linux with `_trace_files_public` set to `TRUE`, the default privileges become `-rw-r--r--`. This way, all users will be able to read the trace files.

From a security point of view, setting the parameter `_trace_files_public` to `TRUE` is problematic only when the access to the database server is not restricted. In providing simple access to the trace files, it is also common to share the directories containing them via SMB, via NFS, or through an HTTP interface. In any case, and for obvious reasons, asking a DBA to manually send a trace file every time one is needed should be avoided as much as possible.

Structure of the Trace Files

A trace file contains information about the database calls executed by a specific process. Actually, when the process ID is reused at the operating system level, a trace file may contain information from several processes as well. Since a process may be used from different sessions (for example, for shared servers or parallel slave processes) and each session may have different session attributes (for example, module name and action name), a trace file can be separated into several logical sections. Figure 3-19 provides an example (both trace files are available for download along with the other files of this chapter).

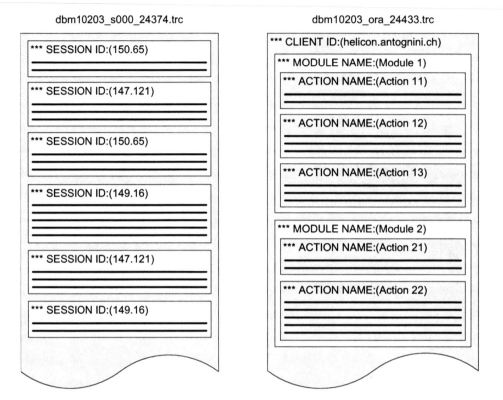

Figure 3-19. *A trace file may be composed of several logical sections. On the left, a trace file of a shared server containing information from three sessions. On the right, a trace file of a dedicated server containing information from one client with two modules and five actions.*

The structure of the trace file shown on the right in Figure 3-19 may be generated with the following PL/SQL block:

```
BEGIN
  dbms_session.set_identifier(client_id=>'helicon.antognini.ch');
  dbms_application_info.set_module(module_name=>'Module 1',
                                   action_name=>'Action 11');
  -- code module 1, action 11
  dbms_application_info.set_module(module_name=>'Module 1',
                                   action_name=>'Action 12');
  -- code module 1, action 12
  dbms_application_info.set_module(module_name=>'Module 1',
                                   action_name=>'Action 13');
  -- code module 1, action 13
  dbms_application_info.set_module(module_name=>'Module 2',
                                   action_name=>'Action 21');
```

```
  -- code module 2, action 21
  dbms_application_info.set_module(module_name=>'Module 2',
                                   action_name=>'Action 22');
  -- code module 2, action 22
END;
```

The tags beginning with the three stars (***), used in Figure 3-19 to mark a section, are the ones used in the trace files. The difference with the trace files is that not only does the database engine repeat some of them for each section, but in addition, a timestamp is added. The following trace file snippet shows an example of content generated by the previous PL/SQL block:

```
...
...
*** ACTION NAME:(Action 11) 2007-07-11 10:59:01.582
*** MODULE NAME:(Module 1) 2007-07-11 10:59:01.582
*** CLIENT ID:(helicon.antognini.ch) 2007-07-11 10:59:01.582
...
...
*** ACTION NAME:(Action 12) 2007-07-11 10:59:03.583
*** MODULE NAME:(Module 1) 2007-07-11 10:59:03.583
...
...
*** ACTION NAME:(Action 13) 2007-07-11 10:59:04.585
*** MODULE NAME:(Module 1) 2007-07-11 10:59:04.585
...
...
*** ACTION NAME:(Action 21) 2007-07-11 10:59:05.585
*** MODULE NAME:(Module 2) 2007-07-11 10:59:05.585
...
...
*** ACTION NAME:(Action 22) 2007-07-11 10:59:06.586
*** MODULE NAME:(Module 2) 2007-07-11 10:59:06.586
...
...
```

As of Oracle Database 10*g*, the format of the trace files has changed in this area. In previous releases, not only is the client ID completely missing but the tags used for module name and action name are also different. The following trace file snippet shows how the information is provided up to Oracle9*i* for the same PL/SQL blocks as before:

```
...
...
APPNAME mod='Module 1' mh=262111370 act='Action 11' ah=810452301
...
...
APPNAME mod='Module 1' mh=262111370 act='Action 12' ah=3880529476
...
...
```

```
APPNAME mod='Module 1' mh=262111370 act='Action 13' ah=3117839477
...
...
APPNAME mod='Module 2' mh=2889377500 act='Action 21' ah=3726166056
...
...
APPNAME mod='Module 2' mh=2889377500 act='Action 22' ah=1514258714
...
...
```

The logical sessions tags you saw earlier are very useful because, thanks to them, it is possible to extract information that is relevant to your needs. For example, if you are investigating a performance problem related to a specific action, you can isolate the part of the trace file related to it. You can do this using the tool described in the next section, TRCSESS.

Using TRCSESS

You can use the command-line tool TRCSESS, which is available as of Oracle Database 10*g*, to extract part of the information contained in one or more trace files, based on the logical sections described earlier. To get a complete list of its arguments, run it without arguments.

```
trcsess [output=<output file name >] [session=<session ID>] [clientid=<clientid>]
        [service=<service name>] [action=<action name>] [module=<module name>]
        <trace file names>
```

```
output=<output file name> output destination default being standard output.
session=<session Id> session to be traced.
Session id is a combination of session Index & session serial number e.g. 8.13.
clientid=<clientid> clientid to be traced.
service=<service name> service to be traced.
action=<action name> action to be traced.
module=<module name> module to be traced.
<trace_file_names> Space separated list of trace files with wild card '*' supported.
```

As you can see, it is possible to specify a session, a client ID, a service name, a module name, and an action name as an argument. For example, to extract the information about *Action 12* from the trace file dbm10203_ora_24433.trc and write the output in a new trace file named action12.trc, you can use the following command:

```
trcsess output=action12.trc action="Action 12" dbm10203_ora_24433.trc
```

Remember that the arguments clientid, service, action, and module are case sensitive. This tool supports trace files generated by early versions as well. However, as you have seen in the previous section, the problem is that up to Oracle9*i*, only the session is identified by the same tags as in Oracle Database 10*g* and later. To get around this problem, you can translate the old tags into the new format with your preferred scripting language. For instance, you can do this using one of the useful Unix command-line utilities. In this particular case, I would personally choose awk. The purpose of the following script is very simple: if a line begins with the tag APPNAME, the line is translated into the new format; otherwise, the input is just echoed to the output.

```
BEGIN {
   FS = "="
}
/^APPNAME/ {
   module = substr($2,2,index($2,"' mh")-2)
   action = substr($4,2,index($4,"' ah")-2)
   if (action) printf "*** ACTION NAME:(%s) O\n", action
   if (module) printf "*** MODULE NAME:(%s) O\n", module
}
!/^APPNAME/ {
  print $0
}
```

The execution of this script, called trcsess.awk, looks like this:

```
awk -f trcsess.awk m9208_ora_5823.trc > m9208_ora_5823.trc2
```

Profilers

Once you have identified the correct trace files, or possibly cut off part of some of them with TRCSESS, it is time to analyze the content. For this purpose, you use a profiler. Its aim is to generate a formatted output based on the content of raw trace files. Oracle distributes with both the database and client binaries such a profiler. Its name is TKPROF (which stands for *Trace Kernel PROfiler*). Even if the output it provides can be useful in several situations, sometimes it is not adequate for quick identification of performance problems. Strangely, Oracle underestimates the importance of such a tool and, consequently, has only marginally improved it since its introduction in Oracle7. A number of commercial and freeware profilers are available, however. I have also developed my own profiler, which is freeware, named TVD$XTAT. Other profilers you may want to consider are Hotsos Profiler,[8] itfprof SQL Analyzer,[9] and OraSRP.[10] Even Oracle (through MetaLink) proposes another profiler, named Trace Analyzer.[11]

In the next two sections, I'll describe two of these profilers. First, I'll cover TKPROF. In spite of its deficiencies, it is the only one that is always available. In fact, you are not allowed in all situations to install another profiler on a database server or download trace files to another machine. In such situations, it can be useful. After covering TKPROF, I'll describe my own profiler. The explanations are based on a trace file generated during the execution of the following PL/SQL block:

---

8. See http://method-r.com for additional information. This product was originally developed by Hotsos (http://www.hotsos.com). As of April 1, 2008, the product is owned, maintained, and supported by Cary Millsap's Method R Corporation, but Hotsos still has the rights to sell it.
9. See http://www.ubtools.com for additional information.
10. See http://www.oracledba.ru/orasrp for additional information.
11. See MetaLink note *Trace Analyzer TRCANLZR* (224270.1) for additional information.

```
DECLARE
  l_channel_id sh.sales.channel_id%TYPE := 3;
BEGIN
  FOR c IN (SELECT cust_id, extract(YEAR FROM time_id), sum(amount_sold)
            FROM sh.sales
            WHERE channel_id = l_channel_id
            GROUP BY cust_id, extract(YEAR FROM time_id))
  LOOP
    NULL;
  END LOOP;
END;
```

Using TKPROF

TKPROF is a command-line tool. Its main purpose is to take a raw trace file as input and generate a formatted text file as output. In addition, it is also able to generate a SQL script to load the data in a database, although this feature is hardly ever used.

The simplest analysis is performed by just specifying an input and an output file. In the following example, the input file is DBM11106_ora_6334.trc, and the output file is DBM11106_ora_6334.txt. Even if the default extension of the output file is prf, I personally always use txt. In my view, it is better to use extensions that mean something to everybody and are usually correctly recognized by any operating system.

```
tkprof DBM11106_ora_6334.trc DBM11106_ora_6334.txt
```

An analysis without specifying further arguments is helpful only when analyzing very small trace files. In most situations, to get a better output, you must specify several arguments.

TKPROF Arguments

If you run TKPROF without arguments, you get a complete list of its arguments with a short description for each of them:

```
Usage: tkprof tracefile outputfile [explain= ] [table= ]
              [print= ] [insert= ] [sys= ] [sort= ]
  table=schema.tablename    Use 'schema.tablename' with 'explain=' option.
  explain=user/password     Connect to ORACLE and issue EXPLAIN PLAN.
  print=integer     List only the first 'integer' SQL statements.
  aggregate=yes|no
  insert=filename   List SQL statements and data inside INSERT statements.
  sys=no            TKPROF does not list SQL statements run as user SYS.
  record=filename   Record non-recursive statements found in the trace file.
  waits=yes|no      Record summary for any wait events found in the trace file.
  sort=option       Set of zero or more of the following sort options:
    prscnt  number of times parse was called
    prscpu  cpu time parsing
```

```
prsela   elapsed time parsing
prsdsk   number of disk reads during parse
prsqry   number of buffers for consistent read during parse
prscu    number of buffers for current read during parse
prsmis   number of misses in library cache during parse
execnt   number of execute was called
execpu   cpu time spent executing
exeela   elapsed time executing
exedsk   number of disk reads during execute
exeqry   number of buffers for consistent read during execute
execu    number of buffers for current read during execute
exerow   number of rows processed during execute
exemis   number of library cache misses during execute
fchcnt   number of times fetch was called
fchcpu   cpu time spent fetching
fchela   elapsed time fetching
fchdsk   number of disk reads during fetch
fchqry   number of buffers for consistent read during fetch
fchcu    number of buffers for current read during fetch
fchrow   number of rows fetched
userid   userid of user that parsed the cursor
```

The function of each argument is as follows:

- explain instructs TKPROF to provide an execution plan for each SQL statement found in the trace file. This is done by executing the SQL statement EXPLAIN PLAN (see Chapter 6 for detailed information about this SQL statement). Obviously, in order to execute a SQL statement, a connection to a database is needed. Consequently, the argument is used to specify the user, password, and, if needed, connect string. The accepted formats are explain=user/password@connect_string and explain=user/password. Be aware that in order to maximize your chances of getting the right execution plans, you should specify a user with access to the same objects and make sure all query optimizer initialization parameters are set to the same value as the one used to generate the trace file. You should also be wary of initialization parameters changed at runtime by the application or with logon triggers. It goes without saying that if you can use the same user, it is even better. In any case, even if all the previous conditions are met, as the execution plans generated by EXPLAIN PLAN do not necessarily match the real ones (the reasons will be explained in Chapter 6), it is not advisable to specify the argument explain. If an invalid user, password, or connect string is specified, the trace file is processed without any interactive error message. Instead, an error like the following will be found in the output file just after the header:

```
error connecting to database using: scott/lion
ORA-01017: invalid username/password; logon denied
EXPLAIN PLAN option disabled.
```

- `table` is used only together with the argument `explain`. Its purpose is, in fact, to specify which table is used by the SQL statement `EXPLAIN PLAN` to generate the execution plans. Usually it is possible to avoid specifying it because TKPROF automatically creates and drops a plan table named `prof$plan_table` in the schema used for the analysis. In any case, if the user is not able to create tables (for example, because the `CREATE TABLE` privilege is lacking), then the argument `table` must be specified. For example, to specify that the table `plan_table` owned by the user `system` must be used, the argument must be set to `table=system.plan_table`. The user performing the analysis must have `SELECT`, `INSERT`, and `DELETE` privileges on the specified table. Also, in this case, errors are made available only in the output file.

▨**Caution** In Oracle Database 10*g* Release 1, because of bug 3451410, TKPROF is not able to automatically create the plan table. Instead, the error ORA-00922 will be found in the output file just after the header. This problem is described in MetaLink note *Tkprof Fails With Error In Create Table Of Explain Plan: Ora-922* (293481.1).

- `print` is used to limit the number of SQL statements provided in the output file. Per default there is no limit. It makes sense to specify this argument only together with the argument `sort` (described in a moment). For example, to get only 10 SQL statements, the argument must be set to `print=10`.

- `aggregate` specifies whether TKPROF handles SQL statements having the same text separately. By default, this is not the case. In other words, all information belonging to a specific SQL statement is aggregated. Note that this is done independently of the number of SQL statements present in the trace file. As is the case with any aggregation, there is a loss of information. In this case, a cursor having multiple children with different execution plans will be handled as a single SQL statement as well. Even if the default is good in many cases, it is sometimes better to specify `aggregate=no` and be able to take a look at single SQL statements.

- `insert` instructs TKPROF to generate a SQL script that can be used to store all information in a database. The name of the SQL script is specified by the argument itself, as in `insert=load.sql`.

- `sys` specifies whether SQL statements executed by the user `sys` (for example, recursive queries against the data dictionary during parse operations) are written to the output file. The default value is `yes`, but most of the time I prefer to set it to `no` to avoid having unnecessary information in the output file. It is unnecessary because you usually have no control over the SQL statements executed recursively by the user `sys`.

- `record` instructs TKPROF to generate a SQL script containing all nonrecursive statements found in the trace file. The name of the SQL script is specified by the argument itself (for example, `record=replay.sql`). According to the documentation, this feature could be used to manually replay the SQL statements. Since bind variables are not handled, this is usually not possible.

- `waits` determines whether information about wait events is added in the output file. Per default, it is added. Personally, I see no good reason for specifying `waits=no` and consequently not having the very important wait events in the output file.

- `sort` specifies the order in which the SQL statements are written to the output file. Per default it is the order in which they are found in the trace file. Basically, by specifying one of the proposed options, you can sort the output according to resource utilization (for example, the number of calls, CPU time, and number of physical reads) or response time (that is, the elapsed time). As you can see for most options (for example, the elapsed time), one value for each type of database call is available: for example, `prsela` for the time spent parsing a cursor, `exeela` for the time spent executing a cursor, and `fchela` for the time spent fetching rows from a cursor. Even if you have many choices and combinations, there is only one sort order that is really useful for investigating performance problems: response time. Therefore, you should specify `sort=prsela,exeela,fchela`. When you specify a comma-separated list of values, TKPROF sums the value of the options passed as arguments. This occurs even if they are incompatible with each other. Note that when a trace file contains several sessions and the argument `aggregate=no` is specified, the SQL statements are sorted independently for each session.

Based on the information just provided, I personally usually run TKPROF with the arguments shown in the following example:

```
tkprof {input trace file} {output file} sys=no sort=prsela,exeela,fchela
```

Now that you have seen how to analyze a trace file with TKPROF, let's take a look at the output file it generates.

Interpreting TKPROF Output

The analysis was done by specifying the following arguments. Note that this is not the way you were just advised to do it. This is only to show you a specific output. Note that both the trace file and the output file are available for download along with the other files for this chapter.

```
tkprof DBM11106_ora_9813.trc DBM11106_ora_9813.txt
      sort=prsela,exeela,fchela print=3 explain=sh/sh aggregate=no
```

The output file begins with a header. Most of its information is static. Nevertheless, there is useful information in it: the name of the trace file, the value of the argument `sort` used for the generation of the output file, and a line that identifies the traced session. This last bit of information is available only because the argument `aggregate=no` was specified. Note that when a trace file contains multiple sessions and the argument `aggregate=no` is specified, this header is repeated and used as a separator between the SQL statements belonging to different sessions.

```
TKPROF: Release 11.1.0.6.0 - Production on Tue Feb 29 10:37:08 2008

Copyright (c) 1982, 2007, Oracle.  All rights reserved.

Trace file: DBM11106_ora_6334.trc
Sort options: prsela  exeela  fchela
```

```
*****************************************************************************
count      = number of times OCI procedure was executed
cpu        = cpu time in seconds executing
elapsed    = elapsed time in seconds executing
disk       = number of physical reads of buffers from disk
query      = number of buffers gotten for consistent read
current    = number of buffers gotten in current mode (usually for update)
rows       = number of rows processed by the fetch or execute call
-----------------------------------------------------------------------------
```

```
*** SESSION ID:(90.6) 2008-02-29 07:43:11.461
```

Any error that occurred while connecting to the database or generating the execution plans is added just after this header.

After the header, the following information is given for every SQL statement: the text of the SQL statement, the execution statistics, information about parsing, the execution plan, and the wait events. The execution plan and wait events are optional and reported only if they are stored in the trace file. Remember, execution plans are stored only when the cursors are closed, and the wait events are stored only if they occurred while the tracing of wait events was enabled.

The text of the SQL statement in some situations is formatted. Unfortunately, the code responsible for this operation does not provide correct formatting in all situations. For instance, in this case the keyword FROM of the function extract is confused with the FROM clause of the SQL statement. Note that the ID of the SQL statement is available only as of Oracle Database 11g.

```
SQL ID : g4h8jndhd8vst
SELECT CUST_ID, EXTRACT(YEAR
FROM
 TIME_ID), SUM(AMOUNT_SOLD) FROM SH.SALES WHERE CHANNEL_ID = :B1 GROUP BY
  CUST_ID, EXTRACT(YEAR FROM TIME_ID)
```

The execution statistics provide data, aggregated by type of database call, in a tabular form. For each of them, the following performance figures are given:

- count is the number of times database calls were executed.

- cpu is the total CPU time in seconds spent processing database calls.

- elapsed is the total elapsed time, in seconds, spent processing database calls. If this value is higher than CPU time, the section about wait events found below the execution statistics provides information about the resources or synchronization points waited for.

- disk is the number of blocks read with physical reads. Be careful, this is not the number of physical I/O operations. The number of physical I/O operations is given in the section about wait events. If this value is larger than the number of logical reads (disk > query + current), this means that blocks spilled into the temporary tablespace. In this case, you can see that at least 870 blocks (2,590–1,720–0) were read from it. This will be confirmed later by the statistics of row source operations and wait events.

- query is the number of blocks read with logical reads from the buffer cache in consistent mode. Usually, this type of logical read is used by queries.

- current is the number of blocks read with logical reads from the buffer cache in current mode. Usually this type of logical read is used by INSERT, DELETE, MERGE, and UPDATE statements.

- rows is the number of rows processed. For queries, this is the number of fetched rows. For INSERT, DELETE, MERGE, and UPDATE statements, this is the number of affected rows. In this case, it is worth noting that 16,348 rows were fetched in 164 fetch calls. This means that on average, each call fetched about 100 rows. Note that 100 is the prefetch size used as of Oracle Database 10g in PL/SQL. (Chapter 11 provides detailed information about the prefetch size.)

call	count	cpu	elapsed	disk	query	current	rows
Parse	1	0.00	0.00	0	0	0	0
Execute	1	0.04	0.19	0	0	0	0
Fetch	164	1.09	4.50	2590	1720	0	16348
total	166	1.13	4.70	2590	1720	0	16348

The following lines summarize basic information about parsing. The first two values (Misses in library cache) provide the number of hard parses that occurred during parse and execute calls. If no hard parse occurred during execute calls, that specific line is missing. The optimizer mode and the user who parsed the SQL statement are shown. Note that the name of the user, in this case ops$cha, is provided only when the argument explain is specified. Otherwise, only the user ID (in this case 33) is shown. The last piece of information is the recursive depth. It is provided only for recursive SQL statements. SQL statements directly executed by an application have a depth of 0. A depth of n (in this case 1) simply means that another SQL statement with depth $n-1$ (in this case 0) has executed this one. In our sample, the SQL statement at depth 0 is the PL/SQL block that was executed by SQL*Plus.

```
Misses in library cache during parse: 1
Misses in library cache during execute: 1
Optimizer mode: ALL_ROWS
Parsing user id: 33  (OPS$CHA)    (recursive depth: 1)
```

After the general information about parsing, you might see the execution plan. Actually, if the argument explain is specified, it may be possible to see two of them. The first one, inaccurately called Row Source Operation, is the execution plan written in the trace file when the cursor was closed and only if it was closed while the tracing was active. This means that if an application reuses cursors without closing them, no execution plan will be written in the trace file for the reused cursors. The second one, called Execution Plan, is generated by TKPROF only when the argument explain is specified. Since it is generated later, it does not necessarily match the first one. In any case, if you see a difference between the two, the first is the correct one.

Chapter 6 describes how to read an execution plan; here I'm describing only the particularities of TKPROF. Both execution plans provide the number of rows returned (not processed—be careful) by each operation in the execution plan in the column Rows. In this example, knowing that the table sales contains 918,843 rows and that according to the trace file only 540,328 rows were returned means that the predicate in the WHERE clause filtered about 41 percent of the rows. After this, the GROUP BY clause further reduced the result set to 16,348 rows.

For each row source operation, the following runtime statistics might also be provided:

- `cr` is the number of blocks read with logical reads in consistent mode.

- `pr` is the number of blocks read with physical reads from the disk.

- `pw` is the number of blocks written with physical writes to the disk.

- `time` is the total elapsed time in microseconds spent processing the operation. Be aware that the value provided by this statistic is not always very precise. In fact, to reduce the overhead, sampling might be used for it.

- `cost` is the estimated cost of the operation. This value is available only as of Oracle Database 11*g*.

- `size` is the estimated amount of data (in bytes) returned by the operation. This value is available only as of Oracle Database 11*g*.

- `card` is the estimated number of rows returned by the operation. This value is available only as of Oracle Database 11*g*.

Note that these values, except for `card`, are cumulative; that is, they include the values of the child row source operations. For example, the number of blocks spilled into the temporary tablespace during the operation HASH GROUP BY is 941 (2,590–1,649). From the previous execution statistics (see the discussion about column "disk"), you were able to estimate only that there were at least 870. Since there are 71 more (941–870), it means that 71 blocks, unrelated to the spill into temporary tablespace, were not found in the buffer cache. This figure also matches the runtime statistics provided by the operation TABLE ACCESS FULL. In fact, the difference between logical reads and physical reads is 71 (1,720–1,649).

```
Rows    Row Source Operation
------  ------------------------------------------------------
 16348  HASH GROUP BY (cr=1720 pr=2590 pw=2590 time=79 us cost=9990 size=11217129
                       card=534149)
540328    PARTITION RANGE ALL PARTITION: 1 28 (cr=1720 pr=1649 pw=1649 time=7744 us
                                               cost=496 size=11217129 card=534149)
540328      TABLE ACCESS FULL SALES PARTITION: 1 28 (cr=1720 pr=1649 pw=1649
                                                     time=4756 us cost=496
                                                     size=11217129 card=534149)


Rows    Execution Plan
------  ------------------------------------------------------
     0 SELECT STATEMENT   MODE: ALL_ROWS
 16348 HASH (GROUP BY)
540328   PARTITION RANGE (ALL) PARTITION: START=1 STOP=28
540328     TABLE ACCESS   MODE: ANALYZED (FULL) OF 'SALES' (TABLE)
               PARTITION: START=1 STOP=28
```

The following section summarizes the wait events for which the SQL statement waited. The following values are provided for each type of wait event:

- `Times Waited` is the number of times a wait event has occurred.

- `Max. Wait` is the maximum wait time in seconds for a single wait event.

- `Total Waited` is the total wait time in seconds for a wait event. Ideally, the sum of the wait time for all wait events should be equal to the difference of the elapsed time and CPU time provided by the execution statistics. The difference, if available, is called *unaccounted-for time*.

UNACCOUNTED-FOR TIME

SQL trace provides information on how much time the database spends on each operation it executes. Ideally, the calculation should be very precise. Unfortunately, it is uncommon to find a trace file that gives exact information for each fraction of a second. Whenever there is a difference between the real elapsed time and the time accounted for in trace files, you have *unaccounted-for time*:

```
unaccounted-for time = real elapsed time - accounted for time
```

The most common reasons for unaccounted-for time are the following:

- The most obvious is the absence of timing information or wait events in the trace files. The former happens when the parameter `timed_statistics` is set to `FALSE`. The latter happens when SQL trace is activated at level 1 or 4. In both cases, the unaccounted-for time is always a positive value. Naturally, correctly enabling extended SQL trace will help you avoid these problems.

- Generally speaking, a process may be in three states: running on a CPU, waiting for the fulfillment of a request made to a device, or waiting for a CPU in the run queue. The instrumentation code is able to calculate the time spent in the first two states, but has no clue about how much time is spent waiting in the run queue. Therefore, in case of CPU starvation, the unaccounted-for time, which is always a positive value, could be quite long. Basically, you can avoid this problem in only two ways: either by increasing the amount of available CPU time or by decreasing the CPU utilization.

- The time measurements performed by the instrumentation code are precise. Nevertheless, there is a small quantization error in every measurement because of the implementation of timers in computer systems. Especially when the measured events are very short, these quantization errors could lead to noticeable unaccounted-for time. Owing to their nature, quantization errors could lead to positive as well as negative values for unaccounted-for time. Unfortunately, you are powerless against them. In practice, however, this problem is rarely the source of large unaccounted-for time since positive errors tend to cancel negative errors.

- If you can eliminate the other three possible reasons listed here, it is likely that the problem is because the instrumentation code does not cover the whole code. For example, the writing of the trace file itself is not accounted for. This is usually not a problem. If the trace files are written to a poorly performing device or the generation of trace information is very high, this can lead to a substantial overhead. In this case, the unaccounted-for time will always be a positive value. To avoid this problem, you should simply write trace files on a device that is able to sustain the necessary throughput. In some rare situations, you may be forced to put the trace files on a RAM disk.

Since these values are highly aggregated, they help you know only which type of resource you have been waiting for. For example, according to the following information, virtually the whole wait time was spent executing physical reads. In fact, db file sequential read is the wait event related to single-block reads, and db file scattered read is the wait event related to multiblock reads (additional information about multiblock reads is given in Chapter 5). In addition, the direct path write temp and direct path read temp waits are related to the spill into the temporary tablespace. Notice how the number of waits, 941, exactly matches the number of physical writes of the operation HASH GROUP BY provided earlier in the row source operations.

```
Elapsed times include waiting on following events:
  Event waited on                               Times    Max. Wait  Total Waited
  ----------------------------------------      Waited   ---------- ------------
  db file sequential read                          32      0.02          0.13
  db file scattered read                          225      0.04          1.76
  direct path write temp                          941      0.04          0.40
  direct path read temp                           941      0.03          1.00
```

In the analysis of the wait events, the key is knowing to which operation they are related. Fortunately, even if there are hundreds of wait event types, the most recurring ones are usually of only a few types. You can find a short description of most of them in the appendixes of the *Oracle Database Reference* manual.

The analysis continues with the next SQL statement. Since the structure of the information is the same as before, I'll comment only when something new or inherently different is present in the output file.

```
DECLARE
  l_channel_id sh.sales.channel_id%TYPE := 3;
BEGIN
  FOR c IN (SELECT cust_id, extract(YEAR FROM time_id), sum(amount_sold)
            FROM sh.sales
            WHERE channel_id = l_channel_id
            GROUP BY cust_id, extract(YEAR FROM time_id))
  LOOP
    NULL;
  END LOOP;
END;
```

The execution statistics for a PL/SQL call are limited. No information about physical and logical reads is available. This is because the resources consumed by the recursive SQL statements (for example, the query analyzed earlier) are not associated to the parent SQL statement. This means that for each SQL statement, you will see only the resources used by the SQL statement itself.

call	count	cpu	elapsed	disk	query	current	rows
Parse	1	0.00	0.04	0	0	0	0
Execute	1	0.00	0.00	0	0	0	1
Fetch	0	0.00	0.00	0	0	0	0
total	2	0.01	0.05	0	0	0	1

Since the PL/SQL block was not executed by the database recursively, the recursive depth is not shown (the recursive depth is 0). Also, no execution plan is available.

```
Misses in library cache during parse: 1
Optimizer mode: ALL_ROWS
Parsing user id: 33  (OPS$CHA)
```

The database waits for SQL*Net message to client while instructing the network layer to send data to the client (be careful, the real time needed to send the data over the network is not included), and the database waits for SQL*Net message from client while waiting for data from the client. Consequently, for each round-trip carried out by the SQL*Net layer, you should see a pair of those wait events. Note that the number of round-trips carried out by lower-level layers might be different. For example, it is not uncommon that at the network layer (for example, IP) a larger number of round-trips are performed because of a smaller packet size.

```
Elapsed times include waiting on following events:
```

Event waited on	Times Waited	Max. Wait	Total Waited
SQL*Net message to client	1	0.00	0.00
SQL*Net message from client	1	0.00	0.00

The next SQL statement is recursively executed by the database engine in order to get information (for example, object statistics) about the objects being used. Among other things, the query optimizer uses such information to figure out the most efficient execution plan. You have confirmation that this SQL statement was executed by the database engine because the user who parsed it is SYS. Since the recursive depth is 2, you can suppose that this SQL statement is needed to parse the SQL statement at depth 1, in other words, the first SQL statement in this output file.

```
SQL ID : 18tv0vxvb6u85
select dimobj#, col#
from
 dimattr$ where detailobj#=:1 union select dimobj#, col# from dimjoinkey$
  where detailobj#=:1 union select dimobj#, col# from dimlevelkey$ where
  detailobj#=:1 order by 2, 1
```

call	count	cpu	elapsed	disk	query	current	rows
Parse	1	0.00	0.00	0	0	0	0
Execute	1	0.00	0.00	0	0	0	0
Fetch	1	0.00	0.03	5	7	0	0
total	3	0.01	0.04	5	7	0	0

```
Misses in library cache during parse: 1
Misses in library cache during execute: 1
Optimizer mode: CHOOSE
Parsing user id: SYS   (recursive depth: 2)
```

Since the user SH has no privileges for the objects referenced in this SQL statement, only the row source operations are shown. See Chapter 6 for detailed information about the privileges needed to execute the SQL statement EXPLAIN PLAN.

```
Rows    Row Source Operation
------  ------------------------------------------------------
     0  SORT UNIQUE (cr=7 pr=5 pw=5 time=0 us cost=9 size=234 card=18)
     0   UNION-ALL  (cr=7 pr=5 pw=5 time=0 us)
     0    TABLE ACCESS BY INDEX ROWID DIMATTR$ (cr=1 pr=1 pw=1 time=0 us cost=2
                                               size=156 card=12)
     0     INDEX RANGE SCAN I_DIMATTR$_2 (cr=1 pr=1 pw=1 time=0 us cost=1
                                               size=0 card=12)(object id 954)
     0    TABLE ACCESS FULL DIMJOINKEY$ (cr=3 pr=2 pw=2 time=0 us cost=2
                                               size=13 card=1)
     0    TABLE ACCESS FULL DIMLEVELKEY$ (cr=3 pr=2 pw=2 time=0 us cost=2
                                               size=65 card=5)
```

```
Elapsed times include waiting on following events:
  Event waited on                            Times   Max. Wait  Total Waited
  ----------------------------------------   Waited  ---------  ------------
  db file sequential read                       5      0.02         0.03
```

After the report of all SQL statements, you can see the overall totals for execution statistics as well as parsing and wait events. The only thing of note in this part is that nonrecursive SQL statements are separated from recursive SQL statements.

```
OVERALL TOTALS FOR ALL NON-RECURSIVE STATEMENTS
```

call	count	cpu	elapsed	disk	query	current	rows
Parse	1	0.00	0.04	0	0	0	0
Execute	2	0.01	0.01	13	55	0	2
Fetch	0	0.00	0.00	0	0	0	0
total	3	0.02	0.05	13	55	0	2

```
Misses in library cache during parse: 1
```

```
Elapsed times include waiting on following events:
  Event waited on                            Times   Max. Wait  Total Waited
  ----------------------------------------   Waited  ---------  ------------
  SQL*Net message to client                     2      0.00         0.00
  SQL*Net message from client                   2      0.00         0.00
  log file sync                                 2      0.00         0.00
```

OVERALL TOTALS FOR ALL RECURSIVE STATEMENTS

call	count	cpu	elapsed	disk	query	current	rows
Parse	313	0.01	0.02	0	0	0	0
Execute	999	0.24	0.45	1	3	4	1
Fetch	1914	1.17	5.13	2733	5294	0	19202
total	3226	1.43	5.60	2734	5297	4	19203

Misses in library cache during parse: 48
Misses in library cache during execute: 48

Elapsed times include waiting on following events:

Event waited on	Times Waited	Max. Wait	Total Waited
db file sequential read	176	0.02	0.70
db file scattered read	225	0.04	1.76
direct path write temp	941	0.04	0.40
direct path read temp	941	0.03	1.00

The following lines summarize the number of SQL statements belonging to the current session, how many of them were executed recursively by the database engine, and how many of them the SQL statement EXPLAIN PLAN was executed for:

```
  3  user  SQL statements in session.
979  internal SQL statements in session.
982  SQL statements in session.
  1  statement EXPLAINed in this session.
```

The output file ends by giving overall information about the trace file. At first, you can see the trace file name, its version, and the value of the argument sort used for the analysis. Then, the overall number of sessions and SQL statements are given. In this specific case, since the argument print=3 was specified, you can deduce that 979 (982–3) SQL statements are missing in the output file. Information about the table used to execute the SQL statement EXPLAIN PLAN is given as well. At the end, the number of lines the trace file is composed of is shown, and, as of Oracle Database 10g, you can see the overall elapsed time for all SQL statements. I would personally prefer to see this last piece of information at the beginning of the output file rather than the end. That is because every time I open a TKPROF output file, I glance at this last line before doing everything else. Knowing how much time is spent for the whole trace file is crucial: without it, you cannot judge the magnitude of the impact of one SQL statement on the total response time.

```
Trace file: DBM11106_ora_9813.trc
Trace file compatibility: 11.01.00
Sort options: prsela  exeela  fchela
       1  session in tracefile.
       3  user  SQL statements in trace file.
```

```
  979  internal SQL statements in trace file.
  982  SQL statements in trace file.
   52  unique SQL statements in trace file.
    1  SQL statements EXPLAINed using schema:
         SH.prof$plan_table
            Default table was used.
            Table was created.
            Table was dropped.
21035  lines in trace file.
    5  elapsed seconds in trace file.
```

Using TVD$XTAT

Trivadis Extended Tracefile Analysis Tool (TVD$XTAT) is a command-line tool. Like TKPROF, its main purpose is to take a raw trace file as input and generate a formatted file as output. The output file can be an HTML or text file.

The simplest analysis is performed by merely specifying an input and an output file. In the following example, the input file is DBM11106_ora_6334.trc, and the output file is DBM11106_ora_6334.html:

```
tvdxtat -i DBM11106_ora_6334.trc -o DBM11106_ora_6334.html
```

Why Is TKPROF Not Enough?

In late 1999, I had my first encounter with extended SQL trace, through MetaLink note *Interpreting Raw SQL_TRACE and DBMS_SUPPORT.START_TRACE output* (39817.1). From the beginning, it was clear that the information it provided was essential for understanding what an application is doing when it is connected to an Oracle database engine. At the same time, I was very disappointed that no tool was available for analyzing extended SQL trace files for the purpose of leveraging their content. I should note that TKPROF at that time did not provide information about wait events. After spending too much time manually extracting information from the raw trace files, I decided to write my own analysis tool: TVD$XTAT.

Currently, TKPROF provides information about wait events, but it still has three major problems that are addressed in TVD$XTAT:

- As soon as the argument sort is specified, the relationship between SQL statements is lost.

- Data is provided only in aggregated form. Consequently, useful information is lost.

- No information about bind variables is provided.

Installation

To install TVD$XTAT, you need to perform the following operations:

1. Download (freeware) TVD$XTAT from http://top.antognini.ch.

2. Uncompress the distribution file into an empty directory of your choice.

3. In the shell script used to start TVD$XTAT (either tvdxtat.cmd or tvdxtat.sh, depending on your operating system), modify the variables java_home and tvdxtat_home. The former references the directory where a Java Runtime Environment (version 1.4.1 or later) is installed. The latter references the directory where the distribution file was uncompressed.

4. Optionally, change the default value of the command-line arguments. To do that, you need to modify the file tvdxtat.properties, which is stored in the subdirectory config. By customizing the default configuration, you can avoid specifying all arguments every time you run TVD$XTAT.

5. Optionally, change the logging configuration. To do that, you have to modify the file logging.properties, which is stored in the directory config. Per default, TVD$XTAT shows errors and warnings. It isn't usually necessary to change these default settings, however.

TVD$XTAT Arguments

If you run TVD$XTAT without arguments, you get a complete list of the available arguments with a short description for each of them. Note that for every argument, there is a short representation (for example, -c) and a long representation (for example, --cleanup).

```
usage: tvdxtat [-a no|yes] [-c no|yes] [-f <int>] [-l <int>]
               [-r 7|8|9|10|11] [-s no|yes] [-t <template>]
               [-w no|yes] -i <input> -o <output>
 -c,--cleanup     remove temporary XML file (no|yes)
 -f,--feedback    display progress every x lines (integer number >= 0, no
                  progress = 0)
 -h,--help        display this help information and exit
 -i,--input       input trace file name (valid extensions are TRC, GZ and
                  ZIP)
 -l,--limit       limit the size of lists (e.g. number of statements) in
                  the output file (integer number >= 0, unlimited = 0)
 -o,--output      output file name (a temporary XML file with the same
                  name but with the extension xml is also created)
 -r,--release     major release of the database engine that generated the
                  input trace file (7|8|9|10|11)
 -s,--sys         report information about SYS recursive statements (no|yes)
 -t,--template    name of the XSL template used to generate the output
                  file (html.xsl|text.xsl)
 -v,--version     print product version and exit
 -w,--wait        report detailed information about wait events (no|yes)
```

The function of each argument is as follows:

- input specifies the name of the input file. The input file must be either a trace file (extension .trc) or a compressed file (extension .gz or .zip) that contains one or several trace files. Note, however, that only a single trace file is extracted from .zip files.

- output specifies the name of the output file. During processing, a temporary XML file is created with the same name as the output file but with the extension .xml. Be careful, if another file with the same name as the output file exists, it will be overwritten.

- cleanup specifies whether the temporary XML file generated during processing is removed at the end. Generally, it should be set to yes. This argument is important only during the development phase to check intermediate results.

- feedback specifies whether progress information is displayed. It is useful during the processing of very large trace files to know the current status of the analysis. The argument specifies the interval (number of lines) at which a new message will be generated. If it is set to 0, no progress information is displayed.

- help specifies whether to display help information. It cannot be used along with other arguments.

- limit sets the maximum number of elements present in lists (for example, the lists used for SQL statements, waits, and bind variables) available in the output file. If it is set to 0, there is no limit.

- release specifies the major release number (that is, 7, 8, 9, 10, or 11) of the Oracle database engine that generated the input trace file.

- sys specifies whether information about recursive SQL statements that are executed by the user SYS are available in the output file. It is commonly set to no.

- template specifies the name of the XSL template used to generate the output file. By default, two templates are available: html.xsl and text.xsl. The former generates an HTML output file, and the latter generates a text output file. The default templates can be modified and new templates can be written as well. In this way, it is possible to fully customize the output file. The templates must be stored in the subdirectory templates.

- version specifies whether to display the version number of TVD$XTAT. It cannot be used along with other arguments.

- wait specifies whether detailed information for wait events is shown. Enabling this feature (that is, setting this argument to yes) might have a significant overhead during processing. Therefore, I suggest you set it initially to no. Afterward, if the basic wait information is not enough, you can run another analysis with it set to yes.

Interpreting TVD$XTAT Output

This section is based on the same trace file already used earlier with TKPROF. Since the output layout of TVD$XTAT is based on the output layout of TKPROF, I'll describe only information specific to TVD$XTAT here. To generate the output file, I used the following parameters. Note that both the trace file and the output file in HTML format are available for download along with the other files of this chapter.

```
tvdxtat -i DBM11106_ora_6334.trc -o DBM11106_ora_6334.html -s no -w yes
```

The output file begins with overall information about the input trace file. The most important information in this part is the interval covered by the trace file and the number of transactions recorded in it.

```
OVERALL INFORMATION

Database Version
----------------
Oracle Database 11g Enterprise Edition Release 11.1.0.6.0 - 64bit Production
With the Partitioning, Oracle Label Security, OLAP, Data Mining
and Real Application Testing options

Analyzed Trace File
-------------------
/u00/app/oracle/diag/rdbms/dbm11106/DBM11106/trace/DBM11106_ora_6334.trc

Interval
--------
Beginning 29 Feb 2008 07:43:11
End       29 Feb 2008 07:43:17
Duration  5.666

Transactions
------------
Committed  1
Rollbacked 0
```

The analysis of the output file starts by looking at the overall resource usage profile. The processing here lasted 5.666 seconds. About 44 percent of this time was spent reading data files (db file scattered read and db file sequential read), about 26 percent was spent running on the CPU, and about 25 percent was spent reading and writing temporary files (direct path read temp and direct path write temp). In summary, most of the time is spent on I/O operations with the rest on CPU. Notice that the unaccounted-for time is explicitly given.

Resource Usage Profile

Component	Total Duration	%	Number of Events	Duration per Event
db file scattered read	1.769	31.224	225	0.008
CPU	1.458	25.730	n/a	n/a
direct path read temp	1.005	17.731	941	0.001
db file sequential read	0.710	12.530	176	0.004
direct path write temp	0.408	7.195	941	0.000
unaccounted-for	0.307	5.425	n/a	n/a
SQL*Net message from client	0.009	0.155	2	0.004
log file sync	0.001	0.010	2	0.000
SQL*Net message to client	0.000	0.000	2	0.000
Total	5.666	100.000		

Note TVD$XTAT always sorts lists according to response time. No option is available to change this behavior because this is the only order that makes sense to investigate performance problems.

Knowing how the database engine spent time gives a general overview only. To continue the analysis, it is essential to find out which SQL statements are responsible for that processing time. For this purpose, a list containing all nonrecursive SQL statements is provided after the overall resource usage profile. In this case, you can see that a single SQL statement (actually, a PL/SQL block) is responsible for about 94 percent of the processing time. Note that in the following list, the total is not 100 percent because the unaccounted-for time is omitted (that is, you simply don't know where this time has gone):

The input file contains 182 distinct statements, 180 of which are recursive.

Only non-recursive statements are reported in the following table.

Statement ID	Type	Total Duration	%	Number of Executions	Duration per Execution
1	PL/SQL	5.333	94.119	1	5.333
35	PL/SQL	0.010	0.184	1	0.010
Total		5.343	94.303		

Naturally, the next step is to get more information about the SQL statement that is responsible for most of the processing time. To reference SQL statements easily, TVD$XTAT generates an ID (the column Statement ID in the previous excerpt) for each SQL statement. In the HTML version of the output file, you can simply click that ID to locate the SQL statement details. In the text version, however, you have to search for the string "STATEMENT 1".

The following information is then given for every SQL statement: general information about the execution environment, the SQL statement, the execution statistics, the execution plan, the bind variables used for the executions, and the wait events. The execution plan, the bind variables, and the wait events are optional and are obviously reported only if they have been recorded in the trace file.

At first, general information about the execution environment and the text of the SQL statement is given. Note that information about the session attributes is displayed only when available. For example, in this case, the attribute action name is not displayed because the application didn't set it. Also note that SQL ID is available as of Oracle Database 11g only.

STATEMENT 1

```
Session ID          90.6
Service Name        DBM11106.antognini.ch
Module Name         SQL*Plus
Parsing User        33
Hash Value          2276506700
SQL ID              3mfcj1a3v1g2c

DECLARE
  l_channel_id sh.sales.channel_id%TYPE := 3;
BEGIN
  FOR c IN (SELECT cust_id, extract(YEAR FROM time_id), sum(amount_sold)
            FROM sh.sales
            WHERE channel_id = l_channel_id
            GROUP BY cust_id, extract(YEAR FROM time_id))
  LOOP
    NULL;
  END LOOP;
END;
```

The execution statistics provide data in a tabular form, aggregated by type of database call. Since the table layout is based on the one generated by TKPROF, the meaning of the columns is the same. There are, however, two additional columns: Misses and LIO. The former is the number of hard parses that occurred during each type of call. The latter is just the sum of the columns Consistent and Current. Also notice that TVD$XTAT provides two tables. The first also includes the statistics about all recursive SQL statements related to the current one. The second, like TKPROF, does not include them.

```
Database Call Statistics with Recursive Statements
--------------------------------------------------
```

Call	Count	Misses	CPU	Elapsed	PIO	LIO	Consistent	Current	Rows
Parse	1	1	0.024	0.162	7	55	55	0	0
Execute	1	0	1.430	5.483	2,726	5,239	5,239	0	1
Fetch	0	0	0.000	0.000	0	0	0	0	0
Total	2	1	1.454	5.645	2,733	5,294	5,294	0	1

```
Database Call Statistics without Recursive Statements
-----------------------------------------------------
```

Call	Count	Misses	CPU	Elapsed	PIO	LIO	Consistent	Current	Rows
Parse	1	1	0.007	0.046	0	0	0	0	0
Execute	1	0	0.011	0.007	0	0	0	0	1
Fetch	0	0	0.000	0.000	0	0	0	0	0
Total	2	1	0.018	0.053	0	0	0	0	1

In this case, little time was spent by the current SQL statement according to the execution statistics. This is also shown by the following resource usage profile. In fact, it shows that almost 100 percent of the time was spent by recursive SQL statements.

```
Resource Usage Profile
----------------------
```

Component	Total Duration	%	Number of Events	Duration per Event
recursive statements	5.312	99.618	n/a	n/a
CPU	0.018	0.338	n/a	n/a
SQL*Net message from client	0.002	0.045	1	0.002
SQL*Net message to client	0.000	0.000	1	0.000
Total	5.333	100.000		

To show which SQL statements these are, the resource usage profile is followed by a list of the recursive SQL statements. From this list, you can see that SQL statement 2, which is a SELECT statement, was responsible for about 98 percent of the response time. Note that all other SQL statements were generated by the database engine itself (for example, during the parse phase) and, therefore, are marked with the label SYS recursive.

10 recursive statements were executed.

Statement ID	Type	Total Duration	%
2	SELECT	5.229	**98.061**
12	SELECT (SYS recursive)	0.030	0.571
17	SELECT (SYS recursive)	0.024	0.453
32	SELECT (SYS recursive)	0.012	0.225
44	SELECT (SYS recursive)	0.006	0.121
57	SELECT (SYS recursive)	0.003	0.056
63	SELECT (SYS recursive)	0.002	0.038
64	SELECT (SYS recursive)	0.002	0.038
70	SELECT (SYS recursive)	0.002	0.037
106	SELECT (SYS recursive)	0.001	0.019
Total		4.819	90.362

Since SQL statement 2 is responsible for most of the response time, you have to drill down further and get its details. The structure is basically the same as for SQL statement 1. There is, however, additional information. In the part that displays the execution environment, you can see the recursive level (remember, the SQL statements executed by the application are at level 0) and the parent SQL statement ID. This second piece of information is essential in order to not lose the relationship between SQL statements (as TKPROF does!).

```
STATEMENT 2

Session ID          90.6
Service Name        DBM11106.antognini.ch
Module Name         SQL*Plus
Parsing User        33
Recursive Level     1
Parent Statement ID 1
Hash Value          1624534809
SQL ID              g4h8jndhd8vst

SELECT CUST_ID, EXTRACT(YEAR FROM TIME_ID), SUM(AMOUNT_SOLD)
FROM SH.SALES
WHERE CHANNEL_ID = :B1
GROUP BY CUST_ID, EXTRACT(YEAR FROM TIME_ID)
```

The SQL statement uses a bind variable. Therefore, if it has been recorded in the trace file, TVD$XTAT will show its datatype and value. If several executions have been performed, bind variables will be grouped (by datatype and value), and the number of executions related to each group will be provided.

```
Bind Variables
--------------

Number of
Execution  Bind  Datatype  Value
----------  -----  ---------  ------
1           1      NUMBER    3
```

Next, you will find the execution plan in the output, if it is available in the trace file. Its format is almost the same as in the output generated by TKPROF.

```
Execution Plan
--------------

Optimizer Mode     ALL_ROWS

Rows     Operation
--------  --------------------------------------------------------------------------
  16,348 HASH GROUP BY (cr=1720 pr=2590 pw=2590 time=79 us cost=9990 size=11217129
                          card=534149)
 540,328   PARTITION RANGE ALL PARTITION: 1 28 (cr=1720 pr=1649 pw=1649 time=7744 us
                                               cost=496 size=11217129 card=534149)
 540,328    TABLE ACCESS FULL SALES PARTITION: 1 28 (cr=1720 pr=1649 pw=1649
                                                   time=4756 us cost=496
                                                   size=11217129 card=534149)
```

As is the case for all SQL statements, the execution plan is followed by the execution statistics, the resource usage profile, and, if available, the recursive SQL statements at level 2 (you are currently looking at a SQL statement at level 1. In this case, you can see that the recursive SQL statements are responsible for only about 15 percent of the response time. Actually, SQL statement 2 is responsible for 4.703 out of 5.476 seconds.

```
Database Call Statistics with Recursive Statements
--------------------------------------------------
```

Call	Count	Misses	CPU	Elapsed	PIO	LIO	Consistent	Current	Rows
Parse	1	1	0.000	0.000	0	0	0	0	0
Execute	1	1	0.326	0.972	136	3,519	3,519	0	0
Fetch	164	0	1.093	4.503	2,590	1,720	1,720	0	16,348
Total	166	2	1.419	**5.476**	2,726	5,239	5,239	0	16,348

```
Database Call Statistics without Recursive Statements
-----------------------------------------------------
```

Call	Count	Misses	CPU	Elapsed	PIO	LIO	Consistent	Current	Rows
Parse	1	1	0.000	0.000	0	0	0	0	0
Execute	1	1	0.045	0.199	0	0	0	0	0
Fetch	164	0	1.093	4.503	2,590	1,720	1,720	0	16,348
Total	166	2	1.138	**4.703**	2,590	1,720	1,720	0	16,348

Resource Usage Profile

Component	Total Duration	%	Number of Events	Duration per Event
db file scattered read	1.769	33.831	225	0.008
CPU	1.138	21.759	n/a	n/a
direct path read temp	1.005	19.211	941	0.001
recursive statements	0.775	**14.812**	n/a	n/a
direct path write temp	0.408	7.796	941	0.000
db file sequential read	0.136	2.592	32	0.004
Total	5.229	100.000		

33 recursive statements were executed.

Statement ID	Type	Total Duration	%
3	SELECT (SYS recursive)	0.135	2.591
4	SELECT (SYS recursive)	0.102	1.948
...			
...			
117	SELECT (SYS recursive)	0.000	0.000
118	SELECT (SYS recursive)	0.000	0.000
Total		0.487	9.319

In the resource usage profiles shown up to now, wait events are just summarized. To have additional information, a histogram like the following is provided for every component of the resource usage profile. In this case, the statistics are related to the wait event db file scattered read of SQL statement 2. Notice how the wait events are grouped by their duration (column Duration). For example, you see that about 49 percent of the wait events lasted between 256 and 512 microseconds. Since a disk needs at least a few milliseconds to physically read some blocks, this means that about half of the I/O operations were served from an operating system or I/O subsystem cache. Since the wait event db file scattered read is associated with multi-block reads, it might also be useful to see the average number of blocks read by an I/O operation (column Blocks per Event).

Duration [μs]	Total Duration	%	Number of Events	%	Duration per Event [μs]	Blocks	Blocks per Event
< 256	0.000	0.027	2	0.889	242	8	4.000
< 512	0.041	2.345	111	**49.333**	374	798	7.189
< 1024	0.005	0.300	8	3.556	663	58	7.250
< 2048	0.001	0.069	1	0.444	1,222	7	7.000
< 4096	0.009	0.487	3	1.333	2,872	22	7.333
< 8192	0.078	4.415	11	4.889	7,100	77	7.000
< 16384	0.482	27.220	41	18.222	11,745	295	7.195
< 32768	0.957	54.090	43	19.111	22,253	316	7.349
< 65536	0.195	11.046	5	2.222	39,084	36	7.200
Total	1.769	100.000	225	100.000	7,863	1,617	7.187

If the display of detailed information is enabled (the argument wait is used for that purpose), further details might be provided in addition to the previous histogram. This strongly depends on the type of wait event. Actually, for many events, no additional information is generated. Wait events related to I/O operations typically provide information at the file level. For example, the following table shows the statistics related to the wait event db file scattered read of SQL statement 2. In this example, you can see that 225 I/O operations were performed on data file 4 in 1.769 seconds. This means that each I/O operation lasted 7.863 milliseconds on average (be careful, the table displays this in microseconds).

File	Total Duration	%	Number of Events	%	Blocks	%	Duration per Event [μs]
4	1.769	100.000	225	100.000	1,617	100.000	7,863

In summary, even if plenty of SQL statements are executed (182 in total), SQL statement 2 is responsible for most of the response time. Therefore, in order to improve performance, the execution of that SQL statement should be avoided or optimized.

Profiling PL/SQL Code

To profile PL/SQL code, the database engine provides an API through the package dbms_profiler. With that package, the profiler integrated in the PL/SQL engine can be enabled and disabled at the session level. While enabled, the following information is gathered for each line of code that is executed:

- The total number of times it has been executed

- The total amount of time that has been spent executing it

- The minimum and maximum amount of time that has been spent executing it

The gathering takes place at session level for all PL/SQL units for which the user has the privilege CREATE. In other words, the privilege to execute a PL/SQL unit is not enough to use the profiler. To maximize the amount of information provided, the PL/SQL unit should be compiled in debug mode. Since native-compiled PL/SQL units are not executed by the PL/SQL engine, no profiling data is gathered for them.

The profiling data is stored in the database tables shown in Figure 3-20. The table plsql_profiler_runs gives information about which profiling sessions have been performed. The table plsql_profiler_units provides the list of units that have been executed for each run. The table plsql_profiler_data gives the profiling data, described earlier, for each line of code that has been executed.

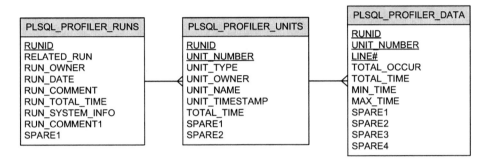

Figure 3-20. *The profiler stores the gathered information in three database tables. Notice that the primary keys consist of the underlined columns.*

Installing the Profiler

To install the package dbms_profiler, execute the script profload.sql as user sys:

```
CONNECT / AS SYSDBA
@?/rdbms/admin/profload.sql
```

The script also creates a public synonym and grants the object privilege EXECUTE to PUBLIC. As of Oracle Database 10g, the package dbms_profiler should already be available because the script profload.sql is executed by one of the main scripts used to create a new database (catproc.sql).

Installing the Output Tables

The package runs with the privileges of the user executing it. Consequently, the output tables do not necessarily need to be created by the user sys. Either the database administrator, as shown here, installs the output tables once and provides the necessary synonyms and privileges to use them or each user installs them in his own schema:

```
CONNECT / AS SYSDBA
@?/rdbms/admin/proftab.sql

CREATE PUBLIC SYNONYM plsql_profiler_runs FOR plsql_profiler_runs;
CREATE PUBLIC SYNONYM plsql_profiler_units FOR plsql_profiler_units;
CREATE PUBLIC SYNONYM plsql_profiler_data FOR plsql_profiler_data;
CREATE PUBLIC SYNONYM plsql_profiler_runnumber FOR plsql_profiler_runnumber;
```

```
GRANT SELECT, INSERT, UPDATE, DELETE ON plsql_profiler_runs TO PUBLIC;
GRANT SELECT, INSERT, UPDATE, DELETE ON plsql_profiler_units TO PUBLIC;
GRANT SELECT, INSERT, UPDATE, DELETE ON plsql_profiler_data TO PUBLIC;
GRANT SELECT ON plsql_profiler_runnumber TO PUBLIC;
```

Gathering the Profiling Data

A profiling analysis starts by enabling the profiler by calling the routine `start_profiler`. While the profiler is enabled, profiling data is gathered for the code executed by the PL/SQL engine. Unless an explicit flush is executed by calling the routine `flush_data`, no profiling data is stored in the output table while the profiler is enabled. The profiler is disabled, and an implicit flush is executed, by calling the routine `stop_profiler`. In addition, it is possible to pause and to resume the profiler by calling the routines `pause_profiler` and `resume_profiler`, respectively. Figure 3-21 shows the states of the profiler and the routines available in `dbms_profiler` that you can use to trigger a change of state.

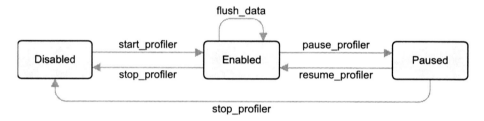

Figure 3-21. *State diagram of the profiler. The package `dbms_profiler` provides routines for changing the state of the profiler—disabled, enabled, or paused.*

    Each routine shown in Figure 3-21 is provided as a function or a procedure. The functions return the processing result status (0 = successful). The procedures generate an exception in case of errors. Except for the routine `start_profiler`, which accepts two comments describing the profiling analysis as a parameter, all other routines are parameterless.

    The following example shows a minimal run aimed at profiling the procedure `perfect_triangles`. The code of the procedure is available in the script `perfect_triangles.sql`. Notice that the `runid` selected while disabling the profiler is used in the next section to reference the profiling data stored in the output table.

```
SQL> ALTER PROCEDURE perfect_triangles COMPILE DEBUG;

SQL> SELECT dbms_profiler.start_profiler AS status
  2  FROM dual;

    STATUS
----------
         0

SQL> execute perfect_triangles(1000)
```

```
SQL> SELECT dbms_profiler.stop_profiler() AS status,
  2          plsql_profiler_runnumber.currval AS runid
  3  FROM dual;

   STATUS     RUNID
---------- ----------
        0        41
```

If the package cannot be manually started, it is also possible to create the following database event triggers to automatically enable and disable the profiler for a whole session. You can find the code to create these triggers in the script dbms_profiler_triggers.sql. To avoid enabling the profiler for all users, I usually suggest creating a role and temporarily granting permission only to the user required for the test. Of course, it is also possible to define the triggers for a single schema or to make other checks based, for example, on the userenv context.

```
CREATE ROLE profile;

CREATE OR REPLACE TRIGGER start_profiler AFTER LOGON ON DATABASE
BEGIN
  IF (dbms_session.is_role_enabled('PROFILE'))
  THEN
    dbms_profiler.start_profiler();
  END IF;
END;
/

CREATE OR REPLACE TRIGGER stop_profiler BEFORE LOGOFF ON DATABASE
BEGIN
  IF (dbms_session.is_role_enabled('PROFILE'))
  THEN
    dbms_profiler.stop_profiler();
  END IF;
END;
/
```

Reporting the Profiling Data

Once the profiling session is over, it is time to report the data generated by the profiler. This is achieved by querying the output tables with a SQL statement, as in the following example. What follows is an excerpt of the output generated by the script dbms_profiler.sql. The query provides only the percentage for the response time for two reasons: first, because we are usually interested in spotting the slowest part of the code, and second, because the timing information, especially when the code is CPU bound, is not very reliable. In fact, for CPU-bound processing, the overhead of the profiler may be very high. In this specific case, which is indeed CPU bound, the processing time increases from 1 second to 5 seconds. Of these 5 seconds, only 2.8 seconds are accounted for by the profiler.

```
SQL> COL line FORMAT 9,999 HEADING LINE#
SQL> COL total_occur FORMAT 9,999,999 HEADING EXEC#
SQL> COL time FORMAT 9,990.9 HEADING TIME%
SQL> COL text FORMAT A100 HEADING CODE

SQL> SELECT s.line,
  2         round(ratio_to_report(p.total_time) OVER ()*100,1) AS time,
  3         total_occur,
  4         s.text
  5  FROM all_source s,
  6      (SELECT u.unit_owner, u.unit_name, u.unit_type,
  7              d.line#, d.total_time, d.total_occur
  8       FROM plsql_profiler_units u, plsql_profiler_data d
  9       WHERE u.runid = &runid
 10       AND d.runid = u.runid
 11       AND d.unit_number = u.unit_number) p
 12  WHERE s.owner = p.unit_owner (+)
 13  AND s.name = p.unit_name (+)
 14  AND s.type = p.unit_type (+)
 15  AND s.line = p.line# (+)
 16  AND s.owner = '&owner'
 17  AND s.name = '&name'
 18  ORDER BY s.line;
Enter value for runid: 41
Enter value for owner: OPS$CHA
Enter value for name: PERFECT_TRIANGLES
```

LINE#	TIME%	EXEC#	CODE
1	0.0	1	PROCEDURE perfect_triangles(p_max IN INTEGER) IS
...			
42	0.0	1,001	FOR long IN 1..p_max
43			LOOP
44	6.8	501,500	FOR short IN 1..long
45			LOOP
46	30.6	500,500	hyp := sqrt(long*long + short*short);
47	13.6	500,500	ihyp := floor(hyp);
48	10.7	500,500	IF hyp-ihyp < 0.01
49			THEN
50	0.3	10,325	IF ihyp*ihyp = long*long + short*short
51			THEN
52	0.1	1,034	IF sides_are_unique(long, short)
53			THEN
54	0.0	179	m := m+1;

```
55       0.0         179              unique_sides(m).long := long;
56       0.0         179              unique_sides(m).short := short;
57       0.0         179              store_dup_sides(long, short);
58       0.0       1,034            END IF;
59       0.0      10,325          END IF;
60       0.0     500,500        END IF;
61       0.0       1,000      END LOOP;
62       0.0           1    END LOOP;
...
69       0.0           1  END perfect_triangles;
```

The GUI Way

In addition to the manual method covered in the previous sections, it is also possible to use one of the graphical interfaces available in third-party products. Such an interface is provided by the major players such as PL/SQL Developer (Allround Automations), SQLDetective (Conquest Software), Rapid SQL (Embarcadero), SQL Insight (Isidian), or Toad and SQL Navigator (Quest Software). All these tools can be used to profile the code, usually by clicking a check box or button before running a test or by simply analyzing the content of the output tables.

As an example, Figure 3-22 shows the information provided by PL/SQL Developer for the profiling session illustrated in the previous sections. Notice the graphical representation in the column Total Time that highlights the major time-consuming lines of code.

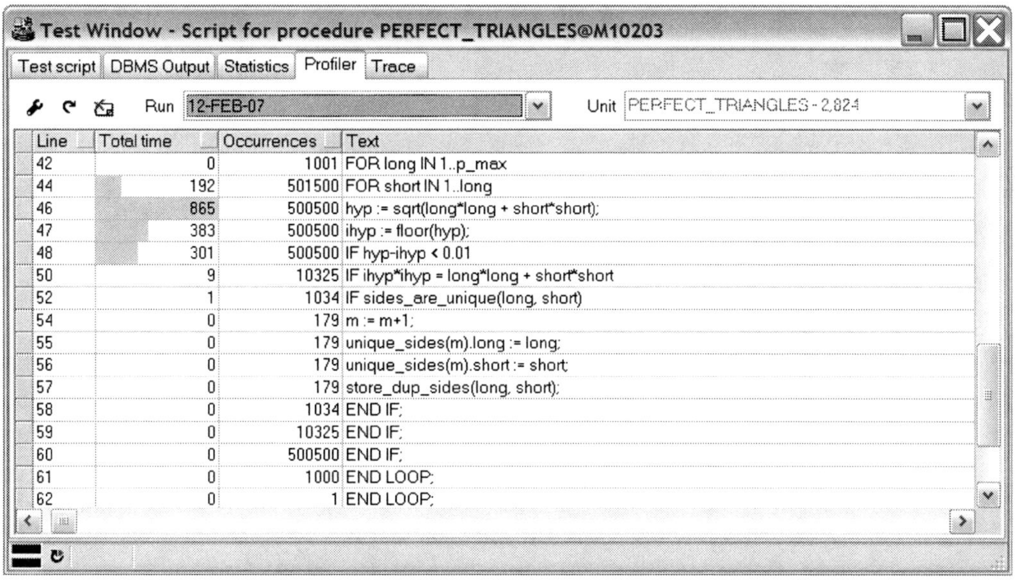

Figure 3-22. *The profiling data displayed in PL/SQL Developer*

On to Chapter 4

This chapter provided a detailed analysis road map for identifying performance problems, while discussing several tools and techniques that can be used with it. Having an analysis road map is really helpful. In the end, however, it is only one approach among many. In any case, the most important point is that only a methodical approach to performance problems leads to a quick and successful identification of the problems. I cannot stress this enough.

That said, the aim is not to investigate performance problems but to avoid them in the first place. Based on my experience, there are two major causes of performance problems: not designing applications for performance and poor configuration of the query optimizer. The latter is critical because every SQL statement executed by the database goes through the query optimizer. In the next two chapters, you will see how such a configuration should be carried out.

PART 3

■■■

Query Optimizer

Make the best use of what is in your power, and take the rest as it happens.

—Epictetus[1]

Every single SQL statement sent to the database before being processed by the SQL engine must be turned into an execution plan. In fact, an application specifies only what data must be processed through SQL statements, not how to process it. The aim of the query optimizer is not only to deliver the SQL engine execution plans describing how to process data but also, and most important, to deliver efficient execution plans. Failing to do so may lead to abysmal performance. Precisely for this reason, a book about database performance must deal with the query optimizer.

The aim of this part, however, is not to cover the internal workings of the query optimizer. Other resources, such as Jonathan Lewis's *Cost-Based Oracle* (Apress, 2006), already do an excellent job in this area. Instead, a very pragmatic approach is presented here, aimed at describing the essential features of the query optimizer you have to know. Chapter 4, for example, discusses the statistics used by the query optimizer. Chapter 5 describes the initialization parameters influencing the behavior of the query optimizer and how to set them. Since sooner or later you will be confronted with SQL statements performing badly, Chapter 6 outlines different methods of obtaining execution plans, as well as how to read them and recognize inefficient ones. Finally, Chapter 7 describes several SQL tuning techniques.

---

1. http://www.quotationspage.com/quote/2525.html

Before going on to Chapter 4, a very important note: up to Oracle9*i*, two main optimizers are available, the *rule-based optimizer* (RBO) and the *cost-based optimizer* (CBO). As of Oracle Database 10*g*, the rule-based optimizer is no longer supported and, therefore, will not be covered here. Throughout this book, when you read the term *query optimizer*, I always mean the cost-based optimizer.

CHAPTER 4

■ ■ ■

System and Object Statistics

System and object statistics are essential because they describe both the system running the database engine and the data stored in the database. In fact, a query optimizer that is aware of only the SQL statement to be processed and the structure of the objects referenced by the SQL statement is not able to provide efficient execution plans. Simply put, it has to be able to quantify the amount of data to be processed.

The aim of this chapter is twofold. First, it describes available system and object statistics. What the query optimizer does with them will be described here for only a few cases. The purpose of most statistics will be explained in Chapter 5. This is because the query optimizer uses statistics and initialization parameters at the same time. Second, this chapter describes how to gather system and object statistics. In practice, this means describing the package dbms_stats.

Overview of the Package dbms_stats

It used to be that object statistics were gathered with the SQL statement ANALYZE. This is no longer the case. For gathering object statistics, the SQL statement ANALYZE is available, but only for purposes of backward compatibility. As of Oracle9*i*, it is recommended that you use the package dbms_stats. In fact, not only does the package dbms_stats provide many more features, but in some situations it provides better statistics as well. For example, the SQL statement ANALYZE provides less control over the gathering of statistics, it does not support external tables, and for partitioned objects it gathers statistics only for each segment and estimates the statistics at the object (table or index) level. For these reasons, I won't cover the SQL statement ANALYZE in this chapter.

It is important to recognize that the package dbms_stats provides a comprehensive set of procedures and functions to manage system statistics and object statistics. For object statistics, since there are a lot of objects in a database, you are also able to manage them at different granularities. In fact, you have the choice between managing the object statistics for the whole database, for the data dictionary, for a single schema, for a single table, for a single index, or for a single table or index partition.

By default, the package dbms_stats modifies the data dictionary. Nevertheless, with most of its procedures and functions, it is also possible to work on a user-defined table stored outside the data dictionary. This is what I call the *backup table*. Since managing statistics means much more than simply gathering them, the package dbms_stats has the following features (see Figure 4-1):

- Gathering statistics and storing them either in the data dictionary or in a backup table

- Locking and unlocking statistics stored in the data dictionary

- Restoring statistics in the data dictionary

- Deleting statistics stored in the data dictionary or a backup table

- Exporting the statistics from the data dictionary to a backup table

- Importing the statistics from a backup table to the data dictionary

- Getting (extracting) statistics stored in the data dictionary or a backup table

- Setting (modifying) statistics stored in the data dictionary or a backup table

Note that moving statistics between databases is performed by means of a generic data movement utility (for example, Data Pump), not with the package dbms_stats itself.

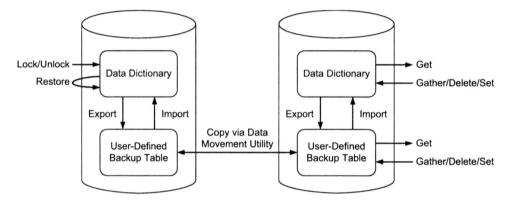

Figure 4-1. *The package dbms_stats provides a comprehensive set of features to manage system statistics and object statistics.*

Depending on the granularity and the operation you want to execute, Table 4-1 shows that the package dbms_stats provides different procedures and functions. For example, if you want to operate on a single schema, the package dbms_stats provides gather_schema_stats, delete_schema_stats, lock_schema_stats, unlock_schema_stats, restore_schema_stats, export_schema_stats, and import_schema_stats.

Table 4-1. *Features Provided by the Package dbms_stats*

Feature	Database	Dictionary*	Schema	Table**	Index**	System
Gather/delete	✓	✓	✓	✓	✓	✓
Lock/unlock*			✓	✓		
Restore*	✓	✓	✓	✓		✓
Export/import	✓	✓	✓	✓	✓	✓
Get/set				✓	✓	✓

* *Available as of Oracle Database 10g.*

** *For partitioned objects, it is possible to limit the processing to a single partition.*

System Statistics

The query optimizer used to base its cost estimations on the number of physical reads needed to execute SQL statements. This method is known as the *I/O cost model*. The main drawback of this method is that single-block reads and multiblock reads are equally costly.[1] Consequently, multiblock read operations, such as full table scans, are artificially favored. Up to Oracle8*i*, especially in OLTP systems, the initialization parameters `optimizer_index_caching` and `optimizer_index_cost_adj` solved this problem (see Chapter 5 for coverage of both initialization parameters). In fact, the default values used to be appropriate for reporting systems and data warehouses only. As of Oracle9*i*, a new costing method, known as the *CPU cost model*, is available to address this flaw. To use the CPU cost model, additional information about the performance of the system where the database engine runs, called *system statistics*, has to be provided to the query optimizer. Essentially, system statistics supply the following information.

- Performance of the I/O subsystem

- Performance of the CPU

Despite its name, the CPU cost model takes into consideration the cost of physical reads as well. But, instead of basing the I/O costs on the number of physical reads only, the performance of the I/O subsystem is also considered. Don't let the name mislead you.

In Oracle9*i*, no system statistics are available per default. This means that, by default, the I/O cost model is used. As of Oracle Database 10*g*, a default set of system statistics is always available. As a result, by default, the CPU cost model is used. Actually, as of Oracle Database 10*g*, the only way to use the I/O cost model is to specify the hint `no_cpu_costing` at the SQL statement level. In all other cases, the query optimizer uses the CPU cost model.[2]

There are two kinds of system statistics, *noworkload statistics* and *workload statistics*. The main difference between the two is the method used to measure the performance of the I/O subsystem. While the former runs a synthetic benchmark, the latter uses an application benchmark. Before discussing the difference between these two approaches in detail, let's see how system statistics are stored in the data dictionary.

APPLICATION VS. SYNTHETIC BENCHMARK

An *application benchmark*, also called a *real benchmark*, is based on the workload produced by the normal operation of a real application. Although it usually provides very good information about the real performance of the system running it, because of its nature, it is not always possible to apply it in a controlled manner.

A *synthetic benchmark* is a workload produced by a program that does no real work. The main idea is that it should simulate (model) an application workload by executing similar operations. Although it can be easily applied in a controlled manner, usually it will not produce performance figures as good as an application benchmark. Nevertheless, it could be useful for comparing different systems.

---

1. Common sense suggests that reading a single block should be faster than reading multiple blocks. Strangely enough, this is not always true in reality. In any case, the important thing is to recognize that there is a difference.
2. There is actually an unsupported way to use the I/O cost model, even in Oracle Database 10g. You set the undocumented initialization parameter `_optimizer_cost_model` to io.

Data Dictionary

System statistics are stored in the data dictionary table aux_stats$. Unfortunately, no data dictionary view is available to externalize them. In this table, there are up to three sets of rows that are differentiated by the following values of the column sname:

- SYSSTATS_INFO is the set containing the status of system statistics and when they were gathered. If they were correctly gathered, the status is set to COMPLETED. If there is a problem during the gathering of statistics, the status is set to BADSTATS, in which case the system statistics are not used by the query optimizer. Two more values may be seen during the gathering of workload statistics: MANUALGATHERING and AUTOGATHERING. In addition, up to Oracle9*i*, the status is set to NOWORKLOAD when noworkload statistics were gathered.

```
SQL> SELECT pname, pval1, pval2
  2  FROM sys.aux_stats$
  3  WHERE sname = 'SYSSTATS_INFO';

PNAME                 PVAL1 PVAL2
--------------- ---------- --------------------
STATUS                      COMPLETED
DSTART                      04-04-2007 14:26
DSTOP                       04-04-2007 14:36
FLAGS                 1
```

- SYSSTATS_MAIN is the set containing the system statistics themselves. Detailed information about them is provided in the next two sections.

```
SQL> SELECT pname, pval1
  2  FROM sys.aux_stats$
  3  WHERE sname = 'SYSSTATS_MAIN';

PNAME                 PVAL1
--------------- ------------
CPUSPEEDNW          1617.6
IOSEEKTIM            10.0
IOTFRSPEED         4096.0
SREADTIM             1.3
MREADTIM             7.8
CPUSPEED          1620.0
MBRC                 7.0
MAXTHR        473982976.0
SLAVETHR       1781760.0
```

- SYSSTATS_TEMP is the set containing values used for the computation of system statistics. It is available only while gathering workload statistics.

Since a single set of statistics exists for a single database, all instances of a RAC system use the same system statistics. Therefore, if the nodes are not equally sized or loaded, it must be carefully decided which node the system statistics are to be gathered on.

System statistics are gathered with the procedure gather_system_stats in the package dbms_stats. Per the default, the permission to execute it is granted to public. As a result, every user can gather system statistics. Nevertheless, to change the system statistics stored in the data dictionary, the role gather_system_statistics, or direct grants on the data dictionary table aux_stats$, are needed. Per the default, the role gather_system_statistics is provided through the role dba.

Noworkload Statistics

As mentioned earlier, the database engine supports two types of system statistics: noworkload statistics and workload statistics. As of Oracle Database 10*g*, noworkload statistics are always available. If you explicitly delete them, they are automatically gathered during the next database start-up. In Oracle9*i*, even if they are gathered, no statistics are stored in the data dictionary. Only the column status in aux_stats$ is set to NOWORKLOAD.

You gather noworkload statistics on an idle system because the database engine uses a synthetic benchmark to generate the load used to measure the performance of the system. To measure the CPU speed, most likely some kind of calibrating operation is executed in a loop. To measure the I/O performance, some reads of different sizes are performed on several datafiles of the database.

To gather noworkload statistics, you set the parameter gathering_mode of the procedure gather_system_stats to noworkload, as shown in the following example:

```
dbms_stats.gather_system_stats(gathering_mode => 'noworkload')
```

Gathering statistics usually takes less than one minute, and the statistics listed in Table 4-2 are computed. Oddly, sometimes it is necessary to repeat the gathering of statistics more than once; otherwise, the default values, which are also available in Table 4-2, are used. Although it is difficult to know what exactly is happening here, I would conjecture that a kind of sanity check, which discards statistics that make little sense, is occurring.

Table 4-2. *Noworkload Statistics Stored in the Data Dictionary*

Name	Description
CPUSPEEDNW	The number of operations per second (in millions) that one CPU is able to process.
IOSEEKTIM	Average time (in milliseconds) needed to locate data on the disk. The default value is 10.
IOTFRSPEED	Average number of bytes per millisecond that can be transferred from the disk. The default value is 4,096.

Workload Statistics

Workload statistics are available only when explicitly gathered. To gather them, you cannot use an idle system because the database engine has to take advantage of the regular database load to measure the performance of the I/O subsystem. On the other hand, the same method as for noworkload statistics is used to measure the speed of the CPU. As shown in Figure 4-2, gathering workload statistics is a three-step activity. The idea is that to compute the average time taken by an operation, it is necessary to know how many times that operation was performed and how much time was spent executing it. For example, with the following SQL statements, I was able to compute the average time for single-block reads (6.2 milliseconds) from one of my test databases, in the same way the package dbms_stats would:

```
SQL> SELECT sum(singleblkrds) AS count, sum(singleblkrdtim)*10 AS time_ms
  2  FROM v$filestat;

    COUNT    TIME_MS
---------- ----------
    22893      36760

SQL> REMARK run a benchmark to generate some I/O operations...

SQL> SELECT sum(singleblkrds) AS count, sum(singleblkrdtim)*10 AS time_ms
  2  FROM v$filestat;

    COUNT    TIME_MS
---------- ----------
    54956     236430

SQL> SELECT round((236430-36760)/(54956-22893),1) AS avg_tim_singleblkrd
  2  FROM dual;

AVG_TIM_SINGLEBLKRD
-------------------
                6.2
```

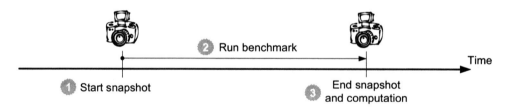

Figure 4-2. *To gather (compute) system statistics, two snapshots of several performance figures are used.*

The three steps illustrated in Figure 4-2 are as follows:

1. A snapshot of several performance figures is taken and stored in the data dictionary table aux_stats$ (for these rows, the column sname is set to SYSSTATS_TEMP). This step is carried out by setting the parameter gathering_mode of the procedure gather_system_stats to start, as shown in the following command:

   ```
   dbms_stats.gather_system_stats(gathering_mode => 'start')
   ```

2. The database engine does not control the database load. Consequently, enough time to cover a representative load has to be waited for before taking another snapshot. It is difficult to provide general advice about this waiting time, but it is common to wait at least 30 minutes.

3. A second snapshot is taken. This step is carried out by setting the parameter gathering_mode of the procedure gather_system_stats to stop, as shown in the following command:

```
dbms_stats.gather_system_stats(gathering_mode => 'stop')
```

4. Then, based on the performance statistics of the two snapshots, the system statistics listed in Table 4-3 are computed. If one of the I/O statistics cannot be computed, it is set to NULL (as of Oracle Database 10g) or -1 (in Oracle9i).

Table 4-3. *Workload Statistics Stored in the Data Dictionary*

Name	Description
CPUSPEED	The number of operations per second (in millions) that one CPU is able to process
SREADTIM	Average time (in milliseconds) needed to perform a single-block read operation
MREADTIM	Average time (in milliseconds) needed to perform a multiblock read operation
MBRC	Average number of blocks read during a multiblock read operation
MAXTHR	Maximum I/O throughput (in bytes per second) for the whole system
SLAVETHR	Average I/O throughput (in bytes per second) for a parallel processing slave

To avoid manually taking the ending snapshot, it is also possible to set the parameter gathering_mode of the procedure gather_system_stats to interval. With this parameter, the starting snapshot is immediately taken, and the ending snapshot is scheduled to be executed after the number of minutes specified by a second parameter named interval. The following command specifies that the gathering of statistics should last 30 minutes:

```
dbms_stats.gather_system_stats(gathering_mode => 'interval',
                              interval      => 30)
```

Note that the execution of the previous command does not take 30 minutes. It just takes the starting snapshot and schedules a job to take the ending snapshot. Up to Oracle Database 10g Release 1, the legacy scheduler (the one managed with the package dbms_job) is used. As of Database 10g Release 2, the new scheduler (the one managed with the package dbms_scheduler) is used. You can see the job by querying the views user_jobs and user_scheduler_jobs, respectively.

The main problem we have in gathering system statistics is choosing the gathering period. In fact, most systems experience a load that is anything but constant, and therefore, the evolution of workload statistics, except for cpuspeed, is equally inconstant. Figure 4-3 shows the evolution of workload statistics that I measured on a production system. To produce the charts, I gathered workload statistics for about four days at intervals of one hour. Consult the scripts `system_stats_` `history.sql` and `system_stats_history_job.sql` for examples of the SQL statements I used for that purpose.

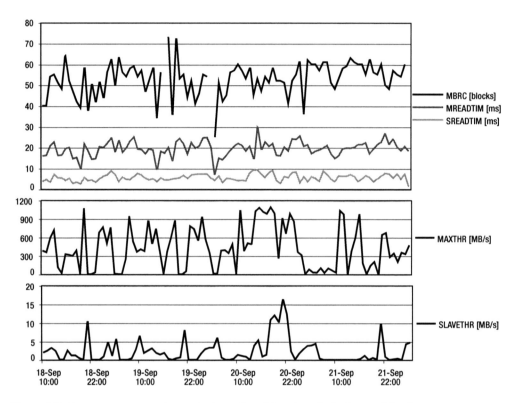

Figure 4-3. *On most systems, the evolution of workload statistics is anything but constant.*

To avoid gathering workload statistics during a period that provides values that are not representative of the load, I see only two approaches. Either we gather workload statistics over a period of several days or we can produce charts like in Figure 4-3 to get values that make sense. I usually advise the latter, because we also get a useful view of the system at the same time. For example, based on the charts shown in Figure 4-3, I suggest using the average values for `mbrc`, `mreadtim`, `sreadtim`, and `cpuspeed` and using the maximum values for `maxthr` and `slavethr`. Then, a PL/SQL block like the following one might be used to manually set the workload statistics. Note that before setting the workload statistics with the procedure `set_system_stats`, the old set of system statistics is deleted with the procedure `delete_system_stats`.

```
BEGIN
  dbms_stats.delete_system_stats();
  dbms_stats.set_system_stats(pname => 'CPUSPEED', pvalue => 772);
  dbms_stats.set_system_stats(pname => 'SREADTIM', pvalue => 5.5);
  dbms_stats.set_system_stats(pname => 'MREADTIM', pvalue => 19.4);
  dbms_stats.set_system_stats(pname => 'MBRC',     pvalue => 53);
  dbms_stats.set_system_stats(pname => 'MAXTHR',   pvalue => 1136136192);
  dbms_stats.set_system_stats(pname => 'SLAVETHR', pvalue => 16870400);
END;
```

This method could also be used if different sets of workload statistics are needed for different periods of the day or week. It must be said, however, that I have never come across a case that required more than one set of workload statistics.

You may have perceived that I do not advise regularly gathering noworkload statistics. I find it much better to fix their value and consider them as initialization parameters.

Impact on the Query Optimizer

When system statistics are available, the query optimizer computes two costs: I/O and CPU. Chapter 5 describes how I/O costs are computed for the most important access paths. Very little information is available about the computation of CPU. Nevertheless, we can imagine that the query optimizer associates a cost to every operation in terms of CPU. For example, as pointed out by Joze Senegacnik, beginning in Oracle Database 10g Release 2, Formula 4-1 is used to compute the CPU cost of accessing a column.

$$cpu\_cost = column\_position \cdot 20$$

Formula 4-1. *The estimated CPU cost to access a column depends on its position in the table. This formula gives the cost of accessing one row. If several rows are accessed, the CPU cost increases proportionally. Chapter 12 provides further information on why the position of a column is relevant.*

The following example, which is an excerpt of the script `cpu_cost_column_access.sql`, shows Formula 4-1 in action. A table with nine columns is created, one row is inserted, and then with the SQL statement EXPLAIN PLAN the CPU cost of independently accessing the nine columns is displayed. Please refer to Chapter 6 for detailed information about this SQL statement. Notice how there is an initial CPU cost of 35,757 to access the table, and then for each subsequent column, a CPU cost of 20 is added. At the same time, the I/O cost is constant. This makes sense because all columns are stored in the very same database block, and therefore the number of physical reads required to read them is the same for all queries.

```
SQL> CREATE TABLE t (c1 NUMBER, c2 NUMBER, c3 NUMBER,
  2                   c4 NUMBER, c5 NUMBER, c6 NUMBER,
  3                   c7 NUMBER, c8 NUMBER, c9 NUMBER);

SQL> INSERT INTO t VALUES (1, 2, 3, 4, 5, 6, 7, 8, 9);
```

```
SQL> EXPLAIN PLAN SET STATEMENT_ID 'c1' FOR SELECT c1 FROM t;
SQL> EXPLAIN PLAN SET STATEMENT_ID 'c2' FOR SELECT c2 FROM t;
SQL> EXPLAIN PLAN SET STATEMENT_ID 'c3' FOR SELECT c3 FROM t;
SQL> EXPLAIN PLAN SET STATEMENT_ID 'c4' FOR SELECT c4 FROM t;
SQL> EXPLAIN PLAN SET STATEMENT_ID 'c5' FOR SELECT c5 FROM t;
SQL> EXPLAIN PLAN SET STATEMENT_ID 'c6' FOR SELECT c6 FROM t;
SQL> EXPLAIN PLAN SET STATEMENT_ID 'c7' FOR SELECT c7 FROM t;
SQL> EXPLAIN PLAN SET STATEMENT_ID 'c8' FOR SELECT c8 FROM t;
SQL> EXPLAIN PLAN SET STATEMENT_ID 'c9' FOR SELECT c9 FROM t;

SQL> SELECT statement_id, cpu_cost AS total_cpu_cost,
  2         cpu_cost-lag(cpu_cost) OVER (ORDER BY statement_id) AS cpu_cost_1_coll,
  3         io_cost
  4  FROM plan_table
  5  WHERE id = 0
  6  ORDER BY statement_id;

STATEMENT_ID TOTAL_CPU_COST CPU_COST_1_COLL IO_COST
------------ -------------- --------------- -------
c1                    35757                       3
c2                    35777              20       3
c3                    35797              20       3
c4                    35817              20       3
c5                    35837              20       3
c6                    35857              20       3
c7                    35877              20       3
c8                    35897              20       3
c9                    35917              20       3
```

The I/O and CPU costs are expressed with different units of measurement. Obviously then, the overall cost of a SQL statement cannot be calculated simply by summing up the costs. To solve this problem, the query optimizer uses Formula 4-2[3] with workload statistics. Simply put, the CPU cost is transformed into the number of single-block reads that can be performed per second.

$$cost \approx io\_cost + \frac{cpu\_cost}{cpuspeed \cdot sreadtim \cdot 1000}$$

Formula 4-2. *The overall costs are based on the I/O costs and the CPU costs.*

To compute the overall cost with noworkload statistics, in Formula 4-2 cpuspeed is replaced by cpuspeednw, and sreadtim is computed using Formula 4-3.

---

3. This formula is available, even if under another form, in the manual *Oracle9i Database Performance Tuning Guide and Reference*. As of Oracle Database 10g, it has disappeared from the manuals.

$$sreadtim = ioseektim + \frac{db\_block\_size}{iotfrspeed}$$

Formula 4-3. *If necessary,* `sreadtim` *is computed based on noworkload statistics and the block size of the database.*

Generally speaking, if workload statistics are available, the query optimizer uses them and ignores noworkload statistics. You should be aware that the query optimizer performs several sanity checks that could disable or partially replace workload statistics.

- When either `sreadtim`, `mreadtim`, or `mbrc` is not available, the query optimizer ignores workload statistics.

- When `mreadtim` is less than or equal to `sreadtim`, the value of `sreadtim` and `mreadtim` is recomputed using Formula 4-3 and Formula 4-4, respectively.

$$mreadtim = ioseektim + \frac{mbrc \cdot db\_block\_size}{iotfrspeed}$$

Formula 4-4. *The computation of* `mreadtim` *based on noworkload statistics and the block size of the database*

System statistics make the query optimizer aware of the system where the database engine is running. This means they are essential for a successful configuration. In other words, it is strongly advisable to always use them. I also recommend freezing them in order to have some stability. Of course, in case of major hardware or software changes, they should be recomputed, and as a result, the whole configuration should be checked. For checking purposes, it is also possible to regularly gather them in a backup table (in other words, using the parameters `statown` and `stattab` of the procedure `gather_system_stats`) and verify whether there is a major difference between the current values and the values stored in the data dictionary.

Object Statistics

Object statistics describe the data stored in the database. For example, they tell the query optimizer how many rows are stored in tables. Without this quantitative information, the query optimizer could never make right decisions, such as finding the right join method for small or large tables (result sets). To illustrate this, consider the following example. Let's say I ask you what the fastest method of transportation is for me to get home from a particular place. Would it be by car, by train, or by plane? Why not by bike? The point is, without considering my actual position and where my home is, you cannot arrive at a meaningful answer. In the same way, without object statistics, the query optimizer has the same problem. It simply cannot generate meaningful execution plans.

The following sections will begin by describing which object statistics are available and where to find them in the data dictionary. Then I'll present the features of the package dbms_stats used to gather, compare, lock, and delete statistics. Then I'll describe a few strategies that I use to manage object statistics, based on the available features.

Note The database engine, through the SQL statement ASSOCIATE STATISTICS, allows user-defined statistics to be associated with columns, functions, packages, types, domain indexes, and index types. When needed, this is a very powerful feature, although in practice, this technique is rarely used. For this reason, it will not be covered here. For information about it, refer to the *Data Cartridge Developer's Guide* manual.

What Object Statistics Are Available?

There are three types of object statistics: table statistics, column statistics, and index statistics. For each type, there are up to three subtypes: table/index-level statistics, partition-level statistics, and subpartition-level statistics. It may be obvious that partition and subpartition statistics exist only when an object is partitioned and subpartitioned, respectively.

Object statistics are shown in the data dictionary views reported in Table 4-4. Of course, for each view there are dba and all versions as well, for example, dba_tables and all_tables.

Table 4-4. *Data Dictionary Views Showing Object Statistics of Relational Tables*

Object	Table/Index-Level Statistics	Partition-Level Statistics	Subpartition-Level Statistics
Tables	user_tab_statistics user_tables*	user_tab_statistics user_tab_partitions*	user_tab_statistics user_tab_subpartitions*
Columns	user_tab_col_statistics user_tab_histograms	user_part_col_statistics user_part_histograms	user_subpart_col_statistics user_subpart_histograms
Indexes	user_ind_statistics user_indexes*	user_ind_statistics user_ind_partitions*	user_ind_statistics user_ind_subpartitions*

* *These views are mainly used only up to Oracle9i. This is because the views user_tab_statistics and user_ind_statistics are available as of Oracle Database 10g only.*

The rest of this section describes the most important object statistics available in the data dictionary. For this purpose, I created a test table with the following SQL statements. These SQL statements, as well as all other queries in this section, are available in the script object_statistics.sql.

```
CREATE TABLE t
AS
SELECT rownum AS id,
       round(dbms_random.normal*1000) AS val1,
       100+round(ln(rownum/3.25+2)) AS val2,
       100+round(ln(rownum/3.25+2)) AS val3,
       dbms_random.string('p',250) AS pad
```

```
FROM all_objects
WHERE rownum <= 1000
ORDER BY dbms_random.value;

UPDATE t SET val1 = NULL WHERE val1 < 0;

ALTER TABLE t ADD CONSTRAINT t_pk PRIMARY KEY (id);

CREATE INDEX t_val1_i ON t (val1);
CREATE INDEX t_val2_i ON t (val2);

BEGIN
  dbms_stats.gather_table_stats(ownname            => user,
                                tabname            => 'T',
                                estimate_percent => 100,
                                method_opt         => 'for all columns size skewonly',
                                cascade            => TRUE);
END;
/
```

Table Statistics

The following query shows how to get the most important table statistics for a table:

```
SQL> SELECT num_rows, blocks, empty_blocks, avg_space, chain_cnt, avg_row_len
  2  FROM user_tab_statistics
  3  WHERE table_name = 'T';
```

NUM_ROWS	BLOCKS	EMPTY_BLOCKS	AVG_SPACE	CHAIN_CNT	AVG_ROW_LEN
1000	44	0	0	0	265

The following is an explanation of the table statistics returned by this query:

- num_rows is the number of rows in the table.

- blocks is the number of blocks below the high watermark in the table.

- empty_blocks is the number of blocks above the high watermark in the table. This value is not computed by the package dbms_stats. It is set to 0.

- avg_space is the average free space (in bytes) in the table data blocks. This value is not computed by the package dbms_stats. It is set to 0.

- chain_cnt is the sum of the rows in the table that are chained or migrated to another block (chained and migrated rows will be described in Chapter 12). This value is not computed by the package dbms_stats. It is set to 0.

- avg_row_len is the average size (in bytes) of a row in the table.

HIGH WATERMARK

The *high watermark* is the boundary between used and unused space in a segment. The used blocks are below the high watermark, and therefore, the unused blocks are above the high watermark. Blocks above the high watermark have never been used or initialized.

In normal circumstances, operations requiring space (for example, INSERT statements) increase the high watermark only if there is no more free space available below the high watermark. A common exception to this is due to direct insert operations because they exclusively use blocks above the high watermark (see Chapter 11).

Operations releasing space (for example, DELETE statements) do not decrease the high watermark. They simply make space available to other operations. If the free space is released at a rate equal to or lower than the rate the space is reused, using the blocks below the high watermark should be optimal. Otherwise, the free space below the high watermark would increase steadily. Long-term, this would cause not only an unnecessary increase in the size of the segment but also suboptimal performance. In fact, full scans access all blocks below the high watermark. This occurs even if they are empty. The segment should be reorganized to solve such a problem.

Column Statistics

The following query shows how to get the most important column statistics for a table:

```
SQL> SELECT column_name AS "NAME",
  2          num_distinct AS "#DST",
  3          low_value,
  4          high_value,
  5          density AS "DENS",
  6          num_nulls AS "#NULL",
  7          avg_col_len AS "AVGLEN",
  8          histogram,
  9          num_buckets AS "#BKT"
 10  FROM user_tab_col_statistics
 11  WHERE table_name = 'T';
```

NAME	#DST	LOW_VALUE	HIGH_VALUE	DENS	#NULL	AVGLEN	HISTOGRAM	#BKT
ID	1000	C102	C20B	.00100	0	4	NONE	1
VAL1	431	C103	C2213E	.00254	503	3	HEIGHT BALANCED	254
VAL2	6	C20202	C20207	.00050	0	4	FREQUENCY	6
VAL3	6	C20202	C20207	.00050	0	4	FREQUENCY	6
PAD	1000	202623436F2943 7334237B426574 336E4A5B302E4F 4B53236932303A 21215F46	7E79514A202D49 4649366C744E25 3F36264C692755 7A57737C6D4B22 59414C44	.00100	0	251	HEIGHT BALANCED	254

LOW_VALUE AND HIGH_VALUE FORMAT

Unfortunately, the columns low_value and high_value are not easily decipherable. In fact, they display the values according to the internal representation used by the database engine to store data. To convert them to human-readable values, there are two possibilities.

First, the package utl_raw provides the functions cast_to_binary_double, cast_to_binary_float, cast_to_binary_integer, cast_to_number, cast_to_nvarchar2, cast_to_raw, and cast_to_varchar2. As the names of the functions suggest, for each specific datatype, there is a corresponding function used to convert the internal value to the actual value. To get the low and high value of the column val1, you can use the following query:

```
SQL> SELECT utl_raw.cast_to_number(low_value) AS low_value,
  2         utl_raw.cast_to_number(high_value) AS high_value
  3  FROM user_tab_col_statistics
  4  WHERE table_name = 'T'
  5  AND column_name = 'VAL1';

LOW_VALUE HIGH_VALUE
--------- ----------
        2       3261
```

Second, the package dbms_stats provides the procedures convert_raw_value (which is overloaded several times), convert_raw_value_nvarchar, and convert_raw_value_rowid. Since procedures cannot be directly used in SQL statements, usually they are used only in PL/SQL programs. In the following example, the PL/SQL block has the same purpose as the previous query:

```
SQL> DECLARE
  2    l_low_value user_tab_col_statistics.low_value%TYPE;
  3    l_high_value user_tab_col_statistics.high_value%TYPE;
  4    l_val1 t.val1%TYPE;
  5  BEGIN
  6    SELECT low_value, high_value
  7    INTO l_low_value, l_high_value
  8    FROM user_tab_col_statistics
  9    WHERE table_name = 'T'
 10    AND column_name = 'VAL1';
 11
 12    dbms_stats.convert_raw_value(l_low_value, l_val1);
 13    dbms_output.put_line('low_value: ' || l_val1);
 14    dbms_stats.convert_raw_value(l_high_value, l_val1);
 15    dbms_output.put_line('high_value: ' || l_val1);
 16  END;
 17  /
low_value: 2
high_value: 3261
```

The following is an explanation of the column statistics returned by this query:

- num_distinct is the number of distinct values in the column.

- low_value is the lowest value in the column. It is shown in the internal representation. Note that for string columns (in the example, the column pad), only the first 32 bytes are used.

- high_value is the highest value in the column. It is shown in the internal representation. Notice that for string columns (in the example, the column pad), only the first 32 bytes are used.

- density is a decimal number between 0 and 1. Values close to 0 indicate that a restriction on that column filters out the majority of the rows. Values close to 1 indicate that a restriction on that column filters almost no rows. If no histogram is present, density is 1/num_distinct. If a histogram is present, the computation differs and depends on the type of histogram.

- num_nulls is the number of NULL values stored in the column.

- avg_col_len is the average column size in bytes.

- histogram indicates whether a histogram is available for the column and, if it is available, which type it is. Valid values are NONE (meaning no histogram), FREQUENCY, and HEIGHT BALANCED. This column is available as of Oracle Database 10g.

- num_buckets is the number of buckets in the histogram. A bucket, or *category* as it is called in statistics, is a group of values of the same kind. As we will see in the next section, histograms are composed of at least one bucket. If no histogram is available, it is set to 1. The maximum number of buckets is 254.

Histograms

The query optimizer starts from the principle that data is uniformly distributed. An example of a uniformly distributed set of data is the one stored in the column id in the test table used throughout the previous sections. In fact, it stores all numbers from 1 up to 1,000 exactly once. In such a case, to find out the number of rows filtered out by a predicate based on that column (for example, id BETWEEN 6 AND 19), the query optimizer requires only the object statistics described in the previous section: the minimum value, the maximum value, and the number of distinct values.

If data is not uniformly distributed, the query optimizer is not able to compute acceptable estimations without additional information. For example, given the data set stored in column val2 (see the output of the following query), how could the query optimizer make a meaningful estimation for a predicate like val2=105? It cannot, because it has no clue that about 50 percent of the rows fulfill that predicate.

```
SQL> SELECT val2 AS val2, count(*)
  2  FROM t
  3  GROUP BY val2
  4  ORDER BY val2;
```

VAL2	COUNT(*)
101	8
102	25
103	68
104	185
105	502
106	212

The additional information needed by the query optimizer to get information about the nonuniform distribution of data is called a *histogram*. Two types of histograms are available: *frequency histograms* and *height-balanced histograms*.

The frequency histogram is what most people understand by the term *histogram*. Figure 4-4 is an example of this type, which shows a common graphical representation of the data returned by the previous query.

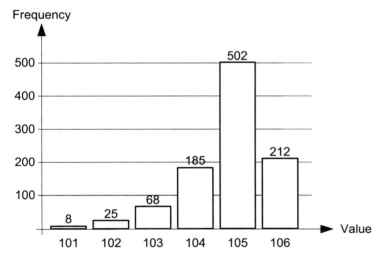

Figure 4-4. *Graphical representation of a frequency histogram based on the set of data stored in column val2.*

The frequency histogram stored in the data dictionary is similar to this representation. The main difference is that instead of the frequency, the cumulated frequency is used. The following query shows the difference between these two values (notice that the column endpoint_number is the cumulated frequency):

```
SQL> SELECT endpoint_value, endpoint_number,
  2           endpoint_number - lag(endpoint_number,1,0)
  3                         OVER (ORDER BY endpoint_number) AS frequency
  4  FROM user_tab_histograms
  5  WHERE table_name = 'T'
  6  AND column_name = 'VAL2'
  7  ORDER BY endpoint_number;
```

```
ENDPOINT_VALUE ENDPOINT_NUMBER  FREQUENCY
-------------- ---------------  ---------
          101               8          8
          102              33         25
          103             101         68
          104             286        185
          105             788        502
          106            1000        212
```

The essential characteristics of a frequency histogram are the following:

- The number of buckets (in other words, the number of categories) is the same as the number of distinct values. For each bucket, a row in the view user_tab_histograms is available.

- The column endpoint_value provides the value itself. Since the datatype of this column is NUMBER, columns based on non-numeric datatypes (such as VARCHAR2, CHAR, NVARCHAR2, NCHAR, and RAW) must be converted. To do this, only the leading 6 bytes (not characters!) are used. This means values stored in histograms are distinguished based only on the leading part. As a result, fixed prefixes might jeopardize the effectiveness of histograms. This is especially true for multibyte character sets where the 6 bytes might be only 3 characters.

- The column endpoint_number provides the cumulated frequency of the value. To get the frequency itself, the value of the column endpoint_number of the previous row must be subtracted.

The following example shows how the query optimizer takes advantage of the frequency histogram to estimate precisely the number of rows returned by a query (the *cardinality*) with a predicate on the column val2. Detailed information about the SQL statement EXPLAIN PLAN is provided in Chapter 6.

```
SQL> EXPLAIN PLAN SET STATEMENT_ID '101' FOR SELECT * FROM t WHERE val2 = 101;
SQL> EXPLAIN PLAN SET STATEMENT_ID '102' FOR SELECT * FROM t WHERE val2 = 102;
SQL> EXPLAIN PLAN SET STATEMENT_ID '103' FOR SELECT * FROM t WHERE val2 = 103;
SQL> EXPLAIN PLAN SET STATEMENT_ID '104' FOR SELECT * FROM t WHERE val2 = 104;
SQL> EXPLAIN PLAN SET STATEMENT_ID '105' FOR SELECT * FROM t WHERE val2 = 105;
SQL> EXPLAIN PLAN SET STATEMENT_ID '106' FOR SELECT * FROM t WHERE val2 = 106;

SQL> SELECT statement_id, cardinality
  2  FROM plan_table
  3  WHERE id = 0;

STATEMENT_ID CARDINALITY
------------ -----------
101                    8
102                   25
103                   68
104                  185
105                  502
106                  212
```

When the number of distinct values is greater than the maximum number of allowed buckets (254), you cannot use frequency histograms because they support a single value per bucket. This is where height-balanced histograms become useful.

To create a height-balanced histogram, think of the following procedure. First, a frequency histogram is created. Then, as shown in Figure 4-5, the values of the frequency histogram are stacked in a pile. Finally, the pile is divided into several buckets of exactly the same height. For example, in Figure 4-5 the pile is split into five buckets.

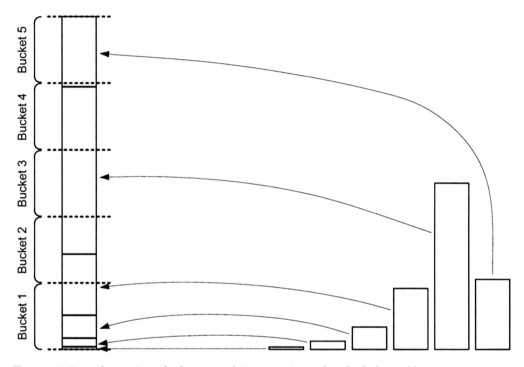

Figure 4-5. *Transformation of a frequency histogram into a height-balanced histogram*

The following query is an example of how to produce such a height-balanced histogram for the column val2. Figure 4-6 shows a graphical representation of the data it returns. Notice how the endpoint value of each bucket is the value at the point where the split occurs. In addition, a bucket 0 is added to store the minimum value.

```
SQL> SELECT count(*), max(val2) AS endpoint_value, endpoint_number
  2  FROM (
  3    SELECT val2, ntile(5) OVER (ORDER BY val2) AS endpoint_number
  4    FROM t
  5  )
  6  GROUP BY endpoint_number
  7  ORDER BY endpoint_number;
```

COUNT(*)	ENDPOINT_VALUE	ENDPOINT_NUMBER
200	104	1
200	105	2
200	105	3
200	106	4
200	106	5

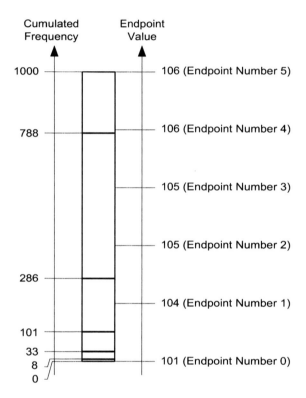

Figure 4-6. *Graphical representation of a height-balanced histogram based on the set of data stored in column val2*

For the case of Figure 4-6, the following query shows the height-balanced histogram stored in the data dictionary. Interestingly enough, not all buckets are stored. This doesn't happen because several adjacent buckets with the same endpoint value are of no use. The result is a kind of compression. In fact, from this data it is possible to infer that bucket 2 has an endpoint value of 105, and bucket 4 has an endpoint value of 106. The values appearing several times in the histogram are called *popular values*.

```
SQL> SELECT endpoint_value, endpoint_number
  2  FROM user_tab_histograms
  3  WHERE table_name = 'T'
  4  AND column_name = 'VAL2'
  5  ORDER BY endpoint_number;
```

```
ENDPOINT_VALUE ENDPOINT_NUMBER
--------------- ---------------
          101               0
          104               1
          105               3
          106               5
```

Here are the main characteristics of height-balanced histograms:

- The number of buckets is less than the number of distinct values. For each bucket, except when they are compressed, a row with the endpoint number is available in the view user_tab_histograms. In addition, the endpoint number 0 indicates the minimum value.

- The column endpoint_value gives the value itself. Since the datatype of the column is NUMBER, non-numeric datatypes (such as VARCHAR2, CHAR, NVARCHAR2, NCHAR, and RAW) must be converted. To do this, only the leading 6 bytes (not characters!) are used.

- The column endpoint_number gives the bucket number.

- The histogram does not store the frequency of the values.

The following example shows the estimation performed by the query optimizer when the height-balanced histogram is in place. Note the lower precision compared to the frequency histogram.

```
SQL> EXPLAIN PLAN SET STATEMENT_ID '101' FOR SELECT * FROM t WHERE val2 = 101;
SQL> EXPLAIN PLAN SET STATEMENT_ID '102' FOR SELECT * FROM t WHERE val2 = 102;
SQL> EXPLAIN PLAN SET STATEMENT_ID '103' FOR SELECT * FROM t WHERE val2 = 103;
SQL> EXPLAIN PLAN SET STATEMENT_ID '104' FOR SELECT * FROM t WHERE val2 = 104;
SQL> EXPLAIN PLAN SET STATEMENT_ID '105' FOR SELECT * FROM t WHERE val2 = 105;
SQL> EXPLAIN PLAN SET STATEMENT_ID '106' FOR SELECT * FROM t WHERE val2 = 106;

SQL> SELECT statement_id, cardinality
  2  FROM plan_table
  3  WHERE id = 0;

STATEMENT_ID CARDINALITY
------------ -----------
101                   50
102                   50
103                   50
104                   50
105                  400
106                  300
```

Considering these essential characteristics of the two types of histograms, it is apparent that frequency histograms are more accurate than height-balanced histograms. The main problem with height-balanced histograms is that sometimes it might be by chance that a value is recognized as popular or not. For example, in the histogram illustrated in Figure 4-6, the split point between buckets 4 and 5 occurs very close to the point where the value changes from 105 to 106.

Therefore, even a small change in the data distribution might lead to a different histogram and to different estimations. The following example illustrates such a case:

```
SQL> UPDATE t SET val2 = 105 WHERE val2 = 106 AND rownum <= 13;

SQL> SELECT endpoint_value, endpoint_number
  2  FROM user_tab_histograms
  3  WHERE table_name = 'T'
  4  AND column_name = 'VAL2'
  5  ORDER BY endpoint_number;

ENDPOINT_VALUE ENDPOINT_NUMBER
-------------- ---------------
           101               0
           104               1
           105               4
           106               5

SQL> EXPLAIN PLAN SET STATEMENT_ID '101' FOR SELECT * FROM t WHERE val2 = 101;
SQL> EXPLAIN PLAN SET STATEMENT_ID '102' FOR SELECT * FROM t WHERE val2 = 102;
SQL> EXPLAIN PLAN SET STATEMENT_ID '103' FOR SELECT * FROM t WHERE val2 = 103;
SQL> EXPLAIN PLAN SET STATEMENT_ID '104' FOR SELECT * FROM t WHERE val2 = 104;
SQL> EXPLAIN PLAN SET STATEMENT_ID '105' FOR SELECT * FROM t WHERE val2 = 105;
SQL> EXPLAIN PLAN SET STATEMENT_ID '106' FOR SELECT * FROM t WHERE val2 = 106;

SQL> SELECT statement_id, cardinality
  2  FROM plan_table
  3  WHERE id = 0;

STATEMENT_ID CARDINALITY
------------ -----------
101                   80
102                   80
103                   80
104                   80
105                  600
106                   80
```

Therefore, in practice, height-balanced histograms may be not only misleading but also may lead to instability in query optimizer estimations.

It is also useful to note that the view user_tab_histograms shows two rows for each column without a histogram. This is because the minimum and maximum values are stored in endpoint numbers 0 and 1, respectively. For example, the content for the column id, which has no histogram, is the following:

```
SQL> SELECT endpoint_value, endpoint_number
  2  FROM user_tab_histograms
  3  WHERE table_name = 'T'
  4  AND column_name = 'ID'
  5  ORDER BY endpoint_number;

ENDPOINT_VALUE ENDPOINT_NUMBER
-------------- ---------------
             1               0
          1000               1
```

Extended Statistics

The column statistics and histograms described in the previous two sections are helpful only when columns are used without being modified in predicates. For example, if the predicate country='Switzerland' is used, with column statistics and histograms in place for the column country, the query optimizer should be able to correctly estimate its selectivity. This is because column statistics and histograms describe the column country itself. On the other hand, if the predicate upper(country)='SWITZERLAND' is used, the query optimizer is no longer able to directly infer the selectivity from the object statistics and histograms. A similar problem occurs when a predicate references several columns. For example, if I apply the predicate country='Denmark' AND language='Danish' to a table containing people from all over the world, it is likely that the two restrictions apply to the same rows for most rows in such a table. In fact, most people speaking Danish live in Denmark, and most people living in Denmark speak Danish. In other words, the two restrictions are almost redundant. Such columns are commonly called *correlated columns* and challenge the query optimizer. This is because no object statistics or histograms describe such a dependency between data, or put another way, the query optimizer actually assumes that data stored in different columns is not interdependent.

As of Oracle Database 11g, it is possible to gather object statistics and histograms on expressions or on groups of columns in order to solve these kinds of problems. These new statistics are called *extended statistics*. Basically, what happens is that a hidden column, called an *extension*, is created, based on either an expression or a group of columns. Then, regular object statistics and histograms are gathered on it.

The definition is carried out with the function create_extended_stats in the package dbms_stats. For example, two extensions are created with the following query. The first one is on upper(pad), and the second one is a column group made up of the columns val2 and val3. In the test table, these contain exactly the same values; in other words, the columns are highly correlated. For the definition, as shown next, the expression or group of columns must be enclosed in parentheses. Note that the function returns a system-generated name for the extension (a 30-byte name starting with SYS_STU).

```
SELECT dbms_stats.create_extended_stats(ownname   => user,
                                         tabname   => 'T',
                                         extension => '(upper(pad))'),
       dbms_stats.create_extended_stats(ownname   => user,
                                         tabname   => 'T',
                                         extension => '(val2,val3)')
FROM dual
```

Obviously, once the extensions are created, the data dictionary provides information about them. The following query, based on the view user_stat_extensions, shows the existing extensions of the test table. There are dba and all versions as well.

```
SQL> SELECT extension_name, extension
  2  FROM user_stat_extensions
  3  WHERE table_name = 'T';

EXTENSION_NAME                     EXTENSION
------------------------------     ---------------
SYS_STUOKSQX64#IO1CKJ5FPGFK3W9     (UPPER("PAD"))
SYS_STUPS77EFBJCOTDFMHM8CHP7Q1     ("VAL2","VAL3")
```

As shown in the output of the next query, the hidden columns have the same name as the extensions. Also notice how the definition of the extension is added to the column.

```
SQL> SELECT column_name, data_type, hidden_column, data_default
  2  FROM user_tab_cols
  3  WHERE table_name = 'T'
  4  ORDER BY column_id;
```

COLUMN_NAME	DATA_TYPE	HIDDEN	DATA_DEFAULT
ID	NUMBER	NO	
VAL1	NUMBER	NO	
VAL2	NUMBER	NO	
VAL3	NUMBER	NO	
PAD	VARCHAR2	NO	
SYS_STUOKSQX64#IO1CKJ5FPGFK3W9	VARCHAR2	YES	UPPER("PAD")
SYS_STUPS77EFBJCOTDFMHM8CHP7Q1	NUMBER	YES	SYS_OP_COMBINED_HASH("VAL2","VAL3")

■Caution Since the extended statistics for a group of columns are based on a hash function (sys_op_combined_hash), they work only with predicates based on equality. In other words, the query optimizer is not able to take advantage of them for predicates based on operators like BETWEEN and < or >.

To drop an extension, the package dbms_stats provides you with the procedure drop_extended_stats. In the following example, the PL/SQL block drops the two extensions previously created:

```
BEGIN
  dbms_stats.drop_extended_stats(ownname   => user,
                                 tabname   => 'T',
                                 extension => '(upper(pad))');
  dbms_stats.drop_extended_stats(ownname   => user,
                                 tabname   => 'T',
                                 extension => '(val2,val3)');
END;
```

It is interesting to note that extended statistics are based on another Oracle Database 11*g* feature called *virtual columns*. A virtual column is a column that does not store data but simply generates its content with an expression based on other columns. This is helpful in case an application makes frequent usage of given expressions. A typical example is applying the function upper to a VARCHAR2 column or the function trunc to a DATE column. If these expressions are frequently used, it makes sense to define them directly in the table as shown in the following example. As you will see in Chapter 9, virtual columns can also be indexed.

```
SQL> CREATE TABLE persons (
  2    name VARCHAR2(100),
  3    name_upper AS (upper(name))
  4  );

SQL> INSERT INTO persons (name) VALUES ('Michelle');

SQL> SELECT name
  2  FROM persons
  3  WHERE name_upper = 'MICHELLE';

NAME
----------
Michelle
```

It is important to recognize that independently of how virtual columns are defined, object statistics and histograms are normally gathered. This way, the query optimizer gets additional statistics about the data.

Index Statistics

Before describing the index statistics, let's briefly review the structure of an index based on Figure 4-7. The block at the top is called the *root block*. This is the block where every lookup starts from. The root block references the *branch blocks*. Note that the root block is also considered a branch block. Each branch block in turn references either another level of branch blocks or, as in Figure 4-7, the *leaf blocks*. The leaf blocks store the keys (in this case, some numeric values between 6 and 89), and the rowids that reference the data. For a given index, there are always the same number of branch blocks between the root block and every leaf block. In other words, the index is always balanced. Note that to support lookups over ranges of values (for example, all values between 25 and 45), the leaf blocks are chained.

Not all indexes have the three types of blocks. In fact, the branch blocks exist only if the root block is not able to store the references of all the leaf blocks. In addition, if the index is very small, it consists of a single block containing all the data usually stored in the root block and the leaf blocks.

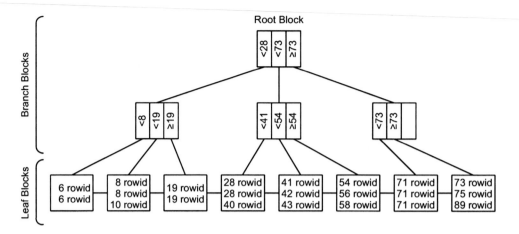

Figure 4-7. *The structure of an index is based on a B⁺-tree.*

The following query shows how to get the most important index statistics for a table:

```
SQL> SELECT index_name AS name,
  2         blevel,
  3         leaf_blocks AS leaf_blks,
  4         distinct_keys AS dst_keys,
  5         num_rows,
  6         clustering_factor AS clust_fact,
  7         avg_leaf_blocks_per_key AS leaf_per_key,
  8         avg_data_blocks_per_key AS data_per_key
  9  FROM user_ind_statistics
 10  WHERE table_name = 'T';
```

NAME	BLEVEL	LEAF_BLKS	DST_KEYS	NUM_ROWS	CLUST_FACT	LEAF_PER_KEY	DATA_PER_KEY
T_VAL2_I	1	2	6	1000	153	1	25
T_VAL1_I	1	2	431	497	479	1	1
T_PK	1	2	1000	1000	980	1	1

The index statistics returned by this query are as follows:

- blevel is the number of branch blocks to be read, including the root block, in order to access a leaf block.

- leaf_blocks is the number of leaf blocks of the index.

- distinct_keys is the number of distinct keys in the index.

- num_rows is the number of keys in the index. For primary keys, this is the same as distinct_keys.

- clustering_factor indicates how many adjacent index entries do not refer to the same data block in the table. If the table and the index are sorted similarly, the clustering factor is low. The minimum value is the number of nonempty data blocks in the table. If the table and the index are sorted differently, the clustering factor is high. The maximum value is the number of keys in the index. I'll discuss the performance impact of these statistics in Chapter 9. The following PL/SQL function, which is available in the script clustering_factor.sql, illustrates how it is computed. Note that this function works only for single-column B-tree indexes.

```
CREATE OR REPLACE FUNCTION clustering_factor (
  p_owner IN VARCHAR2,
  p_table_name IN VARCHAR2,
  p_column_name IN VARCHAR2
) RETURN NUMBER IS
  l_cursor              SYS_REFCURSOR;
  l_clustering_factor   BINARY_INTEGER := 0;
  l_block_nr            BINARY_INTEGER := 0;
  l_previous_block_nr   BINARY_INTEGER := 0;
  l_file_nr             BINARY_INTEGER := 0;
  l_previous_file_nr    BINARY_INTEGER := 0;
BEGIN
  OPEN l_cursor FOR
    'SELECT dbms_rowid.rowid_block_number(rowid) block_nr, '||
    '       dbms_rowid.rowid_to_absolute_fno(rowid, '''||
                                  p_owner||''','''||
                                  p_table_name||''') file_nr '||
    'FROM '||p_owner||'.'||p_table_name||' '||
    'WHERE '||p_column_name||' IS NOT NULL '||
    'ORDER BY ' || p_column_name;
  LOOP
    FETCH l_cursor INTO l_block_nr, l_file_nr;
    EXIT WHEN l_cursor%NOTFOUND;
    IF (l_previous_block_nr <> l_block_nr OR l_previous_file_nr <> l_file_nr)
    THEN
      l_clustering_factor := l_clustering_factor + 1;
    END IF;
    l_previous_block_nr := l_block_nr;
    l_previous_file_nr := l_file_nr;
  END LOOP;
  CLOSE l_cursor;
  RETURN l_clustering_factor;
END;
```

Notice how the values it generates match the statistics stored in the data dictionary:

```
SQL> SELECT i.index_name, i.clustering_factor,
  2          clustering_factor(user, i.table_name, ic.column_name) AS my_clstf
  3  FROM user_indexes i, user_ind_columns ic
  4  WHERE i.table_name = 'T'
  5  AND i.index_name = ic.index_name;

INDEX_NAME   CLUSTERING_FACTOR  MY_CLSTF
-----------  -----------------  ---------
T_PK                       980       980
T_VAL1_I                   479       479
T_VAL2_I                   153       153
```

It is worth mentioning that for bitmap indexes, no real clustering factor is computed. Actually, it is set to the number of keys in the index (that is, the statistic num_rows).

- avg_leaf_blocks_per_key is the average number of leaf blocks that store a single key. This value is derived from other statistics using Formula 4-5.

$$avg\_leaf\_blocks\_per\_key \approx \frac{leaf\_blocks}{distinct\_keys}$$

Formula 4-5. *Computation of the average number of leaf blocks that store a single key*

- avg_data_blocks_per_key is the average number of data blocks in the table referenced by a single key. This value is derived from other statistics using Formula 4-6.

$$avg\_data\_blocks\_per\_key \approx \frac{clustering\_factor}{distinct\_keys}$$

Formula 4-6. *Computation of the average number of data blocks referenced by a single key*

Gathering Object Statistics

Up to Oracle9*i*, the DBA is responsible for gathering object statistics. In fact, by default, no object statistics are available. As of Oracle Database 10*g*, during the creation of the database, a job aimed at automatically gathering the object statistics is created and scheduled. This is a good thing since having up-to-date object statistics should be the rule rather than the exception.

Gathering Statistics with the Package dbms_stats

To gather object statistics, the package dbms_stats contains several procedures. There are several procedures because, depending on the situation, the process of gathering statistics should occur for the whole database, for the data dictionary, for a schema, or for a single object.

- gather_database_stats gathers object statistics for a whole database.

- gather_dictionary_stats gathers object statistics for the data dictionary. Note that the data dictionary is not only composed of the objects stored in the schema sys, but it also includes the other schemas installed by Oracle for optional components. This procedure is available only as of Oracle Database 10*g*.

- gather_fixed_objects_stats gathers object statistics for particular objects called *fixed tables* that are contained in the data dictionary. To know which tables are processed by this procedure, you can use the following query. This procedure is available only as of Oracle Database 10*g*.

```
SELECT name
FROM v$fixed_table
WHERE type = 'TABLE'
```

- gather_schema_stats gathers object statistics for a whole schema.

- gather_table_stats gathers object statistics for one table and, optionally, for its indexes.

- gather_index_stats gathers object statistics for one index.

These procedures provide several parameters that can be grouped into three main categories. With the first group, we specify target objects, with the second group we specify gathering options, and with the third group we specify whether to back up the current statistics before overwriting them. Table 4-5 summarizes which parameter is available with which procedure. The next three sections describe the scope and use of each parameter in detail.

Table 4-5. *Parameters of the Procedures Used for Gathering Object Statistics*

Parameter	Database	Dictionary	Fixed Objects	Schema	Table	Index
Target Objects						
ownname				✓	✓	✓
indname						✓
tabname					✓	
partname					✓	✓
comp_id		✓				
granularity	✓	✓		✓	✓	✓
cascade	✓	✓		✓	✓	
gather_sys	✓					
gather_temp	✓			✓		
options	✓	✓		✓		
objlist	✓	✓		✓		
force				✓	✓	✓
obj_filter_list	✓	✓		✓		
Gathering Options						
estimate_percent	✓	✓		✓	✓	✓
block_sample	✓	✓		✓	✓	
method_opt	✓	✓		✓	✓	
degree	✓	✓		✓	✓	✓

Table 4-5. *Parameters of the Procedures Used for Gathering Object Statistics (Continued)*

Parameter	Database	Dictionary	Fixed Objects	Schema	Table	Index
no_invalidate	✓	✓	✓	✓	✓	✓
Backup Table						
stattab	✓	✓	✓	✓	✓	✓
statid	✓	✓	✓	✓	✓	✓
statown	✓	✓	✓	✓	✓	✓

Target Objects

Target object parameters specify which objects you gather object statistics for.

- ownname specifies the name of the schema to be processed. This parameter is mandatory.

- indname specifies the name of the index to be processed. This parameter is mandatory.

- tabname specifies the name of the table to be processed. This parameter is mandatory.

- partname specifies the name of the partition or subpartition to be processed. If no value is specified, object statistics for all partitions are gathered. The default value is NULL.

- comp_id specifies the ID of the component to be processed. Since the ID of a component cannot be used for gathering statistics, it is transformed internally into a list of schema. To know which schemas are processed for a given component, you can use the following query.[4] Note that the schema sys and system are always processed independently of this parameter. If an invalid value is specified, no error message is returned, and the schemas sys and system are processed regularly. With the default value NULL, all components are processed.

```
SQL> SELECT u.name AS schema_name, r.cid AS comp_id, r.cname AS comp_name
  2  FROM sys.user$ u,
  3       (SELECT schema#, cid, cname
  4        FROM sys.registry$
  5        WHERE status IN (1,3,5)
  6        AND namespace = 'SERVER'
  7        UNION ALL
  8        SELECT s.schema#, s.cid, cname
  9        FROM sys.registry$ r, sys.registry$schemas s
 10        WHERE r.status IN (1,3,5)
 11        AND r.namespace = 'SERVER'
 12        AND r.cid = s.cid) r
 13  WHERE u.user# = r.schema#
```

---

4. Unfortunately, Oracle does not make all necessary information available through data dictionary views. As a result, this query is based on internal tables. The system privilege select any dictionary provides access to the necessary views.

```
 14  ORDER BY u.name, r.cid;

SCHEMA_NAME          COMP_ID COMP_NAME
-------------------  ------- ------------------------------
CTXSYS               CONTEXT Oracle Text
DMSYS                ODM     Oracle Data Mining
EXFSYS               EXF     Oracle Expression Filter
EXFSYS               RUL     Oracle Rule Manager
OLAPSYS              AMD     OLAP Catalog
ORDPLUGINS           ORDIM   Oracle interMedia
ORDSYS               ORDIM   Oracle interMedia
SI_INFORMTN_SCHEMA   ORDIM   Oracle interMedia
SYS                  APS     OLAP Analytic Workspace
SYS                  CATALOG Oracle Database Catalog Views
SYS                  CATJAVA Oracle Database Java Packages
SYS                  JAVAVM  JServer JAVA Virtual Machine
SYS                  XML     Oracle XDK
SYS                  XOQ     Oracle OLAP API
SYSMAN               EM      Oracle Enterprise Manager
WKPROXY              WK      Oracle Ultra Search
WKSYS                WK      Oracle Ultra Search
WK_TEST              WK      Oracle Ultra Search
WMSYS                OWM     Oracle Workspace Manager
XDB                  XDB     Oracle XML Database
```

- granularity specifies at which level statistics for partitioned objects are processed. This parameter accepts the value listed in Table 4-6. Up to Oracle9*i*, the default value is DEFAULT, and as of Oracle Database 10*g*, the default value is AUTO (this default value can be changed; see the sections "Configuring the Package dbms_stats: The 10*g* Way" and "Configuring the Package dbms_stats: The 11*g* Way" later in this chapter).

Table 4-6. *Values Accepted by the Parameter* granularity

Value	Meaning
all	Object, partition, and subpartition statistics are gathered. This value is available only as of Oracle Database 10*g*.
auto	Object and partition statistics are gathered. Subpartition statistics are gathered only if the table is subpartitioned by list or range.
default	Object and partition statistics are gathered. This value is available only up to Oracle9*i*. As of Oracle Database 10*g*, it is replaced by global and partition.
global	Only object statistics are gathered.
global and partition	Object and partition statistics are gathered. This value is available only as of Oracle Database 10*g*.
partition	Only partition statistics are gathered.
subpartition	Only subpartition statistics are gathered.

- cascade specifies whether indexes are processed. This parameter accepts the values TRUE, FALSE, and dbms_stats.auto_cascade. The latter, which is a constant evaluating to NULL, lets the database engine decide whether to gather the index statistics. Up to Oracle9i, the default value is FALSE, and as of Oracle Database 10g, the default value is dbms_stats. auto_cascade (this default value can be changed; see the sections "Configuring the Package dbms_stats: The 10gWay" and "Configuring the Package dbms_stats: The 11gWay" later in this chapter).

- gather_sys specifies whether the schema sys is processed. This parameter accepts the values TRUE and FALSE. The default value is FALSE.

- gather_temp specifies whether temporary tables are processed. Since the package dbms_stats executes a COMMIT at the beginning of the processing, only temporary tables created with on commit preserve rows can be processed. This parameter accepts the values TRUE and FALSE. The default value is FALSE.

- options specifies which, and whether, objects are processed. This parameter accepts the value listed in Table 4-7. The default value is gather.

Table 4-7. *Values Accepted by the Parameter* options

Value	Meaning
gather	All objects are processed.
gather auto	Lets the procedure determine not only which objects are to be processed but also how they are processed. When this value is specified, all parameters except ownname, objlist, stattab, statid, and statown are ignored.
gather stale	Only objects having stale object statistics are processed. Be careful: objects without object statistics are not considered stale.
gather empty	Only objects without object statistics are processed.
list auto	Lists objects that would be processed with the option gather auto.
list stale	Lists objects that would be processed with the option gather stale.
list empty	Lists objects that would be processed with the option gather empty.

STALENESS OF OBJECT STATISTICS

To recognize whether object statistics are stale, the database engine counts the number of rows modified through SQL statements for each object. The result of that counting is externalized through the data dictionary views all_tab_modifications, dba_tab_modifications, and user_tab_modifications. The following query is an example:

```
SQL> SELECT inserts, updates, deletes, truncated
  2  FROM user_tab_modifications
  3  WHERE table_name = 'T';
```

```
 INSERTS    UPDATES   DELETES TRUNCATED
---------- ---------- ---------- ----------
     775      16636        66 NO
```

Based on this information, the package dbms_stats is able to determine whether the statistics associated with a specific object are stale. Up to Oracle Database 10*g*, the statistics are considered stale if at least 10 percent of the rows have been modified. As of Oracle Database 11*g*, you can configure the threshold through the parameter stale_percent. Its default value is 10 percent. Later in this chapter, the section "Configuring the Package dbms_stats: The 11*g* Way" will show how to change it.

In Oracle9*i*, counting is enabled only when it is explicitly specified at the table level. Concretely, this is carried out by specifying the option monitoring through the CREATE TABLE or ALTER TABLE statement. To enable it easily for a whole schema, or even for the whole database, the package dbms_stats provides the procedures alter_schema_tab_monitoring and alter_database_tab_monitoring, respectively. Note that these procedures just execute an ALTER TABLE statement on all available tables. In other words, the setting has no impact on tables created after their execution.

As of Oracle Database 10*g*, the option monitoring is deprecated. Counting is controlled databasewide by the initialization parameter statistics_level. If it is set to either typical (which is the default value) or all, counting is enabled.

- objlist returns, depending on the value of the parameter options, the list of objects that were processed or that would be processed. This is an output parameter based on a type defined in the package dbms_stats. For instance, the following PL/SQL block shows how to display the list of processed objects:

```
SQL> DECLARE
  2     l_objlist dbms_stats.objecttab;
  3     l_index PLS_INTEGER;
  4  BEGIN
  5     dbms_stats.gather_schema_stats(ownname => 'HR',
  6                                    objlist => l_objlist);
  7     l_index := l_objlist.FIRST;
  8     WHILE l_index IS NOT NULL
  9     LOOP
 10       dbms_output.put(l_objlist(l_index).ownname || '.');
 11       dbms_output.put_line(l_objlist(l_index).objname);
 12       l_index := l_objlist.next(l_index);
 13     END LOOP;
 14  END;
 15  /
HR.COUNTRIES
HR.DEPARTMENTS
HR.EMPLOYEES
HR.JOBS
HR.JOB_HISTORY
HR.LOCATIONS
HR.REGIONS
```

- `force` specifies whether locked statistics are overwritten. If this parameter is set to FALSE while a procedure that is designed to process a single table or index is being executed, an error (ORA-20005) is raised. This parameter accepts the values TRUE and FALSE. It is available as of Oracle Database 10*g* Release 2 only. You'll find more information about locked statistics in the section "Locking Object Statistics" later in this chapter.

- `obj_filter_list` specifies to gather statistics only for objects fulfilling at least one of the filters passed as a parameter. It is based on the type objecttab defined in the package dbms_stats itself and is available as of Oracle Database 11*g* only. The following PL/SQL block shows how to gather statistics for all tables of the schema HR and all tables of the schema SH that have a name starting with the letter *C*:

```
DECLARE
  l_filter  dbms_stats.objecttab := dbms_stats.objecttab();
BEGIN
  l_filter.extend(2);
  l_filter(1).ownname := 'HR';
  l_filter(2).ownname := 'SH';
  l_filter(2).objname := 'C%';
  dbms_stats.gather_database_stats(obj_filter_list => l_filter,
                                   options         => 'gather');
END;
```

Gathering Options

The gathering option parameters listed in Table 4-5 specify how the gathering of statistics takes place, which kinds of column statistics are gathered, and whether dependent SQL cursors are invalidated. The options are as follows:

- `estimate_percent` specifies whether sampling is used for gathering statistics. Valid values are decimal numbers between 0.000001 and 100. The value 100, as well as the value NULL, means no sampling. The constant dbms_stats.auto_sample_size, which evaluates to 0, lets the procedure determine the sample size. As of Oracle Database 11*g*, it is recommended to use this value. In passing, note that sampling on external tables is not supported. It is important to understand that the value specified by this parameter is only the minimum percentage used for gathering statistics. In fact, as shown in the following example, the value may be automatically increased if the specified estimate percent is considered too small. Up to Oracle9*i*, the default value is NULL, and as of Oracle Database 10*g*, the default value is dbms_stats.auto_sample_size (this default value can be changed; see the sections "Configuring the Package dbms_stats: The 10*g* Way" and "Configuring the Package dbms_stats: The 11*g* Way" later in this chapter). To speed up the gathering of object statistics, use small estimate percentages; values less than 10 percent are usually good. For large tables, even 0.5 percent, 0.1 percent, or less could be fine. If you are uncertain of your choice, simply try different estimate percentages and compare the gathered statistics. In that way, you may find the best compromise between performance and accuracy. Since values that are too small are automatically increased if the gathering of statistics is performed at the database or schema level, the estimate percentage should be chosen for the biggest tables.

```
SQL> BEGIN
  2    dbms_stats.gather_schema_stats(ownname         => user,
  3                                   estimate_percent => 0.5);
  4  END;
  5  /

SQL> SELECT table_name, sample_size, num_rows,
  2         round(sample_size/num_rows*100,1) AS "%"
  3  FROM user_tables
  4  WHERE num_rows > 0
  5  ORDER BY table_name;

TABLE_NAME                      SAMPLE_SIZE    NUM_ROWS       %
------------------------------  -----------  ----------  -------
CAL_MONTH_SALES_MV                       48          48    100.0
CHANNELS                                  5           5    100.0
COSTS                                  5410       81799      6.6
COUNTRIES                                23          23    100.0
CUSTOMERS                              4700       55648      8.4
FWEEK_PSCAT_SALES_MV                   5262       11155     47.2
PRODUCTS                                 72          72    100.0
PROMOTIONS                              503         503    100.0
SALES                                  4602      920400      0.5
SUPPLEMENTARY_DEMOGRAPHICS             3739        4487     83.3
TIMES                                  1826        1826    100.0
```

- block_sample specifies whether row sampling or block sampling is used for the gathering of statistics. While row sampling is more accurate, block sampling is faster. Therefore, block sampling should be used only when it is sure that data is randomly distributed. This parameter accepts the values TRUE and FALSE. The default value is FALSE.

- method_opt specifies not only whether histograms are gathered but also the maximum number of buckets that should be used in case a histogram is created. In addition, this parameter could also be used to completely disable the gathering of column statistics. The following gathering modes are provided:[5]

  - Gathering column statistics without histograms. To do so, either NULL or an empty string has to be specified.

  - Gathering column statistics and histograms for all[6] columns. All histograms are created with the very same value for the parameter size_clause. The syntax is shown in Figure 4-8. For example, with the value for all columns size 200 a histogram with up to 200 buckets is created for every column.

---

5. For simplicity, I'm not describing all the possible combinations since many of them are redundant or are of no use in practice.
6. Actually, with the options indexed and hidden, it is possible to restrict the statistics gathering to indexed and hidden columns only. As a rule, object statistics should be available for all columns. For this reason, both these options should be avoided (and hence they are shown in the figure in gray). If for some columns there is no need to have object statistics, you should use the syntax described in Figure 4-9 instead.

- Gathering column statistics and histograms only for a subset of columns or for all columns, but with different values for the parameter size_clause. The syntax is shown in Figure 4-9. For example, with the value for columns size 200 col1, col2, col3, col4 size 1, col5 size 1, column statistics are gathered for the five columns, but histograms with up to 200 buckets are gathered only for the columns col1, col2, and col3.

Up to Oracle9*i*, the default value is for all columns size 1; as of Oracle Database 10*g*, the default value is for all columns size auto (this default value can be changed; see the sections "Configuring the Package dbms_stats: The 10*g* Way" and "Configuring the Package dbms_stats: The 11*g* Way" later in this chapter). For simplicity, use either size skewonly or size auto. If it is too slow or the chosen number of buckets is not good (or the needed histogram is not created at all), manually specify the list of columns.

- degree specifies how many slaves are used while gathering statistics for a single object. To use the degree of parallelism defined at the object level, specify the value NULL. To let the procedure determine the degree of parallelism, specify the constant dbms_stats.default_degree. The default value is NULL (as of Oracle Database 10*g*, this default value can be changed; see the sections "Configuring the Package dbms_stats: The 10*g* Way" and "Configuring the Package dbms_stats: The 11*g* Way" later in this chapter). Note that the processing of several objects is serialized. This means parallelization is useful only for speeding up the gathering of statistics on large objects. To parallelize the processing of several objects at the same time, manual parallelization (that is, starting several jobs) is necessary. Refer to Chapter 11 for detailed information about parallel processing. Parallel gathering of object statistics is available only with the Enterprise Edition.

- no_invalidate specifies whether cursors depending on the processed objects are invalidated. This parameter accepts the values TRUE, FALSE, and dbms_stats.auto_invalidate. When the parameter is set to TRUE, the cursors depending on the changed object statistics are not invalidated and, therefore, might be used regularly. On the other hand, if it is set to FALSE, all the cursors are immediately invalidated. With the value dbms_stats.auto_invalidate, which is a constant evaluating to NULL, the cursors are invalidated over a period of time. This last possibility is good for avoiding reparsing spikes. Up to Oracle9*i*, the default value is FALSE; as of Oracle Database 10*g*, the default value is dbms_stats.auto_invalidate (this default value can be changed; see the sections "Configuring the Package dbms_stats: The 10*g* Way" and "Configuring the Package dbms_stats: The 11*g* Way" later in this chapter).

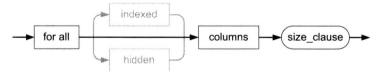

Figure 4-8. *Gathering column statistics and histograms for all columns with a single value for the parameter size_clause (see Table 4-8)*

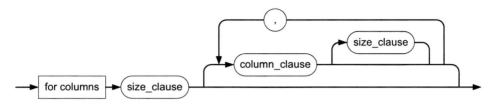

Figure 4-9. *Gathering column statistics and histograms only for a subset of columns or for all columns but with different values of the parameter size_clause (see Table 4-8). For the columns that do not explicitly specify a size_clause, the default size_clause (the first one) is used. If no columns are specified, no column statistics are gathered at all. The column_clause can be a column name, an extension name, or an extension. If an extension that does not exist is specified, a new extension is automatically created.*

Table 4-8. *Values Accepted by the Parameter size_clause*

Value	Meaning
size 1..254	The value specifies the maximum number of buckets. If size 1 is specified, no histograms are created. In any case, column statistics are gathered normally.
size skewonly	Histograms are gathered only for columns with skewed data. The number of buckets is determined automatically.
size auto	Histograms are gathered only for columns with skewed data, such as skewonly, and, in addition, that have been referenced in WHERE clauses. This second condition is based on the *column usage history*. The number of buckets is determined automatically.
size repeat	Refreshes available histograms.

COLUMN USAGE HISTORY

The query optimizer, while generating a new execution plan, tracks which columns are referenced in the WHERE clause. Then, from time to time, this information is stored in the data dictionary table col_usage$.[7] With a query such as the following (which is available in the script col_usage.sql), it is possible to know which columns were referenced in the WHERE clause and for which kind of predicates. The column timestamp indicates the last usage. The other columns are counts of the number of utilizations (not executions, so be careful). Columns that were never referenced in a WHERE clause have no rows in the table col_usage$, so all columns in the output except name are NULL.

---

7. Unfortunately, Oracle does not externalize this information through a data dictionary view, which means this query is based on an internal table. The system privilege select any dictionary provides access to that table.

```
SQL> SELECT c.name, cu.timestamp,
  2          cu.equality_preds AS equality, cu.equijoin_preds AS equijoin,
  3          cu.nonequijoin_preds AS noneequijoin, cu.range_preds AS range,
  4          cu.like_preds AS "LIKE", cu.null_preds AS "NULL"
  5  FROM sys.col$ c, sys.col_usage$ cu, sys.obj$ o, sys.user$ u
  6  WHERE c.obj# = cu.obj# (+)
  7  AND c.intcol# = cu.intcol# (+)
  8  AND c.obj# = o.obj#
  9  AND o.owner# = u.user#
 10  AND o.name = 'T'
 11  AND u.name = user
 12  ORDER BY c.col#;

NAME       TIMESTAMP EQUALITY EQUIJOIN NONEEQUIJOIN RANGE  LIKE   NULL
---------- --------- -------- -------- ------------ ------ ------ ------
ID         14-MAY-07       14       17            0      0      0      0
VAL1       14-MAY-07       15        0            0      0      0      0
VAL2
VAL3       14-MAY-07        7       18            0      0      0      0
PAD        13-MAY-07        0        7            0      1      0      0
```

The package dbms_stats uses this information to determine which columns a histogram is useful for.

Backup Table

The backup table parameters listed in Table 4-5 are supported by all procedures used for gathering object statistics. They instruct the package dbms_stats to back up current statistics in a backup table before overwriting them with the new ones in the data dictionary. The parameters are as follows:

- stattab specifies a table outside the data dictionary where the statistics are stored. The default value is NULL.

- statid is an optional identifier used to recognize multiple sets of object statistics stored in the table specified with the parameter stattab. While every string used to be supported for this identifier, as of Oracle Database 10g Release 2, only valid Oracle identifiers[8] are supported. However, this restriction has been back ported to previous versions as well. For example, it applies to version 9.2.0.8 (but not to 9.2.0.7 or 10.1.0.5). The default value is NULL.

- statown specifies the owner of the table specified with the parameter stattab. The default value is NULL, and therefore the current user is used.

How to create and drop a backup table is described in the section "Creating and Dropping a Backup Table."

---

8. Refer to the *SQL Language Reference* manual of the Oracle documentation for the definition of *identifier.*

Configuring the Package dbms_stats: The 10*g* Way

In Oracle Database 10*g*, you can change the default values of the parameters cascade, estimate_
percent, degree, method_opt, no_invalidate, and granularity. This is possible because the default
values are no longer hard-coded in the signature of the procedures, but rather extracted from
the data dictionary at runtime. The procedure set_param is available for setting default values.
To execute it, you need the system privileges analyze any dictionary and analyze any. The
function get_param is for getting default values. The following example shows how use them.
Note that pname is the parameter name and pval is the parameter value.

```
SQL> execute dbms_output.put_line(dbms_stats.get_param(pname => 'CASCADE'))

DBMS_STATS.AUTO_CASCADE

SQL> execute dbms_stats.set_param(pname => 'CASCADE', pval =>'TRUE')

SQL> execute dbms_output.put_line(dbms_stats.get_param(pname => 'CASCADE'))

TRUE
```

Another parameter that can be set with this method is autostats_target. This parameter
is used only by the job gather_stats_job (described later in this chapter) to determine which
objects the gathering of statistics has to process. Table 4-9 lists the available values. The default
value is AUTO.

Table 4-9. *Values Accepted by the Parameter* autostats_target

Value	Meaning
ALL	All objects are processed.
AUTO	The job determines which objects are processed.
ORACLE	Only objects belonging to the data dictionary are processed.

To get the default value of all parameters without executing the function get_param several
times, you can use the following query:[9]

```
SQL> SELECT sname AS parameter, nvl(spare4,sval1) AS default_value
  2  FROM sys.optstat_hist_control$
  3  WHERE sname IN ('CASCADE','ESTIMATE_PERCENT','DEGREE',
  4                  'METHOD_OPT','NO_INVALIDATE','GRANULARITY');
```

---

9. Unfortunately, Oracle does not externalize this information through a data dictionary view, meaning
   this query is based on an internal table. The system privilege select any dictionary provides access to
   that table.

```
PARAMETER        DEFAULT_VALUE
---------------- --------------------------
CASCADE          DBMS_STATS.AUTO_CASCADE
ESTIMATE_PERCENT DBMS_STATS.AUTO_SAMPLE_SIZE
DEGREE           NULL
METHOD_OPT       FOR ALL COLUMNS SIZE AUTO
NO_INVALIDATE    DBMS_STATS.AUTO_INVALIDATE
GRANULARITY      AUTO
```

To restore the default values to the original setting, the package dbms_stats provides the procedure reset_param_defaults.

Configuring the Package dbms_stats: The 11*g* Way

In Oracle Database 11*g*, the concept of setting default values for parameters, which are called *preferences*, is strongly enhanced compared to Oracle Database 10*g*. In fact, you are not only able to set the global defaults as in Oracle Database 10*g*, but you are also able to set defaults at the schema and table level. In addition, for global defaults, there is the separation between data dictionary objects and user-defined objects. One consequence of these enhancements is that the function get_param and the procedures set_param and reset_param_defaults (introduced in Oracle Database 10*g* and described in the previous section) are already obsolete.

You can change the default values of the parameters cascade, estimate_percent, degree, method_opt, no_invalidate, granularity, publish, incremental, and stale_percent. To change them, the following procedures are available in the package dbms_stats:

- set_global_prefs sets the global preferences. It replaces the procedure set_param.

- set_database_prefs sets the database preferences. The difference between global and database preferences is that the latter are not used for the data dictionary objects. In other words, database preferences are used only for user-defined objects.

- set_schema_prefs sets the preferences for a specific schema.

- set_table_prefs sets the preferences for a specific table.

It is important to be aware that the procedures set_database_prefs and set_schema_prefs do not directly store preferences in the data dictionary. Instead, they are converted into table preferences for all objects available in the database or schema at the time the procedure is called. In practice, only global and table preferences exist. Basically, the procedures set_database_prefs and set_schema_prefs are simple wrappers around the procedure set_table_prefs. This means global preferences are used for new tables.

The following PL/SQL blocks show how to set different values for the parameter cascade. Note that pname is the parameter name, pvalue is the parameter value, ownname is the owner, and tabname is the table name. Once more, be careful because the order of the calls is capital in such a PL/SQL block. In fact, every call overwrites the definition made by the previous call.

```
BEGIN
  dbms_stats.set_database_prefs(pname  => 'CASCADE',
                                pvalue => 'DBMS_STATS.AUTO_CASCADE');
  dbms_stats.set_schema_prefs(ownname => 'SCOTT',
                              pname   => 'CASCADE',
                              pvalue  => 'FALSE');
  dbms_stats.set_table_prefs(ownname => 'SCOTT',
                             tabname => 'EMP',
                             pname   => 'CASCADE',
                             pvalue  => 'TRUE');
END;
```

To get the current setting, the function get_prefs, which replaces the function get_param, is available. The following query shows the effect of the setting performed on the previous PL/SQL blocks. Note that pname is the parameter name, ownname is the owner name, and tabname is the table name. As you can see, depending on which parameters are specified, the function returns the values at a specific level. This searching for preferences is carried out as shown in Figure 4-10.

```
SQL> SELECT dbms_stats.get_prefs(pname => 'cascade') AS global,
  2           dbms_stats.get_prefs(pname   => 'cascade',
  3                                ownname => 'SCOTT',
  4                                tabname =>'EMP') AS emp,
  5           dbms_stats.get_prefs(pname   => 'cascade',
  6                                ownname => 'SCOTT',
  7                                tabname =>'DEPT') AS dept
  8  FROM dual;

GLOBAL                      EMP         DEPT
------------------------- ---------- ----------
DBMS_STATS.AUTO_CASCADE     TRUE        FALSE
```

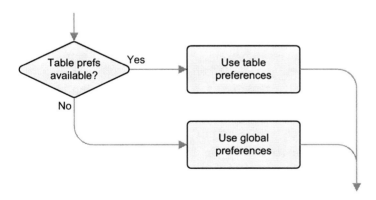

Figure 4-10. *In searching for preferences, table settings take precedence over global preferences.*

To get the global preferences without executing several times the function get_param, as described in the previous section, it is possible to query the internal data dictionary table optstat_hist_control$. To get preferences for tables, it is also possible to run the following query. Notice that even if in the previous PL/SQL block the configuration was performed at the schema level, the data dictionary view dba_tab_stat_prefs shows the setting.

```
SQL> SELECT table_name, preference_name, preference_value
  2  FROM dba_tab_stat_prefs
  3  WHERE owner = 'SCOTT'
  4  AND table_name IN ('EMP','DEPT')
  5  ORDER BY table_name, preference_name;

TABLE_NAME PREFERENCE_NAME PREFERENCE_VALUE
---------- --------------- ----------------
DEPT       CASCADE         FALSE
EMP        CASCADE         TRUE
```

To get rid of preferences, the package dbms_stats provides the following procedures:

- reset_global_pref_defaults resets the global preferences to the default values.

- delete_database_prefs deletes preferences at the database level.

- delete_schema_prefs deletes preferences at the schema level.

- delete_table_prefs deletes preferences at the table level.

The following call shows how to delete the preferences for the schema scott:

```
dbms_stats.delete_schema_prefs(ownname => 'SCOTT',
                               pname   => 'CASCADE')
```

To execute the procedures at the global and database levels, you need to have both the system privileges analyze any dictionary and analyze any. To execute the procedures at a schema or table level, you need to be connected as owner or have the system privilege analyze any.

Working with Pending Statistics

Usually, as soon as gathering statistics is finished, the object statistics are published (that is, made available) to the query optimizer. This means that it is not possible (for testing purposes, for instance) to gather statistics without overwriting the current object statistics. Of course, test databases should be used for testing purposes, but sometimes it is not possible to do so; you might want to do it in production. An example of this is when the data stored in the test database is not the same as the data in the production database.

As of Oracle Database *11g*, it is possible to separate gathering statistics from publishing them, and it is possible to use objects statistics that are unpublished, which are called *pending statistics*, for testing purposes. Here is the procedure (a full example is provided in the script pending_object_statistics.sql):

1. Disable automatic publishing by setting the preference publish to FALSE (the default value is TRUE). As described in the previous section, for other preferences, this can be done at the global, database, schema, or table level. The following example shows how to do it for the table t belonging to the current user:

```
dbms_stats.set_table_prefs(ownname => user,
                           tabname => 'T',
                           pname   => 'PUBLISH',
                           pvalue  => 'FALSE')
```

2. Gather object statistics for the table t belonging to the current user. Since the preference publish is set to FALSE for this table, the newly gathered object statistics are not published. This means the query optimizer keeps using the statistics available before their gathering. At the same time, cursors depending on that table are not invalidated.

```
dbms_stats.gather_table_stats(ownname => user, tabname => 'T')
```

3. To test the impact of the new object statistics on an application or a set of SQL statements, you can set the dynamic initialization parameter optimizer_use_pending_statistics to TRUE at the session level. With this setting, the pending statistics are available for the current session only.

```
ALTER SESSION SET optimizer_use_pending_statistics = TRUE
```

4. If the test is successful, the pending statistics can be published (in other words, made available to all users) by calling the procedure publish_pending_stats. The following example shows how to do it for a single table. If the parameter tabname is set to NULL, all pending statistics of the specified schema are published. This procedure also has two additional parameters. The third, no_invalidate, controls the invalidation of the cursors depending on the modified object statistics. The fourth, force, is used to override a potential lock of the statistics (the section "Locking Object Statistics" later in this chapter describes such locks). Its default value is FALSE, which means that locks are honored by default.

```
dbms_stats.publish_pending_stats(ownname => user, tabname => 'T')
```

5. If the test is not successful, you can delete the pending statistics by calling the procedure delete_pending_stats. If the parameter tabname is not specified or set to NULL, pending statistics for the whole schema specified by the parameter ownname are deleted.

```
dbms_stats.delete_pending_stats(ownname => user, tabname => 'T')
```

To execute the procedures publish_pending_stats and delete_pending_stats, you need to be connected as owner or have the system privilege analyze any.

If you are interested to know the values of the pending statistics, the following data dictionary views provide all the necessary information. For each view there are dba and all versions as well.

- user_tab_pending_stats shows pending table statistics.

- user_ind_pending_stats shows pending index statistics.

- user_col_pending_stats shows pending column statistics.

- user_tab_histgrm_pending_stats shows pending histograms.

The content and structure of these data dictionary views is similar to user_tab_statistics, user_ind_statistics, user_tab_col_statistics, and user_tab_histograms, respectively.

Scheduling Statistics Gathering: The 10*g* Way

The job gather_stats_job is scheduled with the Scheduler.[10] The current configuration, which in the following example is the default configuration of Oracle Database 10*g*, can be displayed with the following queries. The output was generated with the script dbms_stats_job_10g.sql.

```
SQL> SELECT program_name, schedule_name, schedule_type, enabled, state
  2  FROM dba_scheduler_jobs
  3  WHERE owner = 'SYS'
  4  AND job_name = 'GATHER_STATS_JOB';
```

PROGRAM_NAME	SCHEDULE_NAME	SCHEDULE_TYPE	ENABLED	STATE
GATHER_STATS_PROG	MAINTENANCE_WINDOW_GROUP	WINDOW_GROUP	TRUE	SCHEDULED

```
SQL> SELECT program_action, number_of_arguments, enabled
  2  FROM dba_scheduler_programs
  3  WHERE owner = 'SYS'
  4  AND program_name = 'GATHER_STATS_PROG';
```

PROGRAM_ACTION	NUMBER_OF_ARGUMENTS	ENABLED
dbms_stats.gather_database_stats_job_proc	0	TRUE

```
SQL> SELECT w.window_name, w.repeat_interval, w.duration, w.enabled
  2  FROM dba_scheduler_wingroup_members m, dba_scheduler_windows w
  3  WHERE m.window_name = w.window_name
  4  AND m.window_group_name = 'MAINTENANCE_WINDOW_GROUP';
```

WINDOW_NAME	REPEAT_INTERVAL	DURATION	ENABLED
WEEKNIGHT_WINDOW	freq=daily;byday=MON,TUE,WED,THU,FRI; byhour=22;byminute=0; bysecond=0	+000 08:00:00	TRUE
WEEKEND_WINDOW	freq=daily;byday=SAT;byhour=0;byminute=0;bysecond=0	+002 00:00:00	TRUE

---

10. This is the name of the new scheduler available as of Oracle Database 10*g*.

In summary, the configuration is the following:

- The job executes the program gather_stats_prog and is able to run within the window group maintenance_window_group.

- The program gather_stats_prog calls, without parameters, the procedure gather_database_ stats_job_proc in the package dbms_stats. Since no parameters are passed to it, the only way to change its behavior is to change the default configuration of the package dbms_stats, as explained in the section "Configuring the Package dbms_stats: The 10gWay" earlier in this chapter. Note that this procedure is undocumented and tagged "for internal use only."

- The window group maintenance_window_group has two members: the window weeknight_ window and the window weekend_window. The former opens for eight hours every night from Monday to Friday. The latter is open Saturday and Sunday. The gathering of the object statistics takes place when one of these two windows is open.

- The job, the program, and the windows are enabled.

The opening and duration of the default scheduling should be checked and, whenever necessary, be changed to match the expected statistics gathering frequency. If possible, they should match the low-utilization periods.

Every time the job has to be stopped because the window is closed, a trace file is generated, containing the list of all objects that have not been processed. The following is an excerpt of such a trace file:

```
GATHER_STATS_JOB: Stopped by Scheduler.
Consider increasing the maintenance window duration if this happens frequently.
The following objects/segments were not analyzed due to timeout:
  TABLE: "SH"."SALES"."SALES_1995"
  TABLE: "SH"."SALES"."SALES_1996"
  TABLE: "SH"."SALES"."SALES_H1_1997"
...
  TABLE: "SYS"."WRI$_OPTSTAT_AUX_HISTORY".""
  TABLE: "SYS"."WRI$_ADV_OBJECTS".""
  TABLE: "SYS"."WRI$_OPTSTAT_HISTGRM_HISTORY".""
error 1013 in job queue process
ORA-01013: user requested cancel of current operation
```

To enable or disable the job gather_stats_job, the following PL/SQL calls are available:

```
dbms_scheduler.enable(name => 'sys.gather_stats_job')
dbms_scheduler.disable(name => 'sys.gather_stats_job')
```

Per default, only the user sys is able to execute them. Other users need the object privilege alter. After executing the following SQL statement, the user system will be able to alter or drop the job gather_stats_job:

```
GRANT ALTER ON gather_stats_job TO system
```

Scheduling Statistics Gathering: The 11*g* Way

As of Oracle Database 11*g*, the gathering of object statistics is integrated into the automated maintenance tasks scheduled with the Scheduler. As a result, the job gather_stats_job, which is used in Oracle Database 10*g*, no longer exists. The current configuration, which in the following example is the default configuration of Oracle Database 11*g*, can be viewed with the following queries. The output was generated with the script dbms_stats_job_11g.sql.

```
SQL> SELECT task_name, status
  2  FROM dba_autotask_task
  3  WHERE client_name = 'auto optimizer stats collection';

TASK_NAME          STATUS
----------------- -------
gather_stats_prog ENABLED


SQL> SELECT program_action, number_of_arguments, enabled
  2  FROM dba_scheduler_programs
  3  WHERE owner = 'SYS'
  4  AND program_name = 'GATHER_STATS_PROG';

PROGRAM_ACTION                             NUMBER_OF_ARGUMENTS ENABLED
------------------------------------------ ------------------- -------
dbms_stats.gather_database_stats_job_proc                    0 TRUE


SQL> SELECT w.window_name, w.repeat_interval, w.duration, w.enabled
  2  FROM dba_autotask_window_clients c, dba_scheduler_windows w
  3  WHERE c.window_name = w.window_name
  4  AND c.optimizer_stats = 'ENABLED';

WINDOW_NAME       REPEAT_INTERVAL                                    DURATION       ENABLED
----------------- -------------------------------------------------- -------------- -------
MONDAY_WINDOW     freq=daily;byday=MON;byhour=22;byminute=0;         +000 04:00:00  TRUE
                  bysecond=0
TUESDAY_WINDOW    freq=daily;byday=TUE;byhour=22;byminute=0;         +000 04:00:00  TRUE
                  bysecond=0
WEDNESDAY_WINDOW  freq=daily;byday=WED;byhour=22;byminute=0;         +000 04:00:00  TRUE
                  bysecond=0
THURSDAY_WINDOW   freq=daily;byday=THU;byhour=22;byminute=0;         +000 04:00:00  TRUE
                  bysecond=0
FRIDAY_WINDOW     freq=daily;byday=FRI;byhour=22;byminute=0;         +000 04:00:00  TRUE
                  bysecond=0
SATURDAY_WINDOW   freq=daily;byday=SAT;byhour=6;byminute=0;          +000 20:00:00  TRUE
                  bysecond=0
SUNDAY_WINDOW     freq=daily;byday=SUN;byhour=6;byminute=0;          +000 20:00:00  TRUE
                  bysecond=0
```

In summary, the configuration is the following:

- The program gather_stats_prog calls, without parameters, the procedure gather_database_stats_job_proc in the package dbms_stats. Since no parameters are passed to it, the only way to change its behavior is to change the default configuration of the package dbms_stats, as explained in the section "Configuring the Package dbms_stats: The 11g Way" earlier in this chapter. Note that this procedure is undocumented and tagged "for internal use only."

- The window group used by the automatic maintenance task has seven members, one for each day of the week. From Monday to Friday it is open for four hours a day. For Saturday and Sunday, it is open for 20 hours a day. The gathering of the object statistics takes place when one of these windows is open.

- The maintenance task, the program, and the windows are enabled.

The opening and duration of the default scheduling should be checked and, whenever necessary, be changed to match the expected statistics gathering frequency. If possible, they should match the low-utilization periods.

To completely enable or disable the maintenance task, the following PL/SQL calls are available. By setting the parameter windows_name to a non-NULL value, it is also possible to enable or disable the maintenance task for a single window only.

```
dbms_auto_task_admin.enable(client_name => 'auto optimizer stats collection',
                            operation   => NULL,
                            window_name => NULL)

dbms_auto_task_admin.disable(client_name => 'auto optimizer stats collection',
                             operation   => NULL,
                             window_name => NULL)
```

Locking Object Statistics

In some situations, you want to make sure that object statistics cannot be changed for part of the database, either because gathering statistics is not possible, for example because of bugs, or because you have to use object statistics that are not up-to-date for some reason.

As of Oracle Database 10g, it is possible to explicitly lock object statistics. You can do this by executing one of the following procedures in the package dbms_stats. Note that these locks have nothing to do with regular database locks. They are, in fact, simple flags set at the table level in the data dictionary.

- lock_schema_stats locks object statistics for all tables belonging to a schema:

  ```
  dbms_stats.lock_schema_stats(ownname => user)
  ```

- lock_table_stats locks object statistics for a single table:

  ```
  dbms_stats.lock_table_stats(ownname => user, tabname => 'T')
  ```

Naturally, it is also possible to remove the locks. This is carried out by executing one of the following procedures:

- unlock_schema_stats removes locks from object statistics for all tables belonging to a schema; even locks that were set with the procedure lock_table_stats are removed:

  ```
  dbms_stats.unlock_schema_stats(ownname => user)
  ```

- unlock_table_stats removes the lock from object statistics for a single table:

  ```
  dbms_stats.unlock_table_stats(ownname => user, tabname => 'T')
  ```

To execute these four procedures, you need to be connected as owner or have the system privilege analyze any.

When the object statistics of a table are locked, all the object statistics that are table depen-dent (including table statistics, column statistics, histograms, and index statistics on all dependent indexes) are considered to be locked.

When the object statistics of a table are locked, procedures in the package dbms_stats that modify object statistics of a single table (for example gather_table_stats) raise an error (ORA-20005). In contrast, procedures that operate on multiple tables (for example gather_ schema_stats) skip the locked table. As of Oracle Database 10g Release 2, most procedures that modify object statistics can override the lock by setting the parameter force to TRUE. The following example demonstrates that behavior (a full example is provided in the script lock_statistics.sql):

```
SQL> BEGIN
  2    dbms_stats.lock_schema_stats(ownname => user);
  3  END;
  4  /

SQL> BEGIN
  2    dbms_stats.gather_table_stats(ownname => user,
  3                                  tabname => 'T');
  4  END;
  5  /
BEGIN
*
ERROR at line 1:
ORA-20005: object statistics are locked (stattype = ALL)
ORA-06512: at "SYS.DBMS_STATS", line 17806
ORA-06512: at "SYS.DBMS_STATS", line 17827
ORA-06512: at line 2

SQL> BEGIN
  2    dbms_stats.gather_table_stats(ownname => user,
  3                                  tabname => 'T',
  4                                  force   => TRUE);
  5  END;
  6  /
```

```
SQL> BEGIN
  2    dbms_stats.gather_schema_stats(ownname => user);
  3  END;
  4  /
```

To know which tables are locked, you can use a query like the following:

```
SQL> SELECT table_name
  2  FROM user_tab_statistics
  3  WHERE stattype_locked IS NOT NULL;

TABLE_NAME
--------------------
T
```

Be aware that the package dbms_stats isn't the only one that gathers object statistics and, therefore, is affected by locks on object statistics. In fact, the SQL commands ANALYZE, CREATE INDEX, and ALTER INDEX also gather object statistics. The first gathers object statistics when it is explicitly instructed to do so. The other two, by default as of Oracle Database 10g (refer to the sidebar "Compute Statistics Clause"), gather them every time an index is built. Consequently, when the object statistics of a table are locked, these SQL statements may fail. The following example, which is a continuation of the previous one, shows this behavior:

```
SQL> ANALYZE TABLE t COMPUTE STATISTICS;
ANALYZE TABLE t COMPUTE STATISTICS
*
ERROR at line 1:
ORA-38029: object statistics are locked

SQL> CREATE INDEX t_i ON t (pad) COMPUTE STATISTICS;
CREATE INDEX t_i ON t (pad) COMPUTE STATISTICS
                    *
ERROR at line 1:
ORA-38029: object statistics are locked

SQL> CREATE INDEX t_i ON t (pad);

SQL> ALTER INDEX t_pk REBUILD COMPUTE STATISTICS;
ALTER INDEX t_pk REBUILD COMPUTE STATISTICS
*
ERROR at line 1:
ORA-38029: object statistics are locked

SQL> ALTER INDEX t_pk REBUILD;
```

COMPUTE STATISTICS CLAUSE

You can add the COMPUTE STATISTICS clause to the SQL statements CREATE INDEX and ALTER INDEX. It instructs them to gather and store index statistics in the data dictionary, while creating or rebuilding the index. This is useful because the overhead associated with the gathering of statistics while executing these SQL statements is negligible. In Oracle9i, the gathering of statistics is performed only when this clause is specified. As of Oracle Database 10g, whenever statistics are not locked, their gathering is done by default, which means the COMPUTE STATISTICS clause is deprecated and available for backward compatibility only.

Comparing Object Statistics

In the following three common situations, you end up with several sets of object statistics for the very same object:

- When you instruct the package dbms_stats (through the parameters statown, stattab, and statid) to back up current statistics in a user-defined table.

- As of Oracle Database 10g, whenever the package dbms_stats is used to gather statistics. In this case, the package automatically keeps a history of the object statistics instead of simply overwriting them when a new set is gathered. You can find more information about how to manage that history in the section "Statistics History" later in this chapter.

- As of Oracle Database 11g, when you gather pending statistics.

It is not unusual to want to know what the differences between two sets of object statistics are. As of Oracle Database 10g patchset 10.2.0.4, you are no longer required to write queries yourself to make such a comparison. You can simply take advantage of the new functions in the package dbms_stats.

The following example, which is an excerpt of the output generated by the script comparing_object_statistics.sql, shows the kind of report you get. Notice how in the first part, you can see the parameters used for the comparison: the schema and the table name, the definition of two sources (A and B), and a threshold. This last parameter specifies whether to display only the object statistics for which the difference (in percent) between the two sets of statistics exceeds the specified threshold. For example, if you have the two values, 100 and 115, they are recognized as different only if the threshold is set to 15 or less. The default value is 10. To display all statistics, the value 0 can be used.

```
################################################################################

STATISTICS DIFFERENCE REPORT FOR:
.................................

TABLE         : T
OWNER         : OPS$CHA
SOURCE A      : Current Statistics in dictionary
SOURCE B      : Statistics as of 30-NOV-00 01.00.00.000000 AM +02:00
PCTTHRESHOLD  : 10
~~~~~~~~~~~~~~~~~~~~~~~~~~~~~~~~~~~~~~~~~~~~~~~~~~~~~~~~~~~~~~~~~~~~~~~~~~~~~~~~~~~~

TABLE / (SUB)PARTITION STATISTICS DIFFERENCE:
.............................................

OBJECTNAME              TYP SRC ROWS      BLOCKS    ROWLEN     SAMPSIZE
.............................................................................

T                        T   A   10096    66        37         5099
                             B   12584    87        3.7603E+01 5332
~~~~~~~~~~~~~~~~~~~~~~~~~~~~~~~~~~~~~~~~~~~~~~~~~~~~~~~~~~~~~~~~~~~~~~~~~~~~~~~~~~~~

COLUMN STATISTICS DIFFERENCE:
.............................

COLUMN_NAME   SRC NDV    DENSITY     HIST NULLS   LEN MIN  MAX   SAMPSIZ
.............................................................................

ID            A   9902   .000100989  NO   0       4   C102 C302  5001
              B   12546  .000079706  NO   0       5   C102 C3026 5316
VAL1          A   3155   .000458085  YES  0       5   3D434 C22A1 5140
              B   3114   .000480769  YES  0       5   3D434 C2255 5303
VAL2          A   9      .000050114  YES  0       3   C10C  C114  5039
              B   9      .000039482  YES  0       3   C10C  C114  5366
~~~~~~~~~~~~~~~~~~~~~~~~~~~~~~~~~~~~~~~~~~~~~~~~~~~~~~~~~~~~~~~~~~~~~~~~~~~~~~~~~~~~

INDEX / (SUB)PARTITION STATISTICS DIFFERENCE:
.............................................

OBJECTNAME   TYP SRC ROWS    LEAFBLK DISTKEY LF/KY DB/KY CLF    LVL SAMPSIZ
.............................................................................


                          INDEX: T_PK
                          ...........

T_PK          I   A   10000   20      10000   1     1    9820   1   10000
                  B   12500   28      12500   1     1    12148  NUL 12500
################################################################################
```

The following are the functions available in the package dbms_stats:

- diff_table_stats_in_stattab compares the object statistics found in a backup table
  (specified with the parameters ownname and tabname) with the current object statistics
  or another set found in another backup table. The parameters stattab1, statid1, and
  stattab1own are provided to specify the first backup table. The second backup table
  (which is optional) is specified with the parameters stattab2, statid2, and stattab2own.
  If the second backup table is not specified, or set to NULL, the current object statistics
  are compared with the object statistics in the first backup table. The following example
  compares the current object statistics of the table t with a set of object statistics named
  set1 and stored in the backup table mystats:

```
dbms_stats.diff_table_stats_in_stattab(ownname      => user,
                                       tabname      => 'T',
                                       stattab1     => 'MYSTATS',
                                       statid1      => 'SET1',
                                       stattab1own  => user,
                                       pctthreshold => 10)
```

- diff_table_stats_in_history compares the current object statistics for one table, or a
  set from the history, with other object statistics from the history. The parameters time1
  and time2 are provided to specify which statistics are used. If the parameter time2 is not
  specified, or set to NULL, the current object statistics are compared to another set from
  the history. The following example compares the current object statistics of the table t
  with the object statistics of one day ago (for example, prior to a gathering of statistics
  that was executed during the night):

```
dbms_stats.diff_table_stats_in_history(ownname      => user,
                                       tabname      => 'T',
                                       time1        => systimestamp - 1,
                                       time2        => NULL,
                                       pctthreshold => 10)
```

- diff_table_stats_in_pending compares the current object statistics for one table, or a
  set from the history, with the pending statistics. To specify object statistics stored in the
  history, the parameter time_stamp is provided. If this parameter is set to NULL (default),
  current object statistics are compared to pending statistics. The following example
  compares the current statistics of the table t with the pending statistics:

```
dbms_stats.diff_table_stats_in_pending(ownname      => user,
                                       tabname      => 'T',
                                       time_stamp   => NULL,
                                       pctthreshold => 10)
```

Deleting Object Statistics

You can delete object statistics from the data dictionary. Except for testing purposes, this is usually not necessary. Nevertheless, it might happen that a table should not have statistics because you want to take advantage of dynamic sampling (this feature is covered in Chapter 5). In that case, the following procedures are available in the package dbms_stats:

- delete_database_stats

- delete_dictionary_stats

- delete_fixed_objects_stats

- delete_schema_stats

- delete_table_stats

- delete_column_stats

- delete_index_stats

As you can see, for each procedure gather_*_stats, there is a corresponding procedure delete_*_stats. The former ones gather object statistics, and the latter ones delete object statistics. The only exception is the procedure delete_column_stats. As its name suggests, it is used for deleting column statistics and histograms.

Table 4-10 summarizes the parameters available for each of these procedures. Most of them are the same and, therefore, have the same meaning as the parameters used by the procedures gather_*_stats. I will describe here only the parameters that have not already been described with the earlier procedures:

- cascade_parts specifies whether statistics for all underlying partitions are deleted. This parameter accepts the values TRUE and FALSE. The default value is TRUE.

- cascade_columns specifies whether column statistics are deleted as well. This parameter accepts the values TRUE and FALSE. The default value is TRUE.

- cascade_indexes specifies whether index statistics are deleted as well. This parameter accepts the values TRUE and FALSE. The default value is TRUE.

- col_stat_type specifies which statistics are deleted. If it is set to ALL, column statistics and histograms are deleted. If it is set to HISTOGRAM, only histograms are deleted. The default value is ALL. This parameter is available as of Oracle Database 11g.

The following call shows how to delete the histogram of one single column (a full example is found in the script delete_histogram.sql) without modifying the other statistics:

```
dbms_stats.delete_column_stats(ownname      => user,
                               tabname      => 'T',
                               colname      => 'VAL',
                               col_stat_type => 'HISTOGRAM')
```

Table 4-10. *Parameters of the Procedures Used for Deleting Object Statistics*

Parameter	Database	Dictionary	Fixed Objects	Schema	Table	Column	Index
Target Objects							
ownname				✓	✓	✓	✓
indname							✓
tabname				✓	✓	✓	✓
colname						✓	
partname					✓	✓	✓
cascade_parts					✓	✓	✓
cascade_columns					✓		
cascade_indexes					✓		
col_stat_type						✓	
force	✓	✓	✓	✓	✓	✓	✓
Deleting Options							
no_invalidate	✓	✓	✓	✓	✓	✓	
Backup Table							
stattab	✓	✓	✓	✓	✓	✓	
statid	✓	✓	✓	✓	✓	✓	
statown	✓	✓	✓	✓	✓	✓	

Strategies for Keeping Object Statistics Up-to-Date

The package dbms_stats provides many features for managing object statistics. The question is, how and when should we use them to achieve a successful configuration? It is difficult to answer this question. Probably no definitive answer exists. In other words, there is no single method that can be implemented in all situations. Let's examine how to approach the problem.

The general rule, and probably the most important one, is that the query optimizer needs object statistics that describe the data stored in the database. As a result, when data changes, object statistics should change as well. As you may understand, I am an advocate of gathering object statistics regularly. Those who are opposed to this practice argue that if a database is running well, there is no need to regather object statistics. The problem with that approach is that more often than not, some of the object statistics are dependent on the actual data. For example, one statistic that commonly changes is the low/high value of columns. True, there are not many of them that change in typical tables, but usually those that change are critical because they are used over and over again in the application. In practice, I run into many more problems caused by object statistics that are not up-to-date than the other way around.

Obviously, it makes no sense to gather object statistics on data that never changes. Only stale object statistics should be regathered. Therefore, it is essential to take advantage of the feature that logs the number of modifications occurring to each table. In this way, we regather object statistics only for those tables experiencing substantial modifications. By default, a table is considered stale when more than 10 percent of the rows change. This is a good default value. As of Oracle Database 11g, this can be changed if necessary.

The frequency of gathering of statistics is also a matter of opinion. I have seen everything from hourly to monthly or even less frequently as being successful. It really depends on your data. In any case, when the staleness of the tables is used as a basis to regather object statistics, intervals that are too long can lead to an excess of stale objects, which in turn leads to excessive time required for statistics gathering. For this reason, I like to schedule them frequently (in order to spread out the load) and keep single runs as short as possible. If your system has daily or weekly low-utilization periods, then scheduling runs during those periods is usually a good thing. If your system is a true 7×24 system, then it is usually better to use very frequent schedules (many times per day) to spread out the load as much as possible.

If for some good reason object statistics should not be gathered on some tables, as of Oracle Database 10g, you should lock them. In this way, the job that regularly gathers object statistics will simply skip them. This is much better than completely deactivating the job for the whole database. Unfortunately, up to Oracle9i, there is no feature that can be used to achieve the same goal simply. As a workaround, if you schedule a job that takes advantage of table monitoring to trigger the gathering of statistics for a whole schema or even the whole database, you can disable table monitoring on particular tables. In this way, the gathering of statistics will not occur on them.

If you have jobs that load or modify lots of data, you should not wait for a scheduled gathering of object statistics. Simply make the gathering of statistics for the modified objects part of the job itself. In other words, if you know that something has substantially changed, trigger the gathering of statistics immediately.

As of Oracle Database 10g, you should take advantage of the default gathering job as much as possible. For this to meet your requirements, you should check, and if necessary change, the default configuration. Since a configuration at the object level is possible only as of Oracle Database 11g, if you have particular requirements for some tables, you should schedule a job that processes them before the default job. In this way, the default job, which processes only those tables with stale statistics, will simply skip them. Locks might also be helpful to ensure that only a specific job is regathering object statistics on those critical tables.

If gathering statistics leads to inefficient execution plans, you can do two things. The first is to fix the problem by restoring the object statistics that were successfully in use before gathering statistics. The second is to find out why inefficient execution plans are generated by the query optimizer with the new object statistics. To do this, you should first check whether the newly gathered statistics correctly describe the data. For example, it is possible that sampling along with a new data distribution will lead to different histograms. If object statistics are not good, then the gathering itself, or possibly a parameter used for their gathering, is the problem. If the object statistics are in fact good, there are two more possible causes. Either the query optimizer is not correctly configured or the query optimizer is making a mistake. You have little control over the latter, but you should be able to find a solution for the former. In any case, you should avoid thinking too hastily that gathering object statistics is inherently problematic and, as a result, stop gathering them regularly.

The best practice is to gather object statistics with the package dbms_stats. However, there are situations where the correct object statistics may be misleading for the query optimizer. A common example is data for which a history must be kept online for a long time (for instance, in Switzerland some types of data must be kept for at least ten years). In such cases, if the data distribution hardly changes over the time, the object statistics gathered by the package dbms_stats should be fine. In contrast, if the data distribution is strongly dependent on the period and the application frequently accesses only a subset of the data, it could make sense to manually modify (that is, fudge) object statistics to describe the most relevant data. In other words, if you know something that the package dbms_stats ignores or is not able to discover, it is legitimate to inform the query optimizer by fudging the object statistics.

Common Services

The following sections describe several services of the package dbms_stats that are used for both system statistics and object statistics.

Statistics History

As of Oracle Database 10g, whenever system statistics or object statistics are gathered through the package dbms_stats, instead of simply overwriting current statistics with the new statistics, the current statistics are saved in other data dictionary tables that keep a history of all changes occurring within a retention period. The purpose is to be able to restore old statistics in case that new statistics lead to inefficient execution plans.

Up to Oracle9i, you can also implement such a history by taking advantage of a backup table. Nevertheless, it is a good thing that the package dbms_stats automatically takes care of it.

Retention Period and Purging

Statistics are kept in the history for an interval specified by a retention period. The default value is 31 days. You can display the current value by calling the function get_stats_history_retention in the package dbms_stats, as shown here:

```
SQL> SELECT dbms_stats.get_stats_history_retention() AS retention
  2  FROM dual;

 RETENTION
----------
        31
```

To change the retention period, the package dbms_stats provides the procedure alter_stats_history_retention. Here is an example where the call sets the retention period to 14 days:

```
dbms_stats.alter_stats_history_retention(retention => 14)
```

Note that with the procedure alter_stats_history_retention, the following values have a special meaning:

- NULL sets the retention period to the default value.

- 0 disables the history.

- -1 disables the purging of the history.

When the initialization parameter statistics_level is set to typical (the default value) or all, statistics older than the retention period are automatically purged. Whenever manual purging is necessary, the package dbms_stats provides the procedure purge_stats. The following call purges all statistics placed in the history more than 14 days ago:

```
dbms_stats.purge_stats(before_timestamp => systimestamp-14)
```

To execute the procedures alter_stats_history_retention and purge_stats, you need to have the system privilege analyze any dictionary.

Views

If you are interested in knowing when object statistics for a given table were modified, the data dictionary view user_tab_stats_history provides all the necessary information. Of course, there are dba and all versions of that view as well.

Here is an example. With the following query, it is possible to display when the object statistics of the table tab$ in the schema sys where modified:

```
SQL> SELECT stats_update_time
  2  FROM dba_tab_stats_history
  3  WHERE owner = 'SYS' and table_name = 'TAB$';

STATS_UPDATE_TIME
------------------------------------------------
05-MAY-07 06.58.48.005969 AM +02:00
11-MAY-07 10.01.00.898243 PM +02:00
```

Restoring Statistics

Whenever it may be necessary, statistics can be restored from the history. For that purpose, the package dbms_stats provides the following procedures:

- restore_database_stats restores object statistics for the whole database.

- restore_dictionary_stats restores object statistics for the data dictionary.

- restore_fixed_objects_stats restores object statistics for fixed tables.

- restore_system_stats restores system statistics.

- restore_schema_stats restores object statistics for a single schema.

- restore_table_stats restores object statistics for a single table.

In addition to the parameters specifying the target (for example, the schema and table names for the procedure restore_table_stats), all these procedures provide the following parameters:

- `as_of_timestamp` restores the statistics that were in use at a specific time.

- `force` specifies whether locked statistics should be overwritten. Note that locks on statistics are part of the history. This means the information about whether statistics are locked or not is also restored with a restore. The default value is `FALSE`.

- `no_invalidate` specifies whether cursors depending on the overwritten statistics are invalidated. This parameter accepts the values `TRUE`, `FALSE`, and `dbms_stats.auto_invalidate`. The default value is `dbms_stats.auto_invalidate`.

The following call restores the object statistics of the schema SH to the values that were in use one day ago. Since the parameter `force` is set to `TRUE`, the restore is done even if statistics are currently locked.

```
dbms_stats.restore_schema_stats(ownname         => 'SH',
                                as_of_timestamp => systimestamp - 1,
                                force           => TRUE)
```

Creating and Dropping a Backup Table

Throughout the chapter, I've discussed how to take advantage of a backup table. This section describes how to create and drop one.

To create the backup table, the package `dbms_stats` provides the procedure `create_stat_table`. As shown in the following example, its creation is a matter of specifying the owner (with the parameter `ownname`) and the name (with the parameter `stattab`) of the backup table. In addition, the optional parameter `tblspace` specifies in which tablespace the table is created. If the parameter `tblspace` is not specified, by default, the table ends up in the default tablespace of the user.

```
dbms_stats.create_stat_table(ownname  => user,
                             stattab  => 'MYSTATS',
                             tblspace => 'USERS')
```

Since the backup table is used to store different kinds of information, most of its columns are generic. For example, there are 12 columns to store numeric values, named n1 . . . n12, and 5 columns to store string values, named c1 . . . c5.

To drop the table, the package `dbms_stats` provides the procedure `drop_stat_table`. You can also drop it with a regular `DROP TABLE`.

```
dbms_stats.drop_stat_table(ownname => user,
                           stattab => 'MYSTATS')
```

Exporting, Importing, Getting, and Setting Operations

As illustrated in Figure 4-1, the package `dbms_stats` provides several procedures and functions, in addition to the ones used for gathering statistics. I will not describe them here because they are not commonly used in practice. For information about them, refer to the *PL/SQL Packages and Types Reference* manual.

Logging

As of Oracle Database 10g, the procedures in the package dbms_stats working at database, data dictionary, or schema level, log information about their execution in the data dictionary. This logging information is externalized through the data dictionary view dba_optstat_operations. Basically, you are able to know which operations were performed, when they were started, and how long they took. The following example, which is an excerpt taken from a production database, shows that the procedure gather_database_stats is started every day, except on Sunday, and takes between 10 and 17 minutes to run:

```
SQL> SELECT operation, start_time,
  2          (end_time-start_time) DAY(1) TO SECOND(0) AS duration
  3  FROM dba_optstat_operations
  4  ORDER BY start_time DESC;

OPERATION                    START_TIME         DURATION
---------------------------- ------------------ -----------
gather_database_stats(auto)  07-MAY-2007 22:00  +0 00:10:44
gather_database_stats(auto)  05-MAY-2007 06:00  +0 00:12:03
gather_database_stats(auto)  04-MAY-2007 22:00  +0 00:10:03
gather_database_stats(auto)  03-MAY-2007 22:00  +0 00:15:54
gather_database_stats(auto)  02-MAY-2007 22:00  +0 00:10:42
gather_database_stats(auto)  01-MAY-2007 22:00  +0 00:16:40
gather_database_stats(auto)  30-APR-2007 22:00  +0 00:11:56
gather_database_stats(auto)  28-APR-2007 06:00  +0 00:13:56
gather_database_stats(auto)  27-APR-2007 22:00  +0 00:10:50
...
```

The content of the logging table is purged at the same time as the statistics history, and therefore, it has the same retention.

On to Chapter 5

This chapter described what system statistics and object statistics are. While the former provides performance information about the CPU and the I/O subsystem, the latter describes the data stored in the database. In other words, statistics describe the environment in which the query optimizer operates. The chapter also covered how to gather statistics with the package dbms_stats and where to find them in the data dictionary.

This chapter gave little information about the utilization of system statistics and object statistics. Such information will be provided in the next chapter, along with a description of the initialization parameters that configure the query optimizer. After reading that chapter, you should be able to correctly configure the query optimizer and, as a result, get efficient execution plans from it most of the time.

CHAPTER 5

■■■

Configuring the
Query Optimizer

The query optimizer is directly responsible for the performance of SQL statements. For this reason, it makes sense to take some time to configure it correctly. In fact, without an optimal configuration, the query optimizer may generate inefficient execution plans that lead to poor performance.

The configuration of the query optimizer consists not only of several initialization parameters but also of system statistics and object statistics. (I discussed system and object statistics in Chapter 4.) This chapter will describe how these initialization parameters and statistics influence the query optimizer and present a straightforward and pragmatic road map that will help you achieve a successful configuration.

■**Caution** The formulas provided in this chapter, with a single exception, are not published by Oracle. Several tests show that they are able to describe how the query optimizer estimates the cost of a given operation. In any case, they neither claim to be precise nor claim to be correct in all situations. They are provided here to give you an idea of how an initialization parameter or a statistic influences query optimizer estimations.

To Configure or Not to Configure . . .

Adapting a Kenyan proverb[1] to our situation here, I would say "Configuring the query optimizer is costly, but it is worth the expense." In practice, I have seen too many sites that underestimate the importance of a good configuration. From time to time I even have heated discussions with people who say to me, "We don't need to spend time on individually configuring the query optimizer for each database. We already have a set of initialization parameters that we use over and over again on all our databases." My first reply is, frequently, something like this: "Why would Oracle introduce almost two dozen initialization parameters that are specific to the query optimizer if a single set works well on all databases? They know what they are doing. If such a magic configuration existed, they would provide it by default and make the initialization parameters undocumented." I then continue by carefully explaining that such a magic configuration doesn't exist because

- each application has its own requirements and workload profile, and

- each system, which is composed of different hardware and software components, has its own characteristics.

If the people in question are customers, usually I also remind them with "You called me because you have performance problems, right? The application may not be performing at its best in some situations, but the database is also responsible for the present situation . . . So, let's work on the problem."

That said, at least since Oracle9*i* Release 2, the query optimizer works well, meaning it generates good execution plans for most[2] SQL statements. Be careful, though, because this is true only on the condition that the query optimizer is correctly configured and the database has been designed to take advantage of all its features. I cannot stress this enough. Also note that the configuration of the query optimizer includes not only the initialization parameters but the system statistics and object statistics as well.

Configuration Road Map

Since there is no such thing as a magic configuration, we need a solid and reliable procedure to help us. Figure 5-1 sums up the main steps I go through.

---

1. The Kenyan proverb is "Peace is costly, but it is worth the expense." You can find this quote at http://www.quotationspage.com/quote/38863.html.
2. Perfection is unrealizable in software development as in almost any other activity you can imagine. This rule, even if neither you nor Oracle likes it, applies to the query optimizer as well. You should therefore expect that a small percentage of the SQL statements will require manual intervention (this topic is covered in Chapter 7).

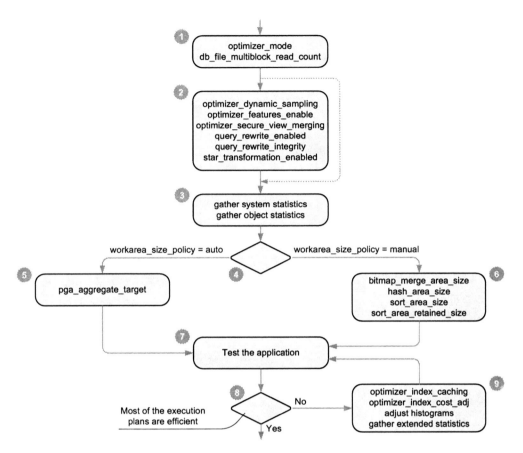

Figure 5-1. *Main steps of the configuration road map*

Here are descriptions of the numbered steps in Figure 5-1.

1. Two initialization parameters should always be adjusted: optimizer_mode and db_file_multiblock_read_count. As you will see later in this chapter, the latter is no longer that important for the query optimizer itself. Nevertheless, the performance of some operations may strongly depend on it.

2. Since the default values of the initialization parameters adjusted in this step are generally good, this step is optional. In any case, the aim of this step is to enable or disable specific features of the query optimizer.

3. Since system statistics and object statistics provide vital information to the query optimizer, they must be gathered.

4. With the initialization parameter `workarea_size_policy`, the choice is made between manual and automatic sizing of work areas provided to operations storing data in memory. Depending on the method chosen, other initialization parameters are set either in step 5 or in step 6.

5. If the sizing of work areas is automatic, the initialization parameter `pga_aggregate_target` is set.

6. If the sizing of work areas is manual, the actual size depends on the type of operation using the memory. Basically, a specific initialization parameter is set for each type of operation.

7. When the first part of the configuration is available, it is time to test the application. During the test, the execution plans are collected for the components that do not provide the required performance. By analyzing these execution plans, you should be able to infer what the problem is. Note that at this stage, it is important to recognize general, not individual, behavior. For example, you may notice that the query optimizer uses too many or too few indexes or does not recognize restrictions correctly.

8. If the query optimizer generates efficient execution plans for most SQL statements, the configuration is good. If not, you proceed to step 9.

9. If the query optimizer tends to use too many or too few indexes or nested loops, it is usually possible to adjust the initialization parameters `optimizer_index_caching` and `optimizer_index_cost_adj` to fix the problem. If the query optimizer makes mistakes in the estimation of cardinalities, it is possible that some histograms are missing or need to be adjusted. As of Oracle Database 11g, extended statistics might also help.

According to Figure 5-1, the initialization parameters set in the steps from 1 to 6 cannot be changed afterward. Of course, this is not written in stone. If you cannot achieve good results by adjusting the index-related initialization parameters or the histograms in step 9, it could be necessary to start over from the beginning. It is also worth mentioning that since several initialization parameters have an impact on system statistics, after changing them it could be necessary to recompute the system statistics.

Set the Right Parameter!

I am quite sure that Oracle does not just randomly provide new initialization parameters. Instead, each initialization parameter is introduced to control a very specific feature or behavior of the query optimizer. At the risk of repeating myself, I must remind you that since Oracle has introduced a parameter, this implies that no value can be applied to all situations. Thus, for each initialization parameter, you must infer a sensible value from both the application workload profile and the system where the database engine runs.

To perform a successful configuration of the query optimizer, it is essential to understand how it works and the impact each initialization parameter has on it. With this knowledge, instead of tweaking the configuration randomly or copying the "good values" from an article you found recently on the Internet, you should do the following:

- Understand the current situation. For instance, why has the query optimizer chosen an execution plan that is suboptimal?

- Determine the goal to be achieved. In other words, what execution plan do you want to achieve?

- Find out which initialization parameters, or possibly which statistics, should be rectified to achieve the goal you set. Of course, in some situations it is not enough to set initialization parameters only. Possibly, it is necessary to modify the SQL statement and/or the database design as well.

The following sections describe how the initialization parameters referenced by the configuration road map of Figure 5-1 work and also give advice on how to find good values for your system. Parameters are divided into two groups: one where only the operation of the query optimizer is affected; the other is where parameters have to do with the *program global area* (PGA).

Query Optimizer Parameters

The following sections describe a number of parameters related to the operation of the query optimizer.

optimizer_mode

The initialization parameter `optimizer_mode` is essential because it specifies how the query optimizer decides which is the most efficient execution plan for executing each SQL statement. It is essential because with it you specify what the word *efficient* means. It may mean "faster," "using fewer resources," or perhaps something else. Since with a database you are processing data, you'll usually want to process it as fast as possible. Therefore, the meaning of *efficient* should be the fastest way to execute a SQL statement without wasting unnecessary resources. What that means for a SQL statement that is always completely executed (for example, an `INSERT` statement) is clear. For a query, on the other hand, there are subtle differences. An application, for example, is not under obligation to fetch all rows returned by a query. In other words, queries might be only partially executed.

Let me give you an example unrelated to Oracle. When I google the term *query optimizer*, I immediately get a page with the first ten results. On the same page, I am informed that there are about 334,000 pages in the result set and that the search took 0.13 seconds. This is a good example of processing that is optimized to deliver the initial data as fast as possible. If I want to access one of the pages, I then click the link. At this point I am usually not interested in getting only the first few lines. I want the whole page to be available and correctly formatted, at which point I will start reading. In this case, the processing should be optimized to provide all data as fast as possible and not only pieces. Every application falls into one of the two categories described earlier. Either fast delivery of the first part of the result set is important or the fast delivery of the whole result set is important.

To choose the value of the initialization parameter `optimizer_mode`, you have to ask yourself whether it is more important for the query optimizer to produce execution plans for the fast delivery of the first row or the fast delivery of the last row:

- If fast delivery of the last row is important, you should use the value all_rows. This configuration is typically used in reporting systems, in OLAP systems, in data warehouses, and with middle-tier components that cache data.

- If fast delivery of the first row(s) is important, you should use the value first_rows_*n* (where *n* is 1, 10, 100, or 1,000 rows). This configuration is typically used for OLTP systems. Notice that the older first row optimizer (that is configured through the value first_rows) should no longer be used. In fact, it is provided for backward compatibility only.

Up to Oracle9*i*, the default value is choose. This means that if object statistics are available for at least one of the objects referenced in the SQL statement that has to be optimized, the value all_rows is used; otherwise, rule is used. In some situations however, even when no object statistics are available, the database engine forces all_rows. This is because, generally speaking, the rule-based optimizer does not support structures added after Oracle7 (for example, partitioned tables). As of Oracle Database 10*g*, the rule-based optimizer has been desupported, and therefore the new default value is all_rows. Consequently, the values choose and rule are no longer supported.

The initialization parameter optimizer_mode is dynamic and can be changed at the instance and session levels. In addition, with one of the following hints, it is possible to set it at the statement level:

- all_rows

- first_rows(*n*) where *n* is any natural number (greater than 0)

optimizer_features_enable

In every database version, Oracle introduces or enables new features in the query optimizer. If you are upgrading to a new database version and want to keep the old behavior of the query optimizer, it is possible to set the initialization parameter optimizer_features_enable to the database version from which you are upgrading. That said, setting it is only a short-term workaround, and sooner or later, the application should be adapted (optimized) for the new database version. In addition, not all new features are disabled by this initialization parameter. For example, if you set it to 9.2.0 in Oracle Database 10*g*, you will not get the 9.2.0 query optimizer. For this reason, I usually advise using the default value, which is the same as the database binaries version.

Valid values for the initialization parameter optimizer_features_enable are database versions such as 9.2.0, 10.1.0.5, or 10.2.0.3. Since the documentation (specifically the *Oracle Database Reference* manual) is not up-to-date for each patch level for this parameter, as of Oracle Database 10*g* Release 2, it is possible to generate the actual supported values with the following SQL statement:

```
SQL> SELECT value
  2  FROM v$parameter_valid_values
  3  WHERE name = 'optimizer_features_enable';
```

```
VALUE
--------------------
8.0.0
8.0.3
8.0.4
...
10.2.0.2
10.2.0.3
10.2.0.3.1
```

Up to Oracle Database 10g Release 1, the view v$parameter_valid_values does not exist. The only workaround I know of to get an up-to-date list is to cause the database engine to generate an error message, as shown in the following example. You can use this trick with other initialization parameters accepting predefined values as well.

```
SQL> ALTER SESSION SET optimizer_features_enable = 'dummy';
ERROR:
ORA-00096: invalid value dummy for parameter optimizer_features_enable, must be
from among 10.1.0.5.1, 10.1.0.5, 10.1.0.4, 10.1.0.3, 10.1.0, 9.2.0, 9.0.1, 9.0.0,
8.1.7, 8.1.6, 8.1.5, 8.1.4, 8.1.3, 8.1.0, 8.0.7, 8.0.6, 8.0.5, 8.0.4, 8.0.3, 8.0.0
```

The initialization parameter optimizer_features_enable is dynamic and can be changed at the instance and session levels. In addition, as of Oracle Database 10g, it is possible to specify a value at the statement level with the hint optimizer_features_enable. The following two examples show the hint used to specify the default value and a specific value, respectively:

- optimizer_features_enable(default)

- optimizer_features_enable('9.2.0')

It is important to note that the initialization parameter optimizer_features_enable disables not only features but bug fixes as well. The script bug5015557.sql provides such an example. If you run it on Oracle Database 10g patchset 10.1.0.5 or higher, you can see how the same query runs correctly with the parameter set to 10.1.0.5 but fails with an ORA-03113 when it is set to 10.1.0.4.

db_file_multiblock_read_count

The maximum I/O size used by the database engine during multiblock reads (for example, full table scans or index fast full scans) is determined by multiplying the values of the initialization parameters db_file_multiblock_read_count and db_block_size. Thus, the maximum number of blocks read during multiblock reads is determined by dividing the maximum I/O size by the block size. In other words, for the default block size, the initialization parameter db_file_multiblock_read_count specifies the maximum number of blocks read. This is "only" a maximum because there are at least three common situations leading to multiblock reads that are smaller than the value specified by this initialization parameter:

- Segment headers are read with single-block reads.

- Physical reads never span several extents.

- Blocks already in the buffer cache, except for direct reads, are not reread from the I/O subsystem.

To illustrate, Figure 5-2 shows the structure of a segment stored in a database. Like any segment, it is composed of extents (in this example, two), and each extent is composed of blocks (in this example, 16). The first block of the first extent is the segment header. Some blocks (4, 9, 10, 19, and 21) are cached in the buffer cache. A database engine process executing a serial full scan (parallel full scans have a particular behavior that will be described in Chapter 11) of this segment is not able to perform a single physical read, even if the initialization parameter db_file_multiblock_read_count is set to a value greater than or equal to 32.

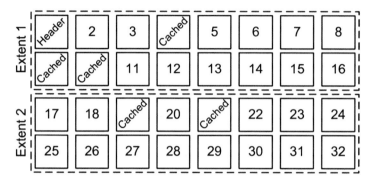

Figure 5-2. *Structure of a data segment*

If the initialization parameter db_file_multiblock_read_count is set to 8, the following physical reads are performed:

- One single-block read of the segment header (block 1).

- One multiblock read of two blocks (2 and 3). More blocks cannot be read because block 4 is cached.

- One multiblock read of four blocks (from 5 to 8). More blocks cannot be read because block 9 is cached.

- One multiblock read of six blocks (from 11 to 16). More blocks cannot be read because block 16 is the last one of the extent.

- One multiblock read of two blocks (17 and 18). More blocks cannot be read because block 19 is cached.

- One single-block read of block 20. More blocks cannot be read because block 21 is cached.

- One multiblock read of eight blocks (from 22 to 29). More blocks cannot be read because the initialization parameter db_file_multiblock_read_count is set to 8.

- One multiblock read of three blocks (from 30 to 32).

In summary, the process performs two single-block reads and six multiblock reads. The average number of blocks read by a multiblock read is about four. The fact that the average size is smaller than eight explains why Oracle introduced the value mbrc in system statistics.

At this point, it is also important to see how the query optimizer computes the cost of multiblock read operations (for example, full table scans or index fast full scans). As pointed out by Wolfgang Breitling in the paper "A Look Under the Hood of CBO: The 10053 Event," when system statistics are not available, the costing is well modeled by Formula 5-1.

$$io\_cost \approx \frac{blocks}{1.6765 \cdot db\_file\_multiblock\_read\_count^{0.6581}}$$

Formula 5-1. *I/O cost of multiblock read operations without system statistics*

When workload system statistics are available, the I/O cost is no longer dependent on the value of the initialization parameter db_file_multiblock_read_count. It is computed by Formula 5-2. Note that mreadtim is divided by sreadtim because the query optimizer normalizes the costs according to single-block reads, as already discussed in the previous chapter (Formula 4-2).

$$io\_cost \approx \frac{blocks}{mbrc} \cdot \frac{mreadtim}{sreadtim}$$

Formula 5-2. *I/O cost of multiblock read operations with workload statistics*

In Formula 5-2, with noworkload statistics, mbrc is replaced by the value of the initialization parameter db_file_multiblock_read_count, sreadtim with the value computed by Formula 4-3, and mreadtim by the value computed by Formula 4-4.

This means that the initialization parameter db_file_multiblock_read_count has a direct impact on the cost of multiblock read operations only when workload statistics are not available. This also means values that are too high may lead to excessive full scans or at least an underestimation of the cost of multiblock read operations. Further, this is another situation where workload statistics are superior to noworkload statistics or no system statistics at all.

Now that you have seen the costing formulas, it is essential that I describe how to find out the value to which this parameter should be set. The most important thing is to recognize that multiblock reads are a performance feature. Therefore, the initialization parameter db_file_multiblock_read_count should be set to achieve best performance. To do so, it is imperative to recognize that higher values do not provide better performance in all cases. In addition, it makes no sense to exceed the maximum physical I/O size supported by the operating system. A simple full table scan with different values gives useful information about the impact of this initialization parameter and, therefore, assists in finding an optimal value. The following PL/SQL block, which is an excerpt of the script assess_dbfmbrc.sql, could be used for that purpose:

```
DECLARE
  l_count PLS_INTEGER;
  l_time PLS_INTEGER;
  l_starting_time PLS_INTEGER;
  l_ending_time PLS_INTEGER;
```

```
BEGIN
  dbms_output.put_line('dbfmbrc seconds');
  FOR l_dbfmbrc IN 1..32
  LOOP
    EXECUTE IMMEDIATE 'ALTER SESSION SET db_file_multiblock_read_count='||l_dbfmbrc;
    l_starting_time := dbms_utility.get_time();
    SELECT /*+ full(t) */ count(*) INTO l_count FROM big_table t;
    l_ending_time := dbms_utility.get_time();
    l_time := round((l_ending_time-l_starting_time)/100);
    dbms_output.put_line(l_dbfmbrc||' '||l_time);
  END LOOP;
END;
```

As you can see, it is not that difficult to do, since the initialization parameter db_file_multiblock_read_count is dynamic and can be changed at the instance and session levels. In any case, be careful not to cache the test table at the database, operating system, and I/O subsystem levels, which would render the test useless. The easiest way to avoid that is to use a table larger than the largest cache available in your system. Note that parallel processing is avoided because usually the database engine uses different system calls to execute parallel full table scans and serial full table scans.

Figure 5-3 shows the characteristics of several systems measured with the previous PL/SQL block:

System 1: Performance increases with a larger I/O size. The gain is important for values up to 8 to 10. Larger values give small benefits.

System 2: Values up to 16 perform poorly (gain less than 10 percent). By switching from 16 to 17, the gain increases by 30 percent. Values larger than 17 provide little benefit. For this system, values smaller than 17 should be avoided.

System 3: The gain is significant for values up to 8. For values between 8 and 16, the gain is stable. By switching from 16 to 17, the gain decreases by 16 percent. For this system, values greater than 16 should be avoided.

System 4: The performance of this system is independent of the I/O size.

As of Oracle Database 10*g* Release 2, it is also possible to instruct the database engine to automatically configure the value of the initialization parameter db_file_multiblock_read_count. To use this feature, simply do not set it. As shown in Formula 5-3, the database engine will then try to set it to a value that allows 1MB physical reads. At the same time, however, a kind of sanity check is applied to reduce the value if the size of the buffer cache is quite small compared to the number of sessions supported by the database.

$$db\_file\_multiblock\_read\_count \approx \min\left(\frac{1048576}{db\_block\_size}, \frac{db\_cache\_size}{sessions \cdot db\_block\_size}\right)$$

Formula 5-3. *Default value of the initialization parameter db_file_multiblock_read_count as of Oracle Database 10g Release 2*

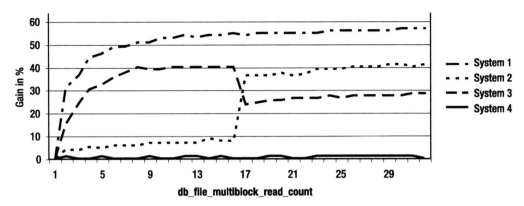

Figure 5-3. *Impact of I/O size on the performance of a full table scan on four different systems*

Since, as described earlier, physical reads with the largest I/O size are not always the ones performing better, I would advise against using this feature. It is better to find out the optimal value case by case.

Note that if noworkload statistics are used with this automatic configuration, mbrc is not replaced by the automatically configured value in Formula 5-2. Instead, the value 8 is used.

optimizer_dynamic_sampling

The query optimizer used to base its estimations solely on object statistics stored in the data dictionary. With dynamic sampling, that has changed. In fact, some statistics may be dynamically gathered during the parse phase as well. This means that to gather additional information, some queries are executed against the referenced objects. Unfortunately, the statistics gathered by dynamic sampling are neither stored in the data dictionary nor stored elsewhere. The only way to virtually reuse them is to reuse the shared cursor itself.

The value (also called *level*) of the initialization parameter optimizer_dynamic_sampling specifies how and when dynamic sampling is used. Table 5-1 summarizes the accepted values and their meanings. Note that the default value depends on the initialization parameter optimizer_features_enable.

- If optimizer_features_enable is set to 10.0.0 or higher, the default is level 2.

- If optimizer_features_enable is set to 9.2.0, the default is level 1.

- If optimizer_features_enable is set to 9.0.1 or lower, dynamic sampling is disabled.

The parameter is dynamic and can be changed at the instance level with the SQL statement ALTER SYSTEM and at session level with the SQL statement ALTER SESSION. In addition, it is possible to specify a value at the statement level with the hint dynamic_sampling. Two options are available with the hint:

- A value can be set for all tables: dynamic_sampling(*level*)

- A value can be set for a specific table only: dynamic_sampling(*table_name level*)

Table 5-1. *Dynamic Sampling Levels and Their Meaning*

Level	When Is Dynamic Sampling Used?	Number of Blocks*
0	Dynamic sampling is disabled.	0
1	Dynamic sampling is used for tables without object statistics. However, this occurs only if the following three conditions are met: the table has no index, it is part of a join (also subquery or nonmergeable view), and it has more blocks than the number of blocks used for the sampling.	32
2	Dynamic sampling is used for all tables without object statistics.	64
3	Dynamic sampling is used for all tables fulfilling the level-2 criterion and, in addition, for which a guess is used to estimate the selectivity of a predicate.	32
4	Dynamic sampling is used for all tables fulfilling the level-3 criterion and, in addition, having two or more columns referenced in the WHERE clause.	32
5	The same as level 4.	64
6	The same as level 4.	128
7	The same as level 4.	256
8	The same as level 4.	1024
9	The same as level 4.	4096
10	The same as level 4.	All

* *This is the number of blocks used for sampling when dynamic sampling is activated with the initialization parameter or the hint without a table name (or alias). When a hint with the table name (or alias) is used, the number of blocks, except for level 10, is computed with the following formula: $32*2^{(level-1)}$.*

Here are some examples (excerpts of the script dynamic_sampling_levels.sql run in version 10.2.0.3) illustrating in which situations the values between 1 and 4 lead to dynamic sampling. The tables used for the tests are created with the following SQL statements. Initially, they have no object statistics. Note that the only difference between the table t_noidx and the table t_idx is that the latter has a primary key.

```
CREATE TABLE t_noidx (id, n1, n2, pad) AS
SELECT rownum, rownum, round(dbms_random.value(1,100)), dbms_random.string('p',1000)
FROM all_objects
WHERE rownum <= 1000

CREATE TABLE t_idx (id PRIMARY KEY, n1, n2, pad) AS
SELECT *
FROM t_noidx
```

The first test queries are the following. The only difference between them is that the first one references the table t_noidx while the second one references the table t_idx.

```
SELECT *
FROM t_noidx t1, t_noidx t2
WHERE t1.id = t2.id AND t1.id < 19

SELECT *
FROM t_idx t1, t_idx t2
WHERE t1.id = t2.id AND t1.id < 19
```

If the level is set to 1, dynamic sampling is performed only for the first query because the table referenced by the second one is indexed. The following is the recursive query used to gather the statistics for table t_noidx on my test database. Some hints have been removed and bind variables replaced with literals to make it easier to read. Note that SQL trace was activated before executing the test query. Then, all I needed to do was inspect the generated trace file to find out which recursive SQL statements were executed.

```
SELECT NVL(SUM(C1),0),
       NVL(SUM(C2),0),
       COUNT(DISTINCT C3),
       NVL(SUM(CASE WHEN C3 IS NULL THEN 1 ELSE 0 END),0)
FROM (
  SELECT 1 AS C1,
         CASE WHEN "T1"."ID"<19" THEN 1 ELSE 0 END AS C2,
         "T1"."ID" AS C3
  FROM "T_NOIDX" SAMPLE BLOCK (20,1) SEED (1) "T1"
) SAMPLESUB
```

Here are the significant points to notice:

- The query optimizer counts the total number of rows, the number of rows in the range specified in the WHERE clause (id < 19), and the number of distinct values and NULL values of the column id.

- The values used in the query must be known. If bind variables are used, the query optimizer must be able to peek the values to perform dynamic sampling.

- The SAMPLE clause is used to perform the sampling. Table t_noidx has 155 blocks on my database, so the sampling percentage is 20 percent (32/155).

If the level is set to 2, dynamic sampling is performed for both test queries since, at that level, dynamic sampling is always used when object statistics are missing. The recursive query used to gather the statistics for both tables is the same as the one shown earlier. The sampling percentage increases because, at that level, it is based on 64 blocks instead of 32. In addition, for table t_idx, the following recursive query is executed as well. Its aim is to scan the index instead of the table like in the previous query. This is done because a quick sampling on the table may miss the rows in the range specified by the predicate present in the WHERE clause. Instead, a quick scan of the index will certainly locate them, if they exist.

```
SELECT NVL(SUM(C1),0), NVL(SUM(C2),0), NVL(SUM(C3),0)
FROM (
  SELECT 1 AS C1, 1 AS C2, 1 AS C3
  FROM "T_IDX" "T1"
  WHERE "T1"."ID"<19 AND ROWNUM <= 2500
) SAMPLESUB
```

The next level of dynamic sampling is 3. Starting with that level, dynamic sampling is also used when object statistics are available in the data dictionary. Before executing further tests, object statistics were gathered with the following PL/SQL block:

```
BEGIN
  dbms_stats.gather_table_stats(ownname    => user,
                                tabname    => 't_noidx',
                                method_opt => 'for all columns size 1');
  dbms_stats.gather_table_stats(ownname    => user,
                                tabname    => 't_idx',
                                method_opt => 'for all columns size 1',
                                cascade    => true);
END;
```

If the level is set to 3 or higher, the query optimizer performs dynamic sampling to estimate the selectivity of a predicate by measuring the selectivity over a sample of the table rows, instead of using the statistics from the data dictionary and possibly hard-coded values. The following two queries illustrate this:

```
SELECT *
FROM t_idx
WHERE id = 19

SELECT *
FROM t_idx
WHERE round(id) = 19
```

For the first one, the query optimizer is able to estimate the selectivity of the predicate id=19 based on the column statistics and histograms. Thus, no dynamic sampling is necessary. Instead, for the second one (except if extended statistics for the expression round(id) are in place), the query optimizer is not able to infer the selectivity of the predicate round(id)=19. In fact, the column statistics and histograms provide information only about the column id itself, not about its rounded values. The query used for the dynamic sampling is the following. As you can see, it has the same structure as one discussed earlier. Column c2 is different because the WHERE clause of the SQL statement leading to dynamic sampling is different. Since an expression is applied to the indexed column (id), even with table t_idx, no sampling on the index is performed in this specific case.

```
SELECT NVL(SUM(C1),0), NVL(SUM(C2),0), COUNT(DISTINCT C3)
FROM (
  SELECT 1 AS C1,
         CASE WHEN ROUND("T_IDX"."ID")=19 THEN 1 ELSE 0 END AS C2,
         ROUND("T_IDX"."ID") AS C3
  FROM "T_IDX" SAMPLE BLOCK (20,1) SEED (1) "T_IDX"
) SAMPLESUB
```

If the level is set to 4 or higher, the query optimizer performs dynamic sampling when two or more columns of the same table are referenced in the WHERE clause. This is useful for improving estimations in the case of correlated columns. The following query provides an example of this. If you look back at the SQL statements used to create the test tables, you will notice that the columns id and n1 contain the same data.

```
SELECT *
FROM t_idx
WHERE id < 19 AND n1 < 19
```

Also in this case, the query optimizer performs dynamic sampling with a query that has the same structure as the previous ones. Once more, the main difference is because of the WHERE clause of the SQL statement that causes dynamic sampling.

```
SELECT NVL(SUM(C1),0), NVL(SUM(C2),0)
FROM (
  SELECT 1 AS C1,
         CASE WHEN "T_IDX"."ID"<19 AND "T_IDX"."N1"<19 THEN 1 ELSE 0 END AS C2
  FROM "T_IDX" SAMPLE BLOCK (20,1) SEED (1) "T_IDX"
) SAMPLESUB
```

Summing up, you can see that level 1 and 2 are usually not very useful. In fact, tables and indexes should have up-to-date object statistics. A common exception is when temporary tables are used. In fact, usually no object statistics are available for them. In any case, be aware that several sessions may share the very same cursor even if their temporary tables contain very different sets of data. Level 3 and higher are useful for improving selectivity estimations of "complex" predicates. Therefore, if the query optimizer is not able to make correct estimations because of "complex" predicates, set the initialization parameter optimizer_dynamic_sampling to 4. Otherwise, leave it at the default value. In any case, as mentioned in Chapter 4, as of Oracle Database 11g, it is possible to gather statistics on expressions and groups of columns. Hence, in many situations it should be possible to avoid dynamic sampling.

optimizer_index_cost_adj

The initialization parameter optimizer_index_cost_adj is used to change the cost of table accesses through index scans. Valid values go from 1 to 10,000. The default is 100. Values greater than 100 make index scans more expensive and as a result favor full table scans. Values less than 100 make index scans less expensive.

To understand the effect of this initialization parameter on the costing formula, it is useful to describe how the query optimizer computes costs related to table accesses based on *index range scans*.

An index range scan is an index lookup of several keys. As shown in Figure 5-4, the following operations are carried out.

1. Access the root block of the index.

2. Go through the branch blocks to locate the leaf block containing the first keys.

3. For each key fulfilling the search criteria, do the following:

    a. Extract the rowid referencing the data block.

    b. Access the data block referenced by the rowid.

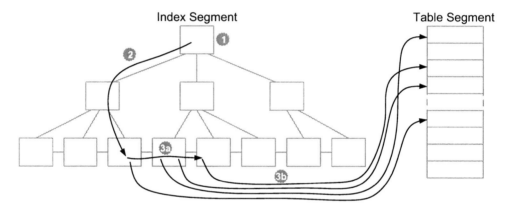

Figure 5-4. *Operations carried out during table accesses based on index range scans*

The number of physical reads performed by an index range scan is equal to the number of branch blocks accessed to locate the leaf block containing the first key (which is the statistic blevel), plus the number of leaf blocks that are scanned (the statistic leaf_blocks multiplied by the selectivity of the operation), plus the number of data blocks accessed via rowid (the clustering_factor multiplied by the selectivity of the operation). This gives you the Formula 5-4 where, in addition, the correction applied by the initialization parameter optimizer_index_cost_adj is taken into consideration.

$$io\_cost \approx (blevel + (leaf\_blocks + clustering\_factor) \cdot selectivity) \cdot \frac{optimizer\_index\_cost\_adj}{100}$$

Formula 5-4. *I/O cost of table accesses based on index range scans*

■**Note** In Formula 5-4, the same selectivity is used to compute the cost of the index access and the cost of the table access. In reality, the query optimizer might use two distinct selectivities for these two distinct costs. This is necessary when only part of the filter is applied through the index access. For example, this happens when an index is composed of three columns and the second one has no restriction.

In summary, you see that the initialization parameter `optimizer_index_cost_adj` has a direct impact on the I/O cost of an index access. When it is set to a value less than the default, all costs decrease proportionally. In some cases this might be a problem because the query optimizer rounds off the results of its estimations. This means that, even if the object statistics of several indexes are different, they may have the same cost as far as the query optimizer is concerned. If several costs are equal in value, the query optimizer decides based on the name of the indexes! It simply takes the first one in alphabetical order. This problem is demonstrated in the following example. Notice how the index used for the INDEX RANGE SCAN operation changes when the initialization parameter `optimizer_index_cost_adj` and the index name changes. This is an excerpt of the output generated by the script `optimizer_index_cost_adj.sql`:

```
SQL> ALTER SESSION SET optimizer_index_cost_adj = 100;

SQL> SELECT * FROM t WHERE val1 = 11 AND val2 = 11;


-------------------------------------------------
| Id  | Operation                   | Name      |
-------------------------------------------------
|   0 | SELECT STATEMENT            |           |
|*  1 |  TABLE ACCESS BY INDEX ROWID| T         |
|*  2 |   INDEX RANGE SCAN          | T_VAL2_I  |
-------------------------------------------------

   1 - filter("VAL1"=11)
   2 - access("VAL2"=11)


SQL> ALTER SESSION SET optimizer_index_cost_adj = 10;

SQL> SELECT * FROM t WHERE val1 = 11 AND val2 = 11;


-------------------------------------------------
| Id  | Operation                   | Name      |
-------------------------------------------------
|   0 | SELECT STATEMENT            |           |
|*  1 |  TABLE ACCESS BY INDEX ROWID| T         |
|*  2 |   INDEX RANGE SCAN          | T_VAL1_I  |
-------------------------------------------------

   1 - filter("VAL2"=11)
   2 - access("VAL1"=11)


SQL> ALTER INDEX t_val1_i RENAME TO t_val3_i;

SQL> SELECT * FROM t WHERE val1 = 11 AND val2 = 11;
```

```
-------------------------------------------------
| Id  | Operation                  | Name     |
-------------------------------------------------
|   0 | SELECT STATEMENT           |          |
|*  1 |   TABLE ACCESS BY INDEX ROWID| T      |
|*  2 |    INDEX RANGE SCAN        | T_VAL2_I |
-------------------------------------------------
```

```
   1 - filter("VAL1"=11)
   2 - access("VAL2"=11)
```

To avoid this kind of instability, I usually do not recommend setting the initialization parameter optimizer_index_cost_adj to low values. It is also important to mention that system statistics provide an adjustment similar to the one provided by this parameter. This means that if system statistics are in place, the default value is usually good. Also notice that system statistics do not have the same drawbacks as this parameter does, because they increase the costs instead of decreasing them.

The initialization parameter optimizer_index_cost_adj is dynamic and can be changed at the instance and session levels.

optimizer_index_caching

The initialization parameter optimizer_index_caching is used to specify the expected amount (in percent) of index blocks cached in the buffer cache during the execution of in-list iterators and nested loop joins. It is important to note that the value of this initialization parameter is used by the query optimizer to adjust its estimations. In other words, it does not specify how much of each of the indexes is actually cached by the database engine. Valid values range from 0 to 100. The default is 0. Values greater than 0 decrease the cost of index scans performed for in-list iterators and in the inner loop of nested loop joins. Because of this, it is used to push the utilization of these operations.

Formula 5-5 shows the correction applied to the index range scan costing formula presented in the previous section (Formula 5-4).

$$io\_cost \approx \left((blevel + leaf\_blocks \cdot selectivity) \cdot \left(1 - \frac{optimizer\_index\_caching}{100} \right) + \right.$$

$$\left. clustering\_factor \cdot selectivity \right) \cdot \frac{optimizer\_index\_cost\_adj}{100}$$

Formula 5-5. *I/O cost of table accesses based on index range scans*

This initialization parameter shares some of the drawbacks described when I talked about the initialization parameter optimizer_index_cost_adj earlier. Nevertheless, its impact is less widespread mainly because of two reasons. First, it is used only for nested loops and in-list iterators. Second, it has no impact on the clustering factor in the costing formula used for index range scans (Formula 5-5). Since the clustering factor is frequently the biggest factor in the costing formula, it is less likely that this initialization parameter leads to wrong decisions. In summary, this initialization parameter has less impact on the query optimizer than the initialization parameter `optimizer_index_cost_adj` does. That said, the default value is usually good.

The initialization parameter `optimizer_index_caching` is dynamic and can be changed at the instance and session levels.

optimizer_secure_view_merging

The initialization parameter `optimizer_secure_view_merging` is available, as of Oracle Database 10*g* Release 2, to control view merging. It can be set to either FALSE or TRUE. The default is TRUE.

- FALSE allows the query optimizer to always do view merging.

- TRUE allows the query optimizer to do view merging only when doing so will not lead to security issues.

To understand the impact of this initialization parameter, and more generally to describe view merging, let's look at the following example (the full example is provided in the script `optimizer_secure_view_merging.sql`).

Say you have a very simple table with one primary key and two more columns:

```
CREATE TABLE t (
  id NUMBER(10) PRIMARY KEY,
  class NUMBER(10),
  pad VARCHAR2(10)
)
```

For security reasons, you want to provide access to this table through the following view. Notice the filter that is applied with the function to partially show the content of the table. How this function is implemented and what it does exactly is not important.

```
CREATE OR REPLACE VIEW v AS
SELECT *
FROM t
WHERE f(class) = 1
```

Another user having access to the view uses it with a query like the following. Notice the restriction on the primary key that makes sure that at most five rows are returned.

```
SELECT id, pad
FROM v
WHERE id BETWEEN 1 AND 5
```

From a performance point of view, the query optimizer now has two choices. The first option is to select all rows from the view and then to apply the filter `id BETWEEN 1 AND 5`. Of course, if the view returns lot of data, the performance will be abysmal even if the query executed by the user provides a restriction on the primary key. The second option is to merge the query of the view with the user's query, as in the following:

```
SELECT id, pad
FROM t
WHERE f(class) = 1
AND id BETWEEN 1 AND 5
```

With this query, the restriction on the primary key can be applied immediately. As a result, the performance will be good, regardless of the amount of data stored in the table. Whenever possible, the query optimizer will take advantage of view merging. Nevertheless, it is not possible in all situations. For example, when the view contains grouping functions in the SELECT clause, set operators, or a hierarchical query, the query optimizer is not able to use view merging. Such a view is called a *nonmergeable view*.

Now that you understand view merging, it is time to see why view merging could be dangerous from a security point of view. Let's say, for example, that the user who has access to the view creates the following PL/SQL function. As you can see, it will just display the value of the input parameters through a call to the package dbms_output:

```
CREATE OR REPLACE FUNCTION spy (id IN NUMBER, pad IN VARCHAR2) RETURN NUMBER AS
BEGIN
  dbms_output.put_line('id='||id||' pad='||pad);
  RETURN 1;
END;
```

With the initialization parameter optimizer_secure_view_merging set to FALSE, you can run two test queries. Both return only the values that the user is allowed to see. In the second one, however, thanks to view merging and the function added to the query, you are able to see data that you should not be able to access.

```
SQL> SELECT id, pad
  2  FROM v
  3  WHERE id BETWEEN 1 AND 5;

        ID PAD
---------- ----------
         1 DrMLTDXxxq
         4 AszBGEUGEL

SQL> SELECT id, pad
  2  FROM v
  3  WHERE id BETWEEN 1 AND 5
  4  AND spy(id, pad) = 1;

        ID PAD
---------- ----------
         1 DrMLTDXxxq
         4 AszBGEUGEL

id=1 pad=DrMLTDXxxq
id=2 pad=XOZnqYRJwI
id=3 pad=nlGfGBTxNk
id=4 pad=AszBGEUGEL
id=5 pad=qTSRnFjRGb
```

With the initialization parameter `optimizer_secure_view_merging` set to `TRUE`, the second query returns the following output. As you can see, the function and the query display the same data.

```
SQL> SELECT id, pad
  2  FROM v
  3  WHERE id BETWEEN 1 AND 5
  4  AND spy(id, pad) = 1;

        ID PAD
---------- ----------
         1 DrMLTDXxxq
         4 AszBGEUGEL

id=1 pad=DrMLTDXxxq
id=4 pad=AszBGEUGEL
```

In summary, with the initialization parameter `optimizer_secure_view_merging` set to `TRUE`, the query optimizer checks whether view merging could lead to security issues. If this is the case, no view merging will be performed, and performance could be suboptimal as a result. For this reason, if you are not using views for security purposes, it is better to set this initialization parameter to `FALSE`.

The initialization parameter `optimizer_secure_view_merging` is dynamic and can be changed at the instance level. It cannot be changed at the session level. Instead, users having either the object privilege `MERGE VIEW` or the system privilege `MERGE ANY VIEW` are not subject to the restrictions imposed by this initialization parameter.

PGA Management

Operations that store data in memory (typically sort operations and hash joins) use *work areas* in order to be executed. These work areas are allocated in the private memory of each server process (PGA). The following sections will describe the initialization parameters devoted to the configuration of these work areas.

Usually, larger work areas provide better performance. Therefore, you should devote the unused memory that is available on the system to PGA. Be careful, though, when changing it. The size of the work areas has an influence on the estimations of the query optimizer as well. You should expect changes not only in performance but also in execution plans. In other words, any modification should be carefully tested if you want to avoid surprises.

Generally speaking, this section does not provide values for the initialization parameter it describes. The only way to find good values for a specific application is to test and measure how much PGA is required to achieve good performance. In fact, the amount of memory has an impact only on performance and not on how an operation works.

workarea_size_policy

The initialization parameter `workarea_size_policy` specifies how the sizing of these work areas is performed. It can be set to one of the following two values:

auto: The sizing of the single work areas is delegated to the *memory manager*. Through the initialization parameter pga_aggregate_target, only the amount of PGA for the whole system is specified. This is the default value as of Oracle Database 10*g*.

manual: Through the initialization parameters bitmap_merge_area_size, hash_area_size, sort_area_size, and sort_area_retained_size, you have full control over the size of the work areas. This is the default value in Oracle9*i*.

In most situations, the memory manager does a good job, so it is highly recommended to delegate the PGA management to it. The following situations are the exceptions:

- In Oracle9*i*, automatic PGA management is not supported with a shared server (formerly called a *multithreaded server*). Only manual PGA management is available. As of Oracle Database 10*g*, automatic PGA management is supported for shared servers as well.

- Up to Oracle Database 10*g* Release 1, the maximum size of work areas is artificially limited (for example, to 100MB for serial operations) and can be increased only by changing undocumented parameters. This is a significant limitation if the size of the work areas needs to be much larger than the limits. As of Oracle Database 10*g* Release 2, the limits automatically increase as available memory increases.

- In rare cases, manual fine-tuning provides better results than automatic PGA management.

The initialization parameter workarea_size_policy is dynamic and can be changed at the instance and session levels. It is also possible to enable automatic PGA management at the system level and then, for special requirements, to switch to manual PGA management at the session level.

pga_aggregate_target

If automatic PGA management is enabled, the initialization parameter pga_aggregate_target specifies (in bytes) the total amount of PGA dedicated to one instance. Values from 10MB up to 4TB are supported. In Oracle9*i*, the default value is 0. As of Oracle Database 10*g*, the default value is 20 percent of the size of the *system global area* (SGA). It is difficult to give any specific advice on what value should be used. On most systems, however, at least a few megabytes per concurrent user are needed.

Note As of Oracle Database 11*g*, the initialization parameters memory_target and memory_max_target might be used to specify the total amount of memory (that is, the SGA + the PGA) used by an instance. When they are set, the instance automatically redistributes memory as needed between the SGA and the PGA. In such a configuration, the initialization parameter pga_aggregate_target is used to set the minimum size of the PGA only.

It is important to understand that the value of the initialization parameter pga_aggregate_target is not a hard limit but is rather a target. As a result, if too small a value is specified, the database engine is free to allocate more memory than the value specified by the initialization parameter pga_aggregate_target. To illustrate this behavior, I executed a query requiring about 60MB of the PGA, with an increasing number of concurrent users (from 1 to 50). The initialization parameter pga_aggregate_target was set to 1GB. This means at most 17 users (1GB/60MB) should be able to get the PGA necessary to execute the whole statement in memory. Figure 5-5 shows the results of the test. As you can see, the system PGA increased up to 1.6GB, which is higher than the configured value. As expected, the system PGA increases proportionally with the number of users only up to 17 concurrent users. With more than 17 users, the system started reducing the amount of the PGA provided to each user.

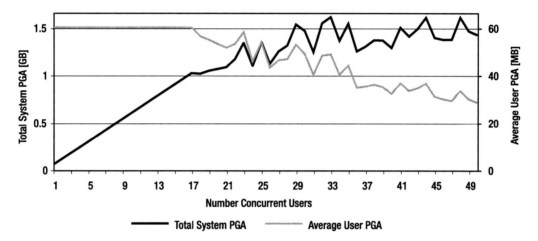

Figure 5-5. *The memory manager automatically adjusts the amount of the PGA provided to users.*

To know whether your system is experiencing an overallocation of the PGA, you can use the following query. If the value of maximum PGA allocated is much higher than the value of aggregate PGA target parameter, then the value of the initialization parameter pga_aggregate_target is probably not suitable.

```
SQL> SELECT name, value, unit
  2  FROM v$pgastat
  3  WHERE name IN ('aggregate PGA target parameter','maximum PGA allocated');

NAME                            VALUE UNIT
------------------------------ ---------- -----
aggregate PGA target parameter 1073741824 bytes
maximum PGA allocated          1648665600 bytes
```

The initialization parameter pga_aggregate_target is dynamic and can be changed only at the instance level.

sort_area_size

If manual PGA management is enabled, the initialization parameter sort_area_size specifies (in bytes) the size of the work areas used for merge joins, sorts, and aggregations (including hash group bys). Be careful: this is the size of one work area, and a single session may allocate several work areas. This implies that the total amount of the PGA used for the whole system depends on the number of allocated work areas and not on the number of sessions. The default value is 64KB. Even though it is practically impossible to give general advice regarding the suggested values, the default is very small, and usually at least 512KB/1MB should be used. Significantly, work areas are not always fully allocated. In other words, the value specified by the initialization parameter sort_area_size is only a limit. Consequently, specifying a value larger than is really needed is not necessarily a problem.

The initialization parameter sort_area_size is dynamic and can be changed at the instance and session levels.

sort_area_retained_size

In the previous section, you saw that the initialization parameter sort_area_size specifies the size of the work areas used for sort operations. Strictly speaking, though, the initialization parameter sort_area_size specifies only the amount of memory used as a temporary work area while the sorting operation takes place. After the last row has been obtained and included in the sorted result stored in the work area, memory is still required only as a buffer to return the sorted result to the parent operation. The initialization parameter sort_area_retained_size specifies (in bytes) the amount of memory retained for that read buffer. This initialization parameter is used only when manual PGA management is enabled. The default value is derived from the initialization parameter sort_area_size. Note that by default, the dynamic performance view v$parameter shows 0.

To set this initialization parameter, you must be aware that if it is set to a value lower than the initialization parameter sort_area_size and the result set does not fit into the retained memory, data is spilled into a temporary segment when the sort operation is completed. This might occur even if the sort operation itself is completely executed in memory! Consequently, it is advisable to use the default value for better performance. Only when the system is really short on memory does it make sense to set this parameter.

The initialization parameter sort_area_retained_size is dynamic and can be changed at the instance and session levels.

hash_area_size

If manual PGA management is enabled, the initialization parameter hash_area_size specifies (in bytes) the size of the work areas used for hash joins. Be aware that this is the size of one work area and that a single session may allocate several work areas. This means that the total amount of the PGA used for the whole system depends on the number of allocated work areas and not on the number of sessions. The default value is twice the value of the initialization parameter sort_area_size. Again, it is difficult to suggest specific values. In any case, for values up to 4MB, it should be set to at least four to five times the value of the initialization parameter sort_area_size. If not, the query optimizer may overestimate the cost of hash joins and, as a result, favor merge joins to them. Again, the work areas are not always fully allocated. In other words, the value specified by the initialization parameter hash_area_size is only a limit. Specifying a value larger than is really required is not necessarily a problem.

The initialization parameter hash_area_size is dynamic and can be changed at the instance and session levels.

bitmap_merge_area_size

If manual PGA management is enabled, the initialization parameter `bitmap_merge_area_size` specifies (in bytes) the size of the work areas used for merging bitmaps related to bitmap indexes. The default value is 1MB. Once again, it is practically impossible to give general advice regarding suggested values. Clearly, larger values might improve performances if a lot of bitmap indexes (for example, because of star transformation—see Chapter 10) are used.

The initialization parameter `bitmap_merge_area_size` is static and cannot be changed at the system or session level. An instance bounce is therefore necessary to change it.

On to Chapter 6

This chapter described how to achieve a good configuration of the query optimizer by setting initialization parameters. You saw that it is essential to understand not only how initialization parameters work but also how object and system statistics influence the query optimizer.

Even with the best configuration in place, the query optimizer may fail to find an efficient execution plan. When the performance of a SQL statement is questioned, the first thing to do is to review the execution plan. The next chapter will discuss how to obtain execution plans and, more important, how to interpret them. I'll present some rules on how to recognize inefficient execution plans as well.

CHAPTER 6
■■■
Execution Plans

An *execution plan* describes the operations carried out by the SQL engine to execute a SQL statement. Every time you have to analyze a performance problem related to a SQL statement, or simply question the decisions taken by the query optimizer, you must know the execution plan. Without it, you are like a blind man with his cane in the middle of the Sahara Desert, groping around trying to find his way. I can't stress enough that the first thing to do while analyzing or questioning the performance of a SQL statement is to get its execution plan.

Whenever you deal with an execution plan, you carry out three basic actions: you obtain it, you interpret it, and you judge its efficiency. The aim of this chapter is to describe in detail how you should perform these three actions.

Obtaining Execution Plans

Basically, Oracle provides four methods to obtain an execution plan:

- Execute the SQL statement EXPLAIN PLAN, and then query the table where the output was written.

- Query a dynamic performance view showing the execution plans cached in the library cache.

- Query an Automatic Workload Repository or Statspack table, showing the execution plans stored in the repository.

- Activate a tracing facility providing execution plans.

No other methods exist. Since all tools displaying execution plans take advantage of one of these methods, the following sections will describe just the basics, instead of focusing on specific tools such as Oracle Enterprise Manager or Quest TOAD. I won't discuss such tools here also because, more often than not, they do not provide all the information you need for a thorough analysis.

SQL Statement EXPLAIN PLAN

The aim of the SQL statement EXPLAIN PLAN is to take a SQL statement as input and to provide its execution plan and some information related to it, as output, in the *plan table*. In other words, with it you can ask the query optimizer which execution plan would be used to execute a given SQL statement.

Syntax and Privileges

Figure 6-1 shows the syntax of the SQL statement EXPLAIN PLAN. The following parameters are available:

- statement specifies for which SQL statement the execution plan should be provided. The following SQL statements are supported: SELECT, INSERT, UPDATE, MERGE, DELETE, CREATE TABLE, CREATE INDEX, and ALTER INDEX.

- id specifies a name to distinguish between several execution plans stored in the plan table. Any string of up to 30 characters is supported. This parameter is optional. The default value is NULL.

- table specifies the name of the plan table where the information about the execution plan is inserted. This parameter is optional. The default value is plan_table. Whenever necessary, it is possible to specify a schema name as well as a database link name with the usual syntax: schema.table@dblink.

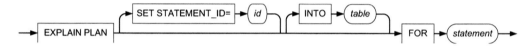

Figure 6-1. *Syntax of the SQL statement* EXPLAIN PLAN

It's important to recognize that the SQL statement EXPLAIN PLAN is a DML statement, not a DDL statement. This means it does not perform an implicit commit of the current transaction. It simply inserts rows into the plan table.

To execute the SQL statement EXPLAIN PLAN, the privileges to execute the SQL statement that is passed as the parameter are needed. Note that when working with views, appropriate privileges on all underlying tables and views are required as well. Since this is counterintuitive, let's look at the following example. Notice how the user is able to execute a query referencing the view user_objects but is not able to execute the SQL statement EXPLAIN PLAN for the very same query.

```
SQL> SELECT count(*) FROM user_objects;

  COUNT(*)
----------
        10

SQL> EXPLAIN PLAN FOR SELECT count(*) FROM user_objects;
EXPLAIN PLAN FOR SELECT count(*) FROM user_objects
                                      *
ERROR at line 1:
ORA-01039: insufficient privileges on underlying objects of the view
```

As pointed out by the error message, the user lacks SELECT privileges on one or several data dictionary tables referenced by the view user_objects.

The Plan Table

The plan table is where the SQL statement EXPLAIN PLAN writes the output. It must exist; otherwise, an error is raised. As of Oracle Database 10*g*, by default, a plan table and a public synonym named plan_table that exposes it to all users are available under the schema SYS. In previous releases or whenever a private table is needed, it is good practice to manually create it with the script utlxplan.sql, available under $ORACLE_HOME/rdbms/admin. If a plan table is manually created, you should not forget to create it again in case of a database upgrade. In fact, it is quite common that new attributes are added with new releases.

It is interesting to notice that the default plan table created as of Oracle Database 10*g* is a global temporary table that stores data up to the end of the session.[1] In this way, several concurrent users working with it do not interfere with each other.

To use a plan table with the SQL statement EXPLAIN PLAN, you need at least INSERT and SELECT privileges. Even though you can perform basic operations without it, the DELETE privilege is usually granted as well.

I will not describe the plan table fully here for the simple reason that you usually do not need to query it directly. For a detailed description of its columns, refer to the *Performance Tuning Guide* manual.[2]

Querying the Plan Table

It may be obvious that you can obtain the execution plan by running queries against the plan table directly. As of Oracle9*i* Release 2, however, there is an easier and much better way to do it—by using the function display in the package dbms_xplan. As shown in the following example, its utilization is simple. In fact, it is enough to call the function in order to display the execution plan generated by the SQL statement EXPLAIN PLAN. Notice how the return value of the function, which is a collection, is converted with the function table.

```
SQL> EXPLAIN PLAN FOR SELECT * FROM emp WHERE deptno = 10 ORDER BY ename;

SQL> SELECT * FROM table(dbms_xplan.display);

PLAN_TABLE_OUTPUT
---------------------------------------------------------------------------

Plan hash value: 150391907


---------------------------------------------------------------------------
| Id  | Operation          | Name | Rows  | Bytes | Cost (%CPU)| Time     |
---------------------------------------------------------------------------
|   0 | SELECT STATEMENT   |      |     5 |   185 |     4  (25)| 00:00:01 |
|   1 |  SORT ORDER BY     |      |     5 |   185 |     4  (25)| 00:00:01 |
|*  2 |   TABLE ACCESS FULL| EMP  |     5 |   185 |     3   (0)| 00:00:01 |
---------------------------------------------------------------------------
```

---

1. In other words, it is a global temporary table created with the option on commit preserve rows.
2. In Oracle9*i*, this manual is entitled *Database Performance Tuning Guide and Reference*.

```
Predicate Information (identified by operation id):
---------------------------------------------------

   2 - filter("DEPTNO"=10)
```

The function display is not limited to being used without parameters. For this reason, later in this chapter I'll cover the package dbms_xplan, exploring all the possibilities, including a description of the generated output.

Bind Variables Trap

The most common mistake I come across in using the SQL statement EXPLAIN PLAN is to specify a SQL statement that is different from the one to be analyzed. Naturally, that could lead to the wrong execution plan. Since the formatting itself has no impact on the execution plan, the difference is usually caused by replacing bind variables. Let's examine the execution plan used by the query in the following PL/SQL procedure:

```
CREATE OR REPLACE PROCEDURE p (p_value IN NUMBER) IS
BEGIN
  FOR i IN (SELECT * FROM emp WHERE empno = p_value)
  LOOP
    -- do something
  END LOOP;
END;
```

A commonly used technique is to copy/paste the query by replacing the PL/SQL variable with a value. You execute a SQL statement in the following way:

```
EXPLAIN PLAN FOR SELECT * FROM emp WHERE empno = 7788
```

The problem is that by replacing the bind variable with a constant, you submit a different SQL statement to the query optimizer. This change—because of SQL profiles, stored outlines, SQL plan baselines, or the method used by the query optimizer to estimate the selectivity of the predicate used in the WHERE clause—might have an impact on the decisions taken by the query optimizer.

The correct approach is to use the same SQL statement. This is possible because bind variables can be used with the SQL statement EXPLAIN PLAN. You should, as an example, execute a SQL statement like the following one. Notice that a colon was simply added before the PL/SQL variable to turn it into a variable for the SQL statement EXPLAIN PLAN.

```
EXPLAIN PLAN FOR SELECT * FROM emp WHERE empno = :p_value
```

Nonetheless, using bind variables with the SQL statement EXPLAIN PLAN has two problems. The first is that, by default, bind variables are declared as VARCHAR2. As a result, to avoid implicit conversions, the database engine automatically adds explicit conversions. You can check this with the information about predicates shown at the end of the output generated by the function display in the package dbms_xplan. In the following output example, the function to_number is used for that purpose:

```
SQL> SELECT * FROM table(dbms_xplan.display);

PLAN_TABLE_OUTPUT
--------------------------------------------------------------------------------
Plan hash value: 4024650034


--------------------------------------------------------------------------------
| Id | Operation                   | Name   | Rows | Bytes | Cost (%CPU)| Time     |
--------------------------------------------------------------------------------
|  0 | SELECT STATEMENT            |        |   1  |   37  |   1   (0)| 00:00:01 |
|  1 |  TABLE ACCESS BY INDEX ROWID| EMP    |   1  |   37  |   1   (0)| 00:00:01 |
|* 2 |   INDEX UNIQUE SCAN         | EMP_PK |   1  |       |   0   (0)| 00:00:01 |
--------------------------------------------------------------------------------


Predicate Information (identified by operation id):
---------------------------------------------------

   2 - access("EMPNO"=TO_NUMBER(:P_VALUE))
```

It is generally good practice to check whether datatypes are correctly handled, for example, by using explicit conversion for all bind variables that are not of type VARCHAR2.

The second problem with using bind variables with the SQL statement EXPLAIN PLAN is that no bind variable peeking is used. Since there is no solution for that problem, it is not guaranteed that the execution plan generated by the SQL statement EXPLAIN PLAN will be the one chosen at runtime. In other words, whenever bind variables are involved, the output generated by the SQL statement EXPLAIN PLAN is unreliable.

Dynamic Performance Views

Four dynamic performance views show information about the cursors present in the library cache:

- v$sql_plan provides basically the same information as the plan table. In other words, it provides execution plans and other related information provided by the query optimizer. The only notable differences between this view and the plan table are due to some columns identifying the cursor related to the execution plan in the library cache.

- v$sql_plan_statistics provides execution statistics, such as the elapsed time and the number of produced rows, for each operation (the *row source operation*) in the view v$sql_plan. Essentially, it provides the runtime behavior of an execution plan. This is an important piece of information because the view v$sql_plan shows the estimations and decisions taken by the query optimizer only at parse time. Since the collection of execution statistics causes a non-negligible overhead, by default they are not collected. To activate the collection, either the initialization parameter statistics_level must be set to all or the hint gather_plan_statistics must be specified in the SQL statement.

- v$sql_workarea provides information about the memory work areas needed to execute a cursor. It gives runtime memory utilization as well as estimations about the amount of memory needed to efficiently execute operations.

- v$sql_plan_statistics_all shows in a single view all the information provided by the views vsql_plan, vsql_plan_statistics, and v$sql_workarea. By using it, you simply avoid manually joining several views.

The cursors in the library cache (and therefore in these views) are identified by three columns: address, hash_value, and child_number. With the columns address and hash_value, you identify the parent cursors. With all three columns, you identify the child cursors. In addition, as of Oracle Database 10g, it is also possible, and more common as well, to use the column sql_id instead of the columns address and hash_value to identify cursors. The advantage of using the column sql_id is that its value depends only on the SQL statement itself. In other words, it never changes for a given SQL statement. On the other hand, the column address is a pointer to the handle of the SQL statement in memory and can change over time. To identify a cursor, basically you are confronted with two search methods. Either you know the session executing a SQL statement or you know the text of the SQL statement. In both cases, once the cursor is identified, you can display information about it.

Identifying Child Cursors

The first common situation you have to face is trying to get information about a SQL statement that is related to a session currently connected to the instance. In this case, you execute the search on the view v$session. The currently executed SQL statement is identified by the columns sql_id (or sql_address and sql_hash_value) and sql_child_number. The last-executed SQL statement is identified by the columns prev_sql_id (or prev_sql_addr and prev_hash_value) and prev_child_number. Notice that the columns sql_id, sql_child_number, and prev_child_number are available only as of Oracle Database 10g. Clearly, in Oracle9i, the missing relation to the child cursors makes it impossible to have a direct mapping between session and cursor, if multiple child cursors exist. To illustrate the use of this method, let's say that a user, Curtis, calls you and complains that he is waiting on a request submitted with an application just a few minutes ago. For this problem, it is useful to query the view v$session directly, as shown in the following example. With that output, you know he is currently running a SQL statement (otherwise, the status would not be ACTIVE) and which cursor is related to his session.

```
SQL> SELECT status, sql_id, sql_child_number
  2  FROM v$session
  3  WHERE username = 'CURTIS';

STATUS    SQL_ID          SQL_CHILD_NUMBER
--------  --------------  ----------------
ACTIVE    1hqjydsjbvmwq                  0
```

The second common situation is when you do know the text of the SQL statement that you want to find more information about. In this case, you execute the search on the view v$sql. The text associated with a cursor is available in the columns sql_text and sql_fulltext. While the first column shows only the first part of the text through a VARCHAR2(1000), the second shows the whole text through a CLOB. For example, if you know that the SQL statement you are looking for contains a literal with the text "online discount," you can use the following query to find out the identifiers of the cursor:

```
SQL> SELECT sql_id, child_number, sql_text
  2  FROM v$sql
  3  WHERE sql_text LIKE '%online discount%' AND sql_text NOT LIKE '%v$sql%';

SQL_ID          CHILD_NUMBER SQL_TEXT
-------------   ------------ -------------------------------------------------------------
1hqjydsjbvmwq              0 SELECT SUM(AMOUNT_SOLD) FROM SALES S, PROMOTIONS P
                             WHERE S.PROMO_ID = P.PROMO_ID AND PROMO_SUBCATEGORY =
                             'online discount'
```

Querying Dynamic Performance Views

To obtain the execution plan, you can run queries directly against the dynamic performance views v$sql_plan and v$sql_plan_statistics_all. As of Oracle Database 10g, however, there is an easier and much better way to do it—you can use the function display_cursor in the package dbms_xplan. As shown in the following example, its use is similar to calling the function display previously discussed. The only difference is that two parameters identifying the child cursor to be displayed are passed to the function.

```
SQL> SELECT * FROM table(dbms_xplan.display_cursor('1hqjydsjbvmwq',0));

PLAN_TABLE_OUTPUT
-------------------------------------------------------------------------------------
SQL_ID  1hqjydsjbvmwq, child number 0
-------------------------------------
SELECT SUM(AMOUNT_SOLD) FROM SALES S, PROMOTIONS P WHERE S.PROMO_ID =
P.PROMO_ID AND PROMO_SUBCATEGORY = 'online discount'

Plan hash value: 265338492

-------------------------------------------------------------------------------
| Id | Operation              | Name       | Rows  | Bytes | Cost (%CPU)| Time     |
-------------------------------------------------------------------------------
|  0 | SELECT STATEMENT       |            |       |       | 517 (100)|          |
|  1 |  SORT AGGREGATE        |            |     1 |    30 |          |          |
|* 2 |   HASH JOIN            |            |  913K |   26M | 517   (4)| 00:00:07 |
|* 3 |    TABLE ACCESS FULL   | PROMOTIONS |    23 |   483 |  17   (0)| 00:00:01 |
|  4 |    PARTITION RANGE ALL |            |  918K | 8075K | 494   (3)| 00:00:06 |
|  5 |     TABLE ACCESS FULL  | SALES      |  918K | 8075K | 494   (3)| 00:00:06 |
-------------------------------------------------------------------------------

Predicate Information (identified by operation id):
-------------------------------------------------

   2 - access("S"."PROMO_ID"="P"."PROMO_ID")
   3 - filter("PROMO_SUBCATEGORY"='online discount')
```

The function display_cursor is not limited to being used without parameters. For this reason, later in this chapter I'll cover the package dbms_xplan, exploring all possibilities, including a description of the generated output.

If you are using Oracle9*i*, the package dbms_xplan does not provide the function display_ cursor. Even in this situation, I would not advise querying the dynamic performance views directly. My advice is to extract the information about the execution plan from the library cache and to insert it into a plan table. This plan table will then be queried with the function display from the package dbms_xplan. The following example shows how:

```
SQL> SELECT address, hash_value, child_number, sql_text
  2  FROM v$sql
  3  WHERE sql_text LIKE '%online discount%' AND sql_text NOT LIKE '%v$sql%';

ADDRESS           HASH_VALUE CHILD_NUMBER SQL_TEXT
---------------- ---------- ------------ -------------------------------------
0000000055DCD888 4132422484            0 SELECT sum(amount_sold) FROM sales s,
                                         promotions p WHERE s.promo_id =
                                         p.promo_id AND promo_subcategory =
                                         'online discount'

SQL> DELETE plan_table;

SQL> INSERT INTO plan_table (operation, options, object_node, object_owner,
  2                          object_name, optimizer, search_columns, id,
  3                          parent_id, position, cost, cardinality, bytes,
  4                          other_tag, partition_start, partition_stop,
  5                          partition_id, other, distribution, cpu_cost,
  6                          io_cost, temp_space, access_predicates,
  7                          filter_predicates)
  8  SELECT operation, options, object_node, object_owner, object_name,
  9         optimizer, search_columns, id, parent_id, position, cost,
 10         cardinality, bytes, other_tag, partition_start, partition_stop,
 11         partition_id, other, distribution, cpu_cost, io_cost, temp_space,
 12         access_predicates, filter_predicates
 13  FROM v$sql_plan
 14  WHERE address = '0000000055DCD888'
 15  AND hash_value = 4132422484
 16  AND child_number = 0;

SQL> SELECT * FROM table(dbms_xplan.display);

PLAN_TABLE_OUTPUT
-----------------------------------------------------------------------
```

```
---------------------------------------------------------------------------
| Id  | Operation             | Name       | Rows   | Bytes | Cost (%CPU)|
---------------------------------------------------------------------------
|   0 | SELECT STATEMENT      |            |        |       |            |
|   1 |  SORT AGGREGATE       |            |      1 |    29 |            |
|*  2 |   HASH JOIN           |            |  64482 | 1826K |   426  (24)|
|*  3 |    TABLE ACCESS FULL  | PROMOTIONS |     24 |   504 |     4  (25)|
|   4 |    PARTITION RANGE ALL|            |        |       |            |
|   5 |     TABLE ACCESS FULL | SALES      |  1016K | 7939K |   398  (19)|
---------------------------------------------------------------------------
```

Predicate Information (identified by operation id):

```
   2 - access("PROMO_ID"="PROMO_ID")
   3 - filter("PROMO_SUBCATEGORY"='online discount')
```

To take advantage of this technique without having to spend time writing long SQL statements, you can use the script `display_cursor_9i.sql`.

Automatic Workload Repository and Statspack

When a snapshot is taken, Automatic Workload Repository (AWR) and Statspack are able to collect execution plans. To get execution plans, queries against the dynamic performance views described in the previous section are executed. Once available, the execution plans may be displayed in reports or, with AWR, by Enterprise Manager. For both AWR and Statspack, the repository table storing the execution plans is mostly the same as the view `v$sql_plan`. Because of this, the techniques described in the previous section apply to it as well.

AWR AND STATSPACK

As of Oracle Database 10*g*, the AWR repository intended to store performance-related information is automatically installed. During normal operation, the database engine is responsible not only for maintaining its content but also for leveraging it for self-tuning purposes. Its purpose is to keep a history of the database workload over the last few weeks. Information about AWR is available in Chapter 5 of the *Performance Tuning Guide* manual.

The predecessor of AWR, called *Statspack*, is neither automatically installed nor maintained. It is just an add-on that a DBA can install in the database. In any case, its purpose is similar to AWR. Information about Statspack is available in Chapter 21 of the Oracle9*i* manual *Database Performance Tuning Guide and Reference*.

The execution plans stored in AWR are available through the view `dba_hist_sql_plan`. To query them, the package `dbms_xplan` provides the function `display_awr`. As for the other functions of this package, their uses are straightforward. The following query is an example. Note that the parameter passed to the function `display_awr` identifies the SQL statement through its `sql_id`.

```
SQL> SELECT * FROM table(dbms_xplan.display_awr('1hqjydsjbvmwq'));

PLAN_TABLE_OUTPUT
--------------------------------------------------------------------------------
SELECT SUM(AMOUNT_SOLD) FROM SALES S, PROMOTIONS P WHERE S.PROMO_ID =
P.PROMO_ID AND PROMO_SUBCATEGORY = 'online discount'

Plan hash value: 265338492
```

Id	Operation	Name	Rows	Bytes	Cost (%CPU)	Time
0	SELECT STATEMENT				517 (100)	
1	SORT AGGREGATE		1	30		
2	HASH JOIN		913K	26M	517 (4)	00:00:07
3	TABLE ACCESS FULL	PROMOTIONS	23	483	17 (0)	00:00:01
4	PARTITION RANGE ALL		918K	8075K	494 (3)	00:00:06
5	TABLE ACCESS FULL	SALES	918K	8075K	494 (3)	00:00:06

The function display_awr is not limited to being used without parameters. For this reason, later in this chapter I'll cover the package dbms_xplan, exploring all possibilities, including a description of the generated output as well.

Statspack stores execution plans in the stats$sql_plan repository table when a level equal to or greater than 6 is used for taking the snapshots. Unfortunately, no feature is provided by the package dbms_xplan to query it. I suggest copying the execution plan in a plan table and displaying it with the function display in the package dbms_xplan (see the technique described in the previous section for the view v$sql_plan in Oracle9*i*).

In addition, for both AWR and Statspack, Oracle provides useful reports for highlighting execution plan changes and resource consumption variation during a period of time for a specific SQL statement. Their names are awrsqrpt.sql and sprepsql.sql, respectively. You will find them under the directory $ORACLE_HOME/rdbms/admin. Note that the script for AWR is available only as of Oracle Database 10*g* Release 2. The following is an excerpt of the output generated by the script awrsqrpt.sql. According to the output, the execution plan of the SQL statement changed during the analyzed period. The average elapsed time went from about 1.5 milliseconds (15,098/10) for the first one to about 0.3 milliseconds (2,780/10) for the second one.

```
SQL ID: 1hqjydsjbvmwq          DB/Inst: DBM11106/DBM11106  Snaps: 143-145
-> 1st Capture and Last Capture Snap IDs
   refer to Snapshot IDs witin the snapshot range
-> SELECT SUM(AMOUNT_SOLD) FROM SALES S, PROMOTIONS P WHERE S.PROMO_ID = ...
```

#	Plan Hash Value	Total Elapsed Time(ms)	Executions	1st Capture Snap ID	Last Capture Snap ID
1	1279966040	15,098	10	144	145
2	265338492	2,780	10	144	145

Plan 1(PHV: **1279966040**)

Execution Plan

```
-----------------------------------------------------------------------------
| Id | Operation             | Name       | Rows  | Bytes | Cost (%CPU)| Time     |
-----------------------------------------------------------------------------
|  0 | SELECT STATEMENT      |            |       |       | 4028 (100)|          |
|  1 |  SORT AGGREGATE       |            |     1 |    30 |           |          |
|  2 |   MERGE JOIN          |            |  913K |   26M | 4028   (2)| 00:00:49 |
|  3 |    SORT JOIN          |            |    23 |   483 |   18   (6)| 00:00:01 |
|  4 |     TABLE ACCESS FULL | PROMOTIONS |    23 |   483 |   17   (0)| 00:00:01 |
|  5 |    SORT JOIN          |            |  918K | 8075K | 4010   (2)| 00:00:49 |
|  6 |     PARTITION RANGE ALL|           |  918K | 8075K |  494   (3)| 00:00:06 |
|  7 |      TABLE ACCESS FULL | SALES     |  918K | 8075K |  494   (3)| 00:00:06 |
-----------------------------------------------------------------------------
```

Plan 2(PHV: **265338492**)

Execution Plan

```
-----------------------------------------------------------------------------
| Id | Operation             | Name       | Rows  | Bytes | Cost (%CPU)| Time     |
-----------------------------------------------------------------------------
|  0 | SELECT STATEMENT      |            |       |       |  517 (100)|          |
|  1 |  SORT AGGREGATE       |            |     1 |    30 |           |          |
|  2 |   HASH JOIN           |            |  913K |   26M |  517   (4)| 00:00:07 |
|  3 |    TABLE ACCESS FULL  | PROMOTIONS |    23 |   483 |   17   (0)| 00:00:01 |
|  4 |    PARTITION RANGE ALL|            |  918K | 8075K |  494   (3)| 00:00:06 |
|  5 |     TABLE ACCESS FULL | SALES      |  918K | 8075K |  494   (3)| 00:00:06 |
-----------------------------------------------------------------------------
```

Tracing Facilities

Several tracing facilities provide information about execution plans. Unfortunately, except for SQL trace (see Chapter 3), all of them are not officially supported. In any case, they may turn out to be useful, so I will cover two of them briefly.

Event 10053

If you are in serious difficulty because of the decisions made by the query optimizer and you want to understand what's going on, event 10053 may help you. Let me warn you, though, that reading the trace files it generates is not an easy task. Luckily, it probably will not be necessary to do it often and then only if you are really interested in the internal workings of the query optimizer.

Usually, you want to analyze one SQL statement at a time. So, in order to generate a trace file, it is common to embed it between the following two SQL statements, thus enabling and disabling the event 10053. Just be careful that the trace file is generated only when a hard parse is performed.

```
ALTER SESSION SET events '10053 trace name context forever'
ALTER SESSION SET events '10053 trace name context off'
```

When event 10053 is enabled, the query optimizer generates a trace file containing plenty of information about the work it carries out. In it you will find the execution environment determined by initialization parameters, system statistics, and object statistics, as well as the estimations performed for the purpose of finding out the most efficient execution plan. Describing the content of the trace file generated by this event is beyond the scope of this book. If necessary, please refer to the following sources:

- Wolfgang Breitling's paper "A Look under the Hood of CBO: The 10053 Event"

- Metalink note "CASE STUDY: Analyzing 10053 Trace Files (338137.1)"

- Chapter 14 of Jonathan Lewis's book *Cost-Based Oracle Fundamentals*

Each server process writes all data about the SQL statements it parses in its own trace file. This means not only that a trace file can contain information for several SQL statements, but also that several trace files will be used whenever the event is enabled in several sessions. For information about the name and location of trace files, refer to the section "Finding Trace Files" in Chapter 3.

Event 10132

You can use event 10132 to cause a trace file to be generated, containing the execution plan related to every hard parse. This may be useful if you want to keep a history of all execution plans for a specific module or application. The following example shows the kind of information stored in the trace file for every SQL statement, principally the SQL statement and its execution plan (which includes information about predicates). Notice that from this output I cut out, in two different places, long lists of parameters and bug fixes that provide information about the execution environment.

```
sql_id=gbxvdrz7jvt80.
Current SQL statement for this session:
SELECT count(n) FROM t WHERE n BETWEEN 6 AND 19


============
Plan Table
============
------------------------------------------+------------------------------------+
| Id  | Operation           | Name   | Rows  | Bytes | Cost  | Time          |
------------------------------------------+------------------------------------+
|  0  | SELECT STATEMENT    |        |       |       |    3 |               |
|  1  |   SORT AGGREGATE    |        |     1 |     4 |      |               |
|  2  |    TABLE ACCESS FULL | T     |    15 |    60 |    3 | 00:00:01      |
------------------------------------------+------------------------------------+
Predicate Information:
----------------------
2 - filter(("N"<=19 AND "N">=6))
```

```
Content of other_xml column
============================
  db_version       : 10.2.0.3
  parse_schema     : OPS$CHA
  plan_hash        : 2966233522
  Outline Data:
  /*+
    BEGIN_OUTLINE_DATA
      IGNORE_OPTIM_EMBEDDED_HINTS
      OPTIMIZER_FEATURES_ENABLE('10.2.0.3')
      ALL_ROWS
      OUTLINE_LEAF(@"SEL$1")
      FULL(@"SEL$1" "T"@"SEL$1")
    END_OUTLINE_DATA
  */

Optimizer environment:
  optimizer_mode_hinted              = false
  optimizer_features_hinted          = 0.0.0
  ...
  ...
  _first_k_rows_dynamic_proration    = true
  _optimizer_native_full_outer_join  = off
  *******************************
  Bug Fix Control Environment
  **************************
  fix   4611850 = enabled
  fix   4663804 = enabled
  ...
  ...
  fix   4908162 = enabled
  fix   5015557 = enabled
Query Block Registry:
********************
SEL$1 0x971d5458 (PARSER) [FINAL]
Optimizer State Dump: call(in-use=23984, alloc=49080),
                      compile(in-use=62200, alloc=108792)
```

The sql_id and all information given after the execution plan itself are available only as of Oracle Database 10g Release 2. The lists of initialization parameters and bug fixes are especially long. For this reason, as of this version, about 12KB of data is written to the trace file even for the simplest SQL statement. The generation of such a trace file might be a significant overhead. You should therefore activate the event 10132 only if you really need it.

The event 10132 can be enabled and disabled in the following ways:

- Enable and disable the event for the current session.

  ```
  ALTER SESSION SET events '10132 trace name context forever'
  ALTER SESSION SET events '10132 trace name context off'
  ```

- Enable and disable the event for the whole database. Warning: this setting does not take effect immediately but only for sessions created after the modification.

  ```
  ALTER SYSTEM SET events '10132 trace name context forever'
  ALTER SYSTEM SET events '10132 trace name context off'
  ```

Each server process writes all data about the SQL statements it parses in its own trace file. This means not only that a trace file can contain information for several SQL statements but also that several trace files will be used whenever the event is enabled in several sessions. For information about the name and location of trace files, refer to the section "Finding Trace Files" in Chapter 3.

Package dbms_xplan

You saw earlier in this chapter that the package dbms_xplan displays execution plans stored in three different places: in the plan table, in the library cache, and in AWR. The following sections describe the functions available in the package for that purpose. To begin with, let's take a look at the output they generate.

Output

The aim of this section is to explain the information contained in the output that is returned by the functions in the package dbms_xplan. To do so, I will use a sample output, generated by the script dbms_xplan_output.sql, that contains all the available sections but not all the information for each section. The problem is that one book page is not wide enough to show you all the information. Therefore, I will choose an output that shows the key information only. Then, if something is missing, I will point it out.

The first section of output is as follows:

```
SQL_ID  cmm8zrzv2v2s5, child number 0
-------------------------------------
SELECT t2.* FROM t t1, t t2 WHERE t1.n = t2.n AND t1.id > 6 AND t2.id
BETWEEN 6 AND 19
```

This section gives the following information about the SQL statement:

- The sql_id identifies the parent cursor. This information is available only when the output is generated by the functions display_cursor and display_awr.

- The child number, along with the sql_id, identifies the child cursor. This information is available only when the output is generated by the function display_cursor.

- The text of the SQL statement is available only when the output is generated by the functions display_cursor and display_awr.

The second section shows the hash value of the execution plan and, in a table, the execution plan itself. Here is an example:

```
Plan hash value: 1338433605
```

```
--------------------------------------------------------------------------------
| Id  | Operation                    | Name | Rows | Bytes | Cost (%CPU)| Time     |
--------------------------------------------------------------------------------
|   0 | SELECT STATEMENT             |      |      |       |  49 (100)|          |
|*  1 |  HASH JOIN                   |      |   14 |  7756 |  49   (3)| 00:00:01 |
|   2 |   TABLE ACCESS BY INDEX ROWID| T    |   14 |  7392 |   4   (0)| 00:00:01 |
|*  3 |    INDEX RANGE SCAN          | T_PK |   14 |       |   2   (0)| 00:00:01 |
|*  4 |   TABLE ACCESS FULL          | T    |  994 | 25844 |  44   (0)| 00:00:01 |
--------------------------------------------------------------------------------
```

In the table, estimations and execution statistics for each operation are provided. The number of columns in the table depends directly on the amount of available information. For example, information about partitioning, parallel processing, or execution statistics is shown only when available. For this reason, two outputs generated by the same function with exactly the same parameters may be different. In this case, you would see the columns that are available by default. Table 6-1 summarizes all the columns you might see.

Table 6-1. *Columns of the Table Containing the Execution Plan*

Column	Description
Basics (Always Available)	
Id	The identifier of each operation (line) in the execution plan. If the number is prefixed by an asterisk, it means that predicate information for that line is available later.
Operation	The operation to be executed. This is also known as the *row source operation*.
Name	The object on which the operation is executed.
Query Optimizer Estimations	
Rows (E-Rows)	The estimated number of rows returned by the operation.
Bytes (E-Bytes)	The estimated amount of data returned by the operation.
TempSpc	The estimated amount of temporary space used by the operation.
Cost (%CPU)	The estimated cost of the operation. The percentage of CPU cost is given in parentheses. Note that this value is cumulated through the execution plan. In other words, the cost of parent operations contains the cost of their child operations.
Time	The estimated amount of time needed to execute the operation (HH:MM:SS).
Partitioning	
Pstart	The number of the first partition to be accessed. Set to either KEY, KEY(I), KEY(MC), KEY(OR), or KEY(SQ) if unknown at parse time.

Table 6-1. *Columns of the Table Containing the Execution Plan (Continued)*

Column	Description
Pstop	The number of the last partition to be accessed. Set to either KEY, KEY(I), KEY(MC), KEY(OR), or KEY(SQ) if unknown at parse time.

Parallel and Distributed Processing

Inst	For distributed processing, the name of the database link used by the operation.
TQ	For parallel processing, the table queue used for the communication between slaves.
IN-OUT	The relationship between parallel or distributed operations.
PQ Distrib	For parallel processing, the distribution used by producers to send data to consumers.

Runtime Statistics*

Starts	The number of times a specific operation was executed.
A-Rows	The actual number of rows returned by the operation.
A-Time	The actual amount of time spent executing the operation (HH:MM:SS.FF).

I/O Statistics*

Buffers	The number of logical read operations performed during the execution.
Reads	The number of physical reads performed during the execution.
Writes	The number of physical writes performed during the execution.

Memory Utilization Statistics

OMem	The estimated amount of memory needed for an optimal execution.
1Mem	The estimated amount of memory needed for one-pass execution.
0/1/M	The number of times the execution was performed in optimal/one-pass/multipass mode.
Used-Mem	The amount of memory used by the operation during the last execution.
Used-Tmp	The amount of temporary space used by the operation during the last execution. This value must be multiplied by 1,024 to be consistent with the other memory utilization columns (for example, 32K means 32MB).
Max-Tmp	The maximum amount of temporary space used by the operation. This value has to be multiplied by 1,024 to be consistent with the other memory utilization columns (for example, 32K means 32MB).

* *Available only when execution statistics are enabled.*

The next section shows the query block names and the object aliases:

```
Query Block Name / Object Alias (identified by operation id):
-------------------------------------------------------------

  1 - SEL$1
  2 - SEL$1 / T2@SEL$1
  3 - SEL$1 / T2@SEL$1
  4 - SEL$1 / T1@SEL$1
```

For each operation in the execution plan, you see which query block it is related to and, optionally, on which object it is executed. This information is essential when, like in this example, the SQL statement references the same table several times. This section is available as of Oracle Database 10g. Query block names will be discussed in more detail along with hints in Chapter 7.

The fourth section is available only as of Oracle Database 10g Release 2. It shows the set of hints that are necessary to force that particular execution plan. This set of hints is called *outline*. Chapter 7 describes how it is possible to store and take advantage of such an outline with stored outlines and SQL plan baselines.

```
Outline Data
-------------

  /*+
      BEGIN_OUTLINE_DATA
      IGNORE_OPTIM_EMBEDDED_HINTS
      OPTIMIZER_FEATURES_ENABLE('10.2.0.3')
      ALL_ROWS
      OUTLINE_LEAF(@"SEL$1")
      INDEX_RS_ASC(@"SEL$1" "T2"@"SEL$1" ("T"."ID"))
      FULL(@"SEL$1" "T1"@"SEL$1")
      LEADING(@"SEL$1" "T2"@"SEL$1" "T1"@"SEL$1")
      USE_HASH(@"SEL$1" "T1"@"SEL$1")
      END_OUTLINE_DATA
  */
```

The next section shows which predicates are applied. For each of them, it is shown where (line) and how (access or filter) they are applied.

```
Predicate Information (identified by operation id):
---------------------------------------------------

  1 - access("T1"."N"="T2"."N")
  3 - access("T2"."ID">=6 AND "T2"."ID"<=19)
  4 - filter("T1"."ID">6)
```

While an access predicate is used to locate rows by taking advantage of an efficient access structure (for example, a hash table in memory like for operation 1 or an index like for operation 3), a filter predicate is applied only after the rows have already been extracted from the structure storing them. Note that this section contains both the predicate present in the SQL statement itself and the predicates that may be generated by the query optimizer or by Virtual Private Database. In the preceding example, you have the following predicates:

- The hash join at line 1 uses the predicate "T1"."N"="T2"."N" to join the two tables. In other words, the access predicate might show a join condition as well. In this specific case, the access predicate is used to specify that the hash table in memory containing the data of table t1 will be probed with the values returned by accessing table t2 (how hash joins work is described in detail in Chapter 10).

- The index scan at line 3 accesses the index t_pk to look up the column id of the table t1. In this case, the access predicate shows on which key the lookup is performed.

- At line 4, all rows in table t3 are read through a full scan. Then, when the rows have been extracted from the blocks, the predicate "T1"."ID">6 is applied to filter them.

The following section shows which columns are returned as output when each operation is executed. It is available as of Oracle Database 10g only. Here is an example:

```
Column Projection Information (identified by operation id):
-------------------------------------------------------------

   1 - (#keys=1) "T2"."N"[NUMBER,22], "T2"."ID"[NUMBER,22],
       "T2"."PAD"[VARCHAR2,1000]
   2 - "T2"."ID"[NUMBER,22], "T2"."N"[NUMBER,22], "T2"."PAD"[VARCHAR2,1000]
   3 - "T2".ROWID[ROWID,10], "T2"."ID"[NUMBER,22]
   4 - "T1"."N"[NUMBER,22]
```

In this case, it is significant to note that while the table access at line 2 returns the columns id, n, and pad, the full scan at line 4 returns only the column n. For this reason, the estimated amount of data (column Bytes) returned from line 2 for each row (7,392/14 = 528 bytes) is much greater than for line 4 (25,844/994 = 26 bytes). Chapter 12 provides further information about the ability of the database engine to partially read a row.

Finally, there is a section providing notes and warnings about the optimization phase, the environment, or the SQL statement itself:

```
Note
-----
dynamic sampling used for this statement
```

Here you are informed that the query optimizer used dynamic sampling to gather object statistics. In Oracle9i Release 2, this section has no header and contains less information (for example, the use of dynamic sampling is not given) than as of Oracle Database 10g.

Function display

The function `display` returns execution plans stored in a plan table. The return value is an instance of the collection `dbms_xplan_type_table`. The elements of the collection are instances of the object type `dbms_xplan_type`. The only attribute of this object type, named `plan_table_output`, is of type `VARCHAR2`.[3] The function has the following input parameters:

- `table_name` specifies the name of the plan table. The default value is `plan_table`. If `NULL` is specified, the default value is used.

- `statement_id` specifies the SQL statement name, optionally given as a parameter, when the SQL statement `EXPLAIN PLAN` is executed. The default value is `NULL`. If the default value is used, the execution plan most recently inserted into the plan table is displayed (provided the parameter `filter_preds` is not specified).

- `format` specifies which information is provided in the output. There are primitive values (`basic`, `typical`, `serial`, `all`, and `advanced`) and, for finer control, additional modifiers (`alias`, `bytes`, `cost`, `note`, `outline`, `parallel`, `partition`, `peeked_binds`, `predicate`, `projection`, `remote`, and `rows`) that can be added to them. If information should be added, modifiers are optionally prefixed by the character + (for example, `basic +predicate`). If information should be removed, modifiers are prefixed by the character – (for example, `typical -bytes`). Multiple modifiers can be specified at the same time (for example, `typical +alias -bytes -cost`). Table 6-2 and Table 6-3 fully describe the primitive values and the modifiers, respectively. The default value is `typical`. The primitive value `advanced` and the modifiers are available as of Oracle Database 10g Release 2 only.

- `filter_preds` specifies a restriction applied while querying the plan table. The restriction is a regular SQL predicate based on one of the columns of the plan table (for example, `statement_id='test3'`). The default value is `NULL`. If the default value is used, the execution plan most recently inserted into the plan table is displayed. This parameter is available as of Oracle Database 10g Release 2.

To use the function `display`, the caller requires only the `EXECUTE` privilege on the package and the `SELECT` privilege on the plan table.

Table 6-2. *Primitive Values Accepted by the* format *Parameter*

Value	Description
`basic`	Displays only the minimum amount of information, basically only the operations and the objects on which they are executed
`typical`	Displays the most relevant information, basically everything except for alias, outline, and column projection information
`serial`	Like `typical`, except that information about parallel processing is not displayed
`all`	Displays all available information except the outline
`advanced`	Displays all available information

---

3. Up to Oracle Database 10g Release 1 it is a `VARCHAR2(200)`. As of Oracle Database 10g Release 2 it is a `VARCHAR2(300)`.

Table 6-3. *Modifiers Accepted by the Parameter format*

Value	Description
alias	Controls the display of the section containing query block names and object aliases.
bytes	Controls the display of the column Bytes in the execution plan table.
cost	Controls the display of the column Cost in the execution plan table.
note	Controls the display of the section containing the notes.
outline	Controls the display of the section containing the outline.
parallel	Controls the display of parallel processing information, specifically, the columns TQ, IN-OUT, and PQ Distrib in the execution plan table.
partition	Controls the display of partitioning information, specifically the columns Pstart and Pstop in the execution plan table.
peeked_binds	Controls the display of the section containing peeked bind variables. Since the current implementation of the SQL statement EXPLAIN PLAN does not perform bind variable peeking, this section was not shown in the previous examples.
predicate	Controls the display of the section containing filter and access predicates.
projection	Controls the display of the section containing column projection information.
remote	Controls the display of SQL statements executed remotely.
rows	Controls the display of the column Rows in the execution plan table.

The following queries, which display the same execution plan, show the main differences between the primitive values basic, typical, and advanced. Here is an excerpt of the output generated by the script display.sql:

```
SQL> SELECT * FROM table(dbms_xplan.display(NULL,NULL,'basic'));

PLAN_TABLE_OUTPUT
-----------------------------------

Plan hash value: 2966233522

-----------------------------------
| Id  | Operation          | Name |
-----------------------------------
|   0 | SELECT STATEMENT   |      |
|   1 |  SORT AGGREGATE    |      |
|   2 |   TABLE ACCESS FULL| T    |
-----------------------------------

SQL> SELECT * FROM table(dbms_xplan.display(NULL,NULL,'typical'));
```

PLAN_TABLE_OUTPUT

Plan hash value: 2966233522

| Id | Operation | Name | Rows | Bytes | Cost (%CPU)| Time |

0	SELECT STATEMENT		1	13	5 (0)	00:00:01
1	SORT AGGREGATE		1	13		
* 2	TABLE ACCESS FULL	T	14	182	5 (0)	00:00:01

Predicate Information (identified by operation id):
----

   2 - filter("N">=6 AND "N"<=19)

Note

   - dynamic sampling used for this statement

SQL> SELECT * FROM table(dbms_xplan.display(NULL,NULL,'advanced'));

PLAN_TABLE_OUTPUT

Plan hash value: 2966233522

| Id | Operation | Name | Rows | Bytes | Cost (%CPU)| Time |

0	SELECT STATEMENT		1	13	3 (0)	00:00:01
1	SORT AGGREGATE		1	13		
* 2	TABLE ACCESS FULL	T	14	182	3 (0)	00:00:01

Query Block Name / Object Alias (identified by operation id):
----

   1 - SEL$1
   2 - SEL$1 / T@SEL$1

Outline Data

```
    /*+
        BEGIN_OUTLINE_DATA
        FULL(@"SEL$1" "T"@"SEL$1")
        OUTLINE_LEAF(@"SEL$1")
        ALL_ROWS
        OPTIMIZER_FEATURES_ENABLE('10.2.0.3')
        IGNORE_OPTIM_EMBEDDED_HINTS
        END_OUTLINE_DATA
    */

Predicate Information (identified by operation id):
---------------------------------------------------

   2 - filter("N">=6 AND "N"<=19)

Column Projection Information (identified by operation id):
-------------------------------------------------------------

   1 - (#keys=0) COUNT(*)[22]

Note
-----
   - dynamic sampling used for this statement
```

The following queries show how to use modifiers to add or remove information from the default output generated by the primitive values basic and typical. Since they are based on the same query as the previous examples, you can compare the outputs to see what is different. This is an excerpt of the output generated by the script display.sql:

```
SQL> SELECT * FROM table(dbms_xplan.display(NULL,NULL,'basic +predicate',NULL));

PLAN_TABLE_OUTPUT
---------------------------------------------------

Plan hash value: 2966233522

------------------------------------
| Id  | Operation           | Name |
------------------------------------
|   0 | SELECT STATEMENT    |      |
|   1 |  SORT AGGREGATE     |      |
|*  2 |   TABLE ACCESS FULL | T    |
------------------------------------

Predicate Information (identified by operation id):
---------------------------------------------------
```

```
   2 - filter("N">=6 AND "N"<=19)

SQL> SELECT *
   2 FROM table(dbms_xplan.display(NULL,NULL,'typical -bytes -note',NULL));


PLAN_TABLE_OUTPUT
-----------------------------------------------------------------

Plan hash value: 2966233522


---------------------------------------------------------------------
| Id  | Operation          | Name | Rows  | Cost (%CPU)| Time     |
---------------------------------------------------------------------
|   0 | SELECT STATEMENT   |      |     1 |     5   (0)| 00:00:01 |
|   1 |  SORT AGGREGATE    |      |     1 |            |          |
|*  2 |   TABLE ACCESS FULL| T    |    14 |     5   (0)| 00:00:01 |
---------------------------------------------------------------------


Predicate Information (identified by operation id):
---------------------------------------------------

   2 - filter("N">=6 AND "N"<=19)
```

Function display_cursor

The function display_cursor returns execution plans stored in the library cache. It is available as of Oracle Database 10g. As for the function display, the return value is an instance of the collection dbms_xplan_type_table. The function has the following input parameters:

- sql_id specifies the parent cursor whose execution plan is returned. The default value is NULL. If the default value is used, the execution plan of the last SQL statement executed by the current session is returned.

- cursor_child_no specifies the child number that, along with sql_id, identifies the child cursor whose execution plan is returned. The default value is 0. If NULL is specified, all child cursors of the parent cursor identified by the parameter sql_id are returned.

- format specifies which information is displayed. The same values are supported as in the parameter format of the function display. In addition, if execution statistics are available (in other words, if the initialization parameter statistics_level is set to all or the hint gather_plan_statistics is specified in the SQL statement), the modifiers described in Table 6-4 are also supported. The default value is typical.

To use the display_cursor function, the caller requires SELECT privileges on the following dynamic performance views: v$session, v$sql, v$sql_plan, and v$sql_plan_statistics_all. The role select_catalog_role and the system privilege select any dictionary provide these privileges, among others.

Table 6-4. *Modifiers Accepted by the Parameter* format

Value	Description
allstats*	This is a shortcut for iostats memstats.
iostats*	Controls the display of I/O statistics.
last*	Per default, the cumulated statistics of all executions are displayed. If this value is specified, only the statistics of the last execution are shown.
memstats*	Controls the display of statistics related to the PGA.
runstats_last	Same as iostats last. Can be used in Oracle Database 10g Release 1 only.
runstats_tot	Same as iostats. Can be used in Oracle Database 10g Release 1 only.

* *This value is available as of Oracle Database 10g Release 2 only.*

The following example shows a query that uses the hint gather_plan_statistics to enable the generation of the execution statistics. The function display_cursor is then instructed to display the I/O statistics for the last execution. Note that only logical read operations (Buffers) are displayed because there were no physical reads or writes. Here is an excerpt of the output generated by the script display_cursor.sql:

```
SQL> SELECT /*+ gather_plan_statistics */ count(*)
  2  FROM t
  3  WHERE mod(n,19) = 0;

  COUNT(*)
----------
        52

SQL> SELECT * FROM table(dbms_xplan.display_cursor(NULL,NULL, 'iostats last'));

PLAN_TABLE_OUTPUT
--------------------------------------------------------------------------------

EXPLAINED SQL STATEMENT:
------------------------
SELECT /*+ gather_plan_statistics */ count(*) FROM t WHERE mod(n,19) = 0

Plan hash value: 2966233522

---------------------------------------------------------------------------------
| Id | Operation          | Name | Starts | E-Rows | A-Rows |   A-Time   | Buffers |
---------------------------------------------------------------------------------
|  1 |  SORT AGGREGATE     |      |      1 |      1 |      1 |00:00:00.01 |     147 |
|* 2 |    TABLE ACCESS FULL| T    |      1 |     10 |     52 |00:00:00.01 |     147 |
---------------------------------------------------------------------------------
```

```
Predicate Information (identified by operation id):
---------------------------------------------------

   2 - filter(MOD("N",19)=0)
```

Function display_awr

The function `display_awr` returns execution plans stored in AWR. It is available as of Oracle Database 10g. As for the function `display`, the return value is an instance of the collection `dbms_xplan_type_table`. The function has the following input parameters:

- `sql_id` specifies the parent cursor whose execution plan is returned. The parameter has no default value.

- `plan_hash_value` specifies the hash value of the execution plan to be returned. The default value is `NULL`. If the default value is used, all execution plans related to the parent cursor identified by the parameter `sql_id` are returned.

- `db_id` specifies on which database the execution plan to be returned was executed. The default value is `NULL`. If the default value is used, the current database is used.

- `format` specifies which information is displayed. The same values as the parameter `format` of the function `display` are supported. The default value is `typical`.

To use the function `display_awr`, the caller requires at least `SELECT` privileges on the following data dictionary views: `dba_hist_sql_plan` and `dba_hist_sqltext`. If the parameter `db_id` is not specified, the `SELECT` privilege on the view `v$database` is necessary as well. The role `select_catalog_role` provides these privileges, among others.

The following queries show the usefulness of the parameter `plan_hash_value` whenever several execution plans exist for a given cursor. Note that while the first query returns two execution plans, the second query returns only one. Here is an excerpt of the output generated by the script `display_awr.sql`:

```
SQL> SELECT *
  2  FROM table(dbms_xplan.display_awr('48vuyqjwpf9wg',NULL,NULL,'basic'));

PLAN_TABLE_OUTPUT
---------------------------------------

SQL_ID 48vuyqjwpf9wg
--------------------
SELECT COUNT(N) FROM T

Plan hash value: 2966233522
```

```
------------------------------------
| Id  | Operation          | Name |
------------------------------------
|   0 | SELECT STATEMENT   |      |
|   1 |  SORT AGGREGATE    |      |
|   2 |   TABLE ACCESS FULL| T    |
------------------------------------
```

```
SQL_ID 48vuyqjwpf9wg
--------------------
SELECT COUNT(N) FROM T
```

Plan hash value: 3776247601

```
---------------------------------------
| Id  | Operation          | Name |
---------------------------------------
|   0 | SELECT STATEMENT   |      |
|   1 |  SORT AGGREGATE    |      |
|   2 |   INDEX FAST FULL SCAN| I    |
---------------------------------------
```

```
SQL> SELECT *
  2  FROM table(dbms_xplan.display_awr('48vuyqjwpf9wg',2966233522,NULL,'basic'));

PLAN_TABLE_OUTPUT
------------------------------------

SQL_ID 48vuyqjwpf9wg
--------------------
SELECT COUNT(N) FROM T
```

Plan hash value: 2966233522

```
------------------------------------
| Id  | Operation          | Name |
------------------------------------
|   0 | SELECT STATEMENT   |      |
|   1 |  SORT AGGREGATE    |      |
|   2 |   TABLE ACCESS FULL| T    |
------------------------------------
```

Several situations lead to multiple execution plans for a given cursor, such as when an index has been added or simply because data (and therefore its object statistics) has changed. Basically, each time the environment that the query optimizer evolves in changes, different execution plans might be generated. Such an output is useful when you are questioning the performance of a SQL statement that you think has been running without problems for some time. The idea is to check whether a SQL statement has been executed with several execution plans over a period of time. If this is the case, infer what could be the reason leading to the change based on the available information.

Interpreting Execution Plans

I have always found it surprising how little documentation there is about how to read execution plans, especially since there seem to be so many people who are unable to correctly read them. I will attempt to address this problem by describing the approach I use when reading an execution plan. Note that details about the different operations are not provided here; rather, I provide the basics you need in order to understand how to walk through execution plans. I'll give detailed information about the most common operations in Part 4. All examples provided in the following sections are excerpts of the output generated by the script execution_plans.sql.

Parent-Child Relationship

An execution plan is a tree describing not only in which order the SQL engine executes operations but also what the relationship between operations is. Each node in the tree is an operation, for example, a table access, a join, or a sort. Between operations (nodes), there is a parent-child relationship. Understanding those relationships is essential to correctly reading an execution plan. The rules governing the parent-child relationship are the following:

- A parent has one or multiple children.

- A child has a single parent.

- The only operation without a parent is the root of the tree.

- When an execution plan is displayed, the children are indented to the right, with respect to their parent. Depending on the method used to display the execution plan, the indentation could be a single space character, two spaces, or something else. It doesn't really matter. The essential point is that all children of a specific parent have the very same indentation.

- A parent is placed before its children (the ID of the parent is less than the ID of the children). If there are several preceding operations for a child, with the same indentation as the parent, the nearest operation is the parent.

The following is a sample execution plan. Note that while only the column Operation is needed to walk through an execution plan, the column Id is shown here to help you identify the operations more easily. The SQL statement used to generate it has been left out intentionally because it doesn't serve our purposes for this section.

```
----------------------------------------
| Id  | Operation                       |
----------------------------------------
|   1 |  UPDATE                         |
|   2 |   NESTED LOOPS                  |
|*  3 |    TABLE ACCESS FULL            |
|*  4 |    INDEX UNIQUE SCAN            |
|   5 |   SORT AGGREGATE                |
|   6 |    TABLE ACCESS BY INDEX ROWID|
|*  7 |     INDEX RANGE SCAN            |
|   8 |   TABLE ACCESS BY INDEX ROWID  |
|*  9 |    INDEX UNIQUE SCAN            |
----------------------------------------
```

Figure 6-2 provides a graphical representation of the execution plan. Using the rules described earlier, you can conclude the following.

- Operation 1 is the root of the tree. It has three children: 2, 5, and 8.

- Operation 2 has two children: 3 and 4.

- Operations 3 and 4 have no children.

- Operation 5 has one child: 6.

- Operation 6 has one child: 7.

- Operation 7 has no children.

- Operation 8 has one child: 9.

- Operation 9 has no children.

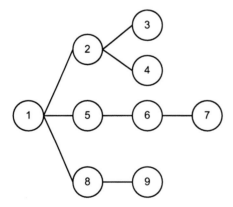

Figure 6-2. *Parent-child relationships between execution plan operations*

Types of Operations

The number of possible operations is high (about 200). Of course, to fully understand an execution plan, you should know what each operation it is made of does. For our purpose of walking through an execution plan, you need to consider only three major types of operations: *stand-alone operations*, *unrelated-combine operations*, and *related-combine operations*. Basically, each type has a particular behavior, and knowing it is sufficient for reading execution plans.

■**Caution** I coined the terms used here for the three types of operations while writing a presentation about the query optimizer a few years ago. Don't expect to find these terms used elsewhere.

In addition to these three types, operations can be separated into blocking operations and nonblocking operations. Simply put, blocking operations process data in bulk, while nonblocking operations process data row by row. For example, a sort operation is blocking because it is able to return the output rows only when all input rows have been fully processed (ordered)—the first output row could be anywhere in the input set. On the other hand, a filter applying a simple restriction is nonblocking because it evaluates each row independently. It goes without saying that for blocking operations, data must be buffered either in memory (PGA) or on disk (temporary tablespace). For simplicity, while walking through an execution plan, you can consider all operations to be blocking. Remember, however, that most of the operations are in fact nonblocking and that the SQL engine, for obvious reasons, tries to avoid the buffering of data as much as possible.

Stand-Alone Operations

I identify all operations having at most one child as *stand-alone operations*. Most operations are of this type. This makes the interpretation of execution plans easier because there are less than 20 operations that are not of this type. The rules governing the working of stand-alone operations are the following:

- Children are executed before their parents. Two optimization techniques presented later in this chapter, however, lead to exceptions to this rule.

- Every child is executed at most once.

- Every child feeds its parent.

Here is an example of a query and its execution plan (Figure 6-3 provides a graphical representation of its parent-child relationships):

```
SELECT deptno, count(*) FROM emp WHERE job = 'CLERK' AND sal < 1200 GROUP BY deptno

-----------------------------------------------------------------------
| Id  | Operation                     | Name       | Starts | A-Rows |
-----------------------------------------------------------------------
|   1 |  HASH GROUP BY                |            |     1  |     2  |
|*  2 |   TABLE ACCESS BY INDEX ROWID | EMP        |     1  |     3  |
|*  3 |    INDEX RANGE SCAN           | EMP_JOB_I  |     1  |     4  |
-----------------------------------------------------------------------

   2 - filter("SAL"<1200)
   3 - access("JOB"='CLERK')
```

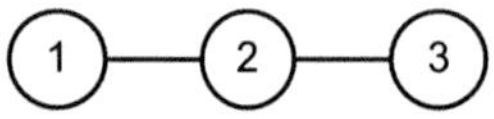

Figure 6-3. *Parent-child relationships between stand-alone operations*

This execution plan consists only of stand-alone operations. By applying the rules described earlier, you find out that the execution plan carries out the operations as follows:

1. Operations 1 and 2 have a single child each (2 and 3, respectively); they they cannot be the first operations being executed. Therefore, the execution starts with operation 3.

2. Operation 3 scans the index emp_job_i by applying the access predicate "JOB"='CLERK'. In doing so, it extracts four rowids (this information is given in the column A-Rows) from the index and passes them to its parent operation (2).

3. Operation 2 accesses the table emp through the four rowids passed from operation 3. For each rowid, a row is read. Then, it applies the filter predicate "SAL"<1200. This filter leads to the exclusion of one row. The data of the remaining three rows are passed to its parent operation (1).

4. Operation 1 performs a GROUP BY on the rows passed from operation 2. The resulting set is reduced to two rows. Since this is the last operation, the data is sent to the caller.

Notice how the column Starts clearly shows that each operation is executed only once.

One of the rules states that child operations are executed before parent operations. This is generally true, but there are situations where smart optimizations are introduced. What can happen is that a parent decides that it makes no sense to completely execute a child or even that it makes no sense to execute it at all. In other words, parents control the execution of children. Let's take a look at two common cases.

Optimization of the Operation COUNT STOPKEY

The operation COUNT STOPKEY is commonly used to execute top-n queries. Its aim is to stop the processing as soon as the required number of rows has been returned to the caller. For example, the aim of the following query is to return only the first ten rows found in the table emp:

```
SELECT * FROM emp WHERE rownum <= 10
```

```
-------------------------------------------------------
| Id | Operation          | Name | Starts | A-Rows |
-------------------------------------------------------
|*  1 | COUNT STOPKEY      |      |     1 |     10 |
|   2 |   TABLE ACCESS FULL| EMP  |     1 |     10 |
-------------------------------------------------------
```

```
  1 - filter(ROWNUM<=10)
```

The important thing to notice in this execution plan is that the number of rows returned by operation 2 is limited to ten. This is true even if operation 2 is a full table scan of a table containing more than ten rows (actually the table contains 14 rows). What happens is that operation 1 stops the processing of operation 2 as soon as the necessary number of rows has been processed. Be careful, though, because nonblocking operations cannot be stopped. In fact, they need to be fully processed before returning rows to their parent operation. For example, in the following query, all rows of the table emp are read because of the ORDER BY clause:

```
SELECT * FROM (SELECT * FROM emp ORDER BY sal DESC) WHERE rownum <= 10
```

```
------------------------------------------------------------
| Id | Operation             | Name | Starts | A-Rows |
------------------------------------------------------------
|*  1 | COUNT STOPKEY         |      |     1 |     10 |
|   2 |   VIEW                |      |     1 |     10 |
|*  3 |    SORT ORDER BY STOPKEY|    |     1 |     10 |
|   4 |      TABLE ACCESS FULL | EMP |     1 |     14 |
------------------------------------------------------------
```

Optimization of the Operation FILTER

The operation FILTER not only applies a filter when its child passes data to it, but in addition, it could decide to completely avoid the execution of a child and all the dependent operations (grandchild and so on) as well. For example, in the following query a predicate that can never be TRUE is present. In practice, such predicates are found when applications dynamically generate part of the SQL statements. Usually, their aim is to completely deactivate part of a SQL statement in particular circumstances.

```
SELECT * FROM emp WHERE job = 'CLERK' AND 1 = 2
```

```
---------------------------------------------------------------------
| Id | Operation                    | Name     | Starts | A-Rows |
---------------------------------------------------------------------
|*  1 | FILTER                       |          |     1 |     0 |
|   2 |   TABLE ACCESS BY INDEX ROWID| EMP      |     0 |     0 |
|*  3 |    INDEX RANGE SCAN          | EMP_JOB_I |    0 |     0 |
---------------------------------------------------------------------
```

```
1 - filter(NULL IS NOT NULL)
3 - access("JOB"='CLERK')
```

According to the rules described earlier, such an execution plan should be carried out by starting the processing of operation 3. In reality, looking at the column Starts tells you that only operation 1 is executed. This optimization simply avoids processing operations 2 and 3 because the data has no chance of going through the filter applied by operation 1 anyway.

Unrelated-Combine Operations

I call all operations having multiple children that are independently executed *unrelated-combine operations*. The following operations are of this type: AND-EQUAL, BITMAP AND, BITMAP OR, BITMAP MINUS, CONCATENATION, CONNECT BY WITHOUT FILTERING, HASH JOIN, INTERSECTION, MERGE JOIN, MINUS, MULTI-TABLE INSERT, SQL MODEL, TEMP TABLE TRANSFORMATION, and UNION-ALL.

The characteristics of unrelated-combine operations are the following:

- Children are executed before their parents.

- Children are executed sequentially, starting from the one with the smallest ID and going to the one with the highest ID. Before starting the processing of a subsequent child, the current one must be completely executed.

- Every child is executed at most once and independently from all other children.

- Every child feeds its parent.

Here is a sample query and its execution plan (see Figure 6-4 for a graphical representation of its parent-child relationships):

```
SELECT ename FROM emp
UNION ALL
SELECT dname FROM dept
UNION ALL
SELECT '%' FROM dual
```

```
-----------------------------------------------------
| Id  | Operation          | Name | Starts | A-Rows |
-----------------------------------------------------
|   1 |  UNION-ALL          |      |      1 |     19 |
|   2 |   TABLE ACCESS FULL| EMP  |      1 |     14 |
|   3 |   TABLE ACCESS FULL| DEPT |      1 |      4 |
|   4 |   FAST DUAL         |      |      1 |      1 |
-----------------------------------------------------
```

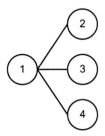

Figure 6-4. *Parent-child relationships of the unrelated-combine operation* UNION-ALL

In this execution plan, the unrelated-combine operation is the UNION-ALL. The other three are stand-alone operations. By applying the rules described earlier, you see that the execution plan carries out the operations as follows:

1. Operation 1 has three children, and, among them, operation 2 is the first in ascending order. Therefore, the execution starts with operation 2.

2. Operation 2 scans the table emp and returns 14 rows to its parent operation (1).

3. When operation 2 is completely executed, operation 3 is started.

4. Operation 3 scans the table dept and returns four rows to its parent operation (1).

5. When operation 3 is completely executed, operation 4 is started.

6. Operation 4 scans the table dual and returns one row to its parent operation (1).

7. Operation 1 builds a single result set of 19 rows based on all data received from its children and sends the data to the caller.

Notice how the column Starts clearly shows that each operation is executed only once.

To walk through the execution plan, all other operations listed earlier have the same behavior as the operation UNION-ALL shown in this example. In short, an unrelated-combine operation sequentially executes its children once. Obviously, the processing performed by the unrelated-combine operation itself is different.

Related-Combine Operations

I refer to all operations having multiple children where one of the children controls the execution of all other children as *related-combine operations*. The following operations are of this type: NESTED LOOPS, UPDATE, FILTER, CONNECT BY WITH FILTERING, and BITMAP KEY ITERATION.

The following are the characteristics of related-combine operations:

- Children are executed before their parents.

- The child with the smallest ID controls the execution of the other children.

- Children are executed going from the one with the smallest ID to the one with the highest ID. Contrary to unrelated-combine operations, however, they are not executed sequentially. Instead, a kind of interleaving is performed.

- Only the first child is executed at most once. All other children may be executed several times or not executed at all.

- Not every child feeds its parent. Some children are used to apply restrictions only.

Even if the operations of this type share the same characteristics, each of them has, to some extent, its own behavior. Let's take a look then at an example for each of them (except for BITMAP KEY ITERATION, which will be covered in Chapter 10).

Operation NESTED LOOPS

This operation is used to join two sets of rows. Consequently, it always has two children, no more, no less. The child with the smallest ID is called the *outer loop* or *driving row source*. The second child is called the *inner loop*. The particular characteristic of this operation is that the inner loop is executed once for each row returned by the outer loop.

The following query and its execution plan are given as an example (Figure 6-5 shows a graphical representation of its parent-child relationships):

```
SELECT *
FROM emp, dept
WHERE emp.deptno = dept.deptno
AND emp.comm IS NULL
AND dept.dname != 'SALES'
```

```
---------------------------------------------------------------------
| Id  | Operation                    | Name     | Starts | A-Rows |
---------------------------------------------------------------------
|   1 |  NESTED LOOPS                |          |      1 |      8 |
|*  2 |   TABLE ACCESS FULL          | EMP      |      1 |     10 |
|*  3 |   TABLE ACCESS BY INDEX ROWID| DEPT     |     10 |      8 |
|*  4 |    INDEX UNIQUE SCAN         | DEPT_PK  |     10 |     10 |
---------------------------------------------------------------------

   2 - filter("EMP"."COMM" IS NULL)
   3 - filter("DEPT"."DNAME"<>'SALES')
   4 - access("EMP"."DEPTNO"="DEPT"."DEPTNO")
```

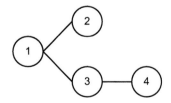

Figure 6-5. *Parent-child relationships of the related-combine operation* NESTED LOOP

In this execution plan, both children of the related-combine operation NESTED LOOPS are stand-alone operations. By applying the rules described earlier, you can see that the execution plan carries out the operations as follows:

1. Operation 1 has two children (2 and 3), and among them, operation 2 is the first in ascending order. Therefore, the execution starts with operation 2 (the outer loop).

2. Operation 2 scans the table emp, applies the filter predicate "EMP"."COMM" IS NULL, and returns the data of ten rows to its parent operation (1).

3. For each row returned by operation 2, the second child of the operation NESTED LOOPS, the inner loop, is executed once. This is confirmed by comparing the column A-Rows of operation 2 with the column Starts of operations 3 and 4.

4. The inner loop is composed of two stand-alone operations. Based on the rules that apply to this type of operation, operation 4 is executed before operation 3.

5. Operation 4 scans the index dept_pk by applying the access predicate "EMP"."DEPTNO"= "DEPT"."DEPTNO". In doing so, it extracts ten rowids from the index over the ten executions and passes them to its parent operation (3).

6. Operation 3 accesses the table dept through the ten rowids passed from operation 4. For each rowid, a row is read. Then it applies the filter predicate "DEPT"."DNAME"<>'SALES'. This filter leads to the exclusion of two rows. It passes the data of the remaining eight rows to its parent operation (1).

7. Operation 1 sends the data of eight rows to the caller.

Operation FILTER

The particular characteristic of this operation is that it supports a varying number of children. If it has a single child, it is considered a stand-alone operation. If it has two or more children, its function is similar to the operation NESTED LOOPS. The first child drives the execution of the other children.

To illustrate, the following query and its execution plan are given (Figure 6-6 shows a graphical representation of its parent-child relationships):

```
SELECT *
FROM emp
WHERE NOT EXISTS (SELECT 0
                  FROM dept
                  WHERE dept.dname = 'SALES' AND dept.deptno = emp.deptno)
AND NOT EXISTS (SELECT 0
                FROM bonus
                WHERE bonus.ename = emp.ename);
```

```
----------------------------------------------------------------
| Id  | Operation                    | Name    | Starts | A-Rows |
----------------------------------------------------------------
|*  1 |  FILTER                      |         |      1 |      8 |
|   2 |    TABLE ACCESS FULL         | EMP     |      1 |     14 |
|*  3 |    TABLE ACCESS BY INDEX ROWID| DEPT   |      3 |      1 |
|*  4 |      INDEX UNIQUE SCAN       | DEPT_PK |      3 |      3 |
|*  5 |    TABLE ACCESS FULL         | BONUS   |      8 |      0 |
----------------------------------------------------------------

  1 - filter( NOT EXISTS (SELECT 0 FROM "DEPT" "DEPT" WHERE "DEPT"."DEPTNO"=:B1
         AND "DEPT"."DNAME"='SALES') AND NOT EXISTS (SELECT 0 FROM "BONUS"
         "BONUS" WHERE "BONUS"."ENAME"=:B2))
  3 - filter("DEPT"."DNAME"='SALES')
  4 - access("DEPT"."DEPTNO"=:B1)
  5 - filter("BONUS"."ENAME"=:B1)
```

■**Caution** The function `display_cursor` in the package `dbms_xplan` sometimes shows wrong predicates. The problem, though, is not the package. It is actually caused by the views `v$sql_plan` and `v$sql_plan_statistics_all` that show wrong information. In this case, the wrongly displayed predicates are the following:

```
  1 - filter(( IS NULL AND  IS NULL))
  3 - filter("DEPT"."DNAME"='SALES')
  4 - access("DEPT"."DEPTNO"=:B1)
  5 - filter("BONUS"."ENAME"=:B1)
```

Note that according to Oracle, this is not a bug. It is just a limitation of the current implementation.

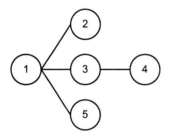

Figure 6-6. *Parent-child relationships of the related-combine operation FILTER*

In this execution plan, the three children of the related-combine operation FILTER are stand-alone operations. Applying the rules described earlier, you see that the execution plan carries out the operations in the following manner:

1. Operation 1 has three children (2, 3 and 5), and operation 2 is the first of them in ascending order. Therefore, the execution starts with operation 2.

2. Operation 2 scans the table emp and returns 14 rows to its parent operation (1).

3. For each row returned by operation 2, the second and third children of the operation FILTER should be executed once. In reality, a kind of caching is implemented to reduce executions to a minimum. This is confirmed by comparing the column A-Rows of operation 2 with the column Starts of operations 3 and 5. Operation 3 is executed three times, once for each distinct value in the column deptno in the table emp. Operation 5 is executed eight times, once for each distinct value in the column empno in the table emp after applying the filter imposed by the operation 3. The following query shows that the number of starts matches the number of distinct values:

```
SQL> SELECT dname, count(*)
  2  FROM emp, dept
  3  WHERE emp.deptno = dept.deptno
  4  GROUP BY dname;

DNAME            COUNT(*)
-------------- ----------
ACCOUNTING              3
RESEARCH                5
SALES                   6
```

4. According to the rules for stand-alone operations, operation 4, which is executed before operation 3, scans the index dept_pk by applying the access predicate "DEPT"."DEPTNO"=:B1. The bind variable (B1) is used to pass the value that is to be checked by the subquery. By doing so over the three executions, it extracts three rowids from the index and passes them to its parent operation (3).

5. Operation 3 accesses the table dept through the rowids passed from its child operation (4) and applies the filter predicate "DEPT"."DNAME"='SALES'. Since this operation is used only to apply a restriction, it returns no data to its parent operation (1). In any case, it is important to note that only one row satisfying the filter predicate was found. Since a NOT EXISTS is used, this matching row is discarded.

6. Operation 5 scans the table bonus and applies the filter predicate "BONUS"."ENAME"=:B1. The bind variable (B1) is used to pass the value to be checked by the subquery. Since this operation is used only to apply a restriction, it returns no data to its parent operation (1). It is, however, important to notice that no row satisfying the filter predicate was found. Since a NOT EXISTS is used, no rows are discarded.

7. Operation 1, after applying the filter predicate implemented with operations 3 and 5, sends the data of eight rows to the caller.

Operation UPDATE

This operation is used when a SQL statement UPDATE is executed. Its particular characteristic is that it supports a varying number of children. Most of the time, it has a single child, and therefore, it is considered a stand-alone operation. Two or more children are available only when subqueries are used in the SET clause. If it has more than one child, its behavior is the same as the operation FILTER. In other words, the first child drives the execution of the other children.

Here is a sample SQL statement and its execution plan (see Figure 6-7 for a graphical representation of its parent-child relationships):

```
UPDATE emp e1
SET sal = (SELECT avg(sal) FROM emp e2 WHERE e2.deptno = e1.deptno),
    comm = (SELECT avg(comm) FROM emp e3)
```

```
---------------------------------------------------------
| Id  | Operation            | Name | Starts | A-Rows |
---------------------------------------------------------
|   1 | UPDATE               | EMP  |    1 |      0 |
|   2 |  TABLE ACCESS FULL   | EMP  |    1 |     14 |
|   3 |  SORT AGGREGATE      |      |    3 |      3 |
|*  4 |   TABLE ACCESS FULL  | EMP  |    3 |     14 |
|   5 |  SORT AGGREGATE      |      |    1 |      1 |
|   6 |   TABLE ACCESS FULL  | EMP  |    1 |     14 |
---------------------------------------------------------
```

```
   4 - filter("E2"."DEPTNO"=:B1)
```

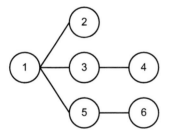

Figure 6-7. *Parent-child relationships of the related-combine operation* UPDATE

In this execution plan, all three children of the related-combine operation UPDATE are stand-alone operations. The rules described earlier indicate that the execution plan carries out the operations as follows:

1. Operation 1 has three children (2, 3, and 5), and operation 2 is the first of the three in ascending order. Therefore, the execution starts with operation 2.

2. Operation 2 scans the table emp and returns 14 rows to its parent operation (1).

3. For each distinct value in the column deptno, the two children (3 and 5) are executed once. Since both these operations are stand-alone, and each has a child, their execution starts with the child operations (4 and 6).

4. Operation 4 scans the table emp and applies the filter predicate "E2"."DEPTNO"=:B1. In doing so over the three executions, it extracts 14 rows and passes them to its parent operation (3).

5. Operation 3 computes the average salary of the rows passed to it from operation 4 and returns the result to its parent operation (1).

6. Operation 6 scans the table emp, extracts 14 rows, and passes them to its parent operation (5). Note that this subquery is executed only once because it is not correlated to the main query.

7. Operation 5 computes the average commission of the rows passed to it from operation 6 and returns the result to its parent operation (1).

8. Operation 1 updates each row passed by operation 2 with the value returned by its other children (3 and 5). Note that even if the UPDATE statement modifies the 14 rows, column A-Rows shows 0 for this operation.

Operation CONNECT BY WITH FILTERING

This operation is used to process hierarchical queries. It is characterized by two child operations. The first one is used to get the root of the hierarchy, and the second one is executed once for each level in the hierarchy.

Here is a sample query and its execution plan (Figure 6-8 shows a graphical representation of its parent-child relationships). Note that the execution plan was generated on Oracle Database 11*g* (the reason will be explained later).

```
SELECT level, rpad('-',level-1,'-')||ename AS ename, prior ename AS manager
FROM emp
START WITH mgr IS NULL
CONNECT BY PRIOR empno = mgr
```

```
---------------------------------------------------------------------
| Id  | Operation                     | Name      | Starts | A-Rows |
---------------------------------------------------------------------
|*  1 |  CONNECT BY WITH FILTERING    |           |      1 |     14 |
|*  2 |   TABLE ACCESS FULL           | EMP       |      1 |      1 |
|   3 |   NESTED LOOPS                |           |      4 |     13 |
|   4 |    CONNECT BY PUMP            |           |      4 |     14 |
|   5 |    TABLE ACCESS BY INDEX ROWID| EMP       |     14 |     13 |
|*  6 |     INDEX RANGE SCAN          | EMP_MGR_I |     14 |     13 |
---------------------------------------------------------------------
```

```
1 - access("MGR"=PRIOR "EMPNO")
2 - filter("MGR" IS NULL)
6 - access("MGR"=PRIOR "EMPNO")
```

Caution This query is another situation where the views v$sql_plan and v$sql_plan_statistics_ all give wrong information. In this case, the wrongly displayed predicates are the following:

```
1 - access("MGR"=PRIOR NULL)
2 - filter("MGR" IS NULL)
6 - access("MGR"=PRIOR NULL)
```

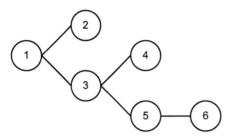

Figure 6-8. *Parent-child relationships of the related-combine operation* CONNECT BY WITH FILTERING

In this execution plan, the first child of the related-combine operation CONNECT BY WITH FILTERING is a stand-alone operation. Instead, the second child is itself a related-combine operation. To read an execution plan in such a situation, you simply apply the basic rules recursively, while descending the tree.

To help you understand the execution plan with a hierarchical query more easily, it is useful to look at the data returned by the query as well:

```
LEVEL ENAME      MANAGER
---------- ---------- ----------
    1 KING
    2 -JONES     KING
    3 --SCOTT    JONES
    4 ---ADAMS   SCOTT
    3 --FORD     JONES
    4 ---SMITH   FORD
    2 -BLAKE     KING
    3 --ALLEN    BLAKE
    3 --WARD     BLAKE
    3 --MARTIN   BLAKE
    3 --TURNER   BLAKE
    3 --JAMES    BLAKE
    2 -CLARK     KING
    3 --MILLER   CLARK
```

Applying the rules described earlier, you can see that the execution plan carries out the operations as follows:

1. Operation 1 has two children (2 and 3), and operation 2 is the first of them in ascending order. Therefore, the execution starts with operation 2.

2. Operation 2 scans the table emp, applies the filter predicate "MGR" IS NULL, and returns the root of the hierarchy to its parent operation (1).

3. Operation 3 is the second child of operation 1. It is therefore executed for each level of the hierarchy—in this case, four times. Naturally, the rules previously discussed for the operation NESTED LOOPS apply for operation 3. The first child, operation 4, is executed, and for each row it returns, the inner loop (composed of operation 5 and its child operation 6) is executed once. Notice, as expected, the match between the column A-Rows of operation 4 with the column Starts of operations 5 and 6.

4. For the first execution, operation 4 gets the root of the hierarchy through the operation CONNECT BY PUMP. In this case, there is a single row (KING) at level 1. With the value in the column mgr, operation 6 does a scan of the index emp_mgr_i by applying the access predicate "MGR"=PRIOR "EMPNO", extracts the rowids, and returns them to its parent operation (5). Operation 5 accesses the table emp with the rowids and returns the rows to its parent operation (3).

5. For the second execution of operation 4, everything works the same as for the first execution. The only difference is that the data from level 2 (JONES, BLAKE, and CLARK) is passed to operation 4 for the processing.

6. For the third execution of operation 4, everything works like in the first one. The only difference is that level 3 data (SCOTT, FORD, ALLEN, WARD, MARTIN, TURNER, JAMES, and MILLER) is passed to operation 4 for the processing.

7. For the fourth and last execution of operation 4, everything works like in the first one. The only difference is that level 4 data (ADAMS and SMITH) is passed to operation 4 for the processing.

8. Operation 3 gets the rows passed from its children and returns them to its parent operation (1).

9. Operation 1 applies the access predicate "MGR"=PRIOR "EMPNO" and sends the 14 rows to the caller.

The execution plan generated on Oracle Database 10g is slightly different. As can be seen, the operation CONNECT BY WITH FILTERING has a third child (operation 8). In this case, it was not executed, however. The value in the column Starts for operation 8 confirms this. Actually, the third child is executed only when the CONNECT BY operation uses temporary space. When that happens, performance might degrade considerably. This problem, which is fixed as of version 10.2.0.4, is known as bug 5065418.

```
---------------------------------------------------------------------
| Id  | Operation                      | Name      | Starts | A-Rows |
---------------------------------------------------------------------
|*  1 |  CONNECT BY WITH FILTERING      |           |      1 |     14 |
|*  2 |   TABLE ACCESS FULL             | EMP       |      1 |      1 |
|   3 |   NESTED LOOPS                  |           |      4 |     13 |
|   4 |    BUFFER SORT                  |           |      4 |     14 |
|   5 |     CONNECT BY PUMP             |           |      4 |     14 |
|   6 |    TABLE ACCESS BY INDEX ROWID  | EMP       |     14 |     13 |
|*  7 |     INDEX RANGE SCAN            | EMP_MGR_I |     14 |     13 |
|   8 |   TABLE ACCESS FULL             | EMP       |      0 |      0 |
---------------------------------------------------------------------
```

Divide and Conquer

In the previous sections, you saw how to read the three types of operations execution plans are composed of. All the execution plans you have seen so far were quite easy (short). More often than not, however, you have to deal with complex (long) execution plans. This is not because most SQL statements are complex but because it is likely that simple SQL statements are correctly optimized by the query optimizer, and as a result, you never have to question their performance.

The essential thing to recognize is that reading long execution plans is no different from reading short ones. All you need is to methodically apply the rules provided in the previous sections. With them, it does not matter how many lines an execution plan has. You simply proceed in the same way.

To show you how to proceed with an execution plan that is longer than a few lines, let's take a look at the operations carried out by the execution plan shown in Figure 6-9 (Figure 6-10 shows a graphical representation of its parent-child relationships). I am not providing the SQL statement used to generate it intentionally. For our purposes, you are simply not interested in the SQL statement. The execution plan, on the other hand, is the key.

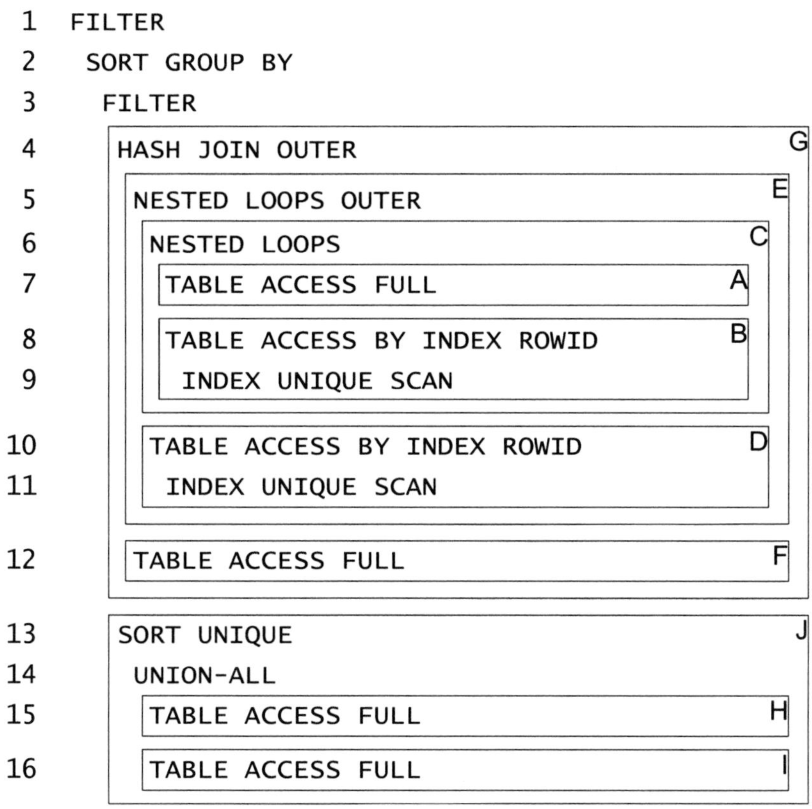

```
 1   FILTER
 2     SORT GROUP BY
 3       FILTER
 4         HASH JOIN OUTER                                    G
 5           NESTED LOOPS OUTER                             E
 6             NESTED LOOPS                               C
 7               TABLE ACCESS FULL                      A
 8               TABLE ACCESS BY INDEX ROWID          B
 9                 INDEX UNIQUE SCAN
10             TABLE ACCESS BY INDEX ROWID              D
11               INDEX UNIQUE SCAN
12           TABLE ACCESS FULL                            F
13         SORT UNIQUE                                       J
14           UNION-ALL
15             TABLE ACCESS FULL                          H
16             TABLE ACCESS FULL                          I
```

Figure 6-9. *An execution plan decomposed in blocks. The numbers on the left identify the operations. The letters on the right identify the blocks.*

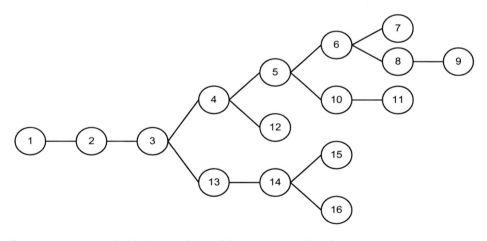

Figure 6-10. *Parent-child relationships of the execution plan shown in Figure 6-9*

Initially, it is necessary to both decompose the execution plan into basic blocks and recognize the order of execution. To do so, you carry out the following steps. To read an execution plan at first, you have to identify the combine operations (both related and unrelated) it is composed of. In other words, you identify each operation having more than one child. In the example in Figure 6-9, the combine operations are the following: 3, 4, 5, 6, and 14. Then, for each child operation of each combine operation, you define a block. Since in Figure 6-9 you have five combine operations and each of them has two children, you have a total of 10 blocks. For example, for operation 3, the first child consists of the lines from 4 to 12 (block G), and the second child consists of the lines from 13 to 16 (block J). Note that in Figure 6-9, each block is delimited by a frame. Finally, you need to find out in what order the blocks are executed. To see how this is done, let's walk through the execution plan shown in Figure 6-9 and apply the rules discussed previously:

1. Operation 1 is a stand-alone operation, and its child (2) is executed before it.

2. Operation 2 is a stand-alone operation, and its child (3) is executed before it.

3. Operation 3 is a related-combine operation, and its children are executed before it. Since the first child block (G) is executed before the second child block (J), let's continue with the first operation (4) of the first child block (G).

4. Operation 4 is an unrelated-combine operation, and its children are executed before it. Since the first child block (E) is executed before the second child block (F), let's continue with the first operation (5) of the first child block (E).

5. Operation 5 is a related-combine operation, and its children are executed before it. Since the first child block (C) is executed before the second child block (D), let's continue with the first operation (6) of the first child block (C).

6. Operation 6 is a related-combine operation, and its children are executed before it. Since the first child block (A) is executed before the second child block (B), let's continue with the first operation (7) of the first child block (A).

7. Operation 7 is a stand-alone operation and has no children. This means that you have finally found the first operation to be executed (hence it's in block A). The operation scans a table and returns the rows to its parent operation (6).

8. Block B is executed for each row returned by block A. In this block, operation 9 scans an index at first, and operation 8 accesses a table with the returned rowids and finally returns the rows to its parent operation (6).

9. Operation 6 performs the join between the rows returned by blocks A and B and then returns the result to its parent operation (5).

10. Block D is executed for each row returned by block C. In other words, it is executed for each row returned by operation 6 to its parent operation (5). In this block, operation 11 scans an index initially. Then, operation 10 accesses a table with the returned rowids and returns the rows to its parent operation (5).

11. Operation 5 performs the join between the rows returned by the blocks C and D and then returns the result to its parent operation (4).

12. Operation 12 (block F) is executed only once. It scans a table and returns the result to its parent operation (4).

13. Operation 4 performs the join between the rows returned by the blocks E and F and then returns the result to its parent operation (3).

14. Block J is basically executed for each row returned by block G. In other words, it is executed for each row returned by operation 4 to its parent operation (3). In this block, operation 15 scans a table at first and returns the rows to its parent operation (14). Then, operation 16 scans a table and returns the rows to its parent operation (14). After that, operation 14 puts the rows returned by its children together and returns the result to its parent operation (13). Finally, operation 13 removes some duplicate rows. Note that this block doesn't return data to its parent. In fact, the parent is a FILTER operation, and the second child is used to apply a restriction only.

15. Once operation 3 has applied the filter with the block J, it returns the result to its parent operation (2).

16. Operation 2 performs a GROUP BY and returns the result to its parent operation (1).

17. Operation 1 applies a filter and returns the result to the caller.

In summary, note that blocks are executed according to their identifier (from A up to J). Some blocks (A, C, E, F, and G) are executed once at most, and others (B, D, H, I, and J) are executed several times depending on how many rows are returned by the operations driving them.

Special Cases

The rules described in the previous sections apply to almost all execution plans. Nevertheless, there are some special cases. Usually you are able to find out what's going on by looking at the operations, the tables on which they are executed, and their runtime behavior (especially the columns Starts and A-Rows). Here are two examples.

For the first example, a query containing a subquery in the SELECT clause is used. The query and its execution plan are the following:

```
SELECT ename, (SELECT dname FROM dept WHERE dept.deptno = emp.deptno)
FROM emp
```

```
-----------------------------------------------------------------
| Id | Operation                   | Name    | Starts | A-Rows |
-----------------------------------------------------------------
|  1 | TABLE ACCESS BY INDEX ROWID | DEPT    |    3   |    3   |
|* 2 |   INDEX UNIQUE SCAN         | DEPT_PK |    3   |    3   |
|  3 | TABLE ACCESS FULL           | EMP     |    1   |   14   |
-----------------------------------------------------------------

   2 - access("DEPT"."DEPTNO"=:B1)
```

The strange thing in this execution plan is the missing parent for operations 1 and 3. If you look carefully at the column Starts, you will notice that although operations 1 and 2 are executed three times, operation 3 is executed only once. This unusual execution plan carries out the operations as follows:

1. Operation 3 scans the table emp and returns all rows. Basically, for each row returned by the operation 3, the subquery should be executed once. However, also in this case the SQL engine caches the results, and therefore, the subquery is executed only once for each distinct value in the column deptno.

2. To execute the subquery, operation 2 does a scan of the index dept_pk by applying the access predicate "DEPT"."DEPTNO"=:B1, extracts the rowids, and returns them to its parent operation (1). The bind variable (B1) is used to pass the value to be checked to the subquery. Then operation 1 accesses the table dept with those rowids.

For the second example, a query containing a NOT IN is used. The query and its execution plan are the following:

```
SELECT deptno
FROM dept
WHERE deptno NOT IN (SELECT deptno FROM emp)
```

```
---------------------------------------------------------
| Id  | Operation          | Name    | Starts | A-Rows |
---------------------------------------------------------
|*  1 |  INDEX FULL SCAN   | DEPT_PK |      1 |      1 |
|*  2 |   TABLE ACCESS FULL| EMP     |      4 |      3 |
---------------------------------------------------------

   1 - filter( NOT EXISTS (SELECT /*+ */ 0 FROM "EMP" "EMP" WHERE
               LNNVL("DEPTNO"<>:B1)))
   2 - filter(LNNVL("DEPTNO"<>:B1))
```

───

▓**Caution** This query is another case where the views v$sql_plan and v$sql_plan_statistics_all show wrong information. In this case, the wrongly displayed predicates are the following:

```
   1 - filter( IS NULL)
   2 - filter(LNNVL("DEPTNO"<>:B1))
```

───

At first sight, this execution plan is composed from two stand-alone operations. If you carefully look at the column Starts, you'll notice something strange. In fact, although the parent operation (1) is executed only once, the child operation (2) is executed four times. Actually, this execution plan carries out the operations as follows:

1. Operation 1, which is the first being executed, scans the index dept_pk.

2. For each value in the column deptno, operation 2 is executed. As shown by the predicates, this operation is because of the subquery NOT EXISTS (SELECT 0 FROM "EMP" "EMP" WHERE LNNVL("DEPTNO"<>:B1)). Notice that the query optimizer transformed the NOT IN into a NOT EXISTS. The bind variable (B1) is used to pass the value to be checked to the subquery.

Please note that these are only two examples of many possible cases. Basically, each time you see something strange, you should be careful to not draw conclusions too quickly.

Recognizing Inefficient Execution Plans

The sad truth is, the only way to be sure that an execution plan is not the most efficient one is to find another one that is faster. Nevertheless, simple checks might reveal clues that suggest an inefficient execution plan. The following sections will describe two checks that I use for that purpose.

Wrong Estimations

The idea behind this check is very simple. The query optimizer computes costs to decide which access paths, join orders, and join methods should be used to get an efficient execution plan. If the computation of the cost is wrong, it is likely that the query optimizer picks out a suboptimal execution plan. In other words, wrong estimations easily lead to making a mistake in the choice of an execution plan.

Judging the cost directly of a SQL statement itself is not feasible in practice. It is much easier to check other estimations performed by the query optimizer, which the computation of the cost is based on: the estimated number of rows (cardinality) returned by an operation. Checking the estimated cardinality is quite easy because you are able, with the function display_ cursor in the package dbms_xplan, for example, to directly compare it with the actual cardinality. As you have just seen, only if the two cardinalities are close did the query optimizer do a good job. One of the central characteristics of this method is that no information about the SQL statement or the database structure is necessary to judge the quality of the execution plan. You simply concentrate on comparing the estimations with the actual data.

Let me illustrate this concept with an example. The following excerpt of the output produced by the script wrong_estimations.sql shows an execution plan with its estimated (E-Rows) and actual (A-Rows) cardinalities. As you can see, the estimation of operation 4 (and consequently of operations 2 and 3) is completely wrong. The query optimizer estimated, for operation 4, a return of only 32 rows instead of 80,016. To make things worse, operation 2 is a related-combine operation. This means that operations 5 and 6, instead of being executed only 32 times as estimated, are in fact executed 80,016 times. This is also confirmed by the value in the column Starts. It is important to note that the estimations for operations 5 and 6 are correct. In fact, before making the comparison, the actual cardinality (A-Rows) must be divided by the number of executions (Starts).

```
SELECT count(t2.col2)
FROM t1 JOIN t2 USING (id)
WHERE t1.col1 = 666
```

```
-----------------------------------------------------------------------
| Id  | Operation                          | Name    | Starts | E-Rows | A-Rows |
-----------------------------------------------------------------------
|   1 |  SORT AGGREGATE                    |         |      1 |      1 |      1 |
|   2 |   NESTED LOOPS                     |         |      1 |     32 |  75808 |
|   3 |    TABLE ACCESS BY INDEX ROWID|     | T1      |      1 |     32 |  80016 |
|*  4 |     INDEX RANGE SCAN               | T1_COL1 |      1 |     32 |  80016 |
|   5 |    TABLE ACCESS BY INDEX ROWID|     | T2      |  80016 |      1 |  75808 |
|*  6 |     INDEX UNIQUE SCAN              | T2_PK   |  80016 |      1 |  75808 |
-----------------------------------------------------------------------
```

```
   4 - access("T1"."COL1"=666)
   6 - access("T1"."ID"="T2"."ID")
```

To understand the problem, you have to carefully analyze why the query optimizer is not able to compute good estimations. The cardinality is computed by multiplying the selectivity by the number of rows in the table. Therefore, if the cardinality is wrong, the problem can have only three possible causes: a wrong selectivity, a wrong number of rows, or a bug in the query optimizer.

In this case, our analysis should start by looking at the estimation performed for operation 4. In other words, the estimation related to the predicate "T1"."COL1"=666. Since the query optimizer bases its estimation on object statistics, let's see whether they describe the current data. With the following query, you are able to get the object statistics for index t1_col1 used for operation 4. At the same time, it is possible to compute the average number of rows per key. This is basically the value used for the query optimizer when no histogram is available.

```
SQL> SELECT num_rows, distinct_keys, num_rows/distinct_keys AS avg_rows_per_key
  2  FROM user_indexes
  3  WHERE index_name = 'T1_COL1';
```

```
  NUM_ROWS DISTINCT_KEYS AVG_ROWS_PER_KEY
---------- ------------- ----------------
    160000          5000               32
```

It is useful to notice that in this case, the average number of rows, 32, is the same as the estimated cardinality in the previous execution plan. To check whether these object statistics are good, you have to compare them with the actual data. So, let's execute the following query on table t1. As you can see, the query not only computes the object statistics of the previous query but also counts the number of rows for which the column col1 is different from 666.

```
SQL> SELECT count(*) AS num_rows, count(DISTINCT col1) AS distinct_keys,
  2          count(nullif(col1,666)) AS rows_per_key_666
  3  FROM t1;
```

```
NUM_ROWS DISTINCT_KEYS ROWS_PER_KEY_666
---------- ------------- ----------------
   160000          5000            79984
```

From the output, you can confirm that not only are the object statistics correct but that the data is also strongly skewed. As a result, a histogram is absolutely essential for correct estimations. With the following query, you can confirm that no histogram exists in this case:

```
SQL> SELECT histogram, num_buckets
  2  FROM user_tab_col_statistics
  3  WHERE table_name = 'T1' AND column_name = 'COL1';

HISTOGRAM       NUM_BUCKETS
--------------- -----------
NONE                      1
```

After gathering the missing histogram, the query optimizer managed to correctly estimate cardinalities and, as a result, considered another execution plan to be the most efficient.

```
--------------------------------------------------------------
| Id | Operation         | Name | Starts | E-Rows | A-Rows |
--------------------------------------------------------------
|  1 | SORT AGGREGATE    |      |      1 |      1 |      1 |
|* 2 |  HASH JOIN        |      |      1 |  80000 |  75808 |
|* 3 |   TABLE ACCESS FULL| T1  |      1 |  80000 |  80016 |
|  4 |   TABLE ACCESS FULL| T2  |      1 |   151K |   151K |
--------------------------------------------------------------
```

Restriction Not Recognized

I must warn you that the check presented in the previous section is superior to this one. I usually use this second check only when I cannot apply the first one. This can happen, for example, while reading an output generated by TKPROF where only the actual cardinalities are available. Of course, it is always possible to generate the estimated cardinality and apply the check described in the previous section. This is bothersome, however, if the number of explain plans is high.

The idea of this check is to verify whether the query optimizer correctly recognized the restriction in the SQL statement and, as a result, applied it as soon as possible. In other words, you check to be sure the execution plan doesn't lead to unnecessary processing.

Let me illustrate this concept with an example. Here, a trace file is generated by the script restriction_not_recognized.sql and then analyzed with TKPROF. The following is an excerpt of the TKPROF output. From it, you can see that the query optimizer decided to start joining table t1 to table t2. This first join returned a result set of 40,000 rows. Later, the result set was joined to table t3. A result set of only 100 rows was generated, even though the operation reading table t3 returned 80,000 rows. This simply means that the query optimizer didn't recognize the restriction and applied it too late when a lot of processing was already being performed.

```
Rows      Row Source Operation
-------   --------------------------------------------------------
      1   SORT AGGREGATE (cr=2337 pr=4254 pw=2133 time=1594879 us)
    100    HASH JOIN  (cr=2337 pr=4254 pw=2133 time=1541152 us)
  40000     HASH JOIN  (cr=1018 pr=1453 pw=645 time=597110 us)
  20000      TABLE ACCESS FULL T1 (cr=329 pr=125 pw=0 time=140064 us)
  40000      TABLE ACCESS FULL T2 (cr=689 pr=683 pw=0 time=640647 us)
  80000     TABLE ACCESS FULL T3 (cr=1319 pr=1313 pw=0 time=321009 us)
```

In this specific case, the problem seems to be related to the estimation of join cardinalities. This is, *en passant,* one of the most difficult tasks the query optimizer has to perform. To check this assumption, you can use the SQL statement EXPLAIN PLAN, for example, to cause the following output to be generated. From it, you can see that the query optimizer expected 79,800 rows from the second join, while there were only 100 at runtime.

```
---------------------------------------------
| Id  | Operation           | Name | Rows  |
---------------------------------------------
|   0 | SELECT STATEMENT    |      |     1 |
|   1 |  SORT AGGREGATE     |      |     1 |
|*  2 |   HASH JOIN         |      | 79800 |
|*  3 |    HASH JOIN        |      | 40000 |
|   4 |     TABLE ACCESS FULL| T1  | 20000 |
|   5 |     TABLE ACCESS FULL| T2  | 40000 |
|   6 |    TABLE ACCESS FULL | T3  | 80000 |
---------------------------------------------
```

When you encounter such problems, there is little that you can do. In fact, there are no object statistics describing the relation between two tables. One possible way to correct a situation of this type is to use a SQL profile. Applying one in this case would give you the following execution plan. (I cover what a SQL profile is, and how it works, in Chapter 7.) For the moment, it is just important to realize that a solution exists. Notice that not only has the order of the join changed (t2 ➤ t3 ➤ t1) but that the access to table t1 is also different.

```
Rows      Row Source Operation
-------   --------------------------------------------------------
      1   SORT AGGREGATE (cr=2210 pr=2708 pw=713 time=561754 us)
    100    NESTED LOOPS  (cr=2210 pr=2708 pw=713 time=336045 us)
    100     HASH JOIN  (cr=2008 pr=2708 pw=713 time=335609 us)
  40000      TABLE ACCESS FULL T2 (cr=689 pr=683 pw=0 time=320792 us)
  80000      TABLE ACCESS FULL T3 (cr=1319 pr=1312 pw=0 time=560235 us)
    100     TABLE ACCESS BY INDEX ROWID T1 (cr=202 pr=0 pw=0 time=5632 us)
    100      INDEX UNIQUE SCAN T1_PK (cr=102 pr=0 pw=0 time=2428 us)
```

It is useful to note that this check can be applied at the same time as the check described in the previous section. In any case, both should point out that something is not good with the estimations performed for the very same operation. Since both checks reveal the same problem, it is better to just use the check described in the previous section whenever possible. The following is an excerpt of the output, comparing the estimations with the actual values:

```
---------------------------------------------------------------
| Id | Operation             | Name | Starts | E-Rows | A-Rows |
---------------------------------------------------------------
|  1 |  SORT AGGREGATE       |      |      1 |      1 |      1 |
|* 2 |   HASH JOIN           |      |      1 |  79800 |    100 |
|* 3 |    HASH JOIN          |      |      1 |  40000 |  40000 |
|  4 |     TABLE ACCESS FULL | T1   |      1 |  20000 |  20000 |
|  5 |     TABLE ACCESS FULL | T2   |      1 |  40000 |  40000 |
|  6 |    TABLE ACCESS FULL  | T3   |      1 |  80000 |  80000 |
---------------------------------------------------------------
```

On to Chapter 7

In this chapter, I described how to obtain execution plans through the SQL statement EXPLAIN PLAN, dynamic performance views, and some tracing facilities. As discussed for the first two techniques, the package dbms_xplan is the tool of choice for extracting and formatting execution plans. With it, you are able to get all the information you need simply, enabling you to understand execution plans. Some rules for interpreting execution plans and for recognizing whether they are efficient were discussed as well.

Clearly, inefficient execution plans should be tuned. The next chapter describes the SQL tuning techniques available for that purpose. Note that there are several techniques since each of them can be applied only in specific circumstances or for the tuning of particular problems only.

CHAPTER 7

■ ■ ■

SQL Tuning Techniques

Whenever the query optimizer is unable to automatically generate an efficient execution plan, some manual tuning is required. For that purpose, Oracle provides several techniques. Table 7-1 summarizes them. The goal of this chapter is not only to describe these techniques in detail but also to explain what each technique can do for you and in which situations you can take advantage of them. To choose one of them, it is essential to ask yourself three basic questions:

- Is the SQL statement known and static?

- Should the measures to be taken have an impact on a single SQL statement or on all SQL statements executed by a single session (or even from the whole system)?

- It is possible to change the SQL statement?

Let me explain why these three questions are so important. First, sometimes the SQL statements are simply unknown because they are generated at runtime and change virtually for each execution. In other situations, the query optimizer is not able to correctly deal with specific constructs (such as a restriction in the WHERE clause that cannot be applied through an index) that are used by lots of SQL statements. In both cases, you have to use techniques that solve the problem at the session or system level, not at the SQL statement level. This fact leads to two main problems. On one hand, as summarized in Table 7-1, several techniques can be used only for specific SQL statements. They are simply not applicable at the session or system level. On the other hand, as explained in Chapter 5, whenever your database schema is good and the configuration of the query optimizer is correctly performed, you usually have to tune a small number of SQL statements. Therefore, you want to avoid techniques impacting the SQL statements for which the query optimizer automatically provides an efficient execution plan.

Second, whenever you deal with an application for which you have no control over the SQL statements (either because the code is not available like in a packaged application or because it generates SQL statements at runtime), you cannot use techniques that require changes to the code. In summary, more often than not, your choice is restricted.

Table 7-1. *SQL Tuning Techniques and Their Impacts*

Technique	System	Session	SQL Statement	Availability
Altering the access structures	✓			All releases
Altering the SQL statement			✓*	All releases
Hints			✓*	All releases
Altering the execution environment		✓	✓*	All releases
SQL profiles			✓	as of 10g[†]
Stored outlines			✓	All releases
SQL plan baselines			✓	As of 11g[‡]

[*] *It is required to change the SQL statement to use this technique.*

[†] *The Tuning Pack and, therefore, Enterprise Edition are required.*

[‡] *Enterprise Edition is required.*

The aim of this chapter is not to describe how to find out what the best execution plan for a given SQL statement is, for example, by explaining in which situation a specific access or join method should be used. This analysis will be covered in Part 4. The purpose of this chapter is solely to describe the available SQL tuning techniques. It is worth mentioning that all SQL tuning techniques, except altering the access structures and altering the execution environment, are based on the fact that the query optimizer is unable to identify an efficient execution plan because of its limitations. Of course, this is true only if the configuration is correctly performed. In this chapter, it will be assumed that the initialization parameters are correctly set and that all the necessary system and object statistics are in place.

Each section that describes a SQL tuning technique is organized in the same way. A short introduction will be followed by a description of how the technique works and when you should use it. All sections end with a discussion of some common pitfalls and fallacies.

Altering the Access Structures

This technique is not tied to a specific feature. It is simply a fact that the response time of a SQL statement is strongly dependent not only on how the processed data is stored but also on how the processed data can be accessed.

How It Works

The first thing you have to do while questioning the performance of a SQL statement is to verify which access structures are in place. Based on the information you find in the data dictionary, you should answer the following questions:

- What is the organization type of the tables involved? Is it heap, index-organized, or external? Or is the table stored in a cluster?

- Are materialized views containing the needed data available?

- What indexes exist on the tables, clusters, and materialized views? Which columns do the indexes contain and in what order?

- How are all these segments partitioned?

Next you have to assess whether the available access structures are adequate to efficiently process the SQL statement you are tuning. For example, during this analysis, you may discover that an additional index is necessary to efficiently support the WHERE clause of the SQL statement. Let's say that you are investigating the performance of the following query:

```
SELECT *
FROM emp
WHERE empno = 7788
```

Basically, the following execution plans can be considered by the query optimizer to execute it. While the first performs a full table scan, the second accesses the table through an index. Naturally, the second can be considered only if the index exists.

```
---------------------------------
| Id | Operation       | Name |
---------------------------------
|  0 | SELECT STATEMENT |     |
|  1 |  TABLE ACCESS FULL| EMP |
---------------------------------


-----------------------------------------------
| Id | Operation                  | Name   |
-----------------------------------------------
|  0 | SELECT STATEMENT           |        |
|  1 |  TABLE ACCESS BY INDEX ROWID| EMP   |
|  2 |   INDEX UNIQUE SCAN        | EMP_PK |
-----------------------------------------------
```

No more information about this topic is provided here because Part 4 will cover when and how the different access structures should be used in detail. For the moment, it is just important to recognize that this is a fundamental SQL tuning technique.

When to Use It

Without the necessary access structures in place, it may be impossible to tune a SQL statement. Therefore, you should consider using this technique whenever you are able to change the access structures. Unfortunately, this is not always possible, such as when you are working with a packaged application and the vendor does not support altering the access structures.

Pitfalls and Fallacies

When altering the access structures, it is essential to carefully consider possible side effects. Generally speaking, every altered access structure introduces both positive and negative consequences. In fact, it is unlikely that the impact of such a measure is restricted to a single SQL statement. There are very few instances where this is not the case. For instance, if you add an index like in the previous example, you have to consider that the index will slow down the execution of every INSERT and DELETE statement on the indexed table as well as every UPDATE statement that modifies the indexed columns. It should also be checked whether the necessary space is available to add access structures. All things considered, it is necessary to carefully determine whether the pros outweigh the cons before altering access structures.

Altering the SQL Statement

SQL is a very powerful and flexible query language. Frequently, you are able to submit the very same request in many different ways. For developers, this is particularly useful. For the query optimizer, however, it is a real challenge to provide efficient execution plans for all sorts of SQL statements. Remember, flexibility is the enemy of performance.

How It Works

Let's say you are selecting all departments without employees in the schema scott. The following four SQL statements, which can be found in the script depts_wo_emps.sql, return the information you are looking for:

```
SELECT deptno
FROM dept
WHERE deptno NOT IN (SELECT deptno FROM emp)

SELECT deptno
FROM dept
WHERE NOT EXISTS (SELECT 1 FROM emp WHERE emp.deptno = dept.deptno)

SELECT deptno FROM dept
MINUS
SELECT deptno FROM emp

SELECT dept.deptno
FROM dept, emp
WHERE dept.deptno = emp.deptno(+) AND emp.deptno IS NULL
```

The purpose of these SQL statements is the same. The results they return are the same as well. Therefore, you might expect the query optimizer to provide the same execution plan in all cases. This is, however, not what happens. In fact, only the second and the fourth use the same execution plan. The others are quite different. Note these execution plans were generated on Oracle Database 10g Release 2. Other versions will probably generate different execution plans.

```
---------------------------------------
| Id | Operation           | Name    |
---------------------------------------
|  0 | SELECT STATEMENT    |         |
|  1 |  INDEX FULL SCAN    | DEPT_PK |
|  2 |   TABLE ACCESS FULL | EMP     |
```

```
----------------------------------------
| Id | Operation          | Name   |
----------------------------------------
|  0 | SELECT STATEMENT   |        |
|  1 |  HASH JOIN ANTI    |        |
|  2 |   INDEX FULL SCAN  | DEPT_PK |
|  3 |   TABLE ACCESS FULL| EMP    |
----------------------------------------

----------------------------------------
| Id | Operation          | Name   |
----------------------------------------
|  0 | SELECT STATEMENT   |        |
|  1 |  MINUS             |        |
|  2 |   SORT UNIQUE NOSORT|       |
|  3 |    INDEX FULL SCAN  | DEPT_PK |
|  4 |   SORT UNIQUE      |        |
|  5 |    TABLE ACCESS FULL| EMP   |
----------------------------------------

----------------------------------------
| Id | Operation          | Name   |
----------------------------------------
|  0 | SELECT STATEMENT   |        |
|  1 |  HASH JOIN ANTI    |        |
|  2 |   INDEX FULL SCAN  | DEPT_PK |
|  3 |   TABLE ACCESS FULL| EMP    |
----------------------------------------
```

Basically, although the method used to access the data is always the same, the method used to combine the data to produce the result set is different. In this specific case, the two tables are very small, and consequently, you wouldn't notice any real performance difference with these three execution plans. Naturally, if you are dealing with much bigger tables, this may not necessarily be the case. Generally speaking, whenever you process a large amount of data, every small difference in the execution plan could lead to substantial differences in the response time or resource utilization.

The key point here is to realize that the very same data can be extracted by means of different SQL statements. Whenever you are tuning a SQL statement, you should ask yourself whether other equivalent SQL statements exist. If they do, compare them carefully to assess which one provides the best performance.

When to Use It

Whenever you are able to change the SQL statement, you should consider this technique. There is no reason for not doing it.

Pitfalls and Fallacies

SQL statements are code. The first rule of writing code is to make it maintainable. In the first place, this means that it should be readable and concise. Unfortunately, with SQL, because of the reasons explained earlier, the simplest or most readable way of writing a SQL statement doesn't always lead to the most efficient execution plan. Consequently, in some situations you may be forced to give up readability and conciseness for performance, although only when it is really necessary and profitable to do so.

Hints

According to the Merriam-Webster online dictionary, a *hint* is an indirect or summary suggestion. In Oracle's parlance, the definition of a hint is a bit different. Simply put, hints are directives added to SQL statements to influence the query optimizer's decisions. In other words, it is something that impels toward an action, not merely suggesting one. It seems to me that Oracle's choice of this word was not the best when naming this feature. In any case, the name is not that important. What hints can do for you is. Just don't let the name mislead you.

■**Caution** Just because a hint is a directive, it doesn't mean that the query optimizer will always use it. Or, seeing it the other way around, just because a hint is not used by the query optimizer, it doesn't imply that a hint is merely a suggestion. As I will describe in a moment, there are cases where a hint is simply not relevant or legal, and therefore, it has no influence over the execution plan generated by the query optimizer.

How It Works

The following sections describe what hints are, which categories of hints exist, and how to use them. The essential thing to note before looking at the details is that using hints is not as trivial as you might think. Actually, in practice, it is quite common to see hints that are incorrectly applied.

What Are Hints?

While optimizing a SQL statement, the query optimizer may have to take a lot of execution plans into account. In theory, it should consider all possible execution plans. In practice, except for simple SQL statements, it is not feasible to consider too many combinations in order to keep the optimization time reasonable. Consequently, the query optimizer excludes some of the execution plans *a priori*. Of course, the decision to completely ignore some of them may be critical, and the query optimizer's credibility is at stake in doing so.

Whenever you specify a hint, your goal is to reduce the number of execution plans considered by the query optimizer. Basically, with a hint you tell the query optimizer which operations should or should not be considered for a specific SQL statement. For instance, let's say the query optimizer has to produce the execution plan for the following query:

```
SELECT *
FROM emp
WHERE empno = 7788
```

If the table emp is a heap table and its column empno is indexed, the query optimizer considers at least two execution plans. The first is to completely read the table emp through a full table scan:

```
-----------------------------------
| Id | Operation        | Name |
-----------------------------------
|  0 | SELECT STATEMENT |      |
|  1 |  TABLE ACCESS FULL| EMP |
-----------------------------------
```

The second is to do an index lookup based on the predicate in the WHERE clause (empno = 7788) and then, through the rowid found in the index, to access the table:

```
-----------------------------------------------
| Id | Operation                   | Name    |
-----------------------------------------------
|  0 | SELECT STATEMENT            |         |
|  1 |  TABLE ACCESS BY INDEX ROWID| EMP     |
|  2 |   INDEX UNIQUE SCAN         | EMP_PK  |
-----------------------------------------------
```

In such a case, to control the execution plan provided by the query optimizer, you could add a hint specifying to use either the full table scan or the index scan. The important thing to understand is that you cannot tell the query optimizer "I want a full table scan on table emp, so search for an execution plan containing it." However, you can tell it "If you have to decide between a full table scan and an index scan on table emp, take a full table scan." This is a slight but fundamental difference. Hints can allow you to influence the query optimizer when it has to choose between several possibilities.

To further emphasize this essential point, let's take an example based on the decision tree shown in Figure 7-1. Note that even if the query optimizer works with decision trees, this is a general example not directly related to Oracle. In Figure 7-1, the aim is to descend the decision tree by starting at the root node (1) and ending at a leaf node (111–123). In other words, the goal is to choose a path going from point A to point B. Let's say that, for some reason, it is necessary to go through node 122. To do so, two hints, in the Oracle parlance, are added to prune the paths from node 12 to the nodes 121 and 123. In this way, the only path going on from node 12 leads to the node 122. But this is not enough to ensure that the path goes through node 122. In fact, if at node 1 it goes through node 11 instead of node 12, the two hints would never have an effect. Therefore, to lead the path through node 122, you should add another hint pruning the path from node 1 to node 11.

Something similar may happen with the query optimizer as well. In fact, hints are evaluated only when they apply to a decision that the query optimizer has to take. No more, no less. For this reason, as soon as you specify a hint, you may be forced to add several of them to ensure it works. And, in practice, as the complexity of the execution plans increases, it is more and more difficult to find all the necessary hints that lead to the desired execution plan.

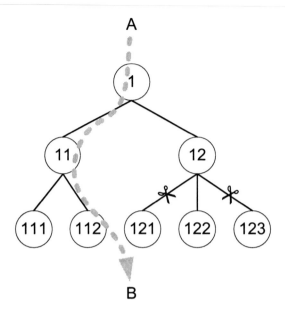

Figure 7-1. *Pruning of a decision tree*

Specifying Hints

Hints are an Oracle extension. To not jeopardize the compatibility of the SQL statements with other database engines, Oracle decided to add them as a special kind of comment. The only differences between comments and hints are the following:

- Hints must follow immediately after DELETE, INSERT, MERGE, SELECT, and UPDATE keywords. In other words, they cannot be specified anywhere in the SQL statement as comments can.

- The first character after the comment delimiter must be a plus sign (+).

Syntactical errors in hints do not raise errors. If the parser does not manage to parse them, they are simply considered real comments. It is also possible to mix comments and hints. Here are two examples that show how to force a full table scan on table emp for the query discussed in the previous section:

```
SELECT /*+ full(emp) */ *
FROM emp
WHERE empno = 7788

SELECT --+ full(emp) you can also add a real comment without invalidating the hint
       *
FROM emp
WHERE empno = 7788
```

Categories of Hints

There are several methods (points of view) of categorizing hints. Personally, I like to group them in the following categories:

- *Initialization parameter hints* overwrite the setting of some initialization parameters defined at the system or session level. I classify the following hints in this category: all_rows, cursor_sharing_exact, dynamic_sampling, first_rows, gather_plan_ statistics, no_cpu_costing, optimizer_features_enable, opt_param, (no_)result_cache, and rule. I'll cover these hints in the section "Altering the Execution Environment" later in this chapter, and I covered the hint gather_plan_statistics in Chapter 6. Note that these hints always overwrite the values set at the instance or session level when they are specified.

- *Query transformation hints* control the utilization of query transformation techniques during the logical optimization. I put the following hints in this category: (no_)eliminate_join, no_expand, (no_)merge, (no_)outer_join_to_inner, (no_)push_pred, (no_)push_subq, no_query_transformation, (no_)rewrite, (no_)unnest, no_xmlindex_ rewrite, no_xml_query_rewrite, and use_concat. I'll cover some of these hints later in this chapter and some others in Chapter 10 and Chapter 11.

- *Access path hints* control the method used to access data (for example, whether an index is used). I classify the following hints in this category: cluster, full, hash, (no_)index, index_asc, index_combine, index_desc, (no_)index_ffs, index_join, (no_)index_ss, index_ss_asc, and index_ss_desc. I'll cover these hints along with access methods in Chapter 9.

- *Join hints* control not only the join method but also the order used to join tables. I put the following hints in this category: leading, (no_)nlj_batching, ordered, (no_)star_transformation, (no_)swap_join_inputs, (no_)use_hash, (no_)use_merge, use_merge_cartesian, (no_)use_nl, and use_nl_with_index. I'll cover these hints along with the join methods in Chapter 10.

- *Parallel processing hints* control how parallel processing is used. I classify the following hints in this category: (no_)parallel, (no_)parallel_index, pq_distribute, and (no_)px_join_filter. I'll cover these hints along with parallel processing in Chapter 11. A possible utilization of the hint pq_distribute is provided along with partition-wise joins in Chapter 10.

- *Other hints* control the utilization of other features that are not related to the previous categories. I classify the following hints in this category: (no_)append, (no_)cache, driving_site, model_min_analysis, (no_)monitor, and qb_name. I'll cover the hint qb_name later in this chapter and some others in Chapter 11.

Although through this book I describe or show plenty of examples of these hints, I will provide neither real references nor their full syntax. Such references are given in Chapter 2 of the *SQL Reference* manual.

It is worth pointing out that a significant number of hints disabling a specific operation or feature (the hints prefixed by no_) are available. This is good because it is sometimes easier to specify which operation or feature should not be used rather than specify which one should be used.

The list of hints just provided is not complete. In fact, there are other hints that are not documented and used only internally by Oracle. You will see some examples in the section "SQL Profiles" later in this chapter. As of Oracle Database 11g, you can select the view v$sql_hint to get what is probably a complete list of all hints.

Validity of Hints

Simple SQL statements have a single query block. Multiple query blocks exist whenever views or constructs such as subqueries, in-line views, and set operators are used. For example, the following query has two query blocks (I'm using the subquery factoring clause instead of defining a real view for illustration purposes only). The first is the main query that references the table dept. The second is the subquery that references the table emp:

```
WITH emps AS (SELECT deptno, count(*) AS cnt
              FROM emp
              GROUP BY deptno)
SELECT dept.dname, emps.cnt
FROM dept, emps
WHERE dept.deptno = emps.deptno
```

Initialization parameter hints are valid for the whole SQL statement. All other hints are valid for a single query block only. Hints valid for a single query block have to be specified in the block they control. For instance, if you want to specify an access path hint for both tables in the earlier query, one hint has to be added into the main query and the other in the subquery. The validity of both is restricted to the query block where they are defined.

```
WITH
  emps AS (SELECT /*+ full(emp) */ deptno, count(*) AS cnt
           FROM emp
           GROUP BY deptno)
SELECT /*+ full(dept) */ dept.dname, emps.cnt
FROM dept, emps
WHERE dept.deptno = emps.deptno
```

Exceptions to this rule are the *global hints*. With them it is possible to reference objects contained in other query blocks (provided they are named) by using the dot notation. For example, in the following SQL statement, the main query contains a hint intended for the subquery. Notice how the subquery name is used for the reference.

```
WITH
  emps AS (SELECT deptno, count(*) AS cnt
           FROM emp
           GROUP BY deptno)
SELECT /*+ full(dept) full(emps.emp) */ dept.dname, emps.cnt
FROM dept, emps
WHERE dept.deptno = emps.deptno
```

The syntax of global hints supports references for more than two levels (for example, for a view referenced in another view). The objects must simply be separated by a dot.

Since subqueries in the WHERE clause are not named, their objects cannot be referenced with global hints. To solve this problem, as of Oracle Database 10*g*, there is another way to achieve the same result. In fact, most hints accept a parameter specifying for which query block they are valid. In this way, the hints may be grouped at the beginning of a SQL statement and simply reference the query block to which they apply. To allow these references, not only does the query optimizer generate a *query block name* for each query block, but it also allows you to specify your own names through the hint qb_name. For instance, in the following query, the two query blocks are called main and sq, respectively. Then, in the hint full, the query block names are referenced by prefixing them with an "at" sign (@). Notice how the access path hint for the table emp of the subquery is specified in the main query.

```
WITH
  emps AS (SELECT /*+ qb_name(sq) */ deptno, count(*) AS cnt
           FROM emp
           GROUP BY deptno)
SELECT /*+ qb_name(main) full(@main dept) full(@sq emp) */ dept.dname, emps.cnt
FROM dept, emps
WHERE dept.deptno = emps.deptno
```

The previous example showed how to specify your own names. Now let's see how you can use the names generated by the query optimizer. First, you have to know what they are. For that you can use the SQL statement EXPLAIN PLAN and the package dbms_xplan, as shown in the following example. Note that the option alias is passed to the function display to make sure that the query block names and aliases are part of the output.

```
SQL> EXPLAIN PLAN FOR
  2  WITH
  3    emps AS (SELECT deptno, count(*) AS cnt
  4             FROM emp
  5             GROUP BY deptno)
  6  SELECT dept.dname, emps.cnt
  7  FROM dept, emps
  8  WHERE dept.deptno = emps.deptno;

SQL> SELECT * FROM table(dbms_xplan.display(NULL, NULL, 'basic +alias'));
```

```
-------------------------------------------------
| Id | Operation                     | Name    |
-------------------------------------------------
|  0 | SELECT STATEMENT              |         |
|  1 |  MERGE JOIN                   |         |
|  2 |   TABLE ACCESS BY INDEX ROWID | DEPT    |
|  3 |    INDEX FULL SCAN            | DEPT_PK |
|  4 |   SORT JOIN                   |         |
|  5 |    VIEW                       |         |
|  6 |     HASH GROUP BY             |         |
```

```
|  7 |         TABLE ACCESS FULL     | EMP    |
-------------------------------------------------

   1 - SEL$2
   2 - SEL$2 / DEPT@SEL$2
   3 - SEL$2 / DEPT@SEL$2
   5 - SEL$1 / EMPS@SEL$2
   6 - SEL$1
   7 - SEL$1 / EMP@SEL$1
```

The system-generated query block names are composed of a prefix followed by an alphanumeric string. The prefix is based on the operation contained in the query block. Table 7-2 summarizes them. The alphanumeric string is a numeration of the query blocks, based on their position (left to right) during the parse of the SQL statement. In the previous example, the main query block is named SEL$2, and the subquery query block is named SEL$1.

Table 7-2. *Prefixes Used in Query Block Names*

Prefix	Used For
CRI$	CREATE INDEX statements
DEL$	DELETE statements
INS$	INSERT statements
MISC$	Miscellaneous SQL statements like LOCK TABLE
MRG$	MERGE statements
SEL$	SELECT statements
SET$	Set operators like UNION and MINUS
UPD$	UPDATE statements

As shown here, the utilization of system-generated query block names is not different from the utilization of user-defined query block names.

```
WITH
  emps AS (SELECT deptno, count(*) AS cnt
           FROM emp
           GROUP BY deptno)
SELECT /*+ full(@sel$2 dept) full(@sel$1 emp) */ dept.dname, emps.cnt
FROM dept, emps
WHERE dept.deptno = emps.deptno
```

I'll make one last comment about the naming of the query blocks generated during the query transformation phase. Since they are not part of the SQL statement during the parse, they cannot be numbered like the others. In such cases, the query optimizer generates an eight-character hash value for them. The following example shows that situation. Here, the system-generated query block name is SEL$5DA710D3.

```
SQL> EXPLAIN PLAN FOR
  2  SELECT deptno
  3  FROM dept
  4  WHERE NOT EXISTS (SELECT 1 FROM emp WHERE emp.deptno = dept.deptno);

SQL> SELECT * FROM table(dbms_xplan.display(NULL,NULL,'basic +alias'));

----------------------------------------
| Id  | Operation         | Name    |
----------------------------------------
|  0  | SELECT STATEMENT  |         |
|  1  |  HASH JOIN ANTI   |         |
|  2  |   INDEX FULL SCAN | DEPT_PK |
|  3  |   TABLE ACCESS FULL| EMP    |
----------------------------------------

   1 - SEL$5DA710D3
   2 - SEL$5DA710D3 / DEPT@SEL$1
   3 - SEL$5DA710D3 / EMP@SEL$2
```

In the previous output, it is interesting to notice that when such a transformation takes place, for some lines in the execution plan there are two query block names. Both can be used in hints. However, the query block name after the transformation (in this case SEL$5DA710D3) is available, from a query optimizer point of view, only when the very same transformation takes place.

When to Use It

The purpose of hints is twofold. First, they are convenient as workarounds when the query optimizer does not manage to automatically generate an efficient execution plan. In such cases, you would use them to get a better execution plan. The important thing to emphasize is that hints are workarounds and, therefore, should not be used as long-term solutions. In some situations, however, they are the only practicable way to solve a problem. Second, hints are useful for assessing the decisions of the query optimizer in that they lead to the generation of alternative execution plans. In such cases, you would use them to do a kind of what-if analysis.

Pitfalls and Fallacies

Every time you want to lock up a specific execution plan through access path hints, join hints, or parallel processing hints, you must carefully specify enough hints to achieve stability. Here, stability means that even if the object statistics and, to some extent, the access structures change, the plan does not change. To lock up a specific execution plan, it is not unusual to have to add not only an access path hint for each table in the SQL statement but also several join hints to control the join methods and order. Note that other types of hints (for example, initialization parameter hints and query transformation hints) are usually not subject to this problem.

While processing a SQL statement, the parser checks the syntax of the hints. In spite of this, no error is raised when a hint is found with invalid syntax. This implies that the parser considers this particular pseudohint to be a comment. From one perspective, this is annoying if it is because of a typing error. On the other hand, this is beneficial because it avoids breaking an already deployed application because of changes to the access structures, which are often referenced in hints (for example, the hint index might reference an index name), or an upgrade to a newer database version. That said, I would welcome a way of validating the hints contained in a SQL statement. For instance, through the EXPLAIN PLAN statement, it should be simple enough to provide a warning (for example, a new note in the dbms_xplan output) in that regard. The only way I know to be able to do this partially is by setting the event 10132. In fact, as of Oracle Database 10g, at the end of the output generated by this event, there is a section dedicated to hints. You can check two things in this section. First, each hint should be listed. If a hint is missing, it means that it has not been recognized as such. Second, check whether a message informing that some hints have errors is present. (The field err is set to a value greater than 0 in such cases.) Note that to get the following output, two initialization parameter hints that conflict with each other were specified.

```
Dumping Hints
=============
atom_hint=(@=0x2a96c1b err=6 resol=1 used=0 token=453 org=1 lvl=2 txt=FIRST_ROWS ())
atom_hint=(@=0x2a96c1f err=6 resol=1 used=0 token=454 org=1 lvl=2 txt=ALL_ROWS ())
********** WARNING: SOME HINTS HAVE ERRORS *********
```

Be aware that with this method, hints having good syntax but referencing wrong objects are not reported as having errors. So, this is not a definitive check that everything is fine.

One of the most common mistakes made in the utilization of hints is related to table aliases. The rule is that when a table is referenced in a hint, the alias should be used instead of the table name, whenever the table has an alias. In the following example, you can see how a table alias (e) is defined for the table emp. In such a case, when the hint full referencing the table uses the table name, the hint has no effect. Notice how in the first example, an index scan is used instead of the wanted full table scan:

```
SQL> EXPLAIN PLAN FOR SELECT /*+ full(emp) */ * FROM emp e WHERE empno = 778

SQL> SELECT * FROM table(dbms_xplan.display(NULL,NULL,'basic +alias'));


-----------------------------------------------
| Id  | Operation                   | Name   |
-----------------------------------------------
|   0 | SELECT STATEMENT            |        |
|   1 |  TABLE ACCESS BY INDEX ROWID| EMP    |
|   2 |   INDEX UNIQUE SCAN         | EMP_PK |
-----------------------------------------------

   1 - SEL$1 / E@SEL$1
   2 - SEL$1 / E@SEL$1

SQL> EXPLAIN PLAN FOR SELECT /*+ full(e) */ * FROM emp e WHERE empno = 7788;
```

```
SQL> SELECT * FROM table(dbms_xplan.display(null,null,'basic'));

---------------------------------
| Id | Operation         | Name |
---------------------------------
|  0 | SELECT STATEMENT  |      |
|  1 |  TABLE ACCESS FULL| EMP  |
---------------------------------
```

Something that should be checked but is frequently forgotten is the impact of hints during upgrades. Since hints are convenient workarounds in situations where the query optimizer does not manage to automatically provide efficient execution plans but their effect depends on the type of decision tree (see Figure 7-1) used by the query optimizer, whenever hinted SQL statements are executed from another database version (and, therefore, from another query optimizer version), they should be carefully checked. In other words, while validating an application against a new database version, the best practice is to reexamine and retest all SQL statements containing hints.

Because views may be used in different contexts, specifying hints in views is usually not recommended. If you really have to add hints in views, make sure that the hints make sense for all modules using them.

Altering the Execution Environment

Chapter 5 described how to configure the query optimizer. The configuration is the default execution environment used by all users connected to the database engine.. Consequently, it must be suitable for most of them. When a database is used by multiple applications (for example, because of database server consolidation) or by a single application with different requirements that depend on the module in use (for example, OLTP during the day and batch during the night), it is not uncommon for a single environment to not be adequate in every situation. In such cases, altering the execution environment at the session level or even at the SQL statement level could be appropriate.

How It Works

Altering the execution environment at the session level is completely different from doing it at the SQL statement level. Because of this, I'll describe the two situations in two distinct subsections. In addition, I'll describe several dynamic performance views displaying the environment related to an instance, a single session, or a child cursor.

Session Level

Most initialization parameters described in Chapter 5 can be changed at the session level with the SQL statement ALTER SESSION. So if you have users or modules requiring a particular configuration, you should simply change the defaults at the session level. For instance, to set up the execution environment, depending on the user connecting to the database, you could use a configuration table and a database trigger, as shown in the following example. You can find the SQL statements in the script exec_env_trigger.sql.

```
CREATE TABLE exec_env_conf (
  username  VARCHAR2(30),
  parameter VARCHAR2(80),
  value     VARCHAR2(512)
);

CREATE OR REPLACE TRIGGER execution_environment AFTER LOGON ON DATABASE
BEGIN
  FOR c IN (SELECT parameter, value
              FROM exec_env_conf
              WHERE username = sys_context('userenv','session_user'))
  LOOP
    EXECUTE IMMEDIATE 'ALTER SESSION SET ' || c.parameter || '=' || c.value;
  END LOOP;
END;
/
```

Then for each user requiring a particular configuration, you insert one row in the configuration table for each initialization parameter. For example, the following two INSERT statements change and define two parameters at the session level when the user ops$cha logs in.

```
INSERT INTO exec_env_conf VALUES ('OPS$CHA', 'optimizer_mode', 'first_rows_10');
INSERT INTO exec_env_conf VALUES ('OPS$CHA', 'optimizer_dynamic_sampling', '0');
```

Of course, you could also define the trigger for a single schema or perform other checks based, for example, on the userenv context.

SQL Statement Level

The execution environment at the SQL statement level is changed through the initialization parameter hints. Since hints are used, the behavior and properties of hints previously described apply in this case as well.

Not all initialization parameters making up the query optimizer configuration can be changed at the SQL statement level. Table 7-3 summarizes which parameters and values have corresponding initialization parameter hints in order to achieve the same configuration at the SQL statement level. Note that for some initialization parameters (for example, cursor_sharing), not all values can be set with hints.

Table 7-3. *Hints That Change the Query Optimizer Configuration at the SQL Statement Level*

Initialization Parameter	Hint
cursor_sharing=exact	cursor_sharing_exact
optimizer_dynamic_sampling=x	dynamic_sampling(x)
optimizer_features_enable=x.y.z	optimizer_features_enable('x.y.z')
optimizer_features_enable not set	optimizer_features_enable(default)
optimizer_index_caching=x	opt_param('optimizer_index_caching' x)

Table 7-3. *Hints That Change the Query Optimizer Configuration at the SQL Statement Level*

Initialization Parameter	Hint
optimizer_index_cost_adj=x	opt_param('optimizer_index_cost_adj' x)
optimizer_mode=all_rows	all_rows
optimizer_mode=first_rows	first_rows
optimizer_mode=first_rows_x	first_rows(x)
optimizer_mode=rule	rule
optimizer_secure_view_merging=x	opt_param('optimizer_secure_view_merging','x')
result_cache_mode=manual	no_result_cache
result_cache_mode=force	result_cache
star_transformation_enabled=x	opt_param('star_transformation_enabled','x')

The hints opt_param and optimizer_features_enable are available as of Oracle Database 10g only. The hints result_cache and no_result_cache are available as of Oracle Database 11g only.

With the hint dynamic_sampling, it is possible not only to overwrite the setting of the initialization parameter optimizer_dynamic_sampling at the SQL statement level but also to specify that dynamic sampling be restricted to a single table in a specific query block only. The whole syntax is the following: dynamic_sampling(@*qbname table level*), where qbname is the query block name, table is the table alias, and level is the dynamic sampling level.

Dynamic Performance Views

As of Oracle Database 10g, there are three dynamic performance views that provide information about the execution environment:

- v$sys_optimizer_env gives information about the execution environment at the instance level. For example, it is possible to find out which initialization parameters are not set to the default value.

```
SQL> SELECT name, value, default_value
  2  FROM v$sys_optimizer_env
  3  WHERE isdefault = 'NO';

NAME                            VALUE  DEFAULT_VALUE
------------------------------- ------ --------------
db_file_multiblock_read_count   16     8
```

- v$ses_optimizer_env gives information about the execution environment for each session. Since no column provides information about whether an initialization parameter has been modified at the system or session level, a query like the following can be used for that purpose:

```
SQL> SELECT name, value
  2  FROM v$ses_optimizer_env
  3  WHERE sid = 161 AND isdefault = 'NO'
  4  MINUS
  5  SELECT name, value
  6  FROM v$sys_optimizer_env;

NAME             VALUE
---------------  --------------
cursor_sharing   force
optimizer_mode   first_rows_10
```

- v$sql_optimizer_env gives information about the execution environment for each child cursor present in the library cache. For example, with a query like the following, it is possible to find out whether two child cursors belonging to the same parent cursor have a different execution environment.

```
SQL> SELECT e0.name, e0.value AS value_child_0, e1.value AS value_child_1
  2  FROM v$sql_optimizer_env e0, v$sql_optimizer_env e1
  3  WHERE e0.sql_id = e1.sql_id
  4  AND e0.sql_id = 'gqpw5sv948u96'
  5  AND e0.child_number = 0
  6  AND e1.child_number = 1
  7  AND e0.name = e1.name
  8  AND e0.value <> e1.value;

NAME                  VALUE_CHILD_0         VALUE_CHILD_1
--------------------  --------------------  --------------
hash_area_size        33554432              131072
optimizer_mode        first_rows_10         all_rows
cursor_sharing        force                 exact
workarea_size_policy  manual                auto
```

When to Use It

Whenever the default configuration is not suitable for part of the application or part of the users, it is a good thing to change it. While changing the initialization parameters at the session level should always be possible, hints can be used only when it is also possible to change the SQL statements.

Pitfalls and Fallacies

Altering the execution environment at the session level is easy when the setting can be centralized either in the database or in the application. Take extra care if you are using a connection pool shared by applications that need a different execution environment. In fact, session parameters are associated with the physical connection. Since the physical connection might have been used by another application, you must set the execution environment every time you get a connection from the pool (which is of course expensive, since additional round-trips to the database are needed). Because of this, if you have applications needing different execution environments, you should use different connection pools as well. In this way, you can have a single configuration for each connection pool, and by defining different users to connect to the database, you may possibly be able to centralize the configuration into a simple database trigger.

Altering the execution environment at the SQL statement level is subject to the same pitfalls and fallacies previously described for hints.

SQL Profiles

As of Oracle Database 10*g*, you can delegate SQL tuning to an extension of the query optimizer called *Automatic Tuning Optimizer*. It might seem strange to delegate this task to the same component that is not able to find an efficient execution plan in the first place. In reality, the two situations are very different. In fact, in normal circumstances the query optimizer is constrained to generate an execution plan very quickly, typically in the subsecond range. Instead, much more time can be given to the Automatic Tuning Optimizer to carry out an efficient execution plan. Further, it is also able to use time-consuming techniques such as what-if analyses and make strong utilization of dynamic sampling techniques to verify its estimations.

The Automatic Tuning Optimizer is exposed through the *SQL Tuning Advisor*. Its aim is to analyze SQL statements and to advise how to enhance their performance by either gathering missing or stale object statistics, creating new indexes, altering the SQL statement, or accepting a SQL profile. The following sections are dedicated to advice related to SQL profiles.

It is essential to understand that SQL profiles, officially, can be generated only through the SQL Tuning Advisor. Nevertheless, as I describe later in this section, you are also able to create them manually. You should be aware that this technique may not be supported by Oracle. For additional information, contact Oracle Support.

How It Works

The following sections describe what SQL profiles are and how to work with them; it will also provide information about their internal workings. To manage them, you can use a graphical interface that is integrated into Enterprise Manager. We will not spend time here looking at it, since in my opinion, if you understand what is going on in the background, you will have no problem using the graphical interface.

What Are SQL Profiles?

A *SQL profile* is an object containing information that helps the query optimizer find an efficient execution plan for a specific SQL statement. It provides information about the execution environment, object statistics, and corrections related to the estimations performed by the query optimizer. One of its main advantages is the ability to influence the query optimizer without modifying the SQL statement or the execution environment of the session executing it. In other words, it is transparent to the application connected to the database engine. To understand how SQL profiles work, let's look at how they are generated and utilized.

Figure 7-2 illustrates the steps carried out during the generation of a SQL profile. Simply put, the user asks the SQL Tuning Advisor to tune a SQL statement, and when a SQL profile is proposed, he accepts it.

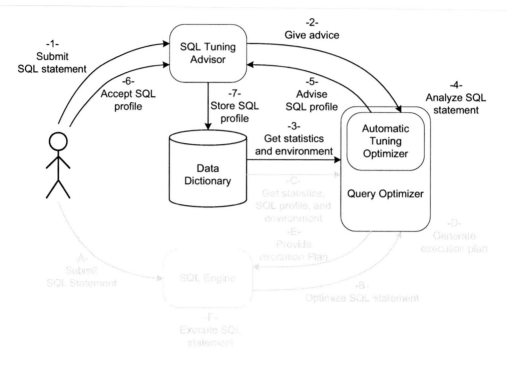

Figure 7-2. *Main steps carried out during the generation of a SQL profile*

Here are the steps in detail:

1. The user passes the poorly performing SQL statement to the SQL Tuning Advisor.

2. The SQL Tuning Advisor asks the Automatic Tuning Optimizer to give advice aimed at tuning the SQL statement.

3. The query optimizer gets the system statistics, the object statistics related to the objects referenced by the SQL statement, and the initialization parameters that set up the execution environment.

4. The SQL statement is analyzed. During this phase, the Automatic Tuning Optimizer performs what-if analyses and partially executes the SQL statement to confirm its guesses.

5. The Automatic Tuning Optimizer returns the SQL profile to the SQL Tuning Advisor.

6. The user accepts the SQL profile.

7. The SQL profile is stored in the data dictionary.

Figure 7-3 illustrates the steps carried out during the utilization of a SQL profile. The important thing is that the utilization is completely transparent to the user.

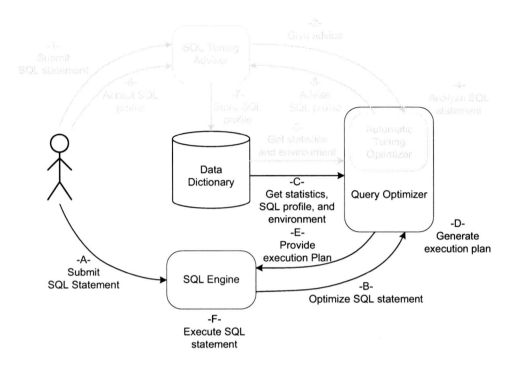

Figure 7-3. *Main steps carried out during the execution of a SQL statement*

Here are the steps in detail:

A. The user sends a SQL statement to be executed to the SQL engine.

B. The SQL engine asks the query optimizer to provide an execution plan.

C. The query optimizer gets the system statistics, the object statistics related to the objects referenced by the SQL statement, the SQL profile, and the initialization parameters that set up the execution environment.

D. The query optimizer analyzes the SQL statement and generates the execution plan.

E. The execution plan is passed to the SQL engine.

F. The SQL engine executes the SQL statement.

The next sections describe in detail the central steps carried out during the generation and utilization of SQL profiles. Special focus is given to the steps that involve the user. Let's start by describing the SQL Tuning Advisor.

SQL Tuning Advisor

The core interface of the SQL Tuning Advisor is available through the package dbms_sqltune. In addition, a graphical interface is integrated in Enterprise Manager. Both interfaces allow you to execute a *tuning task*. They also allow you to review the resulting advice and to accept it. I will not show you here how the graphical user interface works because it is more important to understand what goes on behind the scenes.

To start a tuning task, you have to call the function create_tuning_task and pass as a parameter one of the following (the function is overloaded four times to accept different kinds of parameters):

- The text of a SQL statement

- The reference (sql_id) to a SQL statement stored in the shared pool

- The reference (sql_id) to a SQL statement stored in the Automatic Workload Repository

- The name of a SQL tuning set

SQL TUNING SETS

Simply put, SQL tuning sets are objects that store a set of SQL statements along with their associated execution environments, execution statistics, and, optionally, execution plans. They are available as of Oracle Database 10*g*. SQL tuning sets are managed with the package dbms_sqltune. You can find more information about them in the *Performance Tuning Guide* manual.

To simplify the execution of the function create_tuning_task by taking as a parameter a single SQL statement, I wrote the script tune_last_statement.sql. The idea is that you execute the SQL statement that you want to have analyzed in SQL*Plus and then call the script without parameters. The script gets the reference (sql_id) of the last SQL statement executed by the current session from the view v$session and then creates and executes a tuning task referencing it. The central part of the script is the following anonymous PL/SQL block:

```
DECLARE
  l_sql_id v$session.prev_sql_id%TYPE;
  l_tuning_task VARCHAR2(30);
BEGIN
  SELECT prev_sql_id INTO l_sql_id
  FROM v$session
  WHERE audsid = sys_context('userenv','sessionid');
  l_tuning_task := dbms_sqltune.create_tuning_task(sql_id => l_sql_id);
  dbms_sqltune.execute_tuning_task(:tuning_task);
  dbms_output.put_line(l_tuning_task);
END;
```

The tuning task provides the output of its analysis in several data dictionary views. Instead of querying the views directly, which is a bit bothersome, you can use the function report_tuning_task in the package dbms_sqltune to generate a detailed report about the analysis. The following query shows an example of its utilization. Note that to reference the tuning task, the name of the tuning task returned by the previous PL/SQL block is used.

```
SELECT dbms_sqltune.report_tuning_task('TASK_16467')
FROM dual
```

A report generated by the previous query that advises to use a SQL profile looks like the following. Note that this is an excerpt of the output generated by the script `first_rows.sql`. The first section shows general information about the analysis and the SQL statement. The second section shows findings and recommendations. In this case, the advice is to accept a SQL profile. The last section shows the execution plans before and after applying the advice.

```
GENERAL INFORMATION SECTION
-------------------------------------------------------------------------------
Tuning Task Name                  : TASK_16467
Tuning Task Owner                 : OPS$CHA
Scope                             : COMPREHENSIVE
Time Limit(seconds)               : 42
Completion Status                 : COMPLETED
Started at                        : 07/19/2007 12:45:55
Completed at                      : 07/19/2007 12:45:55
Number of SQL Profile Findings    : 1


-------------------------------------------------------------------------------
Schema Name: OPS$CHA
SQL ID      : f3cq1hxz2d041
SQL Text    : SELECT * FROM T ORDER BY ID


-------------------------------------------------------------------------------
FINDINGS SECTION (1 finding)
-------------------------------------------------------------------------------


1- SQL Profile Finding (see explain plans section below)
--------------------------------------------------------
  A potentially better execution plan was found for this statement.

  Recommendation (estimated benefit: 97.21%)
  ----------------------------------------
  - Consider accepting the recommended SQL profile.
    execute dbms_sqltune.accept_sql_profile(task_name => 'TASK_16467',
            replace => TRUE);


-------------------------------------------------------------------------------
EXPLAIN PLANS SECTION
-------------------------------------------------------------------------------


1- Original With Adjusted Cost
------------------------------
Plan hash value: 961378228
```

```
----------------------------------------------------------------------------------
| Id | Operation          | Name | Rows  | Bytes |TempSpc| Cost (%CPU)| Time     |
----------------------------------------------------------------------------------
|  0 | SELECT STATEMENT   |      | 10000 | 1015K|       |  287   (1)| 00:00:04 |
|  1 |  SORT ORDER BY     |      | 10000 | 1015K| 2232K|  287   (1)| 00:00:04 |
|  2 |   TABLE ACCESS FULL| T    | 10000 | 1015K|       |   47   (0)| 00:00:01 |
----------------------------------------------------------------------------------
```

2- Using SQL Profile

Plan hash value: 1399892806

```
---------------------------------------------------------------------------------
| Id | Operation                  | Name | Rows  | Bytes | Cost (%CPU)| Time     |
---------------------------------------------------------------------------------
|  0 | SELECT STATEMENT           |      |    6  |  624 |    8   (0)| 00:00:01 |
|  1 |  TABLE ACCESS BY INDEX ROWID| T   | 10000 | 1015K|    8   (0)| 00:00:01 |
|  2 |   INDEX FULL SCAN          | T_PK |    6  |      |    2   (0)| 00:00:01 |
---------------------------------------------------------------------------------
```

To use the SQL profile advised by the SQL Tuning Advisor, you have to accept it. The next section describes how you do it. Independently of whether the SQL profile is accepted, once you no longer need the tuning task, you can drop it by calling the procedure drop_tuning_task in the package dbms_sqltune:

```
dbms_sqltune.drop_tuning_task('TASK_16467');
```

Accepting SQL Profiles

The procedure accept_sql_profile in the package dbms_sqltune is used to accept a SQL profile advised by the SQL Tuning Advisor. To accept the SQL profile advised in the previous report, you could use the following PL/SQL call. The parameters task_name and task_owner reference the tuning task that advises the SQL profile. The parameters name and description specify a name and a description for the SQL profile itself. In the example, I use the name of the script generating it as the name. The parameter category is used to group together several SQL profiles for management purposes. It defaults to the value default. The parameter replace specifies whether an already available SQL profile should be replaced. It defaults to FALSE. Finally, the parameter force_match specifies how text normalization is performed. It defaults to FALSE. The next section provides more information about text normalization. The only parameter that is mandatory is task_name. Note that the parameters replace and force_match exist only as of Oracle Database 10g Release 2.

```
dbms_sqltune.accept_sql_profile(
  task_name    => 'TASK_16467',
  task_owner   => 'OPS$CHA',
  name         => 'first_rows',
  description  => 'switch from ALL_ROWS to FIRST_ROWS_n',
  category     => 'TEST',
  replace      => TRUE,
```

```
  force_match => TRUE
);
```

Once accepted, the SQL profile is stored in the data dictionary. The view dba_sql_profiles displays information about it. Since SQL profiles are not tied to a specific user, the views all_sql_profiles and user_sql_profiles do not exist.

```
SQL> SELECT category, sql_text, force_matching
  2  FROM dba_sql_profiles
  3  WHERE name = 'first_rows';

CATEGORY   SQL_TEXT                        FORCE_MATCHING
---------  ------------------------------  ---------------
TEST       SELECT * FROM T ORDER BY ID  YES
```

The function accept_sql_profile that has the same purpose as the procedure accept_sql_profile is available as well. The only difference is that the function returns the name of the SQL profile. This is useful if the name is not specified as an input parameter and the system has to generate it as a result. Actually, in Oracle Database 10g Release 1, only the function is available.

Altering SQL Profiles

You can use the procedure alter_sql_profile in the package dbms_sqltune not only to modify some of the properties specified when the SQL profile was created but also to change its status (either enabled or disabled). With the following PL/SQL call, the SQL profile created by the previous example is disabled. The parameter name identifies the SQL profile to be modified. The parameters attribute_name and value specify the property to be modified and its new value. Note that the parameter attribute_name accepts the values name, description, category, and status. The three parameters are mandatory.

```
dbms_sqltune.alter_sql_profile(
  name             => 'first_rows',
  attribute_name => 'status',
  value            => 'disabled'
);
```

Text Normalization

One of the main advantages of a SQL profile is that although it applies to a specific SQL statement, no modification of the SQL statement itself is needed in order to use it. In fact, the SQL profiles are stored in the data dictionary, and the query optimizer selects them automatically. Figure 7-4 shows what the basic steps carried out during this selection are. First, the SQL statement is normalized to make it not only case insensitive but also independent of the used blank spaces. The signature is computed on the resulting SQL statement. Then, based on that signature, a lookup in the data dictionary is performed. Whenever a SQL profile with the same signature is found, a check is performed to make sure the SQL statement to be optimized and the SQL statement tied to the SQL profile are equivalent. This is necessary because the signature is a hash value, and, therefore, there could be conflicts. If the test is successful, the SQL profile is included in the generation of the execution plan.

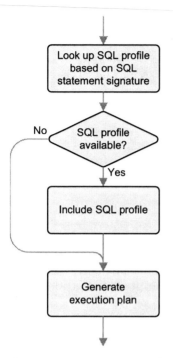

Figure 7-4. *Main steps carried out during the selection of a SQL profile*

If the SQL statement contains literals that change, it is likely that the signature, which is a hash value, changes as well. Because of this, the SQL profile may be useless since it is tied to a very specific SQL statement that will possibly never be executed again. As of Oracle Database 10*g* Release 2, to avoid this problem the database engine is able to remove literals during the normalization phase. This is done by setting the parameter force_match to TRUE while accepting the SQL profile.

To investigate how text normalization works, you can use the function sqltext_to_ signature in the package dbms_sqltune. It takes two parameters, sql_text and force_match, as input. The former specifies the SQL statement, and the latter specifies the kind of text normalization to be used. The following excerpt of the output generated by the script sqltext_to_ signature.sql shows the impact of the parameter force_match on the signature of different, but similar, SQL statements:

- force_match set to FALSE: Blank spaces and case-insensitive.

```
SQL_TEXT                                                 SIGNATURE
--------------------------------------------------- --------------------
SELECT * FROM dual WHERE dummy = 'X'                      7181225531830258335
select  *  from  dual  where  dummy='X'                  7181225531830258335
SELECT * FROM dual WHERE dummy = 'x'                     18443846411346672783
SELECT * FROM dual WHERE dummy = 'Y'                       909903071561515954
SELECT * FROM dual WHERE dummy = 'X' OR dummy = :b1 14508885911807130242
SELECT * FROM dual WHERE dummy = 'Y' OR dummy = :b1  816238779370039768
```

- `force_match` set to `TRUE`: Blank spaces and case- and literal-insensitive. Nevertheless, the substitution of literals is not performed if a bind variable is present in the SQL statement.

```
SQL_TEXT                                                  SIGNATURE
---------------------------------------------------  --------------------
SELECT * FROM dual WHERE dummy = 'X'                 10668153635715970930
select  *  from  dual  where  dummy='X'              10668153635715970930
SELECT * FROM dual WHERE dummy = 'x'                 10668153635715970930
SELECT * FROM dual WHERE dummy = 'Y'                 10668153635715970930
SELECT * FROM dual WHERE dummy = 'X' OR dummy = :b1  14508885911807130242
SELECT * FROM dual WHERE dummy = 'Y' OR dummy = :b1   816238779370039768
```

While accepting SQL profiles through Enterprise Manager, only in Oracle Database 11*g* is it possible to set the value of the parameter `force_match`. In Oracle Database 10*g*, the default value (`FALSE`) is always used.

Activating SQL Profiles

The activation of SQL profiles is controlled at the system and session levels by the initialization parameter `sqltune_category`. It takes as a value either `TRUE`, `FALSE`, or the name of a category specified while accepting the SQL profile. If `TRUE`, the category defaults to the value `default`. For example, the following SQL statement activates the SQL profiles belonging to the category `test` at the session level:

```
ALTER SESSION SET sqltune_category = test
```

The initialization parameter supports a single category. Obviously, this implies that a session is able to activate only a single category at a given time.

Moving SQL Profiles

As of Oracle Database 10*g* Release 2, the package `dbms_sqltune` provides several procedures to move SQL profiles between databases. As shown in Figure 7-5, the following features are provided:

- You can create a staging table through the procedure `create_stgtab_sqlprof`.

- You can copy a SQL profile from the data dictionary to the staging table through the procedure `pack_stgtab_sqlprof`.

- You can change the name and the category of a SQL profile stored in the staging table through the procedure `remap_stgtab_sqlprof`.

- You can copy a SQL profile from the staging table into the data dictionary through the procedure `unpack_stgtab_sqlprof`.

Note that moving the staging table between databases is performed by means of a data movement utility (for example, Data Pump or the legacy export and import utilities) and not with the package `dbms_sqltune` itself.

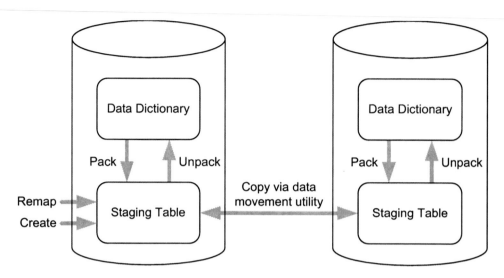

Figure 7-5. *Moving SQL profiles with the package* dbms_sqltune

The following example, which is an excerpt of the script clone_sql_profile.sql, shows how to clone a SQL profile inside a single database. First, the staging table mystgtab is created in the current schema:

```
dbms_sqltune.create_stgtab_sqlprof(
  table_name       => 'MYSTGTAB',
  schema_name      => user,
  tablespace_name  => 'USERS'
);
```

Then, a SQL profile named first_rows is copied from the data dictionary to the staging table:

```
dbms_sqltune.pack_stgtab_sqlprof(
  profile_name        => 'first_rows',
  profile_category    => 'TEST',
  staging_table_name  => 'MYSTGTAB',
  staging_schema_owner => user
);
```

The name of the SQL profile must be changed before copying it back into the data dictionary. At the same time, its category is changed as well.

```
dbms_sqltune.remap_stgtab_sqlprof(
  old_profile_name     => 'first_rows',
  new_profile_name     => 'first_rows-clone',
  new_profile_category => 'CLONE',
  staging_table_name   => 'MYSTGTAB',
  staging_schema_owner => user
);
```

Finally, the SQL profile is copied from the staging table into the data dictionary. Since the parameter replace is set to TRUE, a SQL profile with the same name would be overwritten.

```
dbms_sqltune.unpack_stgtab_sqlprof(
  profile_name          => 'first_rows-clone',
  profile_category      => 'DEFAULT',
  replace               => TRUE,
  staging_table_name    => 'MYSTGTAB',
  staging_schema_owner  => user
);
```

Dropping SQL Profiles

You can use the procedure drop_sql_profile in the package dbms_sqltune to drop a SQL profile from the data dictionary. The parameter name specifies the name of the SQL profile. The parameter ignore specifies whether an error is raised in case the SQL profile does not exist. It defaults to FALSE.

```
dbms_sqltune.drop_sql_profile(
  name   => 'first_rows',
  ignore => TRUE
);
```

Privileges

To create, alter, and drop a SQL profile, the system privileges create any sql profile, drop any sql profile, and alter any sql profile are required, respectively. As of Oracle Database 11g, these three system privileges are deprecated in favor of the system privilege administer sql management object. No object privileges for SQL profiles exist. To use the SQL Tuning Advisor, the system privilege advisor is required.

End users do not require specific privileges to use SQL profiles.

Undocumented Features

How does a SQL profile influence the query optimizer? Oracle provides no real answer to this question in its documentation. It is my belief that the best way to use a feature efficiently is to know how it works. So, let's take a look under the hood. Simply put, a SQL profile stores a set of hints representing the adjustments to be performed by the query optimizer. Some of these hints are documented and already available in Oracle9i. Others are undocumented and are available only as of Oracle Database 10g. In other words, they have probably been implemented for this purpose. All of them are regular hints and, therefore, can be directly added to a SQL statement as well.

The hints stored in the data dictionary cannot be displayed through a data dictionary view. In fact, the only view providing information about SQL profiles, dba_sql_profiles, gives all information except for hints. If you want to know which hints are used for a SQL profile, you have two possibilities. The first is to directly query the data dictionary table sqlprof$attr. The following query shows how to do it for the SQL profile used in the previous examples. In this specific case, there is a single hint, first_rows, that instructs the query optimizer to switch the optimizer mode. This is, of course, done only for the SQL statement associated with the SQL profile.

```
SQL> SELECT attr_val
  2  FROM sys.sqlprof$ p, sys.sqlprof$attr a
  3  WHERE p.sp_name = 'first_rows'
  4  AND p.signature = a.signature
  5  AND p.category = a.category;

ATTR_VAL
-------------------------------------------
FIRST_ROWS(6)
```

If you use Oracle Database 10g Release 2 or later, the second possibility is to move the SQL profile into a staging table, as described in the previous section. Then, with a query like the following, you will get the hints from the staging table. Note that the unnesting through the function `table` is performed because the hints are stored in a varray of VARCHAR2.

```
SQL> SELECT *
  2  FROM table(SELECT attributes
  3              FROM mystgtab
  4              WHERE profile_name = 'first_rows');

COLUMN_VALUE
----------------------------------------
FIRST_ROWS(6)
```

To show you another example of the optimizer mode switch, let's consider the following query, where the hint `rule` forces the query optimizer to work in rule-based mode:

```
SQL> SELECT /*+ rule */ * FROM t ORDER BY id;

-------------------------------------------
| Id | Operation                  | Name |
-------------------------------------------
|  0 | SELECT STATEMENT           |      |
|  1 |  TABLE ACCESS BY INDEX ROWID| T    |
|  2 |   INDEX FULL SCAN          | T_PK |
-------------------------------------------

Note
-----
   - rule based optimizer used (consider using cbo)
```

If you let the SQL Tuning Advisor analyze such a query, as the script `all_rows.sql` does, the advice to create a SQL profile is given. Accepting that advice, a SQL profile containing the following hints is created. Note that two initialization parameter hints (`all_rows` and `optimizer_features_enable`) are used. In addition, to instruct the query optimizer to ignore the hints present in the SQL statement (in this case the hint `rule`), the hint `ignore_optim_embedded_hints` is used.

```
ALL_ROWS
OPTIMIZER_FEATURES_ENABLE(default)
IGNORE_OPTIM_EMBEDDED_HINTS
```

Switching the optimizer mode is not the only thing SQL profiles can do. Another situation in which they are useful is for correcting the wrong cardinality estimations performed by the query optimizer. The script opt_estimate.sql shows such a case. By using the technique described in Chapter 6 for recognizing wrong estimations, you can see in the following example that the estimated cardinality (E-Rows) of several operations is completely different from the actual cardinality (A-Rows):

```
-----------------------------------------------------------------------------
| Id | Operation                      | Name          | Starts | E-Rows | A-Rows |
-----------------------------------------------------------------------------
|  1 | HASH UNIQUE                    |               |      1 |      1 |      1 |
|  2 |  NESTED LOOPS                  |               |      1 |      3 |  26985 |
|* 3 |   TABLE ACCESS BY INDEX ROWID| CH            |      1 |    680 |  26985 |
|* 4 |    INDEX RANGE SCAN            | CH_LANGUAGE_I |      1 |  26985 |  26985 |
|  5 |   TABLE ACCESS BY INDEX ROWID| T             |  26985 |      1 |  26985 |
|* 6 |    INDEX UNIQUE SCAN           | T_PK          |  26985 |      1 |  26985 |
-----------------------------------------------------------------------------
```

If you let the SQL Tuning Advisor analyze such a case and you accept its advice, as the script opt_estimate.sql does, a SQL profile containing the following hints is created. The important thing to note in this case is the presence of the undocumented hint opt_estimate. With that particular hint, it is possible to inform the query optimizer that some of its estimations are wrong and by how much. In fact, the first hint tells the query optimizer to scale up the estimation of the operation at line 3 by about 39 (26,985/680) times. The second hint tells it to scale up the estimation of the operation at line 2 (the join between the two tables) by about 275 times (26,985/3/39—this is not very precise because the 3 was rounded off).

```
OPT_ESTIMATE(@"SEL$1", TABLE, "CH"@"SEL$1", SCALE_ROWS=39.10326263)
OPT_ESTIMATE(@"SEL$1", JOIN, ("T"@"SEL$1", "CH"@"SEL$1"), SCALE_ROWS=275.1560562)
```

With the SQL profile in place, the estimations are precise. Also note that the query optimizer chose another execution plan, which was the purpose of creating a SQL profile in the first place.

```
-----------------------------------------------------------------------------
| Id | Operation                      | Name          | Starts | E-Rows | A-Rows |
-----------------------------------------------------------------------------
|  1 | HASH UNIQUE                    |               |      1 |      1 |      1 |
|* 2 |  HASH JOIN                     |               |      1 |  26985 |  26985 |
|* 3 |   TABLE ACCESS BY INDEX ROWID| CH            |      1 |  26602 |  26985 |
|* 4 |    INDEX RANGE SCAN            | CH_LANGUAGE_I |      1 |  26985 |  26985 |
|  5 |   TABLE ACCESS FULL            | T             |      1 |  27268 |  26985 |
-----------------------------------------------------------------------------
```

Another possible utilization of a SQL profile is when there are objects that have inaccurate or missing object statistics. Of course, that should not happen, but when it does and dynamic sampling cannot be used to provide the query optimizer with the needed information, a SQL profile could be used. The script `object_stats.sql` provides an example of this. The hints making up the SQL profile generated by that script are the following. As the name of the hints suggest, the idea is to provide object statistics either for a table, an index, or a column.

```
TABLE_STATS("SH"."AMOUNT_SOLD_MV", scale, blocks=7 rows=1460)
COLUMN_STATS("SH"."AMOUNT_SOLD_MV", "TIME_ID", scale, length=7 distinct=1460
              nulls=0 min=2450815 max=2452275)
COLUMN_STATS("SH"."AMOUNT_SOLD_MV", "SUMSLD", scale, length=5)
INDEX_STATS("SH"."AMOUNT_SOLD_MV", "I_SNAP$_AMOUNT_SOLD_MV", scale, blocks=8
              index_rows=1460)
```

The last area I will describe in this section about undocumented features is the possibility to manually create a SQL profile. In other words, instead of asking the SQL Tuning Advisor to do an analysis and then, if advised, to accept a SQL profile, you can build a SQL profile yourself. Be careful, though. As I mentioned earlier, I have no idea whether this technique is supported. To be honest, I see no problem using it, because the method used to create the SQL profile is the same as the one used by the database engine when you accept advice provided by the SQL Tuning Advisor. What happens is that the SQL profile is created by calling the undocumented procedure `import_sql_profile` in the package `dbms_sqltune`. The following call is an example. The parameter `sql_text` specifies the SQL statement that the SQL profile is tied to, and the parameter `profile` specifies the list of hints. All other parameters have the same meaning as the parameters of the procedure `accept_sql_profile` previously described.

```
dbms_sqltune.import_sql_profile(
  name        => 'import_sql_profile',
  description => 'SQL profile created manually',
  category    => 'TEST',
  sql_text    => 'SELECT * FROM t ORDER BY id',
  profile     => sqlprof_attr('first_rows(42)',
                              'optimizer_features_enable(default)'),
  replace     => FALSE,
  force_match => FALSE
);
```

When to Use It

You should consider using this technique whenever you are tuning a specific SQL statement and you are not able to change it in the application (for example, when adding hints is not an option). Unfortunately, to use the SQL Tuning Advisor, the Tuning Pack and the Diagnostic Pack must be licensed. Unfortunately, these packs are available only for Enterprise Edition.

Pitfalls and Fallacies

One of the most important properties of SQL profiles is that they are detached from the code. At the same time, that could lead to problems. In fact, since there is no direct reference between the SQL profile and the SQL statement, it is possible that a developer will completely ignore the existence of the SQL profile. Further, if the developer modifies the SQL statement in a way that leads to a modification of its signature, the SQL profile will no longer be used. Similarly, when you deploy an application that needs some SQL profiles to perform correctly, you mustn't forget to install them during the database setup.

If you have to generate a SQL profile, it is good practice to do it in the production environment (if available) and then to move it to another environment for the necessary tests. The problem is that before moving a SQL profile, you have to accept it. Since you do not want to enable it in production without having tested it, you should make sure to accept it by using a category that is different from the one activated through the initialization parameter sqltune_category. In that way, the SQL profile will not be used in the production database. In any case, it is always possible to change the category of a SQL profile later.

You must be aware that SQL profiles are not dropped when the objects they depend on are dropped. This is not necessarily a problem, however. For example, if a table or an index needs to be re-created because it must be reorganized or moved, it is a good thing that the SQL profiles are not dropped; otherwise, it would be necessary to re-create them.

Two SQL statements with the same text have the same signature. This is also true even if they reference objects in different schemas. This means that a single SQL profile could be used for two tables that have the same name but are located in different schemas! You should be very careful, especially if you have a database with multiple copies of the same objects.

Whenever a SQL statement has a SQL profile and a stored outline at the same time (note that stored outlines are covered in the next section), the query optimizer gives precedence to the stored outline instead of using the SQL profile. Of course, this is the case only when the usage of stored outlines is active.

As of Oracle Database 10g Release 2, in order to know whether a SQL profile is used by the query optimizer, you can take advantage of the functions available in the package dbms_xplan. As shown in the following example, the section Note of their output explicitly provides the needed information:

```
SQL> EXPLAIN PLAN FOR SELECT * FROM t ORDER BY id;

SQL> SELECT * FROM table(dbms_xplan.display(NULL,NULL,'basic +note'));


---------------------------------------------
| Id  | Operation                   | Name  |
---------------------------------------------
|   0 | SELECT STATEMENT            |       |
|   1 |  TABLE ACCESS BY INDEX ROWID| T     |
|   2 |   INDEX FULL SCAN           | T_PK  |
---------------------------------------------

Note
-----
   - SQL profile "import_sql_profile" used for this statement
```

Stored Outlines

Stored outlines are designed to provide stable execution plans in case of changes in the execution environment or object statistics. For this reason, this feature is also referred to as *plan stability*. Two important scenarios that can benefit from this feature are reported in the Oracle documentation. The first is the migration from the rule-based optimizer to the cost-based optimizer. The second is the upgrade of an Oracle release to a newer one. In both cases, the idea is to store information about the execution plans while the application is using the old configuration or release and then to use that information to provide the same execution plans against the newer one. In practice, unfortunately, even with stored outlines in place, you may observe changes in execution plans. Probably for this reason, I have never seen a single database where stored outlines were used on a large scale. The definitive confirmation that stored outlines are not always suitable to provide stable execution plans is given by Oracle Database 11*g* itself, since as of this version, stored outlines are deprecated in favor of *SQL plan baselines* (which are covered in the next section). Consequently, in practice, stored outlines are used for specific SQL statements only.

How It Works

The following sections describe what stored outlines are and how to work with them. To manage stored outlines, except with Oracle9*i*, no graphical interface is provided in Enterprise Manager.

What Are Stored Outlines?

A *stored outline* is an object associated to a SQL statement and is designed to influence the query optimizer while it generates execution plans. More concretely, a stored outline is a set of hints or, more precisely, all the hints that are necessary to force the query optimizer to consistently generate a specific execution plan for a given SQL statement.

One of the advantages of a stored outline is that it applies to a specific SQL statement, but to use it, you don't need to modify the SQL statement. In fact, stored outlines are stored in the data dictionary, and the query optimizer selects them automatically. Figure 7-6 shows the basic steps carried out during this selection. First, the SQL statement is normalized by removing blank spaces and converting nonliteral strings to uppercase. The signature of the resulting SQL statement is computed. Then, based on that signature, a lookup in the data dictionary is performed. Whenever a stored outline with the same signature is found, a check is performed to make sure that the SQL statement to be optimized and the SQL statement tied to the stored outline are equivalent. This is necessary because the signature is a hash value, and consequently, there could be conflicts. If the test is successful, the hints making up the stored outline are included in the generation of the execution plan.

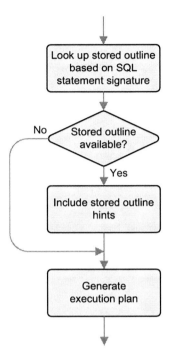

Figure 7-6. *Main steps carried out during the selection of a stored outline*

Creating Stored Outlines

You can use two main methods to create stored outlines. Either you let the database automatically create them or you do it manually. The first method is useful if you want to create a stored outline for each SQL statement executed by a given session or even by the whole system. Nevertheless, as mentioned earlier, this is usually not desirable. Because of this, you will usually create them manually.

To activate the automatic creation, you have to set the initialization parameter create_stored_outlines either to TRUE or to another value specifying a *category*. The purpose of the category is to group together several stored outlines for management purposes. The default category, which is used when the initialization parameter is set to TRUE, is named default. The initialization parameter is dynamic and can be changed at the session and system levels. To disable automatic creation, you have to set the initialization parameter to FALSE.

To manually create a stored outline, you have to use the SQL statement CREATE OUTLINE. The following SQL statement, which is an excerpt of the script outline_from_text.sql, shows the creation of a stored outline named outline_from_text, associated with the category test and based on the query specified in the ON clause:

```
CREATE OR REPLACE OUTLINE outline_from_text
FOR CATEGORY test
ON SELECT * FROM t WHERE n = 1970
```

Once created, you can display information about stored outlines and their properties
through the views user_outlines and user_outline_hints (for both, the all and dba views exist
as well). The view user_outlines displays all information except the hints. The following queries
show the information provided for the stored outline created by the previous SQL statement:

```
SQL> SELECT category, sql_text, signature
  2  FROM user_outlines
  3  WHERE name = 'OUTLINE_FROM_TEXT';

CATEGORY SQL_TEXT                          SIGNATURE
-------- -------------------------------- --------------------------------
TEST     SELECT * FROM t WHERE n = 1970 73DC40455AF10A40D84EF59A2F8CBFFE

SQL> SELECT hint
  2  FROM user_outline_hints
  3  WHERE name = 'OUTLINE_FROM_TEXT';

HINT
--------------------------------------------------------------------------
FULL(@"SEL$1" "T"@"SEL$1")
OUTLINE_LEAF(@"SEL$1")
ALL_ROWS
OPTIMIZER_FEATURES_ENABLE('10.2.0.2')
IGNORE_OPTIM_EMBEDDED_HINTS
```

As of Oracle Database 10g, you are also able to manually create a stored outline by referencing a cursor in the shared pool. The following example, which is an excerpt of the output
generated by the script outline_from_sqlarea.sql, shows how to select the cursor in the
shared pool and to create the stored outline through the procedure create_outline in the
package dbms_outln.

```
SQL> SELECT hash_value, child_number
  2  FROM v$sql
  3  WHERE sql_text = 'SELECT * FROM t WHERE n = 1970';

HASH_VALUE CHILD_NUMBER
---------- ------------
 308120306            0

SQL> BEGIN
  2    dbms_outln.create_outline(
  3      hash_value => '308120306',
  4      child_number => 0,
  5      category => 'test'
  6    );
  7  END;
  8  /
```

The procedure `create_outline` accepts only the three parameters shown in the example. This means that the name of the stored outline is automatically generated. To find out the system-generated name, you have to query the view `user_outlines`. Here is an example where the following query returns the name of the last-created stored outline:

```
SQL> SELECT name
  2  FROM user_outlines
  3  WHERE timestamp = (SELECT max(timestamp) FROM user_outlines);

NAME
------------------------------
SYS_OUTLINE_07072608011150604
```

It is advisable to change the system-generated name to something more useful. The next section describes, among other things, how to do it.

Altering Stored Outlines

To change the name of a stored outline, you have to execute the SQL command `ALTER OUTLINE`:

```
ALTER OUTLINE sys_outline_07072614532024107 RENAME TO outline_from_sqlarea
```

With the SQL command `ALTER OUTLINE` or the procedure `update_by_cat` in the package `dbms_outln`, you are also able to change the category of stored outlines. While the former changes the category of a single stored outline, the latter moves all stored outlines belonging to one category to another one. However, because of bug 5759631, it is not possible with `ALTER OUTLINE` to change the category of a stored outline to `default` (for all other categories, it is not a problem). The following example shows not only what happens if you try to change it but also how to do it with the procedure `update_by_cat`:

```
SQL> ALTER OUTLINE outline_from_text CHANGE CATEGORY TO DEFAULT;
ALTER OUTLINE outline_from_text CHANGE CATEGORY TO DEFAULT
                                                *
ERROR at line 1:
ORA-00931: missing identifier

SQL> execute dbms_outln.update_by_cat(oldcat => 'TEST', newcat => 'DEFAULT')

SQL> SELECT category
  2  FROM user_outlines
  3  WHERE name = 'OUTLINE_FROM_TEXT';

CATEGORY
--------
DEFAULT
```

Finally, with the SQL command ALTER OUTLINE, you are also able to regenerate a stored outline. Regenerating a stored outline is like re-creating it. Usually, you will use this possibility if you want the query optimizer to generate a new set of hints. This could be necessary if you have changed the access structures of the objects related to the stored outline.

```
ALTER OUTLINE outline_from_text REBUILD
```

Activating Stored Outlines

The query optimizer considers only the stored outlines that are active. To be active, a stored outline must meet two conditions. The first is that the stored outlines must be enabled. This is the default when they are created. To enable and disable a stored outline, you use the SQL statement ALTER OUTLINE:

```
ALTER OUTLINE outline_from_text DISABLE
```

```
ALTER OUTLINE outline_from_text ENABLE
```

The second condition is that the category must be activated through the initialization parameter use_stored_outlines at the session or system level. The initialization parameter takes as a value either TRUE, FALSE, or the name of a category. If TRUE is specified, the category defaults to the value default. The following SQL statement activates the stored outlines belonging to the category test at the session level:

```
ALTER SESSION SET use_stored_outlines = test
```

Since the initialization parameter supports a single category, at a given time a session is able to activate only a single category.

Moving Stored Outlines

To move stored outlines, no particular feature is provided. Basically, you have to copy them yourself from one data dictionary to the other. This is easy because the data about the stored outlines is stored in three tables in the schema outln: ol$, hints$, and ol$nodes. You could use the following commands to export and import all available stored outlines:

```
exp tables=(outln.ol$,outln.ol$hints,outln.ol$nodes) file=outln.dmp
```

```
imp full=y ignore=y file=outln.dmp
```

To move a single stored outline (named outline_from_text in this case), you can add the following parameter to the export command:

```
query="WHERE ol_name='OUTLINE_FROM_TEXT'"
```

To move all stored outlines belonging to a category (named test in this case), you can add the following parameter to the export command:

```
query="WHERE category='TEST'"
```

Be careful, because you may have to add some escape characters to successfully pass all parameters, depending on your operating system. For example, on my Linux server I had to execute the following command:

```
exp tables=(outln.ol\$,outln.ol\$hints,outln.ol\$nodes) file=outln.dmp \
    query=\"WHERE ol_name=\'OUTLINE_FROM_TEXT\'\"
```

Editing Stored Outlines

With stored outlines, it is possible to lock up execution plans. However, this is useful only if the query optimizer is able to generate an efficient execution plan that can later be captured and frozen by a stored outline. If this is not the case, the first thing you should investigate is the possibility of modifying the execution environment, the access structures, or the object statistics just for the creation of the stored outline storing an efficient execution plan. For instance, if the execution plan for a given SQL statement uses an index scan that you want to avoid, you could drop the index on a test system, generate a stored outline there, and then move the stored outline in production.

When you find no way to force the query optimizer to automatically generate an efficient execution plan, the last resort is to edit the stored outline yourself. Simply put, you have to modify the hints associated with the stored outline. However, in practice, you cannot simply run a few SQL statements against the *public stored outlines* (which are the kind discussed so far) stored in the data dictionary tables. Instead, you have to carry out the editing as summarized in Figure 7-7. This process is based on the modification of *private stored outlines.* These are like public stored outlines, but instead of being stored in the data dictionary, they are stored in *working tables*. The aim of using these working tables is to avoid modifying the data dictionary tables directly. Therefore, to edit a stored outline, you have to create, modify, and test a private stored outline. Then, when the private stored outline is working correctly, it is published as a public stored outline. The package dbms_outln_edit and a few extensions to the SQL statement CREATE OUTLINE are available for editing stored outlines.

Based on the example available in the script outline_editing.sql, I'll now describe the whole process summarized by Figure 7-7. The purpose is to create and edit a stored outline to have a full table scan instead of an index scan for the following query:

```
SQL> EXPLAIN PLAN FOR SELECT * FROM t WHERE n = 1970;

SQL> SELECT * FROM table(dbms_xplan.display(NULL,NULL,'basic +note'));

---------------------------------------------
| Id  | Operation                  | Name |
---------------------------------------------
|   0 | SELECT STATEMENT           |      |
|   1 |  TABLE ACCESS BY INDEX ROWID| T   |
|   2 |   INDEX RANGE SCAN         | I    |
---------------------------------------------
```

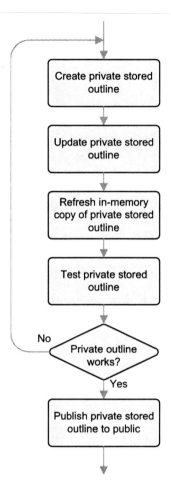

Figure 7-7. *Steps carried out during the editing of a stored outline*

First, you have to create a private stored outline. For that, you have two possibilities. The first is to create a private stored outline from scratch with a SQL statement like the following. The keyword PRIVATE specifies the kind of stored outline to be created.

```
SQL> CREATE OR REPLACE PRIVATE OUTLINE p_outline_editing
  2  ON SELECT * FROM t WHERE n = 1970;
```

The second possibility is to copy a public stored outline already present in the data dictionary by means of a SQL statement like the following. The keywords PRIVATE and PUBLIC specify the kind of stored outline to be copied and created respectively.

```
SQL> CREATE PRIVATE OUTLINE p_outline_editing FROM PUBLIC outline_editing;
```

To successfully execute this command, the working tables must be available. If they are not available, the following error is raised:

```
ORA-18009: one or more outline system tables do not exist
```

As of Oracle Database 10*g*, they are available by default. If you are working with Oracle9*i*, you have to create them manually. The following excerpt of the script `outline_edit_tables.sql` shows an example of how to create them in the schema `system` and give the necessary privileges to `public`:

```
CONNECT / AS SYSDBA

ALTER SESSION SET current_schema = system;

execute dbms_outln_edit.create_edit_tables

CREATE OR REPLACE PUBLIC SYNONYM ol$ FOR system.ol$;
CREATE OR REPLACE PUBLIC SYNONYM ol$hints FOR system.ol$hints;
CREATE OR REPLACE PUBLIC SYNONYM ol$nodes FOR system.ol$nodes;

GRANT SELECT,INSERT,UPDATE,DELETE ON system.ol$ TO public;
GRANT SELECT,INSERT,UPDATE,DELETE ON system.ol$hints TO public;
GRANT SELECT,INSERT,UPDATE,DELETE ON system.ol$nodes TO public;
```

Both methods create a private stored outline in the working tables. Here is the list of hints associated with it:

```
SQL> SELECT hint#, hint_text
  2  FROM ol$hints
  3  WHERE ol_name = 'P_OUTLINE_EDITING';

  HINT# HINT_TEXT
------- -----------------------------------------
      1 INDEX(@"SEL$1" "T"@"SEL$1" ("T"."N"))
      2 OUTLINE_LEAF(@"SEL$1")
      3 ALL_ROWS
      4 OPTIMIZER_FEATURES_ENABLE('10.2.0.2')
      5 IGNORE_OPTIM_EMBEDDED_HINTS
```

Once the private stored outline has been created, you can modify it with regular SQL statements. In this example, the row with the hint `index` is replaced by the hint `full`:

```
SQL> UPDATE ol$hints
  2  SET hint_text = 'FULL(@SEL$1 T)'
  3  WHERE hint# = 1
  4  AND ol_name = 'P_OUTLINE_EDITING';
```

To make sure that the in-memory copy of the stored outline is synchronized with the changes, you should execute the following PL/SQL call:

```
SQL> execute dbms_outln_edit.refresh_private_outline('P_OUTLINE_EDITING')
```

Then, to activate and test the private stored outline, the initialization parameter `use_private_outlines` is set either to `TRUE` or to the name of the category to which the private stored outline belongs. Note how the full table scan in the execution plan and the message in the section `Note` confirm the utilization of the private stored outline.

```
SQL> ALTER SESSION SET use_private_outlines = TRUE

SQL> EXPLAIN PLAN FOR SELECT * FROM t WHERE n = 1970;

SQL> SELECT * FROM table(dbms_xplan.display(NULL,NULL,'basic +note'));


-----------------------------------
| Id  | Operation        | Name |
-----------------------------------
|   0 | SELECT STATEMENT |      |
|   1 |  TABLE ACCESS FULL| T   |
-----------------------------------


Note
-----
   - outline "P_OUTLINE_EDITING" used for this statement
```

Once you are satisfied with the private stored outline, you can publish it as a public stored outline with the following SQL statement:

```
SQL> CREATE PUBLIC OUTLINE outline_editing FROM PRIVATE p_outline_editing;
```

The whole process is a bit awkward. For this reason, the Tuning Pack of Oracle Enterprise Manager 9.2 provides a tool to graphically edit stored outlines. Figure 7-8 shows what it looks like. Basically, a graphical representation of the execution plan is given, and by editing the properties of the nodes, it is possible to modify the execution plan as required. It also gives the possibility of testing the private stored outline before publishing it. Unfortunately, this tool is no longer available in the newer versions of Oracle Enterprise Manager.

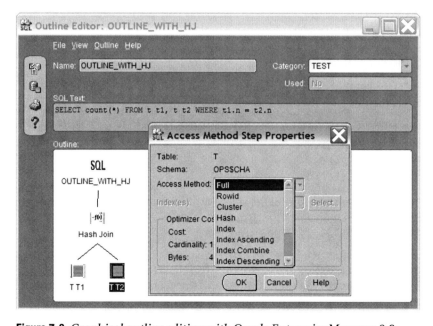

Figure 7-8. *Graphical outline editing with Oracle Enterprise Manager 9.2*

Dropping Stored Outlines

With the SQL command DROP OUTLINE or the procedure drop_by_cat in the package dbms_outln, you are able to drop stored outlines. While the former drops a single stored outline, the latter drops all stored outlines belonging to one category.

```
DROP OUTLINE outline_from_text
```

```
dbms_outln.drop_by_cat(cat => 'TEST')
```

To drop private stored outlines, you have to use the SQL statement DROP PRIVATE OUTLINE.

Privileges

The system privileges required to create, alter, and drop a stored outline are create any outline, drop any outline, and alter any outline, respectively. No object privileges exist for stored outlines.

By default the package dbms_outln is available only to users who either have the role dba or execute_catalog_role. Instead, the package dbms_outln_edit is available to all users (the privilege execute is granted to PUBLIC).

End users do not require specific privileges to use stored outlines.

When to Use It

You should consider using this technique whenever you are tuning a specific SQL statement and you are not able to change it in the application (for example, when adding hints is not an option).

Pitfalls and Fallacies

Oddly enough, the initialization parameter use_stored_outlines cannot be specified in an initialization file (init.ora or spfile.ora). Consequently, the parameter must be set either at the system level every time an instance is bounced or at the session level every time a session is created. In both cases, you could do the setting through a database trigger.

One of the most important properties of stored outlines is that they are detached from the code. Nevertheless, that could lead to problems. In fact, since there is no direct reference between the stored outline and the SQL statement, it is possible that a developer will completely ignore the existence of the stored outline. Additionally, if the developer modifies the SQL statement in a way that leads to a modification of its signature, the stored outline will no longer be used. Similarly, when you deploy an application that needs some stored outlines to perform correctly, during the database setup you mustn't forget to install them.

You must be aware that stored outlines are not dropped when the objects they depend on are dropped. This is not necessarily a problem, however. For example, if a table or an index needs to be re-created because it must be reorganized or moved, it is a good thing that the stored outlines are not dropped; otherwise, it would be necessary to re-create them.

Two SQL statements with the same text have the same signature. That is also true even if they reference objects in different schemas. This means that a single stored outline could be used for two tables with the same name but located in a different schema! Once again, you should be very careful, especially if you have a database with multiple copies of the same objects.

Up to Oracle Database 10*g* Release 1, a stored outline is not able to overwrite the setting of the initialization parameters `optimizer_features_enable`, `query_rewrite_enabled`, and `star_transformation_enabled`. To successfully use stored outlines, their setting must be consistent across execution environments.

As of Oracle Database 10*g* Release 2, to know whether the query optimizer is using a stored outline, you can take advantage of the functions available in the package `dbms_xplan`. In fact, as shown in the following example, the section `Note` of their output explicitly provides the needed information:

```
SQL> EXPLAIN PLAN FOR SELECT * FROM t WHERE n = 1970;

SQL> SELECT * FROM table(dbms_xplan.display(NULL,NULL,'basic +note'));

---------------------------------------------
| Id  | Operation                  | Name |
---------------------------------------------
|   0 | SELECT STATEMENT           |      |
|   1 |  TABLE ACCESS BY INDEX ROWID| T    |
|   2 |   INDEX RANGE SCAN         | I    |
---------------------------------------------

Note
-----
   - outline "OUTLINE_FROM_TEXT" used for this statement
```

Another method that works in all releases is to reset the utilization flag of the stored outline with the procedure `clear_used` in the package `dbms_outln`. Then, by checking the flag before and after an execution that should use the stored outline, you can determine whether the stored outline was in fact used.

```
SQL> execute dbms_outln.clear_used(name => 'OUTLINE_FROM_TEXT')

SQL> SELECT used
  2  FROM user_outlines
  3  WHERE name = 'OUTLINE_FROM_TEXT';

USED
------
UNUSED

SQL> SELECT * FROM t WHERE n = 1970;

SQL> SELECT used
  2  FROM user_outlines
  3  WHERE name = 'OUTLINE_FROM_TEXT';

USED
------
USED
```

You should never need to log in with the account `outln`. Therefore, for security reasons, you should either lock it or change its default password. This is especially important because it owns a dangerous system privilege: `execute any procedure`.

SQL Plan Baselines

As of Oracle Database 11*g*, SQL plan baselines substitute stored outlines. Actually, they can be considered an enhanced version of stored outlines. In fact, not only do they share several characteristics with them, but as stored outlines they are designed to provide stable execution plans in case of changes in the execution environment or object statistics. In addition, as stored outlines, they can be used to tune an application without modifying it.

■ **Note** The only usage mentioned in Oracle documentation is the stabilization of execution plans. For some unknown reason, the possibility of using SQL plan baselines to change the current execution plan (related to a given SQL statement), without modifying the application submitting it, is not mentioned.

How It Works

The following sections describe how SQL plan baselines work. To manage them, a graphical interface is integrated into Enterprise Manager. We will not spend time here looking at it, since in my opinion, if you understand what is going on in the background, you will have no problem at all in using the graphical interface.

What Are SQL Plan Baselines?

A *SQL plan baseline* is an object associated with a SQL statement that is designed to influence the query optimizer while it generates execution plans. More concretely, a SQL baseline contains, among other things, a set of hints. Basically a SQL plan baseline is used to force the query optimizer to consistently generate a specific execution plan for a given SQL statement.

One of the advantages of a SQL plan baseline is that it applies to a specific SQL statement, but to use it, no modification of the SQL statement itself is needed. In fact, the SQL plan baselines are stored in the data dictionary, and the query optimizer selects them automatically. Figure 7-9 shows what the basic steps carried out are during this selection. First, the SQL statement is processed in the conventional way. In other words, the query optimizer generates an execution plan without the support of SQL plan baselines. Then, the SQL statement is normalized to make it both case-insensitive and independent of the blank spaces present in the text. The signature of the resulting SQL statement is computed. Then, based on that signature, a lookup in the data dictionary is performed. Whenever an accepted (trusted) and enabled SQL plan baseline with the same signature is found, a check is performed to make sure that the SQL statement to be optimized and the SQL statement associated with the SQL plan baseline are equivalent. This is necessary because the signature is a hash value, and consequently, there could be conflicts. When the test is successful, the information stored in the SQL plan baseline is used for the generation of the execution plan. Note that if several valid SQL plan baselines are available, the query optimizer takes the one with the lowest cost.

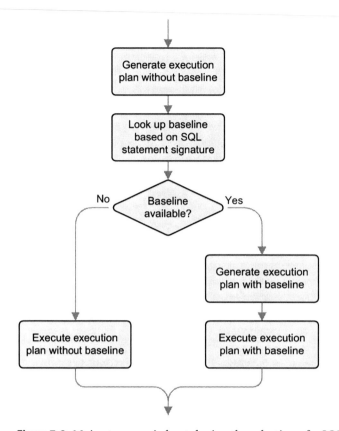

Figure 7-9. *Main steps carried out during the selection of a SQL plan baseline*

Capturing SQL Plan Baselines

You can capture new SQL plan baselines in several ways. Basically, they are created automatically by the database engine or manually by database administrators. The next three sections describe three of these methods.

Automatic Capture

When the dynamic initialization parameter `optimizer_capture_sql_plan_baselines` is set to TRUE, the query optimizer automatically generates new SQL plan baselines. By default, the initialization parameter is set to FALSE. You can change it at the session and system levels.

When the automatic capture is enabled, the query optimizer stores a new SQL plan baseline for each SQL statement that is executed repeatedly (that is, executed at least twice). To that end, it manages a log where it inserts the signature of each SQL statement it works on. This means that the first time a specific SQL statement is executed, its signature is inserted only into the log. Then, when the same SQL statement is executed again, provided a SQL plan baseline does not already exist for it, a new one is stored. If a SQL plan baseline is already associated with a SQL statement, the query optimizer also compares the current execution plan with the execution plan generated with the help of the SQL plan baseline. If they do not match, a new SQL plan baseline that describes the current execution plan is stored. As you have seen before, however, the current execution plan cannot be used. The query optimizer is forced to use the execution plan generated with the help of the SQL plan baseline. Figure 7-10 summarizes the whole process.

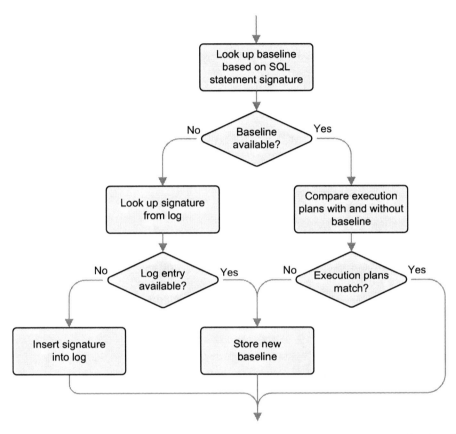

Figure 7-10. *Main steps carried out during the automatic capture of a SQL plan baseline*

When a new SQL plan baseline is stored, it is important to distinguish between two situations:

- If it is the first SQL plan baseline associated with the SQL statement, the SQL plan baseline is stored as *accepted*, and consequently, the query optimizer will be able to use it.

- If at least one SQL plan baseline already exists for the SQL statement, the SQL plan baseline is stored as *nonaccepted*, and as a result, the query optimizer will not be able to use it. The section "Evolving SQL Plan Baselines" will describe how to validate a SQL plan baseline to make it available to the query optimizer.

Load from Library Cache

To manually load SQL plan baselines into the data dictionary based on cursors stored in the library cache, the function load_plans_from_cursor_cache in the package dbms_spm is available.

Actually, the function is overloaded several times to support different methods that identify which cursors have to be processed. The following two main possibilities exist:

- Identify several SQL statements by specifying one of the following attributes:

  - sql_text: Text of the SQL statement. Wildcards (for example, %) are supported with this attribute.

  - parsing_schema_name: Schema name that was used to parse the cursor.

  - module: Name of the module that executed the SQL statement.

  - action: Name of the action that executed the SQL statement.

  To illustrate, the following call, which is an excerpt of the script baseline_from_sqlarea1.sql, creates a SQL plan baseline for each SQL statement stored in the library cache that contains the string MySqlStm in its text:

  ```
  ret := dbms_spm.load_plans_from_cursor_cache(
          attribute_name  => 'sql_text',
          attribute_value => '%MySqlStm%'
      );
  ```

- Identify a single SQL statement by its SQL identifier and, optionally, the hash value of the execution plan. If the hash value is not specified or set to NULL, all execution plans available for the specified SQL statement are loaded. The following call, which is an excerpt of the script baseline_from_sqlarea2.sql, illustrates this:

  ```
  ret := dbms_spm.load_plans_from_cursor_cache(
          sql_id           => '2y5r75r8y3sj0',
          plan_hash_value => NULL
      );
  ```

SQL plan baselines loaded with these functions are stored as accepted and so the query optimizer might immediately take advantage of them.

In the previous examples, the SQL plan baselines are based on the text of the SQL statement found in the library cache. This is relevant only if you want to ensure that the current execution plan will also be used in the future. Sometimes, the purpose of using a SQL plan baseline is to tune a SQL statement without modifying the application. Let's look at an example of such a situation, based on the script baseline_from_sqlarea3.sql.

Let's say one of your applications executes the following SQL statement. The execution plan generated by the query optimizer is based on a full table scan. This is because the SQL statement contains a hint forcing the query optimizer toward this operation.

```
SQL> SELECT /*+ full(t) */ count(pad) FROM t WHERE n = 42;

SQL> SELECT * FROM table(dbms_xplan.display_cursor);
```

```
-----------------------------------
| Id  | Operation        | Name |
-----------------------------------
|   0 | SELECT STATEMENT |      |
|   1 |  SORT AGGREGATE  |      |
|   2 |   TABLE ACCESS FULL| T   |
-----------------------------------
```

You notice that the column on which the restriction is applied (n) is indexed. You then wonder what the performance is when the index is used. So, as shown in the following example, you execute the SQL statement by specifying a hint to ensure that the index is used:

```
SQL> SELECT /*+ index(t) */ count(pad) FROM t WHERE n = 42;

SQL> SELECT * FROM table(dbms_xplan.display_cursor);

SQL_ID  dat4n4845zdxc, child number 0
```

```
------------------------------------------------
| Id  | Operation                  | Name |
------------------------------------------------
|   0 | SELECT STATEMENT           |      |
|   1 |  SORT AGGREGATE            |      |
|   2 |   TABLE ACCESS BY INDEX ROWID| T   |
|   3 |    INDEX RANGE SCAN        | I    |
------------------------------------------------
```

If the second execution plan is more efficient than the first one, your objective is to let the application use it. If you cannot change the application in order to remove or modify the hint, you can take advantage of a SQL plan baseline to solve this problem. To do this, you could create a SQL plan baseline either automatically or manually, as described earlier. In this case, you decide to use the initialization parameter optimizer_capture_sql_plan_baselines.

```
SQL> ALTER SESSION SET optimizer_capture_sql_plan_baselines = TRUE;

SQL> SELECT /*+ full(t) */ count(pad) FROM t WHERE n = 42;

SQL> SELECT /*+ full(t) */ count(pad) FROM t WHERE n = 42;

SQL> ALTER SESSION SET optimizer_capture_sql_plan_baselines = FALSE;
```

Once the SQL plan baseline is created, you check that it is really used. Notice how the package dbms_xplan clearly shows that a SQL plan baseline, identified through a *SQL plan name*, was used to generate the execution plan.

```
SQL> SELECT /*+ full(t) */ count(pad) FROM t WHERE n = 42;

SQL> SELECT * FROM table(dbms_xplan.display_cursor);
```

```
------------------------------------
| Id  | Operation         | Name |
------------------------------------
|   0 | SELECT STATEMENT  |      |
|   1 |  SORT AGGREGATE   |      |
|   2 |   TABLE ACCESS FULL| T   |
------------------------------------
```

Note

   - SQL plan baseline "SYS_SQL_PLAN_8fb2691f3fdbb376" used for this statement

Then, based on the SQL plan name provided by the previous output, you find the identifier of the SQL plan baseline, the *SQL handle*, through the data dictionary view dba_sql_plan_baselines:

```
SQL> SELECT sql_handle
  2  FROM dba_sql_plan_baselines
  3  WHERE plan_name = 'SYS_SQL_PLAN_8fb2691f3fdbb376';

SQL_HANDLE
------------------------------
SYS_SQL_3d1b0b7d8fb2691f
```

Finally, you replace the execution plan used by the SQL plan baseline. To do so, you load the execution plan associated with the SQL statement leading to the index scan and remove the one associated with the full table scan. The former is referenced by the SQL identifier and the hash value, the latter by the SQL handle and SQL plan name.

```
ret := dbms_spm.load_plans_from_cursor_cache(
         sql_id            => 'dat4n4845zdxc',
         plan_hash_value => '3694077449',
         sql_handle        => 'SYS_SQL_3d1b0b7d8fb2691f'
       );

ret := dbms_spm.drop_sql_plan_baseline(
         sql_handle => 'SYS_SQL_3d1b0b7d8fb2691f'
         plan_name  => 'SYS_SQL_PLAN_8fb2691f3fdbb376'
       );
```

To check whether the replacement has correctly taken place, you test the new SQL plan baseline. Notice that even if the SQL statement contains the hint full, the execution plan no longer uses a full table scan.

░**Note** Inappropriate hints occur frequently in practice as the reason for inefficient execution plans. Being able to override them with the technique you have seen in this section is extremely useful.

```
SQL> SELECT /*+ full(t) */ count(pad) FROM t WHERE n = 42;

SQL> SELECT * FROM table(dbms_xplan.display_cursor);

------------------------------------------------
| Id  | Operation                   | Name |
------------------------------------------------
|   0 | SELECT STATEMENT            |      |
|   1 |  SORT AGGREGATE             |      |
|   2 |   TABLE ACCESS BY INDEX ROWID| T   |
|   3 |    INDEX RANGE SCAN         | I    |
------------------------------------------------

Note
-----
   - SQL plan baseline SYS_SQL_PLAN_8fb2691f59340d78 used for this statement
```

To know whether a SQL plan baseline was used for a specific SQL statement, it is also possible to check the column sql_plan_baseline in the dynamic performance view v$sql.

Load from SQL Tuning Set

To load SQL plan baselines from SQL tuning sets, the function load_plans_from_sqlset in the package dbms_spm is available. Loading is simply a matter of specifying the owner and the name of the SQL tuning set. The following call, which is an excerpt of the script baseline_from_sqlset.sql, illustrates this:

```
ret := dbms_spm.load_plans_from_sqlset(
        sqlset_name  => 'test_sqlset',
        sqlset_owner => user
     );
```

SQL plan baselines loaded with this function are stored as accepted, and therefore, the query optimizer is immediately able to take advantage of them.

The most important usage of this function is the upgrade to Oracle Database 11*g*. In fact, it is also possible to load a SQL tuning set created by Oracle Database 10*g*. The scripts baseline_upgrade_10g.sql and baseline_upgrade_11g.sql illustrate this utilization.

Displaying SQL Plan Baselines

General information about the available SQL plan baselines can be displayed through the data dictionary view dba_sql_plan_baselines. To display detailed information about them, the function display_sql_plan_baseline in the package dbms_xplan is available. Note that it works similarly to the other functions in the package dbms_xplan discussed in Chapter 6. The following example shows the kind of information that can be displayed with it:

```
SQL> SELECT *
  2  FROM table(dbms_xplan.display_sql_plan_baseline(
  3              sql_handle => 'SYS_SQL_492bdb47e8861a89'
  4          ));
```

```
--------------------------------------------------------------------------------
SQL handle: SYS_SQL_3d1b0b7d8fb2691f
SQL text: SELECT count(pad) FROM t WHERE n = 42
--------------------------------------------------------------------------------


--------------------------------------------------------------------------------
Plan name: SYS_SQL_PLAN_8fb2691f3fdbb376
Enabled: YES      Fixed: NO      Accepted: YES      Origin: MANUAL-LOAD
--------------------------------------------------------------------------------


Plan hash value: 2966233522


--------------------------------------------------------------------------------
| Id  | Operation          | Name | Rows  | Bytes | Cost (%CPU)| Time      |
--------------------------------------------------------------------------------
|   0 | SELECT STATEMENT   |      |     1 |   505 |    27   (0)| 00:00:01  |
|   1 |  SORT AGGREGATE    |      |     1 |   505 |            |           |
|*  2 |   TABLE ACCESS FULL| T    |     1 |   505 |    27   (0)| 00:00:01  |
--------------------------------------------------------------------------------


Predicate Information (identified by operation id):
---------------------------------------------------

   2 - filter("N"=42)
```

Unfortunately, to display the list of hints associated with a SQL plan baseline, undocumented data dictionary tables must be queried. The following SQL statement shows an example. Note that since hints are stored in XML format, a conversion is necessary to have a readable output.

```
SQL> SELECT extractValue(value(h),'.') AS hint
  2  FROM sys.sqlobj$data od, sys.sqlobj$ so,
  3       table(xmlsequence(extract(xmltype(od.comp_data),'/outline_data/hint'))) h
  4  WHERE so.name = 'SYS_SQL_PLAN_8fb2691f3fdbb376'
  5  AND so.signature = od.signature
  6  AND so.category = od.category
  7  AND so.obj_type = od.obj_type
  8  AND so.plan_id = od.plan_id;

HINT
-------------------------------------------
FULL(@"SEL$1" "T"@"SEL$1")
OUTLINE_LEAF(@"SEL$1")
ALL_ROWS
DB_VERSION('11.1.0.6')
OPTIMIZER_FEATURES_ENABLE('11.1.0.6')
IGNORE_OPTIM_EMBEDDED_HINTS
```

Evolving SQL Plan Baselines

When the query optimizer recognizes that an execution plan different from the one forced by a SQL plan baseline might be more efficient, new nonaccepted SQL plan baselines are automatically added. This will happen even if the query optimizer cannot use them. The idea is to tell you that other and possibly better execution plans exist. To verify whether one of the nonaccepted execution plans will in fact perform better than the ones generated with the help of accepted SQL plan baselines, an *evolution* must be attempted. This is nothing other than asking the query optimizer to run the SQL statement with different execution plans and finding out whether a nonaccepted SQL plan baseline will lead to better performance than an accepted one. If this is in fact the case, the nonaccepted SQL plan baseline is set to accepted. To execute an evolution, the function evolve_sql_plan_baseline in the package dbms_spm is available. To call this function, in addition to identifying the SQL plan baseline with the parameters sql_handle and/or plan_name, the following parameters can be specified:

time_limit: How long, in minutes, the evolution can last. This parameter accepts either a natural number or the constants dbms_spm.auto_limit and dbms_spm.no_limit.

verify: If set to yes (default), the SQL statement is executed to verify the performance. If set to no, no verification is performed, and the SQL plan baselines are simply accepted.

commit: If set to yes (default), the data dictionary is modified according to the result of the evolution. If set to no, provided the parameter verify is set to yes, the verification is performed without modifying the data dictionary.

The return value of the function is a report that provides details about the evolution. The following SQL statement is an example. In this specific case, the SQL plan baseline was evolved.

```
SQL> SELECT dbms_spm.evolve_sql_plan_baseline(
  2            sql_handle => 'SYS_SQL_492bdb47e8861a89',
  3            plan_name  => NULL,
  4            time_limit => 10,
  5            verify     => 'yes',
  6            commit     => 'yes'
  7          )
  8   FROM dual;


-------------------------------------------------------------------------------
                        Evolve SQL Plan Baseline Report
-------------------------------------------------------------------------------

Inputs:
-------
  SQL_HANDLE = SYS_SQL_492bdb47e8861a89
  PLAN_NAME  =
  TIME_LIMIT = 10
  VERIFY     = yes
  COMMIT     = yes
```

```
Plan: SYS_SQL_PLAN_e8861a8959340d78
-----------------------------------
  Plan was verified: Time used .01 seconds.
  Passed performance criterion: Compound improvement ratio >= 25.
  Plan was changed to an accepted plan.

                         Baseline Plan      Test Plan     Improv. Ratio
                         -------------      ---------     -------------
  Execution Status:        COMPLETE         COMPLETE
  Rows Processed:             1                1
  Elapsed Time(ms):           0                0
  CPU Time(ms):               0                0
  Buffer Gets:               75                3               25
  Disk Reads:                 0                0
  Direct Writes:              0                0
  Fetches:                    0                0
  Executions:                 1                1


-------------------------------------------------------------------------
                              Report Summary
-------------------------------------------------------------------------
Number of SQL plan baselines verified: 1.
Number of SQL plan baselines evolved: 1.
```

In addition to the manual evolution just explained, automatic evolution of SQL plan baselines is supported with the Tuning Pack. The idea is simply that an automated task periodically checks whether nonaccepted SQL plan baselines should be evolved.

Altering SQL Plan Baselines

You can use the procedure alter_sql_plan_baseline in the package dbms_spm not only to modify some of the properties specified when the SQL plan baseline was created but also to change its status (either enabled or disabled). The parameters sql_handle and plan_name identify the SQL plan baseline to be modified. At least one of the two must be specified. The parameters attribute_name and attribute_value specify the property to be modified and its new value. The parameter attribute_name accepts the following values:

enabled: This attribute can be set to either yes or no, although a SQL plan baseline can be used by the query optimizer only when set to yes.

fixed: With this attribute set to yes, SQL plan baselines cannot be evolved over time, and they are preferred over nonfixed SQL plan baselines. It can be set to either yes or no.

autopurge: A SQL plan baseline with this attribute set to yes is automatically removed if it is not used over a retention period (the configuration of the retention is discussed later in the section "Dropping SQL Plan Baselines"). It can be set to either yes or no.

plan_name: This attribute is used to change the SQL plan name. It can be any string of up to 30 characters.

description: This attribute is used to attach a description to the SQL plan baseline. It can be any string of up to 500 characters.

In the following call, a SQL plan baseline is disabled:

```
ret := dbms_spm. alter_sql_plan_baseline(
        sql_handle       => 'SYS_SQL_3d1b0b7d8fb2691f',
        plan_name        => 'SYS_SQL_PLAN_8fb2691f3fdbb376',
        attribute_name => 'enabled',
        attribute_value => 'no'
      );
```

Activating SQL Plan Baselines

The query optimizer uses the available SQL plan baselines only when the dynamic initialization parameter optimizer_use_sql_plan_baselines is set to TRUE. The default value is TRUE. You can change it at the session and system levels.

Moving SQL Plan Baselines

The package dbms_spm provides several procedures for moving SQL plan baselines between databases. This is needed when, for example, the SQL plan baselines have to be generated on a development or test database and moved to the production database. As shown in Figure 7-11, the following features are provided:

- You can create a staging table using the procedure create_stgtab_baseline.

- You can copy SQL plan baselines from the data dictionary to the staging table through the function pack_stgtab_baseline.

- You can copy SQL plan baselines from the staging table into the data dictionary through the function unpack_stgtab_baseline.

Notice that moving the staging table between databases is performed by means of a data movement utility (for example, Data Pump or the legacy export and import utilities) and not with the package dbms_spm itself (see Figure 7-11).

The following example, which is an excerpt of the script clone_baseline.sql, shows how to copy a SQL plan baseline from one database into another. First, the staging table mystgtab is created in the current schema.

```
dbms_spm.create_stgtab_baseline(
  table_name       => 'MYSTGTAB',
  table_owner      => user,
  tablespace_name => 'USERS'
);
```

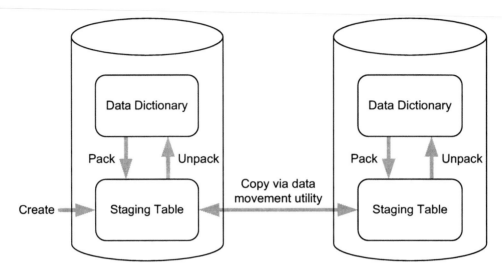

Figure 7-11. *Moving SQL plan baselines with the package dbms_spm*

Then, a SQL plan baseline is copied from the data dictionary into the staging table. You can identify which SQL plan baselines are to be processed in four ways:

- Identify the SQL plan baseline exactly, through the parameters sql_handle and, optionally, plan_name.

- Select all SQL plan baselines that contain a specific string in the text of the SQL statement associated with them. For this purpose, the parameter sql_text, which also supports wildcards (for example, %), is available. Note that the parameter is case-sensitive.

- Select all SQL plan baselines matching one or several of the following parameters: creator, origin, enabled, accepted, fixed, module, and action. If several parameters are specified, all of them must be fulfilled.

- Processing all SQL plan baselines. For that, no parameters are specified.

The following call shows an example where the SQL plan baseline is identified exactly:

```
ret := dbms_spm.pack_stgtab_baseline(
        table_name   => 'MYSTGTAB',
        table_owner  => user,
        sql_handle   => 'SYS_SQL_3d1b0b7d8fb2691f',
        plan_name    => 'SYS_SQL_PLAN_8fb2691f3fdbb376'
      );
```

At this point, the staging table mystgtab is copied by means of a data movement utility from one database into another.

Finally, the SQL plan baseline is copied from the staging table into the data dictionary in the target database. To identify which SQL plan baselines are processed, the same methods as for the function pack_stgtab_baseline are available. The following call shows an example where the SQL plan baselines are identified by the text of the SQL statement associated with them:

```
ret := dbms_spm.unpack_stgtab_baseline(
        table_name  => 'MYSTGTAB',
        table_owner => user,
        sql_text    => '%FROM t%'
      );
```

Dropping SQL Plan Baselines

You can use the procedure drop_sql_plan_baseline in the package dbms_spm to drop a SQL plan baseline from the data dictionary. The parameters sql_handle and plan_name identify the SQL plan baseline to be dropped. At least one of the two must be specified. The following call illustrates this:

```
ret := dbms_spm.drop_sql_plan_baseline(
        sql_handle => 'SYS_SQL_3d1b0b7d8fb2691f',
        plan_name  => 'SYS_SQL_PLAN_8fb2691f3fdbb376'
      );
```

Unused SQL plan baselines that don't have the attribute fixed set to yes are automatically removed after a retention period. The default retention period is 53 weeks. The current value can be displayed through the data dictionary view dba_sql_management_config.

```
SQL> SELECT parameter_value
  2  FROM dba_sql_management_config
  3  WHERE parameter_name = 'PLAN_RETENTION_WEEKS';

PARAMETER_VALUE
---------------
             53
```

You can change the retention period by calling the procedure configure in the package dbms_spm. Values between 5 and 523 weeks are supported. The following example shows how to change it to 12 weeks. If the parameter parameter_value is set to NULL, the default value is restored.

```
dbms_spm.configure(
  parameter_name  => 'plan_retention_weeks',
  parameter_value => 12
);
```

Privileges

When SQL plan baselines are automatically captured (that is, by setting the initialization parameter optimizer_capture_sql_plan_baselines to TRUE), no particular privilege is needed to create them.

The package dbms_spm can be executed only by users with the system privilege administer sql management object (the role dba includes it by default). No object privileges exist for SQL plan baselines.

End users do not require specific privileges to use SQL plan baselines.

When to Use It

You should consider using this technique in two situations. First, you should consider using it whenever you are tuning a specific SQL statement and you are not able to change it in the application (for example, when adding hints is not an option). Second, you should consider using it when, for whatever reason, you are experiencing troublesome instability of execution plans.

Unfortunately, SQL plan baselines are available only with Enterprise Edition.

Pitfalls and Fallacies

You must be aware that SQL plan baselines are not immediately dropped when the objects they depend on are dropped. This is not necessarily a problem, however. For example, if a table or an index needs to be re-created because it must be reorganized or moved, it is a good thing that the SQL plan baselines are not dropped; otherwise, it would be necessary to re-create them. In any case, unused SQL plan baselines will be purged when the retention period ends.

Two SQL statements with the same text have the same signature. This is also true even if they reference objects in different schemas. This means that a single SQL plan baseline could be used for two tables that have the same name but are located in different schemas! You should be very careful, especially if you have a database with multiple copies of the same objects.

SQL plan baselines are stored in the tablespace sysaux. By default, at most 10 percent of the tablespace can be used for them. The current value can be displayed through the data dictionary view dba_sql_management_config:

```
SQL> SELECT parameter_value
  2  FROM dba_sql_management_config
  3  WHERE parameter_name = 'SPACE_BUDGET_PERCENT';

PARAMETER_VALUE
---------------
             10
```

When the threshold is exceeded, a warning message is written in the alert log. To change the default threshold, the procedure configure in the package dbms_spm is available. Values between 1 percent and 50 percent are supported. The following example shows how to change it to 5 percent. If the parameter parameter_value is set to NULL, the default value is restored.

```
dbms_spm.configure(
  parameter_name  => 'space_budget_percent',
  parameter_value => 5
);
```

On to Chapter 8

This chapter described several SQL tuning techniques. Selecting one of them is not always easy. Nevertheless, if you understand the pros and cons of using them, the choice is much easier. That said, in practice your choice is limited because you can't apply all techniques in all situations. This may be either because of technical limits or because there are licensing issues.

This chapter was the last one entirely devoted to the query optimizer. With the next chapter, Part 4 begins. Finally, it is time not only to learn how to efficiently access and join data but also to recognize how to take advantage of the many features designed to improve the performance of SQL statements.

The first chapter in Part 4 is devoted to parsing, which is surely a central step in the execution of SQL statements. It is so important because it is when the query optimizer generates the execution plans. To always have an efficient execution plan, you want to parse every SQL statement executed by the database engine, but conversely, parsing is inherently a very expensive operation. As a result, it must be minimized, and execution plans should be reused as much as possible—but not too much, though. This might mean that the execution plan is not always an efficient one. Once again, in order to take advantage of the database engine in the best possible way, you have to understand how it works and what the pros and cons of the different features are.

PART 4

■■■

Optimization

Performance is your reality. Forget everything else.

—Harold Geneen[1]

Only once you have identified the root cause of a performance problem should you try to solve it. As described in Chapter 3, several kinds of problems exist. Regardless of the problem you are facing, the essential goal to achieve is reducing—or, even better, eliminating—the time spent by the most time-consuming operation. Note that a single operation may be composed of many actions that are executed one by one. For example, many fetches are necessary in order to fully process a query returning a lot of data.

Chapter 8 describes how parsing works, how to identify parsing problems, and how to minimize its impact without jeopardizing performance. Chapter 9 describes how to take advantage of available access structures in order to access data stored in a single table efficiently. Chapter 10 goes beyond accessing a single table, by describing how to join data from several tables together. Chapter 11 deals with parallel processing and the techniques used for speeding up stream inserts and for minimizing the interactions between components. Finally, Chapter 12 describes how some physical storage parameters may also have an observable impact on performance. Simply put, the aim of the chapters in this part is to show how to improve the response time of operations interacting with the SQL engine by taking advantage of the many features provided by the database engine for that purpose.

---

1. You can find this quote at http://www.quotationspage.com/quote/4442.html.

CHAPTER 8

■ ■ ■

Parsing

The impact of parsing on overall performance is extremely variable. In some cases, it is simply not noticeable. In other cases, it is one of the major causes of performance problems. If you have problems with parsing, it usually means the application does not handle it correctly. This is a major problem, because more often than not, to change the behavior of an application, you need to modify the code considerably. Developers need to be aware of the implications of parsing and how to write code in such a way as to avoid, as much as possible, the problems associated with it.

Chapter 2 described the life cycle of a cursor and how parsing works. This chapter describes how to identify, solve, and work around parsing problems. I'll also discuss the overhead associated with parsing. Finally, I'll describe the features provided by common application programming interfaces that reduce parsing activities.

Identifying Parsing Problems

While identifying parsing problems, it is easy to have an attack of compulsive tuning disorder. The problem is that several dynamic performance views contain counters that detail the number of soft parses, hard parses, and executions. These counters, as well as the ratios based on them, are useless because they provide no information about the time spent parsing. Note that with parses this is a real problem because they have no typical duration. In fact, depending on the complexity of the SQL statement and the objects it references, the duration of parses commonly differs by several orders of magnitude. Simply put, such counters tell you only whether the database engine has done a few or many parses, without any information about whether this is a problem. Because of this, in practice they may be useful only for trending purposes.

If you are following the analysis road map described in Chapter 3, it should be clear that the only effective way of identifying parsing problems you should consider is to measure how much time is spent by parsing operations. For this type of analysis, if you are looking for hard facts and not just clues, there is only a single source of information you can use: the output generated by SQL trace. Note that I consider approaches based on the parse time found in dynamic performance views such as v$sesstat and v$sess_time_model to be not particularly valuable, because they generally provide no means of finding out which SQL statements are responsible for the high parse time.

There are two main kinds of parsing problems. The first is associated with parses lasting a very short time. Let's call them *quick parses*. Of course, to be noticeable, a lot of them have to be executed. The second kind of parsing problem is associated with parses lasting a long time. Let's call this type *long parses*. This usually happens when the SQL statement is fairly complex and the query optimizer needs a long time to generate an efficient execution plan. In this case, the number of executions is not relevant.

I'll describe the method used to identify the two kinds of parsing problems in the next two sections. Since there is no real difference in their identification, I'll describe only the first one in full detail.

Quick Parses

The following sections describe how to identify performance problems caused by quick parses. Since Chapter 3 describes two profilers, TKPROF and TVD$XTAT, I'll discuss the same example for the output file of both profilers. The trace file used as an example in this section was generated by executing the Java class stored in the file ParsingTest1.java. The trace file and both output files are available in the file ParsingTest1.zip. Implementations of the same processing in PL/SQL, C (OCI), and C# (ODP.NET) are available as well.

Using TKPROF

As suggested in Chapter 3, TKPROF is executed with the following options:

```
tkprof <trace file> <output file> sys=no sort=prsela,exeela,fchela
```

To start the analysis of the output file, it is always good to take a look at the last few lines. In this specific case, it is important to notice that the processing lasted about 13 seconds, that the application executed 10,000 SQL statements, and that probably almost all SQL statements were different from each other (SQL statements ≈ unique SQL statements).

```
     1  session in tracefile.
 10000  user  SQL statements in trace file.
    62  internal SQL statements in trace file.
 10062  SQL statements in trace file.
 10013  unique SQL statements in trace file.
110627  lines in trace file.
    13  elapsed seconds in trace file.
```

Next, it is time to check how long the first SQL statement listed in the output lasted. Remember, thanks to the option sort that you have specified, the SQL statements were sorted according to their response times. Interestingly enough, the response time (column elapsed) of the first cursor is less than 100th of a second (0.00). In other words, all SQL statements were executed in less than 100th of a second. Actually, on average, an execution lasted 1.3 milliseconds (13/10,000). This means the response time is certainly not due to a few long-running SQL statements but to the high number of SQL statements processed in a short time.

call	count	cpu	elapsed	disk	query	current	rows
Parse	1	0.00	0.00	0	0	0	0
Execute	1	0.00	0.00	0	0	0	0
Fetch	1	0.00	0.00	0	2	0	0
total	3	0.00	0.00	0	2	0	0

In such a situation, to know whether parsing is a problem, you must examine the section providing the overall totals. According to the execution statistics, the parse time was responsible for about 95 percent (4.83/5.10) of the processing time. This clearly shows that the database engine did nothing else besides parsing.

```
call     count     cpu   elapsed     disk      query    current      rows
-------  ------  -------- --------- ---------- ---------- ---------- ----------
Parse    10000     4.83      4.83        0          0          0          0
Execute  10000     0.12      0.13        0          0          0          0
Fetch    10000     0.20      0.13        0      23051          0       3048
-------  ------  -------- --------- ---------- ---------- ---------- ----------
total    30000     5.10      5.10        0      23051          0       3048
```

The following line also shows that each of the 10,000 parses was a hard parse. Note that even if a high percentage of hard parses is usually not wanted, it is not necessarily a problem. It is just a clue that something may be suboptimal.

```
Misses in library cache during parse: 10000
```

The problem with the execution statistics is that about 61 percent (1–5.10/13) of the response time is missing from them. Actually, by looking at the table summarizing the wait events, it can be seen that 5.94 seconds were spent waiting for the client. That still leaves us with about two seconds (13–5.94–5.10) of time still unaccounted for, however.

```
Event waited on                          Times    Max. Wait  Total Waited
---------------------------------------  Waited   ---------- ------------
SQL*Net message to client                10000      0.00         0.00
SQL*Net message from client              10000      0.02         5.94
latch: shared pool                           1      0.00         0.00
```

Since you know that parsing is a problem, it is wise to take a look at the SQL statements. In this case, by looking at a few of them (the following are the top five), it is evident that they are very similar. Only the literals used in the WHERE clauses are different. This is a typical case of where bind variables are not used.

```
SELECT pad FROM t WHERE val = 7650
SELECT pad FROM t WHERE val = 8977
SELECT pad FROM t WHERE val = 3233
SELECT pad FROM t WHERE val = 7777
SELECT pad FROM t WHERE val = 3234
```

The problem in such situations is that TKPROF does not recognize SQL statements that differ only in their literal values. In fact, even when the option aggregate is set to yes, which is the default, only the SQL statements that have the same text are grouped together. This is a major flaw that in real cases makes analyzing parsing problems with TKPROF difficult. To make it a bit easier, it is possible to specify the TKPROF option record. In this way, a file containing only the SQL statements is generated.

```
tkprof <trace file> <output file> sys=no sort=prsela,exeela,fchela record=<sql file>
```

Then you can use command-line utilities such as grep and wc to find out how many similar SQL statements are available. For example, the following command returns the value 10,000:

```
grep "SELECT pad FROM t WHERE val =" <sql file> | wc -l
```

Using TVD$XTAT

TVD$XTAT is executed without specifying particular options:

```
tvdxtat −i <trace file> -o <output file>
```

The analysis of the output file starts by looking at the overall resource usage profile. The processing here lasted about 13 seconds. Of this time, about 45 percent was spent waiting for the client, and about 39 percent was spent running on the CPU. The figures are basically the same as the ones described in the previous section. Only the precision is different. The only additional information in the first section is that the unaccounted-for time is explicitly given.

Component	Total Duration	%	Number of Events	Duration per Event
SQL*Net message from client	5.946	**45.353**	10,000	0.001
CPU	5.132	**39.147**	n/a	n/a
unaccounted-for	2.024	15.436	n/a	n/a
SQL*Net message to client	0.007	0.054	10,000	0.000
latch: shared pool	0.001	0.010	1	0.001
Total	**13.110**	100.000		

By just looking at the summary of nonrecursive SQL statements, you can see that a single SQL statement is responsible for the whole processing. This is a significant difference between TKPROF and TVD$XTAT. In fact, TVD$XTAT recognizes similar SQL statements and reports them together.

Statement ID	Type	Total Duration	%	Number of Executions	Duration per Execution
1	SELECT	11.086	84.564	10,000	0.001
Total		11.086	84.564		

In the output file, only the first SQL statement found during the analysis is shown. In addition, a message informs you about the number of similar SQL statement found:

```
10000 similar SQL statements were detected
```

According to the execution statistics, without recursive statements of the SQL statement number 1, the parse time is responsible for about 95 percent (4.835/5.106) of the processing time. This clearly shows that the database engine did nothing else besides parsing. The slight difference in the execution statistics between the output file of TKPROF and TVD$XTAT is that TVD$XTAT shows the number of misses (in other words, hard parses) next to the number of parse calls.

Call	Count	Misses	CPU	Elapsed	PIO	LIO	Consistent	Current	Rows
Parse	10,000	10,000	4.835	4.835	0	0	0	0	0
Execute	10,000	0	0.122	0.139	0	0	0	0	0
Fetch	10,000	0	0.150	0.131	0	23,051	23,051	0	3,048
Total	30,000	10,000	5.107	5.106	0	23,051	23,051	0	3,048

The problem with these execution statistics is that about 54 percent (1–5.106/11.086) of the response time is missing from them. At any rate, you can see the missing time by looking at the resource usage profile at the SQL statement level shown here; specifically, 5.946 seconds were spent waiting for the client.

Component	Total Duration	%	Number of Events	Duration per Event
SQL*Net message from client	5.946	53.631	10,000	0.001
CPU	5.107	46.067	n/a	n/a
recursive statements	0.025	0.225	n/a	n/a
SQL*Net message to client	0.007	0.064	10,000	0.000
latch: shared pool	0.001	0.012	1	0.001
Total	11.086	100.000		

Summarizing the Problem

The analysis performed by TKPROF and TVD$XTAT shows that the processing performed by the database engine is solely due to parsing. However, on the database side, parsing is responsible for only about 37 percent (4.835/13.110) of the overall response time. This implies that eliminating it should approximately halve the overall response time. The analysis also shows that 10,000 SQL statements like the following one were parsed and executed once:

```
SELECT pad FROM t WHERE val = 3233
```

Since a constantly changing literal value is used, shared cursors in the library cache cannot be reused. In other words, every parse is a hard parse. Figure 8-1 shows a graphical representation of this processing.

Note The processing shown in Figure 8-1 is later referred to as *test case 1*.

It goes without saying that such processing is inefficient. Refer to the section "Solving Parsing Problems" later in this chapter for possible solutions to such a problem.

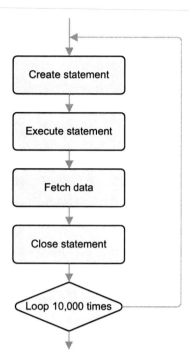

Figure 8-1. *The processing performed by test case 1*

Long Parses

The following sections describe how to identify performance problems caused by long parses. Since Chapter 3 describes two profilers, TKPROF and TVD$XTAT, I'll discuss the same example for the output file of both profilers. The trace file used as an example in this section was generated by executing the script `long_parse.sql`. The trace file and the output files are available in the file `long_parse.zip`.

Using TKPROF

Like for quick parses, the analysis starts at the end of the TKPROF output. In this specific case, it is significant to note that the processing lasted about one second and that the application executed only three SQL statements. All other SQL statements were recursively executed by the database engine.

```
   1  session in tracefile.
   3  user  SQL statements in trace file.
 612  internal SQL statements in trace file.
 615  SQL statements in trace file.
  16  unique SQL statements in trace file.
4931  lines in trace file.
   1  elapsed seconds in trace file.
```

By looking at the execution statistics of the first SQL statement in the output file, it is possible to see not only that it was responsible for the whole response time (about one second) but also that all the time is spent on a single parse:

call	count	cpu	elapsed	disk	query	current	rows
Parse	1	1.07	**1.05**	0	0	0	0
Execute	1	0.00	0.00	0	0	0	0
Fetch	2	0.00	0.00	0	19	0	1
total	4	1.08	**1.06**	0	19	0	1

Using TVD$XTAT

Like for quick parses, the analysis of the TVD$XTAT output starts by looking at the overall resource usage profile. The processing lasted about 1.6 seconds. Of this time, about 71 percent was spent running on the CPU, and 29 percent was spent waiting for the client. Also notice that in this case, the unaccounted-for time is very short and, therefore, completely negligible.

Component	Total Duration	%	Number of Events	Duration per Event
CPU	1.139	**71.281**	n/a	n/a
SQL*Net message from client	0.471	**29.478**	5	0.094
SQL*Net message to client	0.000	0.001	5	0.000
SQL*Net more data from client	0.000	0.001	1	0.000
unaccounted-for	-0.012	-0.761	n/a	n/a
Total	1.598	100.000		

Just by looking at the summary of nonrecursive SQL statements, you can see that three SQL statements were executed. Of them, the first is responsible for almost all the response time.

Statement ID	Type	Total Duration	%	Number of Executions	Duration per Execution
1	SELECT	1.138	71.230	1	1.138
5	PL/SQL	0.003	0.201	1	0.003
13	PL/SQL	0.001	0.063	1	0.001
Total		1.142	71.493		

Notice that in previous figures, the total is not 100 percent because one long-lasting SQL*Net message from client wait was not associated with any cursor. The only way to confirm this is to open the trace file and search for waits belonging to any cursor (such waits are associated with the cursor #0 in the trace file).

```
...
WAIT #0: nam='SQL*Net message to client' ela= 1 driver id=1413697536 ...
WAIT #0: nam='SQL*Net message from client' ela= 465535 driver id=1413697536 ...
WAIT #0: nam='SQL*Net more data from client' ela= 16 driver id=1413697536 ...
...
```

You can confirm this by looking at the following detailed statistics about that type of event. Notice especially that one event lasted about 0.5 seconds, while the overall wait time attributed to the SQL statements is 3 milliseconds.

Duration [μs]	Total Duration	%	Number of Events	%	Duration per Event [μs]
< 1024	0.001	0.131	1	20.000	618
< 2048	0.003	0.585	2	40.000	1,377
< 4096	0.002	0.435	1	20.000	2,050
< 524288	0.466	98.849	1	20.000	465,535
Total	0.471	100.000	5	100.000	94,191

2 statements contributed to this event.

Statement ID	Type	Total Duration	%
1	SELECT	0.002	0.463
5	PL/SQL	0.001	0.253
Total		0.003	0.716

According to the nonrecursive execution statistics of the SQL statement causing the problem, a single parse operation was responsible for about 100 percent (1.056/1.061) of the processing time. This clearly shows that the database engine did nothing else besides parsing.

Call	Count	Misses	CPU	Elapsed	PIO	LIO	Consistent	Current	Rows
Parse	1	1	1.080	1.056	0	0	0	0	0
Execute	1	0	0.001	0.001	0	0	0	0	0
Fetch	2	0	0.003	0.003	0	19	19	0	1
Total	4	1	1.084	1.061	0	19	19	0	1

Summarizing the Problem

The analysis with TKPROF and TVD$XTAT showed that a single SQL statement is responsible for almost the whole response time. In addition, the whole response time is due to parsing for this particular SQL statement. Eliminating it would probably greatly reduce the response time.

Solving Parsing Problems

The obvious way to solve parsing problems is to avoid the parse phase. Unfortunately, this is not always that easy. In fact, depending on whether the parsing problem is related to quick parses or long parses, you have to implement different techniques to solve the problem. I'll discuss these separately in the following sections. In both cases, the examples described in the section "Identifying Parsing Problems" are used as the basis for explaining possible solutions.

░**Note** The following sections describe the impact of parsing by showing the results of different performance tests. The performance figures are intended only to help compare different kinds of processing and to give you a feel for their impact. Remember, every system and every application has its own characteristics. Therefore, the relevance of using each technique might be very different depending on where it is applied.

Quick Parses

This section describes how to take advantage of prepared statements to avoid unnecessary parse operations. Since implementation details depend on the development environment, they are not covered here. Later in this chapter, specifically in the section "Using Application Programming Interfaces," I provide details for PL/SQL, OCI, JDBC, and ODP.NET.

Using Prepared Statements

The first thing to do when a SQL statement causing parsing problems uses literals that are constantly changing is to replace the literals with bind variables. For that, you have to use a *prepared statement*. The aim of using a prepared statement is to share a single cursor for all SQL statements and, consequently, to avoid unnecessary hard parses. Figure 8-2 shows a graphical representation of the processing intended to improve on the performance in test case 1.

░**Note** The processing shown by Figure 8-2 later is referenced as *test case 2*.

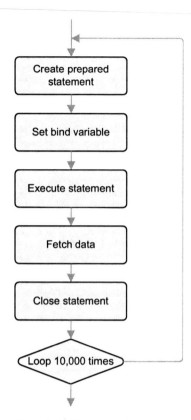

Figure 8-2. *The processing performed by test case 2*

With that enhancement, as shown in Figure 8-3, the response time decreased by about 41 percent compared with test case 1. This was expected because the new code, thanks to the prepared statement, performed only a single hard parse. As a result, most of the processing carried out by the database engine in test case 1 was avoided. Note, however, that 10,000 soft parses were still performed.

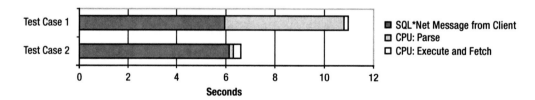

Figure 8-3. *Comparison of the database-side resource usage profile in test case 1 and test case 2 (components that account for less than 1 percent of the response time are not displayed because they would not be visible)*

Reusing Prepared Statements

I suggested in the previous section that using prepared statements is a very good thing. It is even better to reuse them to eliminate not only the hard parses but the soft parses as well. Since in test case 2 the elapsed time for the parses is almost not noticeable, you may ask yourself why. Before giving an answer, I'll show the performance figures related to processing that reuses a single prepared statement. Specifically, Figure 8-4 shows a graphical representation of the processing intended to improve on the performance in test case 2.

Note The processing shown in Figure 8-4 is later referred to as *test case 3*.

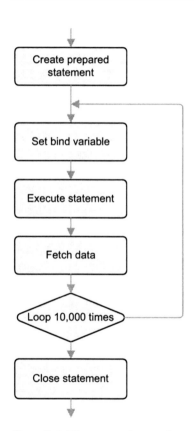

Figure 8-4. *The processing performed by test case 3*

With this enhancement, as shown in Figure 8-5, the response time, compared with test case 1 and test case 2, decreased by about 61 percent and 33 percent, respectively. Significantly, the real difference was made not by the reduction of the CPU time spent to parse (which is already very low in test case 2) but by the reduction of the wait for SQL*Net message from client. This means you are saving resources either in the network or in the client, or possibly both.

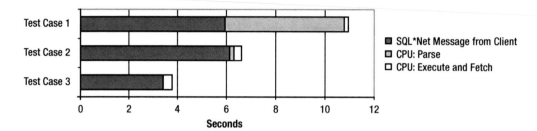

Figure 8-5. *Comparison of the database-side resource usage profile for three test cases (components that account for less than 1 percent of the response time are not displayed because they would not be visible)*

In test case 2, the processing of soft parses at the database level lasted about one-tenth of a second. The question is, where does the improvement come from? It surely doesn't come from the reduction of resource utilization at the database level. You might intuitively think that the gain is because of fewer round-trips between the client and the server. However, by looking at the number of waits for SQL*Net message from client or SQL*Net message to client, you can see that there is no difference among the three test cases. In each case, there are 10,000 round-trips. This is significant because 10,000 executions are performed, and therefore, this implies that in this particular case the parse, execute, and fetch calls are packed into one single SQL*Net message by the client driver. There is, however, a difference in the network layer because of the size of the messages sent between the client and the server. You can use the following query to get information about them:

```
SELECT sn.name, ss.value
FROM v$statname sn, v$sesstat ss
WHERE sn.statistic# = ss.statistic#
AND sn.name LIKE 'bytes%client'
AND ss.sid = 42
```

Figure 8-6 shows the figures for the three test cases. It is important to notice how prepared statements slightly increase the size of the messages received from the database engine. The most important difference, though, is the substantial reduction of the size of the messages both received and sent from the database engine, comparing test case 3 with the other two. This is caused by the data sent over the network in order to open and close a new cursor (for example, in test case 3, the text of the SQL statement is sent only once over the network).

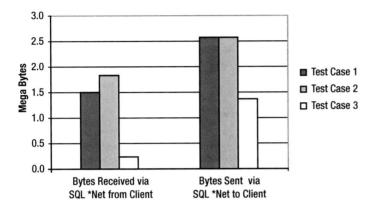

Figure 8-6. *Network traffic for a single execution of the three test cases*

Since the size of the messages sent through the network differs, the response time is expected to depend on the network speed. If the network is fast, the impact of the communication between the client and the server is low or not even noticeable. If the network is slow, the impact may be significant. Figure 8-7 shows the figures for two network speeds. Notice how the time spent by the database engine processing the calls for a given test case does not depend, obviously, on the network speed.

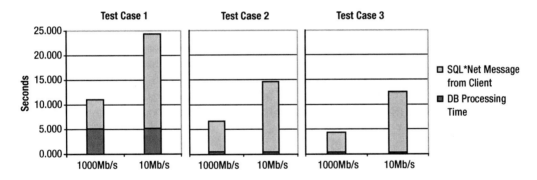

Figure 8-7. *Response time with two network speeds for the three test cases*

Even if the network speed had an impact on the overall response time, it is important to note that the three test cases have a very different impact on the client-side resource utilization, specifically the CPU. Figure 8-8 shows the client-side CPU utilization measured with a profiler. The comparison of the figures for test case 1 and test case 2 shows that the use of bind variables has a small overhead for the client. The comparison of the figures for test case 2 and test case 3 shows that creating and closing SQL statements cause a significant overhead for the client.

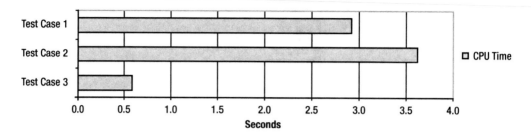

Figure 8-8. *Client-side CPU utilization for the three test cases*

By comparing the results of test case 2 with test case 3, you can see that the reduction of client CPU shown in Figure 8-8 (3.6 − 0.6 = 3.0) nearly matches the reduction in elapsed time unrelated to the database activity in Figure 8-5 (6.1 − 3.4 = 2.7).

Client-Side Statement Caching

This feature is designed to solve performance problems created by applications that cause too many soft parses because cursors are unnecessarily opened and closed. Earlier in this chapter, this problem was indicated by test case 2.

The concept of client-side statement caching is quite simple. Whenever the application closes a cursor, instead of really closing it, the client-side database layer (which is responsible for communicating with the database engine) keeps it open and adds it to a cache. Then, later, if a cursor based on the same SQL statement is opened and parsed again, instead of really opening and parsing it, the cached cursor is reused. Thus, the soft parse should not take place. Basically, the aim is to have an application behaving like test case 3, even if it is written like test case 2.

To take advantage of this feature, it is usually only a matter of enabling it and defining the maximum number of cursors that can be cached by a session. Note that when the cache is full, the least recently used cursors are replaced by newer ones. The activation takes place either by adding some initialization code into the application or by setting a variable in the environment. How this works exactly depends on the programming environment. Later in this chapter, specifically in the section "Using Application Programming Interfaces," details are provided for PL/SQL, OCI, JDBC, and ODP.NET. To set the maximum number of cached cursors, you need to know the application that is being used. If you don't know it, you should analyze the TKPROF or TVD$XTAT output to find out how many SQL statements are subject to a high number of soft parses. In both cases, this is just a first estimation. Afterward, you will have to perform some tests to verify whether the value is good. In any case, it makes no sense to exceed the value of the initialization parameter open_cursors.

As shown in Figure 8-9, test case 2 with client-side statement caching performs almost as well as test case 3. Actually, both executed a single hard parse and a single soft parse. As a result, thanks to statement caching, the client-side processing is greatly reduced.

Figure 8-10 shows, for test case 2, the client-side CPU utilization measured with a profiler, with and without client-side statement caching. From these figures, it is obvious that it is advantageous to use client-side statement caching, not only for the server but also for the client. Actually, in this case, it is the client especially that takes advantage of it.

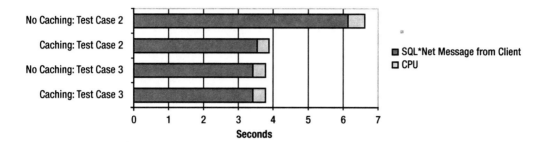

Figure 8-9. *Comparison of the database-side resource usage profile with and without client-side statement caching (components that account for less than 1 percent of the response time are not displayed because they would not be visible)*

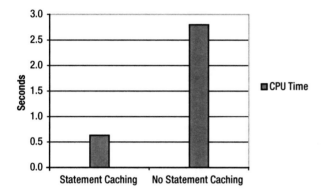

Figure 8-10. *Client-side CPU utilization with and without client-side statement caching*

Summing Up

Utilizing prepared statements with bind variables is crucial in order to avoid unnecessary hard parses. However, when using them, you can expect a small overhead in the client-side CPU utilization and network traffic. You could argue that this overhead will lead to performance problems and, consequently, that prepared statements and bind variables should be used only when really necessary. Since the overhead is almost always negligible, the best practice is to use prepared statements and bind variables whenever possible, as long as they do not lead to inefficient execution plans (refer to Chapters 2 and 4 for detailed information about this topic).

Whenever a prepared statement is frequently used, it is a good idea to reuse it. By doing so, not only do you avoid soft parses, but you reduce the client-side CPU utilization and the network traffic as well. The only problem related to keeping a prepared statement open has to do with memory utilization, on both the client side and the server side. This means that keeping thousands of cursors open per session must be done carefully and only when the necessary memory is available. Also note that the initialization parameter open_cursors limits the number of cursors that can be concurrently kept open by a single session. In case many prepared statements have to be cached, it is probably better to use client-side statement caching with a carefully sized cache instead of manually keeping them open. In this way, the memory pressure may be mitigated by allowing a limited number of prepared statements to be cached.

Long Parses

In case of long parses that are executed only a few times (or as in the previous example only once), it is usually not possible to avoid the parse phase. In fact, the SQL statement must be parsed at least once. In addition, if the SQL statement is rarely executed, a hard parse is probably inevitable because the cursor will be aged out of the library cache between executions. This is especially true if no bind variables are used. Therefore, the only possible solution is to reduce the parsing time itself.

What causes long parse times? Commonly, they're caused by the query optimizer evaluating too many different execution plans. This means that to shorten the parse times, you must reduce the number of evaluated execution plans. This is generally possible only by forcing an execution plan through hints or stored outlines. For example, after creating a stored outline for the SQL statement used as an example in the section "Identifying Parsing Problems," the parse time is reduced by one order of magnitude (see Figure 8-11). A similar effect may be reached by directly specifying hints in the SQL statement, although this is possible only if you are able to modify the code.

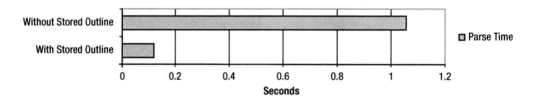

Figure 8-11. *Comparison of the parse time with and without a stored outline*

Working Around Parsing Problems

The previous sections described three test cases related to quick parses. The first is simply a case of poor code writing. The second is much better than the first. The third is the best in most situations. The dilemma is that code has to be modified in order to enhance it, and that, unfortunately, is not always possible. This is either because the code is not available, because of technical barriers (for example, prepared statements are not available in the programming environment), or simply because it is too "expensive" to make all the necessary modifications.

The following sections explain how to work around such problems in order to achieve results similar to those reached by carrying out the right implementation. Even if the performance of such workarounds is not as good as that possible with a correct implementation, in some situations the workaround is much better than doing nothing at all.

■Note The following sections describe the impact of parsing by showing the results of different performance tests. The performance figures are intended only to help compare different kinds of processing and to give you a feel for their impact. Remember, every system and every application has its own characteristics. Therefore, the relevance of using each technique might be very different depending on where it is applied.

Cursor Sharing

This feature is designed to work around performance problems caused by applications that improperly use literals instead of bind variables, which in turn leads to too many hard parses because literals are used instead of bind variables. Earlier in this chapter, I pointed this problem out in test case 1.

The concept of cursor sharing is simple. If an application executes SQL statements containing literals, the database engine automatically replaces the literals with bind variables. Note, however, that no replacement is performed if at least one bind variable is already present in a SQL statement. Thanks to these replacements, hard parses are turned into soft parses for the SQL statements that differ only in the literals. Basically, the goal is to have an application behaving like test case 2, even if it is written like test case 1.

Cursor sharing is controlled through the dynamic initialization parameter `cursor_sharing`. If it is set to `exact`, the feature is disabled. In other words, SQL statements share the same parent cursor only if their text is identical. If `cursor_sharing` is set to `force` or `similar`, the feature is enabled. The default value is `exact`. You can change it at the system and session levels. It is also possible to explicitly disable cursor sharing at the SQL statement level by specifying the hint `cursor_sharing_exact`.

■**Caution** Cursor sharing has a reputation for not being very stable. This is because, over the years, plenty of bugs related to it have been found and fixed. Therefore, my advice is to carefully test applications when cursor sharing is enabled.

Since cursor sharing can be enabled with two values, `force` and `similar`, let's discuss what the difference is between them. For that purpose, test case 1 was executed once for each value of the initialization parameter `cursor_sharing`.

Let's take a look at the results with the value `force`. As shown in Figure 8-12, the database-side resource usage profile in test case 1 (with the value `force`) is similar to the one in test case 2 with `exact`. Actually, both executed a single hard parse and 10,000 soft parses. As a result, thanks to cursor sharing, the parse time was greatly reduced. With the value `force`, there is just a slight increase in the CPU utilization. Since the database engine has to perform more work in order to replace literals with bind variables, this is to be expected.

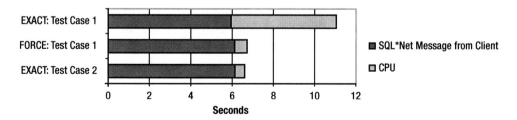

Figure 8-12. *Comparison of the database-side resource usage profile with cursor sharing set to force (components that account for less than 1 percent of the response time are not displayed because they would not be visible)*

The problem related to the value force is that a single child cursor is used for all SQL statements sharing the same text after the replacement of the literals. Consequently, the literals (that are essential for taking advantage of histograms) are peeked only during the generation of the execution plan related to the first submitted SQL statement. Naturally, this could lead to suboptimal execution plans because literals used in subsequent SQL statements will lead to different execution plans. To avoid this problem, the value similar is available. In fact, it checks whether a histogram exists for one of the replaced literals, before reusing a cursor that is already available. If it does exist, a new child cursor is created. If it does not exist, an already available child cursor will be used.

The following are the results with the value similar. Note that all tests up to now were performed with histograms. As shown in Figure 8-13, the database-side resource usage profile in test case 1 with the value similar is even worse than in test case 1 with exact. The problem is not only that 10,000 hard parses were executed but also that the CPU utilization of such parses is higher, because of cursor sharing. Note that after the replacement of literals, all SQL statements have the same text. As a result, the library cache contains a single parent cursor that has many or, in this case, thousands of child cursors.

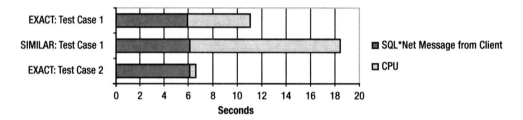

Figure 8-13. *Comparison of the database-side resource usage profile with cursor sharing set to* similar *(components that account for less than 1 percent of the response time are not displayed because they would not be visible)*

In summary, if an application uses literals and cursor sharing is set to similar, the behavior depends on the existence of relevant histograms. If they do exist, similar behaves like exact. If they don't exist, similar behaves like force. This means that if you are facing parsing problems, more often than not, it is pointless to use similar.

Server-Side Statement Caching

This feature is similar to client-side statement caching because it is designed to reduce overhead when too many soft parses are taking place. From a conceptual point of view, the two types of statement caching are similar, except that one is implemented on the server side. From a performance point of view, however, the differences are considerable. In fact, the server-side implementation is far less powerful than the client-side implementation. This is because the server-side implementation reduces the overhead of soft parses on the server side only, and in more than a few circumstances, the overhead of soft parses is much greater on the client than on the server. The only real advantage of the server-side implementation is the ability to cache SQL statements that are executed by PL/SQL or Java code deployed in the database engine.

If an application performs a lot of soft parses, the high pressure on library cache latches and mutexes may lead to a noticeable contention on the database engine as well. The following database-side resource usage profile shows such a situation. Note that to generate it, test case 2 was started while the database engine was processing more than 20,000 parses per second for the same SQL statement. Although this is certainly not a common workload, it helps demonstrate the impact of server-side cursor caching.

Component	Total Duration	%	Number of Events	Duration per Event
SQL*Net message from client	8.283	51.528	10,000	0.001
latch: library cache lock	3.328	20.700	30	0.111
cursor: pin S	2.782	17.304	11	0.253
latch: library cache	1.204	7.488	14	0.086
CPU	0.461	2.867	n/a	n/a
cursor: pin S wait on X	0.011	0.070	1	0.011
SQL*Net message to client	0.007	0.042	10,000	0.000
Total	16.075	100.000		

Whenever the server-side overhead of soft parses is a problem and the application cannot be changed, server-side statement caching may be useful. In this specific case, after enabling it and reapplying the same load, the resulting resource usage profile is the following. Notice how all waits related to library cache latches and mutexes disappeared.

Component	Total Duration	%	Number of Events	Duration per Event
SQL*Net message from client	6.679	94.595	10,000	0.001
CPU	0.375	5.310	n/a	n/a
SQL*Net message to client	0.007	0.095	10,000	0.000
Total	7.061	100.000		

Server-side statement caching is configured through the initialization parameter session_cached_cursors. Its value specifies the maximum number of cursors each session is able to cache. So if it is set to 0, the feature is disabled, and if it is set to a value greater than 0, it is enabled. Up to Oracle Database 10g Release 1, the default value is 0; in Oracle Database 10g Release 2, it is 20; and in Oracle Database 11g, it is 50. At the system level, it can be changed only by bouncing the instance. At the session level, it can be dynamically changed. As for the client-side statement caching, to decide which value to specify for the maximum number of cached cursors, you either need to know the application being used or analyze the TKPROF or TVD$XTAT output to find out how many SQL statements are subject to a high number of soft parses. Then, based on this first estimation, some tests will be necessary to verify whether the value is good. During such tests, it is possible to verify the effectiveness of the cache by looking at the statistics resulting from the following query. Note that the same statistics are available at the system level as well. In any case, you should focus on a single session that has experienced the problematic load in order to find meaningful clues.

```
SQL> SELECT sn.name, ss.value
  2  FROM v$statname sn, v$sesstat ss
  3  WHERE sn.statistic# = ss.statistic#
  4  AND sn.name IN ('session cursor cache hits',
  5                  'session cursor cache count',
  6                  'parse count (total)')
  7  AND ss.sid = 42;

NAME                             VALUE
------------------------------ ----------
session cursor cache hits        9997
session cursor cache count          9
parse count (total)             10008
```

First, compare the number of cached cursors (session cursor cache count) with the value of the initialization parameter session_cached_cursors. If the first is less than the second, it means that incrementing the value of the initialization parameter should have no impact on the number of cached cursors. Otherwise, if the two values are equal, increasing the value of the initialization parameter might be useful in order to cache more cursors. In any case, it makes no sense to exceed the value of the initialization parameter open_cursors. For example, according to the previous statistics, nine cursors are present in the cache. Since the initialization parameter session_cached_cursors was set to 20 during the test, increasing it serves no purpose.

Second, using the additional figures, it is possible to check how many parse calls were optimized because of cached cursors (session cursor cache hits) relative to the total number of parses (parse count (total)). If the two values are close, it probably isn't worthwhile to increase the size of the cache. In the case of the previous statistics, more than 99 percent (9,997/10,008) of the parses are avoided thanks to the cache, so increasing it is probably pointless.

It is also important to notice that in the previous statistics there were "only" 9,997 hits in the cache. Since test case 2 executed the same SQL statement 10,000 times, why weren't there 9,999? The answer is because a cursor is put in the cursor cache only when it has been executed three times. The reason for this is to avoid caching cursors that are executed only once. Getting 9,999 could be possible only when a shareable cursor is already present in the library cache prior to the first parse call.

In summary, server-side statement caching is an important feature. In fact, when correctly sized, it might save some overhead server-side. However, just because this feature is available, there is no excuse for the application to not manage cursors properly in the first place, especially because, as you have already seen, the parsing overhead might be higher on the client side than on the server side.

Using Application Programming Interfaces

The goal of this section is to describe the features related to parsing for different application programming interfaces. As described in the previous sections, to avoid unnecessary hard and soft parses, three central features should be available: bind variables, the ability to reuse statements, and client-side statement caching. Table 8-1 summarizes which of these features are available with which application programming interface. The next sections provide some detailed information for PL/SQL, OCI, JDBC, and ODP.NET.

Table 8-1. *Overview of the Features Provided by Different Application Programming Interfaces*

Application Programming Interface	Bind Variables	Reusing Statements	Client-Side Statement Caching
Java Database Connectivity (JDBC)			
`java.sql.Statement`			(✓)*
`java.sql.PreparedStatement`	✓	✓	✓
Oracle Call Interface (OCI)	✓	✓	✓
Oracle C++ Call Interface (OCCI)	✓	✓	✓§
Oracle Data Provider for .NET (ODP.NET)	✓		✓†
Oracle Objects for OLE (OO4O)	✓		
Oracle Provider for OLE DB	✓		✓‡
PL/SQL			
Static SQL	✓		✓
Native dynamic SQL (`EXECUTE IMMEDIATE`)	✓		✓§
Native dynamic SQL (`OPEN/FETCH/CLOSE`)	✓		
Dynamic SQL with the package `dbms_sql`	✓	✓	
Precompilers	✓	✓	✓
SQLJ	✓		✓

* *Two types of client-side statement caching are supported by JDBC. The class `java.sql.Statement` supports only one of them. For more information, refer to the section about JDBC later in this chapter.*

† *As of Oracle Data Provider for .NET Release 10.1.0.3*

‡ *As of Oracle Database 10g Release 2*

§ *As of Oracle Database 10g Release 1*

PL/SQL

PL/SQL offers different methods for executing SQL statements. The two main categories are static SQL and dynamic SQL. Dynamic SQL can be further divided in three subcategories: `EXECUTE IMMEDIATE`, `OPEN/FETCH/CLOSE`, and the package `dbms_sql`. The only feature related to parsing that is available for all of them is the possibility of using bind variables. In fact, the reutilization of statements and client-side statement caching are only partially available. They are simply not implemented for all methods. The next sections describe the particularities of each of these four categories.

> ■**Note** Since PL/SQL runs in the database engine, it might seem strange to speak about client-side state-ment caching. Nevertheless, from the SQL engine's perspective, PL/SQL is a client. In that client, the concept of client-side statement caching discussed earlier has been implemented.

The PL/SQL blocks provided as examples in this section are excerpts from the scripts ParsingTest1.sql, ParsingTest2.sql, and ParsingTest3.sql implementing test case 1, 2, and 3, respectively.

Static SQL

Static SQL is integrated into the PL/SQL language. As its name implies, it is static, and therefore, the SQL statement must be fully known during compilation. For this reason, the utilization of bind variables is unavoidable if a SQL statement has parameters. For example, with static SQL it is not possible to write a code snippet reproducing test case 1.

You can write static SQL in two ways. The first is based on implicit cursors, so it gives no possibility of controlling the life cycle of a cursor. The following PL/SQL block shows an example implementing test case 2:

```
DECLARE
  l_pad VARCHAR2(4000);
BEGIN
  FOR i IN 1..10000
  LOOP
    SELECT pad INTO l_pad
    FROM t
    WHERE val = i;
  END LOOP;
END;
```

The second way is based on explicit cursors. In this case, some control over the cursors is possible. Nevertheless, the open/parse/execute phases are merged in a single operation (OPEN). This means that only the fetch phase can be controlled. The following PL/SQL block shows an example that implements test case 2 as well:

```
DECLARE
  CURSOR c (p_val NUMBER) IS SELECT pad FROM t WHERE val = p_val;
  l_pad VARCHAR2(4000);
BEGIN
  FOR i IN 1..10000
  LOOP
    OPEN c(i);
    FETCH c INTO l_pad;
    CLOSE c;
  END LOOP;
END;
```

From a performance perspective, the two methods are similar. Although they both prevent bad code from being written (test case 1), they do not allow very efficient code to be written (test case 3). This is because no full control over the cursors is available.

To solve this problem, client-side cursor caching is available. Up to Oracle9*i* version 9.2.0.4, it is always enabled because the maximum number of cached cursors is determined by the initialization parameter open_cursors. Consequently, every cursor that can be opened can also be cached. As of Oracle9*i* version 9.2.0.5, the number of cached cursors is determined by the initialization parameter session_cached_cursors. Up to Oracle Database 10*g* Release 1, the default value of this parameter is 0. However, if it is not explicitly set to 0, the default number of cached cursors is 50. Note that in both cases, an initialization parameter, which is not directly related to client-side statement caching, is "misused" in order to configure it!

Native Dynamic SQL: EXECUTE IMMEDIATE

From a cursor management perspective, native dynamic SQL based on EXECUTE IMMEDIATE is similar to static SQL with implicit cursors. In other words, it is not possible to control the life cycle of a cursor. The following PL/SQL block shows an example implementing test case 2:

```
DECLARE
  l_pad VARCHAR2(4000);
BEGIN
  FOR i IN 1..10000
  LOOP
    EXECUTE IMMEDIATE 'SELECT pad FROM t WHERE val = :1' INTO l_pad USING i;
  END LOOP;
END;
```

Without control over the cursors, it is not possible to write code implementing test case 3. For this reason, client-side cursor caching is used like with static SQL. However, it is available only as of Oracle Database 10*g* Release 1.

Native Dynamic SQL: OPEN/FETCH/CLOSE

From a cursor management perspective, native dynamic SQL based on OPEN/FETCH/CLOSE is similar to static SQL with explicit cursors. In other words, it is possible only to control the fetch phase. The following PL/SQL block shows an example implementing test case 2:

```
DECLARE
  TYPE t_cursor IS REF CURSOR;
  l_cursor t_cursor;
  l_pad VARCHAR2(4000);
BEGIN
  FOR i IN 1..10000
  LOOP
    OPEN l_cursor FOR 'SELECT pad FROM t WHERE val = :1' USING i;
    FETCH l_cursor INTO l_pad;
    CLOSE l_cursor;
  END LOOP;
END;
```

Without full control over the cursors, it is not possible to write code implementing test case 3. In addition, the database engine is not able to take advantage of client-side statement caching with native dynamic SQL based on OPEN/FETCH/CLOSE. This means that the only way to solve a parsing problem caused by code using this method is to rewrite it with EXECUTE IMMEDIATE or the package dbms_sql. As a workaround, you should also consider server-side statement caching.

Dynamic SQL: Package dbms_sql

The package dbms_sql provides full control over the life cycle of cursors. In the following PL/SQL blocks (implementing test case 2), notice how each step is explicitly coded:

```
DECLARE
  l_cursor INTEGER;
  l_pad VARCHAR2(4000);
  l_retval INTEGER;
BEGIN
  FOR i IN 1..10000
  LOOP
    l_cursor := dbms_sql.open_cursor;
    dbms_sql.parse(l_cursor, 'SELECT pad FROM t WHERE val = :1', 1);
    dbms_sql.define_column(l_cursor, 1, l_pad, 10);
    dbms_sql.bind_variable(l_cursor, ':1', i);
    l_retval := dbms_sql.execute(l_cursor);
    IF dbms_sql.fetch_rows(l_cursor) > 0
    THEN
      NULL;
    END IF;
    dbms_sql.close_cursor(l_cursor);
  END LOOP;
END;
```

Since full control over the cursors is given, there is no problem in implementing test case 3. The following PL/SQL block shows an example. Notice how the procedures that prepare (open_cursor, parse, and define_column) and close (close_cursor) the cursor are placed outside the loop to avoid unnecessary soft parses.

```
DECLARE
  l_cursor INTEGER;
  l_pad VARCHAR2(4000);
  l_retval INTEGER;
BEGIN
  l_cursor := dbms_sql.open_cursor;
  dbms_sql.parse(l_cursor, 'SELECT pad FROM t WHERE val = :1', 1);
  dbms_sql.define_column(l_cursor, 1, l_pad, 10);
  FOR i IN 1..10000
  LOOP
    dbms_sql.bind_variable(l_cursor, ':1', i);
    l_retval := dbms_sql.execute(l_cursor);
```

```
    IF dbms_sql.fetch_rows(l_cursor) > 0
    THEN
      NULL;
    END IF;
  END LOOP;
  dbms_sql.close_cursor(l_cursor);
END;
```

The database engine is not able to take advantage of client-side statement caching with the package dbms_sql. So, in order to optimize an application that is suffering because of too many soft parses (as test case 2 is), you must modify it to reuse the cursors (as test case 3 does). As a workaround, you could consider server-side statement caching.

OCI

OCI is a low-level application programming interface. Consequently, it provides full control over the life cycle of cursors. For example, in the following code snippet, which implements test case 2, notice how every step is explicitly coded:

```
for (i=1 ; i<=10000 ; i++)
{
  OCIStmtPrepare2(svc, (OCIStmt **)&stm, err, sql, strlen(sql), NULL, 0,
                  OCI_NTV_SYNTAX, OCI_DEFAULT);
  OCIDefineByPos(stm, &def, err, 1, val, sizeof(val), SQLT_STR, 0, 0, 0,
                  OCI_DEFAULT);
  OCIBindByPos(stm, &bnd, err, 1, &i, sizeof(i), SQLT_INT, 0, 0, 0, 0, 0,
                  OCI_DEFAULT);
  OCIStmtExecute(svc, stm, err, 0, 0, 0, 0, OCI_DEFAULT);
  if (r = OCIStmtFetch2(stm, err, 1, OCI_FETCH_NEXT, 0, OCI_DEFAULT) == OCI_SUCCESS)
  {
    // do something with data...
  }
  OCIStmtRelease(stm, err, NULL, 0, OCI_DEFAULT);
}
```

Since full control over the cursors is available, it is possible to implement test case 3 as well. The following code snippet is an example. Notice how the functions that prepare (OCIStmtPrepare2 and OCIDefineByPos) and close (OCIStmtRelease) the cursor are placed outside the loop to avoid unnecessary soft parses.

```
OCIStmtPrepare2(svc, (OCIStmt **)&stm, err, sql, strlen(sql), NULL, 0,
                OCI_NTV_SYNTAX, OCI_DEFAULT);
OCIDefineByPos(stm, &def, err, 1, val, sizeof(val), SQLT_STR, 0, 0, 0, OCI_DEFAULT);
for (i=1 ; i<=10000 ; i++)
{
  OCIBindByPos(stm, &bnd, err, 1, &i, sizeof(i), SQLT_INT, 0, 0, 0, 0, 0,
                OCI_DEFAULT);
  OCIStmtExecute(svc, stm, err, 0, 0, 0, 0, OCI_DEFAULT);
```

```
    if (r = OCIStmtFetch2(stm, err, 1, OCI_FETCH_NEXT, 0, OCI_DEFAULT) == OCI_SUCCESS)
    {
      // do something with data...
    }
}
OCIStmtRelease(stm, err, NULL, 0, OCI_DEFAULT);
```

OCI not only enables full control of the cursors but also supports client-side statement caching. To use it, it is necessary only to enable statement caching and use the functions OCIStmtPrepare2 and OCIStmtRelease (as the previous examples do). Cursors are added to the cache when the function OCIStmtRelease is called. Then, when a new cursor is created through the function OCIStmtPrepare2, the cache is consulted to find out whether a SQL statement with the same text is present in it. Different methods exist to enable statement caching. Basically, though, it is only a matter of specifying it when the session is opened or retrieved from a pool. For example, if a nonpooled session is opened through the function OCILogon2, it is necessary to specify the value OCI_LOGON2_STMTCACHE as the mode.

```
OCILogon2(env, err, &svc, username, strlen(username), password, strlen(password),
          dbname, strlen(dbname), OCI_LOGON2_STMTCACHE)
```

By default, the size of the cache is 20. The following code snippet shows how to change it to 50 by setting the attribute OCI_ATTR_STMTCACHESIZE on the service context. Note that setting this attribute to 0 disables statement caching.

```
ub4 size = 50;
OCIAttrSet(svc, OCI_HTYPE_SVCCTX, &size, 0, OCI_ATTR_STMTCACHESIZE, err);
```

The C code examples provided in this section are excerpts from the files ParsingTest1.c, ParsingTest2.c, and ParsingTest3.c implementing test case 1, 2, and 3, respectively.

JDBC

java.sql.Statement is the basic class provided by JDBC to execute SQL statements. As shown in Table 8-1, it is not unlikely that parsing problems will arise when using it. In fact, it does not support bind variables, reutilization of cursors, or client-side statement caching. Basically, it is possible only to implement test case 1 with it. The following code snippet demonstrates this:

```
sql = "SELECT pad FROM t WHERE val = ";
for (int i=0 ; i<10000; i++)
{
  statement = connection.createStatement();
  resultset = statement.executeQuery(sql + Integer.toString(i));
  if (resultset.next())
  {
    pad = resultset.getString("pad");
  }
  resultset.close();
  statement.close();
}
```

To avoid all the hard parses performed by the previous code snippet, you must use the class java.sql.PreparedStatement, which is a subclass of java.sql.Statement. The following code snippet shows how to use it to implement test case 2. Notice how the value used for the lookup, instead of being concatenated to the variable sql (as in the previous example), is defined through a bind variable (defined with a question mark in Java and called *placeholder*).

```
sql = "SELECT pad FROM t WHERE val = ?";
for (int i=0 ; i<10000; i++)
{
  statement = connection.prepareStatement(sql);
  statement.setInt(1, i);
  resultset = statement.executeQuery();
  if (resultset.next())
  {
    pad = resultset.getString("pad");
  }
  resultset.close();
  statement.close();
}
```

The next improvement is to avoid the soft parses as well, that is to say, to implement test case 3. As the following code snippet shows, you can achieve this by moving the code for creating and closing the prepared statement outside the loop:

```
sql = "SELECT pad FROM t WHERE val = ?";
statement = connection.prepareStatement(sql);
for (int i=0 ; i<10000; i++)
{
  statement.setInt(1, i);
  resultset = statement.executeQuery();
  if (resultset.next())
  {
    pad = resultset.getString("pad");
  }
  resultset.close();
}
statement.close();
```

JDBC not only allows for the correct handling of prepared statements but also the support of client-side statement caching. According to the JDBC 3.0 specification statement, caching should be transparent when connection pools are used. Actually, the Oracle JDBC drivers provide two extensions to support it without connection pools as well: implicit and explicit statement caching. As the names suggest, while the former requires almost no code change, the latter must be explicitly implemented.

With explicit statement caching, statements are opened and closed by means of Oracle-defined methods. Since this has a huge impact on the code and, compared to implicit statement caching, it is more difficult to write faster code, it is not described here. For more information, refer to the *JDBC Developer's Guide and Reference* manual.

With implicit statement caching, prepared statements are added to the cache when the method `close` is called. Then, when a new prepared statement is instantiated through the method `prepareStatement`, the cache is checked to find out whether a cursor with the same text is already present in it.

The following lines of code show how statement caching is enabled at the connection level. Be careful: setting the size of the cache to a value greater than 0 is a requirement. The casts are necessary because both methods are Oracle extensions.

```
((oracle.jdbc.OracleConnection)connection).setImplicitCachingEnabled(true);
((oracle.jdbc.OracleConnection)connection).setStatementCacheSize(50);
```

Another way to enable implicit statement caching is through the methods `setImplicitCachingEnabled` and `setMaxStatements` of the class `OracleDataSource`. Note that the method `setMaxStatements` is deprecated as of Oracle Database 10*g* Release 2.

By default, all prepared statements are cached with implicit statement caching. When the cache is full, the least recently used one is simply discarded. If necessary, the caching of a specific statement can also be disabled. The following line of code shows how to do it:

```
((oracle.jdbc.OraclePreparedStatement)statement).setDisableStmtCaching(true);
```

The Java code used for the examples in this section is an excerpt from the files `ParsingTest1.java`, `ParsingTest2.java`, and `ParsingTest3.java` that implement test case 1, 2, and 3, respectively.

ODP.NET

ODP.NET provides little control over the life cycle of a cursor. In the following code snippet that implements test case 1, the method `ExecuteReader` triggers parse, execute, and fetch calls at the same time:

```
sql = "SELECT pad FROM t WHERE val = ";
command = new OracleCommand(sql, connection);
for (int i = 0; i < 10000; i++)
{
  command.CommandText = sql + i;
  reader = command.ExecuteReader();
  if (reader.Read())
  {
    pad = reader[0].ToString();
  }
  reader.Close();
}
```

To avoid all the hard parses performed by the previous code snippet, the class `OracleParameter` has to be used for passing parameters (bind variables). The following code snippet shows how to use it to implement test case 2. Notice how the value used for the lookup, instead of being concatenated to the variable `sql` (as in the previous example), is defined through a parameter.

```
String sql = "SELECT pad FROM t WHERE val = :val";
OracleCommand command = new OracleCommand(sql, connection);
OracleParameter parameter = new OracleParameter("val", OracleDbType.Int32);
command.Parameters.Add(parameter);
OracleDataReader reader;
for (int i = 0; i < 10000; i++)
{
  parameter.Value = Convert.ToInt32(i);
  reader = command.ExecuteReader();
  if (reader.Read())
  {
    pad = reader[0].ToString();
  }
  reader.Close();
}
```

With ODP.NET, it is not possible to implement test case 3. However, to achieve the same result, you can use client-side statement caching as of ODP.NET release 10.1.0.3. There are two methods for enabling it and setting the size of the cache. The first, which controls statement caching for all applications using a specific Oracle home, is by setting the following value in the registry. If it is set to 0, statement caching is disabled. Otherwise, statement caching is enabled, and the value specifies the size of the cache (<Assembly_Version> is the full version number of Oracle.DataAccess.dll).

```
HKEY_LOCAL_MACHINE\SOFTWARE\ORACLE\ODP.NET\<Assembly_Version>\StatementCacheSize
```

The second method controls statement caching directly in the code through the attribute Statement Cache Size provided by the class OracleConnection. Basically, it plays the same role as the registry value but for a single connection. The following code snippet shows how to enable statement caching and to set its size to 10:

```
String connectString = "User Id=" + user +
                       ";Password=" + password +
                       ";Data Source=" + dataSource +
                       ";Statement Cache Size=10";
OracleConnection connection = new OracleConnection(connectString);
```

Note that the setting at the connection level overrides the setting in the registry. In addition, when statement caching is enabled, it is possible to disable it at the command level by setting the property AddToStatementCache to false.

The C# code used for the examples in this section is an excerpt from the files ParsingTest1.cs and ParsingTest2.cs that implement test case 1 and 2, respectively.

On to Chapter 9

This chapter described how the database engine parses SQL statements and how to identify, solve, and work around parsing problems. The key message was that by knowing how your application works and the possibilities given by the application programming interface used, you should be able to avoid parsing problems by writing efficient code during the development stage.

Since in the life cycle of a cursor the execution phase follows the parsing of the SQL statement and the binding of variables, it would be useful to outline the different techniques used by the database engine to carry out single-table accesses. The next chapter will discuss this, as well as describe how to take advantage of the different types of indexes and partitioning methods, in order to help speed up the execution of SQL statements.

■ ■ ■

CHAPTER 9

Optimizing Data Access

An execution plan, as described in Chapter 6, is composed of several operations. The most commonly used operations are those that access, filter, and transform data. This chapter specifically deals with data access operations, or, in other words, how the database engine is able to access data. There are basically only two ways to locate data in a table. The first is to scan the whole table. The second is to do a lookup based on a redundant access structure (for example, an index) or on the structure of the table itself (for example, a hash cluster). In addition, in the case of partitioning, access might be restricted to a subset of partitions. This is no different from looking up specific information in this book. Either you read the whole book, you read a single chapter, or you use the index or table of contents to find out where the information you are looking is.

The first part of this chapter describes how to recognize inefficient access paths by looking at runtime statistics provided by either SQL trace or dynamic performance views. The second part describes available access methods and when you should take advantage of them. For each access path, the hint and execution plan operation related to it are described as well.

Note In this chapter, several SQL statements contain hints. This is done not only to show you which hint leads to which access path but also to show you examples of their use. In any case, neither real references nor full syntaxes are provided. You can find these in Chapter 2 of the *SQL Reference* manual.

Identifying Suboptimal Access Paths

Chapter 6 described how to judge the efficiency of an execution plan by checking both the estimations of the query optimizer and whether restrictions are correctly recognized. It is important to understand that even when the query optimizer correctly chooses an execution plan, it does not necessarily mean that this specific execution plan will perform well. It might be that by altering the SQL statement or the access structures (for example, adding an index), an even better execution plan could be taken into consideration. The following sections describe additional checks that can be performed to help recognize an inefficient access path, what might be causing it, and what you can do to avoid the problem.

Identification

The most efficient access path is able to process the data by consuming the least amount of resources. Therefore, to recognize whether an access path is efficient, you have to recognize whether the amount of resources used for its processing is acceptable. To do so, it is necessary to define both how to measure the utilization of resources and what "acceptable" means. In addition, you need to also consider the feasibility of the check. In other words, you also need to consider how much effort is needed to implement a check. It has to be as simple as possible. In fact, a perfect check that takes too much time to be implemented is not acceptable in practice, especially if you need to work on tens, or even hundreds, of SQL statements that are candidates for optimization.

As a side note, keep in mind that this section focuses on efficiency, not on speed alone. It is essential to understand that the most efficient access path is not always the fastest one. As you will see in Chapter 11, with parallel processing, it is sometimes possible to achieve a better response time even though the amount of resources used is higher. Of course, when you consider the whole system, the lower the amount of resources used by SQL statements (in other words, the higher their efficiency is), the more scalable, and faster, the system is. This is true since, by definition, resources are limited.

As a first approximation, the amount of resources used by an access path is acceptable when it is proportional to the amount of returned rows (that is, the number of rows that are returned to the parent operation in the execution plan). In other words, when few rows are returned, the expected utilization of resources is low, and when lots of rows are returned, the expected utilization of resources is high. Consequently, the check should be based on the amount of resources used to return a single row.

In an ideal world, you would like to measure the resource consumption by considering all four main types of resources used by the database engine: CPU, memory, the disk, and the network. Certainly, this can be done, but unfortunately getting and assessing all these figures takes a lot of time and effort and can usually be done only for a limited number of SQL statements in a tuning session. You should also consider that when processing one row, the CPU processing time depends on the speed of the processor, which obviously changes from system to system. Further, the amount of memory used is all but proportional to the number of returned rows, and the disk and network resources are not always used. It is, in fact, not uncommon at all to see long-running SQL statements that use a modest amount of memory and are without disk or network access.

Fortunately, there is a single database metric, which is very easy to collect, that is able to tell you a lot about the amount of work done by the database engine: the number of logical reads, that is, the number of blocks that are accessed in the buffer cache during the execution of a SQL statement. There are four good reasons for this. First, a logical read is a CPU-bound operation and, therefore, reflects CPU utilization very well. Second, a logical read might lead to a physical read, and therefore, by reducing the number of logical reads, it is likely to reduce the I/O operations as well. Third, a logical read is an operation subject to serialization. Since you usually have to optimize for a multiuser load, minimizing the logical reads is good for avoiding scalability problems. Fourth, the number of logical reads is readily available at the SQL statement and execution plan operation levels, in both SQL trace files and dynamic performance views.

Since logical reads are very good at approximating overall resource consumption, you can concentrate (at least for the first round of optimization) on access paths that have a high number of logical reads per returned rows. The following are generally considered good "rules of thumb":

- Access paths that lead to less than about 5 logical reads per returned row are probably good.

- Access paths that lead to up to about 10–15 logical reads per returned row are probably acceptable.

- Access paths that lead to more than about 15–20 logical reads per returned row are probably inefficient. In other words, there is probably room for improvement.

To check the number of logical reads per row, there are basically two methods. The first, which is available as of Oracle Database 10*g* only, is to take advantage of the execution statistics provided by dynamic performance views and displayed using the package `dbms_xplan` (Chapter 6 fully describes this technique). The following execution plan was generated using that method. From it, for each operation, you can see how many rows were returned (column A-Rows) and how many logical reads were performed (column `Buffers`) in order to return them.

```
SELECT * FROM t WHERE n1 BETWEEN 6000 AND 7000 AND n2 = 19
```

```
---------------------------------------------------------------------
| Id  | Operation                   | Name  | Starts | A-Rows | Buffers |
---------------------------------------------------------------------
|*  1 |  TABLE ACCESS BY INDEX ROWID| T     |    1   |    3   |    28   |
|*  2 |   INDEX RANGE SCAN          | T_N2_I|    1   |   24   |     4   |
---------------------------------------------------------------------

   1 - filter(("N1">=6000 AND "N1"<=7000))
   2 - access("N2"=19)
```

The second method is to make use of the information provided by SQL trace (Chapter 3 fully describes this technique). The following is an excerpt of the output generated by TKPROF for the very same query as in the previous example. Note that the number of returned rows (column Rows) and logical reads (attribute cr) match the previous figures.

```
Rows    Row Source Operation
-------  ---------------------------------------------------
     3  TABLE ACCESS BY INDEX ROWID T (cr=28 pr=0 pw=0 time=2 us)
    24   INDEX RANGE SCAN T_N2_I (cr=4 pr=0 pw=0 time=73 us)(object id 13709)
```

Based on the rules of thumb mentioned earlier, the execution plan used as an example is acceptable. In fact, the number of logical reads per returned row for the access path is about 9 (28/3). Let's see what a bad execution plan looks like for the very same SQL statement. Note that it is bad because the number of logical reads per returned row for the access path is about 130 (391/3), not because it contains a full table scan!

```
---------------------------------------------------------------
| Id | Operation          | Name | Starts | A-Rows | Buffers |
---------------------------------------------------------------
|*  1 | TABLE ACCESS FULL| T    |     1 |      3 |     391 |
---------------------------------------------------------------

   1 - filter((("N2"=19 AND "N1">=6000 AND "N1"<=7000))
```

It is important to stress that this section is about access paths. So, you must consider the figures at the access-path level only, not for the whole SQL statement. In fact, the figures at the SQL statement level might be misleading. To understand what the problem might be, let's examine the following query. If only the figures at the SQL statement level (provided by operation 1) are erroneously taken into consideration, 389 logical reads are executed to return a single row. In other words, it would be erroneously classified as inefficient. However, if the figures of the access operation (operation 2) are correctly taken into consideration instead, the ratio between the number of logical reads (389) and the number of returned rows (160) classifies this access path as efficient. The problem in this case is that operation 1 is used to apply the function sum to the rows returned by operation 2. As a result, it always returns a single row and hides the access path performance figures.

```
SELECT sum(n1) FROM t WHERE n2 > 246
```

```
---------------------------------------------------------------
| Id | Operation          | Name | Starts | A-Rows | Buffers |
---------------------------------------------------------------
|   1 | SORT AGGREGATE     |      |     1 |      1 |     389 |
|*  2 |   TABLE ACCESS FULL| T    |     1 |    160 |     389 |
---------------------------------------------------------------

   2 - filter("N2">246)
```

If you really have no choice but to look at the figures at the SQL statement level (for example, because the SQL trace file doesn't contain the execution plan), you will have a hard time using the rules of thumb provided earlier, simply because you don't have enough available data. In this case, however, at least for simple SQL statements, you might try to guess the access path figures and adapt the rule of thumb. For example, you might carefully review the SQL statement to check whether there isn't an aggregation in it, find out how many tables are referenced in the SQL statement, and then increase the limits in the rules of thumb in proportion to the number of referenced tables.

Pitfalls

While examining the number of logical reads, you must be aware of two pitfalls that might distort the figures. The first is related to read consistency, and the second is related to row prefetching.

Read Consistency

For every SQL statement, the database engine has to guarantee the consistency of the processed data. For that purpose, based on current blocks and undo information, consistent copies of blocks might be created at runtime. To execute such an operation, several logical reads are performed. Therefore, the number of logical reads performed by a SQL statement is strongly dependent on the number of blocks that have to be reconstructed. The following excerpt of the output generated by the script read_consistency.sql shows that behavior. Note that the query is the same as the one used in the previous section. According to the execution statistics, the same number of rows was returned (actually it returns the same data). However, a much higher number of logical reads was performed (in total 354 instead of 28). That effect is because of another session that modified the blocks needed to process this query. Since the changes were not committed at the time the query was started, the database engine had to reconstruct the blocks. This led to a much higher number of logical reads.

```
SELECT * FROM t WHERE n1 BETWEEN 6000 AND 7000 AND n2 = 19
```

```
-------------------------------------------------------------------
| Id | Operation                   | Name    | Starts | A-Rows | Buffers |
-------------------------------------------------------------------
|*  1 |  TABLE ACCESS BY INDEX ROWID| T       |    1 |      3 |    354 |
|*  2 |   INDEX RANGE SCAN          | T_N2_I  |    1 |     24 |    139 |
-------------------------------------------------------------------

   1 - filter(("N1">=6000 AND "N1"<=7000))
   2 - access("N2"=19)
```

Row Prefetching

From a performance point of view, you should always avoid row-based processing. For example, when a client retrieves data from a database, it can do it row by row or, better yet, by retrieving several rows at the same time. This technique, known as *row prefetching*, will be fully described in Chapter 11. For the moment, let's just look at its impact on the number of logical reads. Simply put, a logical read is counted each time the database engine accesses a block. With a full table scan, there are two extremes. If row prefetching is set to 1, approximately one logical read per returned row is performed. If row prefetching is set to a number greater than the number of rows stored in each table's single blocks, the number of logical reads is close to the number of the table's blocks. The following excerpt of the output generated by the script row_prefetching.sql shows this behavior. In the first execution, with row prefetching set to 2 (the choice of this value will be explained in the section "Row Prefetching" in Chapter 11), the number of logical reads (5,389) is about half of the number of rows (10,000). In the second execution, since the number of prefetched rows (100) is higher than the average number of rows per block (25), the number of logical reads (489) is about the same as the number of blocks (401).

```
SQL> SELECT num_rows, blocks, round(num_rows/blocks) AS rows_per_block
  2  FROM user_tables
  3  WHERE table_name = 'T';

 NUM_ROWS    BLOCKS  ROWS_PER_BLOCK
--------- --------- ---------------
    10000       401              25

SQL> set arraysize 2

SQL> SELECT * FROM t;


-----------------------------------------------------------------
| Id  | Operation        | Name  | Starts | A-Rows | Buffers |
-----------------------------------------------------------------
|   1 | TABLE ACCESS FULL| T     |      1 |  10000 |    5389 |
-----------------------------------------------------------------


SQL> set arraysize 100

SQL> SELECT * FROM t;


-----------------------------------------------------------------
| Id  | Operation        | Name  | Starts | A-Rows | Buffers |
-----------------------------------------------------------------
|   1 | TABLE ACCESS FULL| T     |      1 |  10000 |     489 |
-----------------------------------------------------------------
```

■**Note** In SQL*Plus, you manage the number of prefetched rows through the system variable `arraysize`. The default value is 15.

Given the dependency of the number of logical reads on row prefetching, whenever you execute a SQL statement for testing purposes in a tool such as SQL*Plus, you should carefully set row prefetching like the application does. In other words, the tool you use for the tests should prefetch the same number of rows as the application. Failing to do so may cause severely misleading results.

When aggregation operations are executed, the SQL engine uses row prefetching internally. As a result, when aggregations are part of the execution plan, the number of logical reads of an access path is very close to the number of blocks. In other words, every time the SQL engine accesses a block, it extracts all rows contained in it. The following example illustrates this:

```
SQL> set arraysize 2

SQL> SELECT sum(n1) FROM t;

-----------------------------------------------
| Operation        | Name | A-Rows | Buffers |
-----------------------------------------------
|  SORT AGGREGATE  |      |      1 |     389 |
|   TABLE ACCESS FULL| T   |  10000 |     389 |
-----------------------------------------------
```

Causes

There are several main causes of inefficient access paths:

- No suitable access structures (for example, indexes) are available.

- A suitable access structure is available, but the syntax of the SQL statement does not allow the query optimizer to use it.

- The table or the index is partitioned, but no pruning is possible. As a result, all partitions are accessed.

- The table or the index, or both, is not partitioned.

In addition to the examples in the previous list, two additional situations lead to inefficient access paths:

- When the query optimizer makes wrong estimations because of a lack of statistics, because of statistics that are not up-to-date, or because a wrong query optimizer configuration is in place. I won't cover that here, since I will assume that the necessary statistics are in place and that the query optimizer is correctly configured (Chapters 4 and 5 fully described these two topics).

- When the query optimizer is itself the problem, for example, when there are internal bugs or limitations in how it works. I will not deal with this either, since bugs or query optimizer limitations are responsible for a very limited number of problems.

Solutions

As described in the previous sections, to efficiently execute a SQL statement, the objective is to minimize the number of logical reads or, in other words, to determine which access path accesses fewer blocks. To reach this objective, it may be necessary to add new access structures (for example, indexes) or change the physical layout (for example, partition some tables or their indexes). Given a SQL statement, there are many combinations of access structures and physical layouts. Luckily, to make the choice easier, it is possible to classify SQL statements (or better, data access operations) in two main categories with regard to selectivity:

- Operations with weak (high) selectivity

- Operations with strong (low) selectivity

The selectivity is important because the access structures and layouts that work well with operations with very weak selectivity work badly for operations with very strong selectivity, and vice versa. Be careful, however, that there is no fixed boundary between these two categories. Instead, it depends on the operation, on the data it processes, and on how this data is stored. For example, both data distribution and the number of rows per block strongly impact performance. In other words, it is absolutely wrong to say that selectivity up to 0.1 (or any other value you could think of) is necessarily strong, and above this value, it is necessarily weak. In spite of this, it may be said that, in practice, the limit commonly ranges between 0.05 and 0.25. As Figure 9-1 shows, only for values very close to 0 or 1 can you be certain.

Figure 9-1. *There is no fixed limit between strong and weak selectivity.*

It is essential to understand that for determining the category of an operation, the absolute number of rows it returns is not relevant. Only the selectivity is. For example, knowing that an operation returns 500,000 rows is not relevant at all to choosing an access path. In contrast, knowing that the operation has a selectivity of 0.001 clearly puts it in the strong selectivity category.

The category is important in order to have a clue to the type of access path that should lead to an efficient execution plan. Figure 9-2 broadly correlates the selectivity with the access path that is usually optimal. Operations with strong selectivities are executed efficiently when a suitable index is in place. As you will see later in this chapter, in some situations a rowid access or hash cluster might also be helpful. On the other hand, operations with very poor selectivities are processed efficiently by reading the whole table. In between these two possibilities, partitioned tables and hash clusters play an important role.

Figure 9-2. *Specific access paths work efficiently only for a specific range of selectivity.*

Let's take a look at two tests to demonstrate this. In the first test, a single row is retrieved, while in the second, thousands of rows are retrieved.

Retrieving a Single Row

The aim of this test, which is based on the script access_structures_1.sql, is to compare the number of logical reads necessary to retrieve a single row, with the following access structures in place:

- A heap table with a primary key

- An index-organized table

- A single-table hash cluster that has the primary key as the cluster key

> **Note** This chapter describes only how to take advantage of different types of segments (for example, tables, clusters, and indexes) to minimize the number of logical reads performed during the processing of SQL statements. You can find basic information about them in the manual *Oracle Database Concepts* in the chapter "Schema Objects."

The queries used for the tests are the following. Note that the column id is the primary key of the table. A row with the value 6 exists, and the variable rid stores the rowid of that row.

```
SELECT * FROM sales WHERE id = 6

SELECT * FROM sales WHERE rowid = :rid
```

Since the number of logical reads depends on the height of the index, the test is performed while 10; 10,000; and 1,000,000 rows are being stored in the table. Figure 9-3 summarizes the results. They illustrate four main facts:

- For all access structures, a single logical read is performed through a rowid (obviously, to read the block where the row is stored, you cannot do less work than this).

- For the heap table, at least two logical reads are necessary: one for the index and one for the table. As the number of rows increases, the height of the index increases, and the number of logical reads increases as well.

- An access through the index-organized table requires one less logical read than through the heap table.

- For the single-table hash cluster, not only is the number of logical reads independent of the number of rows, but in addition, it always leads to a single logical read.

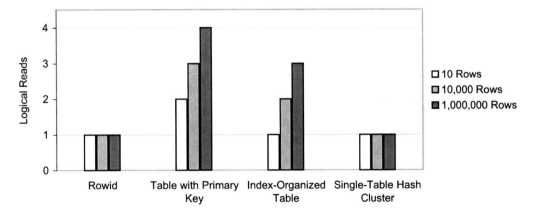

Figure 9-3. *Different access structures lead to different numbers of logical reads.*

In summary, for retrieving a single row, a "regular" table with an index is the worst-performing access structure. However, as I will describe later in this chapter, "regular" tables are the most commonly used because you can take advantage of the other access structures only in specific situations.

Retrieving Thousands of Rows

The purpose of this test, which is based on the script `access_structures_1000.sql`, is to compare the number of logical reads necessary to retrieve thousands of rows with the following access structures in place:

- Nonpartitioned table without an index.

- List-partitioned table. The column `prod_category` is the partition key.

- Single-table hash cluster. The column `prod_category` is the cluster key.

- Nonpartitioned table with an index on the column `prod_category`. For this test, two different physical distributions of the rows in the table segment (and hence, different clustering factors) were tested.

The test data set consists of 918,843 rows. The following query shows the distribution of the values for the column `prod_category`:

```
SQL> SELECT prod_category, count(*), ratio_to_report(count(*)) over() AS selectivity
  2  FROM sales
  3  GROUP BY prod_category
  4  ORDER BY count(*);

PROD_CATEGORY     COUNT(*) SELECTIVITY
--------------- ---------- -----------
Hardware            15357        .017
Photo               95509        .104
Electronics        116267        .127
Peripherals        286369        .312
Software/Other     405341        .441
```

The queries used for the tests are the following:

```
SELECT sum(amount_sold) FROM sales WHERE prod_category = 'Hardware'

SELECT sum(amount_sold) FROM sales WHERE prod_category = 'Photo'

SELECT sum(amount_sold) FROM sales WHERE prod_category = 'Electronics'

SELECT sum(amount_sold) FROM sales WHERE prod_category = 'Peripherals'

SELECT sum(amount_sold) FROM sales WHERE prod_category = 'Software/Other'

SELECT sum(amount_sold) FROM sales
```

■**Caution** The queries used for the test are based on an aggregation. Therefore, because of row prefetching, the ratio between the logical reads and the number of rows is always very low. Anyway, the aim of this test is to show the differences between the different access structures.

For each of them, the number of logical reads was measured. Figure 9-4 summarizes the results, which lead to four main facts:

- The number of logical reads needed to read the nonpartitioned table without an index is independent of the selectivity. Therefore, it is efficient only when the selectivity is weak.

- The number of logical reads needed to read a single partition of the list-partitioned table is proportional to the selectivity, since the table has been partitioned according to the column `prod_category`. Therefore, in all situations, a minimal number of logical reads is carried out.

- The number of logical reads needed to read the single-table hash cluster is proportional only to the selectivity for medium and high values. (As you will see later, hash clusters might be very useful when the selectivity is very strong. In this test, however, they are at a disadvantage because of the nonuniform data distribution.)

- The number of logical reads needed to read the table through an index is highly dependent on the physical distribution of data. Therefore, knowing only the selectivity is not enough to find out whether such an access path might process data efficiently.

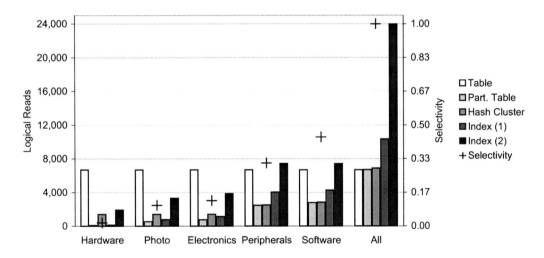

Figure 9-4. *Specific access paths work efficiently only for a specific range of selectivity.*

Now that you have seen what the main available options are that can access data efficiently in different situations, it is time to describe in detail the access paths used to process SQL statements with weak and strong selectivity.

SQL Statements with Weak Selectivity

To process data efficiently, SQL statements with weak (that is, high) selectivity have to use either a full table scan or a full partition scan. However, there are plenty of situations where only full table scans come into play. There are three main reasons for this. First, partitioning is an Enterprise Edition option. So, you won't be able to take advantage of it if you are using Standard Edition or, of course, if you don't have a license to use it. Second, even if you are allowed to use the partitioning option, not all tables will be partitioned in practice. Third, a table might be partitioned by only a limited number of columns. As a result, even if the table is partitioned, not all SQL statements that reference a table will be able to take advantage of partitioning, unless all of them reference the partitioning key(s), which is usually not the case in practice.

In particular situations, both full table scans and full partition scans might be avoided by replacing them with full index scans. In such cases, the idea is to take advantage of indexes not for the purpose of searching for particular values but simply because they are smaller than tables.

Full Table Scans

It is possible to perform a full table scan on all tables. Although there are no particular requirements for doing this type of scan, on occasion it may be the only access path possible. The following query is an example. Note that in the execution plan, the operation TABLE ACCESS FULL corresponds to the full table scan. The example also shows how to force a full table scan with the hint full.

```
SELECT /*+ full(t) */ * FROM t WHERE n2 = 19
```

```
-----------------------------------
| Id  | Operation         | Name |
-----------------------------------
|   1 |  TABLE ACCESS FULL| T    |
-----------------------------------
```

During a full table scan, the database engine reads all of the table's blocks below the high watermark sequentially. So, the number of logical reads depends on the number of *blocks*, not on the number of *rows*. This might be suboptimal, especially if the table contains a lot of empty or almost-empty blocks. Clearly, a block has to be read to know whether it contains data. One of the most common scenarios that can lead to a table with a lot of sparsely populated blocks is when tables are subject to more deletes than inserts. The following example, which is an excerpt of the output generated by the script full_scan_hwm.sql, illustrates this:

- At the beginning, a query leads to 390 logical reads in order to return 24 rows.

  ```
  SQL> SELECT * FROM t WHERE n2 = 19;

  SQL> SELECT last_output_rows, last_cr_buffer_gets, last_cu_buffer_gets
    2  FROM v$session s, v$sql_plan_statistics p
    3  WHERE s.prev_sql_id = p.sql_id
    4  AND s.prev_child_number = p.child_number
    5  AND s.sid = sys_context('userenv','sid')
    6  AND p.operation_id = 1;
  ```

```
LAST_OUTPUT_ROWS LAST_CR_BUFFER_GETS LAST_CU_BUFFER_GETS
---------------- -------------------- --------------------
              24                  390                    0
```

- Then, almost all rows (9,976 out of 10,000) are deleted. However, the number of logical reads needed to execute the query does not change. In other words, a lot of completely empty blocks were uselessly accessed.

```
SQL> DELETE t WHERE n2 <> 19;

9976 rows deleted.

SQL> SELECT * FROM t WHERE n2 = 19;

SQL> SELECT last_output_rows, last_cr_buffer_gets, last_cu_buffer_gets
  2  FROM v$session s, v$sql_plan_statistics p
  3  WHERE s.prev_sql_id = p.sql_id
  4  AND s.prev_child_number = p.child_number
  5  AND s.sid = sys_context('userenv','sid')
  6  AND p.operation_id = 1;


LAST_OUTPUT_ROWS LAST_CR_BUFFER_GETS LAST_CU_BUFFER_GETS
---------------- -------------------- --------------------
              24                  390                    0
```

- To lower the high watermark, a reorganization of the table is necessary. As of Oracle Database 10g, you can do this with the following SQL statements. Note that row movement must be activated because rows might get a new rowid during the reorganization.

```
SQL> ALTER TABLE t ENABLE ROW MOVEMENT;

SQL> ALTER TABLE t SHRINK SPACE;
```

- After the reorganization, the query performs only four logical reads in order to return 24 rows:

```
SQL> SELECT * FROM t WHERE n2 = 19;

SQL> SELECT last_output_rows, last_cr_buffer_gets, last_cu_buffer_gets
  2  FROM v$session s, v$sql_plan_statistics p
  3  WHERE s.prev_sql_id = p.sql_id
  4  AND s.prev_child_number = p.child_number
  5  AND s.sid = sys_context('userenv','sid')
  6  AND p.operation_id = 1;


LAST_OUTPUT_ROWS LAST_CR_BUFFER_GETS LAST_CU_BUFFER_GETS
---------------- -------------------- --------------------
              24                    4                    0
```

Remember that the number of logical reads performed by a full table scan strongly depends on the setting for row prefetching. Refer to the section "Row Prefetching" earlier in this chapter for an example of this.

Full Partition Scans

When the selectivity is very weak (that is, close to 1), full table scans are the most efficient way to access data. As soon as the selectivity decreases, many blocks are unnecessarily accessed by full table scans. Since the use of indexes is not beneficial with weak selectivity, partitioning is the only option available to reduce the number of logical reads. The motive for using partitioning is to take advantage of the query optimizer's ability to exclude the processing of partitions that contain processing-irrelevant data *a priori*. This feature is called *partition pruning*.

There are two basic prerequisite conditions in order to capitalize on partition pruning for a given SQL statement. First, and obviously, a table must be partitioned. Second, a restriction or a join condition on the partition key must be specified in the WHERE clause of the SQL statement. If these two requirements are met, the query optimizer is able to replace a full table scan by one or several full partition scans. In practice, however, things are not that easy. In fact, the query optimizer has to deal with several particular situations that might, or might not, lead to partition pruning. To understand these situations better, the following sections detail partition pruning basics, as well as more advanced pruning techniques such as OR, multicolumn, subquery, and join-filter pruning. These are followed by some practical advice on how to implement partitioning. Note that partitioned indexes are also discussed in the "SQL Statements with Strong Selectivity" section later in this chapter.

Range Partitioning

To illustrate how partition pruning works, let's examine several examples based on the script pruning_range.sql. The test table is range partitioned and created with the following SQL statement. To be able to show all types of partition pruning, the partition key is composed of two columns: n1 and d1. The table is partitioned by month (based on column d1), and for each month, there are four different partitions (based on column n1). This means there are 48 partitions per year. Figure 9-5 is a graphical representation of the test table.

```
CREATE TABLE t (
  id NUMBER,
  d1 DATE,
  n1 NUMBER,
  n2 NUMBER,
  n3 NUMBER,
  pad VARCHAR2(4000),
  CONSTRAINT t_pk PRIMARY KEY (id)
)
PARTITION BY RANGE (n1, d1) (
  PARTITION t_jan_2007_1 VALUES LESS THAN (1, to_date('2007-02-01','yyyy-mm-dd')),
  PARTITION t_feb_2007_1 VALUES LESS THAN (1, to_date('2007-03-01','yyyy-mm-dd')),
  PARTITION t_mar_2007_1 VALUES LESS THAN (1, to_date('2007-04-01','yyyy-mm-dd')),
  ...
```

```
   PARTITION t_oct_2007_4 VALUES LESS THAN (4, to_date('2007-11-01','yyyy-mm-dd')),
   PARTITION t_nov_2007_4 VALUES LESS THAN (4, to_date('2007-12-01','yyyy-mm-dd')),
   PARTITION t_dec_2007_4 VALUES LESS THAN (4, to_date('2008-01-01','yyyy-mm-dd'))
)
```

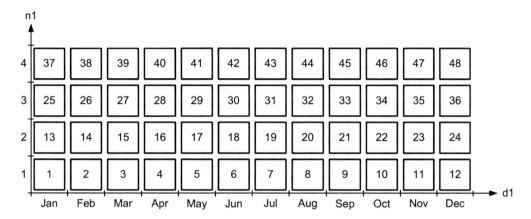

Figure 9-5. *The test table is composed of 48 partitions per year.*

Each partition can be identified by either its name or its "position" in the table (the latter is shown in Figure 9-5). Of course, the mapping between these two values is available in the data dictionary. The following query shows how to get it from the data dictionary view user_tab_partitions:

```
SQL> SELECT partition_name, partition_position
  2  FROM user_tab_partitions
  3  WHERE table_name = 'T'
  4  ORDER BY partition_position;

PARTITION_NAME PARTITION_POSITION
-------------- ------------------
T_1_JAN_2007                    1
T_1_FEB_2007                    2
T_1_MAR_2007                    3
...
T_4_OCT_2007                   46
T_4_NOV_2007                   47
T_4_DEC_2007                   48
```

With such a table, if a restriction is applied to the partition key, the query optimizer recognizes it and whenever possible excludes partitions containing data that is processing-irrelevant. This is possible because the data dictionary contains the boundaries of the partitions, and therefore, the query optimizer can compare them to the restriction or join condition specified in the WHERE clause. Because of limitations, however, this is not always possible. The next subsections show different examples that point out how and when the query optimizer is able to use partition pruning.

PARTITION RANGE SINGLE

In the following SQL statement, the WHERE clause contains two restrictions: one for each column of the partition key. In this type of situation, the query optimizer recognizes that only a single partition contains relevant data. As a result, the operation PARTITION RANGE SINGLE appears in the execution plan. It is essential to understand that its child operation (TABLE ACCESS FULL) is not a full table scan over the whole table. Instead, only a single partition is accessed. This is confirmed by the value of the column Starts as well. Which partition is accessed is specified by the columns Pstart and Pstop. Figure 9-6 is a graphical representation of this behavior.

```
SELECT * FROM t WHERE n1 = 3 AND d1 = to_date('2007-07-19','yyyy-mm-dd')
```

```
---------------------------------------------------------------
| Id  | Operation            | Name | Starts | Pstart| Pstop |
---------------------------------------------------------------
|  1  |  PARTITION RANGE SINGLE|      |    1 |    31 |    31 |
|* 2  |    TABLE ACCESS FULL   | T    |    1 |    31 |    31 |
---------------------------------------------------------------

   2 - filter("D1"=TO_DATE('2007-07-19 00:00:00', 'yyyy-mm-dd hh24:mi:ss') AND
           "N1"=3)
```

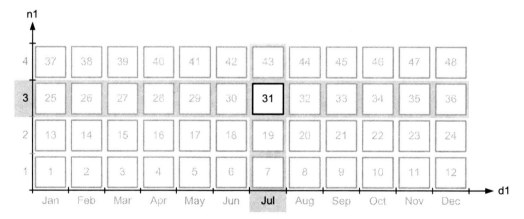

Figure 9-6. *Representation of a PARTITION RANGE SINGLE operation*

As the output of the following query shows, the partition numbers in the columns Pstart and Pstop match the values in the column partition_position in the data dictionary view user_tab_partitions.

```
SQL> SELECT partition_name, partition_position, num_rows
  2  FROM user_tab_partitions
  3  WHERE table_name = 'T'
  4  ORDER BY partition_position;

PARTITION_NAME PARTITION_POSITION  NUM_ROWS
-------------- ------------------ ----------
T_1_JAN_2007                    1        212
T_1_FEB_2007                    2        192
T_1_MAR_2007                    3        212
...
T_3_JUN_2007                   30        206
T_3_JUL_2007                   31        212
T_3_AUG_2007                   32        213
...
T_4_OCT_2007                   46        212
T_4_NOV_2007                   47        206
T_4_DEC_2007                   48        212
```

Whenever a bind variable is used in a restriction, the query optimizer is no longer able to determine which partitions need to be accessed at parse time. In such cases, partition pruning is performed at runtime. The execution plan does not change, but the values of the columns Pstart and Pstop are set to KEY. This indicates that partition pruning occurs, but that at parse time, the query optimizer ignores which partition contains relevant data.

```
SELECT * FROM t WHERE n1 = :n1 AND d1 = to_date(:d1,'yyyy-mm-dd')


----------------------------------------------------------------
| Id  | Operation             | Name  | Starts | Pstart| Pstop |
----------------------------------------------------------------
|   1 |  PARTITION RANGE SINGLE|      |      1 |  KEY  |  KEY  |
|*  2 |    TABLE ACCESS FULL   | T    |      1 |  KEY  |  KEY  |
----------------------------------------------------------------

   2 - filter("N1"=TO_NUMBER(:N1) AND "D1"=TO_DATE(:D1,'yyyy-mm-dd'))
```

If you are working with Oracle9*i*, you should be very careful because the operation PARTITION RANGE SINGLE is not always shown as part of the execution plan. Consequently, the plan might be easily misunderstood. For example, if, in the previous query, you replace bind variables with literal values, the following execution plan results. From this, without the columns Pstart and Pstop, you would think that no partition pruning takes place, even though, as in this case, a single partition is accessed! Note that when the same query uses a bind variable instead of a literal value, the execution plan contains the operation PARTITION RANGE SINGLE as expected.

```
SELECT * FROM t WHERE n1 = 3 AND d1 = to_date('2007-07-19','yyyy-mm-dd')


-------------------------------------------------------------
| Id  | Operation          | Name    | Pstart| Pstop |
-------------------------------------------------------------
|*  1 |  TABLE ACCESS FULL  | T       |   31  |   31  |
-------------------------------------------------------------

   1 - filter("T"."D1"=TO_DATE('2007-07-19 00:00:00', 'yyyy-mm-dd hh24:mi:ss') AND
              "T"."N1"=3)
```

PARTITION RANGE ITERATOR

The execution plans described in the previous section contain the operation PARTITION RANGE SINGLE. This was because the query optimizer recognizes that only a single partition contains processing-relevant data. Obviously, there are situations where several partitions have to be accessed. For example, in the following query, the restriction uses a less-than condition (<) instead of being based on an equality condition (=) Thus, the operation becomes a PARTITION RANGE ITERATOR, and the columns Pstart and Pstop show the range of partitions that are accessed (see Figure 9-7). In addition, the column Starts shows that operation 1 is executed only once, but operation 2 is executed once per partition. In other words, seven full partition scans are executed.

```
SELECT * FROM t WHERE n1 = 3 AND d1 < to_date('2007-07-19','yyyy-mm-dd')


---------------------------------------------------------------------
| Id  | Operation             | Name | Starts | Pstart| Pstop |
---------------------------------------------------------------------
|   1 |  PARTITION RANGE ITERATOR|     |   1  |   25  |   31  |
|*  2 |   TABLE ACCESS FULL      | T   |   7  |   25  |   31  |
---------------------------------------------------------------------

   2 - filter("N1"=3 AND
              "D1"<TO_DATE('2007-07-19 00:00:00', 'yyyy-mm-dd hh24:mi:ss'))
```

The operation PARTITION RANGE ITERATOR is also used when a restriction is based on the leading part of the partition key only. The following query illustrates this, where the restriction is applied to the first column of the partition key. Note that partition 37 is accessed as well. This is because rows that have column n1 equal to 3 would be stored in that partition if column d1 had a value later than the 31st of January 2007.

```
SELECT * FROM t WHERE n1 = 3


---------------------------------------------------------------------
| Id  | Operation             | Name | Starts | Pstart| Pstop |
---------------------------------------------------------------------
|   1 |  PARTITION RANGE ITERATOR|     |   1  |   25  |   37  |
|*  2 |   TABLE ACCESS FULL      | T   |  13  |   25  |   37  |
---------------------------------------------------------------------

   2 - filter("N1"=3)
```

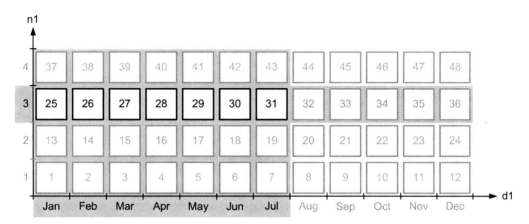

Figure 9-7. *Representation of a PARTITION RANGE ITERATOR operation*

As the name of this operation implies, it works only with a continuous range of partitions. When a noncontinuous range is used, the operation presented in the next section comes into play.

PARTITION RANGE INLIST

If a restriction is based on one or several IN conditions that are composed of more than one element, a specific operation, PARTITION RANGE INLIST, appears in the execution plan. With this operation, the columns Pstart and Pstop do not give precise information about which partitions are accessed. Instead, they show the value KEY(I). This indicates that partition pruning occurs separately for every value in the IN condition. In addition, the column Starts shows how many partitions are accessed (in this case twice).

```
SELECT * FROM t WHERE n1 IN (1,3) AND d1 = to_date('2007-07-19','yyyy-mm-dd')


---------------------------------------------------------------
| Id  | Operation             | Name | Starts | Pstart| Pstop |
---------------------------------------------------------------
|  1  | PARTITION RANGE INLIST|      |    1   |KEY(I) |KEY(I) |
|* 2  |   TABLE ACCESS FULL    | T   |    2   |KEY(I) |KEY(I) |
---------------------------------------------------------------

   2 - filter("D1"=TO_DATE('2007-07-19 00:00:00', 'yyyy-mm-dd hh24:mi:ss') AND
             ("N1"=1 OR "N1"=3))
```

In this specific case, based on the WHERE clause, you infer that only partitions 7 and 31 are accessed. Figure 9-8 illustrates this.

Of course, if the values in the IN condition are sufficiently spread, it is possible that most of the partitions are accessed. In cases where the query optimizer recognizes that all partitions are accessed, the operation in the next section applies.

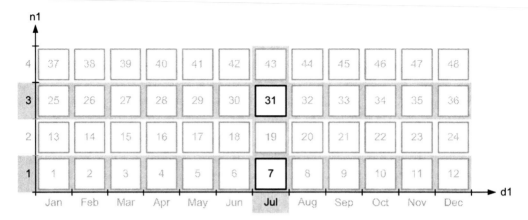

Figure 9-8. *Representation of a PARTITION RANGE INLIST operation*

PARTITION RANGE ALL

If no restriction is applied to the partition key, all partitions must be accessed. In such a case, the execution plan contains the operation PARTITION RANGE ALL, and the columns Starts, Pstart, and Pstop clearly show that all partitions are accessed.

```
SELECT * FROM t WHERE n3 BETWEEN 6000 AND 7000
```

```
-------------------------------------------------------------
| Id | Operation          | Name | Starts | Pstart| Pstop |
-------------------------------------------------------------
|  1 | PARTITION RANGE ALL|      |    1 |    1 |   48 |
|* 2 |   TABLE ACCESS FULL | T    |   48 |    1 |   48 |
-------------------------------------------------------------

   2 - filter("N3">=6000 AND "N3"<=7000)
```

This very same execution plan is also used when inequalities are used as restrictions on the partition key. The following query is an example:

```
SELECT * FROM t WHERE n1 != 3 AND d1 != to_date('2007-07-19','yyyy-mm-dd')
```

Another case where the very same execution plan is used is when a restriction on the partition key is based on an expression or function. For example, in the following query, one is added to column n1, and column d1 is modified through the function to_char.

```
SELECT * FROM t WHERE n1 + 1 = 4 AND to_char(d1,'yyyy-mm-dd') = '2007-07-19'
```

This means that to take advantage of partition pruning, not only should you have a restriction based on the partition key, but you should also not apply an expression or function to it. If applying an expression is a must, as of Oracle Database 11g, it is possible to choose a virtual column as the partition key.

PARTITION RANGE EMPTY

A particular operation, PARTITION RANGE EMPTY, appears in execution plans when the query optimizer recognizes that no partition is able to store processing-relevant data. For example, the following query is looking for data that has no partition where it could be stored (column n1 is out of range). It is also important to note that not only are the columns Pstart and Pstop set to the value INVALID, but in addition, only operation 1 is executed (consuming no resource at all since, basically, it is a no-op operation).

```
SELECT * FROM t WHERE n1 = 5 AND d1 = to_date('2007-07-19','yyyy-mm-dd')
```

```
-------------------------------------------------------------
| Id  | Operation            | Name | Starts | Pstart| Pstop |
-------------------------------------------------------------
|  1  |  PARTITION RANGE EMPTY|      |      1 |INVALID|INVALID|
|* 2  |   TABLE ACCESS FULL   | T    |      0 |INVALID|INVALID|
-------------------------------------------------------------

   2 - filter("N1"=5 AND
           "D1"=TO_DATE('2008-07-19 00:00:00', 'yyyy-mm-dd hh24:mi:ss'))
```

PARTITION RANGE OR

Up to Oracle Database 10g Release 1, a WHERE clause that contains several predicates (on the partition key) that are combined by OR conditions might lead to a full table scan. In other words, the query optimizer is not always able to take advantage of partition pruning. As of Oracle Database 10g Release 2, thanks to *OR pruning*, this limitation no longer applies. The following query is an example of such a situation. When this type of pruning is used, the operation PARTITION RANGE OR appears in the execution plan. Also note that the columns Pstart and Pstop are set to the value KEY(OR). In the following example, according to the column Starts, 18 partitions are accessed. There are 18 because although the restriction applied to column n1 causes partitions 25 to 37 to be accessed, the restriction applied to column d1 causes partitions 1, 3, 15, 27, and 39 to be accessed (partition 1 is necessary in order to find out whether there are rows with column n1 containing values less than 1).

```
SELECT * FROM t WHERE n1 = 3 OR d1 = to_date('2007-03-06','yyyy-mm-dd')
```

```
-------------------------------------------------------------
| Id  | Operation          | Name | Starts | Pstart| Pstop |
-------------------------------------------------------------
|  1  |  PARTITION RANGE OR|      |      1 |KEY(OR)|KEY(OR)|
|* 2  |   TABLE ACCESS FULL| T    |     18 |KEY(OR)|KEY(OR)|
-------------------------------------------------------------

   2 - filter("N1"=3 OR
           "D1"=TO_DATE('2007-03-06 00:00:00', 'yyyy-mm-dd hh24:mi:ss'))
```

PARTITION RANGE SUBQUERY

In the previous sections, all restrictions used for partition pruning were based on literal values or bind variables. However, it is not uncommon for restrictions to actually be join conditions. Whenever a join is based on a partition key, the query optimizer has to choose between three strategies. Naturally, it ought to choose the strategy that will lower costs.

▨Note Chapter 10 covers the join methods in detail.

The first strategy is to elude partition pruning. The following query (note that the table tx is a copy of the table t; the only difference is that table tx is not partitioned) illustrates this, where no partition pruning on the table t is performed. In fact, since operation 4 is a PARTITION RANGE ALL, operation 5 is processed for all partitions. In this particular example, this execution plan is highly inefficient. This is especially the case given that the selectivity of the query is very strong.

```
SELECT * FROM tx, t WHERE tx.d1 = t.d1 AND tx.n1 = t.n1 AND tx.id = 19
```

```
---------------------------------------------------------------------
| Id  | Operation                     | Name  | Starts | Pstart| Pstop |
---------------------------------------------------------------------
|*  1 |  HASH JOIN                    |       |     1 |       |       |
|   2 |   TABLE ACCESS BY INDEX ROWID | TX    |     1 |       |       |
|*  3 |    INDEX UNIQUE SCAN          | TX_PK |     1 |       |       |
|   4 |   PARTITION RANGE ALL         |       |     1 |    1 |    48 |
|   5 |    TABLE ACCESS FULL          | T     |    48 |    1 |    48 |
---------------------------------------------------------------------
```

```
    1 - access("TX"."D1"="T"."D1" AND "TX"."N1"="T"."N1")
    3 - access("TX"."ID"=19)
```

This strategy is always available. Nevertheless, it could lead to poor performance if the selectivity of the join condition is not close to 1, or, in other words, in situations where partition pruning should be used.

The second strategy is to execute the join with the operation NESTED LOOPS and define the table, which the partition pruning should occur on, as the second child. In fact, as discussed in Chapter 6, the operation NESTED LOOPS is a related-combine operation, and therefore, its first child controls the execution of the second child. The following example shows such a situation. Note that the operation PARTITION RANGE ITERATOR and the values of the columns Pstart and Pstop confirm that partition pruning takes place. According to the column Starts, a single partition is accessed. In this specific case, the following execution plan is, therefore, far more efficient than the one used by the first strategy:

```
SELECT * FROM tx, t WHERE tx.d1 = t.d1 AND tx.n1 = t.n1 AND tx.id = 19
```

```
-------------------------------------------------------------------
| Id | Operation                      | Name  | Starts | Pstart| Pstop |
-------------------------------------------------------------------
|  1 |  NESTED LOOPS                   |       |    1 |       |       |
|  2 |   TABLE ACCESS BY INDEX ROWID| TX    |    1 |       |       |
|* 3 |    INDEX UNIQUE SCAN           | TX_PK |    1 |       |       |
|  4 |   PARTITION RANGE ITERATOR     |       |    1 |  KEY  |  KEY  |
|* 5 |    TABLE ACCESS FULL           | T     |    1 |  KEY  |  KEY  |
-------------------------------------------------------------------
```

```
  3 - access("TX"."ID"=19)
  5 - filter(("TX"."D1"="T"."D1" AND "TX"."N1"="T"."N1"))
```

This strategy performs well only if the number of rows returned by the first child of the operation NESTED LOOP (in this case operation 2) is low. Otherwise, it is even possible that the same partition is accessed several times by the second child (in this case operation 4).

The third strategy is to execute the join with the operation HASH JOIN or MERGE JOIN. No regular partition pruning based on the join condition is possible, however, with these join methods. In fact, as discussed in Chapter 6, they are unrelated-combine operations, and consequently, the two children are executed separately. In such cases, the query optimizer can take advantage of another type of partition pruning, the *subquery pruning*. The idea here is to find out which partitions of the second child should be accessed, by executing a recursive query (on the table accessed by the first child) to retrieve the columns used in the join condition that maps to the partition keys of the second child. Then, by consulting the partition definitions of the second child stored in the data dictionary, the partitions to be accessed by the second child are identified, and so it is possible to scan only them. The following query shows an example of this. Note that the operation PARTITION RANGE SUBQUERY and the value of the columns Pstart and Pstop confirm that partition pruning takes place. According to the column Starts, a single partition is accessed.

```
SELECT * FROM tx, t WHERE tx.d1 = t.d1 AND tx.n1 = t.n1 AND tx.id = 19
```

```
-------------------------------------------------------------------
| Id | Operation                      | Name  | Starts | Pstart  | Pstop   |
-------------------------------------------------------------------
|* 1 |  HASH JOIN                      |       |    1 |         |         |
|  2 |   TABLE ACCESS BY INDEX ROWID| TX    |    1 |         |         |
|* 3 |    INDEX UNIQUE SCAN           | TX_PK |    1 |         |         |
|  4 |   PARTITION RANGE SUBQUERY     |       |    1 | KEY(SQ) | KEY(SQ) |
|  5 |    TABLE ACCESS FULL           | T     |    1 | KEY(SQ) | KEY(SQ) |
-------------------------------------------------------------------
```

```
  1 - access("TX"."D1"="T"."D1" AND "TX"."N1"="T"."N1")
  3 - access("TX"."ID"=19)
```

What actually happens here is that in order to find out which partitions have to be accessed, the operation PARTITION RANGE SUBQUERY executes the following query recursively. This recursive query retrieves the number of the partitions that contain relevant data with the function tbloridx$part$num. With this information, operation 5 can take advantage of partition pruning. For example, in this case, only partition 37 needs to be scanned:

```
SQL> SELECT DISTINCT tbl$or$idx$part$num("T", 0, 1, 0, "N1", "D1") AS part_num
  2  FROM (SELECT "TX"."N1" "N1", "TX"."D1" "D1"
  3           FROM "TX" "TX"
  4           WHERE "TX"."ID"=19)
  5  ORDER BY 1;

  PART_NUM
----------
        37
```

Clearly, it makes sense to use this third technique only when the overhead caused by the execution of the recursive query is less than the gain because of partition pruning. For the query used in this example, the efficiency of the execution plans resulting from the second and third strategies are very similar. Nevertheless, if selectivity were weaker, the execution plan resulting from the third strategy would be more efficient.

Note that the operation PARTITION RANGE SUBQUERY has been introduced in Oracle Database 10g Release 2. In previous releases, where subquery pruning is also available, the operation PARTITION RANGE ITERATOR is used instead. The only way to recognize subquery pruning up to Oracle Database 10g Release 1 is to check whether the columns Pstart and Pstop contain the value KEY(SQ).

PARTITION RANGE JOIN-FILTER

Subquery pruning is a useful optimization technique. However, as discussed in the previous section, part of the SQL statement is executed twice. To avoid this double execution, Oracle Database 11g provides another type of partition pruning, the *join-filter pruning* (aka *bloom-filter pruning*). To understand how it works, let's look at the execution plan generated by the same query as the one used to describe subquery pruning. Note that several new things appear: the operation PART JOIN FILTER CREATE; the operation PARTITION RANGE JOIN-FILTER; and, in the columns Name, Pstart, and Pstop, the string :BF0000.

```
SELECT * FROM tx, t WHERE tx.d1 = t.d1 AND tx.n1 = t.n1 AND tx.id = 19
```

Id	Operation	Name	Starts	Pstart	Pstop
* 1	HASH JOIN		1		
2	PART JOIN FILTER CREATE	:BF0000	1		
3	TABLE ACCESS BY INDEX ROWID	TX	1		
* 4	INDEX UNIQUE SCAN	TX_PK	1		
5	PARTITION RANGE JOIN-FILTER		1	:BF0000	:BF0000
6	TABLE ACCESS FULL	T	1	:BF0000	:BF0000

```
1 - access("TX"."N1"="T"."N1" AND "TX"."D1"="T"."D1")
4 - access("TX"."ID"=19)
```

The execution plan is executed as follows:

- Operations 3 and 4 access table tx through the index tx_pk.

- Based on the data returned by operation 3, operation 2 creates a memory structure (a bloom filter) based on values from columns tx.d1 and tx.n1.

- Based on the memory structure created by operation 2, operation 5 is able to take advantage of partition pruning and, therefore, is able to access only the partitions that contain relevant data. In this case, a single partition is accessed (see column Starts).

PARTITION RANGE MULTI-COLUMN

If the partition key is composed of several columns, it is important to observe what happens when a restriction is not defined for every column. The main question is, does the query optimizer take advantage of partition pruning? The answer depends on which release you are using. In fact, in earlier versions, the query optimizer uses partition pruning only when restrictions are applied to the leading part of the partition key. For example, if a partition key consists of the three columns c1, c2, and c3, partition pruning is possible only if a restriction on c1 or on both c1 and c2 is specified. This means that a restriction on both c2 and c3 does not lead to partition pruning. This restriction has been removed in Oracle Database 10*g* Release 2 thanks to *multicolumn pruning*. Later, it was also back ported in the patchset 9.2.0.8 and 10.1.0.5. The concept of multicolumn pruning is quite simple: independently of which columns a restriction is defined on, partition pruning always occurs.

Let's see this feature in action on the same test table we have used before. Since the partition key of the test table is composed of two columns, there are two cases to consider: the restriction is applied to either the first column or the second column. The following query is an example of the former:

```
SELECT * FROM t WHERE n1 = 3
```

```
-----------------------------------------------------------------
| Id  | Operation             | Name | Starts | Pstart| Pstop |
-----------------------------------------------------------------
|   1 | PARTITION RANGE ITERATOR|     |     1 |    25 |    37 |
|*  2 |    TABLE ACCESS FULL  | T    |      13 |    25 |    37 |
-----------------------------------------------------------------

   2 - filter("N1"=3)
```

The following query is an example of the latter. Note that the operation PARTITION RANGE MULTI-COLUMN and the value of the columns Pstart and Pstop confirm that partition pruning takes place; however, no information is provided about which partitions are accessed.

```
SELECT * FROM t WHERE d1 = to_date('2007-07-19','yyyy-mm-dd')

-------------------------------------------------------------------------
| Id  | Operation                    | Name | Starts | Pstart| Pstop |
-------------------------------------------------------------------------
|   1 |  PARTITION RANGE MULTI-COLUMN|      |     1  |KEY(MC)|KEY(MC)|
|*  2 |    TABLE ACCESS FULL         | T    |     8  |KEY(MC)|KEY(MC)|
-------------------------------------------------------------------------

   2 - filter("D1"=TO_DATE('2007-07-19 00:00:00', 'yyyy-mm-dd hh24:mi:ss'))
```

It is also important to note that the operation PARTITION RANGE MULTI-COLUMN was first introduced in Oracle Database 10*g* Release 2. In previous releases, where multicolumn pruning is also available, the operation PARTITION RANGE ITERATOR is used instead. Thus, the only way to recognize multicolumn pruning in previous releases is to check whether the columns Pstart and Pstop contain the value KEY(MC).

Hash and List Partitioning

The previous section covered range partitioning only. Anyway, with hash and list partitioning, most of the techniques described for range partitioning are available as well.

The following are the operations available with hash partitioning. Note that only OR and multicolumn pruning are missing. The script pruning_hash.sql provides examples of execution plans that contain these operations:

- PARTITION HASH SINGLE

- PARTITION HASH ITERATOR

- PARTITION HASH INLIST

- PARTITION HASH ALL

- PARTITION HASH SUBQUERY

- PARTITION HASH JOIN-FILTER

The following are the operations available with list partitioning. Note that only multicolumn pruning is missing. This is obvious, since the partition key is always composed of a single column with list partitioning. The script pruning_list.sql provides examples of execution plans containing these operations:

- PARTITION LIST SINGLE

- PARTITION LIST ITERATOR

- PARTITION LIST INLIST

- PARTITION LIST ALL

- PARTITION LIST EMPTY

- PARTITION LIST OR

- PARTITION LIST SUBQUERY

- PARTITION LIST JOIN-FILTER

Composite Partitioning

There is little that can be said about composite partitioning. Basically, everything that applies at the partition level applies at the subpartition level as well. Nevertheless, it makes sense to illustrate at least one example. The following test table is partitioned by range (based on column d1) and subpartitioned by list (based on column n1). The following SQL statement, which is an excerpt of the script pruning_composite.sql, was used to create the table. Note that also in this case, there are 48 partitions per year.

```
CREATE TABLE t (
  id NUMBER,
  d1 DATE,
  n1 NUMBER,
  n2 NUMBER,
  n3 NUMBER,
  pad VARCHAR2(4000),
  CONSTRAINT t_pk PRIMARY KEY (id)
)
PARTITION BY RANGE (d1)
SUBPARTITION BY LIST (n1)
SUBPARTITION TEMPLATE (
  SUBPARTITION sp_1 VALUES (1),
  SUBPARTITION sp_2 VALUES (2),
  SUBPARTITION sp_3 VALUES (3),
  SUBPARTITION sp_4 VALUES (4)
)(
  PARTITION t_jan_2007 VALUES LESS THAN (to_date('2007-02-01','yyyy-mm-dd')),
  PARTITION t_feb_2007 VALUES LESS THAN (to_date('2007-03-01','yyyy-mm-dd')),
  PARTITION t_mar_2007 VALUES LESS THAN (to_date('2007-04-01','yyyy-mm-dd')),
  ...
  PARTITION t_oct_2007 VALUES LESS THAN (to_date('2007-11-01','yyyy-mm-dd')),
  PARTITION t_nov_2007 VALUES LESS THAN (to_date('2007-12-01','yyyy-mm-dd')),
  PARTITION t_dec_2007 VALUES LESS THAN (to_date('2008-01-01','yyyy-mm-dd'))
)
```

Figure 9-9 is a graphical representation of this test table. If you compare it with the previous one (see Figure 9-5), the only difference is that there is no single value that identifies the position of subpartitions throughout the table. In fact, the position of a subpartition is based on its "parent" partition.

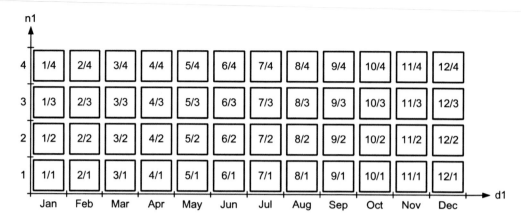

Figure 9-9. *The test table is composed of 48 partitions per year.*

Of course, the mapping between name and position is available in the data dictionary also in this case. The following query shows how to get it from the data dictionary views user_tab_partitions and user_tab_subpartitions:

```
SQL> SELECT subpartition_name, partition_position, subpartition_position
  2  FROM user_tab_partitions p, user_tab_subpartitions s
  3  WHERE p.table_name = 'T'
  4  AND s.table_name = p.table_name
  5  AND s.partition_name = p.partition_name
  6  ORDER BY p.partition_position, s.subpartition_position;

SUBPARTITION_NAME  PARTITION_POSITION SUBPARTITION_POSITION
-----------------  ------------------ ---------------------
T_JAN_2007_SP_1                     1                     1
T_JAN_2007_SP_2                     1                     2
T_JAN_2007_SP_3                     1                     3
T_JAN_2007_SP_4                     1                     4
T_FEB_2007_SP_1                     2                     1
...
T_NOV_2007_SP_4                    11                     4
T_DEC_2007_SP_1                    12                     1
T_DEC_2007_SP_2                    12                     2
T_DEC_2007_SP_3                    12                     3
T_DEC_2007_SP_4                    12                     4
```

The following query is an example of a restriction at both the partition and subpartition levels. The operations are those described in the previous sections. Operation 1 applies at the partition level, and operation 2 applies at the subpartition level. At the partition level, partitions 1 to 7 are accessed. For each of them, only subpartition 3 is accessed. Figure 9-10 shows this behavior. Notice how the values in the columns Pstart and Pstop match the result of the previous query when executed against the data dictionary.

```
SELECT * FROM t WHERE d1 < to_date('2007-07-19','yyyy-mm-dd') AND n1 = 3
```

```
-----------------------------------------------------------------
| Id  | Operation               | Name | Starts | Pstart| Pstop |
-----------------------------------------------------------------
|   1 |  PARTITION RANGE ITERATOR|      |      1 |     1 |     7 |
|   2 |    PARTITION LIST SINGLE |      |      7 |     3 |     3 |
|*  3 |      TABLE ACCESS FULL   | T    |      7 |   KEY |   KEY |
-----------------------------------------------------------------
```

```
   3 - filter("D1"<TO_DATE(' 2007-07-19 00:00:00', 'syyyy-mm-dd hh24:mi:ss'))
```

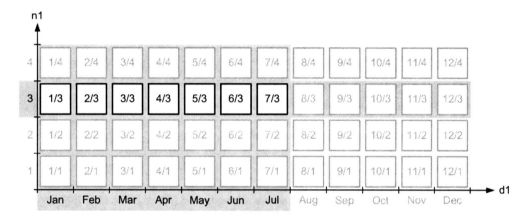

Figure 9-10. *Representation of composite partition pruning*

Design Considerations

As you have seen in the previous sections, the query optimizer can take advantage of partition pruning in a wide range of situations. Table 9-1 summarizes when partition pruning occurs for each type of partitioning method and for the most common SQL conditions.

Table 9-1. *Conditions That Lead to Partition Pruning**

Condition	Range	List	Hash
Equality (=)	✓	✓	✓
IN	✓	✓	✓
BETWEEN, >, >=, <, or <=	✓	✓	
IS NULL	✓	✓	

* Inequality (!= or <>), NOT IN, and NOT NULL conditions and restrictions based on expressions and functions do not lead to partition pruning.

Choosing the partition key and the partitioning method is probably the most important decision you have to make while working on the design of a partitioned table. The objective is to take advantage of partition pruning in order to process as many SQL statements as possible. In addition, one partition should ideally contain only the data you expect to be processed by a single SQL statement. For example, if there are frequent SQL statements processing data by the day, you should partition by the day. Or, if there are frequent SQL statements that process data by country, you should partition the data by country. If you do this incorrectly, you will never be able to take advantage of partition pruning. The following four characteristics of your application have to be considered very carefully, since they are the ones that impact the partitioning strategy the most:

- What columns the restrictions are expected to be applied on and with what frequency

- What kind of data will be stored in those columns

- What the SQL conditions used in those restrictions will be

- Whether data must be regularly purged and what criterion to base the purge on

The first and the fourth are essential for choosing the partition key. The second and the third are for choosing the partitioning method. Let's discuss them in detail.

Knowing which columns the restrictions are applied on is essential because no partition pruning is possible if no restriction is applied to the partition key. In other words, based on this criterion, you restrict the choice between a limited number of columns. In practice, it is quite common for several, possibly very different, restrictions to be applied by different SQL statements. Therefore, you must know the frequency of utilization of the different SQL statements as well. In this way, you can decide which restrictions are the most important to optimize. In any case, you should consider only those restrictions that have weak selectivity. In fact, restrictions with strong selectivity can be optimized with other access structures (for example, indexes).

Once the columns to be potentially used in the partition key are known, it is time to take a look at the data they store. The idea is to find out which partitioning method would be applicable to them. For that, it is essential to recognize two things. First, only range and list partitioning allow the grouping together of "related" data (for example, all of July's sales or all European countries) or an exact mapping of specific values with specific partitions. Second, each partitioning method is suitable only for a very specific kind of data:

- *Range* is suitable for values that are sequential by nature. Typical examples are time stamps and numbers generated by a sequence.

- *List* is suitable when the number of distinct values is both well known and limited in number. Typical examples are all kinds of status information (for example, enabled, disabled, processed) and attributes that describe people (for example, sex, marital status) or things (for example, country and postal codes, currencies, categories, format).

- *Hash* is suitable for all kinds of data for which the number of distinct values is much higher than the number of partitions (for example, customer number).

The partitioning method has to be both suitable for the kind of data and suitable for the restrictions applied to the columns making up the partition key. Here, the restrictions related to hash partitioning described in Table 9-1 should be taken into consideration. In addition, note that even though it is technically possible to use range conditions on list-partitioned tables, it is not uncommon for such conditions to *not* lead to partition pruning. In fact, data in a list-partitioned table is by nature not sequential.

If regular purging activities take place, you should also take into consideration whether they can be implemented by taking advantage of partitioning. Dropping a partition is much faster than deleting the data it contains. Such a strategy is usually possible only when range partitioning is used.

Once the partition key has been chosen, it is necessary to decide whether the partition key can be modified. Such a modification typically means moving the row into another partition and, consequently, changing its rowid. Usually, a row never changes its rowid. So if it is a possibility, not only must row movement be enabled at the table level to allow the database engine to make such a critical modification, but the application also needs to use rowids with special care.

One final, but in my honest opinion very important remark, is to prevent the most common mistake I have experienced in projects that implement partitioning. The mistake is designing and implementing the database and the application without implementing partitioning and then, afterward, partitioning it. More often than not, such an approach is doomed to fail. I strongly recommend planning the use of partitioning from the beginning of a project. If you think you will be able to easily introduce it later, if necessary, you may be in for a big surprise.

Full Index Scans

The database engine can use indexes not only to extract lists of rowids and use them as pointers to read the corresponding rows from the table, but it can also directly read the column values that are part of the index keys, thus avoiding following the rowid and accessing the table altogether. Thanks to this very important optimization, when an index contains all the data needed to process a query, a full table scan or full partition scan might be replaced by a *full index scan*. And since an index segment is usually much smaller than a table segment, this is useful for reducing the number of logical reads.

Full index scans are useful in three main situations. The first is when an index stores all the columns used by a query. For example, since column n1 is indexed in the test table, the following query can take advantage of a full index scan. The following execution plan confirms that no table access is performed (note that all examples in this section are based on the script index_full_scan.sql):

```
SELECT /*+ index(t t_n1_i) */ n1 FROM t WHERE n1 IS NOT NULL
```

```
-------------------------------------------------------
| Id | Operation      | Name   | Starts | Buffers |
-------------------------------------------------------
|* 1 |  INDEX FULL SCAN| T_N1_I |    1 |    689 |
-------------------------------------------------------

   1 - filter("N1" IS NOT NULL)
```

It is essential to understand that this execution plan is possible because the condition available in the WHERE clause (n1 IS NOT NULL) makes sure that the index stores all the data required for the processing (a NOT NULL constraint on column n1 would have the same effect because it makes sure that no NULL values are inserted). Otherwise, since single-column B-tree indexes do not store NULL values, a full table scan would be executed.

The operation INDEX FULL SCAN, which can be forced by the hint index as shown in the previous example, scans an index according to its structure. The advantage of this is that the retrieved data is sorted according to the index key. The disadvantage is that if the index blocks are not found in the buffer cache, they are read from the data files with single-block reads. Since a full index scan may read a lot of data, this is usually inefficient. To improve the performance in such cases, *index fast full scans* can be used. The following execution plan shows an example:

```
SELECT /*+ index_ffs(t t_n1_i) */ n1 FROM t WHERE n1 IS NOT NULL


----------------------------------------
| Id | Operation           | Name    |
----------------------------------------
|* 1 |   INDEX FAST FULL SCAN| T_N1_I |
----------------------------------------

   1 - filter("N1" IS NOT NULL)
```

The peculiarity of the operation INDEX FAST FULL SCAN, which can be forced by the hint index_ffs, is that if the index blocks are not found in the buffer cache, they are read from the data files with multiblock reads, like full table scans do for tables. During such a scan, the root and the branch blocks can simply be discharged because all data is stored in the leaf blocks (usually root and branch blocks are only a tiny fraction of the index segment, so even if they are read uselessly, the overhead is usually negligible). As a consequence, the index structure is not considered for the access, and therefore, the retrieved data is not sorted according to the index key.

The second case is similar to the previous one. The only difference is that the data has to be delivered in the same order as it is stored in the index. For example, as shown in the following query, this is the case because an ORDER BY clause is specified. Since the order matters, only the operation INDEX FULL SCAN can be used to avoid the sort operation.

```
SELECT /*+ index(t t_n1_i) */ n1 FROM t WHERE n1 IS NOT NULL ORDER BY n1


----------------------------------
| Id | Operation      | Name    |
----------------------------------
|* 1 |   INDEX FULL SCAN| T_N1_I |
----------------------------------

   1 - filter("N1" IS NOT NULL)
```

Since the operation INDEX FULL SCAN is less efficient than the operation INDEX FAST FULL SCAN, the former is used only when the order matters.

Per default, an index scan is performed in ascending order. Consequently, the hint index instructs the query optimizer to behave in this way also. To explicitly specify the scan order, you can use the hints index_asc and index_desc. The following query shows how. The scan in descending order is shown in the execution plan:

```
SELECT /*+ index_desc(t t_n1_i) */ n1 FROM t WHERE n1 IS NOT NULL ORDER BY n1 DESC
```

```
--------------------------------------------
| Id  | Operation               | Name  |
--------------------------------------------
|*  1 |   INDEX FULL SCAN DESCENDING| T_N1_I |
--------------------------------------------
```

```
   1 - filter("N1" IS NOT NULL)
```

The third case is related to the function count. If a query contains it, the query optimizer tries to take advantage of an index in order to avoid a full table scan. The following query is an example. Notice that the operation SORT AGGREGATE is used to execute the function count.

```
SELECT /*+ index_ffs(t t_n1_i) */ count(n1) FROM t
```

```
----------------------------------------
| Id  | Operation               | Name  |
----------------------------------------
|   1 |   SORT AGGREGATE         |       |
|   2 |     INDEX FAST FULL SCAN| T_N1_I |
----------------------------------------
```

When a count against a *nullable* column is processed, the query optimizer is able to pick out any index containing that column. When either a count(*) or a count against a *not-nullable* column is processed, the query optimizer is able to pick out any index that contains at least a not-nullable column (this is necessary since only in this case the number of index entries is guaranteed to be the same as the number of rows). Therefore, it picks out the smaller index of a not-nullable column.

Even though the examples in this section are based on B-tree indexes, most techniques apply to bitmap indexes as well. There are only two differences. First, bitmap indexes cannot be scanned in descending order (this is a limitation due to the implementation). Second, bitmap indexes always store NULL values. Because of this, they can be used in more situations than B-tree indexes. The following queries show examples that are analogous to the previous ones:

```
SELECT /*+ index(t t_n2_i) */ n2 FROM t WHERE n2 IS NOT NULL
```

```
--------------------------------------
| Id  | Operation               |
--------------------------------------
|   1 |   BITMAP CONVERSION TO ROWIDS|
|*  2 |     BITMAP INDEX FULL SCAN  |
--------------------------------------
```

```
   2 - filter("N2" IS NOT NULL)
```

```
SELECT /*+ index_ffs(t t_n2_i) */ n2 FROM t WHERE n2 IS NOT NULL


---------------------------------------
| Id  | Operation                     |
---------------------------------------
|  1  |  BITMAP CONVERSION TO ROWIDS  |
|* 2  |   BITMAP INDEX FAST FULL SCAN |
---------------------------------------

   2 - filter("N2" IS NOT NULL)
```

```
SELECT /*+ index(t t_n2_i) */ n2 FROM t WHERE n2 IS NOT NULL ORDER BY n2


--------------------------------------
| Id  | Operation                    |
--------------------------------------
|  1  |  BITMAP CONVERSION TO ROWIDS |
|* 2  |   BITMAP INDEX FULL SCAN     |
--------------------------------------

   2 - filter("N2" IS NOT NULL)
```

```
SELECT /*+ index_ffs(t t_n2_i) */ count(n2) FROM t


---------------------------------------
| Id  | Operation                     |
---------------------------------------
|  1  |  SORT AGGREGATE               |
|  2  |   BITMAP CONVERSION TO ROWIDS |
|  3  |    BITMAP INDEX FAST FULL SCAN|
---------------------------------------
```

SQL Statements with Strong Selectivity

To efficiently process SQL statements with strong selectivity, the data should be accessed through a rowid, an index, or a single-table hash cluster.[1] These three possibilities are described in the next sections.

Rowid Access

The most efficient way to access a row is to directly specify its rowid in the WHERE clause. However, to take advantage of that access path, you have to get the rowid first, store it, and then reuse it for further accesses. In other words, it is a method that can be considered only if a row is accessed at least two times. In practice, this is something that happens quite frequently when SQL

---

1. Actually, there are also multitable hash clusters and index clusters. They are not described here since they are rarely used in practice.

statements have strong selectivity. For example, applications used to manually maintain data (in other words, not batch jobs) commonly access the same rows at least two times: at least once to show the current data and at least a second time to store the modifications. In such cases, it makes sense to carefully take advantage of the efficiency of rowid accesses.

Good examples demonstrating such an implementation are offered by two of Oracle's tools: Forms and SQL Developer. For instance, when SQL Developer displays data, it gets both the data itself as well as the rowids. For the table emp of the user scott, the tool executes the following query. Note that the first column in the SELECT clause is the rowid.

```
SELECT ROWID,"EMPNO","ENAME","JOB","MGR","HIREDATE","SAL","COMM","DEPTNO"
FROM "SCOTT"."EMP"
```

Later, the rowid can be used to access each specific row directly. For example, if you open the Single Record View dialog box (see Figure 9-11), edit the column comm, and commit the modification, the following SQL statement is executed. As you can see, the tool uses the rowid to reference the modified row instead of the primary key (thus saving the overhead of reading several blocks from the primary key index).

```
UPDATE "SCOTT"."EMP" SET COMM = '1000' WHERE ROWID = 'AAADGZAAEAAAAAoAAH'
```

Figure 9-11. *The SQL Developer's dialog box used to display, browse, and edit data*

Using the rowid is very good from a performance point of view because the row can be accessed directly, without the help of a secondary access structure such as an index. The following is an execution plan that is related to such a SQL statement:

```
-------------------------------------------------------
| Id  | Operation                   | Name  | Starts |
-------------------------------------------------------
|  1  |  UPDATE                      | EMP   |    1   |
|  2  |    TABLE ACCESS BY USER ROWID| EMP   |    1   |
-------------------------------------------------------
```

Note that the operation TABLE ACCESS BY USER ROWID is exclusively used when the rowid is directly passed as a parameter or literal. In the next section, you will see that when a rowid is extracted from an index, the operation TABLE ACCESS BY INDEX ROWID is used instead. The effectiveness of these table accesses is the same; the two operations are used only to distinguish the source of the rowid.

When a SQL statement specifies several rowids through an IN condition, an addition operation, INLIST ITERATOR, appears in the execution plan. The following query is an example. Note that operation 1 (the parent) simply indicates that operation 2 (the child) is processed several times. According to the value of the column Starts of operation 2, it is processed twice. In other words, the table emp is accessed twice through a rowid.

```
SELECT *
FROM emp
WHERE rowid IN ('AAADGZAAEAAAAAoAAH', 'AAADGZAAEAAAAAoAAI')
```

```
---------------------------------------------------------
| Id  | Operation                  | Name | Starts |
---------------------------------------------------------
|   1 |   INLIST ITERATOR          |      |      1 |
|   2 |    TABLE ACCESS BY USER ROWID| EMP  |      2 |
---------------------------------------------------------
```

Note The operation INLIST ITERATOR is not specific to rowid accesses. It is a general operation used when an IN condition is present in a WHERE clause. It means that the list of objects specified in the IN clause is iterated on and passed, one by one, to the child operation.

In summary, whenever specific rows are accessed at least two times, you should consider getting the rowid during the first access and then take advantage of it for subsequent accesses.

Index Access

Index accesses are by far the most often used access paths for SQL statements with strong selectivity. To take advantage of them, it is necessary to apply at least one of the restrictions present in the WHERE clause through an index. To do this, it is essential to not only index columns used in WHERE clauses that provide strong selectivity but also to understand which type of conditions might be applied efficiently through an index. The database engine supports different types of indexes. Before describing the properties and access paths supported by B-tree and bitmap indexes in detail, it is important to discuss the clustering factor or, in other words, why the distribution of data impacts the performance of an index scan (see Figure 9-4).

Note Although the database engine supports domain indexes for complex data such as PDF documents or images, this is not covered in this book. Refer to *Oracle Database Documentation* for further information.

Clustering Factor

As described in Chapter 4, the clustering factor indicates how many adjacent index keys do not refer to the same data block in the table (bitmap indexes are an exception because their clustering factor is always set to the number of keys in the index; see Chapter 4). Here is a mental picture that might help. If the whole table is accessed through an index and in the buffer cache there is a single buffer to store the data blocks, the clustering factor is the number of physical reads performed against the table. For example, the clustering factor of the index shown in Figure 9-12 is 10 (notice that there are 12 rows and only two adjacent index keys, which are highlighted, refer to the same data block).

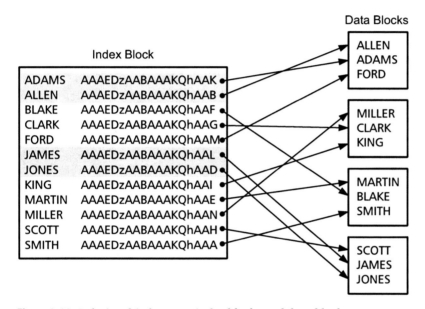

Figure 9-12. *Relationship between index blocks and data blocks*

From a performance point of view, you should avoid row-based processing. As discussed previously in this chapter, the database engine, thanks to row prefetching, also tries to avoid it as much as possible. In fact, when several rows have to be extracted from the same block, instead of accessing the block (that is, doing a logical read) once per row, all rows are extracted in a single access. To emphasize this point, let's look at an example based on the script clustering_factor.sql. The following is the test table created by the script:

```
SQL> CREATE TABLE t (
  2    id NUMBER,
  3    pad VARCHAR2(4000),
  4    CONSTRAINT t_pk PRIMARY KEY (id)
  5  );

SQL> INSERT INTO t
  2    SELECT rownum AS id, dbms_random.string('p',500) AS pad
  3    FROM dual
  4    CONNECT BY level <= 1000;
```

Since the values of the column id are inserted in increasing order, the clustering factor of the index that supports the primary key is close to the number of blocks in the table. In other words, it is very good.

```
SQL> SELECT blocks, num_rows
  2  FROM user_tables
  3  WHERE table_name = 'T';

   BLOCKS   NUM_ROWS
---------- ----------
       73       1000

SQL> SELECT blevel, leaf_blocks, clustering_factor
  2  FROM user_indexes
  3  WHERE index_name = 'T_PK';

   BLEVEL LEAF_BLOCKS CLUSTERING_FACTOR
---------- ----------- -----------------
        1           2                72
```

It is now useful to look at the number of logical reads performed when the whole table is accessed through the primary key (a hint is used to force such an execution plan). The first test is performed with row prefetching set to 2. Hence, at least 500 calls to the database engine must be performed to retrieve the 1,000 rows. This behavior can be confirmed by looking at the number of logical reads (column Buffers): 503 on the index and 572 (1,075 – 503) on the table. Basically, for each call, two rowids were extracted from the index block, and their data was found in the same data block almost every time, thanks to the good clustering factor.

```
SQL> set arraysize 2

SQL> SELECT /*+ index(t t_pk) */ * FROM t;
```

Id	Operation	Name	Starts	A-Rows	Buffers
1	TABLE ACCESS BY INDEX ROWID	T	1	1000	1075
2	INDEX FULL SCAN	T_PK	1	1000	503

The second test is performed with row prefetching set to 100. Hence, at least 10 calls to the database engine are enough to retrieve all rows. Also in this case, this behavior is confirmed by looking at the number of logical reads: 13 on the index and 82 (95 – 13) on the table. Basically, for each call, 10 rowids were extracted from the index block, and their data was often found in the same data block.

```
SQL> set arraysize 100

SQL> SELECT /*+ index(t t_pk) */ * FROM t;
```

```
-------------------------------------------------------------------------
| Id | Operation                   | Name | Starts | A-Rows | Buffers |
-------------------------------------------------------------------------
|  1 |  TABLE ACCESS BY INDEX ROWID| T    |    1 |   1000 |     95 |
|  2 |   INDEX FULL SCAN           | T_PK |    1 |   1000 |     13 |
-------------------------------------------------------------------------
```

It is worth noting that in the previous two examples, the number of logical reads performed on the table is equal to the sum of the clustering factor and the number of calls (that is, the number of rows divided by the prefetching size). However, this is not always the case.

Now let's perform the same test with a much higher clustering factor. To achieve this, an ORBER BY clause is added to the INSERT statement. The only statistic that is changed is the clustering factor. Notice that it is close to the number of rows. In other words, it is very bad.

```
SQL> INSERT INTO t
  2  SELECT rownum AS id, dbms_random.string('p',500) AS pad
  3  FROM dual
  4  CONNECT BY level <= 1000
  5  ORDER BY dbms_random.value;

SQL> SELECT blocks, num_rows
  2  FROM user_tables
  3  WHERE table_name = 'T';

    BLOCKS   NUM_ROWS
---------- ----------
        73       1000

SQL> SELECT blevel, leaf_blocks, clustering_factor
  2  FROM user_indexes
  3  WHERE index_name = 'T_PK';

    BLEVEL LEAF_BLOCKS CLUSTERING_FACTOR
---------- ----------- -----------------
         1           2               990
```

The following are the numbers of logical reads for the two tests. On one hand, for both tests the number of logical reads on the index has not changed. This makes sense because it is close to the number of calls to the database engine. On the other hand, for both tests the number of logical reads on the table is close to the number of rows. This is reasonable because two adjacent rowids in the index almost never refer to the same block.

```
SQL> set arraysize 2

SQL> SELECT /*+ index(t t_pk) */ * FROM t;
```

```
-------------------------------------------------------------------------
| Id  | Operation                   | Name  | Starts | A-Rows | Buffers |
-------------------------------------------------------------------------
|  1  |  TABLE ACCESS BY INDEX ROWID| T     |   1    |  1000  |  1497   |
|  2  |   INDEX FULL SCAN           | T_PK  |   1    |  1000  |   502   |
-------------------------------------------------------------------------
```

```
SQL> set arraysize 100

SQL> SELECT /*+ index(t t_pk) */ * FROM t;
```

```
-------------------------------------------------------------------------
| Id  | Operation                   | Name  | Starts | A-Rows | Buffers |
-------------------------------------------------------------------------
|  1  |  TABLE ACCESS BY INDEX ROWID| T     |   1    |  1000  |  1003   |
|  2  |   INDEX FULL SCAN           | T_PK  |   1    |  1000  |    13   |
-------------------------------------------------------------------------
```

In summary, row prefetching is less effective with a high clustering factor, and therefore, a higher number of logical reads is performed. The impact of clustering factor on the resource consumption is so high that the query optimizer (as described in Chapter 5, specifically, Formula 5-5) uses the clustering factor to compute the cost related to index accesses.

B-tree Indexes vs. Bitmap Indexes

Simply put, there are some situations where only B-tree indexes can be considered. If you are not in one of those situations, bitmap indexes should be taken into consideration most of the time. Table 9-2 summarizes the features that you need to take into account when deciding between B-tree and bitmap indexes.

Table 9-2. *Essential Features Supported by B-tree and Bitmap Indexes*

Feature	B-tree	Bitmap
Primary and unique key	✓	
Row-level locking	✓	
Efficient space management while processing DML statements	✓	✓*
Efficient combination of several indexes		✓
Star transformation		✓

* Only as of Oracle Database 10g. Problems related to previous releases are documented in MetaLink note "Understanding Bitmap Indexes Growth while Performing DML operations on the Table" (260330.1).

> **Note** Bitmap indexes are available only in Enterprise Edition.

The use of bitmap indexes is mainly limited by two situations. First, only B-tree indexes can be used for primary and unique keys. There is simply no choice here. Second, only B-tree indexes support row-level locking since locks in (B-tree and bitmap) indexes are internally set for an index entry. Because a single bitmap index entry might index thousands of rows, a modification of a bitmap-indexed column may prevent the concurrent modification of thousands of other rows (those referenced by the same index entry), which may greatly inhibit scalability. A third problem that occurs only prior to Oracle Database 10*g* is because bitmap indexes have space management problems. These lead to (too) frequent index rebuilds. Consequently, up to Oracle9*i*, they are used only for columns that are rarely modified.

In addition, if you want to take advantage of either the efficient combination of several indexes or of the star transformation, you need to use bitmap indexes.

Note that Table 9-2 provides no comment regarding the selectivity of the index or the cardinality of the indexed column. This is despite that many books and papers about bitmap indexes contain advice like the following:

These indexes are suitable for low cardinality data. Through compression techniques, they can generate a large number of rowids with minimal I/O. Combining bitmap indexes on non-selective columns allows efficient AND and OR operations with a great number of rowids with minimal I/O.

*—Oracle Database Performance Tuning Guide 11*g *Release 1*

Honestly, in my opinion, such information is at the very least misleading. The fact is, a SQL statement with weak selectivity can never be efficiently executed by getting a list of rowids from an index. This is because the time needed to build the list of rowids is much smaller, both for B-tree and for bitmap indexes, than the time needed to access the table with them in such situations. That said, it is true that bitmap indexes behave better than B-tree indexes with low cardinality data. But be careful, *better* does not necessarily mean *efficient*. For example, a *bad* product is not *good* simply because it is better than a *very bad* product. It may be that combining bitmap indexes is very efficient, but, once again, building a list of rowids is just the beginning. The rows still have to be accessed. In addition, I should also mention OR. If you think about it, you will realize that combining several nonselective conditions with OR can lead only to even weaker selectivity, while the goal is to increase it if you want to use indexes. In conclusion, forget about selectivity and cardinality when you have to choose between a B-tree index and a bitmap index.

In addition to the differences summarized in Table 9-2, B-tree indexes and bitmap indexes do not show the same efficiency when dealing with the same SQL conditions. Actually, bitmap indexes are usually more powerful. Table 9-3 summarizes, for both types of indexes, their ability to cope with different types of conditions. The aim of the following sections is to provide some examples regarding this. I'll also describe different properties and limitations. All examples are based on the script conditions.sql. The test table and its indexes were created with the following SQL statements:

```
CREATE TABLE t (
  id NUMBER,
  d1 DATE,
  n1 NUMBER,
  n2 NUMBER,
  n3 NUMBER,
  n4 NUMBER,
  n5 NUMBER,
  n6 NUMBER,
  c1 VARCHAR2(20),
  c2 VARCHAR2(20),
  pad VARCHAR2(4000),
  CONSTRAINT t_pk PRIMARY KEY (id)
);

INSERT INTO t
SELECT rownum AS id,
       trunc(to_date('2007-01-01','yyyy-mm-dd')+rownum/27.4) AS d1,
       nullif(1+mod(rownum,19),10) AS n1,
       nullif(1+mod(rownum,113),10) AS n2,
       nullif(1+mod(rownum,61),10) AS n3,
       nullif(1+mod(rownum,19),10) AS n4,
       nullif(1+mod(rownum,113),10) AS n5,
       nullif(1+mod(rownum,61),10) AS n6,
       dbms_random.string('p',20) AS c1,
       dbms_random.string('p',20) AS c2,
       dbms_random.string('p',255) AS pad
FROM dual
CONNECT BY level <= 10000
ORDER BY dbms_random.value;

CREATE INDEX i_n1 ON t (n1);
CREATE INDEX i_n2 ON t (n2);
CREATE INDEX i_n3 ON t (n3);
CREATE INDEX i_n123 ON t (n1, n2, n3);
CREATE BITMAP INDEX i_n4 ON t (n4);
CREATE BITMAP INDEX i_n5 ON t (n5);
CREATE BITMAP INDEX i_n6 ON t (n6);
CREATE INDEX i_c1 ON t (c1);
CREATE BITMAP INDEX i_c2 ON t (c2);
```

Table 9-3. *Conditions That Lead to an Index Range Scan*

Condition	B-tree	Bitmap
Equality (=)	✓	✓
IS NULL	✓*	✓
Inequality (!=, <>) and IS NOT NULL		✓†
Range (BETWEEN, >, >=, < and <=)	✓	✓
IN	✓	✓
LIKE	✓	✓

Applicable to composite indexes only when at least one condition is not based on IS NULL or an inequality

† *Applicable only when several bitmaps are combined*

Equality Conditions and B-tree Indexes

With B-tree indexes, equality conditions are carried out with one of two operations. The first, INDEX UNIQUE SCAN, is used exclusively with unique indexes. As the name suggests, at most one rowid is returned with it. The following query is an example. The execution plan confirms, through the access predicate of operation 2, that the condition on the column id is applied with the index t_pk. Then, operation 1 uses the rowid extracted from the index to access the table t. This is carried out with the operation TABLE ACCESS BY INDEX ROWID. Notice that both operations are executed only once.

```
SELECT /*+ index(t) */ * FROM t WHERE id = 6
```

```
-----------------------------------------------------------------
| Id  | Operation                   | Name  | Starts | A-Rows |
-----------------------------------------------------------------
|   1 |  TABLE ACCESS BY INDEX ROWID| T     |    1 |      1 |
|*  2 |   INDEX UNIQUE SCAN         | T_PK  |    1 |      1 |
-----------------------------------------------------------------

   2 - access("ID"=6)
```

■**Note** In this section, to force index scans, the hint index is used by specifying the name of the table only. When it is used in this way, the query optimizer is free to choose one of the indexes from those available. In all the examples, a single predicate is present in the WHERE clause. For this reason, the query optimizer always chooses the index based on the column referenced in that predicate. The best practice, however, is to explicitly specify which index should be used. I give some examples in the next section.

The second operation, INDEX RANGE SCAN, is used with nonunique indexes. The only difference between this operation and the previous one is that it can extract many rowids (527 in the example), not just one.

```
SELECT /*+ index(t) */ * FROM t WHERE n1 = 6
```

```
---------------------------------------------------------------
| Id | Operation                   | Name | Starts | A-Rows |
---------------------------------------------------------------
|  1 | TABLE ACCESS BY INDEX ROWID| T    |    1 |   527 |
|* 2 |   INDEX RANGE SCAN          | I_N1 |    1 |   527 |
---------------------------------------------------------------
```

```
   2 - access("N1"=6)
```

Per default, an index scan is performed in ascending order. Therefore, the hint index instructs the query optimizer to behave in that way also. To explicitly specify the scan order, it is possible to use the hints index_asc and index_desc. The following query shows how. In the execution plan, the scan in descending order is shown through the operation INDEX RANGE SCAN DESCENDING. Note that both operations return the same data. Only the order is different.

```
SELECT /*+ index_desc(t) */ * FROM t WHERE n1 = 6
```

```
---------------------------------------------------------------
| Id | Operation                     | Name | Starts | A-Rows |
---------------------------------------------------------------
|  1 | TABLE ACCESS BY INDEX ROWID   | T    |    1 |   527 |
|* 2 |   INDEX RANGE SCAN DESCENDING | I_N1 |    1 |   527 |
---------------------------------------------------------------
```

```
   2 - access("N1"=6)
       filter("N1"=6)
```

Descending scans for equality conditions are pointless, however, from a practical point of view. The section on range conditions describes when such an access path is in fact useful.

Equality Conditions and Bitmap Indexes

With bitmap indexes, equality conditions are carried out in three operations. In order of execution, the first operation is BITMAP INDEX SINGLE VALUE, which scans the index and applies the restriction. As the name suggests, this operation looks for a single value. The second operation, BITMAP CONVERSION TO ROWIDS, converts the bitmaps it gets from the first operation, into a list of rowids. The third operation accesses the table with the list of rowids built by the second operation. Note that all three operations are executed only once.

```
SELECT /*+ index(t i_n4) */ * FROM t WHERE n4 = 6
```

```
---------------------------------------------------------------
| Id | Operation                   | Name   | Starts | A-Rows |
---------------------------------------------------------------
|  1 |  TABLE ACCESS BY INDEX ROWID | T     |      1 |    527 |
|  2 |   BITMAP CONVERSION TO ROWIDS|       |      1 |    527 |
|* 3 |    BITMAP INDEX SINGLE VALUE | I_N4  |      1 |      1 |
---------------------------------------------------------------
```

```
   3 - access("N4"=6)
```

▓**Caution** In this section, in order to force index scans, the hint `index` is used by specifying both the name
of the table and the name of the index. In other words, the hint specifies which index should be used. When
it is used in this way, the hint is valid only if an index with that name exists. Since the name of an index can
be easily changed (for example, with the SQL statement `ALTER INDEX RENAME`), in practice it is also very
easy for hints with that syntax to be invalidated by mistake.

IS NULL Conditions and B-tree Indexes

With B-tree indexes, IS NULL conditions can be applied only through composite B-tree indexes
when several SQL conditions are applied and at least one of them is not based on IS NULL or an
inequality. The following query demonstrates this. The execution plan confirms, through the
access predicate of operation 2, that the condition on column n2 is applied using the index
i_n123. Also notice that operation 2 returns only 5 rows, while for the example in the previous
section, which doesn't have the restriction n2 IS NULL, the range scan returned 527 rows.

```
SELECT /*+ index(t) */ * FROM t WHERE n1 = 6 AND n2 IS NULL
```

```
-----------------------------------------------------------
| Id | Operation                   | Name    | Starts | A-Rows |
-----------------------------------------------------------
|  1 |  TABLE ACCESS BY INDEX ROWID| T       |      1 |      5 |
|* 2 |   INDEX RANGE SCAN          | I_N123  |      1 |      5 |
-----------------------------------------------------------
```

```
   2 - access("N1"=6 AND "N2" IS NULL)
```

As the following example shows, the very same execution plan is also used when the
condition IS NULL is specified for the leading column of the index.

```
SELECT /*+ index(t) */ * FROM t WHERE n1 IS NULL AND n2 = 8
```

```
-----------------------------------------------------------------
| Id  | Operation                  | Name   | Starts | A-Rows |
-----------------------------------------------------------------
|   1 |  TABLE ACCESS BY INDEX ROWID| T      |     1 |     4 |
|*  2 |   INDEX RANGE SCAN          | I_N123 |     1 |     4 |
-----------------------------------------------------------------
```

```
   2 - access("N1" IS NULL AND "N2"=8)
       filter("N2"=8)
```

Single-column indexes, however, cannot be used to apply IS NULL conditions. This is because the NULL values are not stored in the index. Therefore, the query optimizer is simply not able to take advantage of an index in such a case. Even if you try to force its utilization with the hint index, a full table scan is performed.

```
SELECT /*+ index(t i_n1) */ * FROM t WHERE n1 IS NULL
```

```
---------------------------------------------------
| Id  | Operation         | Name | Starts | A-Rows |
---------------------------------------------------
|*  1 |  TABLE ACCESS FULL| T    |     1 |    526 |
---------------------------------------------------
```

```
   1 - filter("N1" IS NULL)
```

IS NULL Conditions and Bitmap Indexes

With bitmap indexes, IS NULL conditions are carried out in the same way as equality conditions. This is possible because the bitmap index stores NULL values in the same way as any other value.

```
SELECT /*+ index(t i_n4) */ * FROM t WHERE n4 IS NULL
```

```
-----------------------------------------------------------------
| Id  | Operation                  | Name  | Starts | A-Rows |
-----------------------------------------------------------------
|   1 |  TABLE ACCESS BY INDEX ROWID | T     |     1 |    526 |
|   2 |   BITMAP CONVERSION TO ROWIDS|       |     1 |    526 |
|*  3 |    BITMAP INDEX SINGLE VALUE | I_N4  |     1 |      1 |
-----------------------------------------------------------------
```

```
   3 - access("N4" IS NULL)
```

Range Conditions and B-tree Indexes

With B-tree indexes, range conditions are carried out in the same way as equality conditions on nonunique indexes, or, in other words, with the operation INDEX RANGE SCAN. For range conditions, the index type (that is, its uniqueness) is not relevant. Since it is a range scan, several rowids could always be returned. For example, the following query shows a range condition that is applied to the column that the primary key consists of:

```
SELECT /*+ index(t (t.id)) */ * FROM t WHERE id BETWEEN 6 AND 19
```

```
--------------------------------------------------------------
| Id  | Operation                   | Name  | Starts | A-Rows |
--------------------------------------------------------------
|   1 |  TABLE ACCESS BY INDEX ROWID| T     |     1  |    14  |
|*  2 |   INDEX RANGE SCAN          | T_PK  |     1  |    14  |
--------------------------------------------------------------

   2 - access("ID">=6 AND "ID"<=19)
```

Note In this section, several hints are used to force index scans by specifying the name of the table and on which columns the index has to be created. The advantage of this compared to the method where the index name is specified is that the hint does not depend on the index name. This gives greater robustness to the hint. Note that this syntax is available as of Oracle Database 10*g*.

As mentioned in the previous section, the index scan is performed in ascending order per default. This means that when an ORDER BY is applied to the same column as the range condition, the result set is already sorted. As a result, no explicit sort is carried out. However, when the ORDER BY is required in descending order, an explicit sort needs to be executed, as the following query illustrates. The sort is carried out by operation 1, SORT ORDER BY. Notice how the index scan in ascending order is forced by the hint index_asc.

```
SELECT /*+ index_asc(t (t.id)) */ *
FROM t
WHERE id BETWEEN 6 AND 19
ORDER BY id DESC
```

```
--------------------------------------------------------------
| Id  | Operation                   | Name  | Starts | A-Rows |
--------------------------------------------------------------
|   1 |  SORT ORDER BY              |       |     1  |    14  |
|   2 |   TABLE ACCESS BY INDEX ROWID| T    |     1  |    14  |
|*  3 |    INDEX RANGE SCAN         | T_PK  |     1  |    14  |
--------------------------------------------------------------

   3 - access("ID">=6 AND "ID"<=19)
```

The same query can naturally take advantage of a descending index scan to avoid the explicit sort. Here is an example, where the operation SORT ORDER BY is no longer present in the execution plan:

```
SELECT /*+ index_desc(t (t.id)) */ *
FROM t
WHERE id BETWEEN 6 AND 19
ORDER BY id DESC
```

```
-----------------------------------------------------------------
| Id  | Operation                     | Name | Starts | A-Rows |
-----------------------------------------------------------------
|   1 |  TABLE ACCESS BY INDEX ROWID  | T    |      1 |     14 |
|*  2 |   INDEX RANGE SCAN DESCENDING | T_PK |      1 |     14 |
-----------------------------------------------------------------
```

```
   2 - access("ID">=6 AND "ID"<=19)
```

Range Conditions and Bitmap Indexes

With bitmap indexes, range conditions are carried out in the same way as equality conditions. The only difference is that the operation BITMAP INDEX RANGE SCAN is used instead of the operation BITMAP INDEX SINGLE VALUE.

```
SELECT /*+ index(t (t.n4)) */ * FROM t WHERE n4 BETWEEN 6 AND 19
```

```
-----------------------------------------------------------------
| Id  | Operation                    | Name | Starts | A-Rows |
-----------------------------------------------------------------
|   1 |  TABLE ACCESS BY INDEX ROWID | T    |      1 |   6840 |
|   2 |   BITMAP CONVERSION TO ROWIDS|      |      1 |   6840 |
|*  3 |    BITMAP INDEX RANGE SCAN    | I_N4 |      1 |     13 |
-----------------------------------------------------------------
```

```
   3 - access("N4">=6 AND "N4"<=19)
```

With bitmap indexes, since there is no concept of ascending and descending scans, it is not possible to avoid, and thereby optimize, ORDER BY operations.

IN Conditions

IN conditions do not have a specific access path. Instead, in the execution plan, the operation INLIST ITERATOR points out that part of the execution plan is executed several times because of an IN condition. The following three queries show how the operation used for the index scan itself depends on the index type. The first is a unique index, the second is a nonunique index, and the third is a bitmap index. Basically, an IN condition is just a series of equality conditions. Note that operations related to the index and table access are executed once for each value in the IN list (see column Starts).

```
SELECT /*+ index(t t_pk) */ * FROM t WHERE id IN (6, 8, 19, 28)
```

```
-----------------------------------------------------------
| Id  | Operation                    | Name  | Starts | A-Rows |
-----------------------------------------------------------
|  1  | INLIST ITERATOR              |       |    1 |      4 |
|  2  |   TABLE ACCESS BY INDEX ROWID| T     |    4 |      4 |
|* 3  |     INDEX UNIQUE SCAN        | T_PK  |    4 |      4 |
-----------------------------------------------------------
```

   3 - access("ID"=6 OR "ID"=8 OR "ID"=19 OR "ID"=28)

```
SELECT /*+ index(t i_n1)) */ * FROM t WHERE n1 IN (6, 8, 19, 28)
```

```
-----------------------------------------------------------
| Id  | Operation                    | Name  | Starts | A-Rows |
-----------------------------------------------------------
|  1  | INLIST ITERATOR              |       |    1 |   1579 |
|  2  |   TABLE ACCESS BY INDEX ROWID| T     |    4 |   1579 |
|* 3  |     INDEX RANGE SCAN         | I_N1  |    4 |   1579 |
-----------------------------------------------------------
```

   3 - access("N1"=6 OR "N1"=8 OR "N1"=19 OR "N1"=28)

```
SELECT /*+ index(t i_n4) */ * FROM t WHERE n4 IN (6, 8, 19, 28)
```

```
-----------------------------------------------------------
| Id  | Operation                    | Name  | Starts | A-Rows |
-----------------------------------------------------------
|  1  | INLIST ITERATOR              |       |    1 |   1579 |
|  2  |   TABLE ACCESS BY INDEX ROWID | T     |    4 |   1579 |
|  3  |     BITMAP CONVERSION TO ROWIDS|     |    4 |   1579 |
|* 4  |       BITMAP INDEX SINGLE VALUE | I_N4 |   4 |      3 |
-----------------------------------------------------------
```

   4 - access(("N4"=6 OR "N4"=8 OR "N4"=19 OR "N4"=28))

LIKE Conditions

Provided that patterns do not begin with a wildcard (the underscore and the percent characters), LIKE conditions are carried out in the same way as range conditions. Otherwise, a full table scan or a full index scan cannot be avoided. The following examples show this behavior. The first two queries retrieve all rows that begin with the letter *A*, for columns c1 and c2, respectively. Hence, a range scan is possible. The third and forth queries retrieve all rows that contain the letter *A* in any position for columns c1 and c2, respectively. Hence, a full index scan is performed.

```
SELECT /* index(t i_c1) */ * FROM t WHERE c1 LIKE 'A%'


-------------------------------------------------------
| Id  | Operation                  | Name  | A-Rows |
-------------------------------------------------------
|   1 |  TABLE ACCESS BY INDEX ROWID| T    |    119 |
|*  2 |   INDEX RANGE SCAN          | I_C1 |    119 |
-------------------------------------------------------

   2 - access("C1" LIKE 'A%')
       filter("C1" LIKE 'A%')

SELECT /* index(t i_c2) */ * FROM t WHERE c2 LIKE 'A%'


----------------------------------------------------------------
| Id  | Operation                  | Name  | Starts | A-Rows |
----------------------------------------------------------------
|   1 |  TABLE ACCESS BY INDEX ROWID | T    |     1 |    108 |
|   2 |   BITMAP CONVERSION TO ROWIDS|      |     1 |    108 |
|*  3 |    BITMAP INDEX RANGE SCAN   | I_C2 |     1 |    108 |
----------------------------------------------------------------

   3 - access("C2" LIKE 'A%')
       filter(("C2" LIKE 'A%' AND "C2" LIKE 'A%'))

SELECT /* index(t i_c1) */ * FROM t WHERE c1 LIKE '%A%'


----------------------------------------------------------------
| Id  | Operation                  | Name  | Starts | A-Rows |
----------------------------------------------------------------
|   1 |  TABLE ACCESS BY INDEX ROWID| T    |     1 |   1921 |
|*  2 |   INDEX FULL SCAN           | I_C1 |     1 |   1921 |
----------------------------------------------------------------

   2 - filter("C1" LIKE '%A%')

SELECT /* index(t i_c2) */ * FROM t WHERE c2 LIKE '%A%'


----------------------------------------------------------------
| Id  | Operation                  | Name  | Starts | A-Rows |
----------------------------------------------------------------
|   1 |  TABLE ACCESS BY INDEX ROWID | T    |     1 |   1846 |
|   2 |   BITMAP CONVERSION TO ROWIDS|      |     1 |   1846 |
|*  3 |    BITMAP INDEX FULL SCAN    | I_C2 |     1 |   1846 |
----------------------------------------------------------------

   3 - filter("C2" LIKE '%A%')
```

Min/Max Functions and B-tree Indexes

To execute queries containing the functions min and max efficiently, two specific operations are available with B-tree indexes. The first, INDEX FULL SCAN (MIN/MAX), is used when a query does not specify a range condition. In spite of its name, however, it performs no full index scan. It simply gets either the rightmost or the leftmost index key.

```
SELECT /*+ index(t t_pk) */ min(id) FROM t
```

```
----------------------------------------------------------------
| Id  | Operation                  | Name  | Starts  | A-Rows |
----------------------------------------------------------------
|   1 |   SORT AGGREGATE           |       |     1 |       1 |
|   2 |     INDEX FULL SCAN (MIN/MAX)| T_PK |     1 |       1 |
----------------------------------------------------------------
```

The second, INDEX RANGE SCAN (MIN/MAX), is used when the query specifies a condition on the same column used in the function:

```
SELECT /*+ index(t t_pk) */ min(id) FROM t WHERE id > 42
```

```
----------------------------------------------------------------
| Id  | Operation                  | Name  | Starts  | A-Rows |
----------------------------------------------------------------
|   1 |   SORT AGGREGATE           |       |     1 |       1 |
|   2 |     FIRST ROW              |       |     1 |       1 |
|*  3 |       INDEX RANGE SCAN (MIN/MAX)| T_PK |  1 |    1 |
----------------------------------------------------------------
```

```
   3 - access("ID">42)
```

Unfortunately, this optimization technique cannot be applied when both functions (min and max) are used in the same query. In this type of situation, an index full scan is performed. The following query is an example:

```
SELECT /*+ index(t t_pk) */ min(id), max(id) FROM t
```

```
-----------------------------------------------------
| Id  | Operation       | Name  | Starts  | A-Rows |
-----------------------------------------------------
|   1 | SORT AGGREGATE  |       |     1 |       1 |
|   2 |   INDEX FULL SCAN| T_PK |     1 |   10000 |
-----------------------------------------------------
```

Min/Max Functions and Bitmap Indexes

For bitmap indexes, no specific operation is available to execute the functions min and max. The same operations used for equality conditions and range conditions are used.

Function-based Indexes

To take advantage of indexes, one of the fundamental rules to follow is to never modify the values returned by an indexed column in the WHERE clause. Otherwise, the query optimizer will be unable to use an index created on the referenced columns. For example, if an index exists on column c1, a restriction like upper(c1)='SELDON' cannot be applied efficiently through the index built on column c1. This should be pretty obvious, since you can search only for a value that is stored in an index, rather than something else. The following example, as the others in this section, is based on the script fbi.sql:

```
SQL> CREATE INDEX i_c1 ON t (c1);

SQL> SELECT * FROM t WHERE upper(c1) = 'SELDON';


-----------------------------------
| Id  | Operation          | Name |
-----------------------------------
|*  1 |   TABLE ACCESS FULL| T    |
-----------------------------------

    1 - filter(UPPER("C1")='SELDON')
```

In other words, every time an indexed column is passed as an argument to a function, or involved in an expression, it is impossible to use the index built on that column for an index range scan. The only exception is when constraints ensure that an index contains the necessary information. In this specific case, two constraints on column c1 provide that information to the query optimizer:

```
SQL> ALTER TABLE t ADD CONSTRAINT t_c1_upper CHECK (c1 = upper(c1));

SQL> ALTER TABLE t MODIFY (c1 NOT NULL);

SQL> SELECT * FROM t WHERE upper(c1) = 'SELDON';


---------------------------------------------
| Id  | Operation                  | Name |
---------------------------------------------
|   0 | SELECT STATEMENT           |      |
|   1 |   TABLE ACCESS BY INDEX ROWID| T  |
|*  2 |    INDEX RANGE SCAN         | I_C1 |
---------------------------------------------

    2 - access("C1"='SELDON')
        filter(UPPER("C1")='SELDON')
```

Obviously, you want to take advantage of an index if a restriction leads to strong selectivity. For that purpose, if it is not possible to modify the WHERE clause or specify constraints, you can create a *function-based index*. Simply put, this is an index created on the return value of a function or the result of an expression.

```
SQL> CREATE INDEX i_c1_upper ON t (upper(c1));

SQL> SELECT * FROM t WHERE upper(c1) = 'SELDON';


----------------------------------------------------
| Id  | Operation                    | Name         |
----------------------------------------------------
|   1 |  TABLE ACCESS BY INDEX ROWID | T            |
|*  2 |   INDEX RANGE SCAN           | I_C1_UPPER   |
----------------------------------------------------

   2 - access(UPPER("C1")='SELDON')
```

■ **Note** Up to Oracle9i Release 2 patchset 9.2.0.3, in order to create a function-based index, a user requires the system privilege `query rewrite`. In addition, the query optimizer takes such an index into consideration only when the initialization parameter `query_rewrite_enabled` is set to `TRUE` and the initialization parameter `query_rewrite_integrity` is set to either `trusted` or `stale_tolerated`. As described in MetaLink note "Bug 2799028" (2799028.8), these requirements are no longer necessary as of patchset 9.2.0.4.

As of Oracle Database 11g, to avoid repeating a function or expression in the index as well as in several or possibly many SQL statements, it is possible to create a virtual column based on the function or expression. In this way, the index can be created directly on the virtual column, and the code can be made transparent to the definition. The following example shows how to add, index, and use a virtual column that applies the function upper to the column c1:

```
SQL> ALTER TABLE t ADD (c1_upper AS (upper(c1)));

SQL> CREATE INDEX i_c1_upper ON t (c1_upper);

SQL> SELECT * FROM t WHERE c1_upper = 'SELDON';


----------------------------------------------------
| Id  | Operation                    | Name         |
----------------------------------------------------
|   1 |  TABLE ACCESS BY INDEX ROWID | T            |
|*  2 |   INDEX RANGE SCAN           | I_C1_UPPER   |
----------------------------------------------------

   2 - access("C1_UPPER"='SELDON')
```

An additional advantage of using virtual columns, as you have seen in Chapter 4, is that object statistics are gathered for them by the package `dbms_stats`. With them, the query optimizer is able to correctly estimate the cardinalities of restrictions based on virtual columns.

Even though the examples in this chapter are based on B-tree indexes, function-based bitmap indexes are supported as well.

Linguistic Indexes

Per default, the database engine performs *binary comparisons* for the purpose of comparing character strings. With them, characters are compared according to their binary value. Consequently, two character strings are considered equal only when the numeric code of each corresponding character is identical.

As of Oracle Database 10*g* Release 2, the database engine is also able to perform *linguistic comparisons*. With these comparisons, the numeric code of each character does not have to be identical in order to match. For example, it is possible to instruct the database engine to consider equal lowercase and uppercase characters, or characters with and without accents.

> ▓**Note** Linguistic comparisons are partially available in previous versions as well. However, not all operators and functions respect them. Therefore, to avoid inconsistent or misleading results, I recommend using them only with Oracle Database 10*g* Release 2 or later. This section will not deal with the features available up to Oracle Database 10*g* Release 1.

To manage this behavior of the SQL operators, the initialization parameter nls_comp is available. It can be set to one of the following values:

binary: Binary comparisons are used. This is the default.

linguistic: Linguistic comparisons are used. The initialization parameter nls_sort specifies the linguistic sort sequence (and therefore the rules) that applies to the comparisons. The accepted values are binary (which is not useful for linguistic comparisons) and most of the values accepted by the initialization parameter nls_language.

ansi: This value is available for backward compatibility only. linguistic should be used instead.

The dynamic initialization parameters nls_comp and nls_sort can be set at the instance and session levels. At the session level, they can be set with the SQL statement ALTER SESSION, as well as be defined on the client side at the operating system level (for example, in Microsoft Windows with an entry in the registry).

As an example, let's consider a table storing the following data (the table and the test queries are available in the script linguistic_index.sql):

```
SQL> SELECT c1 FROM t;

C1
--------------------
Leon
Léon
LEON
LÉON
```

Per default, binary comparisons are performed. To use linguistic comparisons, it is necessary to set the initialization parameter nls_comp to linguistic, and the linguistic sort sequence (and therefore the rules) used for the comparisons must be specified through the initialization parameter nls_sort. The following example uses generic_m, an ISO standard for Latin-based characters:

```
SQL> ALTER SESSION SET nls_comp = linguistic;

SQL> ALTER SESSION SET nls_sort = generic_m;

SQL> SELECT c1 FROM t WHERE c = 'LEON';

C1
--------------------
LEON
```

As expected, nothing particular happens with the previous setting. The useful feature is provided by two extensions of generic_m. The first is generic_m_ci. With it, as shown in the following query, the comparisons are case insensitive:

```
SQL> ALTER SESSION SET nls_sort = generic_m_ci;

SQL> SELECT c1 FROM t WHERE c = 'LEON';

C1
--------------------
Leon
LEON
```

The second is generic_m_ai. With it, as shown in the following query, the comparisons are case and accent insensitive:

```
SQL> ALTER SESSION SET nls_sort = generic_m_ai;

SQL> SELECT c1 FROM t WHERE c = 'LEON';

C1
--------------------
Leon
Léon
LEON
LÉON
```

From a functional point of view, this is excellent. By setting two initialization parameters, you are able to control the behavior of the SQL operators. Let's see what happens, though, in the following example, when the initialization parameter nls_comp is set to linguistic:

```
SQL> CREATE INDEX i_c1 ON t (c1);

SQL> ALTER SESSION SET nls_sort = generic_m_ai;

SQL> ALTER SESSION SET nls_comp = binary;
```

```
SQL> SELECT /*+ index(t) */ * FROM t WHERE c1 = 'LEON';

---------------------------------------------
| Id  | Operation                  | Name  |
---------------------------------------------
|   1 |  TABLE ACCESS BY INDEX ROWID| T     |
|*  2 |    INDEX RANGE SCAN          | I_C1  |
---------------------------------------------

   2 - access("C1"='LEON')

SQL> ALTER SESSION SET nls_comp = linguistic;

SQL> SELECT /*+ index(t) */ * FROM t WHERE c1 = 'LEON';

-----------------------------------
| Id  | Operation       | Name  |
-----------------------------------
|*  1 |  TABLE ACCESS FULL| T     |
-----------------------------------

   1 - filter(NLSSORT("C1",'nls_sort=''GENERIC_M_AI''')=HEXTORAW('022601FE02380232'))
```

Obviously, when the initialization parameter nls_comp is set to linguistic, the index is no longer used. The reason is indicated by the last line of the output. No lookup in the index is possible because a function, nlssort, is silently applied to the indexed column c1. Hence, for that purpose, a function-based index is necessary to avoid a full table scan. It is essential to recognize that the definition of the index must contain the same value as the initialization parameter nls_sort. Therefore, if several languages are in use, several indexes ought to be created.

```
SQL> CREATE INDEX i_c1_linguistic ON t (nlssort(c1,'nls_sort=generic_m_ai'));

SQL> ALTER SESSION SET nls_sort = generic_m_ai;

SQL> ALTER SESSION SET nls_comp = linguistic;

SQL> SELECT /*+ index(t) */ * FROM t WHERE c1 = 'LEON';

------------------------------------------------------------
| Id  | Operation                  | Name            |
------------------------------------------------------------
|   1 |  TABLE ACCESS BY INDEX ROWID| T               |
|*  2 |    INDEX RANGE SCAN          | I_C1_LINGUISTIC |
------------------------------------------------------------

   2 - access(NLSSORT("C1",'nls_sort=''GENERIC_M_AI''')=HEXTORAW('022601FE02380232'))
```

Up to Oracle Database 10*g* Release 2, another limitation is that in order to apply a LIKE operator, the database engine is not able to take advantage of linguistic indexes. In other words, a full index scan or full table scan cannot be avoided. This limitation is no longer available as of Oracle Database 11*g*.

Even though the examples in this section are based on B-tree indexes, linguistic bitmap indexes are supported as well.

In summary, linguistic comparison is a powerful feature that is transparent for SQL statements. However, the database engine is able to apply them efficiently only when a set of adapted indexes is available. Since the setting at the client level might impact the utilization of the indexes, it is essential to plan its use carefully.

Composite Indexes

So far, with one exception, I've discussed only indexes that have an index key consisting of a single column. Indexes, however, can have many columns (the limit is 32 for B-tree indexes and 30 for bitmap indexes). Indexes with multiple columns are called *composite indexes* (sometimes the terms *concatenated indexes* or *multicolumn indexes* are used also). In this regard, B-tree indexes and bitmap indexes have completely different behaviors. Thus, they will be discussed separately.

B-tree Indexes

The purpose of composite indexes is twofold. First, they can be used to apply a primary key or unique key constraint composed of several columns. Second, they can be used to apply a restriction composed of several SQL conditions combined with AND. Be careful because when several SQL conditions are combined with OR, composite indexes cannot be used efficiently!

Naturally, it is important to discuss how to use composite indexes for applying restrictions. The following query is used for this:

```
SELECT * FROM t WHERE n1 = 6 AND n2 = 42 AND n3 = 11
```

Let's begin by looking at what happens when a single column index is used.

With an index built on column n1, 527 rowids are returned from the index scan. Since the index stores only the data related to column n1, only the predicate n1=6 can be applied efficiently through the index by operation 2. The other two predicates are applied as a filter by operation 1. Because of the many rowids returned by operation 2, the execution generates 327 logical reads in total. This is unacceptable when retrieving a single row.

```
---------------------------------------------------------------------
| Id  | Operation                  | Name  | Starts | A-Rows | Buffers |
---------------------------------------------------------------------
|*  1 |  TABLE ACCESS BY INDEX ROWID| T    |     1 |      1 |    327 |
|*  2 |   INDEX RANGE SCAN          | I_N1  |     1 |    527 |      4 |
---------------------------------------------------------------------

   1 - filter(("N3"=11 AND "N2"=42))
   2 - access("N1"=6)
```

With an index built on column n2, the situation is basically the same as in the previous example. The only improvement is that fewer rowids (89) are returned by the index scan. Therefore, much fewer logical reads (85) are performed in total.

```
--------------------------------------------------------------------------
| Id  | Operation                    | Name  | Starts | A-Rows | Buffers |
--------------------------------------------------------------------------
|*  1 |  TABLE ACCESS BY INDEX ROWID | T     |    1 |     1 |     85 |
|*  2 |   INDEX RANGE SCAN           | I_N2  |    1 |    89 |      4 |
--------------------------------------------------------------------------

   1 - filter(("N3"=11 AND "N1"=6))
   2 - access("N2"=42)
```

With an index built on column n3, the situation is still similar to the previous ones. In fact, the index scan returns plenty of rowids (164). The total number of logical reads (141) is still too high.

```
--------------------------------------------------------------------------
| Id  | Operation                    | Name  | Starts | A-Rows | Buffers |
--------------------------------------------------------------------------
|*  1 |  TABLE ACCESS BY INDEX ROWID | T     |    1 |     1 |    141 |
|*  2 |   INDEX RANGE SCAN           | I_N3  |    1 |   164 |      4 |
--------------------------------------------------------------------------

   1 - filter(("N2"=42 AND "N1"=6))
   2 - access("N3"=11)
```

In summary, none of the three indexes is able to apply the predicates efficiently. The selectivities of the three restrictions taken one by one are too high. This observation is in line with the object statistics stored in the data dictionary. In fact, the number of distinct values for each column is low, as demonstrated by the following query:

```
SQL> SELECT column_name, num_distinct
  2  FROM user_tab_columns
  3  WHERE table_name = 'T' AND column_name IN ('ID', 'N1', 'N2', 'N3');

COLUMN_NAME   NUM_DISTINCT
------------  ------------
ID                   10000
N1                      18
N2                     112
N3                      60
```

In such situations, it is more efficient to apply the various conditions with a single index built on several columns. For example, the following execution plan shows what happens if a composite index is created on the three columns. It is essential to understand that with this index, the number of logical reads is lower because the index scan returns only rows that fulfill the whole WHERE clause.

```
-------------------------------------------------------------------
| Id  | Operation                   | Name    | Starts | A-Rows | Buffers |
-------------------------------------------------------------------
|   1 |  TABLE ACCESS BY INDEX ROWID| T       |    1 |    1 |      4 |
|*  2 |   INDEX RANGE SCAN          | I_N123  |    1 |    1 |      3 |
-------------------------------------------------------------------
```

```
   2 - access("N1"=6 AND "N2"=42 AND "N3"=11)
```

At this point, it is crucial to recognize that the database engine is able to use an index even when not all columns on which the index is built are referenced in the WHERE clause. The basic requirement is that a condition should be applied to the leading column of the index key. For example, with the index i_n123 used in the previous example, the conditions on the columns n2 or n3 are optional. The following query shows an example where no condition on column n2 is present:

```
SELECT * FROM t WHERE n1 = 6 AND n3 = 11
```

```
-------------------------------------------------------------------
| Id  | Operation                   | Name    | Starts | A-Rows | Buffers |
-------------------------------------------------------------------
|   1 |  TABLE ACCESS BY INDEX ROWID| T       |    1 |    1 |      8 |
|*  2 |   INDEX RANGE SCAN          | I_N123  |    1 |    1 |      7 |
-------------------------------------------------------------------
```

```
   2 - access("N1"=6 AND "N3"=11)
       filter("N3"=11)
```

There are cases where the index can even be used (efficiently) when there is no condition on the leading column of the index key. Such an operation is called an *index skip scan*. However, it makes sense to use it only when the leading column has a very low number of distinct values because an independent index range scan is performed for each value of the leading column. The following query shows such an example. Notice the hint index_ss and the operation INDEX SKIP SCAN.

```
SELECT /*+ index_ss(t i_n123) */ * FROM t WHERE n2 = 42 AND n3 = 11
```

```
-------------------------------------------------------------------
| Id  | Operation                   | Name    | Starts | A-Rows | Buffers |
-------------------------------------------------------------------
|   1 |  TABLE ACCESS BY INDEX ROWID| T       |    1 |    2 |     33 |
|*  2 |   INDEX SKIP SCAN           | I_N123  |    1 |    2 |     31 |
-------------------------------------------------------------------
```

```
   2 - access("N2"=42 AND "N3"=11)
       filter(("N2"=42 AND "N3"=11))
```

Since descending index skip scans are supported for "regular" index scans (using the operation INDEX SKIP SCAN DESCENDING), you can use the two hints index_ss_asc and index_ss_desc to control the order of the scan.

Speaking of composite indexes, I believe it is necessary to mention the most common mistake I come across when dealing with them, as well as the most frequently asked question. The mistake is related to overindexation. The misconception is that the database engine is able to take advantage of an index only when all columns comprising the index key are used in the WHERE clause. As you have just seen in several examples, this is not the case. This misconception usually leads to the creation of several indexes on the same table, with the same leading column—for instance, one index with columns n1, n2, and n3 and another with columns n1 and n3. The second is generally superfluous. Note that superfluous indexes are a problem because not only do they slow down SQL statements that modify the indexed data, but also because they waste space unnecessarily.

The most frequently asked question is, how do I choose the order of the columns? For example, if an index key is composed of columns n1, n2, and n3, what is the best order? When all indexed columns are present in a WHERE clause, the efficiency of the index is independent of the order of the columns in the index. Therefore, the best order is the one that maximizes the chances of using the index as frequently as possible when not all indexed columns are present in WHERE clauses. In other words, it should be possible to use an index for the greatest number of SQL statements. To make sure this is the case, the leading column should be the one that is more frequently (ideally speaking, of course) specified in WHERE clauses. Whenever several columns are used with equal frequency, there are two opposing approaches that can be followed:

- The leading column should be the one with the highest number of distinct values. This would be useful if a restriction is applied only on that particular column in future SQL statements. In other words, you maximize the chances that the index could be selected by the query optimizer.

- The leading column should be the one with the lowest number of distinct values. This could be useful to achieve a better compression ratio for the index.

INDEX COMPRESSION

One important difference between B-tree and bitmap indexes is the compression used to store the keys in the index leaf blocks. While bitmap indexes are always compressed, B-tree indexes are compressed only when requested.

In a noncompressed B-tree index, every key is fully stored. In other words, if several keys have the same value, the value is repeatedly stored for each key. Consequently, in nonunique indexes, it is common to have the same value stored several times in the same leaf block. To eliminate these repeated occurrences, you can compress the index keys. You can do this by (re)building the index with the parameter COMPRESS and, optionally, the number of columns that need to be compressed. For example, the index i_n123 is composed of three columns: n1, n2, and n3. With COMPRESS 1, you specify to compress only column n1; with COMPRESS 2, you specify to compress columns n1 and n2; and with COMPRESS 3, you specify to compress all three columns. When the number of columns to be compressed is not specified, for nonunique indexes all columns are compressed, and for unique indexes the number of columns minus one are compressed.

Since columns are compressed from left to right, columns should be ordered by decreasing selectivity to achieve the best compression. However, you should reorder the columns of an index only when this doesn't prevent the query optimizer from using the index.

B-tree index compression is not activated per default because it doesn't always reduce the size of indexes. Actually, in some situations, the index might become larger with compression! Because of this, you should enable compression only if there is a real advantage to doing so. You have two options for checking the expected compression ratio for a given index. First, you can build the index once without compression and then again with compression, and then you compare the size. Second, you can let the SQL statement ANALYZE INDEX perform an analysis to find out the optimal number of columns to compress and how much space can be saved with the optimal compression. The following example shows such an analysis for the index i_n123. Note that the output of the analysis is written in the table index_stats. In this case, you are informed that by compressing two columns you can save 17 percent of the space currently occupied by the index.

```
SQL> ANALYZE INDEX i_n123 VALIDATE STRUCTURE;

SQL> SELECT opt_cmpr_count, opt_cmpr_pctsave FROM index_stats;

OPT_CMPR_COUNT OPT_CMPR_PCTSAVE
-------------- ----------------
             2               17
```

The following SQL statements show not only how to implement the compression of the index i_n123 but also how to check the result of the compression:

```
SQL> SELECT blocks FROM index_stats;

    BLOCKS
----------
        40

SQL> ALTER INDEX i_n123 REBUILD COMPRESS 2;

SQL> ANALYZE INDEX i_n123 VALIDATE STRUCTURE;

SQL> SELECT blocks FROM index_stats;

    BLOCKS
----------
        32
```

From a performance point of view, the key advantage of compressed indexes is that because of their smaller size, fewer logical reads are needed to perform index range scans and index full scans. The disadvantage, however, is the increasing likelihood of suffering from block contention (this topic is covered in Chapter 12).

Bitmap Indexes

Composite bitmap indexes are rarely created. This is because several indexes can be combined efficiently in order to apply a restriction. To see how powerful bitmap indexes are, let's look at several queries.

The first query takes advantage of three bitmap indexes that are combined with AND in order to apply three equality conditions. Note that the hint index_combine forces this type of plan. First, operation 4 scans the index based on column n5 by looking for the rows that fulfill the restriction on that column. The resulting bitmaps are passed to operation 3. Then, operations 5 and 6 perform the same scan on the indexes created on columns n6 and n4, respectively. Once the three index scans are completed, operation 3 computes the AND of the three sets of bitmaps. Finally, operation 2 converts the resulting bitmap into a list of rowids, and then they are used by operation 1 to access the table.

```
SELECT /*+ index_combine(t i_n4 i_n5 i_n6) */ *
FROM t
WHERE n4 = 6 AND n5 = 42 AND n6 = 11
```

```
-------------------------------------------------------------------------------
| Id | Operation                      | Name | Starts | A-Rows | Buffers |
-------------------------------------------------------------------------------
|  1 | TABLE ACCESS BY INDEX ROWID    | T    |    1   |   1    |    7    |
|  2 |  BITMAP CONVERSION TO ROWIDS   |      |    1   |   1    |    6    |
|  3 |   BITMAP AND                   |      |    1   |   1    |    6    |
|* 4 |    BITMAP INDEX SINGLE VALUE   | I_N5 |    1   |   1    |    2    |
|* 5 |    BITMAP INDEX SINGLE VALUE   | I_N6 |    1   |   1    |    2    |
|* 6 |    BITMAP INDEX SINGLE VALUE   | I_N4 |    1   |   1    |    2    |
-------------------------------------------------------------------------------
```

```
   4 - access("N5"=42)
   5 - access("N6"=11)
   6 - access("N4"=6)
```

The second query is very similar to the first one. The only difference is because of the OR instead of the AND. Notice how only operation 3 has changed in the execution plan.

```
SELECT /*+ index_combine(t i_n4 i_n5 i_n6) */ *
FROM t
WHERE n4 = 6 OR n5 = 42 OR n6 = 11
```

```
-------------------------------------------------------------------------------
| Id | Operation                      | Name | Starts | A-Rows | Buffers |
-------------------------------------------------------------------------------
|  1 | TABLE ACCESS BY INDEX ROWID    | T    |    1   |  767   |   396   |
|  2 |  BITMAP CONVERSION TO ROWIDS   |      |    1   |  767   |    7    |
|  3 |   BITMAP OR                    |      |    1   |   1    |    7    |
|* 4 |    BITMAP INDEX SINGLE VALUE   | I_N4 |    1   |   1    |    3    |
|* 5 |    BITMAP INDEX SINGLE VALUE   | I_N6 |    1   |   1    |    2    |
|* 6 |    BITMAP INDEX SINGLE VALUE   | I_N5 |    1   |   1    |    2    |
-------------------------------------------------------------------------------
```

```
4 - access("N4"=6)
5 - access("N6"=11)
6 - access("N5"=42)
```

The third query is similar to the first one. This time, the only difference is because of the condition n4!=6 instead of n4=6. Since the execution plan is quite different, let's look at it in detail. Initially, operation 6 scans the index based on column n5 by looking for the rows fulfilling the condition n5=42 on that column. The resulting bitmaps are passed to operation 5. Then, operation 7 performs the same scan on the index created on column n6 for the condition n6=11. Once the two index scans are completed, operation 5 computes the AND of the two sets of bitmaps and passes the resulting bitmaps to operation 4. Next, operation 8 scans the index based on column n4 by looking for rows fulfilling the condition n4=6 (which is the opposite of what is specified in the WHERE clause). The resulting bitmaps are passed to operation 4, which subtracts them from the bitmaps delivered by operation 5. Then, operations 9 and 3 perform the same scan for the condition n4 IS NULL. This is necessary because NULL values do not fulfill the condition n4!=6. Finally, operation 2 converts the resulting bitmap into a list of rowids, which are then used by operation 1 to access the table.

```
SELECT /*+ index_combine(t i_n4 i_n5 i_n6) */ *
FROM t
WHERE n4 != 6 AND n5 = 42 AND n6 = 11
```

```
--------------------------------------------------------------------------
| Id | Operation                      | Name | Starts | A-Rows | Buffers |
--------------------------------------------------------------------------
|  1 | TABLE ACCESS BY INDEX ROWID    | T    |   1    |   1    |    9    |
|  2 |  BITMAP CONVERSION TO ROWIDS   |      |   1    |   1    |    8    |
|  3 |   BITMAP MINUS                 |      |   1    |   1    |    8    |
|  4 |    BITMAP MINUS                |      |   1    |   1    |    6    |
|  5 |     BITMAP AND                 |      |   1    |   1    |    4    |
|* 6 |      BITMAP INDEX SINGLE VALUE | I_N5 |   1    |   1    |    2    |
|* 7 |      BITMAP INDEX SINGLE VALUE | I_N6 |   1    |   1    |    2    |
|* 8 |     BITMAP INDEX SINGLE VALUE  | I_N4 |   1    |   1    |    2    |
|* 9 |    BITMAP INDEX SINGLE VALUE   | I_N4 |   1    |   1    |    2    |
--------------------------------------------------------------------------
```

```
6 - access("N5"=42)
7 - access("N6"=11)
8 - access("N4"=6)
9 - access("N4" IS NULL)
```

In summary, bitmap indexes can be combined efficiently, as well as have several SQL conditions applied during combinations. In a few words, they are very flexible. Because of these characteristics, they are essential for reporting systems where the queries are not known (fixed) in advance.

Bitmap Plans for B-tree Indexes

The bitmap plans described in the previous section perform so well that they can also be applied to B-tree indexes. The idea is that the database engine is able to build a kind of in-memory bitmap index based on the data returned by B-tree index scans. The following query, which is the same as the one used in the part about composite B-tree indexes, is an example. Note that the BITMAP CONVERSION FROM ROWIDS operations are responsible for the conversion in the execution plan.

```
SELECT /*+ index_combine(t i_n1 i_n2 i_n3) */ *
FROM t
WHERE n1 = 6 AND n2 = 42 AND n3 = 11
```

```
---------------------------------------------------------------------------
| Id  | Operation                     | Name | Starts | A-Rows | Buffers |
---------------------------------------------------------------------------
|   1 |  TABLE ACCESS BY INDEX ROWID  | T    |    1   |    1   |   10    |
|   2 |   BITMAP CONVERSION TO ROWIDS |      |    1   |    1   |    9    |
|   3 |    BITMAP AND                 |      |    1   |    1   |    9    |
|   4 |     BITMAP CONVERSION FROM ROWIDS|   |    1   |    1   |    3    |
|*  5 |      INDEX RANGE SCAN         | I_N2 |    1   |   89   |    3    |
|   6 |     BITMAP CONVERSION FROM ROWIDS|   |    1   |    1   |    3    |
|*  7 |      INDEX RANGE SCAN         | I_N3 |    1   |  164   |    3    |
|   8 |     BITMAP CONVERSION FROM ROWIDS|   |    1   |    1   |    3    |
|*  9 |      INDEX RANGE SCAN         | I_N1 |    1   |  527   |    3    |
---------------------------------------------------------------------------
```

```
   5 - access("N2"=42)
   7 - access("N3"=11)
   9 - access("N1"=6)
```

■ **Caution** The query optimizer is not always able to correctly estimate the cost of this conversion. The costs related to it might be underestimated. As a result, the conversion might be performed even if it is not appropriate to do so. If this leads to problems, you can disable the feature by setting the undocumented initialization parameter _b_tree_bitmap_plans to FALSE.

Index-only Scans

A useful optimization technique related to indexes is that the database engine can extract lists of rowids from indexes to access tables as well as get column data stored in the indexes. Therefore, when an index contains all data needed to process a query, an *index-only scan* can be executed. This is useful for reducing the number of logical reads. In fact, an index-only scan does not access the table. This could be especially useful if the clustering factor of the index is high. The following query illustrates this. Notice that no table access is performed.

```
SELECT c1 FROM t WHERE c1 LIKE 'A%'
```

```
---------------------------------------------------------------
| Id | Operation       | Name | Starts | A-Rows | Buffers |
---------------------------------------------------------------
|* 1 |  INDEX RANGE SCAN| I_C1 |      1 |    119 |       6 |
---------------------------------------------------------------

   1 - access("C1" LIKE 'A%')
       filter("C1" LIKE 'A%')
```

If the SELECT clause references the column n1 instead of c1, the query optimizer is not able
to take advantage of the index-only scan. Notice, in the following example, how the query
performed 124 logical reads (5 against the index and 119 against the table; in other words, one
for each rowid get from the index) to retrieve 119 rows:

```
SELECT n1 FROM t WHERE c1 LIKE 'A%'
```

```
---------------------------------------------------------------------
| Id | Operation                  | Name | Starts | A-Rows | Buffers |
---------------------------------------------------------------------
|  1 |  TABLE ACCESS BY INDEX ROWID| T    |      1 |    119 |     124 |
|* 2 |   INDEX RANGE SCAN          | I_C1 |      1 |    119 |       5 |
---------------------------------------------------------------------

   2 - access("C1" LIKE 'A%')
       filter("C1" LIKE 'A%')
```

In this type of situation, in order to take advantage of index-only scans, you might add
columns to an index even if they are not used to apply a restriction. The idea is to create a
composite index with an index key that is composed of all columns that are referenced in the
SQL statement, not only those in the WHERE clause. In other words, you "misuse" the index to
store redundant data and, therefore, minimize the number of logical reads. Note, however,
that the leading column of the index must be one of the columns that are referenced in the
WHERE clause. In this specific case, this means that a composite index on the columns c1 and n1
is created. With that index in place, the very same query retrieves the same rows with only four
logical reads instead of 124.

```
-------------------------------------------------------------------
| Id | Operation       | Name    | Starts | A-Rows | Buffers |
-------------------------------------------------------------------
|* 1 |  INDEX RANGE SCAN| I_C1_N1 |      1 |    119 |       4 |
-------------------------------------------------------------------

   1 - access("C1" LIKE 'A%')
       filter("C1" LIKE 'A%')
```

Even though the examples in this section are based on B-tree indexes, index-only scans
are available for bitmap indexes as well.

Index-organized Tables

One particular way to achieve an index-only scan is to create an index-organized table. The central idea of this kind of table is, in fact, to avoid having a table segment at all. Instead, all data is stored in an index segment based on the primary key. It is also possible to store part of the data in an overflow segment. By doing so, however, the benefit of using an index-organized table vanishes (unless the overflow segment is rarely accessed). The same happens when a *secondary index* (that is, another index in addition to the primary key) is created: two segments need to be accessed. Hence, there is no benefit in using it. For these reasons, you should consider using index-organized tables only when two requirements are met. First, the table is normally accessed through the primary key. Second, all data can be stored in the index structure (a row can take at most 50 percent of a block). In all other cases, it makes little sense to use them.

A row in an index-organized table is not referenced by a *physical rowid*. Instead, it is referenced by a *logical rowid*. This kind of rowid is composed of two parts: first, a guess referencing the block that contains the row (key) at the time it is inserted, and second, the value of the primary key. A visit to the index-organized table by logical rowid at first follows the guess, hoping to find the row still in the insert-time block, but since the guess is not updated when block splits occurs, it might become stale when DML statements are executed. If the guess is correct, with a logical rowid, it is possible to access one row with a single logical read (see Figure 9-3). In case the guess is wrong, the number of logical reads would be equal to or greater than two (one for the useless access through the guess, plus the regular access with the primary key). Naturally, to have the best performance, it is capital to have correct guesses. To assess the correctness of such guesses, the column pct_direct_access, which is updated by the package dbms_stats, is available in the view user_indexes. The value provides the percentage of correct guess for a specific index. The following example, which is an excerpt of the script iot_guess.sql, shows not only the impact of stale guesses on the number of logical reads but also how to rectify this type of suboptimal situation (note that the index i is a secondary index):

```
SQL> SELECT pct_direct_access
  2  FROM user_indexes
  3  WHERE index_name = 'I';

PCT_DIRECT_ACCESS
-----------------
               76

SQL> SELECT /*+ index(t i) */ count(pad) FROM t WHERE n > 0;
```

```
-----------------------------------------------
| Id | Operation           | Name | Buffers |
-----------------------------------------------
|  1 |  SORT AGGREGATE      |      |   1496 |
|  2 |    INDEX UNIQUE SCAN | T_PK |   1496 |
|  3 |     INDEX RANGE SCAN | I    |      6 |
-----------------------------------------------
```

```
SQL> ALTER INDEX i UPDATE BLOCK REFERENCES;
```

```
SQL> execute dbms_stats.gather_index_stats(ownname=>user, indname=>'i')

SQL> SELECT pct_direct_access
  2  FROM user_indexes
  3  WHERE index_name = 'I';

PCT_DIRECT_ACCESS
-----------------
              100

SQL> SELECT /*+ index(t i) */ count(pad) FROM t WHERE n > 0;

---------------------------------------------
| Id | Operation          | Name  | Buffers |
---------------------------------------------
|  1 |  SORT AGGREGATE     |       |   1006  |
|  2 |    INDEX UNIQUE SCAN| T_PK  |   1006  |
|  3 |     INDEX RANGE SCAN| I     |      6  |
---------------------------------------------
```

In addition to avoiding accessing a table segment, index-organized tables provide two more advantages that should not be underestimated. The first is that data is always clustered, and therefore, range scans based on the primary key can always be performed efficiently, and not only when the clustering factor is low like with heap-organized tables. The second advantage is that range scans based on the primary key always return the data in the order in which the data is stored in the primary key index. This could be useful for optimizing ORDER BY operations.

Global, Local, or Nonpartitioned Indexes?

With partitioned tables, it is common to create local partitioned indexes. The main advantage of doing so is to reduce the dependencies between indexes and table partitions. For example, it makes things much easier when new partitions are added, dropped, or exchanged. Simply put, creating local indexes is generally good. Nevertheless, there are situations where it is not possible or not advisable to do so.

The first problem is related to primary keys and unique indexes. In fact, to be based on local indexes, their keys must contain the partition key. Although this is sometimes possible, more often than not there is no such possibility without distorting the logical database design. This is especially true when range partitioning is used. So, in my opinion, this should be considered only as a last resort. You should never mess up the logical design. Since the logical design cannot be changed, only two other possibilities remain. The first is to create a nonpartitioned index. The second is to create a global partitioned index. The latter should be implemented only if there is a real advantage in doing so. Since such indexes are commonly hash partitioned, however (which, by the way, is possible only since Oracle Database 10*g*), it is advantageous to do it only for very large indexes or for indexes experiencing a very high load. In summary, it is not uncommon at all to create nonpartitioned indexes in order to support primary keys and unique keys.

The second problem with local partitioned indexes is that they can make the performance worse for SQL statements that are unable to take advantage of partition pruning. The causes of such situations were described in the section "Range Partitioning" earlier in this chapter. The impact on index scans might be very high. The following example, based on the range-partitioned table in Figure 9-5, shows what the problem might be. At first, a nonpartitioned index is created. With it, a query retrieves one row by performing four logical reads. This is good. Notice that the operation TABLE ACCESS BY GLOBAL INDEX ROWID indicates that the rowid comes from a global or nonpartitioned index.

```
SQL> CREATE INDEX i ON t (n3);

SQL> SELECT * FROM t WHERE n3 = 3885;

1 row selected.
```

Id	Operation	Name	Starts	Pstart	Pstop	Buffers
1	TABLE ACCESS BY GLOBAL INDEX ROWID	T	1	ROWID	ROWID	4
* 2	INDEX RANGE SCAN	I	1			3

```
   2 - filter("N3"=3885)
```

For the second part of this test, the index is re-created. This time it is a local index. Since the table has 48 partitions, the index will have 48 partitions as well. Since the test query does not contain a restriction based on the partition key, no partition pruning can be performed. This is confirmed not only by the operation PARTITION RANGE ALL but also by the columns Pstart and Pstop. Also notice that the operation TABLE ACCESS BY LOCAL INDEX ROWID indicates that the rowid comes from a local partitioned index. The problem with this execution plan is that instead of executing a single index scan like in the previous case, this time an index scan is performed for each partition (notice the column Starts for operations 2 and 3). Therefore, even if only a single row is retrieved, 50 logical reads are necessary.

```
SQL> CREATE INDEX i ON t (n3) LOCAL;

SQL> SELECT * FROM t WHERE n3 = 3885;

1 row selected.
```

Id	Operation	Name	Starts	Pstart	Pstop	Buffers
1	PARTITION RANGE ALL		1	1	48	50
2	TABLE ACCESS BY LOCAL INDEX ROWID	T	48	1	48	50
* 3	INDEX RANGE SCAN	I	48	1	48	49

```
   3 - access("N3"=3885)
```

In summary, without partition pruning, the number of logical reads increases proportionally to the number of partitions. Therefore, as already pointed out previously, sometimes it could be better to use a nonpartitioned index than a partitioned one. Or, as a compromise, it could be good to have a limited number of partitions. Note, however, that sometimes you have no choice. For example, bitmap indexes can be created only as local indexes.

Single-table Hash Cluster Access

In practice, too few databases take advantage of single-table hash clusters. As a matter of fact, when they are correctly sized and accessed through an equality condition on the cluster key, they provide excellent performance. There are two reasons for this. First, they need no separate access structure (for example, an index) to locate data. In fact, the cluster key is enough to locate it. Second, all data related to a cluster key is clustered together. These two advantages were also demonstrated by the tests summarized in Figures 9-3 and 9-4 earlier in this chapter.

Single-table hash clusters are dedicated to the implementation of lookup tables that are frequently (ideally, always) accessed through a specific key. Basically, this is the same utilization you can get from index-organized tables. However, there are some major differences between the two. Table 9-4 lists the main advantages and disadvantages of single-table hash clusters compared to index-organized tables. The crucial disadvantage is that single-table hash clusters need to be accurately sized to take advantage of them.

Table 9-4. *Single-table Hash Clusters Compared to Index-organized Tables*

Advantages	Disadvantages
Better performance (if accessed through cluster key and sizing is done correctly)	Careful sizing needed to avoid hash collisions and waste of space
Cluster key might be different from primary key	Partitioning not supported
	LOB columns not supported

When a single-table hash cluster is accessed through the cluster key, the operation TABLE ACCESS HASH appears in the execution plan. What it does is to access the block(s) containing the required data directly through the cluster key. The following excerpt of the output generated by the script hash_cluster.sql illustrates this:

```
SELECT * FROM t WHERE id = 6

-------------------------------------------------------------
| Id  | Operation       | Name | Starts | A-Rows | Buffers |
-------------------------------------------------------------
|*  1 |  TABLE ACCESS HASH| T  |      1 |      1 |       1 |
-------------------------------------------------------------

   1 - access("ID"=6)
```

In addition to the equality condition, the only other condition that enables access to data through the cluster key is the IN condition. When it is specified, the operation CONCATENATION appears in the execution plan. Each child of that operation is executed once to get a particular cluster key.

```
SELECT * FROM t WHERE id IN (6, 8, 19, 28)
```

```
-----------------------------------------------------------------
| Id | Operation            | Name | Starts | A-Rows | Buffers |
-----------------------------------------------------------------
|  1 |  CONCATENATION        |      |    1  |    4  |      4  |
|* 2 |   TABLE ACCESS HASH|  T   |      |    1  |    1  |      1  |
|* 3 |   TABLE ACCESS HASH|  T   |      |    1  |    1  |      1  |
|* 4 |   TABLE ACCESS HASH|  T   |      |    1  |    1  |      1  |
|* 5 |   TABLE ACCESS HASH|  T   |      |    1  |    1  |      1  |
-----------------------------------------------------------------
```

```
    2 - access("ID"=28)
    3 - access("ID"=19)
    4 - access("ID"=8)
    5 - access("ID"=6)
```

It is important to stress that all other conditions would lead to a full table scan, if no index is available. For example, the following query, that contains a range condition in the WHERE clause, uses an index:

```
SELECT * FROM t WHERE id < 6
```

```
-----------------------------------------------------------------------
| Id | Operation                     | Name | Starts | A-Rows | Buffers |
-----------------------------------------------------------------------
|  1 | TABLE ACCESS BY INDEX ROWID|  T   |      1  |    5  |      5  |
|* 2 |   INDEX RANGE SCAN           | T_PK |      1  |    5  |      3  |
-----------------------------------------------------------------------
```

```
    2 - access("ID"<6)
```

On to Chapter 10

This chapter described not only the importance of selectivity in choosing an efficient access path but also the different methods that are available for processing data stored in a single table. For that purpose, SQL statements with weak selectivity should use either full table scans, full partition scans, or full index scans. I also discussed that in order to process SQL statements with strong selectivity efficiently, the access paths of choice are based on rowids, indexes, and single-table hash clusters.

So far, I've discuss only those SQL statements that process a single table. In practice, it is quite common for several tables to be joined together. To address this area, the next chapter will describe the three basic join methods as well as their pros and cons, so you will know when and how to use the appropriate join method.

■■■

CHAPTER 10

Optimizing Joins

When a SQL statement references several tables, the query optimizer has to determine, in addition to the access path for each table, which order the tables are joined in and which join methods are used. The goal of the query optimizer is to minimize the amount of processing by filtering out unneeded data as soon as possible.

This chapter starts by defining key terms and explaining how the three basic join methods (nested loop join, merge join, and hash join) work. Some advice follows on how to choose the join methods. Finally, the chapter describes optimization techniques such as partition-wise joins and transformations.

Note In this chapter, several SQL statements contain hints. This is done not only to show you which hint leads to which execution plan but also to show you examples of their utilization. In any case, neither real references nor full syntaxes are provided. You can find these in the *SQL Reference* manual in Chapter 2.

Definitions

To avoid misunderstandings, the following sections define some terms and concepts used through this chapter. Specifically, I'll cover the different types of join trees, the difference between restrictions and join conditions, and the different types of joins.

Join Trees

All join methods supported by the database engine process only two sets of data at a time. These are called *left input* and *right input*. They are named in this way because when a graphical representation (see Figure 10-1) is used, one of the inputs is placed on the left of the join (T1) and the other on the right (T2). Note that in this graphical representation, the node on the left is executed before the node on the right.

When more than two sets of data must be joined, the query optimizer evaluates *join trees*. The types of join trees employed by the query optimizer are described in the next four sections.

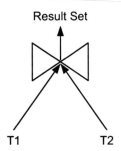

Figure 10-1. *Graphical representation of a join between two sets of data*

Left-Deep Trees

A *left-deep tree*, as shown in Figure 10-2, is a join tree where every join has a table (that is, not a result set generated by a previous join) as its right input. This is the join tree most commonly used by the query optimizer.

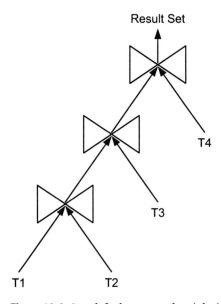

Figure 10-2. *In a left-deep tree, the right input is always a table.*

The following execution plan illustrates the join tree depicted in Figure 10-2. Note that the second child (that is, the right input) of each join operation (that is, lines 5, 6, and 7) is a table.

```
-------------------------------------
| Id  | Operation         | Name |
-------------------------------------
|   1 |   HASH JOIN       |      |
|   2 |     HASH JOIN     |      |
```

```
|   3 |      HASH JOIN         |     |
|   4 |        TABLE ACCESS FULL|  T1 |
|   5 |        TABLE ACCESS FULL|  T2 |
|   6 |      TABLE ACCESS FULL  |  T3 |
|   7 |    TABLE ACCESS FULL    |  T4 |
-----------------------------------------
```

Right-Deep Trees

A *right-deep tree*, as shown in Figure 10-3, is a join tree where every join has a table in its left input. This join tree is rarely used by the query optimizer.

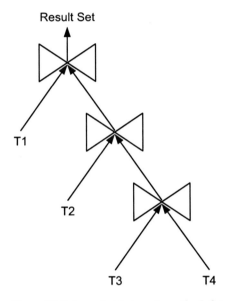

Figure 10-3. *In a right-deep tree, the left input is always a table.*

The following execution plan illustrates the join tree depicted in Figure 10-3. Note that the first child (that is, the left input) of each join operation (that is, lines 2, 4, and 6) is a table.

```
-----------------------------------------
| Id  | Operation             | Name |
-----------------------------------------
|   1 |  HASH JOIN            |      |
|   2 |    TABLE ACCESS FULL  | T1   |
|   3 |    HASH JOIN          |      |
|   4 |      TABLE ACCESS FULL| T2   |
|   5 |      HASH JOIN        |      |
|   6 |        TABLE ACCESS FULL| T3 |
|   7 |        TABLE ACCESS FULL| T4 |
-----------------------------------------
```

Zig-zag Trees

A *zig-zag tree*, as shown in Figure 10-4, is a join tree where every join has at least one table as input, but the input based on the table is sometimes on the left and sometimes on the right. This type of join tree is not commonly used by the query optimizer.

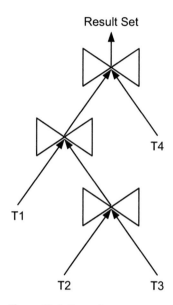

Figure 10-4. *In a zig-zag tree, at least one of the two inputs is a table.*

The following execution plan illustrates the join tree depicted in Figure 10-4:

```
---------------------------------------
| Id  | Operation           | Name |
---------------------------------------
|*  1 |  HASH JOIN          |      |
|*  2 |   HASH JOIN         |      |
|   3 |    TABLE ACCESS FULL | T1  |
|*  4 |    HASH JOIN        |      |
|   5 |     TABLE ACCESS FULL| T2  |
|   6 |     TABLE ACCESS FULL| T3  |
|   7 |   TABLE ACCESS FULL  | T4  |
---------------------------------------
```

Bushy Trees

A *bushy tree*, as shown in Figure 10-5, is a join tree that might have a join with two inputs that are not tables. In other words, the structure of the tree is completely free. The query optimizer chooses this type of join tree only if it has no other possibility. This usually happens when unmergeable views or subqueries are present.

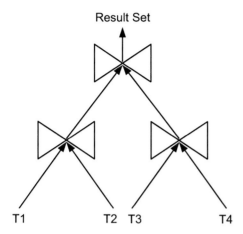

Figure 10-5. *The structure of a bushy tree is completely free.*

The following execution plan illustrates the join tree depicted in Figure 10-5. Notice that the children of join operation 1 are result sets of two other join operations.

```
-------------------------------------
| Id | Operation          | Name |
-------------------------------------
|  1 |  HASH JOIN         |      |
|  2 |   VIEW             |      |
|  3 |    HASH JOIN       |      |
|  4 |     TABLE ACCESS FULL| T1  |
|  5 |     TABLE ACCESS FULL| T2  |
|  6 |   VIEW             |      |
|  7 |    HASH JOIN       |      |
|  8 |     TABLE ACCESS FULL| T3  |
|  9 |     TABLE ACCESS FULL| T4  |
-------------------------------------
```

Types of Joins

There are two syntax types for specifying joins. The legacy syntax, which was specified by the very first SQL standard (SQL-86), uses both the FROM clause and the WHERE clause to specify joins. Instead, the newer syntax, supported as of Oracle9*i* and available for the first time in SQL-92, uses only the FROM clause to specify a join. The newer syntax is sometimes called *ANSI join syntax*. However, both syntax types are valid from a SQL standard point of view. With Oracle, for historical reasons, the most commonly used syntax is the legacy one. In fact, not only are many developers and DBAs used to it, but many applications were developed using it as well. Nevertheless, the newer syntax offers possibilities that the legacy syntax does not support. The following sections provide examples based on both syntaxes. All queries used here as examples are provided in the script join_types.sql.

> **Note** The join types described in this section are not mutually exclusive. A given join may fall into more than one category. For example, it is perfectly plausible to conceive of a theta join that is also a self-join.

Cross Joins

A *cross join*, also called *Cartesian product*, is the operation that combines every row of one table with every row of another table. This type of operation is carried out in the two situations illustrated with the following queries. The first uses the legacy join syntax (no join condition is specified):

```
SELECT emp.ename, dept.dname
FROM emp, dept
```

The second uses the new join syntax (the CROSS JOIN is used):

```
SELECT emp.ename, dept.dname
FROM emp CROSS JOIN dept
```

In reality, cross joins are rarely needed. Nevertheless, the latter syntax is better to document the developer's intention. Cross joins have the advantage of being explicitly specified. In fact, with the former it is not clear whether the person who wrote the SQL statement forgot a WHERE clause.

Theta Joins

A *theta join* is equivalent to performing a selection over the result set of a cross join. In other words, instead of returning a combination of every row from one table with every row from another table, only the rows satisfying a join condition are returned. The following two queries are examples of this type of join:

```
SELECT emp.ename, salgrade.grade
FROM emp, salgrade
WHERE emp.sal BETWEEN salgrade.losal AND salgrade.hisal
```

```
SELECT emp.ename, salgrade.grade
FROM emp JOIN salgrade ON emp.sal BETWEEN salgrade.losal AND salgrade.hisal
```

Theta joins are also called *inner joins*. In the previous query using the new join syntax, the keyword INNER was assumed, but it can be explicitly coded as in the following example:

```
SELECT emp.ename, salgrade.grade
FROM emp INNER JOIN salgrade ON emp.sal BETWEEN salgrade.losal AND salgrade.hisal
```

Equi-joins

An *equi-join* (aka *natural join*) is a special type of theta join where only equality operators are used in the join condition. The following two queries are examples:

```
SELECT emp.ename, dept.dname
FROM emp, dept
WHERE emp.deptno = dept.deptno

SELECT emp.ename, dept.dname
FROM emp JOIN dept ON emp.deptno = dept.deptno
```

Self-joins

A *self-join* is a special type of theta join where a table is joined to itself. The following two queries are examples of this. Notice that the table emp is referenced twice in the FROM clause.

```
SELECT emp.ename, mgr.ename
FROM emp, emp mgr
WHERE emp.mgr = mgr.empno

SELECT emp.ename, mgr.ename
FROM emp JOIN emp mgr ON emp.mgr = mgr.empno
```

Outer Joins

An *outer join* extends the result set of a theta join. In fact, with an outer join, all rows of one table (the *preserved table*) are returned even if no matching value is found in the other table. The value NULL is associated with the returned columns of the table that do not contain matching rows. For instance, the queries in the previous section (self-joins) do not return all rows of the table emp because the employee KING, who is the president, has no manager. To specify an outer join with the legacy syntax, an Oracle extension (based on the operator (+)) must be used. The following query is an example:

```
SELECT emp.ename, mgr.ename
FROM emp, emp mgr
WHERE emp.mgr = mgr.empno(+)
```

To specify an outer join with the new syntax, several possibilities exist. For example, the following two queries are equivalent to the previous one:

```
SELECT emp.ename, mgr.ename
FROM emp LEFT JOIN emp mgr ON emp.mgr = mgr.empno

SELECT emp.ename, mgr.ename
FROM emp mgr RIGHT JOIN emp ON emp.mgr = mgr.empno
```

The following query shows that, like for the theta join, the keyword OUTER might be added to explicitly specify that it is an outer join:

```
SELECT emp.ename, mgr.ename
FROM emp LEFT OUTER JOIN emp mgr ON emp.mgr = mgr.empno
```

In addition, with the new join syntax, it is possible to specify that all rows of both tables be returned by means of a *full outer join*. In other words, rows of both tables that have no matching row in the other table are preserved. The following query is an example:

```
SELECT mgr.ename AS manager, emp.ename AS subordinate
FROM emp FULL OUTER JOIN emp mgr ON emp.mgr = mgr.empno
```

As of Oracle Database 10g, it is also possible to specify a *partitioned outer join.*[1] Be careful, the word *partitioned* is not related to the physical partitioning of objects discussed in Chapter 9. Instead, its meaning is that data is divided at runtime into several subsets. The idea is to perform an outer join not between two tables but between one table and subsets of another table. For example, in the following query, the table emp is divided into subsets based on the column job. Then, each subset is outer joined with the table dept.

```
SELECT dept.dname, count(emp.empno)
FROM dept LEFT JOIN emp PARTITION BY (emp.job) ON emp.deptno = dept.deptno
WHERE emp.job = 'MANAGER'
GROUP BY dept.dname
```

Semi-joins

A *semi-join* between two tables returns rows from one table when matching rows are available in the other table. Contrary to a theta join, rows from the left input are returned once at most. In addition, data from the right input is not returned at all. The join condition is written with IN or EXISTS. The following two queries are examples:

```
SELECT deptno, dname, loc
FROM dept
WHERE deptno IN (SELECT deptno FROM emp)
```

```
SELECT deptno, dname, loc
FROM dept
WHERE EXISTS (SELECT deptno FROM emp WHERE emp.deptno = dept.deptno)
```

Anti-joins

An *anti-join* is a special type of semi-join, where only rows from one table without matching rows in the other table are returned. The join condition is usually written with NOT IN or NOT EXISTS. The following two queries are examples:

```
SELECT deptno, dname, loc
FROM dept
WHERE deptno NOT IN (SELECT deptno FROM emp)
```

```
SELECT deptno, dname, loc
FROM dept
WHERE NOT EXISTS (SELECT deptno FROM emp WHERE emp.deptno = dept.deptno)
```

---

1. Note that this type of outer join is not specified in SQL:2003. However, it is expected to be specified in the next version of the SQL standard.

Restrictions vs. Join Conditions

To choose a join method, it is essential to understand the difference between *restrictions* (aka *filtering conditions*) and *join conditions*. From a syntactical point of view, the two might be confused only when the legacy join syntax is used. In fact, with the legacy join syntax, the WHERE clause is used to specify both the restrictions and the join conditions. Instead, with the new join syntax, the restrictions are specified in the WHERE clause, and the join conditions are specified in the FROM clause. The following pseudo SQL statement illustrates this:

```
SELECT *
FROM <table1> [OUTER] JOIN <table2> ON ( <join conditions> )
WHERE <restrictions>
```

From a conceptual point of view, a SQL statement containing join conditions and restrictions is executed in the following way:

- The two sets of data are joined based on the join conditions.

- The restrictions are applied to the result set returned by the join.

In other words, a join condition is specified to avoid a cross join while joining two sets of data. It is not intended to filter out the result set. Instead, a restriction is specified to filter the result set returned by a previous operation (for example, a join). For example, in the following query, the join condition is emp.deptno=dept.deptno, and the restriction is dept.loc='DALLAS':

```
SELECT emp.ename
FROM emp, dept
WHERE emp.deptno = dept.deptno
AND dept.loc = 'DALLAS'
```

From an implementation point of view, it is not unusual that the query optimizer misuses restrictions and join conditions. On one hand, join conditions might be used to filter out data. On the other hand, restrictions might be evaluated before join conditions to minimize the amount of data to be joined. For example, the previous query might be executed with the following execution plan. Notice how the restriction dept.loc='DALLAS' (operation 2) is applied before the join condition emp.deptno=dept.deptno (operation 1).

```
-----------------------------------
| Id | Operation        | Name |
-----------------------------------
|* 1 |  HASH JOIN        |      |
|* 2 |   TABLE ACCESS FULL| DEPT |
|  3 |   TABLE ACCESS FULL| EMP  |
-----------------------------------

  1 - access("EMP"."DEPTNO"="DEPT"."DEPTNO")
  2 - filter("DEPT"."LOC"='DALLAS')
```

Nested Loop Joins

The following sections describe how nested loop joins work. First, I describe their general behavior, and then I give some examples of two-table and four-table joins. Finally, I describe some optimization techniques (for example, block prefetching). All examples are based on the script `nested_loops_join.sql`.

Concept

The two sets of data processed by a nested loop join are called *outer loop* (aka *driving row source*) and *inner loop*. The outer loop is the left input, and the inner loop is the right input. As illustrated in Figure 10-6, while the outer loop is executed once, the inner loop is executed once for each row returned by the outer loop.

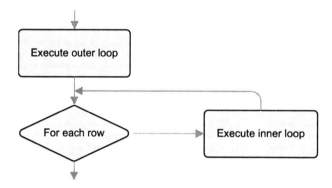

Figure 10-6. *Overview of the processing performed by a nested loop join*

Nested loop joins have the following specific characteristics:

- The left input (outer loop) is executed only once. The right input (inner loop) is potentially executed many times.

- They are able to return the first row of the result set before completely processing all rows.

- They can take advantage of indexes to apply both restrictions and join conditions.

- They support all types of joins.

Two-table Join

The following is a simple execution plan processing a nested loop join between two tables. The example also shows how to force a nested loop by using the hints `leading` and `use_nl`. The former indicates accessing table `t1` first. In other words, it specifies which table is accessed in the outer loop. The latter specifies which join method is used to join the data returned by the inner loop (that is, table t2) to table t1. It is essential to note that the hint use_nl contains no reference to table t1.

```
SELECT /*+ leading(t1) use_nl(t2) full(t1) full(t2) */ *
FROM t1, t2
WHERE t1.id = t2.t1_id
AND t1.n = 19
```

```
-------------------------------------
| Id  | Operation           | Name |
-------------------------------------
|   0 | SELECT STATEMENT    |      |
|   1 |  NESTED LOOPS       |      |
|*  2 |   TABLE ACCESS FULL| T1    |
|*  3 |   TABLE ACCESS FULL| T2    |
-------------------------------------
```

```
   2 - filter("T1"."N"=19)
   3 - filter("T1"."ID"="T2"."T1_ID")
```

As described in Chapter 6, the operation NESTED LOOPS is of type related combine. This means the first child (the outer loop) controls the execution of the second child (the inner loop). In this case, the processing of the execution plan can be summarized as follows:

- All rows in table t1 are read through a full scan, and then the restriction n=19 is applied.

- The full scan of table t2 is executed as many times as the number of rows returned by the previous step.

Clearly, when operation 2 returns more than one row, this kind of execution plan is inefficient and, therefore, almost never chosen by the query optimizer. For this reason, in this specific example, it is necessary to specify two access hints (full) in order to force the query optimizer to use this execution plan. On the other hand, if the outer loop returns a single row and the selectivity of the inner loop is high, the full scan of table t2 might be good. To illustrate, let's create the following unique index on column n for table t1:

```
CREATE UNIQUE INDEX t1_n ON t1 (n)
```

With this index in place, the previous query can be executed with the following execution plan. Note that because of operation 3 (INDEX UNIQUE SCAN), the inner loop is guaranteed to be executed no more than once.

```
SELECT /*+ ordered use_nl(t2) index(t1) full(t2) */ *
FROM t1, t2
WHERE t1.id = t2.t1_id
AND t1.n = 19
```

```
---------------------------------------------
| Id  | Operation                   | Name |
---------------------------------------------
|   0 | SELECT STATEMENT            |      |
|   1 |   NESTED LOOPS              |      |
|   2 |    TABLE ACCESS BY INDEX ROWID| T1  |
|*  3 |     INDEX UNIQUE SCAN       | T1_N |
|*  4 |    TABLE ACCESS FULL        | T2   |
---------------------------------------------
```

```
   3 - access("T1"."N"=19)
   4 - filter("T1"."ID"="T2"."T1_ID")
```

As discussed in the previous chapter, if the selectivity of the inner loop is very low, it makes sense to use an index scan for the inner loop. Since the nested loop join is a related-combine operation, for the inner loop it is even possible to take advantage of the join condition for that purpose. For example, in the following execution plan, operation 5 does a lookup using the value of column t1.id that is returned by operation 3:

```sql
SELECT /*+ ordered use_nl(t2) index(t1) index(t2) */ *
FROM t1, t2
WHERE t1.id = t2.t1_id
AND t1.n = 19
```

```
---------------------------------------------------
| Id  | Operation                   | Name       |
---------------------------------------------------
|   0 | SELECT STATEMENT            |            |
|   1 |   NESTED LOOPS              |            |
|   2 |    TABLE ACCESS BY INDEX ROWID| T1       |
|*  3 |     INDEX UNIQUE SCAN       | T1_N       |
|   4 |    TABLE ACCESS BY INDEX ROWID| T2       |
|*  5 |     INDEX RANGE SCAN        | T2_T1_ID   |
---------------------------------------------------
```

```
   3 - access("T1"."N"=19)
   5 - access("T1"."ID"="T2"."T1_ID")
```

In summary, if the inner loop is executed several (or many) times, only access paths that have good selectivity and lead to very few logical reads make sense.

Four-table Join

The following execution plan is an example of a typical left-deep tree, implemented with nested loop joins (refer to Figure 10-2 for a graphical representation). Notice how each table is accessed through indexes. The example also shows how to force a nested loop by using the hints ordered and use_nl. The former specifies to access the tables in the same order as they appear in the FROM clause. The latter specifies which join method is used to join the other tables to the first table or to the result sets of the previous join operations.

```
SELECT /*+ ordered use_nl(t2 t3 t4) */ t1.*, t2.*, t3.*, t4.*
FROM t1, t2, t3, t4
WHERE t1.id = t2.t1_id
AND t2.id = t3.t2_id
AND t3.id = t4.t3_id
AND t1.n = 19
```

```
-------------------------------------------------------
| Id  | Operation                      | Name     |
-------------------------------------------------------
|  0  | SELECT STATEMENT               |          |
|  1  |  NESTED LOOPS                  |          |
|  2  |   NESTED LOOPS                 |          |
|  3  |    NESTED LOOPS                |          |
|  4  |     TABLE ACCESS BY INDEX ROWID| T1       |
|* 5  |      INDEX RANGE SCAN          | T1_N     |
|  6  |     TABLE ACCESS BY INDEX ROWID| T2       |
|* 7  |      INDEX RANGE SCAN          | T2_T1_ID |
|  8  |    TABLE ACCESS BY INDEX ROWID | T3       |
|* 9  |     INDEX RANGE SCAN           | T3_T2_ID |
| 10  |   TABLE ACCESS BY INDEX ROWID  | T4       |
|* 11 |    INDEX RANGE SCAN            | T4_T3_ID |
-------------------------------------------------------
```

```
  5 - access("T1"."N"=19)
  7 - access("T1"."ID"="T2"."T1_ID")
  9 - access("T2"."ID"="T3"."T2_ID")
 11 - access("T3"."ID"="T4"."T3_ID")
```

The processing of this type of execution plan can be summarized as follows (this description assumes that no row prefetching is used):

1. When the first row is fetched (in other words, not when the query is parsed or executed), the processing starts by getting the first row that fulfills the restriction t1.n=19 from table t1.

2. Based on the data found in table t1, table t2 is looked up. Note that the database engine takes advantage of the join condition t1.id=t2.t1_id to access table t2. In fact, no restriction is applied to that table. Only the first row that fulfills the join condition is returned to the parent operation.

3. Based on the data found in table t2, table t3 is looked up. Also in this case, the database engine takes advantage of a join condition, t2.id=t3.t2_id, to access table t3. Only the first row that fulfills the join condition is returned to the parent operation.

4. Based on the data found in table t3, table t4 is looked up. Here too, the database engine takes advantage of a join condition, t3.id=t4.t3_id, to access table t4. The first row that fulfills the join condition is immediately returned to the client.

5. When the subsequent rows are fetched, the same actions are performed as for the first fetch. Obviously, the processing is restarted from the position of the last match (that could be the second row that matches in table t4, if any). It is essential to stress that data is returned as soon as a row that fulfills the request is found. In other words, it is not necessary to fully execute the join before returning the first row.

Block Prefetching

In normal circumstances, each access path based on single-block processing (for example, rowid access and index range scan) leads to single-block physical reads in case of a cache miss. For nested loop joins, especially when many rows are processed, this could be very inefficient. In fact, it is not unusual that nested loop joins access several adjacent blocks with several single-block physical reads.

To improve the efficiency of nested loop joins, the database engine is able to take advantage of block prefetching. The goal of this optimization technique is to substitute several single-block physical reads performed on adjacent blocks, with one multiblock physical read. This is true for both indexes and tables.

Looking at an access path cannot tell you whether the database engine will use prefetching. The only way is to look at the physical reads performed by the server process, specifically, the wait events associated with them:

- The event db file sequential read is associated with single-block physical reads. Therefore, if it occurs, either no block prefetching is being used or it is not possible to use it (for example, because the required blocks are already in the buffer cache).

- The event db file scattered read is associated with multiblock physical reads. Therefore, if it occurs for rowid accesses or index range scans, it means that block prefetching is being used.

It is important to notice that you have no control over the utilization of block prefetching. The database engine decides whether to take advantage of it.

▪**Caution** As described in MetaLink note *Table Prefetching Causes Intermittent Wrong Results in 9iR2,10gR1, and 10gR2* (406966.1), up to Oracle Database 10g Release 2, table prefetching might cause wrong results. I strongly advise you to review the note to find out whether the problem applies to the version you are using.

Alternate Execution Plans

As discussed in the section "Two-table Join," the following execution plan can be used to execute a nested loop join:

```
-------------------------------------------------
| Id  | Operation                   | Name      |
-------------------------------------------------
|   0 | SELECT STATEMENT            |           |
|   1 |  NESTED LOOPS               |           |
|   2 |   TABLE ACCESS BY INDEX ROWID| T1       |
|*  3 |    INDEX UNIQUE SCAN        | T1_N      |
|   4 |   TABLE ACCESS BY INDEX ROWID| T2       |
|*  5 |    INDEX RANGE SCAN         | T2_T1_ID  |
-------------------------------------------------
```

```
    3 - access("T1"."N"=19)
    5 - access("T1"."ID"="T2"."T1_ID")
```

In practice, in recent versions this type of execution plan is used only when either the outer loop or the inner loop is based on an index unique scan. Let's see what happens if the index t1_n on column n is defined as follows (nonunique):

```
CREATE INDEX t1_n ON t1 (n)
```

With this index in place, the following execution plan would be used. Notice the different position of the rowid access in table t2. In the previous plan, it is operation 4, while in the following it is operation 1. It is peculiar that the child of the rowid access (operation 1) is the nested loop join (operation 2). From our perspective, the two execution plans do the same work. The following execution plan is probably implemented in order to take advantage of internal optimizations such as block prefetching.

```
-------------------------------------------------
| Id  | Operation                   | Name      |
-------------------------------------------------
|   0 | SELECT STATEMENT            |           |
|   1 |  TABLE ACCESS BY INDEX ROWID | T2       |
|   2 |   NESTED LOOPS              |           |
|   3 |    TABLE ACCESS BY INDEX ROWID| T1      |
|*  4 |     INDEX RANGE SCAN        | T1_N      |
|*  5 |    INDEX RANGE SCAN         | T2_T1_ID  |
-------------------------------------------------
```

```
    4 - access("T1"."N"=19)
    5 - access("T1"."ID"="T2"."T1_ID")
```

As of Oracle Database 11g, the following execution plan might be observed instead of the previous one. Note that even if the query is always the same (that is, a two-table join), the execution plan contains two nested loop joins! A simple performance test showed an improvement of about 10 percent using it. This is probably because of a new internal optimization that applies only to the new execution plan. To control this new execution plan, the hints nlj_batching and no_nlj_batching are available.

```
---------------------------------------------------
| Id  | Operation                    | Name      |
---------------------------------------------------
|   0 | SELECT STATEMENT             |           |
|   1 |  NESTED LOOPS                |           |
|   2 |   NESTED LOOPS               |           |
|   3 |    TABLE ACCESS BY INDEX ROWID| T1       |
|*  4 |     INDEX RANGE SCAN         | T1_N      |
|*  5 |     INDEX RANGE SCAN         | T2_T1_ID  |
|   6 |    TABLE ACCESS BY INDEX ROWID| T2       |
---------------------------------------------------

   4 - access("T1"."N"=19)
   5 - access("T1"."ID"="T2"."T1_ID")
```

Merge Joins

The following sections describe how merge joins (aka sort-merge joins) work. I begin by describing their general behavior and give some examples of two-table and four-table joins. Finally, I describe the work areas used during processing. All examples are based on the script merge_join.sql.

Concept

When processing a merge join, both sets of data are read and sorted according to the columns of the join condition. Once these operations are completed, the data contained in the two work areas is merged, as illustrated in Figure 10-7.

Merge joins are characterized by the following properties:

- Each child is executed only once.

- Both inputs must be sorted according to the columns of the join condition.

- Because of the sort operations, both inputs must be fully read and sorted before returning the first row of the result set.

- All types of joins are supported.

▪**Caution** There are situations, for example, when merge joins are used to execute cross joins, where two of the properties just described don't apply. First, the two inputs mustn't be sorted. Second, the first row can be immediately returned. I do not further describe these cases in this chapter because they are not common.

Merge joins are not used very often. The reason is that in most situations either nested loop joins or hash joins perform better than merge joins. Nevertheless, this join method is essential because it is the only one that supports all types of joins.

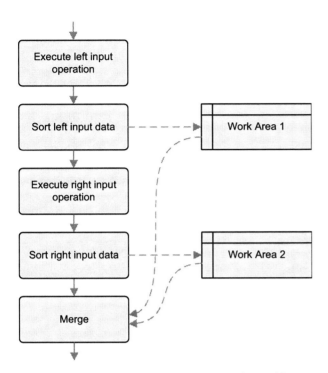

Figure 10-7. *Overview of the processing performed by a merge join*

Two-table Join

The following is a simple execution plan processing a merge join between two tables. The example also shows how to force a merge join by using the hints ordered and use_merge.

```
SELECT /*+ ordered use_merge(t2) */ *
FROM t1, t2
WHERE t1.id = t2.t1_id
AND t1.n = 19
```

```
-------------------------------------
| Id  | Operation            | Name  |
-------------------------------------
|   0 | SELECT STATEMENT     |       |
|   1 |  MERGE JOIN          |       |
|   2 |   SORT JOIN          |       |
|*  3 |    TABLE ACCESS FULL | T1    |
|*  4 |   SORT JOIN          |       |
|   5 |    TABLE ACCESS FULL | T2    |
-------------------------------------

   3 - filter("T1"."N"=19)
   4 - access("T1"."ID"="T2"."T1_ID")
       filter("T1"."ID"="T2"."T1_ID")
```

As described in Chapter 6, the operation MERGE JOIN is of type unrelated combine. This means the two children are processed only once and independently of each other. In this case, the processing of the execution plan can be summarized as follows:

- All rows in table t1 are read through a full scan, the restriction n=19 is applied, and the resulting rows are sorted according to the columns used as the join condition (id).

- All rows in table t2 are read through a full scan and sorted according to the columns used as the join condition (t1_id).

- The two sets of data are joined together, and the resulting rows are returned. Note that the join itself is straightforward because the two sets of data are sorted according to the same value (the columns used in the join condition).

The most important limitation of the operation MERGE JOIN (like for the other unrelated-combine operations) is its inability to take advantage of indexes to apply join conditions. In other words, indexes can be used only as an access path to evaluate restrictions (if available) before sorting the inputs. Therefore, in order to choose the access path, you have to apply the methods discussed in Chapter 9 to both tables. For instance, if the restriction n=19 provides good selectivity, it could be useful to create an index to apply it.

```
CREATE INDEX t1_n ON t1 (n)
```

In fact, with this index in place, the following execution plan might be used. You should notice that table t1 is no longer accessed through a full table scan.

```
-----------------------------------------------
| Id  | Operation                    | Name  |
-----------------------------------------------
|   0 | SELECT STATEMENT             |       |
|   1 |  MERGE JOIN                  |       |
|   2 |   SORT JOIN                  |       |
|   3 |    TABLE ACCESS BY INDEX ROWID| T1   |
|*  4 |     INDEX RANGE SCAN         | T1_N  |
|*  5 |   SORT JOIN                  |       |
|   6 |    TABLE ACCESS FULL         | T2    |
-----------------------------------------------

   4 - access("T1"."N"=19)
   5 - access("T1"."ID"="T2"."T1_ID")
       filter("T1"."ID"="T2"."T1_ID")
```

To execute merge joins, a non-negligible amount of resources may be spent on sort operations. To improve performance, the query optimizer avoids performing sort operations whenever it saves resources. But, of course, this is possible only when the data is already sorted according to the columns used as the join condition. This happens in two situations. The first is when an index range scan taking advantage of an index built on the columns used as the join condition is used. The second is when a step preceding the merge join (for example, another merge join) already sorted the data in the right order. For example, in the following execution plan, notice how table t1 is accessed through the index t1_pk (which is built on the column id used as the join condition). As a result, for the left input, the sort operation (SORT JOIN) can be avoided.

```
-------------------------------------------------
| Id  | Operation                    | Name  |
-------------------------------------------------
|   0 | SELECT STATEMENT             |       |
|   1 |  MERGE JOIN                  |       |
|*  2 |   TABLE ACCESS BY INDEX ROWID| T1    |
|   3 |    INDEX FULL SCAN           | T1_PK |
|*  4 |   SORT JOIN                  |       |
|   5 |    TABLE ACCESS FULL         | T2    |
-------------------------------------------------

   2 - filter("T1"."N"=19)
   4 - access("T1"."ID"="T2"."T1_ID")
       filter("T1"."ID"="T2"."T1_ID")
```

Four-table Join

The following execution plan is an example of a typical left-deep tree implemented with merge joins (refer to Figure 10-2 for a graphical representation). The example also shows how to force a merge join by means of the hints leading and use_merge. Note that the hint leading supports several tables as of Oracle Database 10*g* only.

```
SELECT /*+ leading(t1 t2 t3) use_merge(t2 t3 t4) */ t1.*, t2.*, t3.*, t4.*
FROM t1, t2, t3, t4
WHERE t1.id = t2.t1_id
AND t2.id = t3.t2_id
AND t3.id = t4.t3_id
AND t1.n = 19
```

```
-----------------------------------------
| Id  | Operation               | Name  |
-----------------------------------------
|   0 | SELECT STATEMENT        |       |
|   1 |  MERGE JOIN             |       |
|   2 |   SORT JOIN             |       |
|   3 |    MERGE JOIN           |       |
|   4 |     SORT JOIN           |       |
|   5 |      MERGE JOIN         |       |
|   6 |       SORT JOIN         |       |
|*  7 |        TABLE ACCESS FULL| T1    |
|*  8 |       SORT JOIN         |       |
|   9 |        TABLE ACCESS FULL| T2    |
```

```
|* 10 |      SORT JOIN             |      |
| 11 |        TABLE ACCESS FULL  | T3   |
|* 12 |    SORT JOIN             |      |
| 13 |      TABLE ACCESS FULL    | T4   |
-----------------------------------------

  7 - filter("T1"."N"=19)
  8 - access("T1"."ID"="T2"."T1_ID")
      filter("T1"."ID"="T2"."T1_ID")
 10 - access("T2"."ID"="T3"."T2_ID")
      filter("T2"."ID"="T3"."T2_ID")
 12 - access("T3"."ID"="T4"."T3_ID")
      filter("T3"."ID"="T4"."T3_ID")
```

The processing is not really different from the two-table join discussed in the previous section. However, it is important to emphasize that data is sorted several times. In fact, each join condition is based on different columns. For example, the data resulting from the join between table t1 and table t2, which is sorted according to the column id of table t1, is sorted again by operation 4 according to the column id of table t2. The same happens with the data returned by operation 3. In fact, it has to be sorted according to the column id of table t3. In summary, to process this type of execution plan, six sorts have to be performed, and all of them have to be performed before being able to return a single row.

Work Areas

To process a merge join, up to two work areas in memory are used to sort data. If a sort is completely processed in memory, it is called an *in-memory sort*. If a sort needs to spill temporary data to the disk, it is called an *on-disk sort*. From a performance point of view, it should be obvious that in-memory sorts should be faster than on-disk sorts. The next sections discuss how these two types of sorts work. I'll also discuss how to recognize which one is used to process a SQL statement, based on the output of the package dbms_xplan.

I discussed work area configuration (sizing) in Chapter 5. As you might recall from that section, there are two sizing methods. Which one is used depends on the value of the initialization parameter workarea_size_policy. The two methods are as follows:

auto: The database engine automatically does the sizing of the work areas. The total amount of PGA dedicated to one instance is limited by the initialization parameter pga_aggregate_target or, as of Oracle Database 11g, by the initialization parameter memory_target.

manual: The initialization parameter sort_area_size limits the maximum size of a single work area. In addition, the initialization parameter sort_area_retained_size controls how the PGA is released when the sort is over.

In-memory Sorts

The processing of an in-memory sort is straightforward. The data is loaded into a work area, and the sorting takes place. It is important to stress that all data must be loaded into the work area, not only the columns referenced as the join condition. Therefore, to avoid wasting a lot of memory, only the columns that are really necessary should be added to the SELECT clause. To illustrate this point, let's look at two examples based on the four-table join discussed in the previous section.

In the following example, all columns in all tables are referenced in the SELECT clause. In the execution plan, the two columns, OMem and Used-Mem, provide information about the work areas. The former is the estimated amount of memory needed for an in-memory sort. The latter is the actual amount of memory used by the operation during execution. The value between brackets (that is, the zero) means that the sorts were fully processed in memory.

```
SELECT t1.*, t2.*, t3.*, t4.*
FROM t1, t2, t3, t4
WHERE t1.id = t2.t1_id
AND t2.id = t3.t2_id
AND t3.id = t4.t3_id
AND t1.n = 19
```

```
-----------------------------------------------------------
| Id | Operation             | Name | OMem  | Used-Mem   |
-----------------------------------------------------------
|  1 | MERGE JOIN            |      |       |            |
|  2 |  SORT JOIN            |      | 24576 |22528  (0)  |
|  3 |   MERGE JOIN          |      |       |            |
|  4 |    SORT JOIN          |      |  4096 | 4096  (0)  |
|  5 |     MERGE JOIN        |      |       |            |
|  6 |      SORT JOIN        |      |  2048 | 2048  (0)  |
|  7 |       TABLE ACCESS FULL| T1  |       |            |
|  8 |      SORT JOIN        |      | 11264 |10240  (0)  |
|  9 |       TABLE ACCESS FULL| T2  |       |            |
| 10 |    SORT JOIN          |      | 106K  |96256  (0)  |
| 11 |     TABLE ACCESS FULL | T3  |       |            |
| 12 |  SORT JOIN            |      | 974K  | 865K  (0)  |
| 13 |   TABLE ACCESS FULL   | T4  |       |            |
-----------------------------------------------------------
```

In the following example, only one of the columns already referenced in the WHERE clause is referenced in the SELECT clause. It is important to note that except for operation 6, smaller work areas were used for all other sorts and that this was true even though the execution plan was the same in both cases. Also notice that the query optimizer's estimations (column Omem) take this difference into consideration.

```
SELECT t1.id, t2.id, t3.id, t4.id
FROM t1, t2, t3, t4
WHERE t1.id = t2.t1_id
AND t2.id = t3.t2_id
AND t3.id = t4.t3_id
AND t1.n = 19
```

```
-----------------------------------------------------------
| Id  | Operation            | Name |  OMem | Used-Mem    |
-----------------------------------------------------------
|   1 |  MERGE JOIN          |      |       |             |
|   2 |   SORT JOIN          |      |  4096 |  4096  (0)  |
|   3 |    MERGE JOIN        |      |       |             |
|   4 |     SORT JOIN        |      |  2048 |  2048  (0)  |
|   5 |      MERGE JOIN      |      |       |             |
|   6 |       SORT JOIN      |      |  2048 |  2048  (0)  |
|   7 |        TABLE ACCESS FULL| T1  |       |             |
|   8 |       SORT JOIN      |      |  4096 |  4096  (0)  |
|   9 |        TABLE ACCESS FULL| T2  |       |             |
|  10 |     SORT JOIN        |      | 36864 | 32768  (0)  |
|  11 |      TABLE ACCESS FULL | T3  |       |             |
|  12 |   SORT JOIN          |      |  337K |  299K (0)   |
|  13 |    TABLE ACCESS FULL | T4  |       |             |
-----------------------------------------------------------
```

On-disk Sorts

When a work area is too small to contain all data, the database engine processes the sort in several steps. These steps are detailed in the following list. The actual number of steps depends, obviously, not only on the amount of data but also on the size of the work areas.

1. The data is read from the table and stored in the work area. While storing it, a structure is built that organizes the data according to the sort criteria. In this example, the data is sorted according to the column id. This is step 1 in Figure 10-8.

2. When the work area is full, part of its content is spilled into a temporary segment in the user's temporary tablespace. This type of data batch is called a *sort run*. Note that all data is stored not only in the work area but also in the temporary segment. This is step 2 in Figure 10-8.

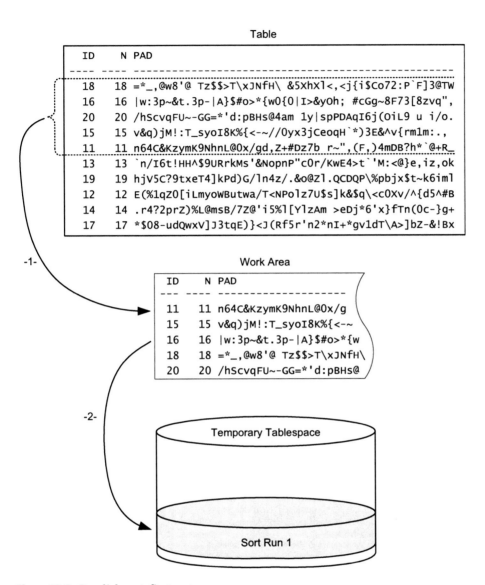

Figure 10-8. *On-disk sort, first sort run*

3. Since data has been spilled into the temporary segment, some free space is available in the work area. Therefore, it is possible to continue reading and storing the input data in the work area. This is step 3 in Figure 10-9.

4. When the work area is full again, another sort run is stored in the temporary segment. This is step 4 in Figure 10-9.

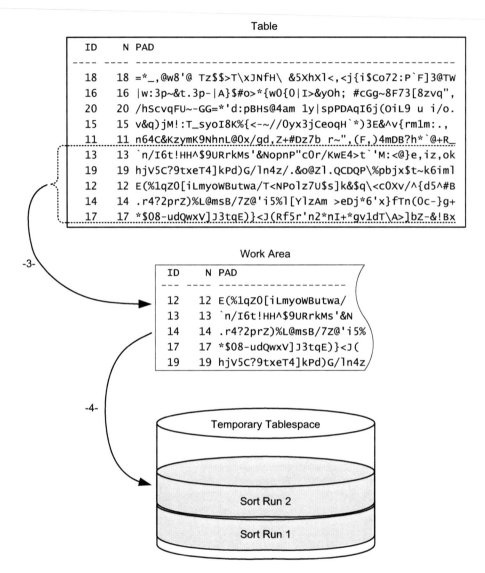

Figure 10-9. *On-disk sort, second sort run*

5. When all data has been sorted and stored in the temporary segment, it is time to merge it. The merge phase is necessary because each sort run is sorted independently of each other. To perform the merge, some data from each sort run is read. For example, while the row with id equal to 11 is stored in sort run 1, the row with id equal to 12 is stored in sort run 2. In other words, the merge takes advantage of the fact that data was sorted before spilling it into the temporary segment, in order to read each sort run sequentially. This is step 5 in Figure 10-10.

6. As soon as some data sorted in the right way is available, it can be returned to the parent operation. This is step 6 in Figure 10-10.

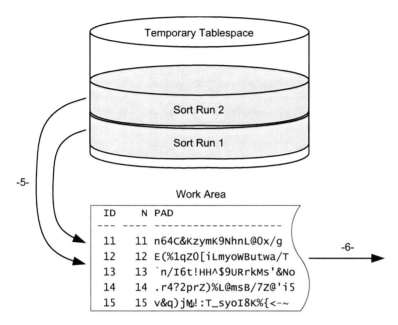

Figure 10-10. *On-disk sort, merge phase*

In the example just described, the data has been written and read into/from the temporary segment only once. This type of sort is called a *one-pass sort*. When the size of the work area is much smaller than the amount of data to be sorted, several merge phases are necessary. In such a situation, the data is written and read into/from the temporary segment several times. This kind of sort is called a *multipass sort*. Obviously, from a performance point of view, a one-pass sort should be faster than a multipass sort.

To recognize the two types of sorts, you can use the output generated by the package dbms_xplan. Let's take a look at an output based on the four-table join already used in the previous section. In this output, two additional columns are displayed: 1Mem and Used-Tmp. The former is the estimated amount of memory needed for a one-pass sort. The latter is the actual size of the temporary segment used by the operation during the execution. If no value is available, it means that an in-memory sort has been performed. Also, note how the values between brackets are no longer 0 for the operations using temporary space. Their value is set to the number of passes executed for the sort. In other words, while operation 10 was a one-pass sort, operation 12 was a multipass (nine-pass) sort.

```
SELECT t1.*, t2.*, t3.*, t4.*
FROM t1, t2, t3, t4
WHERE t1.id = t2.t1_id
AND t2.id = t3.t2_id
AND t3.id = t4.t3_id
AND t1.n = 19
```

```
-------------------------------------------------------------------------
| Id | Operation             | Name | OMem | 1Mem | Used-Mem | Used-Tmp|
-------------------------------------------------------------------------
|  1 | MERGE JOIN            |      |      |      |          |         |
|  2 |  SORT JOIN            |      | 37888| 37888|32768 (0) |         |
|  3 |   MERGE JOIN          |      |      |      |          |         |
|  4 |    SORT JOIN          |      |  5120|  5120| 4096 (0) |         |
|  5 |     MERGE JOIN        |      |      |      |          |         |
|  6 |      SORT JOIN        |      |  3072|  3072| 2048 (0) |         |
|  7 |       TABLE ACCESS FULL| T1  |      |      |          |         |
|  8 |      SORT JOIN        |      | 23552| 23552|20480 (0) |         |
|  9 |       TABLE ACCESS FULL| T2  |      |      |          |         |
| 10 |     SORT JOIN         |      |  108K|  108K|74752 (1) |   1024  |
| 11 |      TABLE ACCESS FULL| T3  |      |      |          |         |
| 12 |    SORT JOIN          |      | 1251K|  576K|74752 (9) |   2048  |
| 13 |     TABLE ACCESS FULL | T4  |      |      |          |         |
-------------------------------------------------------------------------
```

■**Caution** Usually, the output of the package dbms_xplan displays values about the size of memory in bytes. Unfortunately, as pointed out in Chapter 6, the values in the column Used-Tmp must be multiplied by 1,024 to have bytes. For example, in the previous output operations 10 and 12 used 1MB and 2MB of temporary space, respectively.

Hash Joins

This section describes how hash joins work. A description of their general behavior and some examples of two-table and four-table joins are given first, followed by a description of the work areas used during processing. Finally, a particular optimization technique, index joins, is described. All examples are based on the script hash_join.sql.

Concept

The two sets of data processed by a hash join are called *build input* and *probe input*. The build input is the left input, and the probe input is the right input. As illustrated in Figure 10-11, using every row of the build input, a hash table in memory (or temporary space, if not enough memory is available) is built. Note that the hash key used for that purpose is computed based on the columns used as the join condition. Once the hash table contains all data from the build input, the processing of the probe input begins. Every row is probed against the hash table in order to find out whether it fulfills the join condition. Obviously, only matching rows are returned.

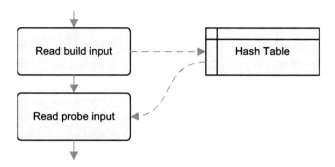

Figure 10-11. *Overview of the processing performed by a hash join*

Hash joins are characterized by the following properties:

- Each child is executed only once.

- The hash table is built on the left input only. Consequently, it is usually built on the smallest input.

- Before returning the first row, only the left input must be fully processed.

- Cross joins, theta joins, and partitioned outer joins are not supported.

Two-table Joins

The following is a simple execution plan processing a hash join between two tables. The example also shows how to force a hash join by means of the hints `leading` and `use_hash`.

```
SELECT /*+ leading(t1) use_hash(t2) */ *
FROM t1, t2
WHERE t1.id = t2.t1_id
AND t1.n = 19
```

```
-----------------------------------
| Id | Operation          | Name |
-----------------------------------
|  0 | SELECT STATEMENT   |      |
|* 1 |  HASH JOIN         |      |
|* 2 |   TABLE ACCESS FULL| T1   |
|  3 |   TABLE ACCESS FULL| T2   |
-----------------------------------

   1 - access("T1"."ID"="T2"."T1_ID")
   2 - filter("T1"."N"=19)
```

As described in Chapter 6, the operation HASH JOIN is of type unrelated combine. This means that the two children are processed only once and independently of each other. In this case, the processing of the execution plan can be summarized as follows:

- All rows of the table t1 are read through a full scan, the restriction n=19 is applied, and a hash table is built with the resulting rows. To build the hash table, a hash function is applied to the columns used as the join condition (id).

- All rows of the table t2 are read through a full scan, the hash function is applied to the columns used as the join condition (t1_id), and the hash table is probed. If a match is found, the resulting row is returned.

The most important limitation to the operation HASH JOIN (as for other unrelated-combine operations) is the inability to take advantage of indexes to apply join conditions. This means that indexes can be used as the access path only if restrictions are available. Consequently, in order to choose the access path, it is necessary to apply the methods discussed in Chapter 9 to both tables. For instance, if the restriction n=19 provides good selectivity, it could be useful to create an index to apply it.

```
CREATE INDEX t1_n ON t1 (n)
```

In fact, with this index in place, the following execution plan might be used. Note that the table t1 is no longer accessed through a full table scan.

```
---------------------------------------------
| Id  | Operation                  | Name  |
---------------------------------------------
|   0 | SELECT STATEMENT           |       |
|*  1 |  HASH JOIN                  |       |
|   2 |   TABLE ACCESS BY INDEX ROWID| T1   |
|*  3 |    INDEX RANGE SCAN         | T1_N  |
|   4 |   TABLE ACCESS FULL         | T2    |
---------------------------------------------

   1 - access("T1"."ID"="T2"."T1_ID")
   3 - access("T1"."N"=19)
```

Four-table Joins

The following execution plan is an example of a typical left-deep tree implemented with hash joins (refer to Figure 10-2 for a graphical representation). The example also shows how to force a hash join by using the hints leading and use_hash.

```
SELECT /*+ leading(t1 t2 t3) use_hash(t2 t3 t4) */ t1.*, t2.*, t3.*, t4.*
FROM t1, t2, t3, t4
WHERE t1.id = t2.t1_id
AND t2.id = t3.t2_id
AND t3.id = t4.t3_id
AND t1.n = 19
```

```
-------------------------------------
| Id  | Operation              | Name |
-------------------------------------
|   0 | SELECT STATEMENT       |      |
|*  1 |  HASH JOIN             |      |
|*  2 |   HASH JOIN            |      |
|*  3 |    HASH JOIN           |      |
|*  4 |     TABLE ACCESS FULL| T1   |
|   5 |     TABLE ACCESS FULL| T2   |
|   6 |    TABLE ACCESS FULL  | T3   |
|   7 |   TABLE ACCESS FULL   | T4   |
-------------------------------------

   1 - access("T3"."ID"="T4"."T3_ID")
   2 - access("T2"."ID"="T3"."T2_ID")
   3 - access("T1"."ID"="T2"."T1_ID")
   4 - filter("T1"."N"=19)
```

The processing of this type of execution plan is summarized here:

- Table t1 is read through a full scan, the restriction n=19 is applied, and a hash table containing the resulting rows is created.

- Table t2 is read through a full scan, and the hash table created in the previous step is probed. Then, a hash table containing the resulting rows is created.

- Table t3 is read through a full scan, and the hash table created in the previous step is probed. Then a hash table containing the resulting rows is created.

- Table t4 is read through a full scan, and the hash table created in the previous step is probed. The resulting rows are returned. The first row can be returned only when the tables t1, t2, and t3 have been fully processed. Instead, it is not necessary to fully process table t4 in order to return the first row.

One peculiar property of hash joins is that they also support right-deep and zig-zag trees. The following execution plan is an example of the former (refer to Figure 10-3 for a graphical representation). Compared to the previous example, only the hints specified in the SQL statement are different.

```
SELECT /*+ leading(t3 t4 t2) use_hash(t1 t2 t4) */ t1.*, t2.*, t3.*, t4.*
FROM t1, t2, t3, t4
WHERE t1.id = t2.t1_id
AND t2.id = t3.t2_id
AND t3.id = t4.t3_id
AND t1.n = 19
```

```
-------------------------------------
| Id | Operation            | Name |
-------------------------------------
|  0 | SELECT STATEMENT     |      |
|* 1 |  HASH JOIN           |      |
|* 2 |   TABLE ACCESS FULL  | T1   |
|* 3 |   HASH JOIN          |      |
|  4 |    TABLE ACCESS FULL | T2   |
|* 5 |    HASH JOIN         |      |
|  6 |     TABLE ACCESS FULL| T3   |
|  7 |     TABLE ACCESS FULL| T4   |
-------------------------------------
```

```
  1 - access("T1"."ID"="T2"."T1_ID")
  2 - filter("T1"."N"=19)
  3 - access("T2"."ID"="T3"."T2_ID")
  5 - access("T3"."ID"="T4"."T3_ID")
```

One of the differences between the two execution plans (that is, the left-deep tree and the right-deep tree) is the number of active work areas (that is, hash tables) that are being used at a given time. With a left-deep tree, at most two work areas are available at the same time. In addition, when the last table is processed, only a single work area is needed. On the other hand, in a right-deep tree, during almost the entire execution, a number of work areas (that are equal to the number of joins) are allocated and probed.

The dynamic performance view v$sql_workarea_active provides information about the active work areas. The following query shows the work areas used by one session that is currently executing the previous execution plan. While the column operation_id is used to relate the work areas to an operation in the execution plan, the column actual_mem_used shows the size (in bytes) and the columns tempseg_size and tablespace give information about the utilization of temporary space.

```
SQL> SELECT operation_id, operation_type, actual_mem_used, tempseg_size, tablespace
  2  FROM v$session s, v$sql_workarea_active w
  3  WHERE s.sid = w.sid
  4  AND s.sid = 87;

OPERATION_ID OPERATION_TYPE ACTUAL_MEM_USED TEMPSEG_SIZE TABLESPACE
------------ -------------- --------------- ------------ ----------
           1 HASH-JOIN                57344
           3 HASH-JOIN               178176
           5 HASH-JOIN               196608      1048576 TEMP
```

Work Areas

To process a hash join, a work area in memory is used to store the hash table. If the work area is large enough to store the whole hash table, the hash join is fully processed in memory. If the work area is not large enough, data is spilled into a temporary segment. I explained how to recognize whether a join is fully executed in memory earlier in the chapter.

I discussed work area configuration (sizing) in Chapter 5. As you might recall, there are two methods to perform the sizing. Which one you use depends on the value of the initialization parameter `workarea_size_policy`.

auto: The database engine automatically does the sizing of the work areas. The total amount of the PGA dedicated to one instance is limited by the initialization parameter `pga_aggregate_target` or, as of Oracle Database 11*g*, by the initialization parameter `memory_target`.

manual: The initialization parameter `hash_area_size` limits the maximum size of a single work area.

Index Joins

Index joins can be executed only with hash joins. Because of this, they can be considered a special case of hash joins. Their purpose is to avoid expensive table scans by joining two or more indexes belonging to the same table. This may be very useful when a table has many indexed columns and few of them are referenced by a SQL statement. The following query is an example. Note how the query references a single table, but in spite of what you might expect, a join is executed instead of a single table access. It is also important to notice that the join condition between the two data sets is based on the rowids. The example also shows how to force an index join through the hint `index_join`.

```
SELECT /*+ index_join(t4 t4_n t4_pk) */ id, n
FROM t4
WHERE id BETWEEN 10 AND 20
AND n < 100
```

```
-----------------------------------------------
| Id  | Operation          | Name              |
-----------------------------------------------
|   0 | SELECT STATEMENT   |                   |
|*  1 |  VIEW              | index$_join$_001  |
|*  2 |   HASH JOIN        |                   |
|*  3 |    INDEX RANGE SCAN| T4_N              |
|*  4 |    INDEX RANGE SCAN| T4_PK             |
-----------------------------------------------

   1 - filter("ID"<=20 AND "N"<100 AND "ID">=10)
   2 - access(ROWID=ROWID)
   3 - access("N"<100)
   4 - access("ID">=10 AND "ID"<=20)
```

Outer Joins

The three basic join methods described in the previous sections support outer joins. When an outer join is executed, the only difference visible in the execution plan is the keyword OUTER that is appended to the join operation. To illustrate, the following SQL statement is executed, because of hints, with an outer hash join. Notice that even if the SQL statement is written with the new join syntax, the predicate uses the Oracle proprietary syntax based on the operator (+).

```
SELECT /*+ leading(t1) use_hash(t2) */ *
FROM t1 LEFT JOIN t2 ON (t1.id = t2.t1_id)


-----------------------------------
| Id  | Operation          | Name |
-----------------------------------
|   0 | SELECT STATEMENT   |      |
|*  1 |  HASH JOIN OUTER    |      |
|   2 |   TABLE ACCESS FULL| T1   |
|   3 |   TABLE ACCESS FULL| T2   |
-----------------------------------


   1 - access("T1"."ID"="T2"."T1_ID"(+))
```

An important limitation of the outer joins is that the preserved table (for example, the table t1 in the previous SQL statement) must be the left input of the join operation. However, as of Oracle Database 10*g*, that limitation has been partially removed. In fact, the database engine supports a *right*-outer hash join. The following execution plan, based on the same SQL statement as the previous one, illustrates this. In practice, the query optimizer chooses to build the hash table on the smallest result set. Of course, this is useful in order to limit the size of the work area. In this case, since table t1 is smaller than table t2, for illustration purposes it is necessary to force the query optimizer to swap the two join inputs with the hint swap_join_inputs.

```
SELECT /*+ leading(t1) use_hash(t2) swap_join_inputs(t2) */ *
FROM t1 LEFT JOIN t2 ON (t1.id = t2.t1_id)


---------------------------------------
| Id  | Operation           | Name |
---------------------------------------
|   0 | SELECT STATEMENT    |      |
|*  1 |  HASH JOIN RIGHT OUTER|    |
|   2 |   TABLE ACCESS FULL  | T2   |
|   3 |   TABLE ACCESS FULL  | T1   |
---------------------------------------


   1 - access("T1"."ID"="T2"."T1_ID"(+))
```

Consequently, whenever the query optimizer has to generate an execution plan for a SQL statement containing an outer join, its options are limited. The only exception is given by hash joins as of Oracle Database 10*g*.

Choosing the Join Method

To choose a join method, you must consider the following issues:

- The optimizer goal, that is, first-rows and all-rows optimization

- The type of join to be optimized and the selectivities of the predicates

- Whether to execute the join in parallel

The next sections discuss, based on these three criteria, how to choose a join method, or more specifically, how to choose between a nested loop join, a merge join, and a hash join.

First-rows Optimization

With first-rows optimization, the overall response time is a secondary goal of the query optimizer. The response time to return the first rows is far and away its most important goal. Therefore, for a successful first-rows optimization, joins should return rows as soon as the first matches are found and not after all rows have been processed. For this purpose, nested loop joins are often the best choice. Hash joins, which support partial execution to only some extent, are useful now and then. In contrast, merge joins are rarely suitable for a first-rows optimization.

All-rows Optimization

With an all-rows optimization, the response time to return the entire result set is the most important goal of the query optimizer. Therefore, for a successful all-rows optimization, joins should be completely executed as fast as possible. To choose the best join method, the absolute amount of processed/returned rows is not significant. What is central is the relative amount of processed/returned rows, that is, the selectivity. Two main cases can be distinguished:

- When selectivity is high, hash joins are often the best choice.

- When selectivity is low, nested loops are often the best choice. Usually, hash joins and merge joins are considered only if selectivity is the result of restrictions instead of join conditions.

Generally speaking, merge joins are considered only when either the result sets are already sorted or hash joins cannot be used because of technical limitations (see the next section).

Supported Join Methods

To choose a join method, it is essential to know which type of join has to be executed. In fact, not all join methods support all types of joins. Table 10-1 summarizes which methods are available in which situation.

Table 10-1. *Types of Joins Supported by Each Join Method*

Join	Nested Loop Join	Hash Join	Merge Join
Cross join	✓		✓
Theta join	✓		✓
Equi-join	✓	✓	✓
Semi/anti-join	✓	✓	✓
Outer join	✓	✓	✓
Partitioned outer join	✓		✓

Parallel Joins

All join methods can be executed in parallel. However, as shown in Figure 10-12, they scale differently. Depending on the degree of parallelism, one method might be faster than the other. So to pick out the best join method, it is essential to know both whether parallel processing is used and what the degree of parallelism is. Note that Chapter 11 covers parallel processing.

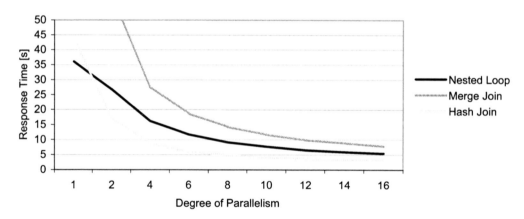

Figure 10-12. *Comparison of the performance with different degrees of parallelism. This figure shows a two-table join (50K and 94M rows) executed on a system with 8 CPU.*

Partition-wise Joins

A *partition-wise join* (which should not be confused with a partitioned outer join) is an optimization technique that the query optimizer applies to merge and hash joins only. Partition-wise joins are used to reduce the amount of CPU, memory, and, in case of RAC, network resources used to process joins. The basic idea is to divide a large join into several smaller joins. Partition-wise joins can be full or partial. The following sections describe these two alternatives. All queries used as examples are provided in the script pwj.sql.

Note Partition-wise joins require partitioned tables. Consequently, they are available only when the Partitioning option in Enterprise Edition is used.

Full Partition-wise Joins

To illustrate the operation of a full partition-wise join, let's begin by describing how a join without this optimization is performed. Figure 10-13 shows a join between two partitioned tables. A single join of all rows of the two tables is executed by a single server process.

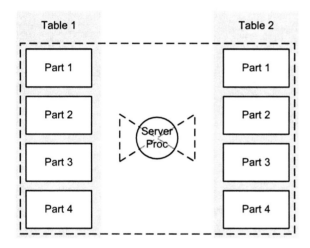

Figure 10-13. *Joining two partitioned tables without a partition-wise join*

When the two tables are equi-partitioned on their join keys, the database engine is able to take advantage of a full partition-wise join. Instead of executing a single large join, it performs, as shown in Figure 10-14, several smaller joins (in this case 4). Note that this is possible because the tables are partitioned in the same way. Because of this, every row that is stored in, for example, partition 1 of table 1, can have matching rows only in partition 1 of table 2.

One of the most useful things about decomposing a large join into several smaller joins is the possibility of parallelizing the execution. In fact, the database engine is able to start a separate slave process for each join. For example, in Figure 10-14 the server process coordinates four slave processes to execute the full partition-wise join. (Chapter 11 provides more information about parallel processing.)

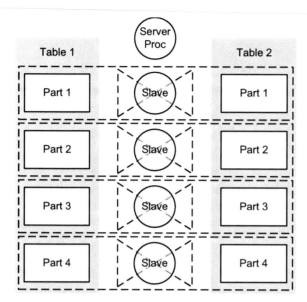

Figure 10-14. *Joining two tables with a full partition-wise join*

Figure 10-15 shows the results of a performance test based on the script pwj_
performance.sql. The purpose of the test was to reproduce an execution like the one illustrated
in Figure 10-14 or, specifically, a join of two tables with four partitions. In this particular case,
the tables contained 1,000,000 and 10,000,000 rows, respectively. Note that the degree of the
parallel executions was equal to the number of partitions, that is, four.

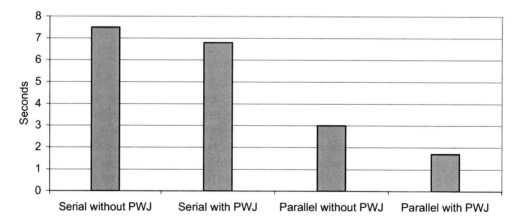

Figure 10-15. *Response time of a two-table join with and without full partition-wise join*

To recognize whether a full partition-wise join is used, it is necessary to look at the execution plan. If the partition operation appears before the join operation, it means that a full partition-wise join is being used. In the following execution plan, the partition operation `PARTITION HASH ALL` appears before the join operation `HASH JOIN`. Notice how you can use the hint `pq_distribute` to force a full partition-wise join.

```
SELECT /*+ ordered use_hash(t2p) pq_distribute(t2p none none) */ *
FROM t1p, t2p
WHERE t1p.id = t2p.id
```

```
-------------------------------------
| Id  | Operation           | Name  |
-------------------------------------
|  0  | SELECT STATEMENT    |       |
|  1  |  PARTITION HASH ALL |       |
|  2  |   HASH JOIN         |       |
|  3  |    TABLE ACCESS FULL| T1P   |
|  4  |    TABLE ACCESS FULL| T2P   |
-------------------------------------
```

The previous execution plan shows a serial full partition-wise join. The following shows the execution plan used with parallel processing for the very same SQL statement. Also in this case, the partition operation `PX PARTITION HASH ALL` appears before the join operation `HASH JOIN`. (Chapter 11 provides more information about the operations used for parallel processing.)

```
---------------------------------------------
| Id  | Operation            | Name       |
---------------------------------------------
|  0  | SELECT STATEMENT     |            |
|  1  |  PX COORDINATOR      |            |
|  2  |   PX SEND QC (RANDOM) | :TQ10000  |
|  3  |    PX PARTITION HASH ALL|         |
|  4  |     HASH JOIN        |            |
|  5  |      TABLE ACCESS FULL | T1P      |
|  6  |      TABLE ACCESS FULL | T2P      |
---------------------------------------------
```

Since full partition-wise joins require two equi-partitioned tables, special care is necessary to use this optimization technique during physical database design. In other words, it is capital to equi-partition tables that are expected to be frequently subject to massive joins. If you don't equi-partition them, you won't be able to benefit from full partition-wise joins.

It is also important to note that all partitioning methods are supported and that a full partition-wise join is able to join partitions to subpartitions. To illustrate, let's say you have two tables: `sales` and `customers`. The join key is `customer_id`. If both tables are hash partitioned, have the same number of partitions, and both use the join key as the partition key, it is possible to take advantage of full partition-wise joins. Keep in mind that it is often a requirement to partition a table like `sales` (in other words, a table containing historical data) with range partitioning. In such a situation, it is possible to composite the partition table `sales`: at the partition level with a range and at the subpartition level with a hash in order to meet both requirements. Thus, the full partition-wise join is performed between the hash partitions of the table `customers` with the subpartitions of the table `sales`.

Partial Partition-wise Joins

In contrast to full partition-wise joins, partial partition-wise joins are not required to have two equi-partitioned tables. In addition, only one table must be partitioned according to the join key; the other table (that can be partitioned or not) is dynamically partitioned based on the join key. Another characteristic of partial partition-wise joins is that they can be executed only in parallel. Figure 10-16 illustrates a partial partition-wise join. In this case, one of the tables is not partitioned at all. During execution, the database engine starts two sets of parallel slaves. The first reads the nonpartitioned table (table 2) and distributes the data according to the join key. The second receives the data from the first set, and each slave reads one partition of the partitioned table and then performs its part of the join.

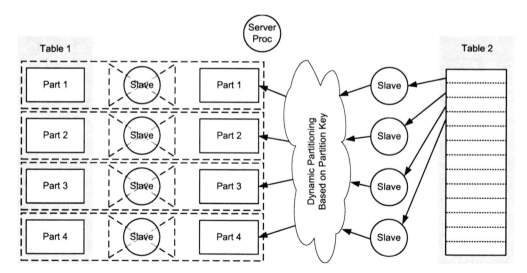

Figure 10-16. *Joining two tables with a partial partition-wise join*

To recognize whether a partial partition-wise join is used, it is necessary to look at the execution plan. If the PX SEND operation is of type PARTITION (KEY), it means that a partial partition-wise join is being used. In the following example, operation 7 provides that information:

```
SELECT /*+ ordered use_hash(t2p) pq_distribute(t2p none partition) */ *
FROM t1p, t2p
WHERE t1p.id = t2p.id
```

```
--------------------------------------------------
| Id  | Operation                   | Name     |
--------------------------------------------------
|   0 | SELECT STATEMENT            |          |
|   1 |  PX COORDINATOR             |          |
|   2 |   PX SEND QC (RANDOM)       | :TQ10001 |
|   3 |    HASH JOIN BUFFERED       |          |
|   4 |     PX PARTITION HASH ALL   |          |
|   5 |      TABLE ACCESS FULL      | T1P      |
|   6 |     PX RECEIVE              |          |
|   7 |      PX SEND PARTITION (KEY)| :TQ10000 |
|   8 |       PX BLOCK ITERATOR     |          |
|   9 |        TABLE ACCESS FULL    | T2P      |
--------------------------------------------------
```

In practice, partial partition-wise joins do not necessarily lead to improved performance. In fact, regular joins might be faster than partial partition-wise joins. In other words, using partial partition-wise joins might be detrimental to performance. For this reason, you will seldom see the query optimizer using this optimization technique.

Transformations

The query optimizer relies on transformations to enhance query performance. The goal is to generate semantically equivalent SQL statements (that is, those that produce the same results) that either are easier to optimize or have a wider search space. Some of the transformations are performed whenever technically possible, because the query optimizer assumes they always lead to better performance. Some others, called *cost-based transformations*, are applied only if the transformation leads to cheaper costs. The next sections describe four transformations related to joins: the elimination of superfluous joins, the conversion of outer joins into inner joins, subquery unnesting, and star transformation.

Join Elimination

In some specific situations, as of Oracle Database 10*g* Release 2, the query optimizer is able to completely avoid executing a join even if a SQL statement explicitly calls for it. This optimization technique is called *join elimination*. This transformation is especially useful when views containing joins are used. Note, however, that join elimination does not work only with views. It can be applied to SQL statements without views as well.

Let's take a look at an example, based on the script `join_elimination.sql`, that illustrates this optimization technique. The following SQL statement defines the view. Notice that between table t1 and table t2, there is a master-child relationship. In fact, table t2, with its column t1_id, references the primary key of table t1.

```
CREATE VIEW v AS
SELECT t1.id AS t1_id, t1.n AS t1_n, t2.id AS t2_id, t2.n AS t2_n
FROM t1, t2
WHERE t1.id = t2.t1_id
```

When all the columns are referenced, as shown in the following example, the join is regularly executed. No surprise here.

```
SELECT * FROM v
```

```
-----------------------------------
| Id  | Operation        | Name |
-----------------------------------
|   0 | SELECT STATEMENT |      |
|*  1 |  HASH JOIN       |      |
|   2 |   TABLE ACCESS FULL| T1 |
|   3 |   TABLE ACCESS FULL| T2 |
-----------------------------------

   1 - access("T1"."ID"="T2"."T1_ID")
```

However, as illustrated in the next example, when only columns defined in the child table are referenced, the query optimizer is able to eliminate the join. It can do so because there is a validated foreign key constraint that guarantees that all rows in table t2 reference one row in table t1.

```
SELECT t2_id, t2_n FROM v
```

```
-----------------------------------
| Id  | Operation        | Name |
-----------------------------------
|   0 | SELECT STATEMENT |      |
|   1 |  TABLE ACCESS FULL| T2 |
-----------------------------------
```

Outer Join to Inner Join

If an outer join is superfluous, the query optimizer can convert it into an inner join. The following example, based on the script `outer_to_inner.sql`, illustrates this transformation. The execution plan belonging to the first SQL statement, because of the hint no_outer_join_to_inner (which is available as of Oracle Database 11g only), implements an outer join (HASH JOIN OUTER). In other words, no transformation is applied. In the execution plan belonging to the second SQL statement, not only is the join not an outer join, but no predicate is applied for the restriction t2.id IS NOT NULL.

```
SELECT /*+ no_outer_join_to_inner */ *
FROM t1, t2
WHERE t1.id = t2.t1_id(+)
AND t2.id IS NOT NULL


---------------------------------------
| Id  | Operation            | Name |
---------------------------------------
|   0 | SELECT STATEMENT     |      |
|*  1 |  FILTER              |      |
|*  2 |   HASH JOIN OUTER    |      |
|   3 |    TABLE ACCESS FULL | T1   |
|   4 |    TABLE ACCESS FULL | T2   |
---------------------------------------

   1 - filter("T2"."ID" IS NOT NULL)
   2 - access("T1"."ID"="T2"."T1_ID"(+))

SELECT *
FROM t1, t2
WHERE t1.id = t2.t1_id(+)
AND t2.id IS NOT NULL


---------------------------------------
| Id  | Operation            | Name |
---------------------------------------
|   0 | SELECT STATEMENT     |      |
|*  1 |  HASH JOIN           |      |
|   2 |   TABLE ACCESS FULL  | T1   |
|   3 |   TABLE ACCESS FULL  | T2   |
---------------------------------------

   1 - access("T1"."ID"="T2"."T1_ID")
```

Obviously, the quality of this kind of SQL statement should be questioned. In any case, it is a good thing that the query optimizer recognizes such odd situations and avoids performing unnecessary processing.

Subquery Unnesting

Simply put, the purpose of subquery unnesting is to transform semi- and anti-join subqueries into regular joins. In this way, the query optimizer is able to take advantage of all available join methods. In fact, without subquery unnesting, the basic method for their execution is based on the operation FILTER. The following example, based on the script subquery_unnesting.sql, illustrates this. The operation FILTER, as described in Chapter 6, is a related-combine operation. Because of this, the subquery (lines 3 and 4) is executed once for every row (actually, as described in Chapter 6, once for every distinct value of the column t2.t1_id) returned by the main query (line 2).

```
SELECT *
FROM t2
WHERE EXISTS (SELECT /*+ no_unnest */ 1
              FROM t1
              WHERE t2.t1_id = t1.id
              AND t1.pad IS NOT NULL)
```

```
-----------------------------------------------
| Id  | Operation                    | Name  |
-----------------------------------------------
|   0 | SELECT STATEMENT             |       |
|*  1 |  FILTER                      |       |
|   2 |   TABLE ACCESS FULL          | T2    |
|*  3 |   TABLE ACCESS BY INDEX ROWID| T1    |
|*  4 |    INDEX UNIQUE SCAN         | T1_PK |
-----------------------------------------------
```

```
    1 - filter( EXISTS (SELECT /*+ NO_UNNEST */ 0 FROM "T1" "T1" WHERE
            "T1"."ID"=:B1 AND "T1"."PAD" IS NOT NULL))
    3 - filter("T1"."PAD" IS NOT NULL)
    4 - access("T1"."ID"=:B1)
```

To generate this execution plan, it is necessary to specify, in the subquery, the hint no_unnest. In other words, I had to force the query optimizer not to use the optimization technique covered in this section, subquery unnesting. In fact, without the hint no_unnest, the query optimizer unnests the subquery and produces the following execution plan. Note that the semi-join is implemented with the operation HASH JOIN SEMI. As a result, the table t1 (line 3) is accessed only once.

```
-----------------------------------------
| Id  | Operation         | Name  |
-----------------------------------------
|   0 | SELECT STATEMENT  |       |
|*  1 |  HASH JOIN SEMI    |       |
|   2 |   TABLE ACCESS FULL| T2    |
|*  3 |   TABLE ACCESS FULL| T1    |
-----------------------------------------
```

```
    1 - access("T2"."T1_ID"="T1"."ID")
    3 - filter("T1"."PAD" IS NOT NULL)
```

Even if in this example a hash join is used, note that the query optimizer might choose to use other join methods as well.

Unnesting a subquery can be summarized in two steps. The first step, as shown in the following query, is to rewrite the subquery as an inline view. Note that this is not a valid SQL statement because the operator implementing the semi-join (s=) is not available in SQL (it is used only internally by the query optimizer).

```
SELECT *
FROM t2, (SELECT id FROM t1 WHERE pad IS NOT NULL) sq
WHERE t2.t1_id s= sq.id
```

The second step, as shown here, is to rewrite the inline view in a regular join:

```
SELECT *
FROM t2, t1
WHERE t2.t1_id s= t1.id
AND t1.pad IS NOT NULL
```

Although the previous example is based on a semi-join, the same optimization technique is used for anti-joins. Note though that such transformations cannot always be applied. For example, subquery unnesting is not available if the subquery contains a set operator, some type of aggregations, or the pseudocolumn `rownum`.

Star Transformation

The *star transformation* is an optimization technique used with *star schemas* (aka dimensional models). This type of schema is composed of one large central table, the *fact table*, and of several other tables, the *dimension tables*. Its main characteristic is that the fact table references the dimension tables. Figure 10-17 is an example based on the sample schema SH (the *Sample Schemas* manual describes this fully).

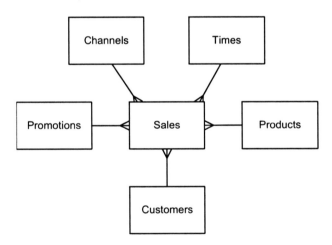

Figure 10-17. *A typical star schema*

The following is a typical query executed against a star schema:

```
SELECT c.cust_state_province, t.fiscal_month_name, sum(s.amount_sold) AS amount_sold
FROM sales s, customers c, times t, products p
WHERE s.cust_id = c.cust_id
AND s.time_id = t.time_id
AND s.prod_id = p.prod_id
```

```
AND c.cust_year_of_birth BETWEEN 1970 AND 1979
AND p.prod_subcategory = 'Cameras'
GROUP BY c.cust_state_province, t.fiscal_month_name
ORDER BY c.cust_state_province, sum(s.amount_sold) DESC
```

To optimize this query against the star schema, the query optimizer should do the following:

1. Start evaluating each dimension table that has restrictions on it.

2. Assemble a list with the resulting dimension keys.

3. Use this list to extract the matching rows from the fact table.

Unfortunately, this approach cannot be implemented with regular joins. On the one hand, the query optimizer can join only two data sets at one time. On the other hand, joining two dimension tables leads to a Cartesian product. To solve this problem, the database engine implements the star transformation.

▓**Caution** Although the star transformation was initially introduced with Oracle8 in 1997 and was strongly enhanced in Oracle8*i* two years later—that is, some time ago—its stability has always been a problem. Probably every patchset released since its introduction fixes bugs related to it. Whenever something goes wrong, ORA-07445, ORA-00600, or incorrect results are generated. That said, I have successfully used this feature since Oracle8*i* Release 2. My advice is simply to test it carefully. If it works, the improvement in performance will be considerable. If not, at least you would know it before going into production.

You need to meet two basic requirements to take advantage of star transformation. First, the feature must be enabled. You use the initialization parameter star_transformation_enabled to control it. Note that, per default, the feature is disabled since the parameter is set to FALSE. To enable it, you should set it to either temp_disable or TRUE. Second, there must be a single-column bitmap index for each foreign key on the fact table. Actually, the query optimizer is also able to convert B-tree indexes into bitmap indexes on the fly. However, if you want to use the star transformation, it is more efficient to create bitmap indexes in the first place.

When the initialization parameter star_transformation_enabled is set to temp_disable, the following execution plan is used for the sample SQL statement. This example, like the following ones, is based on the script star_transformation.sql.

```
---------------------------------------------------------------------
| Id  | Operation                      | Name        |              |
---------------------------------------------------------------------
|   0 | SELECT STATEMENT               |             |              |
|   1 |  SORT ORDER BY                 |             |              |
|   2 |   HASH GROUP BY                |             |              |
|*  3 |    HASH JOIN                   |             |              |
|   4 |     TABLE ACCESS FULL          | TIMES       |              |
|*  5 |     HASH JOIN                  |             |              |
```

```
|   6 |       PARTITION RANGE ALL                  |                            |
|   7 |         TABLE ACCESS BY LOCAL INDEX ROWID| SALES                        |
|   8 |          BITMAP CONVERSION TO ROWIDS     |                            |
|   9 |           BITMAP AND                     |                            |
|  10 |            BITMAP MERGE                   |                            |
|  11 |             BITMAP KEY ITERATION         |                            |
|  12 |              BUFFER SORT                  |                            |
|  13 |               TABLE ACCESS BY INDEX ROWID| PRODUCTS                     |
|* 14 |                INDEX RANGE SCAN          | PRODUCTS_PROD_SUBCAT_IX     |
|* 15 |              BITMAP INDEX RANGE SCAN     | SALES_PROD_BIX              |
|  16 |            BITMAP MERGE                   |                            |
|  17 |             BITMAP KEY ITERATION         |                            |
|  18 |              BUFFER SORT                  |                            |
|* 19 |               TABLE ACCESS FULL          | CUSTOMERS                    |
|* 20 |              BITMAP INDEX RANGE SCAN     | SALES_CUST_BIX              |
|* 21 |       TABLE ACCESS FULL                  | CUSTOMERS                    |
--------------------------------------------------------------------------
```

```
 3 - access("S"."TIME_ID"="T"."TIME_ID")
 5 - access("S"."CUST_ID"="C"."CUST_ID")
14 - access("P"."PROD_SUBCATEGORY"='Cameras')
15 - access("S"."PROD_ID"="P"."PROD_ID")
19 - filter("C"."CUST_YEAR_OF_BIRTH">=1970 AND "C"."CUST_YEAR_OF_BIRTH"<=1979)
20 - access("S"."CUST_ID"="C"."CUST_ID")
21 - filter("C"."CUST_YEAR_OF_BIRTH">=1970 AND "C"."CUST_YEAR_OF_BIRTH"<=1979)
```

Since this execution plan contains some peculiar operations, let's take a detailed look at its operation:

1. The execution starts with operation 4, the full scan of the dimension table times. With the data returned from it, a hash table is built. This is necessary for operation 3, the hash join.

2. Operations 13 and 14 access the dimension table products and apply the restriction p.prod_subcategory='Cameras'.

3. Operation 12, BUFFER SORT, stores the data returned by operation 13 in a buffer.

4. Operation 11, BITMAP KEY ITERATION, is a related-combine operation. For each row returned by its first child (operation 12), the second child (operation 15) is executed once. In this case, a lookup based on the bitmap index defined on the fact table is performed. Note that this lookup can be done only using a bitmap index. That's why you need to have a bitmap index for each foreign key column on the fact table.

5. Operation 10, BITMAP MERGE, merges the bitmaps passed to it by its child operation. This operation is necessary because one index key from a bitmap index might cover only part of the indexed table.

6. Operations 16 to 20 process the dimension table customers in the same way as the dimension table products is processed by operations 10 to 15. In fact, every dimension that a restriction is applied to is processed in the same way.

7. Operation 9, BITMAP AND, combines the bitmaps passed from its two child operations (10 and 16) and keeps only the matching entries.

8. Operation 8, BITMAP CONVERSION TO ROWIDS, converts the bitmaps passed from its child operation (9) in rowids of the fact table sales.

9. Operation 7 accesses the fact table with the rowids passed by its child operation (8).

10. With the rows returned by operation 7, a hash table is built. This is necessary for operation 5, the hash join. Note that operation 6 is merely informative, telling you that all partitions are processed.

11. Operation 21 does a full scan of the dimension table customers and applies the restriction c.cust_year_of_birth BETWEEN 1970 AND 1979. For each resulting row, the hash tables of the two hash joins (operations 3 and 5) are probed. If matching rows are found, they are passed to operation 2.

12. Operation 2, HASH GROUP BY, processes the GROUP BY clause and passes the resulting rows to operation 1.

13. Finally, operation 1, SORT ORDER BY, processes the ORDER BY clause.

In summary, the following steps are performed to execute a star transformation:

• The dimension tables are "joined" to the corresponding bitmap index on the fact table. This operation is necessary only for the dimension tables that have restrictions applied to them, in this case, the tables products and customers.

• The resulting bitmaps are merged and converted to rowids. Then, the fact table is accessed through the rowids.

• The dimension tables are joined to the data selected from the fact table. This operation is necessary only for the dimensions that have columns referenced outside the WHERE clause, in this case, for the tables times and, again, customers (this is why the table customers appears twice in the execution plan).

You can apply two additional optimization techniques to this basic behavior: temporary tables and bitmap-join indexes.

The purpose of temporary tables is to avoid the double processing of dimension tables. For example, in the previous execution plan, not only is the dimension table customers accessed twice with a full scan (operations 19 and 21), but the predicate applied to it is also executed twice. The idea is to access the dimension only once, apply the predicates, and store the resulting row in a temporary table. This optimization technique is enabled when the initialization parameter star_transformation_enabled is set to TRUE. The following execution plan, which is based on the same SQL statement as before, is an example. Notice the creation of the temporary table sys_temp_0fd9d6600_2d2eac (operations from 1 to 3) and its utilization (operations 22 and 24).

```
---------------------------------------------------------------------------
| Id  | Operation                           | Name                        |
---------------------------------------------------------------------------
|   0 | SELECT STATEMENT                    |                             |
|   1 |  TEMP TABLE TRANSFORMATION          |                             |
|   2 |   LOAD AS SELECT                    | SYS_TEMP_0FD9D6600_2D2EAC   |
|*  3 |    TABLE ACCESS FULL                | CUSTOMERS                   |
|   4 |   SORT ORDER BY                     |                             |
|   5 |    HASH GROUP BY                    |                             |
|*  6 |     HASH JOIN                       |                             |
|   7 |      TABLE ACCESS FULL              | TIMES                       |
|*  8 |      HASH JOIN                      |                             |
|   9 |       PARTITION RANGE ALL           |                             |
|  10 |        TABLE ACCESS BY LOCAL INDEX ROWID| SALES                   |
|  11 |         BITMAP CONVERSION TO ROWIDS |                             |
|  12 |          BITMAP AND                 |                             |
|  13 |           BITMAP MERGE              |                             |
|  14 |            BITMAP KEY ITERATION     |                             |
|  15 |             BUFFER SORT             |                             |
|  16 |              TABLE ACCESS BY INDEX ROWID| PRODUCTS                |
|* 17 |               INDEX RANGE SCAN      | PRODUCTS_PROD_SUBCAT_IX     |
|* 18 |             BITMAP INDEX RANGE SCAN | SALES_PROD_BIX              |
|  19 |           BITMAP MERGE              |                             |
|  20 |            BITMAP KEY ITERATION     |                             |
|  21 |             BUFFER SORT             |                             |
|  22 |              TABLE ACCESS FULL      | SYS_TEMP_0FD9D6600_2D2EAC   |
|* 23 |             BITMAP INDEX RANGE SCAN | SALES_CUST_BIX              |
|  24 |       TABLE ACCESS FULL             | SYS_TEMP_0FD9D6600_2D2EAC   |
---------------------------------------------------------------------------
```

```
 3 - filter("C"."CUST_YEAR_OF_BIRTH">=1970 AND "C"."CUST_YEAR_OF_BIRTH"<=1979)
 6 - access("S"."TIME_ID"="T"."TIME_ID")
 8 - access("S"."CUST_ID"="CO")
17 - access("P"."PROD_SUBCATEGORY"='Cameras')
18 - access("S"."PROD_ID"="P"."PROD_ID")
23 - access("S"."CUST_ID"="CO")
```

The second optimization technique is based on bitmap-join indexes. The idea is to avoid the "join" between the dimension table and the corresponding bitmap index on the fact tables. For this purpose, the bitmap-join index must be created on the fact table and index one or several columns of the dimension table. For example, the following indexes are necessary to apply the restrictions c.cust_year_of_birth BETWEEN 1970 AND 1979 and p.prod_subcategory='Cameras', respectively:

```
CREATE BITMAP INDEX sales_cust_year_of_birth_bix ON sales (c.cust_year_of_birth)
FROM sales s, customers c
WHERE s.cust_id = c.cust_id
LOCAL
```

```
CREATE BITMAP INDEX sales_prod_subcategory_bix ON sales (p.prod_subcategory)
FROM sales s, products p
WHERE s.prod_id = p.prod_id
LOCAL
```

With these two indexes in place, the following execution plan results. Note that the method used to produce the rowids (lines 9 to 13) is much more straightforward than the one used in the previous examples. Actually, instead of accessing the dimension tables and joining them to the bitmap indexes on the fact table, it is enough to access the bitmap-join indexes. This is possible because the value of the associated dimension row is already present in the bitmap-join index of the fact table.

```
----------------------------------------------------------------------------
| Id  | Operation                              | Name                       |
----------------------------------------------------------------------------
|   0 | SELECT STATEMENT                       |                            |
|   1 |  SORT ORDER BY                         |                            |
|   2 |   HASH GROUP BY                        |                            |
|*  3 |    HASH JOIN                           |                            |
|   4 |     TABLE ACCESS FULL                  | TIMES                      |
|*  5 |     HASH JOIN                          |                            |
|*  6 |      TABLE ACCESS FULL                 | CUSTOMERS                  |
|   7 |      PARTITION RANGE ALL               |                            |
|   8 |       TABLE ACCESS BY LOCAL INDEX ROWID| SALES                      |
|   9 |        BITMAP CONVERSION TO ROWIDS     |                            |
|  10 |         BITMAP AND                     |                            |
|* 11 |          BITMAP INDEX SINGLE VALUE     | SALES_PROD_SUBCATEGORY_BIX |
|  12 |          BITMAP MERGE                  |                            |
|* 13 |           BITMAP INDEX RANGE SCAN      | SALES_CUST_YEAR_OF_BIRTH_BIX |
----------------------------------------------------------------------------

 3 - access("S"."TIME_ID"="T"."TIME_ID")
 5 - access("S"."CUST_ID"="C"."CUST_ID")
 6 - filter("C"."CUST_YEAR_OF_BIRTH">=1970 AND "C"."CUST_YEAR_OF_BIRTH"<=1979)
11 - access("S"."SYS_NC00009$"='Cameras')
13 - access("S"."SYS_NC00008$">=1970 AND "S"."SYS_NC00008$"<=1979)
```

The star transformation is a cost-based transformation. Therefore, when enabled, the query optimizer decides not only whether it makes sense to use it but also whether temporary tables and/or bitmap-join indexes are useful for efficient SQL statement execution. The utilization of this feature can also be controlled with the hints star_transformation and no_star_ transformation. However, be careful because even if the hint star_transformation is specified, there is no guarantee that the star transformation will take place. This behavior is also clearly documented.

On to Chapter 11

This chapter described two main subjects related to joins. First, it covered the methods used by the database engine to perform joins (nested loop joins, merge joins, and hash joins) and when it makes sense to use each of them. Second, it covered some transformations that the query optimizer applies to increase the search space.

Now that I've discussed the basic access path and join methods, it is time to look at advanced optimization techniques. In the next chapter, I discuss materialized views, result caching, parallel processing, and direct-path inserts. All of these features are not used that often, but when correctly applied, they can greatly improve performance. It's time to go beyond accesses and join optimization.

■ ■ ■

Beyond Data Access and Join Optimization

The optimization of data accesses and joins must be performed before considering the advanced optimization techniques presented in this chapter. In fact, the optimization techniques described here are intended only to further improve performance when it is not possible to achieve it otherwise. In other words, you should fix the basics first, and then, if the performance is still not acceptable, you can consider special means.

This chapter describes how materialized views, result caches, parallel processing, direct-path inserts, row prefetching, and the array interface work and how they can be used to improve performance. Each section that describes an optimization technique is organized in the same way. A short introduction is followed by a description of how the technique works and when you should use it. All sections end with a discussion of some common pitfalls and fallacies.

Note In this chapter, several SQL statements contain hints in order to show you examples of their utilization. In any case, neither real references nor full syntaxes are provided. You can find these in Chapter 2 of the *SQL Reference* manual.

Note This chapter shows the results of different performance tests. The performance figures are intended only to help you compare different kinds of processing and to give you a feel for their impact. Remember, every system and every application has its own characteristics. Therefore, the relevance of using each technique might be very different, depending on where it is applied.

Materialized View

A *view* is a virtual table based on the result set returned by the query specified at view creation time. Every time that a view is accessed, the query is executed. To avoid executing the query for every access, the result set of the query can be stored in a *materialized view*. In other words, materialized views simply transform and duplicate data that is already stored elsewhere.

■**Note** Materialized views can also be used in distributed environments in order to replicate data between databases. This usage is not covered in this book.

How It Works

The following sections describe what a materialized view is and how it works. After describing the concepts that materialized views are based on, query rewrite and refreshes are covered in detail.

Concepts

Let's say you have to improve the performance of the following query (available in the script mv.sql), which is based on the sample schema sh (the *Sample Schemas* manual describes this fully).

```
SELECT p.prod_category, c.country_id,
       sum(s.quantity_sold) AS quantity_sold,
       sum(s.amount_sold) AS amount_sold
FROM sales s, customers c, products p
WHERE s.cust_id = c.cust_id
AND s.prod_id = p.prod_id
GROUP BY p.prod_category, c.country_id
ORDER BY p.prod_category, c.country_id
```

If you judge the efficiency of the execution plan by applying the methods and rules described in Chapters 6 and 9, you find that everything is fine. The estimations are excellent, and the number of logical reads per returned row of the different access paths is very low.

```
---------------------------------------------------------------------
| Id  | Operation              | Name      | E-Rows | A-Rows | Buffers |
---------------------------------------------------------------------
|   1 |  SORT GROUP BY         |           |     68 |     81 |    3844 |
|*  2 |   HASH JOIN            |           |   918K |   918K |    3844 |
|   3 |    TABLE ACCESS FULL   | PRODUCTS  |     72 |     72 |      11 |
|*  4 |    HASH JOIN           |           |   918K |   918K |    3833 |
|   5 |     TABLE ACCESS FULL  | CUSTOMERS |  55500 |  55500 |    1457 |
|   6 |     PARTITION RANGE ALL|           |   918K |   918K |    2376 |
|   7 |      TABLE ACCESS FULL | SALES     |   918K |   918K |    2376 |
---------------------------------------------------------------------

   2 - access("S"."PROD_ID"="P"."PROD_ID")
   4 - access("S"."CUST_ID"="C"."CUST_ID")
```

The "problem" is that lots of data is processed before the aggregation takes place. The performance cannot be improved by just changing an access path or a join method, since they are already as optimal as they can be; in other words, their full potential is already exploited. It is time then to apply an advanced optimization technique. Let's create a materialized view based on the query to be optimized.

A materialized view is created with the CREATE MATERIALIZED VIEW statement. In the simplest case, you have to specify a name and the query on which the materialized view is based. Note that the tables on which the materialized view is based are called *base tables* (aka *master tables*). The following SQL statement and Figure 11-1 illustrate this (notice that the ORDER BY clause used in the original query is omitted):

```
CREATE MATERIALIZED VIEW sales_mv
AS
SELECT p.prod_category, c.country_id,
       sum(s.quantity_sold) AS quantity_sold,
       sum(s.amount_sold) AS amount_sold
FROM sales s, customers c, products p
WHERE s.cust_id = c.cust_id
AND s.prod_id = p.prod_id
GROUP BY p.prod_category, c.country_id
```

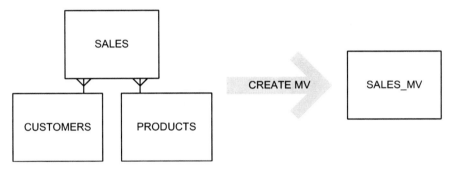

Figure 11-1. *Creation of a materialized view*

■**Note** When you create a materialized view based on a query containing the ORDER BY clause, the rows are sorted according to the ORDER BY clause only during the creation of the materialized view. Later, during refreshes, this sorting criterion is not maintained. This is also because the ORDER BY clause is not included in the definition that is stored in the data dictionary.

When you execute the previous SQL statement, the database engine creates a materialized view (which is only an object in the data dictionary; in other words, it is only metadata) and a *container table*. The container table is a "regular" table that has the same name as the materialized view. It is used to store the result set returned by the query.

You can query the container table as you would with any other table. The following SQL statement shows an example of this. Notice that the number of logical reads, compared to the original query, has dropped from 3,844 to 3. Also notice that the access path MAT_VIEW ACCESS FULL clearly states that a materialized view is accessed. This access path exists as of Oracle Database 10*g* only. In previous versions, a regular TABLE ACCESS FULL is used instead, although this is merely a naming convention used to conveniently point out that a materialized view is being used. In reality, the two access paths are absolutely the same.

```
SELECT *
FROM sales_mv
ORDER BY prod_category, country_id
```

```
-----------------------------------------------------------------
| Id  | Operation             | Name      | E-Rows | A-Rows | Buffers |
-----------------------------------------------------------------
|  1  | SORT ORDER BY         |           |    81  |   81   |    3    |
|  2  |   MAT_VIEW ACCESS FULL| SALES_MV  |    81  |   81   |    3    |
-----------------------------------------------------------------
```

Directly referencing the container table is always an option. But if you want to improve the performance of an application without modifying the SQL statements it executes, there is a second powerful possibility: use *query rewrite*.

The concept of query rewrite is straightforward. When the query optimizer receives a query to be optimized, it can decide to use it as is (in other words, to *not* use query rewrite), or it can choose to rewrite it so as to use a materialized view that contains all, or a part of, the data that is required to execute the query. Figure 11-2 illustrates this. The decision, of course, is based on the cost estimated by the query optimizer for the execution plans, with and without query rewrite. The execution plan with the lower cost is used to execute the query. The hints rewrite and no_rewrite are available to influence the query optimizer's decisions.

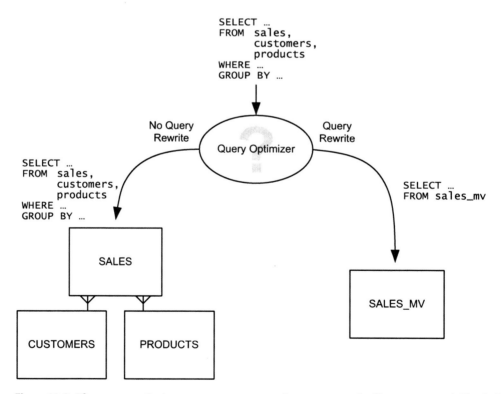

Figure 11-2. *The query optimizer can use query rewrite to automatically use a materialized view.*

To take advantage of query rewrite, it must be enabled at two levels. First, you have to set the dynamic initialization parameter query_rewrite_enabled to TRUE. Second, you have to enable it for the materialized view.

```
ALTER MATERIALIZED VIEW sales_mv ENABLE QUERY REWRITE
```

Once query rewrite is enabled, if you submit the original query, the optimizer considers the materialized view as a candidate for query rewrite; in this case, the query optimizer does, in fact, rewrite the query to use the materialized view. Notice that the access path MAT_VIEW REWRITE ACCESS FULL clearly states that query rewrite takes place. Once again, this access path is available as of Oracle Database 10*g* only. In previous versions, a regular TABLE ACCESS FULL is used instead, even though it is merely a naming convention used to indicate conveniently that a materialized view is used; the two access paths are absolutely the same.

```
SELECT p.prod_category, c.country_id,
       sum(s.quantity_sold) AS quantity_sold,
       sum(s.amount_sold) AS amount_sold
FROM sales s, customers c, products p
WHERE s.cust_id = c.cust_id
AND s.prod_id = p.prod_id
GROUP BY p.prod_category, c.country_id
ORDER BY p.prod_category, c.country_id
```

```
---------------------------------------------------------------------------
| Id | Operation                     | Name     | E-Rows | A-Rows | Buffers |
---------------------------------------------------------------------------
|  1 |   SORT ORDER BY               |          |     81 |     81 |       3 |
|  2 |    MAT_VIEW REWRITE ACCESS FULL| SALES_MV |     81 |     81 |       3 |
---------------------------------------------------------------------------
```

In summary, with query rewrite, the query optimizer is able to automatically use a materialized view that contains the data required to execute a query. As an analogy, it is similar to what happens when you add an index to a table. You (usually) don't have to modify the SQL statements to take advantage of it. Thanks to the data dictionary, the query optimizer knows that such an index exists, and if it is useful for executing a SQL statement more efficiently, the query optimizer will use it. The same goes for materialized views.

When the base tables are modified through DML or DDL statements, the materialized view (actually, the container table) may contain *stale* data ("stale" means "old," that is, data that is no longer equal to the result set of the materialized view query, if executed on the new content of the base tables now). For this reason, as shown in Figure 11-3, after modifying the base tables, a *refresh* of the materialized view has to be performed. You can choose how and when the refresh of a materialized view is performed.

Now that I have introduced the basic concepts, let me describe, in more detail, which parameters can be specified during the creation of materialized views and how query rewrite and refreshes work.

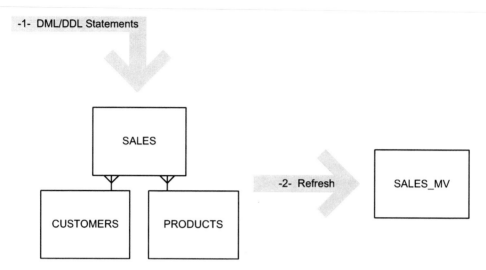

Figure 11-3. *After modifying the base tables, the materialized view has to be refreshed.*

Parameters

As you saw in the previous section, you can create a materialized view without specifying parameters. However, you can fully customize its creation:

- You can specify physical properties such as partitioning, compression, tablespace, and storage parameters for the container table. In this regard, the container table is handled like any other table. Owing to this, you can apply the techniques discussed in Chapter 9 to further optimize data access.

- When the materialized view is created, the query is executed, and the result set is inserted into the container table. This is because the parameter build immediate is used by default. Two additional possibilities exist: first, to defer the insertion of the rows to the first refresh by specifying the parameter build deferred, and second, to reuse an already existing table as the container table by specifying the parameter on prebuilt table.

- By default, query rewrite is disabled. To enable it, you must specify the parameter enable query rewrite.

- To improve the performance of fast refreshes (which are described later in this chapter) an index is created on the container table, by default. To suppress the creation of this index, you can specify the parameter using no index. This is useful, for example, for avoiding index maintenance overhead, which might be far from negligible, if you never want to perform fast refreshes.

The following SQL statement shows an example that is based on the same query as earlier, but where several of the parameters that have just been described are specified:

```
CREATE MATERIALIZED VIEW sales_mv
PARTITION BY HASH (country_id) PARTITIONS 8
TABLESPACE users
BUILD IMMEDIATE
USING NO INDEX
ENABLE QUERY REWRITE
AS
SELECT p.prod_category, c.country_id,
       sum(s.quantity_sold) AS quantity_sold,
       sum(s.amount_sold) AS amount_sold
FROM sales s, customers c, products p
WHERE s.cust_id = c.cust_id
AND s.prod_id = p.prod_id
GROUP BY p.prod_category, c.country_id
```

In addition, you can also specify how the materialized view is refreshed. The section "Materialized View Refreshes" provides detailed information on this topic.

Query Rewrite

The query optimizer is able to take advantage of query rewrite whenever a SELECT clause is present in a SQL statement, or, to be more specific, in the following cases:

- SELECT ... FROM ...

- CREATE TABLE ... AS SELECT ... FROM ...

- INSERT INTO ... SELECT ... FROM ...

- Subqueries

In addition, as already described, query rewrite is used only when two requirements are fulfilled. First, the dynamic initialization parameter query_rewrite_enabled must be set to TRUE (the default value is TRUE only as of Oracle Database 10g). Second, the materialized view must be created with the parameter enable query rewrite.

Once these requirements are met, every time the query optimizer generates an execution plan, it has to find out whether a materialized view that contains the required data can be used to rewrite a SQL statement. For that purpose, it uses one of three methods:

- *Full-text-match query rewrite*: The text of the query passed to the query optimizer is compared to the text of the query of each available materialized view. If they match, the materialized view obviously contains the required data. Note that the comparison is less strict than the one commonly used by the database engine: it is case insensitive (except for literals) and ignores blank spaces (for example, new lines and tabs) and the ORDER BY clause.

- *Partial-text-match query rewrite*: The comparison is similar to the one used for full-text-match query rewrite. With this one, however, differences in the SELECT clause are permitted. For example, if the materialized view stores three columns and only two of them are referenced by the query to be optimized, the materialized view contains all the required data, and therefore a query rewrite is possible.

- *General query rewrite*: To find a matching materialized view, general query rewrite does a kind of semantic analysis. For that purpose, it makes extensive use of constraints and dimensions to infer the semantic relations between data in the base tables. The purpose is to apply query rewrite even if the query passed to the query optimizer is quite different from the one associated with the matching materialized view. In fact, it is quite common for a well-designed materialized view to be used to rewrite many (and possibly very different) SQL statements.

DIMENSIONS

The query optimizer uses constraints stored in the data dictionary to infer data relations that enable general query rewrite to be used to the fullest extent possible. Sometimes, other very useful relationships, not covered by constraints, exist between columns in the same table or even in different tables. This is especially true for denormalized tables (such as the table `times` in the schema `sh`). To provide such information to the query optimizer, it is possible to use a *dimension*. Because of it, it is possible to specify 1:n relations with *hierarchies* and 1:1 relations with *attributes*. Both hierarchies and attributes are based on *levels*, which are, simply put, columns in a table. The following SQL statement illustrates this:

```
CREATE DIMENSION times_dim
LEVEL day IS times.time_id
LEVEL month IS times.calendar_month_desc
LEVEL quarter IS times.calendar_quarter_desc
LEVEL year IS times.calendar_year
HIERARCHY cal_rollup (day CHILD OF month CHILD OF quarter CHILD OF year)
ATTRIBUTE day DETERMINES (day_name, day_number_in_month)
ATTRIBUTE month DETERMINES (calendar_month_number, calendar_month_name)
ATTRIBUTE quarter DETERMINES (calendar_quarter_number)
ATTRIBUTE year DETERMINES (days_in_cal_year)
```

Detailed information about dimensions is available in the *Data Warehousing Guide* manual.

Full-text-match and partial-text-match query rewrites can be applied very quickly. But since their decisions are based on a simple text match, they are not very flexible. As a result, they are able to rewrite only a limited number of queries. In contrast, general query rewrite is much more powerful. The downside is that the overhead of applying it is much higher. For this reason, the query optimizer applies the methods in an increasing order of complexity (and thereby parse overhead) until a matching materialized view is found. This process is illustrated in Figure 11-4.

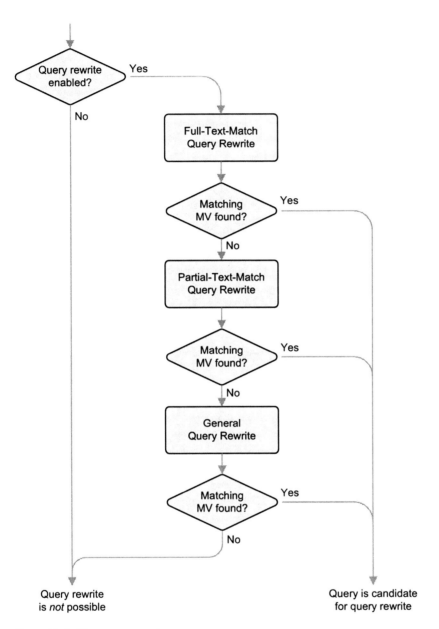

Figure 11-4. *The query rewrite process*

The following example, based on the script mv_rewrite.sql, shows general query rewrite in action. Notice that the query is similar to the one used in the previous section to define the materialized view sales_mv. There are three differences. First, the SELECT clause is different. In any case, the materialized view contains all the necessary data. Second, an ORDER BY clause is specified. Third, the table customers is not referenced. However, thanks to a validated foreign key constraint on table sales that references table customers, the query optimizer can determine that there is no loss of data by omitting that join. Therefore, it can use the materialized view sales_mv.

```
SQL> SELECT upper(p.prod_category) AS prod_category,
  2         sum(s.amount_sold) AS amount_sold
  3  FROM sales s, products p
  4  WHERE s.prod_id = p.prod_id
  5  GROUP BY p.prod_category
  6  ORDER BY p.prod_category;
```

```
----------------------------------------------------
| Id  | Operation                      | Name      |
----------------------------------------------------
|  1  |   SORT GROUP BY                |           |
|  2  |     MAT_VIEW REWRITE ACCESS FULL| SALES_MV |
----------------------------------------------------
```

It is important to note that per default, the query optimizer does not use constraints that are not validated. As a result, if such nonvalidated constraints exist, the query optimizer is not able to use general query rewrite. Since, with this specific query, full-text-match query rewrite and partial-text-match query rewrite cannot be used, no query rewrite occurs. The following example illustrates this. Notice that this is the same query used in the previous example. Only the status of the constraint sales_customer_fk has changed.

```
SQL> ALTER TABLE sales MODIFY CONSTRAINT sales_customer_fk NOVALIDATE;
```

```
SQL> SELECT upper(p.prod_category) AS prod_category,
  2         sum(s.amount_sold) AS amount_sold
  3  FROM sales s, products p
  4  WHERE s.prod_id = p.prod_id
  5  GROUP BY p.prod_category
  6  ORDER BY p.prod_category;
```

```
--------------------------------------------------
| Id  | Operation               | Name           |
--------------------------------------------------
|  1  |   SORT GROUP BY         |                |
|  2  |    HASH JOIN            |                |
|  3  |     VIEW                | VW_GBC_5       |
|  4  |      HASH GROUP BY      |                |
|  5  |       PARTITION RANGE ALL|               |
|  6  |        TABLE ACCESS FULL | SALES         |
|  7  |      TABLE ACCESS FULL  | PRODUCTS       |
--------------------------------------------------
```

Especially for data marts, it is not uncommon to use constraints that, although not validated by the database engine, are known to be fulfilled by the data, thanks to the way we (carefully) maintain our tables. At the same time, it is also not uncommon to have materialized views that, although considered stale by the database engine, are known to be safe for rewriting queries.

To take advantage of general query rewrites in such situations, you can use the dynamic initialization parameter query_rewrite_integrity. With it, you can specify whether only enforced constraints (and therefore, validated by the database engine) are to be used and whether a materialized view containing stale data is to be used. The parameter can be set to the following three values:

- enforced: Only materialized views containing fresh data are considered for query rewrite. In addition, only validated constraints are used for general query rewrite. This is the default value.

- trusted: Only materialized views containing fresh data are considered for query rewrite. In addition, dimensions and constraints that are enabled with novalidate and marked with rely are trusted for general query rewrite.

- stale_tolerated: All existing materialized views, including those with stale data, are considered for query rewrite. In addition, dimensions and constraints that are enabled with novalidate and marked with rely are trusted for general query rewrite.

The following example shows how to use general query rewrite without validating the constraint. As shown, the constraint is marked with rely, and the integrity level is set to trusted.

```
SQL> ALTER TABLE sales MODIFY CONSTRAINT sales_customer_fk RELY;

SQL> ALTER SESSION SET query_rewrite_integrity = trusted;

SQL> SELECT upper(p.prod_category) AS prod_category,
  2          sum(s.amount_sold) AS amount_sold
  3  FROM sales s, products p
  4  WHERE s.prod_id = p.prod_id
  5  GROUP BY p.prod_category
  6  ORDER BY p.prod_category;

---------------------------------------------------
| Id | Operation                   | Name    |
---------------------------------------------------
|  1 |  SORT GROUP BY              |         |
|  2 |    MAT_VIEW REWRITE ACCESS FULL| SALES_MV |
---------------------------------------------------
```

If you are in trouble because one of your SQL statements is not using query rewrite and you don't understand why, you can use the procedure explain_rewrite in the package dbms_mview to find out what the problem is. The following PL/SQL block is an example of how it is used. Notice that the parameter query specifies the query that should be rewritten, the parameter mv specifies the materialized view that should be used for the rewrite, and the parameter statement_id specifies an arbitrary character string that is used to identify the information stored in the output table rewrite_table.

```
SQL> ALTER SESSION SET query_rewrite_integrity = enforced;

SQL> DECLARE
  2    l_query CLOB := 'SELECT upper(p.prod_category) AS prod_category,
  3                            sum(s.amount_sold) AS amount_sold
  4                     FROM sales s, products p
  5                     WHERE s.prod_id = p.prod_id
  6                     GROUP BY p.prod_category, p.prod_status
  7                     ORDER BY p.prod_category';
  8  BEGIN
  9    dbms_mview.explain_rewrite(
 10      query        => l_query,
 11      mv           => 'sales_mv',
 12      statement_id => '42'
 13    );
 14  END;
 15  /
```

Note The table `rewrite_table` does not exist per default. You can create it in the schema used for the analysis by executing the script `utlxrw.sql` stored under `$ORACLE_HOME/rdbms/admin`.

The output of the procedure, given in the table `rewrite_table`, gives the reasons why the query rewrite doesn't happen. The output is composed of messages that are documented in the *Error Messages* manual.

```
SQL> SELECT message
  2  FROM rewrite_table
  3  WHERE statement_id = '42';

MESSAGE
-----------------------------------------------------------------------
QSM-01150: query did not rewrite
QSM-01110: query rewrite not possible with materialized view SALES_MV
because it contains a join between tables (SALES and CUSTOMERS) that is
not present in the query and that potentially eliminates rows needed by
the query
QSM-01052: referential integrity constraint on table, SALES, not VALID
in ENFORCED integrity mode
```

It is also essential to understand that not all query rewrite methods can be applied to all materialized views. Certain materialized views support full-text-match query rewrite only. Others support only full-text-match and partial-text-match query rewrites. In general, as the complexity (given, for example, by the utilization of constructs such as set operators and hierarchical queries) of materialized views increases, less often are advanced query rewrite methods supported. The restrictions also depend on the Oracle database engine version. So instead of providing a list of what is supported (such a list is already available in the *Data Warehousing Guide* manual), I will show you how to find out, given a specific case, which query rewrite methods are supported. To illustrate, let's re-create the materialized view with the following SQL statement. Notice that, compared to the previous examples, I have added only p.prod_status to the GROUP BY clause (in practice, executing such a SQL statement is usually pointless, but, as you will see shortly, it is an easy way to partially deactivate query rewrite).

```
CREATE MATERIALIZED VIEW sales_mv
ENABLE QUERY REWRITE
AS
SELECT p.prod_category, c.country_id,
       sum(s.quantity_sold) AS quantity_sold,
       sum(s.amount_sold) AS amount_sold
FROM sales s, customers c, products p
WHERE s.cust_id = c.cust_id
AND s.prod_id = p.prod_id
GROUP BY p.prod_category, c.country_id, p.prod_status
```

To display the query rewrite methods supported by a materialized view, you can query the view user_mviews as shown in the following example. In this case, according to the column rewrite_enabled, query rewrite is enabled at the materialized view level, and according to the column rewrite_capability, only text-match query rewrite is supported (in other words, general query rewrite is not).

```
SQL> SELECT rewrite_enabled, rewrite_capability
  2  FROM user_mviews
  3  WHERE mview_name = 'SALES_MV';

REWRITE_ENABLED REWRITE_CAPABILITY
--------------- ------------------
Y               TEXTMATCH
```

Note that the column rewrite_capability can have only one of the following values: none, textmatch, or general. If general query rewrite is supported (and, consequently, the other two methods as well), the information provided by the view user_mviews is enough. However, as in this case, if the value textmatch is shown, it would be useful to know at least two more things. First, which of the two types of text match query rewrite is supported? Only full-text-match query rewrite or also partial-text-match query rewrite? Second, why isn't general query rewrite supported?

To answer these questions, you can use the procedure explain_mview in the package dbms_mview, as shown in the following example. Notice that the parameter mv specifies the name of the materialized view, and the parameter stmt_id specifies an arbitrary string that is used to identify the information stored in the output table mv_capabilities_table.

```
dbms_mview.explain_mview(mv => 'sales_mv', stmt_id => '42')
```

■**Note** The table mv_capabilities_table is not available per default. You can create it in the schema used for the analysis by executing the script utlxmv.sql stored under $ORACLE_HOME/rdbms/admin.

The output of the procedure, found in the table mv_capabilities_table, shows whether the materialized view sales_mv supports the three query rewrite modes. If it doesn't, the column msgtxt indicates the reason why a specific query rewrite mode is not supported. In this case, notice that the problem is caused by at least one column that is referenced in the GROUP BY clause only. Upon inspecting the SQL statement, you can immediately identify the column: p.prod_status.

```
SQL> SELECT capability_name, possible, msgtxt
  2  FROM mv_capabilities_table
  3  WHERE statement_id = '42'
  4  AND capability_name IN ('REWRITE_FULL_TEXT_MATCH',
  5                          'REWRITE_PARTIAL_TEXT_MATCH',
  6                          'REWRITE_GENERAL')
  7  ORDER BY seq;

CAPABILITY_NAME            POSSIBLE MSGTXT
-------------------------- -------- ----------------------------------------
REWRITE_FULL_TEXT_MATCH    Y
REWRITE_PARTIAL_TEXT_MATCH N        grouping column omitted from SELECT list
REWRITE_GENERAL            N        grouping column omitted from SELECT list
```

Refreshes

When a table is modified, its dependent materialized view becomes stale. Therefore, a refresh is necessary to make the materialized view fresh. When you create a materialized view, you can specify how and when refreshes will take place.

To specify how the database engine performs refreshes, you can choose from these methods:

- REFRESH COMPLETE: The whole content of the container table is deleted, and all data is reloaded from the base tables. Obviously, this method is always supported. You should use it only when a sizable part of a base table has been modified.

- REFRESH FAST: The content of the container table is reused, and only the modifications are propagated to the container table. If little data has been modified in the base tables, this is the method you should use. This method is available only if several requirements are fulfilled. If one of them is not fulfilled, either the REFRESH FAST is refused as a valid parameter of the materialized view or an error is raised. Fast refreshes are covered in detail in the next sections.

- REFRESH FORCE: At first, a fast refresh is attempted. If it doesn't work, a complete refresh is performed. This is the default method.

- NEVER REFRESH: The materialized view is never refreshed. If a refresh is attempted, it terminates with the error ORA-23538: cannot explicitly refresh a NEVER REFRESH materialized view. You should use this method to make sure that a refresh will never be performed.

You can choose the point in time when the refresh of a materialized view occurs in two different ways:

- ON DEMAND: The materialized view is refreshed when explicitly requested (either manually or by running a job at a regular interval). This means that the materialized view may contain stale data during the period of time from the modification of the base tables to the refresh of the materialized view.

- ON COMMIT: The materialized view is automatically refreshed in the same transaction that modifies the base table(s). In other words, the materialized view always contains fresh data as far as the other sessions are concerned.

You can combine the options to specify how and when a materialized view is refreshed and use them with both the CREATE MATERIALIZED VIEW and ALTER MATERIALIZED VIEW statements. Here is an example of this:

```
ALTER MATERIALIZED VIEW sales_mv REFRESH FORCE ON DEMAND
```

It is even possible to create a materialized view with the options REFRESH COMPLETE ON COMMIT. However, it is very unlikely that such a configuration is useful in practice.

To display the parameters associated with a materialized view, whether it is fresh, and how and when it was last refreshed, you can query the view user_mviews:

```
SQL> SELECT refresh_method, refresh_mode, staleness,
  2         last_refresh_type, last_refresh_date
  3  FROM user_mviews
  4  WHERE mview_name = 'SALES_MV';

REFRESH_METHOD REFRESH_MODE STALENESS LAST_REFRESH_TYPE LAST_REFRESH_DATE
-------------- ------------ --------- ----------------- -------------------
FORCE          DEMAND       FRESH     COMPLETE          02.04.2008 20:38:31
```

When you choose to manually refresh a materialized view, you use one of the following procedures in the package dbms_mview:

- refresh: This procedure refreshes the materialized views specified as a comma-separated list through the parameter list. For example, the following call refreshes the materialized views sales_mv and cal_month_sales_mv in the schema sh:

  ```
  dbms_mview.refresh(list => 'sh.sales_mv,sh.cal_month_sales_mv')
  ```

- refresh_all_mviews: This procedure refreshes all materialized views stored in the database except those that are marked to never be refreshed. The output parameter number_of_failures returns the number of failures that occurred during processing.

  ```
  dbms_mview.refresh_all_mviews(number_of_failures => :r)
  ```

- refresh_dependent: This procedure refreshes the materialized views that depend on the base tables that are specified as a comma-separated list through the parameter list. The output parameter number_of_failures returns the number of failures that occurred during processing. For example, the following call refreshes all materialized views depending on the table sales that are stored in the schema sh:

  ```
  dbms_mview.refresh_dependent(number_of_failures => :r, list => 'sh.sales')
  ```

All these procedures also support the parameters method and atomic_refresh. The former specifies how the refresh is done ('c' for complete, 'f' for fast, and '?' for force), and the latter specifies whether the refresh is performed in a single transaction. If the parameter atomic_refresh is set to FALSE, no single transaction is used. As a result, for complete refreshes, the materialized views are truncated instead of being deleted. On one hand, the refresh is faster. On the other hand, if another session queries the materialized view while a refresh is running, the query might return a wrong result (no rows selected).

Caution   In Oracle9*i*, because of bug 3168840, even if the parameter atomic_refresh is set to TRUE (the default in all versions), during a complete refresh of a single materialized view, a TRUNCATE statement is executed. If several materialized views are refreshed at the same time however, the refresh works atomically as expected. Therefore, to work around this bug, it is possible to create a refresh group containing the materialized view you have to refresh and a "dummy" materialized view that is created only to have a second one. You can use the script atomic_refresh.sql to reproduce this behavior.

In case you want to automate a refresh on demand, with both CREATE MATERIALIZED VIEW and ALTER MATERIALIZED VIEW, you can also specify the time of the first refresh (START WITH clause) and an expression that evaluates to the time of subsequent ones (NEXT clause). For example, in the following SQL statement, a refresh is scheduled every ten minutes starting from the time the SQL statement is executed:

```
ALTER MATERIALIZED VIEW sales_mv REFRESH COMPLETE ON DEMAND
START WITH sysdate NEXT sysdate+to_dsinterval('0 00:10:00')
```

To schedule the refreshes, a job based on the package dbms_job is submitted. Notice that the package dbms_refresh is used instead of the package dbms_mview. Since the package dbms_refresh is also affected by bug 3168840, this job might be useless in Oracle9*i*, and you could be forced to schedule your own job to work around the bug.

```
SQL> SELECT what, interval
  2  FROM user_jobs;

WHAT                                     INTERVAL
---------------------------------------- -----------------------------------
dbms_refresh.refresh('"SH"."SALES_MV"'); sysdate+to_dsinterval('0 00:10:00')
```

REFRESH GROUPS

The package dbms_refresh is used to manage *refresh groups*. A refresh group is simply a collection of one or more materialized views. A refresh performed with the procedure refresh in the package dbms_refresh is performed in a single transaction (atomic_refresh is set to TRUE). This behavior is necessary if the consistency between several materialized views is to be guaranteed. This also means that either all materialized views contained in the group are successfully refreshed or the whole refresh is rolled back.

Fast Refreshes with Materialized View Logs

During a fast refresh, the content of the container table is reused and only the modifications are propagated from the base tables to the container table. Obviously, the database engine is able to propagate the modifications only if they are known. For that purpose, you have to create a *materialized view log* on each base table in order to enable fast refreshes (partition change tracking fast refreshes, which are discussed in the next section, are an exception to this). For example, the materialized view sales_mv requires materialized view logs on the tables sales, customers, and products, in order to be fast refreshed. Simply put, a materialized view log is a table that is automatically maintained by the database engine that tracks the modifications that occur on a base table.

In addition to materialized view logs, an internal log table is used for direct-path inserts. You don't need to create it since it is automatically installed when the database is created. To display its content, you can query the view all_sumdelta.

In the simplest case, you create the materialized view logs with SQL statements like the following (this example is based on the script mv_refresh_log.sql). Note that the clause WITH ROWID is added to specify how rows are identified in the materialized view log, that is, how to identify the base table row whose modification is tracked by each materialized view log row. It is also possible to create materialized view logs that identify rows with the primary key or the object ID. However, for the purposes of this chapter, the rows have to be identified by their rowid.

```
SQL> CREATE MATERIALIZED VIEW LOG ON sales WITH ROWID;

SQL> CREATE MATERIALIZED VIEW LOG ON customers WITH ROWID;

SQL> CREATE MATERIALIZED VIEW LOG ON products WITH ROWID;
```

Just as materialized views have an associated container table, every materialized view log also has an associated table where the modifications to the base table are logged. The following query shows how to display its name:

```
SQL> SELECT master, log_table
  2  FROM user_mview_logs
  3  WHERE master IN ('SALES', 'CUSTOMERS', 'PRODUCTS');

MASTER       LOG_TABLE
----------   ----------------
CUSTOMERS    MLOG$_CUSTOMERS
PRODUCTS     MLOG$_PRODUCTS
SALES        MLOG$_SALES
```

For most materialized views, such a basic materialized view log is not enough to support fast refreshes. There are additional requirements to be fulfilled. Since these requirements are strongly dependent on the query associated with the materialized view and the Oracle database engine's version, instead of providing a list (which is available in the *Data Warehousing Guide* manual), I will show you how to find out, given a specific case, what these requirements are. To do this, you can use the same method used to find out what the supported query rewrite modes are (see the earlier section "Query Rewrite"). In other words, you can use the procedure explain_mview in the package dbms_mview as shown in the following example:

```
SQL> execute dbms_mview.explain_mview(mv => 'sales_mv', stmt_id => '42')
```

The output of the procedure is provided in the table mv_capabilities_table. To see whether the materialized view can be fast refreshed, you can use a query like the following. Notice that in the output, the column possible is always set to N. This means that no fast refresh is possible. In addition, the columns msgtxt and related_text indicate the cause of the problem.

```
SQL> SELECT capability_name, possible, msgtxt, related_text
  2  FROM mv_capabilities_table
  3  WHERE statement_id = '42'
  4  AND capability_name LIKE 'REFRESH_FAST_AFTER%'
  5  ORDER BY seq;
```

CAPABILITY_NAME	POSSIBLE	MSGTXT	RELATED_TEXT
REFRESH_FAST_AFTER_INSERT	N	mv log must have new values	SH.PRODUCTS
REFRESH_FAST_AFTER_INSERT	N	mv log does not have all necessary columns	SH.PRODUCTS
REFRESH_FAST_AFTER_INSERT	N	mv log must have new values	SH.CUSTOMERS
REFRESH_FAST_AFTER_INSERT	N	mv log does not have all necessary columns	SH.CUSTOMERS
REFRESH_FAST_AFTER_INSERT	N	mv log must have new values	SH.SALES
REFRESH_FAST_AFTER_INSERT	N	mv log does not have all necessary columns	SH.SALES
REFRESH_FAST_AFTER_ONETAB_DML	N	SUM(expr) without COUNT(expr)	AMOUNT_SOLD
REFRESH_FAST_AFTER_ONETAB_DML	N	SUM(expr) without COUNT(expr)	QUANTITY_SOLD
REFRESH_FAST_AFTER_ONETAB_DML	N	see the reason why REFRESH_FAST_AFTER_INSERT is disabled	
REFRESH_FAST_AFTER_ONETAB_DML	N	COUNT(*) is not present in the select list	
REFRESH_FAST_AFTER_ONETAB_DML	N	SUM(expr) without COUNT(expr)	
REFRESH_FAST_AFTER_ANY_DML	N	mv log does not have sequence #	SH.PRODUCTS
REFRESH_FAST_AFTER_ANY_DML	N	mv log does not have sequence #	SH.CUSTOMERS
REFRESH_FAST_AFTER_ANY_DML	N	mv log does not have sequence #	SH.SALES
REFRESH_FAST_AFTER_ANY_DML	N	see the reason why REFRESH_FAST_AFTER_ONETAB_DML is disabled	

Some of the problems are related to the materialized view logs, others to the materialized view. Simply put, the database engine needs much more information to perform a fast refresh.

To solve the problems related to the materialized view logs, you must add some options to the CREATE MATERIALIZED VIEW LOG statements. For the problem mv log does not have all necessary columns, you have to specify that every column referenced in the materialized view be stored in the materialized view log. For the problem mv log must have new values, you have to add the INCLUDING NEW VALUES clause. With this option, materialized view logs store both old and new values (by default only old ones are stored). For the problem mv log does not have sequence, it is necessary to add the SEQUENCE clause. With this option, a sequential number is associated to each row stored in the materialized view log. The following are the redefined materialized view logs:

```
SQL> CREATE MATERIALIZED VIEW LOG ON sales WITH ROWID, SEQUENCE
  2 (cust_id, prod_id, quantity_sold, amount_sold) INCLUDING NEW VALUES;

SQL> CREATE MATERIALIZED VIEW LOG ON customers WITH ROWID, SEQUENCE
  2 (cust_id, country_id) INCLUDING NEW VALUES;

SQL> CREATE MATERIALIZED VIEW LOG ON products WITH ROWID, SEQUENCE
  2 (prod_id, prod_category) INCLUDING NEW VALUES;
```

To solve materialized view problems, some new columns, based on the function count, have to be added when the materialized view is created. The following SQL statement shows the definition that includes the new columns:

```
SQL> CREATE MATERIALIZED VIEW sales_mv
  2 REFRESH FORCE ON DEMAND
  3 AS
  4 SELECT p.prod_category, c.country_id,
  5        sum(s.quantity_sold) AS quantity_sold,
  6        sum(s.amount_sold) AS amount_sold,
  7        count(*) AS count_star,
  8        count(s.quantity_sold) AS count_quantity_sold,
  9        count(s.amount_sold) AS count_amount_sold
 10 FROM sales s, customers c, products p
 11 WHERE s.cust_id = c.cust_id
 12 AND s.prod_id = p.prod_id
 13 GROUP BY p.prod_category, c.country_id;
```

After redefining the materialized view logs and the materialized view, a further analysis using the procedure explain_mview shows that fast refreshes are possible in all situations (column possible is always set to Y). So, let's test how fast the refresh is by inserting data into two tables and then executing a fast refresh:

```
SQL> INSERT INTO products
  2 SELECT 619, prod_name, prod_desc, prod_subcategory,  prod_subcategory_id,
  3        prod_subcategory_desc, prod_category, prod_category_id,
  4        prod_category_desc, prod_weight_class, prod_unit_of_measure,
  5        prod_pack_size, supplier_id, prod_status, prod_list_price,
  6        prod_min_price, prod_total, prod_total_id, prod_src_id,
  7        prod_eff_from, prod_eff_to, prod_valid
  8 FROM products
  9 WHERE prod_id = 136;

1 row created.

SQL> INSERT INTO sales
  2 SELECT 619, cust_id, time_id, channel_id, promo_id, quantity_sold, amount_sold
  3 FROM sales
  4 WHERE prod_id = 136;
```

```
710 rows created.

SQL> COMMIT;

SQL> execute dbms_mview.refresh(list => 'sh.sales_mv', method => 'f')

PL/SQL procedure successfully completed.

Elapsed: 00:00:00.32
```

In this case, the fast refresh lasted 0.32 seconds. That's more than one order of magnitude less than the complete refresh, which is good. If you are not satisfied with the performance of a fast refresh, you should use SQL trace to investigate why it's taking too long. Then, by applying the techniques described in Chapter 9, you might be able to speed it up by adding indexes or by partitioning the segment.

Fast Refreshes with Partition Change Tracking

Tables that store historical data are frequently range partitioned by day, week, or month. In other words, partitioning is based on the column that stores timing information. Therefore, it happens regularly that new partitions are added, data is loaded into them, and older ones are dropped (it is common to keep online only a specific number of partitions). After performing these operations, all dependent materialized views are stale and thus should be refreshed.

The problem is that fast refreshes with materialized view logs (those described in the previous section) cannot be executed after a partition management operation such as CREATE PARTITION or DROP PARTITION. If such a refresh is started, the error ORA-32313: REFRESH FAST of "SH"."SALES_MV" unsupported after PMOPs is raised. Of course, it is always possible to execute a complete refresh. However, if there are many partitions and only one or two of them have been modified, the refresh time might be unacceptable.

To solve this problem, fast refreshes with partition change tracking (PCT) are available. The idea is that the database engine is able to track the staleness at partition level, and not only at table level. In other words, it is able to skip the refresh for all the partitions that have not been altered. To use this refresh method, the materialized view must fulfill some requirements. Basically, the database engine must be able to map the rows that are stored in the materialized view to the base table partitions. This is possible if the materialized view contains one of the following:

- Partition key

- Rowid

- Partition marker

- Join-dependent expression (as of Oracle Database 10*g* only)

It should be obvious what the first two are; let's look at examples of the third and fourth.

A partition marker is nothing other than a partition identifier generated by the function pmarker in the package dbms_mview. To generate the partition marker, the function uses the rowid passed as a parameter. The following example, based on the script mv_refresh_pct.sql, shows how to create a materialized view containing a partition marker:

```
CREATE MATERIALIZED VIEW sales_mv
REFRESH FORCE ON DEMAND
AS
SELECT p.prod_category, c.country_id,
       sum(s.quantity_sold) AS quantity_sold,
       sum(s.amount_sold) AS amount_sold,
       count(*) AS count_star,
       count(s.quantity_sold) AS count_quantity_sold,
       count(s.amount_sold) AS count_amount_sold,
       dbms_mview.pmarker(s.rowid) AS pmarker
FROM sales s, customers c, products p
WHERE s.cust_id = c.cust_id
AND s.prod_id = p.prod_id
GROUP BY p.prod_category, c.country_id, dbms_mview.pmarker(s.rowid)
```

■**Note** Since the function pmarker is called for each row, don't underestimate the time needed to call it. On my system, creating the materialized view takes 2.5 times longer with the partition marker than without it.

The materialized view contains a *join-dependent expression* when the partition key is used to join another table. In the example used in this section, it means that a join with the table times has to be added to the materialized view. The following SQL statement provides an example:

```
CREATE MATERIALIZED VIEW sales_mv
REFRESH FORCE ON DEMAND
AS
SELECT p.prod_category, c.country_id, t.fiscal_year,
       sum(s.quantity_sold) AS quantity_sold,
       sum(s.amount_sold) AS amount_sold,
       count(*) AS count_star,
       count(s.quantity_sold) AS count_quantity_sold,
       count(s.amount_sold) AS count_amount_sold
FROM sales s, customers c, products p, times t
WHERE s.cust_id = c.cust_id
AND s.prod_id = p.prod_id
AND s.time_id = t.time_id
GROUP BY p.prod_category, c.country_id, t.fiscal_year
```

With either the partition marker or the join-dependent expression in place, an analysis using the function explain_mview in the package dbms_mview shows that a fast refresh based on partition change tracking is possible. However, it's possible only for modifications performed on the table sales:

```
SQL> SELECT capability_name, possible, msgtxt, related_text
  2  FROM mv_capabilities_table
  3  WHERE statement_id = '42'
  4  AND capability_name IN ('PCT_TABLE','REFRESH_FAST_PCT')
  5  ORDER BY seq;

CAPABILITY_NAME  POSSIBLE MSGTXT                          RELATED_TEXT
---------------- -------- ------------------------------- -------------
PCT_TABLE        Y                                        SALES
PCT_TABLE        N        relation is not a partitioned CUSTOMERS
                          table
PCT_TABLE        N        relation is not a partitioned PRODUCTS
                          table
REFRESH_FAST_PCT Y
```

When to Use It

Materialized views are redundant access structures. Like all redundant access structures, they are useful for accessing data efficiently, but they impose an overhead to keep them up-to-date. If you compare materialized views to indexes, both the improvement and the overhead of materialized views may be much higher than those of indexes. Clearly, the two concepts are aimed at solving different problems. Simply put, you should use materialized views only if the pros of improving data access exceed the cons of managing redundant copies of the data (such as indexes, of course).

In general, I see two uses of materialized views:

- To improve the performance of large aggregations and/or joins for which the ratio between the number of logical reads and the number of returned rows is very high.

- To improve the performance of single-table accesses that are neither performed efficiently with a full table scan nor performed efficiently with an index range scan. Basically, these are accesses with an average selectivity that would require partitioning, but if it is not possible to take advantage of partitioning (Chapter 9 discusses when this is not possible), materialized views might be helpful.

Materialized views are commonly used in data warehouses to build stored aggregates. There are two reasons for this. First, data is mostly read-only; therefore, the overhead of refreshing materialized views can be minimized and segregated in time windows while the database is dedicated to modifying the tables only. Second, in such environments, the improvement may be huge. In fact, it is common to see queries based on large aggregates or joins that require an unacceptable amount of resources to be processed without materialized views.

Even if data warehouses are the primary environment where materialized views are used, I have been successful in implementing them in OLTP systems as well. This may be beneficial for tables that are frequently queried and undergo, in comparison, relatively few modifications. In such environments, to refresh materialized views, it is common to use fast refreshes on commit in order to guarantee subsecond refresh times and always-fresh materialized views.

Pitfalls and Fallacies

You should *not* use the new join syntax (aka ANSI join syntax) with materialized views. If you do use it, some query rewrite and fast refresh capabilities are not supported. Therefore, I advise you to simply avoid that syntax, if possible. Note that the documentation does not mention these restrictions.

Since fast refreshes are not always faster than complete refreshes, you should not use them in all situations. One specific case is when lots of data is modified in the base tables. In addition, you should not underestimate the overhead of maintaining the materialized view log while modifying the base tables. Hence, you should assess the pros and cons of using fast refreshes carefully.

When creating a materialized view log, you must be very careful with the use of commas. Can you identify what is wrong with the following SQL statement?

```
SQL> CREATE MATERIALIZED VIEW LOG ON products WITH ROWID, SEQUENCE,
  2  (prod_id, prod_category) INCLUDING NEW VALUES;
CREATE MATERIALIZED VIEW LOG ON products WITH ROWID, SEQUENCE,
*
ERROR at line 1:
ORA-12026: invalid filter column detected
```

The problem is the comma between the keyword SEQUENCE and the filter list (in other words, the list of columns between brackets). If the comma is present, the option PRIMARY KEY is implied, and that option cannot be specified in this case because the primary key (the column prod_id) is already in the filter list. The following is the correct SQL statement. Notice that only the comma has been removed.

```
SQL> CREATE MATERIALIZED VIEW LOG ON products WITH ROWID, SEQUENCE
  2  (prod_id, prod_category) INCLUDING NEW VALUES;

Materialized view log created.
```

Result Caching

Caching is one of the most common techniques used in computer systems to improve performance. Both hardware and software make extensive use of it. The Oracle database engine is no exception. For example, it caches data file blocks in the buffer cache, data dictionary information in the dictionary cache, and cursors in the library cache. As of Oracle Database 11*g*, *result caches* are also available.

■**Note** Result caches are available in Enterprise Edition only.

How It Works

The Oracle database engine provides three result caches:

- The *server result cache* (aka *query result cache*) is a server-side cache that stores query result sets.

- The *PL/SQL function result cache* is a server-side cache that stores the return value of PL/SQL functions.

- The *client result cache* is a client-side cache that stores query result sets.

The next sections describe how these caches work and what you have to do to take advantage of them. Note that, by default, result caches are not used.

Server Result Cache

The server result cache is used to avoid the reexecution of queries. Simply put, the first time a query is executed, its result set is stored in the shared pool. Then, for subsequent executions of the same query, the result set is served directly from the result cache instead of being recalculated. Note that two queries are considered equal and, therefore, can use the same cached result, only if they have the same text (differences in blank spaces and capitalization are allowed, though). In addition, if bind variables are present, their values must all be the same. This is necessary because, quite obviously, bind variables are input parameters that are passed to the query, and hence, the result set is usually different for different bind variable values. Also note that the result cache is stored in the shared pool, and all sessions connected to a given instance share the same cache entries.

To provide you with an example, let's execute the query already used twice in the section on materialized views. Note that the hint result_cache is specified in the query to enable the result cache. The first execution takes 1.78 seconds. Notice that in the execution plan the operation RESULT CACHE confirms that the result cache is enabled for the query. However, the column Starts in the execution plan clearly shows that all operations have been executed at least once. The execution of all operations is necessary because this is the first execution of the query, and consequently, the result cache does not contain the result set yet.

```
SQL> SELECT /*+ result_cache */
  2         p.prod_category, c.country_id,
  3         sum(s.quantity_sold) AS quantity_sold,
  4         sum(s.amount_sold) AS amount_sold
  5  FROM sales s, customers c, products p
  6  WHERE s.cust_id = c.cust_id
  7  AND s.prod_id = p.prod_id
  8  GROUP BY p.prod_category, c.country_id
  9  ORDER BY p.prod_category, c.country_id;

Elapsed: 00:00:01.78
```

```
--------------------------------------------------------------------------------
| Id  | Operation              | Name                          | Starts | A-Rows |
--------------------------------------------------------------------------------
|   1 |  RESULT CACHE          | fxtfk2w8kgrhm6c5j1y73twrgp    |     1  |    81  |
|   2 |   SORT GROUP BY        |                               |     1  |    81  |
|*  3 |    HASH JOIN           |                               |     1  |   918K |
|   4 |     TABLE ACCESS FULL  | PRODUCTS                      |     1  |    72  |
|*  5 |     HASH JOIN          |                               |     1  |   918K |
|   6 |      TABLE ACCESS FULL | CUSTOMERS                     |     1  |  55500 |
|   7 |      PARTITION RANGE ALL|                              |     1  |   918K |
|   8 |       TABLE ACCESS FULL | SALES                        |    28  |   918K |
--------------------------------------------------------------------------------
```

The second execution takes 0.07 seconds. This time the column `Starts` in the execution plan shows that all operations, except for `RESULT CACHE`, have not been executed. In other words, the result set for the query is served directly from the result cache.

```
SQL> SELECT /*+ result_cache */
  2          p.prod_category, c.country_id,
  3          sum(s.quantity_sold) AS quantity_sold,
  4          sum(s.amount_sold) AS amount_sold
  5  FROM sales s, customers c, products p
  6  WHERE s.cust_id = c.cust_id
  7  AND s.prod_id = p.prod_id
  8  GROUP BY p.prod_category, c.country_id
  9  ORDER BY p.prod_category, c.country_id;
```

Elapsed: 00:00:00.07

```
--------------------------------------------------------------------------------
| Id  | Operation              | Name                          | Starts | A-Rows |
--------------------------------------------------------------------------------
|   1 |  RESULT CACHE          | fxtfk2w8kgrhm6c5j1y73twrgp    |     1  |    81  |
|   2 |   SORT GROUP BY        |                               |     0  |     0  |
|*  3 |    HASH JOIN           |                               |     0  |     0  |
|   4 |     TABLE ACCESS FULL  | PRODUCTS                      |     0  |     0  |
|*  5 |     HASH JOIN          |                               |     0  |     0  |
|   6 |      TABLE ACCESS FULL | CUSTOMERS                     |     0  |     0  |
|   7 |      PARTITION RANGE ALL|                              |     0  |     0  |
|   8 |       TABLE ACCESS FULL | SALES                        |     0  |     0  |
--------------------------------------------------------------------------------
```

In the execution plan, it is interesting to note that a name, the *cache ID*, is associated with the operation `RESULT CACHE`. If you know the cache ID, you can query the view v$result_cache_objects to display information about the cached data. The following query shows that the cached result set has been published (in other words, available for use), when the result cache was created, how much time (in hundredths of seconds) it took to build it, how many rows are stored in it, and how many times it has been referenced. Other views that provide information about the result cache are v$result_cache_dependency, v$result_cache_memory, and v$result_cache_statistics.

```
SQL> SELECT status, creation_timestamp, build_time, row_count, scan_count
  2  FROM v$result_cache_objects
  3  WHERE cache_id = 'fxtfk2w8kgrhm6c5j1y73twrgp';

STATUS     CREATION_TIMESTAMP    BUILD_TIME ROW_COUNT SCAN_COUNT
---------  -------------------   ---------- --------- ----------
Published  08.04.2008 23:51:38          168        81          1
```

To guarantee the consistency of the results (that is, that the result set is the same whether it is served from the result cache or calculated from the database content), every time that something changes in the objects referenced by a query, the cache entries dependent on it are invalidated (an exception with remote objects will be discussed shortly). This is the case even if no real changes occur. For example, even a SELECT FOR UPDATE, immediately followed by a COMMIT, leads to the invalidation of the cache entries that depend on the selected table.

The following are the dynamic initialization parameters that control the server result cache:

- result_cache_max_size specifies (in bytes) the amount of shared pool memory that can be used for the result cache. If it is set to 0, the feature is disabled. The default value, which is greater than 0, is derived from the size of the shared pool. Memory allocation is dynamic, and therefore, this initialization parameter specifies only the upper limit. You can display the currently allocated memory by using a query like the following:

```
SQL> SELECT name, sum(bytes)
  2  FROM v$sgastat
  3  WHERE name LIKE 'Result Cache%'
  4  GROUP BY rollup(name);

NAME                         SUM(BYTES)
-------------------------    ----------
Result Cache                     196888
Result Cache: Bloom Fltr           2048
Result Cache: Cache Mgr             152
Result Cache: Memory Mgr            200
Result Cache: State Objs           2896
                                 202184
```

- result_cache_mode specifies in which situation the result cache is used. You can set it either to manual, which is the default, or to force. With manual, the result cache is used only if the hint result_cache is specified. With force, the result cache is used for all queries that do not contain the hint no_result_cache. Since in most situations you want to use the result cache for a limited number of queries, I advise you to leave this initialization parameter to its default value and to add the hint result_cache only when necessary.

- `result_cache_max_result` specifies (in percent) the amount of `result_cache_max_size` that any single result can use. The default value is 5. Values from 0 to 100 are allowed. Results that exceed this limit are invalidated.

- `result_cache_remote_expiration` specifies (in minutes) the temporal validity of a result based on remote objects. This is necessary because the invalidation of results based on remote objects is not performed when the remote objects have been changed. Instead, the results are invalidated when the temporal validity defined by this initialization parameter is elapsed. The default value is 0, which means that the caching of queries based on remote objects is disabled.

The initialization parameters `result_cache_max_size` and `result_cache_max_result` can be changed at the system level only. The other two, `result_cache_mode` and `result_cache_remote_expiration`, can also be changed at the session level.

■**Caution** Setting the initialization parameter `result_cache_remote_expiration` to a value greater than 0 can lead to stale results. Therefore, you should use values greater than 0 only if you fully understand and accept the implications of doing so.

There are a few, albeit obvious, limitations with the utilization of the result cache:

- Queries that reference nondeterministic functions, sequences, and temporary tables are not cached.

- Queries that violate read consistency are not cached. For example, the result set created by a session with outstanding transactions on the referenced tables cannot be cached.

- Queries that reference data dictionary views are not cached.

DBMS_RESULT_CACHE

You can use the package `dbms_result_cache` to manage the result cache. To do this, it provides the following subprograms:

- `bypass` temporarily disables (or enables) the result cache at the session or system level.

- `flush` removes all the objects from the result cache.

- `invalidate` invalidates all result sets that are dependent on a given database object.

- `invalidate_object` invalidates a single cache entry.

- `memory_report` produces a report on memory utilization.

- `status` shows the status of the result cache.

PL/SQL Function Result Cache

The PL/SQL function result cache is similar to the server result cache, but it supports PL/SQL functions. It also shares the same memory structures as the server result cache. Its purpose is to store the return value of functions (and only functions—the result cache cannot be used with procedures) in the result cache. Obviously, functions with different input values are cached in separate cache entries. The following example, which is an excerpt of the output generated by the script result_cache_plsql.sql, shows a function for which the result cache is enabled. To enable it, the clause RESULT_CACHE is specified. Optionally, the clause RELIES_ON can also specify on which table(s) the return value of the function depends. This information is critical to the invalidation of the cache entries.

```
SQL> CREATE OR REPLACE FUNCTION f(p IN NUMBER)
  2    RETURN NUMBER
  3    RESULT_CACHE RELIES_ON (t)
  4  IS
  5    l_ret NUMBER;
  6  BEGIN
  7    SELECT count(*) INTO l_ret
  8    FROM t
  9    WHERE id = p;
 10    RETURN l_ret;
 11  END;
 12  /
```

In the following example, the function is called 10,000 times without result cache (with the procedure bypass, the cache is temporarily disabled). The execution takes 4.76 seconds.

```
SQL> execute dbms_result_cache.bypass(bypass_mode => TRUE, session => TRUE)

SQL> SELECT count(f(1)) FROM t;

COUNT(F(1))
-----------
      10000

Elapsed: 00:00:04.76
```

Now, let's call the function 10,000 times again, but this time with the result cache enabled. The execution takes only 0.04 seconds.

```
SQL> execute dbms_result_cache.bypass(bypass_mode => FALSE, session => TRUE)

SQL> SELECT count(f(1)) FROM t;

COUNT(F(1))
-----------
      10000

Elapsed: 00:00:00.04
```

■**Caution** If the clause RELIES_ON is not specified, or contains wrong information, no invalidation will occur because of modifications that take place in the objects on which the function depends. Consequently, stale results can occur.

There are a few limitations to the utilization of the PL/SQL function result cache. The result cache cannot be used for the following functions:

- Functions with OUT and/or IN OUT parameters

- Functions that are defined with invoker's rights

- Pipelined table functions

- Functions called from anonymous blocks

- Functions with IN parameters or return values of the following types: LOBs, REF CURSOR, objects, and records

In addition, note that unhandled exceptions are not stored in the result cache. In other words, if the function raises an exception and the exception is propagated to the caller, the next call of the same function will be executed again.

Client Result Cache

The client result cache is a client-side cache that stores the result sets of queries. Its purpose and working is similar to the server result cache. Compared to server-side implementation, there are two important differences. First, it avoids the client/server round-trips needed to execute SQL statements. This is a big advantage. Second, the invalidations are based on a polling mechanism, and therefore, consistency cannot be guaranteed. This is a big disadvantage.

To implement polling, a client has to regularly execute database calls to check the database engine to see whether one of its cached result sets has to be invalidated. To minimize the overhead associated with polling, every time a client executes a database call for another reason, it checks the validity of the cached result sets as well. In this way, database calls that are used exclusively for the invalidation of the cached result sets are avoided for clients that are steadily executing "regular" database calls.

Even if this is a client-side cache, you have to enable it on the server side. The following are the initialization parameters that control the client result cache:

- client_result_cache_size specifies (in bytes) the maximum amount of memory that every client process can use for the result cache. If it is set to 0, which is the default, the feature is disabled. This initialization parameter is static and can be set only at the instance level. An instance bounce is therefore necessary to change it.

- client_result_cache_lag specifies (in milliseconds) the maximum time lag between two database calls. In other words, it specifies how long stale result sets can remain in the client-side cache. The default value is 3,000. This initialization parameter is static and can be set only at the instance level. An instance bounce is therefore necessary to change it.

In addition to the server-side configuration, the following parameters can be specified in the client's `sqlnet.ora` file:

- `oci_result_cache_max_size` overrides the server-side setting that is specified with the initialization parameter `client_result_cache_size`. Note, however, that if the client result cache is disabled on the server side, this parameter cannot enable it.

- `oci_result_cache_max_rset_size` specifies (in bytes) the maximum amount of memory any single result set can use.

- `oci_result_cache_max_rset_rows` specifies the maximum number of rows any single result set can store.

When to Use It

If you are dealing with a performance problem that is caused by an application that executes the same operation over and over again, you have to reduce either the frequency of execution or the response time of the operation. Ideally, you should do both. However, sometimes (for example, when the application's code cannot be modified) you can implement only the latter. To reduce response time, you should initially employ the techniques presented in Chapters 9 and 10. If this is not enough, only then should advanced optimization techniques, such as result caches, be considered. Basically, result caches are effective given two conditions. First, the same data is queried more often than it is modified. Second, there is enough memory to store the results.

In most situations, you should not enable the result caches for all queries. In fact, most of the time, only specific queries can benefit from the result cache. For the others, result cache management is simply pure overhead that might also overstress the cache. Also keep in mind that server-side caches are shared by all sessions, so their access is synchronized (they can become a point of serialization like any shared resource). Therefore, you should enable result caches only for the queries requiring them. In other words, the hint `result_cache` should be added selectively and only when it is really necessary to improve performance.

The server result cache does not completely avoid the overhead of executing a query. This means that if a query already performs relatively few logical reads per row (and no physical reads) without using the result cache, it will not be much faster when using it. Remember, both the buffer cache and the result cache are stored in the same shared memory.

The PL/SQL function result cache is especially useful for functions that are frequently used in SQL statements. In fact, it is not uncommon for such functions to be called for every row that is processed or returned, while the input parameters are different on only a few rows. However, functions that are frequently called from PL/SQL can also take advantage of the result cache.

Because of the problem with consistency, the client result cache should be used only for read-only or read-mostly tables.

Finally, note that you can take advantage of server and client result caches at the same time. However, for the queries executed by the client, you cannot choose to bypass the client result cache and use the server result cache only. In other words, both result caches are used.

Pitfalls and Fallacies

As pointed out in the previous sections, the consistency of the results is not guaranteed in the following cases:

- When the initialization parameter `result_cache_remote_expiration` is set to a value greater than 0 and queries via database link are executed

- When PL/SQL functions that do not specify (or wrongly specify) the clause `RELIES_ON` are defined

- When the client result cache is used

In this case it is, therefore, best to avoid result caches, unless you fully understand and accept the implications of each of these situations.

Parallel Processing

When you submit a SQL statement to a database engine, by default it is executed serially by a single server process. Therefore, even if the server running the database engine has several CPUs, your SQL statement runs on a single CPU. The purpose of parallel processing is to distribute the execution of a single SQL statement over several CPUs.

■**Note** Parallel processing is available in Enterprise Edition only.

How It Works

Before describing the specifics of how queries, DML statements, and DDL statements are executed in parallel, it is important to understand the basics of parallel processing, understand how to configure an instance to take advantage of parallel processing, and understand how to control the degree of parallelism.

■**Note** Because, as of Oracle Database 10*g*, the execution plans related to parallel processing are much more descriptive, I will show execution plans generated on only that version in the following sections. If you want to compare them with the Oracle9*i* execution plans, you can run the scripts available for download.

Basics

Without parallel processing, a SQL statement is executed serially by a single server process that, in turn, runs on a single CPU. This means that the amount of resources used for the execution of a SQL statement is restricted by the amount of processing a single CPU can do. For example, as illustrated in Figure 11-5, if a SQL statement executes a data access operation that scans a whole segment (which is probably an I/O bound operation if most of the data is read from the disk) independently of the total throughput the I/O subsystem can deliver, the response time is limited by the bandwidth that a single CPU can use. This bandwidth can of course be limited because of hardware limitations of the data access path between the CPU and the disk but also because the execution is serial: when the server process is on the CPU, by definition it is not accessing the disk (asynchronous I/O are an exception to this) and thus not taking advantage of the total throughput the I/O subsystem can deliver.

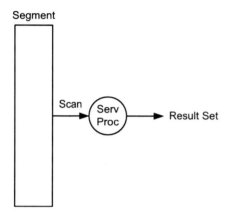

Figure 11-5. *Serially executed SQL statements are processed by a single server process.*

The following SQL statement with the related execution plan shows an example of the processing illustrated in Figure 11-5:

```
SELECT * FROM t
```

```
-----------------------------------
| Id | Operation      | Name |
-----------------------------------
|  0 | SELECT STATEMENT |      |
|  1 |  TABLE ACCESS FULL| T    |
-----------------------------------
```

The aim of parallel processing is to split one large task into several smaller subtasks. If there is a parallel processed SQL statement, this basically means there are several *slave processes* that cooperate to execute a single SQL statement. The coordination of the slave processes is under the control of the server process associated to the session that submits the SQL statement. Because of this role, it is commonly called the *query coordinator*. The query coordinator is responsible for acquiring the slave processes, assigning a subtask to each of them, collecting and combining the partial result sets they deliver, and returning the final result set to the client. For example, in the case of a SQL statement that requires a scan of a whole segment, the query coordinator can instruct each of the slave processes to scan part of the segment and to deliver the necessary data to it. Figure 11-6 illustrates this. Since each of the four slave processes is able to run on a different CPU, in this case the response time is no longer limited by the bandwidth that a single CPU can use.

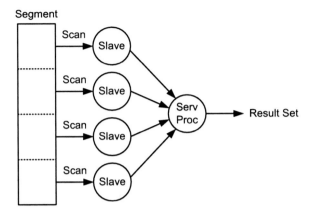

Figure 11-6. *Parallel executed SQL statements are processed by a set of slave processes coordinated by a server process (aka query coordinator).*

In a parallel scan like the one illustrated in Figure 11-6, the work is distributed among the slave processes in units of work called *granules.* Each slave process, at a given time, works on a single granule. If there are more granules than slave processes, when a slave process has finished working on a granule, it will receive another one to work on until all granules have been processed. The database engine can use two types of granules:

- A *partition granule* is a whole partition or subpartition. Obviously, this type of granule can be used only with partitioned segments.

- A *block range granule* is a range of blocks from a segment dynamically defined at runtime (not at parse time).

Since the definition of partition granules is static (only the number, because of partition pruning, can change), block range granules tend to be used most of the time. Their main advantage is that they allow, in most situations, an even distribution of the work to the slave processes. In fact, with partition granules, the distribution of the work is highly dependent not only on the ratio of the number of slave processes to the number of partitions but also on the amount of data stored in each partition. If work is not evenly distributed, some of the slave processes could work much more than others, and therefore, this could lead to a longer response time. As a result, the overall efficiency of the parallel execution might be jeopardized.

The following execution plan shows an example of the processing illustrated in Figure 11-6. Operation 4 (TABLE ACCESS FULL) scans part of table t. Which part it scans depends on its parent operation, 3 (PX BLOCK ITERATOR). This is the operation related to block range granules. Then, operation 2 (PX SEND QC) sends the retrieved data to the query coordinator. Note that in the execution plan, you identify the operations executed by a set of slave processes by looking at the column TQ. In this execution plan, operations 2 to 4 have the same value (Q1,00) and so are executed by the same set of slave processes (note that based on the execution plan, you cannot know how many slave processes belong to the set). Also notice the parallel to serial (P->S) communication between the slave processes and the query coordinator (QC) in operation 2. This is necessary because, as shown in Figure 11-6, four slave processes send data to the query coordinator.

```
SELECT * FROM t
```

```
---------------------------------------------------------------------
| Id  | Operation              | Name     |   TQ  |IN-OUT| PQ Distrib |
---------------------------------------------------------------------
|   0 | SELECT STATEMENT       |          |       |      |            |
|   1 |  PX COORDINATOR        |          |       |      |            |
|   2 |   PX SEND QC (RANDOM)| :TQ10000 | Q1,00 | P->S | QC (RAND)  |
|   3 |    PX BLOCK ITERATOR  |          | Q1,00 | PCWC |            |
|   4 |     TABLE ACCESS FULL| T        | Q1,00 | PCWP |            |
---------------------------------------------------------------------
```

Data access operations are not the only operations that can be executed in parallel. In fact, among other things, the database engine is able to parallelize inserts, joins, aggregations, and sorts. When a SQL statement executes two or more independent operations (for example, a scan and a sort), it is common for the database engine to use two sets of slave processes. For example, as illustrated in Figure 11-7, if a SQL statement executes a scan and then a sort, one set is used for the scan and another set is used for the sort.

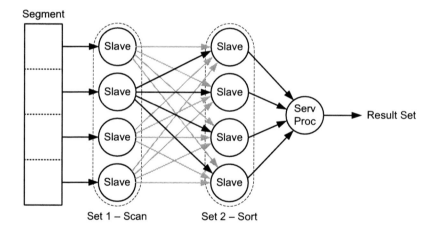

Figure 11-7. *Several sets of slave processes can be used to execute a SQL statement.*

The parallelization of a single operation is referred to as *intra-operation parallelism*. For example, in Figure 11-7, intra-operation parallelism (with four slaves) is used twice: once for the scan and once for the sort. When several sets of slave processes are used to execute a SQL statement, the parallelization is referred to as *inter-operation parallelism*. For example, in Figure 11-7, inter-operation parallelism is used between set 1 (scan) and set 2 (sort).

When inter-operation parallelism is used, communication between the sets of slave processes takes place. In Figure 11-7, set 1 reads data from the segment and sends it to set 2 for the sort. The slave processes that send data are called *producers*. The slave processes that receive data are called *consumers*. Depending on the operation executed by the producers and the consumers, rows are distributed using one of the following methods:

- *Broadcast*: Each producer sends all rows to each consumer.

- *Round-robin*: Producers send each row to a single consumer one at a time, like when dealing cards. As a result, rows are evenly distributed among consumers.

- *Range*: Producers send specific ranges of rows to different consumers. Dynamic range partitioning is performed to determine which row has to be sent to which consumer. For example, for a sort, this method range partitions the rows based on the columns used in the ORDER BY clause.

- *Hash*: Producers send rows to consumers as determined by a hash function. Dynamic hash partitioning is performed to determine which row is to be sent to which consumer. For example, for an aggregation, this method may hash partitions the rows based on the columns used in the GROUP BY clause.

- *QC Random*: Each producer sends all rows to the query coordinator. The order is not important (hence, random). This is the most commonly used distribution to communicate with the query coordinator.

- *QC Order*: Each producer sends all rows to the query coordinator. The order is important. For example, this is used by a sort executed in parallel to send data to the query coordinator.

RELATIONSHIP BETWEEN PARALLEL OPERATIONS

The following relationships between parallel operations are used in execution plans executed in parallel:

- Parallel to serial (P->S): A parallel operation sends data to a serial operation. For example, this is used in every execution plan to send data to the query coordinator.

- Parallel to parallel (P->P): A parallel operation sends data to another parallel operation. This is used when there are two sets of slave processes.

- Parallel combined with parent (PCWP): An operation is executed in parallel by the same slave processes that also execute in parallel with the parent operation in the execution plan. Therefore, no communication takes place.

- Parallel combined with child (PCWC): An operation is executed in parallel by the same slave processes that also execute in parallel with the child operation in the execution plan. Therefore, no communication takes place.

- Serial to parallel (S->P): A serial operation sends data to a parallel operation. Since most of the time this is inefficient, it should be avoided. There are two main reasons. First, a single process might not be able to produce data as fast as several processes can consume it. If it is the case, the consumers spend much of their time waiting for data instead of doing real work. Second, unnecessary communication is needed to send data from the operation executed serially and the operation executed in parallel.

In the output generated by the package dbms_xplan, the relationship between parallel operations is provided in the column IN-OUT.

The following execution plan is an example of the processing illustrated in Figure 11-7. Operations 5 to 7 have the same value for the column TQ (Q1,00), which means they are executed by one set of slave processes (set 1 in Figure 11-7). On the other hand, operations 2 to 4 have another value (Q1,01) and so are executed by another set of slave processes (set 2 in Figure 11-7). Set 1, the producer, scans table t based on block range granules and sends the retrieved data to set 2. In turn, set 2, the consumer, receives the data, sorts it, and sends the sorted result set to the query coordinator. Set 1 and set 2 do their processing concurrently. Since they are communicating with each other, the set that processes data faster waits for the other one. For example, in the following execution plan, it is not unlikely that set 2 is able to consume data much faster than set 1 is able to produce it. If it is the case, set 2 spends a lot of time waiting for set 1.

```
SELECT * FROM t ORDER BY id
```

```
-------------------------------------------------------------------------
| Id | Operation            | Name      |   TQ  |IN-OUT| PQ Distrib |
-------------------------------------------------------------------------
|  0 | SELECT STATEMENT     |           |       |      |            |
|  1 |  PX COORDINATOR      |           |       |      |            |
|  2 |   PX SEND QC (ORDER) | :TQ10001  | Q1,01 | P->S | QC (ORDER) |
|  3 |    SORT ORDER BY     |           | Q1,01 | PCWP |            |
|  4 |     PX RECEIVE       |           | Q1,01 | PCWP |            |
|  5 |      PX SEND RANGE   | :TQ10000  | Q1,00 | P->P | RANGE      |
|  6 |       PX BLOCK ITERATOR |        | Q1,00 | PCWC |            |
|  7 |        TABLE ACCESS FULL| T       | Q1,00 | PCWP |            |
-------------------------------------------------------------------------
```

A producer sends data to a consumer through a memory structure in the SGA called a *table queue*. For each producer-consumer pair, there is a table queue. For example, in Figure 11-7, there are a total of 16 table queues for the communication between the two sets of slaves. In addition, four table queues are used for the communication between set 2 and the server process. Producers write into table queues with the operation PX SEND. Consumers read from them with the operation PX RECEIVE—query coordinators are an exception because they use the operation PX COORDINATOR.

Configuration

The maximum number of slave processes per instance is limited. For this reason, an instance maintains a pool of slave processes. A query coordinator requests slave processes from the pool; then it uses them to execute one SQL statement, and finally, when the execution is complete, it returns them to the pool. The following initialization parameters are set to configure the pool:

- parallel_min_servers specifies the number of slave processes that are started at instance startup. These slave processes are always available and don't need to be started when a server process requires them. The slave processes exceeding this minimum are dynamically started when required and, once returned to the pool, stay idle for five minutes. If they are not reused in that period, they are shut down. By default, this initialization parameter is set to 0. This means that no slave processes are created at startup. I advise changing this value only if some SQL statements are waiting too long for the startup of the slave processes. The wait event related to this operation is os thread startup.

- `parallel_max_servers` specifies the maximum number of slave processes available in the pool. It is difficult to give advice on how to set this parameter. Nevertheless, a value of 8–10 times the number of cores (in other words, the value of the initialization parameter `cpu_count`) is a good starting point. The default value depends on several other initialization parameters, the version, and the platform.

To display the status of the pool, you can use the following query:

```
SQL> SELECT *
  2  FROM v$px_process_sysstat
  3  WHERE statistic LIKE 'Servers%';

STATISTIC          VALUE
------------------ -----
Servers In Use         4
Servers Available      8
Servers Started       46
Servers Shutdown      34
Servers Highwater     12
Servers Cleaned Up     0
```

The table queues used for communication between processes are memory structures that can be allocated from either the shared pool or the large pool. However, it is *not* recommended to use the shared pool for them. The large pool, which is specialized for nonreusable memory structures, is a much better choice. There are two situations that lead to a utilization of the large pool for table queues:

- Automatic SGA management is enabled through the initialization parameter `sga_target` or, as of Oracle Database 11*g*, `memory_target`.

- The initialization parameter `parallel_automatic_tuning` is set to `TRUE`. Note that this initialization parameter is deprecated as of Oracle Database 10*g*. However, if you do *not* want to use automatic SGA management, setting it is the only way to use the large pool for parallel processing as of Oracle Database 10*g*.

■**Note** Despite its name, the initialization parameter `parallel_automatic_tuning` does only two simple things. First, it changes the default value of several initialization parameters related to parallel processing. Second, it instructs the database engine to use the large pool for the table queues.

Each table queue is composed of up to three (four with RAC) buffers. The size of each buffer (in bytes) is set through the initialization parameter `parallel_execution_message_size`. The default size is either 2,152 bytes or, if `parallel_automatic_tuning` is set to `TRUE`, 4,096 bytes. This is usually too small. For the best performance, you should set it to the highest supported value. Depending on the platform you are using, this could be either 16KB, 32KB, or 64KB.

When increasing it, you should make sure that the necessary memory is available. You can use Formula 11-1 to compute the minimum amount of the large pool that should be available for a non-RAC instance.

$$large\_pool\_size \geq parallel\_max\_servers^2 \cdot parallel\_execution\_message\_size \cdot 3$$

Formula 11-1. *The amount of the large pool used by non-RAC instances for table queues (for RAC instances multiply by 4 instead of by 3)*

To display how much of the large pool is currently in use by an instance, you can run the following query:

```
SQL> SELECT *
  2  FROM v$sgastat
  3  WHERE name = 'PX msg pool';

POOL        NAME         BYTES
---------- ----------- -------
large pool PX msg pool 1032960
```

Degree of Parallelism

The number of slave processes used for intra-operation parallelism is called *degree of parallelism* (DOP). A degree of parallelism is associated to each table and index. It is used by default for the operations referencing it. Its default value is 1, which means that no parallel processing is used. As shown in the following SQL statements, the degree of parallelism is set with the PARALLEL clause, either when an object is created or later:

```
CREATE TABLE t (id NUMBER, pad VARCHAR2(1000)) PARALLEL 4

ALTER TABLE t PARALLEL 2

CREATE INDEX i ON t (id) PARALLEL 4

ALTER INDEX i PARALLEL 2
```

■**Caution** It is quite common to use parallel processing to improve the performance of maintenance tasks or batch jobs that create tables or indexes. For that purpose, the PARALLEL clause is specified. Be aware, however, that when this clause is used, the degree of parallelism is used not only during the creation of the table or index but also later for the operations executed on it. Therefore, if you want to use parallel processing only during the creation of a table or index, it is essential that you alter the degree of parallelism once created.

To disable parallel processing, either the degree of parallelism is set to 1 or the NOPARALLEL clause is specified:

```
ALTER TABLE t PARALLEL 1

ALTER INDEX i NOPARALLEL
```

Note When the PARALLEL clause is used without specifying a degree of parallelism (for example, ALTER TABLE t PARALLEL), a system default value is used. To compute this default value, the database engine multiplies the number of available CPUs (the value of the initialization parameters cpu_count) by the number of slave processes that a CPU is expected to handle (the initialization parameter parallel_threads_per_cpu—on most platforms, the default value of this parameter is 2). Most of the time, the default degree of parallelism is too high. Therefore, I usually advise to specify a value.

To override the degree of parallelism defined at the table and index levels, it is possible to use the hints parallel, no_parallel (noparallel in Oracle9*i*), parallel_index, and no_parallel_index (noparallel_index in Oracle9*i*). The first two override the setting at the table level, and the third and fourth override it at the index level. Examples of their utilization are provided in the next sections. When a different degree of parallelism is specified for different tables or indexes used in a SQL statement, a single degree of parallelism is calculated by the database engine and used for the whole SQL statement. The rules are fully documented in the manuals, but usually, the degree of parallelism chosen is simply the maximum of the ones specified at the table or index level.

Since the degree of parallelism defines the number of slave processes for intra-operation parallelism, when inter-operation parallelism is used, the number of slave processes used to execute a SQL statement is twice the degree of parallelism. This is because at most two sets of slave processes are active at any given time, and the degree of parallelism of each set must be equal.

As described in the previous section, the maximum number of slave processes in the pool is limited by the initialization parameter parallel_max_servers. It is therefore essential to understand that the degree of parallelism specified at the table and index levels defines only how many slave processes the query coordinator requests from the pool and not how many slave processes are actually provided to it. In fact, the database engine, depending on how many slave processes are already running at the time the query coordinator requests some of them, might not be able to fulfill the request. For example, if the maximum number of slave processes is set to 40, for the execution plan illustrated in Figure 11-7 (that requires eight slave processes) only 5 concurrent SQL statements (40/8) can be executed with the required degree of parallelism. When the limit is reached, there are two possibilities: either the degree of parallelism is downgraded (in other words, reduced) or an error (ORA-12827: insufficient parallel query slaves available) is returned to the server process. To configure which one of these two possibilities is used, you have to set the initialization parameter parallel_min_percent. It can be set to an integer value ranging from 0 to 100. There are three main situations:

- *0*: This value (which is the default) specifies that the degree of parallelism can be silently downgraded. In other words, the database engine can provide as many slave processes as possible. If less than two slave processes are available, the execution is serialized. This means that the SQL statements are always executed, and the error ORA-12827 is never raised.

- *1–99*: The values ranging from 1 to 99 define a limit for the downgrade. At least the specified percentage of the slave processes must be provided; otherwise, the error ORA-12827 is raised. For example, if it is set to 25 and 16 slave processes are requested, at least 4 (16*25/100) must be provided to avoid the error.

- *100*: With this value, either all the requested slave processes are provided or the error ORA-12827 is raised.

The following example (based on the script px_dop1.sql), executed while no other parallel execution was running, illustrates this:

```
SQL> show parameter parallel_max_servers

NAME                     TYPE     VALUE
--------------------- -------- ------
parallel_max_servers  integer  40

SQL> ALTER TABLE t PARALLEL 50;

SQL> ALTER SESSION SET parallel_min_percent = 80;

SQL> SELECT count(pad) FROM t;

  COUNT(*)
----------
    100000

SQL> ALTER SESSION SET parallel_min_percent = 81;

SQL> SELECT count(pad) FROM t;
SELECT count(pad) FROM t
*
ERROR at line 1:
ORA-12827: insufficient parallel query slaves available
```

Another initialization parameter that influences the number of slave processes assigned to a server process is parallel_adaptive_multi_user. It accepts two values:

- FALSE: If the pool is not exhausted, the requested number of slave processes is assigned to the server process. This is the default value in Oracle9*i*.

- TRUE: As the number of already assigned slave processes increases, the requested degree of parallelism is automatically reduced, even if there are still enough servers in the pool to satisfy the required degree of parallelism. This is the default value as of Oracle Database 10*g*.

To illustrate the impact of the initialization parameter parallel_adaptive_multi_user, let's take a look at the number of slave processes allocated when an increasing number of parallel operations are executed at short intervals. For this purpose, the following shell script was used. Its purpose is to start 15 parallel operations with a degree of parallelism of 8 (this is the default at the table level) at intervals of 5 seconds.

```
sql="select * from t;"
for i in 1 2 3 4 5 6 7 8 9 10 11 12 13 14 15
do
  sqlplus -s $user/$password <<<$sql &
  sleep 5
done
```

Figure 11-8 summarizes the results measured on Oracle Database 10g. With the initialization parameter `parallel_adaptive_multi_user` set to `FALSE`, the number of allocated slave processes is proportional to the number of executed parallel operations up to the limit imposed by the initialization parameter `parallel_max_servers` (80 in this case). With the initialization parameter `parallel_adaptive_multi_user` set to `TRUE`, starting from four concurrent parallel operations, the degree of parallelism decreases, and therefore, fewer slave processes than requested are allocated.

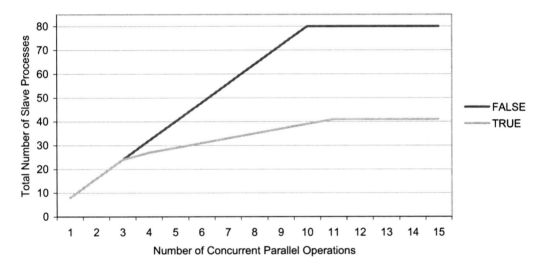

Figure 11-8. *Impact of the initialization parameter* `parallel_adaptive_multi_user`

In Figure 11-8 it is important to note that when the initialization parameter `parallel_adaptive_multi_user` is set to `TRUE`, the pool is not exhausted. This is because the reduction factor computed by the algorithm that is responsible for adapting the degree of parallelism is based on the default degree of parallelism and not on the requested degree of parallelism. Because of that, I usually advise setting the initialization parameter `parallel_adaptive_multi_user` to `FALSE`.

If you want to know how many operations were downgraded on a running instance, and by how much, you can execute the following query. Obviously, when you see too many downgrades, especially when many operations are serialized, you should question the configuration.

```
SQL> SELECT name, value
  2  FROM v$sysstat
  3  WHERE name like 'Parallel operations%';

NAME                                        VALUE
------------------------------------------- ------
Parallel operations not downgraded              8
Parallel operations downgraded to serial       18
Parallel operations downgraded 75 to 99 pct     0
Parallel operations downgraded 50 to 75 pct    14
Parallel operations downgraded 25 to 50 pct     0
Parallel operations downgraded 1 to 25 pct      0
```

Parallel Queries

The following operations, in both queries and subqueries, can be executed in parallel:

- Full table scans, full partition scans, and fast full index scans

- Index full and range scans, but only if the index is partitioned (at a given time, a partition can be accessed by a single slave process only; as a side effect, the degree of parallelism is limited by the number of accessed partitions)

- Joins (Chapter 10 provides some examples)

- Set operators

- Sorts

- Aggregations

■**Note** Full table scans, full partition scans, and fast full index scans executed in parallel use direct reads and, therefore, bypass the buffer cache. However, index full and range scans do regular physical reads.

Parallel queries are *enabled* by default. At the session level, you can enable and disable them with the following SQL statements:

```
ALTER SESSION ENABLE PARALLEL QUERY
```

```
ALTER SESSION DISABLE PARALLEL QUERY
```

In addition, it is also possible to enable parallel queries and, at the same time, override the degree of parallelism defined at the table or index level with the following SQL statement:

```
ALTER SESSION FORCE PARALLEL QUERY PARALLEL 4
```

Be aware, however, that hints have precedence over the setting at the session level. On one hand, even if parallel queries are disabled at the session level, hints can force a parallel execution. The only way to really turn off parallel queries is to set the initialization parameter parallel_max_servers to 0. On the other hand, even if a parallel degree is forced at the session level, hints can lead to another degree of parallelism. To check whether parallel queries are enabled or disabled at the session level, you can execute a query like the following one (the column pq_status is set to either ENABLED, DISABLED, or FORCED):

```
SELECT pq_status
FROM v$session
WHERE sid = sys_context('userenv','sid')
```

The following execution plan shows an example with a parallel index range scan, a parallel full table scan, and a parallel hash join. It is based on the script px_query.sql. Notice the hints: the hint parallel_index is used for an index access, the hint parallel is used for a table scan. Both hints specify a degree of parallelism of 2. In addition, the hint pq_distribute is used to specify the distribution method. The column TQ contains three values, which means that three sets of slave processes are used to perform this execution plan. Operation 8 scans index i1 in parallel (this is possible because index i1 is partitioned). Then, operation 7, with the rowid extracted from index i1, accesses table t1. As shown in operation 6, partition granules are used for these two operations. Then, the data is sent with a hash distribution to the consumers (the slave processes of set Q1,02). When the consumers receive the data (operation 4), they pass it to operation 3 to build the hash table for the hash join. As soon as all the data of table t1 is fully processed, the parallel full scan of table t2 can start. This is performed in operation 12. As shown in operation 11, block range granules are used for this operation. Then, the data is sent with a hash distribution to the consumers (the slave processes of the set Q1,02). When the consumers receive data (operation 9), they pass it to operation 3 to probe the hash table. Finally, operation 2 (PX SEND QC) sends the rows fulfilling the join condition to the query coordinator. Figure 11-9 illustrates this execution plan.

```
SELECT /*+ leading(t1) use_hash(t2)
           index(t1) parallel_index(t1 2)
           full(t2) parallel(t2 2)
           pq_distribute(t2 hash,hash) */ *
FROM t1, t2
WHERE t1.id > 9000
AND t1.id = t2.id+1
```

```
--------------------------------------------------------------------------------
| Id  | Operation                          | Name      |   TQ  |IN-OUT| PQ Distrib |
--------------------------------------------------------------------------------
|   0 | SELECT STATEMENT                   |           |       |      |            |
|   1 |  PX COORDINATOR                    |           |       |      |            |
|   2 |   PX SEND QC (RANDOM)              | :TQ10002  | Q1,02 | P->S | QC (RAND)  |
|*  3 |    HASH JOIN BUFFERED              |           | Q1,02 | PCWP |            |
|   4 |     PX RECEIVE                     |           | Q1,02 | PCWP |            |
|   5 |      PX SEND HASH                  | :TQ10000  | Q1,00 | P->P | HASH       |
|   6 |       PX PARTITION HASH ALL        |           | Q1,00 | PCWC |            |
|   7 |        TABLE ACCESS BY INDEX ROWID | T1        | Q1,00 | PCWP |            |
|*  8 |         INDEX RANGE SCAN           | I1        | Q1,00 | PCWP |            |
|   9 |     PX RECEIVE                     |           | Q1,02 | PCWP |            |
|  10 |      PX SEND HASH                  | :TQ10001  | Q1,01 | P->P | HASH       |
|  11 |       PX BLOCK ITERATOR            |           | Q1,01 | PCWC |            |
|* 12 |        TABLE ACCESS FULL           | T2        | Q1,01 | PCWP |            |
--------------------------------------------------------------------------------
```

```
 3 - access("T1"."ID"="T2"."ID"+1)
 8 - access("T1"."ID">9000)
12 - filter("T2"."ID"+1>9000)
```

According to the execution plan and Figure 11-9, three sets of slave processes are used (since the requested degree of parallelism is 2, six slave processes in total). Actually, only two sets are allocated from the pool (in other words, four slave processes). This is possible because the set used for scanning table t1 (Q1,00) never works concurrently with the set used for scanning table t2 (Q1,01). Therefore, the query coordinator simply (re)uses the same slave processes for these two sets.

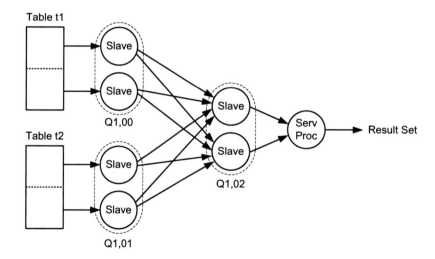

Figure 11-9. *Three sets of slave processes execute a query in parallel.*

Parallel DML Statements

The following DML statements can be executed in parallel:

- DELETE

- INSERT with a subquery (since it makes no sense to execute in parallel INSERT statements of a single row, INSERT statements with the VALUES clause cannot be parallelized)

- MERGE

- UPDATE

■**Note** INSERT statements and MERGE statements (for the part inserting data) executed in parallel use direct-path inserts. Therefore, they are subject to the pros and cons of direct-path inserts. I'll describe them in the section "Direct-Path Insert" later in this chapter.

DML statements cannot be executed in parallel when

- a table has a trigger;

- a table has either a foreign key constraint referencing itself, a foreign key constraint with delete cascade, or a deferred constraint;

- an object column is modified; or

- a clustered or temporary table is modified.

Parallel DML statements are *disabled* by default (be careful, this is the opposite of parallel queries). At the session level, you can enable and disable them with the following SQL statements:

```
ALTER SESSION ENABLE PARALLEL DML

ALTER SESSION DISABLE PARALLEL DML
```

In addition, it is also possible to force the parallel execution to a specific degree of parallelism with the following SQL statement:

```
ALTER SESSION FORCE PARALLEL DML PARALLEL 4
```

In contrast to what happens with parallel queries, hints alone cannot enable parallel DML statements. In other words, parallel processing of DML statements must be absolutely enabled at the session level to take advantage of it. To check whether parallel DML statements are enabled or disabled at the session level, you can execute a query like the following (the column pdml_status is set to either ENABLED, DISABLED, or FORCED):

```
SELECT pdml_status
FROM v$session
WHERE sid = sys_context('userenv','sid')
```

Except for INSERT statements, parallel queries must also be enabled to execute DML statements in parallel. In fact, DML statements are basically composed of two operations: the first finds the rows to be modified, and the second modifies them. The problem is that if the part that finds the rows is not executed in parallel, the part that modifies the rows cannot be parallelized. To illustrate this behavior, let's look at several examples based on the script px_dml.sql.

- When both parallel queries and DML statements are disabled, no operation is parallelized.

```
SQL> ALTER SESSION DISABLE PARALLEL QUERY;

SQL> ALTER SESSION DISABLE PARALLEL DML;

SQL> ALTER TABLE t PARALLEL 2;

SQL> UPDATE t SET id = id + 1;
```

```
------------------------------------
| Id | Operation          | Name |
------------------------------------
|  0 | UPDATE STATEMENT   |      |
|  1 |  UPDATE            | T    |
|  2 |   TABLE ACCESS FULL| T    |
------------------------------------
```

- When only parallel queries are enabled, the update part of the DML statement is not executed in parallel. In fact, only operations 3 to 5 are executed by slave processes. Therefore, operation 1 (UPDATE) is executed serially by the query coordinator.

```
SQL> ALTER SESSION ENABLE PARALLEL QUERY;

SQL> ALTER SESSION DISABLE PARALLEL DML;

SQL> ALTER TABLE t PARALLEL 2;

SQL> UPDATE t SET id = id + 1;
```

```
-------------------------------------------------------------------------
| Id | Operation             | Name     |   TQ  |IN-OUT| PQ Distrib |
-------------------------------------------------------------------------
|  0 | UPDATE STATEMENT      |          |       |      |            |
|  1 |  UPDATE               | T        |       |      |            |
|  2 |   PX COORDINATOR      |          |       |      |            |
|  3 |    PX SEND QC (RANDOM)| :TQ10000 | Q1,00 | P->S | QC (RAND)  |
|  4 |     PX BLOCK ITERATOR |          | Q1,00 | PCWC |            |
|  5 |      TABLE ACCESS FULL| T        | Q1,00 | PCWP |            |
-------------------------------------------------------------------------
```

- When both parallel queries and DML statements are enabled, the update part (operation 3) can also be executed in parallel. In this case, only one set of slave processes is used (operations 2 to 5 have the same value in the column TQ). This implies that the same slave process scans the table and modifies the rows.

```
SQL> ALTER SESSION ENABLE PARALLEL QUERY;

SQL> ALTER SESSION ENABLE PARALLEL DML;

SQL> ALTER TABLE t PARALLEL 2;

SQL> UPDATE t SET id = id + 1;
```

```
---------------------------------------------------------------------
| Id | Operation              | Name     |   TQ  |IN-OUT| PQ Distrib |
---------------------------------------------------------------------
|  0 | UPDATE STATEMENT       |          |       |      |            |
|  1 |  PX COORDINATOR        |          |       |      |            |
|  2 |   PX SEND QC (RANDOM)  | :TQ10000 | Q1,00 | P->S | QC (RAND)  |
|  3 |    UPDATE              | T        | Q1,00 | PCWP |            |
|  4 |     PX BLOCK ITERATOR  |          | Q1,00 | PCWC |            |
|  5 |      TABLE ACCESS FULL | T        | Q1,00 | PCWP |            |
---------------------------------------------------------------------
```

Parallel DDL Statements

Parallel DDL statements are supported for tables and indexes. The following are operations that are typically parallelized:

- CREATE TABLE AS SELECT (CTAS) statements

- Creation and rebuild of indexes

- Creation and validation of constraints

In addition, partition-management operations such as SPLIT and MOVE can be parallelized for partitioned tables and indexes. Usually, DDL statements that can take advantage of parallel processing provide the PARALLEL clause (as you will see shortly, constraints are an exception) to specify whether parallel processing is used and, if it is used, the degree of parallelism. Hints cannot be used to specify the degree of parallelism.

Parallel DDL statements are *enabled* by default. At the session level you can enable and disable them with the following SQL statements:

```
ALTER SESSION ENABLE PARALLEL DDL

ALTER SESSION DISABLE PARALLEL DDL
```

It is also possible to force parallel executions with a specific degree of parallelism (for DDL statements that support it) using the following SQL statement:

```
ALTER SESSION FORCE PARALLEL DDL PARALLEL 4
```

To check whether parallel DDL statements are enabled or disabled at the session level, you can execute a query like the following (the column pddl_status is set to either ENABLED, DISABLED, or FORCED):

```
SELECT pddl_status
FROM v$session
WHERE sid = sys_context('userenv','sid')
```

The following sections show, for the three main types of DML statements that can be executed in parallel, several examples based on the script px_ddl.sql.

CTAS Statements

A CTAS statement is composed of two operations that process data: the query used to retrieve data from the source tables and the insert into the target table. Each part can be executed either serially or in parallel independently of the other. However, if parallel processing is used, it is common to parallelize both operations. The following execution plans illustrate this:

- *Parallelization of insert:* Only operations 2 to 5 are executed in parallel. The query coordinator scans table t1 and distributes its content to the slave processes using the round-robin method. Since the query coordinator communicates with several slave processes, the relationship between the operations is serial to parallel (S->P). A set of slave processes receives the data and performs the insert (operation LOAD AS SELECT) in parallel.

  ```
  CREATE TABLE t2 PARALLEL 2 AS SELECT /*+ no_parallel(t1) */ * FROM t1
  ```

Id	Operation	Name	TQ	IN-OUT	PQ Distrib
0	CREATE TABLE STATEMENT				
1	PX COORDINATOR				
2	PX SEND QC (RANDOM)	:TQ10001	Q1,01	P->S	QC (RAND)
3	LOAD AS SELECT		Q1,01	PCWP	
4	BUFFER SORT		Q1,01	PCWC	
5	PX RECEIVE		Q1,01	PCWP	
6	PX SEND ROUND-ROBIN	:TQ10000		S->P	RND-ROBIN
7	TABLE ACCESS FULL	T1			

- *Parallelization of query:* Only operations 3 to 5 are executed in parallel. The slave processes scan table t1 in parallel based on block range granules and send its content to the query coordinator, which is the reason for the parallel to serial (P->S) relationship. The query coordinator executes the insert (operation LOAD AS SELECT).

```
CREATE TABLE t2 NOPARALLEL AS SELECT /*+ parallel(t1 2) */ * FROM t1
```

```
-------------------------------------------------------------------
| Id | Operation               | Name       |  TQ  |IN-OUT| PQ Distrib |
-------------------------------------------------------------------
|  0 | CREATE TABLE STATEMENT |            |        |      |            |
|  1 |  LOAD AS SELECT         |            |        |      |            |
|  2 |   PX COORDINATOR        |            |        |      |            |
|  3 |    PX SEND QC (RANDOM)  | :TQ10000   | Q1,00 | P->S | QC (RAND)  |
|  4 |     PX BLOCK ITERATOR   |            | Q1,00 | PCWC |            |
|  5 |      TABLE ACCESS FULL  | T1         | Q1,00 | PCWP |            |
-------------------------------------------------------------------
```

- *Parallelization of both operations*: The slave processes scan table t1 in parallel based on block range granules and insert the data they get in the target table directly. Two important things should be highlighted. First, the query coordinator is not directly involved in the processing of data. Second, the data is not sent through a table queue (except for a negligible amount of information sent to the query coordinator by operation 2, no communication takes place).

```
CREATE TABLE t2 PARALLEL 2 AS SELECT /*+ parallel(t1 2) */ * FROM t1
```

```
-------------------------------------------------------------------
| Id | Operation               | Name       |  TQ  |IN-OUT| PQ Distrib |
-------------------------------------------------------------------
|  0 | CREATE TABLE STATEMENT |            |        |      |            |
|  1 |  PX COORDINATOR         |            |        |      |            |
|  2 |   PX SEND QC (RANDOM)   | :TQ10000   | Q1,00 | P->S | QC (RAND)  |
|  3 |    LOAD AS SELECT        |            | Q1,00 | PCWP |            |
|  4 |     PX BLOCK ITERATOR   |            | Q1,00 | PCWC |            |
|  5 |      TABLE ACCESS FULL  | T1         | Q1,00 | PCWP |            |
-------------------------------------------------------------------
```

Creation and Rebuild of Indexes

You can create and rebuild indexes in parallel. To do this, two sets of slave processes work together. The first set reads the data to be indexed. The second set sorts the data it receives from the first set and builds the index. The following SQL statement is an example. Notice how the first set executes operations 6 to 8 (Q1,00) and the second executes operations 2 to 5 (Q1,01). Data is distributed between the two sets using the range method and a parallel to parallel (P->P) relationship.

```
CREATE INDEX i1 ON t1 (id) PARALLEL 4
```

```
----------------------------------------------------------------------------
| Id | Operation               | Name      |    TQ  |IN-OUT| PQ Distrib |
----------------------------------------------------------------------------
|  0 | CREATE INDEX STATEMENT  |           |        |      |            |
|  1 |  PX COORDINATOR         |           |        |      |            |
|  2 |   PX SEND QC (ORDER)    | :TQ10001  | Q1,01  | P->S | QC (ORDER) |
|  3 |    INDEX BUILD NON UNIQUE| I1       | Q1,01  | PCWP |            |
|  4 |     SORT CREATE INDEX   |           | Q1,01  | PCWP |            |
|  5 |      PX RECEIVE         |           | Q1,01  | PCWP |            |
|  6 |       PX SEND RANGE     | :TQ10000  | Q1,00  | P->P | RANGE      |
|  7 |        PX BLOCK ITERATOR |          | Q1,00  | PCWC |            |
|  8 |         TABLE ACCESS FULL| T1       | Q1,00  | PCWP |            |
----------------------------------------------------------------------------
```

A rebuild of an index leads to a very similar execution plan:

```
ALTER INDEX i1 REBUILD PARALLEL 4
```

```
----------------------------------------------------------------------------
| Id | Operation               | Name      |    TQ  |IN-OUT| PQ Distrib |
----------------------------------------------------------------------------
|  0 | ALTER INDEX STATEMENT   |           |        |      |            |
|  1 |  PX COORDINATOR         |           |        |      |            |
|  2 |   PX SEND QC (ORDER)    | :TQ10001  | Q1,01  | P->S | QC (ORDER) |
|  3 |    INDEX BUILD NON UNIQUE| I1       | Q1,01  | PCWP |            |
|  4 |     SORT CREATE INDEX   |           | Q1,01  | PCWP |            |
|  5 |      PX RECEIVE         |           | Q1,01  | PCWP |            |
|  6 |       PX SEND RANGE     | :TQ10000  | Q1,00  | P->P | RANGE      |
|  7 |        PX BLOCK ITERATOR |          | Q1,00  | PCWC |            |
|  8 |         INDEX FAST FULL SCAN| I1    | Q1,00  | PCWP |            |
----------------------------------------------------------------------------
```

Creation and Validation of Constraints

When constraints (such as foreign keys and check constraints) are created or validated, the data already stored in the table must be validated. For that purpose, the database engine executes a recursive query. For example, let's say that you execute the following SQL statement:

```
ALTER TABLE t ADD CONSTRAINT t_id_nn CHECK (id IS NOT NULL)
```

Recursively, the database engine executes a query like the following one to validate the data stored in the table (note that if the query returns no row, the data is valid):

```
SELECT rowid
FROM t
WHERE NOT (id IS NOT NULL)
```

As a result, if table t has a degree of parallelism of 2 or higher, the database engine executes the query in parallel.

> ■**Note** The degree of parallelism defined at the table level is used for the recursive query, regardless of whether at the session level the parallel queries and DDL statements are enabled, forced, or disabled. In other words, the SQL statement ALTER SESSION … PARALLEL has no influence on the recursive query.

When you define a primary key constraint, the database engine is not able to create the index in parallel. To avoid this limitation, you have to create the (unique) index before defining the constraint. The following SQL statements show an example:

```
CREATE UNIQUE index t_pk ON t (id) PARALLEL 2

ALTER TABLE t ADD CONSTRAINT t_pk PRIMARY KEY (id)
```

When to Use It

Parallel processing should be used only when two conditions are met. First, you can use it when plenty of free resources (CPU, memory, and I/O bandwidth) are available. Remember, the aim of parallel processing is to reduce the response time by distributing the work usually done by a single process (and hence a single CPU) to several processes (and hence several CPUs). Second, you can use it for SQL statements that take more than a dozen seconds to execute serially; otherwise, the time and resources needed to initialize and terminate the parallel environment (mainly, the slave processes and the table queues) might be higher than the time gained by the parallelization itself. The actual limit depends on the amount of resources that are available. Therefore, in some situations, only SQL statements that take more than a few minutes, or even longer, are good candidates for being executed in parallel. It is important to stress that if these two conditions are not met, the performance could decrease instead of increase.

If parallel processing is commonly used for many SQL statements, the degree of parallelism should be set at the table and/or index levels. On the other hand, if it is used only for specific batches or reports, it is usually better to enable it at the session level or through hints.

Pitfalls and Fallacies

It is very important to understand that the hints parallel and parallel_index do not force the query optimizer to use parallel processing. Instead, they override the degree of parallelism defined at the table or index level. This change, in turn, allows the query optimizer to consider parallel processing with the specified degree of parallelism. This means that the query optimizer considers execution plans with and without parallel processing and, as usual, picks out the one with the lower cost. Let me stress this point by showing you an example based on the script px_dop2.sql. As shown in the following SQL statements, the cost associated with a full table scan decreases proportionally to the degree of parallelism:

```
SQL> EXPLAIN PLAN SET STATEMENT_ID 'dop1' FOR
  2  SELECT /*+ full(t) parallel(t 1) */ * FROM t WHERE id > 90000;

SQL> EXPLAIN PLAN SET STATEMENT_ID 'dop2' FOR
  2  SELECT /*+ full(t) parallel(t 2) */ * FROM t WHERE id > 90000;
```

```
SQL> EXPLAIN PLAN SET STATEMENT_ID 'dop3' FOR
  2  SELECT /*+ full(t) parallel(t 3) */ * FROM t WHERE id > 90000;

SQL> EXPLAIN PLAN SET STATEMENT_ID 'dop4' FOR
  2  SELECT /*+ full(t) parallel(t 4) */ * FROM t WHERE id > 90000;

SQL> SELECT statement_id, cost
  2  FROM plan_table
  3  WHERE id = 0
  4  ORDER BY statement_id;

STATEMENT_ID   COST
-------------  -----
dop1            430
dop2            238
dop3            159
dop4            119
```

If the SQL statement is executed without hints and the degree of parallelism is set to 1, the query optimizer chooses an index range scan. Notice that the cost associated with this execution plan (178) is lower than the cost of the full table scan with a degree of parallelism up to 2. In contrast, with a degree of parallelism equal or higher than 3, the full table scan is cheaper.

```
SQL> SELECT * FROM t WHERE id > 9000;

-----------------------------------------------------------
| Id | Operation                   | Name | Cost (%CPU)|
-----------------------------------------------------------
|  0 | SELECT STATEMENT            |      |  178    (0)|
|  1 |  TABLE ACCESS BY INDEX ROWID| T    |  178    (0)|
|  2 |   INDEX RANGE SCAN          | I    |   24    (0)|
-----------------------------------------------------------
```

Now, let's see what happens when only the hint parallel is added to the SQL statement, in other words, when no access path hints are used. What happens is that the query optimizer picks out a serial index range scan when the degree of parallelism is set to 2 but chooses a parallel full table scan when the degree of pallelism is set to 3. Basically, the hints parallel and parallel_index simply allow the query optimizer to consider parallel processing; they do not force parallel processing.

```
SQL> SELECT /*+ parallel(t 2) */ * FROM t WHERE id > 90000;

-----------------------------------------------------------
| Id | Operation                   | Name | Cost (%CPU)|
-----------------------------------------------------------
|  0 | SELECT STATEMENT            |      |  178    (0)|
|  1 |  TABLE ACCESS BY INDEX ROWID| T    |  178    (0)|
|  2 |   INDEX RANGE SCAN          | I    |   24    (0)|
-----------------------------------------------------------
```

```
SQL> SELECT /*+ parallel(t 3) */ * FROM t WHERE id > 90000;

--------------------------------------------------------
| Id | Operation              | Name      | Cost (%CPU)|
--------------------------------------------------------
|  0 | SELECT STATEMENT       |           |   159   (0)|
|  1 |  PX COORDINATOR        |           |           |
|  2 |   PX SEND QC (RANDOM)  | :TQ10000  |   159   (0)|
|  3 |    PX BLOCK ITERATOR   |           |   159   (0)|
|  4 |     TABLE ACCESS FULL  | T         |   159   (0)|
--------------------------------------------------------
```

To achieve an efficient parallelization, it is critical that the amount of work is evenly distributed among all slave processes. In fact, all slave processes belonging to a set have to wait until all others have finished. Simply put, a parallel operation is as fast as the slowest slave process. If you want to check the actual distribution for a SQL statement, you can use the dynamic performance view v$pq_tqstat. Basically, the view provides one row for each slave process and for each PX SEND and PX RECEIVE operation in the execution plan. Just be careful that information is provided only for the current session and only for the last SQL statement executed in parallel. I'll now describe an example based on the output generated by the script px_tqstat.sql. The mapping between the two outputs is performed with column TQ of the execution plan and columns dfo_number and tq_id of the view v$pq_tqstat. In fact, for the producers, dfo_number is the number prefixed by the letter Q, and tq_id is the number following the comma. For example, Q1,00 maps to dfo_number equals 1 and tq_id equals 0. In addition, PX SEND operations map to producers, and PX RECEIVE operations map to consumers.

```
SQL> SELECT * FROM t t1, t t2 WHERE t1.id = t2.id;

--------------------------------------------------------------------------------
| Id | Operation                | Name     |   TQ  |IN-OUT| PQ Distrib |
--------------------------------------------------------------------------------
|  0 | SELECT STATEMENT         |          |       |      |            |
|  1 |  PX COORDINATOR          |          |       |      |            |
|  2 |   PX SEND QC (RANDOM)    | :TQ10001 | Q1,01 | P->S | QC (RAND)  |
|  3 |    HASH JOIN             |          | Q1,01 | PCWP |            |
|  4 |     PX RECEIVE           |          | Q1,01 | PCWP |            |
|  5 |      PX SEND PARTITION (KEY)| :TQ10000 | Q1,00 | P->P | PART (KEY) |
|  6 |       PX BLOCK ITERATOR  |          | Q1,00 | PCWC |            |
|  7 |        TABLE ACCESS FULL | T        | Q1,00 | PCWP |            |
|  8 |     PX PARTITION HASH ALL|          | Q1,01 | PCWC |            |
|  9 |      TABLE ACCESS FULL   | T        | Q1,01 | PCWP |            |
--------------------------------------------------------------------------------

SQL> SELECT dfo_number, tq_id, server_type, process, num_rows, bytes
  2  FROM v$pq_tqstat
  3  ORDER BY dfo_number, tq_id, server_type DESC, process;
```

DFO_NUMBER	TQ_ID	SERVER_TYPE	PROCESS	NUM_ROWS	BYTES
1	0	Producer	P002	54952	6009713
1	0	Producer	P003	45048	4921468
1	0	Consumer	P000	20238	2213326
1	0	Consumer	P001	79762	8717855
1	1	Producer	P000	20238	4426604
1	1	Producer	P001	79762	17435710
1	1	Consumer	QC	100000	21862314

In this case, you can get the following information:

- Operation 5 has sent 54,952 rows with the slave process P002 and 45,048 rows with the slave process P003.

- Operation 4 has received the data sent by operation 5: 20,238 rows with the slave process P000 and 79,762 rows with the slave process P001. This shows that the distribution based on the partition key doesn't work very well in this specific case.

- Operation 2 has sent to the query coordinator 20,238 rows with the slave process P000 and 79,762 rows with the slave process P001. As a result of the previous distribution, this one is also suboptimal.

- Operation 1, which is executed by the query coordinator, has received 100,000 rows.

Each slave process opens its own session to the instance. This means that if you want to monitor or trace the processing performed to execute a single SQL statement, you cannot focus on a single session. Instead, you have to aggregate execution statistics coming from several sessions. For example, with SQL trace, every slave process generates its own trace file (the command-line tool TRCSESS might be useful in such a situation). One of the main problems related to this is that the query coordinator ignores the execution statistics of the slave processes working for it. The following execution plan illustrates this. Notice how the values of the columns Starts, A-Rows, and Buffers are set to 0 except for the operation executed by the query coordinator (PX COORDINATOR).

Id	Operation	Name	Starts	A-Rows	Buffers
1	PX COORDINATOR		1	100K	14
2	PX SEND QC (RANDOM)	:TQ10001	0	0	0
3	HASH JOIN		0	0	0
4	PX RECEIVE		0	0	0
5	PX SEND PARTITION (KEY)	:TQ10000	0	0	0
6	PX BLOCK ITERATOR		0	0	0
7	TABLE ACCESS FULL	T	0	0	0
8	PX PARTITION HASH ALL		0	0	0
9	TABLE ACCESS FULL	T	0	0	0

The session executing a parallel DML statement (and only that session—for other sessions, the uncommitted data is not even visible) cannot access the modified table without committing (or rolling back) the transaction. SQL statements executed before committing (or rolling back) terminate with an ORA-12838: cannot read/modify an object after modifying it in parallel error. Here is an example:

```
SQL> UPDATE t SET id = id + 1;

SQL> SELECT count(*) FROM t;
SELECT count(*) FROM t
                    *
ERROR at line 1:
ORA-12838: cannot read/modify an object after modifying it in parallel

SQL> COMMIT;

SQL> SELECT count(*) FROM t;

  COUNT(*)
----------
    100000
```

Direct-Path Insert

The Oracle database engine provides two types of INSERT statements to load data into a table: *conventional inserts* and *direct-path inserts*. Conventional inserts, as the name suggests, are the ones that are generally used. Direct-path inserts, instead, are used only when the database engine is explicitly instructed to do so. The aim of direct-path inserts is to efficiently load large amounts of data (they can have poorer performance than conventional inserts for small amounts of data). They are able to achieve this goal because their implementation is optimized for performance at the expense of functionality. For this reason, they are subject to more requirements and restrictions than conventional inserts. I'll now discuss how direct-path inserts work, when they should be used, and some common pitfalls and fallacies related to them.

How It Works

It is essential to understand that direct-path inserts are not supported for all types of INSERT statements. Actually, only INSERT INTO … SELECT … statements (including multitable inserts), MERGE statements (for the part inserting data), and applications using the OCI direct-path interface (for example, the SQL*Loader utility) are able to take advantage of them. This means that "regular" INSERT statements that use the VALUES clause do not support this feature.

You have two ways to make an INSERT INTO … SELECT … statement use a direct-path insert:

- Specify the hint append in the SQL statement: INSERT /*+ append */ INTO … SELECT ….

- Execute the SQL statement in parallel. Note that in this case, both the INSERT and the SELECT can be parallelized independently. To take advantage of direct-path inserts, at least the INSERT part must be parallelized.

To improve efficiency and, thereby, performance, a direct-path insert uses direct writes to load data directly above the high watermark of the modified segment. This fact has important implications:

- The buffer cache, because of direct writes, is bypassed.

- Concurrent DELETE, INSERT, MERGE, and UPDATE statements, as well as the (re)build of indexes on the modified table, are not permitted. Naturally, table locks are obtained to guarantee this.

- The blocks containing free space below the high watermark are not taken into consideration. This means that even if DELETE statements are regularly executed in order to purge data, the size of the segment would increase constantly.

One of the reasons that direct-path inserts lead to better performance is that only minimal undo is generated for the table segment. In fact, undo is generated only for space management operations (for example, to increase the high watermark and add a new extent to the segment), and not for the rows contained in the blocks that are inserted by direct-path. If the table is indexed, however, undo is normally generated for the index segments. If you want to avoid the undo related to index segments as well, you can make the indexes unusable before the load and rebuild them when the load is finished. Especially in ETL jobs, this is common practice; also, it's popular because it may be faster to rebuild the index than to let the database engine do the maintenance at the end of the load.

To further improve performance, you can also use *minimal logging*. The aim of minimal logging is to minimize redo generation. This is optional, but it is often essential to greatly reduce response time. You can instruct minimal logging to be used by setting the parameter nologging at the table or partition level. The essential thing to understand is that minimal logging is supported only for direct-path inserts and some DDL statements. In fact, redo is always generated for all other operations.

Note You should use nologging and, thereby, minimize redo generation only if you fully understand the implications of doing so. In fact, media recovery cannot be performed for blocks modified with minimal logging. This means that if media recovery is performed, the database engine can only mark those blocks as logically corrupted, since media recovery needs to access the redo information in order to reconstruct the block's contents. Naturally, as said previously, redo information is not stored when using nologging. As a result, SQL statements that access objects containing such blocks terminate with an ORA-26040: Data block was loaded using the NOLOGGING option error. Therefore, you should use minimal logging only if you either can manually reload data or are willing to make a backup after the load.

Figure 11-10 shows an example of the improvement you can achieve with direct-path inserts. These figures were measured by starting the script dpi_performance.sql on my test system.

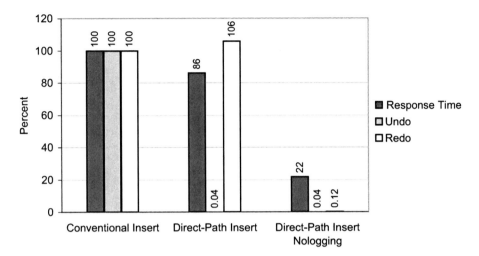

Figure 11-10. *Comparison of loading data with and without direct-path inserts (table without indexes)*

Notice that in Figure 11-10, the undo generation for both direct-path inserts is negligible. This is because the modified table is not indexed. Figure 11-11 shows the figures of the same test but with a primary key in place. As expected, undo for the index segment is generated.

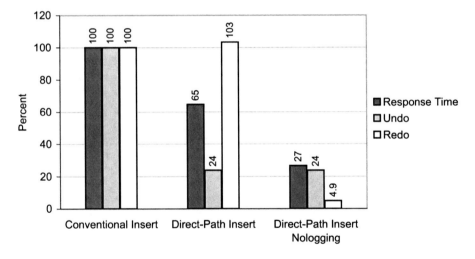

Figure 11-11. *Comparison of loading data with and without direct-path inserts (table with primary key)*

Direct-path inserts do not support all objects that conventional inserts do. Their functionality is restricted. If the database engine is not able to execute a direct-path insert, the operation is silently converted into a conventional insert. This happens when one of the following conditions is met:

- An enabled INSERT trigger is present on the modified table. (Note that DELETE and UPDATE triggers have no impact on direct-path inserts.)

- An enabled foreign key is present on the modified table (foreign keys of other tables that point to the modified table are not a problem).

- The modified table is index organized.

- The modified table is stored in a cluster.

- The modified table contains object type columns.

When to Use It

You should use direct-path inserts whenever you have to load a large amount of data and the restrictions that apply to direct-path inserts are not a concern for you.

If performance is your primary goal, you might also consider using minimal logging (nologging). As previously explained, however, you should use this possibility only if you fully understand and accept the implications of doing so and if you take necessary measures to not lose data in the process.

Pitfalls and Fallacies

Even if minimal logging is *not* used, a database running in noarchivelog mode doesn't generate redo for direct-path inserts.

It is not possible to use minimal logging for segments stored in a database or a tablespace in *force logging* mode. In fact, force logging overrides the parameter nologging. Note that force logging is particularly useful with standby databases and streams. To successfully use them, redo logs need to contain information about all modifications.

During a direct-path insert, the high watermark is not increased. This operation is performed only when the transaction is committed. Therefore, the session executing a direct-path insert (and only that session—for other sessions, the uncommitted data above the high watermark is not even visible) cannot access the modified table after the load, without committing (or rolling back) the transaction. SQL statements executed before committing (or rolling back) terminate with an ORA-12838: cannot read/modify an object after modifying it in parallel error. Here is an example:

```
SQL> INSERT /*+ append */ INTO t SELECT * FROM t;

100000 rows created.

SQL> SELECT count(*) FROM t;
SELECT count(*) FROM t
                      *
ERROR at line 1:
ORA-12838: cannot read/modify an object after modifying it in parallel

SQL> COMMIT;
```

```
SQL> SELECT count(*) FROM t;

  COUNT(*)
----------
    200000
```

The text associated with the error ORA-12938 may be confusing also because it is generated even if no parallel processing is used.

Row Prefetching

When an application fetches data from a database, it can do it row by row or, better yet, by fetching numerous rows at the same time. Fetching numerous rows at a time is called *row prefetching.*

How It Works

The concept of row prefetching is straightforward. Every time an application asks the driver to retrieve a row from the database, several rows are prefetched with it and stored in client-side memory. In this way, several subsequent requests do not have to execute database calls to fetch data. They can be served from the client-side memory. As a result, the number of round-trips to the database decreases proportionally to the number of prefetched rows. Hence, the overhead of retrieving result sets with numerous rows may be strongly reduced. As an example, Figure 11-12 shows you the response time of retrieving 100,000 rows by increasing the number of prefetched rows up to 50. The Java class RowPrefetchingPerf.java was used for this test.

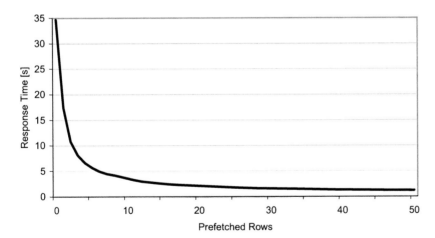

Figure 11-12. *The time needed to retrieve a result set containing numerous rows is strongly dependent on the number of prefetched rows.*

It is essential to understand that the poor performance of the retrieval without row prefetching (in other words, row by row processing) is *not* caused by the database engine. Instead, it is the application that causes it and in turn suffers from it. This becomes obvious when looking at the execution statistics generated with SQL trace for the nonprefetching case. The following figures show that even if the client-side elapsed time lasted about 35 seconds (see Figure 11-12), only 2.79 seconds were spent processing the query on the database side!

call	count	cpu	elapsed	disk	query	current	rows
Parse	1	0.00	0.00	0	0	0	0
Execute	1	0.00	0.00	0	0	0	0
Fetch	100001	2.66	2.79	0	100005	0	100000
total	100003	2.66	2.79	0	100005	0	100000

Even if row prefetching is much more important for the client, the database also profits from it. In fact, row prefetching greatly reduces the number of logical reads. The following execution statistics show the reduction when 50 rows are prefetched:

call	count	cpu	elapsed	disk	query	current	rows
Parse	1	0.00	0.00	0	123	1	0
Execute	1	0.00	0.00	0	0	0	0
Fetch	2001	0.10	0.11	0	4369	0	100000
total	2003	0.11	0.12	0	4492	1	100000

The next sections provide some basic information on how to take advantage of row prefetching with PL/SQL, OCI, JDBC, and ODP.NET.

PL/SQL

As of Oracle Database 10g, if at compile time the dynamic initialization parameter plsql_optimize_level is set to 2 or higher, row prefetching is used for cursor FOR loops. For example, the query in the following PL/SQL block prefetches 100 rows at a time. Note that the number of prefetched rows cannot be changed.

```
BEGIN
  FOR c IN (SELECT * FROM t)
  LOOP
    -- process data
    NULL;
  END LOOP;
END;
```

■ **Note** The default value of the initialization parameter plsql_optimize_level is 2 as of Oracle Database 10g Release 2. However, it is 0 in Oracle Database 10g Release 1.

It is essential to understand that row prefetching is automatically used for cursor FOR loops only. To use row prefetching with other types of cursors, the BULK COLLECT clause must be used. Its utilization with an implicit cursor is shown here:

```
DECLARE
  TYPE t_t IS TABLE OF t%ROWTYPE;
  l_t t_t;
BEGIN
  SELECT * BULK COLLECT INTO l_t
  FROM t;
  FOR i IN l_t.FIRST..l_t.LAST
  LOOP
    -- process data
    NULL;
  END LOOP;
END;
```

With the previous PL/SQL block, all rows of the result set are returned in a single fetch. If the number of rows is high, a lot of memory is required. Therefore, in practice, either you know that the number of rows that will be returned is limited or you set a limit for a single fetch with the LIMIT clause. The following PL/SQL block shows how to fetch 100 rows at a time:

```
DECLARE
  CURSOR c IS SELECT * FROM t;
  TYPE t_t IS TABLE OF t%ROWTYPE;
  l_t t_t;
BEGIN
  OPEN c;
  LOOP
    FETCH c BULK COLLECT INTO l_t LIMIT 100;
    EXIT WHEN l_t.COUNT = 0;
    FOR i IN l_t.FIRST..l_t.LAST
    LOOP
      -- process data
      NULL;
    END LOOP;
  END LOOP;
  CLOSE c;
END;
```

Row prefetching is supported by the package dbms_sql, native dynamic SQL, and the RETURNING clause. However, as in the previous two examples, it must be explicitly enabled (for example, with BULK COLLECT).

OCI

With OCI, row prefetching is controlled by two statement attributes: OCI_ATTR_PREFETCH_ROWS and OCI_ATTR_PREFETCH_MEMORY. The former limits the number of fetched rows. The latter limits the amount of memory (in bytes) used to fetch the rows. The following code snippet shows how to call the function OCIAttrSet to set these attributes. The C program row_prefetching.c provides a complete example.

```
ub4 rows = 100;
OCIAttrSet(stm,                      // statement handle
           OCI_HTYPE_STMT,           // type of handle being modified
           &rows,                    // attribute's value
           sizeof(rows),             // size of the attribute's value
           OCI_ATTR_PREFETCH_ROWS,   // attribute being set
           err);                     // error handle

ub4 memory = 10240;
OCIAttrSet(stm,                      // statement handle
           OCI_HTYPE_STMT,           // type of handle being modified
           &memory,                  // attribute's value
           sizeof(memory),           // size of the attribute's value
           OCI_ATTR_PREFETCH_MEMORY, // attribute being set
           err);                     // error handle
```

When both attributes are set, the limit that is reached first is honored. To switch row prefetching off, you must set both attributes to zero.

JDBC

Row prefetching is enabled with the Oracle JDBC driver by default. You can change the default number of fetched rows, 10, in two ways. The first is to specify the property defaultRowPrefetch when opening a connection to the database with either the class OracleDataSource or the class OracleDriver. The following code snippet shows an example, where the user, the password, and the number of prefetched rows are set for an OracleDataSource object. Note that in this case, because defaultRowPrefetch is set to 1, row prefetching is disabled.

```
connectionProperties = new Properties();
connectionProperties.put("user", user);
connectionProperties.put("password", password);
connectionProperties.put("defaultRowPrefetch", "1");
dataSource.setConnectionProperties(connectionProperties);
```

The second is to override the default value at the connection level by using the method setFetchSize in the class Statement. The following code snippet shows an example where the method setFetchSize is used to set the number of fetched rows to 100. The Java program RowPrefetching.java provides a complete example.

```
sql = "SELECT id, pad FROM t";
statement = connection.prepareStatement(sql);
statement.setFetchSize(100);
resultset = statement.executeQuery();
```

```
while (resultset.next())
{
  id = resultset.getLong("id");
  pad = resultset.getString("pad");
  // process data
}
resultset.close();
statement.close();
```

ODP.NET

The default fetch size of ODP.NET (65,536) is defined in bytes, *not* rows. You can change
this value through the property FetchSize provided by the classes OracleCommand and
OracleDataReader. The following code snippet is an example of how to set the value for fetching
100 rows. Notice how the property RowSize of the class OracleCommand is used to compute the
amount of memory needed to store the 100 rows. The C# program RowPrefetching.cs provides
a complete example.

```
sql = "SELECT id, pad FROM t";
command = new OracleCommand(sql, connection);
reader = command.ExecuteReader();
reader.FetchSize = command.RowSize * 100;
while (reader.Read())
{
  id = reader.GetDecimal(0);
  pad = reader.GetString(1);
  // process data
}
reader.Close();
```

As of Oracle Data Provider for .NET Release 10.2.0.3, you can also change the default fetch
size through the following registry entry (<Assembly_Version> is the full version number of
Oracle.DataAccess.dll):

```
HKEY_LOCAL_MACHINE\SOFTWARE\ORACLE\ODP.NET\<Assembly_Version>\FetchSize
```

When to Use It

Anytime more than one row has to be fetched, it makes sense to use row prefetching.

Pitfalls and Fallacies

When OCI libraries are used, it is not always possible to fully disable row prefetching. For example,
with the JDBC OCI driver or with SQL*Plus, the minimum number of fetched rows is two. In
practice, this is not a problem, but there may be some confusion as to why, for example, in
spite of setting the system variable arraysize to 1 in SQL*Plus, you see that two rows are fetched.

If an application displays, let's say, 10 rows at time, it is usually pointless to prefetch 100 rows
from the database. The number of prefetched rows should ideally be the same as the number
of rows needed by an application at a given time.

Array Interface

In the previous section, you have seen that when an application fetches data from a database, it can do it row by row or, even better, by using row prefetching. The same concept applies to the situations where the application passes data to the database engine or, in other words, during the binding of input variables. For this purpose, the *array interface* is available.

How It Works

The array interface allows you to bind arrays instead of scalar values. This is very useful when a specific DML statement needs to insert or modify numerous rows. Instead of executing the DML statement separately for each row, you can bind all necessary values as arrays and execute it only once, or if the number of rows is high, you can split the execution into smaller batches. As a result, the number of round-trips to the database decreases proportionally to the number of executions. Figure 11-13 shows the response time of inserting 100,000 rows by increasing the size of the arrays up to 50. The Java class ArrayInterfacePerf.java was used for this test.

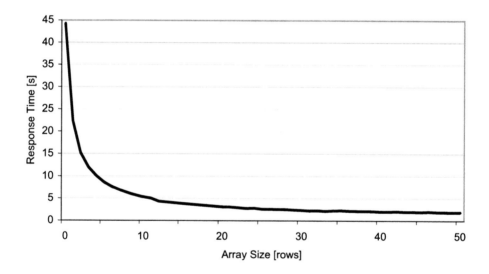

Figure 11-13. *The time needed to load data into the database is strongly dependent on the number of rows processed by each execution.*

It is essential to understand that poor performance of the load without array processing (in other words, row by row processing) is *not* due to the database engine. Instead, it is the application that causes and suffers from it. You can clearly see this by looking at the execution statistics generated with SQL trace. The following figures show that even if the client-side elapsed time lasted about 44 seconds (see Figure 11-13), only 3.16 seconds were spent processing the database side inserts.

call	count	cpu	elapsed	disk	query	current	rows
Parse	1	0.00	0.00	0	0	0	0
Execute	100000	3.07	3.16	1	1498	113131	100000
Fetch	0	0.00	0.00	0	0	0	0
total	100001	3.07	3.16	1	1498	113131	100000

Even if the array interface is much more effective for the client, the database also profits from it. In fact, the array interface reduces the number of logical reads. The following execution statistics show the reduction when the rows are inserted in batches of 50:

call	count	cpu	elapsed	disk	query	current	rows
Parse	1	0.00	0.00	0	0	0	0
Execute	2000	0.45	1.23	2	2858	15677	100000
Fetch	0	0.00	0.00	0	0	0	0
total	2001	0.45	1.23	2	2858	15677	100000

The next sections provide some basic information on how to take advantage of the array interface with PL/SQL, OCI, JDBC, and ODP.NET.

PL/SQL

To use the array interface in PL/SQL, the FORALL statement is available. With it, you can execute a DML statement that binds arrays to pass data to the database engine. The following PL/SQL block shows how to insert 100,000 rows with a single execution. Notice that the first part of the code is used only to prepare the arrays. The FORALL statement with the INSERT statement takes only two lines.

```
DECLARE
  TYPE t_id IS TABLE OF t.id%TYPE;
  TYPE t_pad IS TABLE OF t.pad%TYPE;
  l_id t_id := t_id();
  l_pad t_pad := t_pad();
BEGIN
  -- prepare data
  l_id.extend(100000);
  l_pad.extend(100000);
  FOR i IN 1..100000
  LOOP
    l_id(i) := i;
    l_pad(i) := rpad('*',100,'*');
  END LOOP;
  -- insert data
  FORALL i IN l_id.FIRST..l_id.LAST
    INSERT INTO t VALUES (l_id(i), l_pad(i));
END;
```

It is important to note that even if the syntax is based on the keyword FORALL, this is not a loop. All rows are sent in a single database call.

The array interface is supported not only in this case, but the package dbms_sql and native dynamic SQL also support it.

OCI

To take advantage of the array interface with OCI, no specific function is needed. In fact, the functions used to bind the variables, OCIBindByPos and OCIBindByName, and the function used to execute the SQL statement, OCIStmtExecute, have the ability to work with arrays as parameters. The C program array_interface.c provides an example.

JDBC

To use the array interface with JDBC, *batch updates* are available. As shown in the following code snippet, which inserts 100,000 rows in a single execution, you can add an "execution" to a batch by executing the method addBatch. When the whole batch containing several executions is then ready, it can be submitted to the database engine by executing the method executeBatch. Both methods are available in the class Statement and, consequently, in the subclasses PreparedStatement and CallableStatement as well. The Java program ArrayInterface.java provides a complete example.

```
sql = "INSERT INTO t VALUES (?, ?)";
statement = connection.prepareStatement(sql);
for (int i=1 ; i<=100000 ; i++)
{
  statement.setInt(1, i);
  statement.setString(2, "... some text ...");
  statement.addBatch();
}
statement.executeBatch();
statement.close();
```

ODP.NET

To use the array interface with ODP.NET, it is enough to define parameters based on arrays and to set the property ArrayBindCount to the number of values stored in the arrays. The following code snippet, which inserts 100,000 rows in a single execution, illustrates this. You can find a complete example in the C# program ArrayInterface.cs.

```
Decimal[] idValues = new Decimal[100000];
String[] padValues = new String[100000];

for (int i=0 ; i<100000 ; i++)
{
  // initialize arrays
}
```

```
id = new OracleParameter();
id.OracleDbType = OracleDbType.Decimal;
id.Value = idValues;

pad = new OracleParameter();
pad.OracleDbType = OracleDbType.Varchar2;
pad.Value = padValues;

sql = "INSERT INTO t VALUES (:id, :pad)";
command = new OracleCommand(sql, connection);
command.ArrayBindCount = 100000;
command.Parameters.Add(id);
command.Parameters.Add(pad);
command.ExecuteNonQuery();
```

When to Use It

Anytime more than one row has to be inserted or modified, it makes sense to use the array interface.

Pitfalls and Fallacies

In the execution statistics generated through SQL trace, there is no explicit information about the utilization of the array processing. However, if you know the SQL statement, by looking at the ratio between the number of modified rows and the number of executions, you should be able to identify whether array processing was used. For example, in the following execution statistics, a plain INSERT statement, which was executed only once, inserted 2,342 rows. Something like that is possible only when the array interface is used.

```
INSERT INTO T VALUES (:B1 , :B2 )
```

call	count	cpu	elapsed	disk	query	current	rows
Parse	1	0.00	0.00	0	0	0	0
Execute	1	0.00	0.00	0	78	522	2342
Fetch	0	0.00	0.00	0	0	0	0
total	2	0.00	0.00	0	78	522	2342

On to Chapter 12

This chapter described some advanced optimization techniques aimed at improving performance. Some of them (materialized views, result caches, parallel processing, and direct-path inserts) should be used only if with "regular" optimization techniques it is not possible to achieve the required performance. In contrast, others (row prefetching and array processing) should always be used if possible.

Although this chapter mainly described optimization techniques that are not commonly used, the next (and last) chapter, describes techniques that basically apply to every table stored in a database. In fact, when you perform the translation from logical design to physical design, for every table it is necessary to decide how data is physically stored.

■ ■ ■

Optimizing the Physical Design

During the translation from the logical design to the physical design, you must make four kinds of decisions. First, for each table, you have to decide not only whether you should use a heap table, a cluster, or an index-organized table but also whether it has to be partitioned. Second, you must consider whether you should utilize redundant access structures such as indexes and materialized views. Third, you have to decide how to implement the constraints (not *whether* you have to implement them). Fourth, you have to decide how data will be stored in blocks, including the order of the columns, what datatypes are to be used, how many rows per block should be stored, or whether compression should be activated. This chapter focuses on the fourth topic only. For information about the others, especially the first two, refer to Chapters 9, 10, and 11.

The aim of this chapter is to explain why the optimization of the physical design should not be seen as a fine-tuning activity but as a basic optimization technique. The chapter starts by discussing why choosing the correct column order and the correct datatype is essential. It continues by explaining what row migration and row chaining are, how to identify problems related to them, and how to avoid row migration and row chaining in the first place. Then, it describes a common performance issue experienced by systems with a high workload: block contention. Finally, it describes how to take advantage of data compression to improve performance.

Optimal Column Order

Little care is generally taken to find the optimal column order for a table. Depending on the situation, this might have no impact at all or may cause a significant overhead. To understand what situations this might cause significant overhead in, it is essential to describe how the database engine stores rows into blocks.

A row stored into a block has a very simple format (see Figure 12-1). First, there is a header (H) recording some properties about the row itself, such as whether it is locked or how many columns it contains. Then, there are the columns. Because every column might have a different size, each of them consists of two parts. The first is the length (Ln) of the data. The second is the data (Dn) itself.

Figure 12-1. *Format of a row stored in a database block (H=row header, Ln=length of column n, Dn=data of column n)*

The essential thing to understand in this format is that the database engine doesn't know the offset of the columns in a row. For example, if it has to locate column 3, it has to start by locating column 1. Then, based on the length of column 1, it locates column 2. Finally, based on the length of column 2, it locates column 3. So whenever a row has more than a few columns, a column near the beginning of the row might be located much faster than a column near the end of the row. To better understand this, you can perform the following test, based on the script `column_order.sql`, to measure the overhead associated with the search of a column:

1. Create a table with 250 columns:

   ```
   CREATE TABLE t (n1 NUMBER, n2 NUMBER, ..., n249 NUMBER, n250 NUMBER)
   ```

2. Insert 10,000 rows. Every column of every row stores the same value.

3. Measure the response time for the following query, executed 1,000 times in a loop, for each column.

   ```
   SELECT count(<col>) FROM t
   ```

Figure 12-2 summarizes the results of this test run on my test server. It is important to note that the query referencing the first column (position 1) performs about five times faster than the query referencing the 250th column (position 250). This is because the database engine optimizes every access and thus avoids locating and reading columns that are not necessary for the processing. For example, the query `SELECT count(n3) FROM t` stops walking the row when the third column is located. Figure 12-2 also reports, at position 0, the figure for `count(*)`, which does not need to access any column at all.

Because of this, the general rule is to place intensively accessed columns first. However, in order to take advantage of this, you should be careful to access (reference) only the columns that are really needed. In any case, from a performance point of view, selecting not-needed columns (or worse, as it is sadly very often done, referencing all columns using a `SELECT *` even if only some of them are actually needed by the application) is bad, not only because there is an overhead when reading them from blocks, as you have just seen, but also because more memory is needed to temporarily store them on the server and on the client and because more time and resources are needed to send data over the network. Simply put, every time data is processed, there is an overhead.

In practice, the overhead related to the position of the columns is (more) noticeable in one of the following situations:

- When tables have many columns and SQL statements frequently reference very few of the ones located at the end of the row.

- When many rows are read from a single block, such as during a full table scan. This is because more often than not, the overhead for locating and accessing a block is by far more significant than the one for locating and accessing the columns if few rows are read.

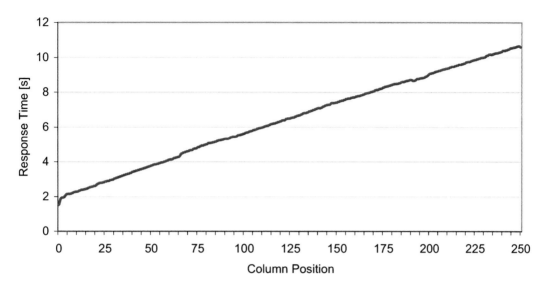

Figure 12-2. *The position of a column in a row vs. the amount of processing needed to access it*

Since trailing NULL values are not stored, it makes sense to place columns expected to contain NULL values at the end of the table. In this way, the number of physically stored columns and consequently the average size of the rows might decrease.

Optimal Datatype

In recent years, I have witnessed a worrying trend in physical design. This trend can be called *wrong datatype selection*. At first glance, choosing the datatype for a column seems like a very straightforward decision to make. Nevertheless, in a world where software architects spend a lot of time discussing high-level things such as agile software development, SOA, Ajax, or persistence frameworks and seem to forget about low-level ones, I am convinced it is essential to get back to the basics and discuss why datatype selection is important.

Pitfalls in Datatype Selection

To illustrate wrong datatype selection, I will present five examples of typical problems that I have encountered over and over again. Even though this may all seem very basic, you can be sure that there is a huge number of systems that are now running and suffering because of these problems.

The first problem caused by wrong datatype selection is wrong or lacking validation of data when it is inserted or modified in the database. For example, if a column is supposed to store numeric values, choosing a character datatype for it calls for an external validation. In other words, the database engine is not able to validate the data. It leaves it to the application to do. Even if such a validation is easy to implement, bear in mind that every time the same piece of code is spread to several locations, instead of being centralized in the database, sooner or later there will be a mismatch in functionality (typically, in some locations the validation may be forgotten, or maybe the validation changes later and its implementation is updated only in some locations). The example I'm presenting is related to the initialization parameter `nls_numeric_characters`. Remember that this initialization parameter specifies the characters used as decimals and group separators. For example, in Switzerland it is usually set to ".,", and therefore the value pi is formatted as follows: 3.14159. Instead, in Germany it is commonly set to ",.", and therefore the same value is formatted as follows: 3,14159. Sooner or later, running an application with different client-side settings of this initialization parameter will cause an `ORA-01722: invalid number` error if conversions take place because of using a wrong datatype in the database. And by the time you notice this, your database will be filled with `VARCHAR2` columns containing both formats, and therefore a painful data reconciliation will have to be performed.

The second problem caused by wrong datatype selection is loss of information. In other words, during the conversion of the original (correct) datatype to the database datatype, information gets lost. For example, imagine what happens when the date and time of an event is stored with a `DATE` datatype instead of a `TIMESTAMP WITH TIME ZONE` datatype. Fractional seconds and time zone information get lost. Although the former leads to a very small error (less than one second), the latter might be a bigger problem. In one case that I witnessed, a customer's data was always generated using local standard time (without daylight saving time adjustments) and stored directly in the database. The problems arose when, for reporting purposes, a correction for daylight saving time had to be applied. A function designed to make a conversion between two time zones was implemented. Its signature was the following:

```
new_time_dst(in_date DATE, tz1 VARCHAR2, tz2 VARCHAR2) RETURN DATE
```

Calling such a function once was very fast. The problem was calling it thousands of times for each report. The response time increased by a factor of 25 as a result. Clearly, with the correct datatype, everything would not only be faster but also easier (the conversion would be performed automatically).

The third problem caused by wrong datatype selection is that things do not work as expected. Let's say you have to range partition a table, based on a `DATE` or `TIMESTAMP` column storing date and time information. This is usually no big deal. The problem arises if the column used as the partition key contains the numeric representation of the datetime value based on some format mask, or an equivalent string representation, instead of plain `DATE` or `TIMESTAMP` values. If the conversion from the datetime values to the numeric values is performed with a format mask like `YYYYMMDDHH24MISS`, the definition of the range partitions is still possible. However, if the conversion is based on a format mask like `DDMMYYYYHH24MISS`, you have no chance of solving the problem without changing the datatype or format of the column since the numeric (or string) order does not match the natural datetime value order (as of Oracle Database 11g, it might be possible to work around the problem by implementing virtual column–based partitioning).

The fourth problem caused by wrong datatype selection is related to the query optimizer. This is probably the least obvious of this short list and also the one leading to the subtlest problems. The reason for this is that with the wrong datatypes the query optimizer will perform wrong estimates and, consequently, will choose suboptimal access paths. Frequently, when something like that happens, most people blame the query optimizer that "once again" is not doing its job correctly. In reality, the problem is that information is hidden from it, so the query optimizer cannot do its job correctly. To better understand this problem, take a look at the following example, which is based on the script wrong_datatype.sql. Here, you are checking the estimated cardinality of similar restrictions based on three columns that store the same set of data (the date of each day in 2008) but that are based on different datatypes. As you can see, the query optimizer is able to make a precise estimation (the correct cardinality is 29) only for the column that is correctly defined.

```
SQL> CREATE TABLE t (d DATE, n NUMBER(8), c VARCHAR2(8));

SQL> INSERT INTO t (d)
  2  SELECT trunc(sysdate,'year')+level-1
  3  FROM dual
  4  CONNECT BY level <= 366;

SQL> UPDATE t
  2  SET n = to_number(to_char(d,'YYYYMMDD')), c = to_char(d,'YYYYMMDD');

SQL> SELECT *
  2  FROM t
  3  ORDER BY d;

D                 N C
---------- --------- ---------
01-JAN-08    20080101 20080101
02-JAN-08    20080102 20080102
...
30-DEC-08    20081230 20081230
31-DEC-08    20081231 20081231

SQL> execute dbms_stats.gather_table_stats(ownname=>user, tabname=>'t')

SQL> EXPLAIN PLAN SET STATEMENT_ID = 'd' FOR
  2  SELECT *
  3  FROM t
  4  WHERE d BETWEEN to_date('20080201','YYYYMMDD')
  5              AND to_date('20080229','YYYYMMDD');

SQL> EXPLAIN PLAN SET STATEMENT_ID = 'n' FOR
  2  SELECT *
  3  FROM t
  4  WHERE n BETWEEN 20080201 AND 20080229;

SQL> EXPLAIN PLAN SET STATEMENT_ID = 'c' FOR
  2  SELECT *
  3  FROM t
  4  WHERE c BETWEEN '20080201' AND '20080229';
```

```
SQL> SELECT statement_id, cardinality
  2  FROM plan_table
  3  WHERE id = 0;

STATEMENT_ID CARDINALITY
------------ -----------
d                     30
n                     11
c                     11
```

The fifth problem is also related to the query optimizer. This one, however, is because of implicit conversion (as a general rule, you should always avoid implicit conversion). What might happen is that an implicit conversion prevents the query optimizer from choosing an index. To illustrate this problem, the same table as in the previous example is used. For this table, an index based on the column of datatype VARCHAR2 is created. If a WHERE clause contains a restriction on that column that uses a character string, the query optimizer picks out the index. However, if the restriction uses a number (the developer "knows" that only numeric values are stored in it), a full table scan is used (notice, in the second SQL statement, that the implicit conversion based on the function to_number prevents the index from being used).

```
SQL> CREATE INDEX i ON t (c);

SQL> SELECT *
  2  FROM t
  3  WHERE c = '20080229';

-----------------------------------------------
| Id  | Operation                   | Name |
-----------------------------------------------
|   0 | SELECT STATEMENT            |      |
|   1 |  TABLE ACCESS BY INDEX ROWID| T    |
|*  2 |   INDEX RANGE SCAN          | I    |
-----------------------------------------------

   2 - access("C"='20080229')

SQL> SELECT *
  2  FROM t
  3  WHERE c = 20080229;

-----------------------------------
| Id  | Operation         | Name |
-----------------------------------
|   0 | SELECT STATEMENT  |      |
|*  1 |  TABLE ACCESS FULL| T    |
-----------------------------------

   1 - filter(TO_NUMBER("C")=20080229)
```

In summary, there are plenty of good reasons for selecting your datatypes correctly. Doing so may just save you a lot of problems.

Best Practices in Datatype Selection

As discussed in the previous section, the key principle is that every datatype should store only values for which it has been designed. For instance, a number must be stored in a numeric datatype and not in a character string datatype. In addition, whenever several datatypes exist (for example, several datatypes that may store character strings), it is important to choose the one that is able to fully store the data in the most efficient way. In other words, you should avoid losing information or performance.

The following sections provide some information (mainly related to performance) that you should consider when selecting a datatype. They cover the four main categories of built-in datatypes: numbers, datetimes, character strings, and bit strings.

Numbers

The main datatype used to store floating-point numbers and integers is NUMBER. It is a variable-length datatype. This means it is possible to specify, through the *precision* and *scale*, the accuracy used to store data. Whenever it is used to store integers or whenever full accuracy is not needed, it is important to specify the scale in order to save space. The following example shows how the same value takes either 21 bytes or 2 bytes depending on the scale:

```
SQL> CREATE TABLE t (n1 NUMBER, n2 NUMBER(*,2));

SQL> INSERT INTO t VALUES (1/3, 1/3);

SQL> SELECT * FROM t;

                                        N1    N2
---------------------------------------- ----
 .3333333333333333333333333333333333333333   .33

SQL> SELECT vsize(n1), vsize(n2) FROM t;

 VSIZE(N1)  VSIZE(N2)
---------- ----------
        21          2
```

Since the internal format is proprietary, a CPU cannot directly process them. Instead, they are processed by internal Oracle library routines. For this reason, the NUMBER datatype is not efficient when supporting number-crunching loads. To solve this problem, as of Oracle Database 10*g*, two new datatypes are available: BINARY_FLOAT and BINARY_DOUBLE. They have two advantages over the NUMBER datatype. First, they implement the IEEE 754 standard, so a CPU can directly process them. Second, they are fixed-length datatypes. Table 12-1 summarizes the differences between these datatypes.

Table 12-1. *Comparison Between Number Datatypes*

Property	NUMBER(precision,scale)	BINARY_FLOAT*	BINARY_DOUBLE*
Range of values	±1.0E126	±3.40E38	±1.79E308
Size	1–22 bytes	4 bytes	8 bytes
Support ±infinity	Yes	Yes	Yes
Support NAN	No	Yes	Yes
Advantages	Accuracy Precision and scale can be specified	Speed Fixed length	Speed Fixed length

* *Available as of Oracle Database 10g*

Character Strings

There are three basic datatypes used for storing character strings: VARCHAR2, CHAR, and CLOB. The first two support up to 4,000 and 2,000 bytes, respectively (note that the max length is specified in bytes, not characters). The third supports up to 4GB in Oracle9i and even more as of Oracle Database 10g. The main difference between VARCHAR2 and CHAR is that the former is of variable length, while the latter is of fixed length. This means CHAR is usually used when the length of the character string is known. However, my advice is to always use VARCHAR2 because it provides better performance than CHAR. CLOB should be used only when character strings are expected to be larger than the maximum of VARCHAR2. As of Oracle Database 11g, there are two storage methods for CLOB: basicfile and securefile. For better performance, you should use securefile.

The three basic datatypes store character strings according to the database character set. In addition, three other datatypes, NVARCHAR2, NCHAR, and NCLOB, are available to store character strings according to the *national character set* (a secondary Unicode character set defined at the database level). These three datatypes have the same characteristics as the basic ones with the same name. Only their character set is different.

LONG is another character string datatype, even though it has been deprecated in favor of CLOB. You should no longer use it; it is provided for backward compatibility only.

Datetimes

The datatypes used to store datetime values are DATE, TIMESTAMP, TIMESTAMP WITH TIME ZONE, and TIMESTAMP WITH LOCAL TIME ZONE. All of them store the following information: year, month, day, hours, minutes, and seconds. The length of this part is fixed at 7 bytes. The three datatypes based on TIMESTAMP might also store the fractional part of seconds (0–9 digits, per default 6). This part is of variable length: 0–4 bytes. Lastly, TIMESTAMP WITH TIME ZONE stores the time zone in two additional bytes. Since all of them store different information, the best-suited datatype is the one that takes the minimum amount of space for storing the required data.

Bit Strings

Two datatypes are used for storing bit strings: RAW and BLOB. The first supports up to 2,000 bytes. The second should be used only when bit strings are expected to be larger than 2,000 bytes. As of Oracle Database 11g, there are two storage methods for BLOB: basicfile and securefile. For better performance, you should use securefile.

Another bit string datatype is LONG RAW, but it has been deprecated in favor of BLOB. You should no longer use it; it is provided for backward compatibility only.

Row Migration and Row Chaining

Migrated and chained rows are often confused. In my opinion, this is because of two main reasons. First, it is because they share some characteristics, so it is easy to confuse them. Second, it is because Oracle, in its documentation and in the implementation of its software, has never been very consistent in distinguishing them. So before describing how to detect and avoid them, it is essential to briefly describe what the differences between the two are.

Migration vs. Chaining

When rows are inserted into a block, the database engine reserves some free space for future updates. You define the amount of free space reserved for updates using the parameter PCTFREE. To illustrate, I inserted six rows in the block depicted in Figure 12-3. Since the limit set through PCTFREE has been reached, this block is no longer available for inserts.

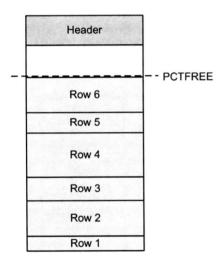

Figure 12-3. *Inserts leave some free space for future updates.*

When a row is updated and its size increases, the database engine tries to find enough free space in the block where it is stored. When not enough free space is available, the row is split into two pieces. The first piece (containing only control information, such as a rowid to the second piece) remains in the original block. This is necessary to avoid changing the rowid. Note that this is crucial because rowids might not only be permanently stored in indexes by the database engine but also be temporarily stored in memory by clients. The second piece, containing all the data, goes into another block. This kind of row is called a *migrated row*. For example, in Figure 12-4, row 4 has been migrated.

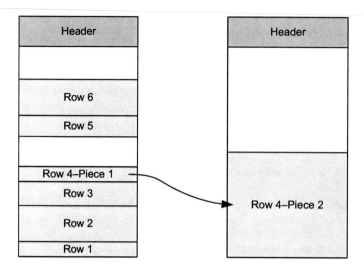

Figure 12-4. *Updated rows that can no longer be stored in the original block are migrated to another one.*

When a row is too big to fit into a single block, it is split into two or more pieces. Then, each piece is stored in a different block, and a chain between the pieces is built. This type of row is called a *chained row*. To illustrate, Figure 12-5 shows a row that is chained over three blocks.

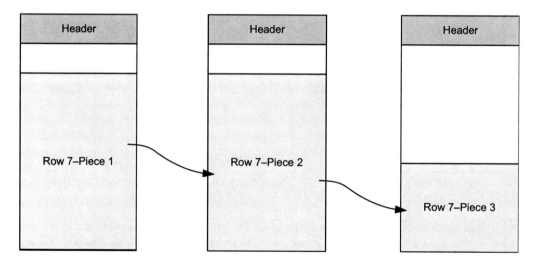

Figure 12-5. *A chained row is split into two or more pieces.*

There is a second situation that causes row chaining: tables with lots of columns. In fact, the database engine is not able to store more than 255 columns in a row piece. Consequently, whenever more than 255 columns have to be stored, the row is split into several pieces. This situation is particular, in that several pieces belonging to the same row can also be stored in a single block. This is called *intra-block row chaining*. Figure 12-6 shows a row with three pieces (since it has 654 columns).

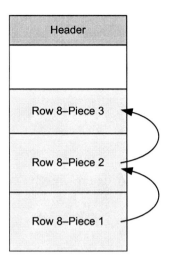

Figure 12-6. *Tables with more than 255 columns might cause intra-block row chaining.*

Note that migrated rows are caused by updates, while chained rows are caused either by inserts or by updates. When chained rows are caused by updates, the rows might be migrated and chained at the same time.

Problem Description

The impact on performance caused by row migration depends on the access path used to read the rows. If they are accessed by rowid, the cost doubles. In fact, both row pieces have to be accessed separately. Instead, there is no overhead if they are accessed through full scans. This is because the first row piece, which contains no data, is simply skipped.

The impact on performance caused by chaining is independent of the access path. In fact, every time the first piece is found, it is necessary to read all the other pieces through the rowid as well. There is one exception, however. As discussed in the section "Optimal Column Order," when only part of a row is needed, not all pieces may need to be accessed. For example, if only columns stored in the first piece are needed, there is no need to access all other pieces.

An overhead that applies to both migration and chaining is related to row-level locking. Every row piece has to be locked. This means that the overhead due to the lock increases proportionally with the number of pieces.

Problem Identification

There are two main techniques for detecting migrated and chained rows. Unfortunately, neither is based on response time. This means no information about the real impact of the problem is available. The first, which is based on the views v$sysstat and v$sesstat, merely gives a clue that somewhere in the database there are either migrated or chained rows. The idea is to check the statistic that gives the number of fetches that read more than one row piece (including intra-block chained rows), namely, table fetch continued row. To assess the relative impact of row chaining and migration, this statistic could also be compared with table scan rows gotten and table fetch by rowid. In contrast, the second technique gives precise information about the migrated and chained rows. Unfortunately, it requires the execution of the SQL statement ANALYZE TABLE <table_name> LIST CHAINED ROWS for each table potentially containing chained or migrated rows. If chained or migrated rows are found, their rowid is inserted into the table chained_rows. Then, based on the rowids, as shown in the following query, it is possible to estimate the size of the rows and, from that, by comparing their size with the block size, recognize whether they are migrated or chained.

```
SELECT vsize(<col1>) + vsize(<col2>) + ... + vsize(<coln>)
FROM <table>
WHERE rowid = '<rowid>'
```

Alternatively, as a rough estimation, it is also possible to look at the column avg_row_len in the table dba_tables. If the average column length is larger than the block size, it is likely that the rows are chained.

Caution The column chain_cnt of the table dba_tables should provide the number of chained and migrated rows. Unfortunately, this statistic is not gathered by the package dbms_stats. It is simply set to 0. Although the only way to populate it with correct values is to execute the SQL statement ANALYZE TABLE <table_name> COMPUTE STATISTICS, this will cause all object statistics for the analyzed table to be overwritten. This is not recommended practice.

Solutions

The measures applied to avoid migration are different from those applied for chaining. Because of this, let me stress that you have to determine whether the problem is caused by migration or chaining before taking measures.

Avoiding row migration is possible. It is only a matter of correctly setting PCTFREE or, in other words, of reserving enough free space to fully store the modified rows in the original blocks. This way, if you have determined that you are experiencing row migration, you should increase the current values of PCTFREE. To choose a good value, you should estimate the average row growth. To do that, you should know their average size at the time when they are inserted and their average size once they are no longer being updated.

To remove migrated rows from a table, there are two possibilities. First, you can completely reorganize the table with export/import or ALTER TABLE MOVE. Second, you can copy only the migrated rows into a temporary table and then delete and reinsert them into the original table. The second approach is especially useful when a small percentage of the rows are migrated and there is not enough time or resources to fully reorganize the table.

Avoiding row chaining is much more difficult. The obvious measure to apply is to use a larger block size. Sometimes, however, even the largest block size is not large enough. In addition, if chaining is due to the number of columns being greater than 255, only a redesign can help. Therefore, in some situations, the only possible workaround to this problem is to place infrequently accessed columns at the end of the table and thereby avoid accessing all pieces every time.

Block Contention

Block contention, which is when multiple processes vie for access to the same blocks at the same time, can lead to poor application performance. Block contention can sometimes be alleviated by manipulating the physical storage parameters for a table or for an index.

Problem Description

The buffer cache is shared among all processes belonging to an instance. As a result, several processes might concurrently read or modify the very same block stored in the buffer cache. To avoid conflicting accesses, each process, before being able to access a block in the buffer cache, has to hold a pin on it (there are exceptions to this rule, but it is not important to discuss them for the purpose of this section). A *pin*, which is a short-term lock, is taken in either shared or exclusive mode. On a given block, several processes might hold a pin in shared mode (for example, if they all need to read the block only), while only a single process can hold it in exclusive mode (needed to modify the block). Whenever a process needs a pin in a mode conflicting with other pins held by other processes, it has to wait. It is confronted with *block contention*.

■ **Note** Before being able to pin or unpin a block, a process has to get the `cache buffers chains` latch protecting the block. Because of that, it might happen that block contention is masked by contention for the latch.

System-wide information about block contention is available through the view v$waitstat (the following query shows an example of the information it provides). The essential thing to understand about this view is that the column class is referring to the block type, not to the type of data or structure for which it is waited. For example, if there is contention due to freelists contained in a segment header block, the waits are reported under the class segment header and not under the class free list.

```
SQL> SELECT * FROM v$waitstat;

CLASS                 COUNT       TIME
------------------ ---------- ----------
data block            102011       5162
sort block                 0          0
save undo block            0          0
segment header         76053        719
save undo header           0          0
free list               3265         12
extent map                 0          0
1st level bmb           6318        352
2nd level bmb            185          3
3rd level bmb              0          0
bitmap block               0          0
bitmap index block         0          0
file header block        389       2069
```

unused	0	0
system undo header	1	1
system undo block	0	0
undo header	3244	70
undo block	38	2

Problem Identification

If you are following the analysis road map described in Chapter 3, the only effective way to identify block contention problems is to measure how much time is lost because of them. The best way to get this information is by means of a profiler. For that purpose, you should check the wait event related to block contention, namely, buffer busy waits. In fact, processes that experience block contention wait for that event. As a result, if this event shows up as a relevant component in the resource usage profile, the application is suffering because of block contention. To analyze such a situation, you need the following information:

- The SQL statement that experienced the waits

- The class of the blocks on which the waits occurred

- The segment on which the waits occurred

Since Chapter 3 describes two profilers, TKPROF and TVD$XTAT, I discuss in the next two sections the same example for the output of both profilers. The trace file used as an example was generated by executing the script buffer_busy_waits.sql. The trace file and both output files are available in the file buffer_busy_waits.zip.

Using TKPROF

The output file generated by TKPROF shows that one SQL statement, an UPDATE statement, is responsible for almost the whole response time. The following excerpt shows its execution statistics. For 10,000 executions, an elapsed time of 5.69 seconds and a CPU time of 0.94 seconds were measured.

```
UPDATE T SET D = SYSDATE WHERE ID = :B1 AND N10 = ID
```

call	count	cpu	elapsed	disk	query	current	rows
Parse	1	0.00	0.00	0	0	0	0
Execute	10000	0.94	5.69	0	31934	29484	10000
Fetch	0	0.00	0.00	0	0	0	0
total	10001	0.94	5.69	0	31934	29484	10000

Since the CPU time is only 16.5 percent of the response time, it is necessary to analyze the waits that occurred during the processing to find out how the time was spent. The following excerpt shows precisely that information. You can see that the greatest consumer is the event buffer busy waits with 4.64 seconds. Also notice that in this specific case, there is minimal contention for the latch cache buffers chains. In other words, the SQL statement experienced block contention.

Event waited on	Times Waited	Max. Wait	Total Waited
buffer busy waits	4466	0.01	4.64
latch: In memory undo latch	152	0.00	0.02
latch: cache buffers chains	584	0.00	0.04
wait list latch free	2	0.01	0.02
latch: undo global data	3	0.00	0.00
latch free	3	0.00	0.00
latch: enqueue hash chains	3	0.00	0.00

As described before, in order to analyze buffer busy waits events, it is essential to know the class of the block and the segment on which the waits occurred. This information is not available in the TKPROF output. You have to manually extract it from the raw trace file. This is bothersome (especially because there are many waits; in this case, there are 4,466). Because of this, I advise using TVD$XTAT for that purpose.

Using TVD$XTAT

Naturally, the output of TVD$XTAT points out that an UPDATE statement is suffering from block contention as well. As shown in the following excerpt, the first part of the output is similar to the one generated by TKPROF. It also reveals that the greatest response time component is the event buffer busy waits.

Call	Count	Misses	CPU	Elapsed	PIO	LIO	Consistent	Current	Rows
Parse	1	1	0.000	0.000	0	0	0	0	0
Execute	10,000	1	0.942	5.694	0	61,418	31,934	29,484	10,000
Fetch	0	0	0.000	0.000	0	0	0	0	0
Total	10,001	2	0.942	5.694	0	61,418	31,934	29,484	10,000

Component	Duration	%	Events	Event
buffer busy waits	4.649	81.753	4,466	0.001
CPU	0.942	16.563	n/a	n/a
latch: cache buffers chains	0.043	0.752	584	0.000
latch: In memory undo latch	0.025	0.445	152	0.000
wait list latch free	0.024	0.425	2	0.012
recursive statements	0.003	0.053	n/a	n/a
latch free	0.000	0.005	3	0.000
latch: undo global data	0.000	0.002	3	0.000
latch: enqueue hash chains	0.000	0.002	3	0.000
Total	5.686	100.000		

The additional information provided by TVD$XTAT is a list containing the blocks on which the waits occurred. The following excerpt shows what such a list looks like in the case being analyzed here. You can see from it that more than 99 percent of the buffer busy waits events occurred on block 23,725 in file 4. Also notice that the block experiencing contention is a data block.

File	Block Number	Total Duration	%	Number of Events	%	Class/Reason
4	23,725	4.628	99.544	4,102	91.850	**data block** (1)
2	9	0.003	0.068	31	0.694	undo header (17)
2	121	0.003	0.058	40	0.896	undo header (31)
2	105	0.003	0.055	34	0.761	undo header (29)
2	89	0.002	0.051	25	0.560	undo header (27)
2	137	0.002	0.051	31	0.694	undo header (33)
2	57	0.002	0.040	38	0.851	undo header (23)
2	73	0.002	0.039	39	0.873	undo header (25)
2	153	0.002	0.037	35	0.784	undo header (35)
2	25	0.002	0.037	45	1.008	undo header (19)
2	41	0.001	0.020	43	0.963	undo header (21)
2	7,418	0	0.000	1	0.022	undo block (26)
2	7,674	0	0.000	1	0.022	undo block (28)
2	7,927	0	0.000	1	0.022	undo block (36)
Total		4.649	100.000	4,466	100.000	

> **Note** For each block that has experienced block contention, either the reason for the contention or the class of the block is given. This is because up to Oracle9*i*, the trace files contain the former and, as of Oracle Database 10*g*, they contain only the latter. This is not specific to the files generated by SQL trace. Actually, the dynamic performance views that give information about wait events were modified in the same way as well.

Based on this information, you can find out the name of the segment on which the waits occurred with a query like the following (be careful, as executing this query might be resource-intensive):

```
SQL> SELECT owner, segment_name, segment_types
  2  FROM dba_extents
  3  WHERE file_id = 4
  4  AND 23725 BETWEEN block_id AND block_id+blocks-1;

OWNER     SEGMENT_NAME  SEGMENT_TYPE
--------  ------------- -------------
OPS$CHA   T             TABLE
```

In summary, the whole analysis provided the following information:

- The SQL statement that experienced the waits is an UPDATE statement.

- The waits occurred, most of the time, on a single data block.

- The segment on which the waits occurred is the table t in the schema ops$cha, in other words, the table on which the UPDATE statement was executed.

Solutions

By identifying the SQL statement, the block class, and the segment that experienced the waits, it should be possible to identify the root cause of the problem. Let's discuss some typical cases for common block classes.

Contention for Data Blocks

All the blocks that make up a table or index segments that are not used for storing metadata (for example, segment headers) are called *data blocks*. Contention for them has two main causes. The first is when the frequency of table or index scans on a given segment is very high. The second is when the frequency of executions is very high. At first glance, both are the same thing. Why they are in fact different requires some explanation. In the first case, the problem is because of inefficient execution plans causing frequent table or index scans over the same blocks. Usually it is because of inefficient related-combine operations (for example, nested loop joins). Here, even two or three SQL statements executed concurrently might be enough to cause contention. Instead, in the second case, the problem is the execution of several SQL statements accessing the same block at the same time. In other words, it is the number of SQL statements executed concurrently against (few) blocks that is the problem. It might be that both happen at the same time. If this is the case, take care of solving the first problem before facing the second one. In fact, the second problem might disappear when the first is gone.

To solve the first problem, SQL tuning is necessary. An efficient execution plan must be executed in place of the inefficient one. Of course, in some situations, that is easier said than done. Nevertheless, this is really what you have to achieve.

To solve the second problem, several approaches are available. Which one you have to use depends on the type of the SQL statement (that is, DELETE, INSERT, SELECT,[1] and UPDATE) and on the type of the segment (that is, table or index). However, before starting, you should always ask one question when the frequency of execution is high: is it really necessary to execute those SQL statements against the same data so often? Actually, it is not unusual to see applications (that implement some kind of polling, for example) that unnecessarily execute the same SQL statement too often. If the frequency of execution cannot be reduced, there are the following possibilities. Note that in all situations, the goal is to spread the activities over a greater number of blocks in order to solve the problem.

---

1. SELECT statements modify blocks in two situations: first, when the option FOR UPDATE is specified, and second, when deferred block cleanout occurs.

- If there is contention for a table's blocks because of DELETE, SELECT, and UPDATE state-ments, you should reduce the number of rows per block. Note that this is the opposite of the common best practice to fit the maximum number of rows per block. To store fewer rows per block, either a higher PCTFREE or a smaller block size can be used.

- If there is contention for a table's blocks because of INSERT statements and freelist segment space management is in use, the number of freelists can be increased. In fact, the goal of having several freelists is precisely to spread concurrent INSERT statements over several blocks. Another possibility is to move the segment into a tablespace with automatic segment storage management.

- If there is contention for an index's blocks, there are two possible solutions. First, the index can be created with the option REVERSE. Note, however, that this method does not help if the contention is on the root block of the index. Second, the index can be hash partitioned, based on the leading column of the index key (this creates multiple root blocks and so helps with root block contention if a single partition is accessed). Because global hash-partitioned indexes are available as of Oracle Database 10*g* only, this is not an option with Oracle9*i*.

The important thing to note about reverse indexes is that range scans on them cannot apply restrictions based on range conditions (for example, BETWEEN, >, or <=). Of course, equality predicates are supported. The following example, based on the script reserve_index.sql, shows that the query optimizer no longer uses the index after rebuilding it with the option REVERSE.

```
SQL> SELECT * FROM t WHERE n < 10;


---------------------------------------------
| Id | Operation                 | Name |
---------------------------------------------
|  0 | SELECT STATEMENT          |      |
|  1 |  TABLE ACCESS BY INDEX ROWID| T  |
|  2 |   INDEX RANGE SCAN        | T_I  |
---------------------------------------------

SQL> ALTER INDEX t_i REBUILD REVERSE;

SQL> SELECT * FROM t WHERE n < 10;


-----------------------------------
| Id | Operation        | Name |
-----------------------------------
|  0 | SELECT STATEMENT |      |
|  1 |  TABLE ACCESS FULL| T   |
-----------------------------------
```

Note that hints do not help in such a situation either. The database engine is simply not able to apply a range condition with an index range scan with a reverse index. Therefore, as the following example illustrates, if you try to force the query optimizer to use an index access, an index full scan will be used.

```
SQL> SELECT /*+ index(t) */ * FROM t WHERE n < 10;

-------------------------------------------
| Id  | Operation                 | Name  |
-------------------------------------------
|   0 | SELECT STATEMENT          |       |
|   1 |  TABLE ACCESS BY INDEX ROWID| T   |
|   2 |   INDEX FULL SCAN         | T_I   |
-------------------------------------------
```

Contention for Segment Header Blocks

Every table and index segment has a header block. This block contains the following metadata: information about the high watermark of the segment, a list of the extents making up the segment, and information about the free space. To manage the free space, the header block contains (depending on the type of segment space management that is in use) either freelists or a list of blocks containing automatic segment space management information. Typically, contention for a segment header block is experienced when its content is modified by several processes concurrently. Note that the header block is modified in the following situations:

- If INSERT statements make it necessary to increase the high watermark

- If INSERT statements make it necessary to allocate new extents

- If DELETE, INSERT, and UPDATE statements make it necessary to modify a freelist

A possible solution for these situations is to partition the segment in order to spread the load over several segment header blocks. Most of the time, this might be achieved with hash partitioning, although, depending on the load and the partition key, other partitioning methods might work as well. However, if the problem is because of the second or third situation, other solutions exist. For the second, you should use bigger extents. In this way, new extents would seldom be allocated. For the third, which does not apply to tablespaces using automatic segment space management, freelists can be moved into other blocks by means of freelist groups. In fact, when several freelist groups are used, the freelists are no longer located in the segment header block (they are spread on a number of blocks equal to the value specified with the parameter FREELIST GROUPS, so you will have less contention on them—you are not simply moving the contention to another place!). Another possibility is to use a tablespace with automatic segment space management instead of freelist segment space management.

■**Note** One of the long-lasting myths about the Oracle database engine is that freelist groups are useful only when Real Application Clusters is in use. This is *wrong*. Freelist groups are useful in every database. I stress this point because I have read and heard wrong information about this too many times.

Contention for Undo Header and Undo Blocks

Contention for these types of blocks occurs in two situations. The first, and only for undo header blocks, is when few undo segments are available and lots of transactions are concurrently committed (or rolled back). This should be a problem only if you are using manual undo management. In other words, it usually happens if the database administrator has manually created the rollback segments. To solve this problem, you should use automatic undo management. The second situation is when several sessions modify and query the same blocks at the same time. As a result, lots of consistent read blocks have to be created, and this requires you to access both the block and its associated undo blocks. There is little that can be done about this situation, other than reducing the concurrency for the data blocks, thereby reducing the ones for the undo blocks at the same time.

Contention for Extent Map Blocks

As discussed in the section "Contention for Segment Header Blocks," the segment header blocks contain a list of the extents that make up the segment. If the list does not fit in the segment header, it is distributed over several blocks: the segment header block and one or more extent map blocks. Contention for a segment header block is experienced when concurrent INSERT statements have to constantly allocate new extents. To solve this problem, you should use bigger extents.

Contention for Freelist Blocks

As discussed in the section "Contention for Segment Header Blocks," freelists can be moved into other blocks, called *freelist blocks*, by means of freelist groups. Contention for a freelist block is experienced when concurrent DELETE, INSERT, or UPDATE statements have to modify the freelists. To solve this problem, you should increase the number of freelist groups. Another possibility is to use a tablespace with automatic segment space management instead of freelist segment space management.

Data Compression

The common goal of compressing data is to save disk space. Since we are dealing with performance, in this section I will speak about another advantage of data compression that is frequently forgotten: improving response time.

Note Data compression is a feature available in Enterprise Edition only.

The idea is quite simple. If a SQL statement has to process a lot of data through a full table (or partition) scan, it is likely that the main contributor to its resource usage profile is related to I/O operations. In such a situation, decreasing the amount of data to be read from the disk will increase performance. Actually, the performance should increase almost proportionally to the compression factor. The following example, based on the script data_compression.sql, illustrates this:

```
SQL> CREATE TABLE t NOCOMPRESS AS
  2  SELECT rownum AS n, rpad(' ',500,mod(rownum,15)) AS pad
  3  FROM dual
  4  CONNECT BY level <= 2000000;

SQL> execute dbms_stats.gather_table_stats(ownname=>user, tabname=>'t')

SQL> SELECT table_name, blocks FROM user_tables WHERE table_name = 'T';

TABLE_NAME                       BLOCKS
------------------------------ ----------
T                                143486

SQL> SELECT count(n) FROM t;

  COUNT(*)
----------
   2000000

Elapsed: 00:00:12.68

SQL> ALTER TABLE t MOVE COMPRESS;

SQL> execute dbms_stats.gather_table_stats(ownname=>user, tabname=>'t')

SQL> SELECT table_name, blocks FROM user_tables WHERE table_name = 'T';

TABLE_NAME                       BLOCKS
------------------------------ ----------
T                                 27274

SQL> SELECT count(n) FROM t;

  COUNT(*)
----------
   2000000

Elapsed: 00:00:02.76

SQL> SELECT 143486/27274, 12.68/2.76 FROM dual;

143486/27274 12.68/2.76
------------ ----------
  5.26090782  4.5942029
```

To take advantage of data compression for full-scan operations as shown in the example, it essential to have spare CPU resources. This is not because of the CPU overhead of "uncompressing" the blocks (which is very small; they are not compressed using a zip-like algorithm) but simply because the operations performed by the SQL engine (in the previous example, accessing the blocks and doing the count) are executed in a shorter period of time. For example, on my test system, the CPU utilization during the execution of the test query was about 7 percent without compression and 11 percent with compression.

To use data compression, the following requirements must be fulfilled:

- The table cannot have more than 255 columns.

- The table cannot be created with the parameter `rowdependencies`.

It is important to note that although data compression does have some advantages, it also has several drawbacks. The most significant is that the database engine, up to Oracle Database 10g, compresses data blocks only when data is inserted through the direct path interface. Hence, it will compress data blocks only with the following operations:

- `CREATE TABLE ... COMPRESS ... AS SELECT ...`

- `ALTER TABLE ... MOVE COMPRESS`

- `INSERT /*+ append */ INTO ... SELECT ...`

- `INSERT /*+ parallel(...) */ INTO ... SELECT ...`

- Loads performed by applications using the OCI direct-path interface (for example, the SQL*Loader utility)

The result is that data inserted through regular `INSERT` statements is inserted in noncompressed blocks. Another disadvantage is that not only do `UPDATE` statements commonly lead to migrated rows stored in noncompressed blocks but also that the free space in compressed blocks caused by `DELETE` statements is never reused. For these reasons, I suggest using data compression only on segments that are (mostly) read-only. For example, in a partitioned table storing a long history where only the last few partitions are modified, it could be useful to compress the partitions that are (mostly) read-only. Data marts and completely refreshed materialized views are also good candidates for data compression.

As of Oracle Database 11g, the following two compression methods are available:

`compress for direct_load operations`: This method is equivalent to the compression method used up to Oracle Database 10g (that is, it is equivalent to specifying `compress`).

`compress for all operations`: This method partially overcomes some of the limitations of the previous one. However, the Advanced Compression option is required.

Since the new compression method is dynamic (data might be compressed not when it is inserted but later when the block storing it is modified), it is difficult to give advice about its utilization. Actually, there are still several situations in which the new compression method is not better than the old one. To figure out whether the new compression method is able to correctly handle data that is not (mostly) read-only, I strongly advise you to carefully test it with the expected load.

Appendixes

APPENDIX A

■ ■ ■

Downloadable Files

This appendix lists all the files used throughout the book. It also describes the test environment, which is important because some scripts will work correctly only when a specific configuration is in place.

Test Environment

My test server is a Dell PowerEdge 1900, equipped with a quad-core Xeon processor (E5320, 1.86GHz), 4GB of memory, two mirrored SATA disks (Samsung Spinpoint, 300GB, 7,200rpm) for the operating system and all other applications, and four striped SAS disks (Seagate Cheetah, 73GB, 15,000rpm) for the database files. The server is connected to my workstation and to the other test clients through a gigabit network and switch.

The operating system is CentOS[1] 4.4 x86_64. The following versions of the Oracle database engine are installed (actually, these are all the versions that are currently available for this platform):

- *Oracle9i Release 2*: 9.2.0.4, 9.2.0.6, 9.2.0.7, 9.2.0.8

- *Oracle Database 10g Release 1*: 10.1.0.3, 10.1.0.4, 10.1.0.5

- *Oracle Database 10g Release 2*: 10.2.0.1, 10.2.0.2, 10.2.0.3, 10.2.0.4

- *Oracle Database 11g Release 1*: 11.1.0.6

For each version, I installed two databases: Enterprise Edition without options and Enterprise Edition with all options.

Files Available for Download

Figure A-1 shows the structure of the distribution file you can download from http://top.antognini.ch. For each chapter (except Chapter 1), there is a directory containing the files related to it. In addition, for each database, there is a directory containing the files I used to build it.

---

1. See http://www.centos.org for additional information.

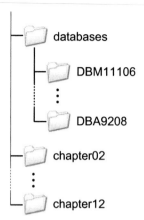

Figure A-1. *The directory structure of the distribution file*

Databases

Scripts were generated using the Database Configuration Assistant. For all databases, only the initialization parameters related to the name of the database, the location of the files, and the memory utilization are set. All other initialization parameters were left at the default value. The only exception is the initialization parameter remote_os_authent, which is set to TRUE. Note that you should never use this value for a database, except in a "playground" (a system that has no value and contains no data of any importance whatsoever).

The names of the databases define the type of the installation. For example, the names of the two databases shown in Figure A-1 mean the following:

- DBM11106: Database without options (M stands for "minimal") of version 11.1.0.6

- DBA9208: Database with all options (A stands for "all") of version 9.2.0.8

Every script has been tested against every database. If a specific script doesn't work in one of them, the header of the script indicates when this is the case.

Chapter 2

The files listed in Table A-1 are available for download for Chapter 2.

Table A-1. *Files for Chapter 2*

File Name	Description
bind_variables.sql	This script shows how and when bind variables lead to the sharing of cursors.
bind_variables_peeking.sql	This script shows the pros and cons of bind variable peeking.
selectivity.sql	This scripts provides the examples shown in the section "Defining Selectivity."
sharable_cursors.sql	This script shows examples of parent and child cursors that cannot be shared.

Chapter 3

The files listed in Table A-2 are available for download for Chapter 3.

Table A-2. *Files for Chapter 3*

File Name	Description
DBM11106_ora_6334.trc	This is the sample trace file used as the basis for explaining the TKPROF and TVD$XTAT output.
DBM11106_ora_6334.txt	This is the TKPROF output of the trace file DBM11106_ora_9813.trc used as the basis for explaining the format of the file generated by TKPROF.
DBM11106_ora_6334.html	This is the TVD$XTAT output of the trace file DBM11106_ora_9813.trc used as the basis for explaining the format of the file generated by TVD$XTAT.
dbm10203_ora_24433.trc	This is the sample trace file depicted in Figure 3-19. It shows how information is stored regarding multiple sections generated by a single session.
dbm10203_s000_24374.trc	This is the sample trace file shown in Figure 3-19. It shows how information is stored regarding three sessions connected through a shared server.
dbms_profiler.sql	This script shows how to profile a PL/SQL procedure and how to display the generated information.
dbms_profiler_triggers.sql	You can use this script to create two triggers enabling and disabling the PL/SQL profiler.
LoggingPerf.java	You can use this Java class to compare the average execution time of the methods info and isInfoEnabled of the log4j class Logger.
makefile.mk	This is the makefile I used to compile the C program given as an example.
map_session_to_tracefile.sql	You can use this script to map a session ID to a trace file.
perfect_triangles.sql	You can use this script to create the PL/SQL procedure perfect_triangles used as an example in the "Gathering the Profiling Data" section.
session_attributes.c	This C program shows how to set the client identifier, client information, module name, and action name through OCI.
SessionAttributes.cs	This C# class shows how to set the client identifier through ODP.NET.
SessionAttributes.java	This Java class shows how to set the client identifier, module name, and action name through JDBC.
trcsess.awk	You can use this awk script to make SQL trace files generated with Oracle9*i* compatible with the command-line tool trcsess.

Chapter 4

The files listed in Table A-3 are available for download for Chapter 4.

Table A-3. *Files for Chapter 4*

File Name	Description
clustering_factor.sql	This script creates a function that illustrates how the clustering factor is computed.
comparing_object_statistics.sql	This script shows how to compare current object statistics with object statistics stored in the history that are pending and stored in a backup table.
cpu_cost_column_access.sql	This script shows the CPU cost estimated by the query optimizer when accessing a column, depending on its position in the table.
dbms_stats_job_10g.sql	This script shows the actual configuration of the job aimed at automatically gathering object statistics, which is installed and scheduled during the creation of a 10*g* database.
dbms_stats_job_11g.sql	This script shows the actual configuration of the job aimed at automatically gathering object statistics, which is installed and scheduled during the creation of an 11*g* database.
delete_histogram.sql	This script shows how to delete a single histogram, without modifying the other statistics.
lock_statistics.sql	This script shows the working and behavior of locked object statistics.
mreadtim_lt_sreadtim.sql	This script shows the correction performed by the query optimizer when mreadtim is smaller or equal to sreadtim.
object_statistics.sql	This script provides an overview of all object statistics.
pending_object_statistics.sql	This script shows how to use pending statistics to test a new set of object statistics before publishing them.
system_stats_history_job.sql	This script can be used to create a table and a job to store the evolution of workload statistics over several days.
system_stats_history.sql	This script is used to extract workload statistics from the history table created by the script system_stats_history_job.sql. The output can be imported into the spreadsheet system_stats_history.xls.
system_stats_history.xls	This Excel spreadsheet can be used to compute average values and to draw charts showing trends of workload statistics extracted with the script system_stats_history.sql.

Chapter 5

The files listed in Table A-4 are available for download for Chapter 5.

Table A-4. *Files for Chapter 5*

File Name	Description
assess_dbfmbrc.sql	This script is used to test the performance of multiblock reads for different values of the initialization parameter db_file_multiblock_read_count. The idea is to determine the value of this parameter that provides optimal performance.
bug5015557.sql	This script shows that the initialization parameter optimizer_features_enable disables bug fixes as well as regular features.
dynamic_sampling_levels.sql	This script shows examples of queries taking advantage of dynamic sampling, for levels going from 1 to 4.
optimizer_index_caching.sql	This script shows the working and drawbacks of the initialization parameter optimizer_index_caching.
optimizer_index_cost_adj.sql	This script shows the drawbacks of setting the initialization parameter optimizer_index_cost_adj.
optimizer_secure_view_merging.sql	This script shows the working and drawbacks of the initialization parameter optimizer_secure_view_merging.

Chapter 6

The files listed in Table A-5 are available for download for Chapter 6.

Table A-5. *Files for Chapter 6*

File Name	Description
dbms_xplan_output.sql	This script generates a sample output containing the main information provided by the functions of dbms_xplan.
display.sql	This script shows examples of how to use the function display in the package dbms_xplan.
display_awr.sql	This script shows examples of how to use the function display_awr in the package dbms_xplan.
display_cursor.sql	This script shows examples of how to use the function display_cursor in the package dbms_xplan.
display_cursor_9i.sql	This script displays the execution plan of a cursor stored in the library cache. The cursor is identified by address, hash value, and child number.
execution_plans.sql	This script shows the different types of operations that execution plans are composed of.
parent_vs_child_cursors.sql	This script shows the relationship between a parent cursor and its children's cursors.

Table A-5. *Files for Chapter 6 (Continued)*

File Name	Description
restriction_not_recognized.sql	This script generates the output used for showing how to recognize inefficient execution plans, by checking actual cardinalities.
wrong_estimations.sql	This script generates the output used for showing how to recognize inefficient execution plans by looking at wrong estimations.

Chapter 7

The files listed in Table A-6 are available for download for Chapter 7.

Table A-6. *Files for Chapter 7*

File Name	Description
all_rows.sql	This script shows how it is possible to switch the optimizer mode from rule to all_rows with a SQL profile.
baseline_automatic.sql	This script shows how the query optimizer automatically captures a SQL plan baseline.
baseline_from_sqlarea1.sql	This script shows how to manually load a SQL plan baseline from the library cache. The cursor is identified by the text of the SQL statement associated with it.
baseline_from_sqlarea2.sql	This script shows how to manually load a SQL plan baseline from the library cache. The cursor is identified by the SQL identifier of the SQL statement associated with it.
baseline_from_sqlarea3.sql	This script shows how to tune an application without changing its code. A SQL plan baseline is used for that purpose.
baseline_from_sqlset.sql	This script shows how to manually load a SQL plan baseline from a SQL tuning set.
baseline_upgrade_10g.sql	This script shows how to create and export a SQL tuning set on Oracle Database 10*g*. It is used along with the script baseline_upgrade_11g.sql to show how to stabilize execution plans during an upgrade to Oracle Database 11*g*.
baseline_upgrade_11g.sql	This script shows how to import and load a SQL tuning set into a SQL plan baseline. It is used along with the script baseline_upgrade_10g.sql to show how to stabilize execution plans during an upgrade from Oracle Database 10*g* to Oracle Database 11*g*.
clone_baseline.sql	This script shows how to move SQL plan baselines between two databases.
clone_sql_profile.sql	This script shows how to create a copy of a SQL profile.
depts_wo_emps.sql	This script was used to generate the execution plans used as examples in the section "Altering the Access Structures."

Table A-6. *Files for Chapter 7*

File Name	Description
exec_env_trigger.sql	This script creates a configuration table and a database trigger to control the execution environment at the session level.
first_rows.sql	This script shows how it is possible to switch the optimizer mode from all_rows to first_rows with a SQL profile.
object_stats.sql	This script shows how it is possible to provide object statistics to the query optimizer with a SQL profile.
opt_estimate.sql	This script shows how it is possible to enhance the cardinality estimations performed by the query optimizer with a SQL profile.
outline_editing.sql	This script shows how to manually edit a stored outline.
outline_edit_tables.sql	This script creates the working tables and public synonym necessary to edit private outlines.
outline_from_sqlarea.sql	This script shows how to manually create a stored outline by referencing a cursor in the shared pool.
outline_from_text.sql	This script shows how to manually create a stored outline as well as how to manage and use it.
outline_with_ffs.sql	This script tests whether a stored outline is able to overwrite the setting of the initialization parameter optimizer_features_enable.
outline_with_hj.sql	This script tests whether a stored outline is able to overwrite the setting of the initialization parameter hash_join_enabled.
outline_with_rewrite.sql	This script tests whether a stored outline is able to overwrite the setting of the initialization parameter query_rewrite_enabled.
outline_with_star.sql	This script tests whether a stored outline is able to overwrite the setting of the initialization parameter star_transformation_enabled.
tune_last_statement.sql	This script is used to instruct the SQL Tuning Advisor to analyze the last SQL statement executed by the current session. When the processing is over, the analysis report is shown.

Chapter 8

The files listed in Table A-7 are available for download for Chapter 8.

Table A-7. *Files for Chapter 8*

File Name	Description
bind_variables.sql	This script shows how and when bind variables lead to the sharing of cursors.
bind_variables_peeking.sql	This script shows the pros and cons of bind variable peeking.
lifecycle.sql	This script shows the difference between implicit and explicit cursor management.
long_parse.sql	This script is used to carry out a parse lasting about one second. It also shows how to create a stored outline to avoid such a long parse.
long_parse.zip	This compressed archive contains two trace files generated by the execution of the script long_parse.sql. For each trace file, the output files generated by TKPROF and TVD$XTAT are available as well.
ParsingTest1.c, ParsingTest2.c, and ParsingTest3.c	These files contain C (OCI) implementations of test case 1, 2, and 3, respectively.
ParsingTest1.cs and ParsingTest2.cs	These files contain C# (ODP.NET) implementations of test case 1 and 2, respectively.
ParsingTest1.java, ParsingTest2.java, and ParsingTest3.java	These files contain Java implementations of test case 1, 2, and 3, respectively.
ParsingTest1.sql, ParsingTest2.sql, and ParsingTest3.sql	These scripts provide PL/SQL implementations of test case 1, 2, and 3, respectively.
ParsingTest1.zip, ParsingTest2.zip, and ParsingTest3.zip	These compressed archives contain several trace files generated by the execution of the Java implementation of test case 1, 2, and 3, respectively. For each trace file, the output files generated by TKPROF and TVD$XTAT are available as well.

Chapter 9

The files listed in Table A-8 are available for download for Chapter 9.

Table A-8. *Files for Chapter 9*

File Name	Description
access_structures_1.sql	This script compares the performance of different access structures in order to read a single row. It was used to generate the figures in Figure 9-3.
access_structures_1000.sql	This script compares the performance of different access structures in order to read thousands of rows. It was used to generate the figures in Figure 9-4.
conditions.sql	This script shows how you can use B-tree and bitmap indexes to apply several types of conditions.
fbi.sql	This script shows an example of a function-based index.
full_scan_hwm.sql	This script shows that full table scans read all blocks up to the high watermark.
index_full_scan.sql	This script shows examples of full index scans.
iot_guess.sql	This script shows the impact of stale guesses on logical reads.
linguistic_index.sql	This script shows an example of a linguistic index.
pruning_composite.sql	This script shows several examples of partition pruning applied to a composite-partitioned table.
pruning_hash.sql	This script shows several examples of partition pruning applied to a hash-partitioned table.
pruning_list.sql	This script shows several examples of partition pruning applied to a list-partitioned table.
pruning_range.sql	This script shows several examples of partition pruning applied to a range-partitioned table.
read_consistency.sql	This script shows how the number of logical reads might change because of read consistency.
row_prefetching.sql	This script shows how the number of logical reads might change because of row prefetching.

Chapter 10

The files listed in Table A-9 are available for download for Chapter 10.

Table A-9. *Files for Chapter 10*

File Name	Description
block_prefetching.sql	This script shows block prefetching for data and index blocks.
hash_join.sql	This script provides several examples of hash joins.
join_elimination.sql	This script provides an example of join elimination.
join_trees.sql	This script provides an example for each type of join tree.
join_types.sql	This script provides an example for each type of join.
nested_loops_join.sql	This script provides several examples of nested loop joins.
merge_join.sql	This script provides several examples of merge joins.
outer_join.sql	This script provides several examples of outer joins.
outer_to_inner.sql	This script provides an example of an outer join transformed into an inner join.
pwj.sql	This script provides several examples of partition-wise joins.
pwj_performance.sql	This script is used to compare the performance of different partition-wise joins. It was used to generate the figures found in Figure 10-15.
star_transformation.sql	This script provides several examples of star transformation.
subquery_unnesting.sql	This script provides several examples of subquery unnesting.

Chapter 11

The files listed in Table A-10 are available for download for Chapter 11.

Table A-10. *Files for Chapter 11*

File Name	Description
array_interface.sql, array_interface.c, ArrayInterface.cs, and ArrayInterface.java	These scripts provide examples of implementing the array interface with PL/SQL, OCI, JDBC, and ODP.NET.
ArrayInterfacePerf.java	This script shows that the array interface can greatly improve the response time of a large load. It was used to generate Figure 11-13.
atomic_refresh.sql	This script can be used to reproduce bug 3168840 in Oracle9*i*. The bug causes refreshes not to work correctly if a single materialized view is refreshed.

Table A-10. *Files for Chapter 11*

File Name	Description
dpi.sql	This script shows the behavior of direct-path inserts related to the utilization of the buffer cache, the generation of redo and undo, and the support of triggers and foreign keys.
dpi_performance.sql	This script is used to compare direct-path inserts with conventional inserts. It was used to generate Figure 11-10 and Figure 11-11.
makefile.mk	This is the makefile I used to compile the C programs given as an example.
mv.sql	This script shows the basic concepts of materialized views.
mv_refresh_log.sql	This script shows how fast refreshes based on materialized view logs work.
mv_refresh_pct.sql	This script shows how fast refreshes based on partition change tracking work.
mv_rewrite.sql	This script shows several examples of query rewrite.
px_ddl.sql	This script shows several examples of parallel DDL statements.
px_dml.sql	This script shows several examples of parallel DML statements.
px_dop1.sql	This script shows the impact of the initialization parameter parallel_min_percent.
px_dop2.sql	This script shows that hints do not force the query optimizer to use parallel processing. They simply override the default degree of parallelism.
px_query.sql	This script shows several examples of parallel queries.
px_tqstat.sql	This script shows what kind of information the dynamic performance view v$pq_tqstat displays.
result_cache_query.sql	This script shows an example of a query that takes advantage of the server result cache.
result_cache_plsql.sql	This script shows an example of a PL/SQL function that implements the PL/SQL function result cache.
row_prefetching.sql, row_prefetching.c, RowPrefetching.cs, RowPrefetching.java	These scripts provide examples of implementing row prefetching with PL/SQL, OCI, JDBC, and ODP.NET.
RowPrefetchingPerf.java	This script shows that row prefetching can greatly improve the response time of a query that retrieves many rows. It was used to generate Figure 11-12.

Chapter 12

The files listed in Table A-11 are available for download for Chapter 12.

Table A-11. *Files for Chapter 12*

File Name	Description
buffer_busy_waits.sql	This script shows an example of processing that causes plenty of buffer busy waits events.
buffer_busy_waits.zip	This file contains the trace files and the output of TKPROF and TVD$XTAT used in the section "Block Contention."
column_order.sql	This script shows that the position of a column in a row determines the amount of processing needed to access it. The script was used to generate the values represented in Figure 12-2.
data_compression.sql	This script shows that the performance of I/O bound processing might be improved thanks to data compression.
reverse_index.sql	This script shows that range scans on reverse indexes cannot be used to apply restrictions based on range conditions.
wrong_datatype.sql	This script shows that the decisions of the query optimizer are badly affected by the utilization of wrong datatypes.

APPENDIX B

Bibliography

Adams, Steve, "Oracle Internals and Advanced Performance Tuning." Miracle Master Class, 2003.

Alomari, Ahmed, *Oracle8i & Unix Performance Tuning*. Prentice Hall PTR, 2001.

Antognini, Christian, "Tracing Bind Variables and Waits." SOUG Newsletter, 2000.

Antognini, Christian, "When should an index be used?" SOUG Newsletter, 2001.

Antognini, Christian, Dominique Duay, Arturo Guadagnin, and Peter Welker, "Oracle Optimization Solutions." Trivadis TechnoCircle, 2004.

Antognini, Christian, "CBO: A Configuration Roadmap." Hotsos Symposium, 2005.

Antognini, Christian, "SQL Profiles." Trivadis CBO Days, 2006.

Antognini, Christian, "Oracle Data Storage Internals." Trivadis Traning, 2007.

Booch, Grady, *Object-Oriented Analysis and Design with Applications*. Addison-Wesley, 1994.

Brady, James, "A Theory of Productivity in the Creative Process." IEEE Computer Graphics and Applications, 1986.

Breitling, Wolfgang, "A Look Under the Hood of CBO: the 10053 Event." Hotsos Symposium, 2003.

Breitling, Wolfgang, "Histograms—Myths and Facts." Trivadis CBO Days, 2006.

Breitling, Wolfgang, "Joins, Skew and Histograms." Hotsos Symposium, 2007.

Brown, Thomas, "Scaling Applications through Proper Cursor Management." Hotsos Symposium, 2004.

Chaudhuri, Surajit, "An Overview of Query Optimization in Relational Systems." ACM Symposium on Principles of Database Systems, 1998.

Dageville, Benoît and Mohamed Zait, "SQL Memory Management in Oracle9i." VLDB Conference, 2002.

Dageville, Benoît et al, "Automatic SQL Tuning in Oracle 10g." VLDB Conference, 2004.

Database Language – SQL. ANSI, 1992.

Database Language – SQL – Part 2: Foundation. ISO/IEC, 2003.

Date, Chris, *Database In Depth*. O'Reilly, 2005.

Dell'Era, Alberto, "Join Over Histograms." 2007.

Dyke, Julian, "Library Cache Internals." 2006.

Ellis, Jon and Linda Ho, *JDBC 3.0 Specification*. Sun Microsystems, 2001.

Engsig, Bjørn, "Efficient use of bind variables, cursor_sharing and related cursor parameters." Miracle White Paper, 2002.

Foote, Richard, Richard Foote's Oracle blog (http://richardfoote.wordpress.com).

Green, Connie and John Beresniewicz, "Understanding Shared Pool Memory Structures." UKOUG Conference, 2006.

Goldratt, Eliyahu, *Theory of Constraints*. North River Press, 1990.

Gongloor, Prabhaker, Sameer Patkar, "Hash Joins, Implementation and Tuning." Oracle Technical Report, 1997.

Gülcü Ceki, *The complete log4j manual*. QOS.ch, 2003.

Jain, Raj, *The Art of Computer Systems Performance Analysis*. Wiley, 1991.

Kolk, Anjo, "The Life of an Oracle Cursor and its Impact on the Shared Pool." AUSOUG Conference, 2006.

Knuth, Donald, *The Art of Computer Programming, Volume 3 – Sorting and Searching*. Addison-Wesley, 1998.

Kyte, Thomas, *Effective Oracle by Design*. McGraw-Hill/Osborne, 2003.

Lahdenmäki, Tapio and Michael Leach, *Relational Database Index Design and the Optimizers*. Wiley, 2005.

Lewis, Jonathan, *Cost-Based Oracle Fundamentals*. Apress, 2006.

Lewis, Jonathan, "Hints and how to use them." Trivadis CBO Days, 2006.

Lewis, Jonathan, Oracle Scratchpad (http://jonathanlewis.wordpress.com).

Lilja, David, *Measuring Computer Performance*. Cambridge Universtity Press, 2000.

Machiavelli Niccoló, *Il Principe*. Einaudi, 1995.

Mahapatra, Tushar and Sanjay Mishra, *Oracle Parallel Processing*. O'Reilly, 2000.

Menon, R.M., *Expert Oracle JDBC Programming*. Apress, 2005.

Mensah, Kuassi, *Oracle Database Programming using Java and Web Services*. Digital Press, 2006.

Merriam-Webster online dictionary (http://www.merriam-webster.com)

Millsap, Cary, "Why You Should Focus on LIOs Instead of PIOs." 2002.

Millsap, Cary with Jeff Holt, *Optimizing Oracle Performance*. O'Reilly, 2003.

Moerkotte, Guido, *Building Query Compilers*. 2006.

Nørgaard, Mogens et al, *Oracle Insights: Tales of the Oak Table*. Apress, 2004.

Oracle Corporation, "EVENT: 10046 'enable SQL statement tracing (including binds/waits).'" MetaLink note 21154.1, 2003.

Oracle Corporation, "Remove Functional Index need for QUERY_REWRITE/QUERY_REWRITE_ENABLED." MetaLink note 2799028.8, 2003.

Oracle Corporation, "Understanding Bitmap Indexes Growth while Performing DML operations on the Table." MetaLink note 260330.1, 2004.

Oracle Corporation, "Delete or Update running slow—db file scattered read waits on index range scan." MetaLink note 296727.1, 2005.

Oracle Corporation, "Interpreting Raw SQL_TRACE and DBMS_SUPPORT.START_TRACE output." MetaLink note 39817.1, 2007.

Oracle Corporation, "Table Prefetching causes intermittent Wrong Results in 9iR2, 10gR1, and 10gR2." MetaLink note 406966.1, 2007.

Oracle Corporation, "Tracing Sessions in Oracle Using the DBMS_SUPPORT Package." MetaLink note 62160.1, 2007.

Oracle Corporation, "Trace Analyzer TRCANLZR—Interpreting Raw SQL Traces with Binds and/or Waits generated by EVENT 10046." MetaLink note 224270.1, 2008.

Oracle Corporation, "The DBMS_SUPPORT Package." MetaLink note 62294.1, 2002.

Oracle Corporation, "Oracle JDBC Thin Driver generates different Execution Plan." MetaLink note 273635.1, 2007.

Oracle Corporation, "Handling and resolving unshared cursors/large version_counts." MetaLink note 296377.1, 2007.

Oracle Corporation, "CASE STUDY: Analyzing 10053 Trace Files." MetaLink note 338137.1, 2006.

Oracle Corporation, *Oracle9i Documentation, Release 2.*

Oracle Corporation, *Oracle Database Documentation, 10g Release 1.*

Oracle Corporation, *Oracle Database Documentation, 10g Release 2.*

Oracle Corporation, *Oracle Database Documentation, 11g Release 1.*

Oracle Corporation, *Oracle Database 10g: Performance Tuning,* Oracle University, 2006.

Oracle Corporation, "Query Optimization in Oracle Database 10g Release 2." Oracle white paper, 2005.

Oracle Corporation, "SQL Plan Management in Oracle Database 11g." Oracle white paper, 2007.

Quest Software, *JProbe Profiler: Developer's Guide, Version 7.0.1.*

Quest Software, *PerformaSure: User's Guide, Version 4.4.*

Senegacnik, Joze, "Advanced Management of Working Areas in Oracle 9i/10g." Collaborate, 2006.

Senegacnik, Joze, "How Not to Create a Table." Miracle Database Forum, 2006.

Shee, Richmond, "If Your Memory Serves You Right." IOUG Live! Conference, 2004.

Shee, Richmond, Kirtikumar Deshpande and K Gopalakrishnan, *Oracle Wait Interface: A Pratical Guide to Performance Diagnostics & Tuning.* McGraw-Hill/Osborne, 2004.

Shirazi, Jack, *Java Performance Tuning.* O'Reilly, 2003.

Sun Microsystems, *Java 2 Platform Standard Edition 5.0 Development Kit* documentation.

Vargas, Alejandro, "10g Questions and Answers." 2007.

Wikipedia encyclopedia (http://www.wikipedia.org).

Williams, Mark, *Pro .NET Oracle Programming.* Apress, 2005.

Williams, Mark, "Improve ODP.NET Performance." *Oracle Magazine*, 2006.

Wustenhoff, Edward, *Service Level Agreement in the Data Center.* Sun BluePrints, 2002.

Zait, Mohamed, "Oracle10g SQL Optimization." Trivadis CBO Days, 2006.

Index

You Need the Companion eBook

CPSIA information can be obtained at www.ICGtesting.com
Printed in the USA
LVOW110258131211

259149LV00007B/5/P